WITHDRAWN

Mass
Communication
Education

Mass Communication Education

EDITED BY
MICHAEL D. MURRAY
ROY L. MOORE

Iowa State Press
A Blackwell Publishing Company

Iowa State Press
2121 State Avenue, Ames, Iowa 50014

Orders: 1-800-862-6657
Office: 1-515-292-0140
Fax: 1-515-292-3348
Web site: www.iowastatepress.com

Authorization to photocopy items for internal or personal use, or the internal or personal use of specific clients, is granted by Iowa State Press, provided that the base fee of $.10 per copy is paid directly to the Copyright Clearance Center, 222 Rosewood Drive, Danvers, MA 01923. For those organizations that have been granted a photocopy license by CCC, a separate system of payments has been arranged. The fee code for users of the Transactional Reporting Service is 0-8138-0274-1/2003 $.10.

Printed on acid-free paper in the United States of America

First edition, 2003

Library of Congress Cataloging-in-Publication Data

Mass communication education/edited by Michael D. Murray, Roy L. Moore—1st ed.
     p. cm.
Includes bibliographical references.
   ISBN 0-8138-0274-1 (alk. paper)
   1. Mass media—Study and teaching (Higher)—United States. 2. Journalism—Study and teaching (Higher)—United States. I. Murray, Michael D. II. Moore, Roy L.
   P91.5.U5 M37 2003
   302.23'071'173—dc21

                                                                            2002154436

The last digit is the print number: 9 8 7 6 5 4 3 2 1

Dedication

This book is dedicated to our first teachers and mentors: our parents, Austin and Marcella Murray, Chester and Essie Moore.

Contents

Preface

Because you picked up this book, it is quite likely that you are already well aware that there are at least two competing traditions in mass communication education. Some folks argue that there are actually two divisions or "camps," sometimes armed, or at least at odds over the two underlying philosophies behind what we, as mass communication educators do, in developing curriculum and teaching our classes.

The evolving distinctions emerge from historic differences between preparing students for the journalistic workplace and the study of the broader field of mass communication, including advertising, broadcasting and public relations. New technological innovations have accelerated an interest in applied communication. Thus we have included a chapter to address what has come to be termed *communication convergence*. We hope that in a small way this book contributes to the movement toward convergence in the field.

The need to address improvements and new directions is important because at various times and places the two traditions or approaches to the field have appeared to the general public as at war. In fact, the term *mass communication* is sometimes viewed with disdain by those trained as journalists, accelerating the debate over whether practical skills or research should dominate the curriculum. We include chapters that focus on both areas. Many higher education leaders take the position that, within the context of a university education, the mission of faculty should be directed toward problem solving.

The debate over what mass communication educators should be doing was crystallized in 2002 when the President of Columbia University called off the search for a new dean of its esteemed School of Journalism founded by Joseph Pulitzer. This was done as a means of trying to obtain a clearer vision of how graduate-level education in the field, the focus of that school, might effectively address broader societal needs while achieving a better "fit" at that particular institution. Some discussion ensued about how the curriculum of journalism students might be altered to include the study of other academic fields. This was put forward with the hope that the students in that highly regarded master's degree program will be permitted to take courses in fields that might expose them to areas on which they might eventually report.

Thus this book comes at a good time. Although the book is by no means definitive, our goal is to light the way toward a better understanding. We hope to offer some insight into the debate and, for some of the road warriors in the battle, perhaps provide some direction toward reconciliation. This book is all about teaching. We understand that any work of this kind, while not viewed as "high" scholarship, will in some way serve as a tribute to the great teachers we had ourselves—those whom we try to emulate. We know of no other collective work offering an emphasis on mass communication courses that has as much range and depth of focus on media education, especially with a wealth of individuals willing to share their expertise and especially their use of new media sources.

With all of this in mind, we offer the contributors, the chapter authors, and their sources a great deal of gratitude. The road to publishing this work was slightly bumpier than one might expect. When we co-authored a work on nonprint resources for the Association for Education in Journalism and Mass Communication a quarter century ago, no truly online resources existed. When we published an overview of what a handful of people were doing a few decades ago, no one was using the Internet. Just a decade ago, for a review of descriptions of coursework by individual instructors, looking primarily at what they did themselves in the classroom, cooperative developments under way at that time were still unappreciated. While this work goes in another direction and focuses specifically on what a wide range of people are doing in each of their courses, we have no doubt that the next decade will find even greater change.

We recognize that some rather radical differences exist, particularly at those institutions where tradition has well served those schools and the nation. Our objective is to move beyond debates over direction and focus instead on what is being currently accomplished in a wide variety of institutions. We think this book is also timely because we recognize that various pressures are moving higher education toward an uncritical culture that we deplore, a mind-set that encourages faculty, like many counterparts in journalism, to give "customers" what they want instead of what we know they need.

This book identifies a wide variety of approaches and examines courses in some detail, often using both course instructors and their online resources as primary source material. Our primary objective is improved teaching. We have taken a series of snapshots of how courses are being approached at some schools. It is by no means comprehensive or scientific but does achieve our goal to go beyond the wide range of organizational efforts to produce a collection of syllabi to explain further what individual professors provide students.

Preparing such a book has its unique challenges. First, coursework in the field is in constant flux. The book makes it clear that the impact of the integration of the so-called new media into the classroom is not yet fully understood. Indeed, many of the instructors contacted and used as major sources for this project expressed some degree of dissatisfaction with what they were doing currently in the classroom and online, anticipating changes even as they were describing their current methods. These are, of course, the kind of people with whom we love to talk, since they are looking forward at a critical time, rather than looking back in the proverbial rear-view mirror.

The editors thank everyone who made this project possible, especially contributing authors who are varied in background and in terms of their relationship to this project. The authors were sometimes asked to venture beyond their own institutions to reach individuals who might provide important insights into key classroom issues. We thank the multitude of course instructors who shared their vision and, in many cases, took the authors on a virtual tour of their classroom. We are grateful to the hundreds of instructors who made their course material available to the various chapter authors and then, in many cases, were willing to follow-up with telephone interviews regarding their methods and the passion they hold for their work.

Some of the contributors started out as participants in panels at meetings of the American Communication Association (ACA), the Association for Education in Journalism and Mass Communication (AEJMC), the American Journalism Historians Association (AJHA), the Broadcast Education Association (BEA), and the National Communication Association (NCA) more than six years ago. The participation of the University of Kentucky doctoral program in Communication in a national program to enhance teaching, the Preparing Future Faculty (PFF) initiative, played a role as did a fellowship supported by the American Council on Education (ACE) at the University of Georgia.

While the goal for some of the Web-based projects was to merely provide a preliminary laundry list of course syllabi in select areas, the objective was effectively met and encouraged this more elaborate project. Members of the International Radio and Television Society (IRTS) board, including Joyce Tudryn and Michelle Marsala, encouraged the development of this book through their annual faculty seminars. A significant number of contributors attended those meetings focusing most recently on new media sources. Fellowships and financial support from the IRTS in the name of Dr. Frank Stanton as well as Stephen Coltrin Awards from that organization also provided tangible and much moral support.

A few of the contributors to the book also worked on an early BEA Syllabus project, still available at that organization's Web site, www.beaweb.org. Members of the BEA board provided support, including Dom Caristi, a major contributor to this book, and Lynne Gross, California State University at Fullerton, the subject of an important essay. BEA administrator Louisa Nielsen, and the president of the organization at the time, Dr. Donald Godfrey, were also supportive of this project.

Dr. Godfrey, a close friend and co-collaborator on this and other books, was willing to encourage additional authors and educators, such as Val Limburg of the Edward R. Murrow School at Washington State University, to take what was a mere listing of syllabi to the next level. A distinguished teacher in his own right, Dr. Limburg wrote what turned out to be a prototype chapter for the book. We are also grateful to Barbara Cloud of the University of Nevada, Las Vegas, who was helpful in identifying important contributors, including Erika Engberg and Gary Larson of UNLV, who wrote and then rewrote early course-review segments.

We also thank the many thoughtful individuals, including Jerry Allen, who made recommendations for author essays concerning the mentors to be profiled in this book. In many ways, this turned out to be one of the most interesting, yet sensitive, aspects of the project because, in offering a less clinical approach, we opened up a fascinating area of interpersonal interaction. We discovered that many of the assumptions that we had about mentors were unfounded. For example, the role of research was critical to success, as were role models and friends, to a generation of scholars. And, while no means definitive, the broadening of our mission to include an analysis of information and approaches across curricula helps the cause. By examining the particular methods and the influence of some of the leaders in mass communication education, the book offers a more up-to-date and comprehensive treatment of the field.

In this regard, we thank Dr. Joe Foote, Dean at Arizona State University, former president of both the BEA and the AEJMC, who has been an important figure in the movement toward addressing the traditional divergence in the field. He offered a great deal of encouragement with this particular project and he contributed to a panel at a meeting of the NCA that spurred us to look especially at new technology in mass communication courses.

Some of our contributors were gently coaxed to write essays about their mentors, which turned out to be a gratifying and even emotion-laden assignment. As the book was being developed, it became clear that certain individuals held a great deal of special sway when it came to personal influence on teaching. As we emulate our best teachers and vow to do for our own students what they did for us, the challenge of that task becomes clearer and more daunting. While in no way definitive, these essays point the way and credit individuals who have invested heavily in a profession and their students.

Another former AEJMC and AJHA president, Dr. Maurine Beasley of the University of Maryland, also contributed to the work in many ways, including authorship. She encouraged others within both of those organizations to support this project as it moved through many stages of development. We are especially grateful for her special efforts to broaden the content of the book, including the mass communication history chapter, in which she worked with one of her graduate students, Kim Wilmot Voss.

The editors thank two very understanding wives, Pamela Moore and Carol Murray, very distinguished educators in their own right, for their support. We have also been very lucky in our own professors. We have been greatly influenced by our memories of such people as Steve Chaffee, Jack McLeod, Bruce Westley, Lewis Donohew, Robert A. Johnston, S.J., Jerry Allen, Loren Reid, Paul Nelson, Joe Wolfe, Keith Sanders, Edward C. Lambert, and William Stephenson. We have an excellent cohort of colleagues in our previous teaching assignments at Virginia Tech, the University of North Carolina at Chapel Hill, Georgia State University, and the University of Louisville, as well as our current institutions.

We appreciate the support of J. David Johnson, Dean of the College of Communications and Information Studies, and Richard Wilson, Acting Director of the School of Journalism and Telecommunications at the University of Kentucky. We thank John Hylton, the Dean of the College of Fine Arts and Communication at the University of Missouri at St. Louis, and former Chancellor Blanche M. Touhill. We are grateful to the staff at the Iowa State Press and especially Project Manager Judi Brown, Copyeditor John Flukas, and our key contact on this particular project, Mark Barrett, a true gentleman.

Michael D. Murray
Roy L. Moore

Editors

Michael D. Murray is Curators' Distinguished Teaching Professor at the University of Missouri at St. Louis. He received his doctorate in Communication from the University of Missouri at Columbia and taught at Virginia Tech and the University of Louisville. He is author or editor of five books, numerous articles, and received many teaching awards. These include those of the Broadcast Division of the Association for Education in Journalism and Mass Communication (AEJMC), the Mass Communication Division of the National Communication Association (NCA), and the American Communication Association's (ACA) Theodore Clevenger Award for Teaching Excellence. He has been Fellow of the International Radio and Television Society (IRTS) and received the Missouri Governor's Teaching Excellence Award.

Roy L. Moore is a Professor and Associate Dean for Graduate Studies in the College of Communications and Information Studies at the University of Kentucky. He earned his doctorate in Mass Communication from the University of Wisconsin at Madison and his J.D. in Law from Georgia State University. He is a prolific author and a practicing attorney specializing in libel and First Amendment issues. His textbooks include *Mass Communication Law and Ethics* and *The Law of Advertising and Public Relations*, co-authored with Ron Farrar and Erik Collins. He chaired Law and Mass Communications and Society Divisions of the Association of Education in Journalism and Mass Communication. He served as American Council on Education Fellow at the University of Georgia and was designated as a "Great Teacher" by the University of Kentucky Alumni Association.

Contributors

Sean Aday is an Assistant Professor at the School of Media and Public Affairs at George Washington University in Washington, D.C. His principal research focuses on political communication, specifically the role of the press in the political process, media effects, and public opinion. Aday received his Bachelor's of Science in Journalism from Northwestern University's Medill School of Journalism. After working as a journalist, he received his master's and doctorate from the Walter Annenberg School for Communication at the University of Pennsylvania.

Philip J. Auter received his doctorate from the University of Kentucky. He joined the Mass Communication program at the University of Louisiana after teaching at the University of West Florida. He serves as the research chair of the Radio-Television Division of the Association for Education in Journalism and Mass Communication and was past chair of the Research Division of the Broadcast Education Association. Auter teaches TV production and broadcast news and conducts audience research. He has experience in broadcast, print and online media.

Mary E. Beadle is a Professor of Communications and also serves as the Dean of the Graduate School at John Carroll University in Cleveland. She received her doctorate from Kent State University and is a former chair of the Communication Department at Walsh University in Canton, Ohio. She is a specialist in media history and international media. She has conducted communication seminars in Latin America and Russia and is co-editor of *Indelible Images: Women in Local Television*.

Maurine H. Beasley, Professor of Journalism at the University of Maryland, holds bachelor's degrees from the University of Missouri at Columbia, a master's degree from Columbia University, and a doctorate from George Washington University. She is a past president of both the Association for Education in Journalism and Mass Communication and the American Journalism Historians Association. She has published eight books, including *The Eleanor Roosevelt Encyclopedia* and *Taking Their Place: A Documentary History of Women and Journalism*.

Dave Bennett, who teaches journalism at Indiana State University in Terre Haute, has received fellowships from the American Society of Newspaper Editors, the Gannett Foundation, and the Poynter Institute for Media Studies. He has developed programs in China and South Korea and served as a military journalist, government reporter, environmental writer, and Associated Press wire-service reporter and editor. He recently wrote a series on capital punishment for the *Tribune-Star* (Indiana).

Gretchen Bisplinghoff teaches in the Department of Communication at Northern Illinois University. She has a doctorate in Film from Northwestern University, where

she was a founding member of the Feminar (Feminist Film Seminar), which sponsored the Rodgers Feminist Film Criticism Conference (the first national conference
on feminist film criticism) and of the Women's Caucus of the Society for Cinema
Studies. She is co-author of two books on the careers of directors Roman Polanski and
Robert Altman and has published on Irish cinema and the image of women in film.

Fred R. Blevens is Professor and Associate Dean at the Gaylord College of Journalism and Mass Communication at the University of Oklahoma. His previous
appointments have been at Southwest Texas State, Texas A&M, and Ball State universities. He has been recognized with numerous teaching awards, including the Freedom
Forum's 2001 Teacher of the Year. He is co-author of *Twilight of Press Freedom*.
Before joining academe Blevens was a journalist. He holds bachelor's and master's
degrees from Ball State University and a doctorate in Journalism from the University
of Missouri.

Bonnie Brennen is Associate Professor at the University of Missouri School of
Journalism. Her interest in cultural labor history grows out of her professional media
work. She received her doctorate in 1993 from the University of Iowa and is the author
of *For the Record: An Oral History of Rochester* and *New York; Newsworkers* (2001)
and co-editor, with Hanno Hardt, of *Picturing the Past: Media, History & Photography* and *Newsworkers: Towards a History of the Rank and File*.

Dom Caristi, who is Associate Professor of Telecommunications at Ball State University, has been a Fellow of the National Association of Television Program Executives and also the Radio-Television News Directors Foundation. In 1995, he was a
Fulbright Professor at the University of Ljubljana in Slovenia. He received his doctorate from the University of Iowa and has published works in Quorum Books, *Journal of
Broadcasting & Electronic Media*, *Suffolk University Law Review*, *Telecommunications Policy* and *Feedback*, a publication of the Broadcast Education Association.

David A. Copeland, who is the A. J. Fletcher Professor of Communication at Elon
University, is the author of three books and many works on the press, early America,
and religion. He is editor of the book *Debating the Issues in the Press of the Time* and
co-editor of *Media History Monographs*. Past president of the American Journalism
Historians Association, he was Carnegie Foundation for Advancement of Teaching
Professor and received an Exemplary Teaching Award. His doctorate in Mass Communication Research is from the University of North Carolina.

Dale Cressman, who teaches at Brigham Young University and is a doctoral candidate at the University of Utah, taught at Lyndon State College and Utah State University. His work has earned many awards, including a regional Emmy from the National
Academy of Television Arts and Sciences, the result of a visit to Russia and a film on
traditions. He has worked as news producer and TV-station manager in Indiana, Texas,
Wisconsin, and Utah. A native of Saskatchewan, he was editor for the Canadian
Broadcasting Corporation and also a newspaper reporter.

Frank E. X. Dance is the John Evans Professor of Human Communication Studies
at the University of Denver and teaches a course in the Digital Media Studies (DMS)
program at that institution. He has authored or co-authored over 10 books and 60 refereed articles. He is past president of the National Communication Association
(NCA), past president of the International Communication Association (ICA), and

past editor of the *Journal of Communication* and *Communication Education.* He is a Fellow of the International Communication Association and received his doctorate from Northwestern University.

William R. Davie, who received his doctorate from the University of Texas, is Broadcasting Coordinator at the University of Louisiana. He served as liaison between the Radio-Television News Directors Association and the Association for Education in Journalism and Mass Communication. He is past head of the AEJMC Radio-Television Division and former chair of the Broadcast Education Association's News Division. He was Fellow in the Excellence in Journalism Education Project funded by the Knight Foundation. He has contributed to many works and co-authored *Principles of Electronic Media.*

David Davies teaches at the University of Southern Mississippi, where he has also served as department chairperson. He has been a newspaper reporter as well as a radio news director. He completed his doctorate at the University of Alabama and has taught at Ohio State University and Ohio Wesleyan University. He edited the book *The Press and Race*, and his chapter, "The Contemporary Newspaper, 1945–Present," appears in *The Age of Mass Communication.* His articles have also appeared in a number of places, including *American Journalism.*

Erika Engstrom worked in radio and television news in Orlando and Gainesville, Florida. She holds a doctorate in Mass Communication from the University of Florida. She has taught courses in Broadcast Newswriting and Television Production since 1986 and currently serves as an associate professor in the Hank Greenspun School of Communication at the University of Nevada, Las Vegas.

Douglas Ferguson graduated from The Ohio State University with a bachelor's and master's in Communication. He spent 13 years as a programmer and manager of an NBC television affiliate in Ohio before completing his doctorate at Bowling Green State University. After a dozen years teaching in Ohio, he went to the College of Charleston as the inaugural chair of the Department of Communication. He has co-written three books on the television industry and numerous articles and papers.

John P. Ferré is a Professor of Communication at the University of Louisville, where he investigates ethical, religious, and historical dimensions of mass media. He received his doctorate from the University of Illinois. In addition to numerous articles and reviews, he has written several books, including *Good News: Social Ethics and the Press* with Clifford G. Christians and P. Mark Fackler. In 1996, he received the Krieghbaum Under-40 Award for Outstanding Achievement from the Association for Education in Journalism and Mass Communication. In 2001 he was named Distinguished Teaching Professor.

Donald G. Godfrey is Professor in the Cronkite School of Journalism and Mass Communication at Arizona State University. He has worked in commercial radio, educational and commercial television, and corporate communications. He holds a doctorate from the University of Washington and is author or editor of eight books, including the biography of inventor *Philo T. Farnsworth: The Father of Television*, and numerous articles. He has served as President of the Broadcast Education Association and Council of Communication Associations. His students have received awards in all major contests in the field.

W. Glenn Griffin is an Assistant Professor of Advertising at Pennsylvania State University. He holds a doctorate in advertising from the University of Texas at Austin, and his research deals with creativity theory, cognitive psychology, and advertising education. His research has been published in the *Journal of Advertising Education* and *Journalism and Mass Communication Educator*. He coached the National Student Advertising Competition team at the University of Alabama, 1996–1999. Prior to faculty assignments he was art director and copywriter.

Max V. Grubb received his doctorate in Mass Communication from Ohio University. Prior to receiving his doctorate he spent 15 years in broadcast sales and management. He has also worked in public broadcasting and is currently on the board of directors of WDBX-FM. He has served on international media programs and conducts management training workshops for the U.S. State Department's Telecommunication Training Institute. He is currently an assistant professor in the Department of Radio-Television in the College of Mass Communication and Media Arts at Southern Illinois University at Carbondale.

Walt Harrington, who is a Professor of Journalism at the University of Illinois at Urbana at Champaign, was a writer for the *Washington Post Magazine* for nearly 15 years. His book *Crossings: A White Man's Journey Into Black America* was the winner of the Gustavus Myers Award for the Study of Human Rights in the United States. He is the editor of *Intimate Journalism: The Art and Craft of Reporting Everyday Life*. His most recent book is *The Everlasting Stream: A True Story of Rabbits, Guns, Friendship, and Family*.

Karie Hollerback is an Instructor of Advertising and teaches mass communication theory and research, advertising design, techniques of advertising, and media planning in the Mass Communication Department at Southeast Missouri State University in Cape Girardeau, Missouri, where she received her master's of science degree.

Liese L. Hutchinson, APR, is an Assistant Professor of Communication and teaches a variety of public relations courses at Saint Louis University. She has taught at the Maastricht Center for Transatlantic Studies in the Netherlands. She is recipient of the Robert A. Johnston S.J. Award for Teaching Excellence. Active as a PR consultant, she has more than 15 years experience, is an accredited member of the Public Relations Society of America, and is her chapter's ethics officer and past president. She received a Fulbright grant to teach at Concordia International University in Estonia in 2003.

Donald J. Jung is an Assistant Professor of Advertising at Southeast Missouri State University at Cape Girardeau. He is responsible for teaching Principles of Advertising, Copy Writing and Advertising Campaigns, as well as directing the Senior Seminar in Mass Communication. He received his doctorate in Communication from Purdue University and has served as a Fellow of the International Radio and Television Society.

Elliot King is an Associate Professor of Communication at Loyola College, where he founded the Digital Media Lab. He is the co-author of *The Online Journalist* and four other books about the use of new communication technology. He has served as the chair of the AEJMC History Division Joint Conference and as an officer in divisions of American Journalism Historians Association. Former managing editor of the *Journal of Magazine and New Media Research*, he is editorial director of *Database Trends and Applications Magazine*.

John A. Kline is Provost Emeritus of the USAF Air University. He received his doctorate from the University of Iowa and taught at the University of New Mexico. He served as Director of Graduate Studies at the University of Missouri at Columbia before accepting a position in 1975 as a civilian professor at the USAF Air University. He graduated from Harvard University's program in national security and became Provost of the USAF Air University in 1991, a position he held for 10 years. Currently a writer and speaker, he conducts training workshops.

Gary Larson spent almost 20 years in broadcasting before earning his doctorate from the University of Minnesota in 1997. He has written about media history, mediated construction of reality, and the rhetoric of visual communication. An Assistant Professor of Communication Studies, Larson teaches broadcast news production courses in the Greenspun School of Communication at the University of Nevada, Las Vegas.

Frederic Leigh is Associate Director and Clinical Professor in the Cronkite School of Journalism and Mass Communication at Arizona State University. In addition to administrative service, he teaches broadcasting courses and serves as advisor of the campus radio station. His professional experience includes a decade in public radio, and his publications include numerous journal articles, book chapters, a historical dictionary of American radio, and an electronic media textbook. He holds bachelor's and master's degrees in communication arts and a doctorate in higher education administration.

Val E. Limburg is Professor and head of broadcasting in the Edward R. Murrow School of Communication at Washington State University in Pullman. His books include *Electronic Media Ethics* and *Mass Media Literacy* (1989). His articles appear in the *Journal of Mass Media Ethics, Contemporary Media Issues,* and *Media Management Review* and in several media encyclopedias, 1997–99. He served as an officer of the Washington State Association of Broadcasters and on the Board of Directors of the Broadcast Education Association.

Rebecca Ann Lind, who is Associate Professor and Director of Undergraduate Studies at the University of Illinois at Chicago, has taught a variety of courses, including Race and Gender in Media, Processes and Effects of Mass Communication, Media Ethics, and Mass Communication Theory. Her research interests are audience studies, race and gender in media, new media, and media ethics. She has published numerous articles, received many grants, and is active in leadership for both the National Communication Association and the Broadcast Education Association.

Walter S. McDowell, who teaches at the University of Miami, taught previously in the School of Mass Communication and Media Arts at Southern Illinois University and completed his doctorate in Mass Communication at the University of Florida. He has 20 years of experience in broadcasting, including a dozen years as Director of Marketing and Creative Services at ABC affiliate, WFTV Orlando, Florida.

Thomas L. McPhail is a Professor of Communication and Fellow in the Center for International Studies at the University of Missouri at St. Louis. He recently published one of the most authoritative books in international communication entitled *Global Communication: Theories, Stakeholders, and Trends.* In addition to numerous articles, he previously published *Electronic Colonialism* and *Communication: The Canadian*

Experience, co-authored with Brenda McPhail. This latter book has a major section on the theories of Marshall McLuhan.

Robert Musburger is the former Director of the School of Communication at the University of Houston, where he teaches courses in media history and production. He holds a doctorate from Florida State University and spent 20 years in commercial broadcasting as a producer-director of news and documentaries and hosted a weekly program on radio and the web. He is widely published, including *Electronic News-gathering: A Guide to ENG, Single Camera Video Production*, and the co-authored text *Introduction to Media Production: From Analog to Digital*. He is active in the Broadcast Education Association and the Society of Motion Picture and Television Engineers.

Yorgo Pasadeos is Professor and Associate Dean of Graduate Studies at the College of Communication and Information Sciences, the University of Alabama. He holds a doctorate in Mass Communication from the University of Texas at Austin. He teaches graduate and undergraduate courses in advertising, research methods, and international communication. His research interests are in advertising informativeness, international information flow, media performance, and bibliometrics.

John J. Pauly received his doctorate from the University of Illinois. He teaches and researches the areas of media history, mass communication and society, and qualitative research methods. He served as editor of *American Journalism*, was a Fellow at the Center for Twentieth Century Studies at the University of Wisconsin at Milwaukee, and received a Fellowship for College Teachers from the National Endowment for the Humanities. His research has appeared in many journals, including *Critical Studies in Mass Communication* and *Communication Research*.

Michael J. Porter is an Associate Professor in the Department of Communication and Director of Special Degree Programs in the College of Arts and Science at the University of Missouri at Columbia. He has also had responsibility for overseeing the Wakonse teaching program for professors at the University of Missouri, where he teaches courses in television criticism, media in society, and mass communication theory. His research focuses on narrative theory and media literacy. He received his doctorate from the University of Iowa.

Alf Pratte is Professor of Journalism at Brigham Young University. A former reporter for *Honolulu Star-Bulletin*, *Salt Lake City Tribune*, and *Deseret News*, he is author of *Gods within the Machine: A History of the American Society of Newspaper Editors*. He is a founder and a past president of the American Journalism Historians Association. His articles have appeared in *Journalism Quarterly*, *American Journalism*, *Journalism History*, *Journal of Communication Inquiry*, *Radio Studies*, *Newspaper Research Journal*, *Media Ethics*, *Media History Digest*, *Quill*, *Editor & Publisher*, and the *Masthead*.

Sonny Rhodes has 25 years of professional experience as a daily newspaper reporter and editor, most recently working as features copy desk chief at the *Arkansas Democrat-Gazette* in Little Rock. He is currently an assistant professor at the University of Arkansas at Little Rock, where he has served as adjunct faculty several times since 1990. He received his Master's in Arts in Journalism degree from the University of Mississippi. His specialty areas are reporting, editing, mass media, and society.

Susan Plumb Salas is Director of Broadcasting at Pepperdine University in Malibu, California, where she teaches radio-television production and theory courses. She holds a Master's in Arts degree in Telecommunications from the University of Iowa and a Master's of Fine Arts in Film Producing from the American Film Institute in Los Angeles. She has produced over 100 national and regional commercials for major advertising agencies and studios. She has also appeared in over 200 commercials and guest starred in many popular TV series.

B. William Silcock teaches broadcast news at Arizona State University. He completed his doctorate at the University of Missouri, where he also taught and directed the Radio-Television News Director's Management Seminar for News Executives and was program director for the State Department's Office of International Broadcasting workshops. He has been a Fulbright Scholar at the University of Stockholm and City University Dublin. He conducted research on international news and served as editor to *Euro-Reporter*, a magazine produced in Brussels by students from Sweden, France, Holland and Ireland.

Lowndes F. (Rick) Stephens is the J. Rion McKissick Professor of Journalism at the University of South Carolina. He received bachelor's and master's degrees from the University of Kentucky and his doctorate from the University of Wisconsin at Madison. He served as associate dean at the University of South Carolina and acting director of the USC Center for Mass Communication Research. His professional experience includes teaching at the University of North Dakota, where he directed the communications research center, and also work as an economist and researcher for private and governmental agencies.

Penelope Bradley Summers teaches journalism at Northern Kentucky University. She is a former Scripps Howard Fellow and has taught Media Law for the past 10 years. She has worked as a newspaper reporter and editor, radio reporter and news documentary producer, television public affairs writer and associate television producer, and worked professionally in advertising and public relations. She is active in the Association for Education in Journalism and Mass Communications and has served as Media Law Clerk and program chair, and she currently serves as head of the Law Division for that organization.

Bernell E. Tripp is an Associate Professor of Journalism at the University of Florida, where she teaches reporting, magazine and feature writing, media history, and methods. She has written a book and numerous book chapters on the 19th-century African-American press, the abolitionist press, and the antebellum press. She is three-time winner of the J. William Snorgrass Award for Minority Research, selected from papers presented at the conference of the American Journalism Historians Association. She is that organization's president and received her doctorate from the University of Alabama.

Max Utsler joined the William Allen White School of Journalism and Mass Communications at the University of Kansas in 1983. He received his undergraduate degree from Knox College and his master's and doctorate in Journalism from the University of Missouri at Columbia. In television he served as an assistant news director, producer and reporter. He has received a number of awards for both television programming and corporate video.

Kimberly Wilmot Voss is currently an Assistant Professor at the University of Wisconsin–Stout in Menomonie, where she teaches a variety of courses for the Department of English. She is also a doctoral candidate at the University of Maryland at College Park, with a specialty in journalism history and interests in the role of women in the mass media.

S. Scott Whitlow serves as Coordinator of the Advertising Sequence and previously served as Director of Internships for the School of Journalism and Telecommunications at the University of Kentucky. She has consulted and conducted research for many groups and has been awarded her College's Excellence in Teaching Award, a Lexington Ad Club's "Pacesetter Award," and Pilot International's Kentucky Professional Woman of the Year. She holds a doctorate from Southern Illinois University at Carbondale and has published in *Journalism Quarterly*, *Journalism Educator*, *Mass Comm Review*, and *Educational Communication*.

PART I

Starting Out, Yesterday, Today and Tomorrow

CHAPTER 1

Introduction

Michael D. Murray and Roy L. Moore

In a *New York Times* commentary in 2002, the father of a high school student recounted his visits to various colleges and universities in preparation for his son's decision about which higher education institution he would attend, or rather which school would select him for admission. During the visits the father and his son checked out some of the nation's top schools. The father also described the anxiety accompanying the admittance decision by select institutions, with the Ivy League schools among those most favored and potentially challenging.

The father named names in the commentary, discussing how, during one college visit, he had seen a videotape in which students from a prestigious, highly selective, science-oriented institution attempted to counter the prevailing stereotype of that school as a haven for academic nerds. The father described how, after viewing the tape during the on-campus visit, he had left that school's auditorium to walk around the physical plant, observing many student "nerds" grazing in full view. So much for that "select" segment of the sales pitch.

In the same article, the father also reviewed the more substantive promises some highly selective schools make to impress students and their families with the quality of education they might receive, should they be fortunate enough to be chosen by one of these schools. The promises included small class size, undergraduate instruction by senior, full professors, and the chance to network with future leaders in a given field. Many of these areas have been institutionalized by having chaired professorships tied to undergraduate instruction and, certainly, the last category—networking prospects—assumes that other high-achieving high school students would be enrolling with the prospective applicant.

Other promised highlights included internship and cooperative business programs as well as the opportunity to be mentored by or perhaps even assist senior faculty members with specialized research assignments or working with them on major long-term grants, journal articles and books.

The editors of this text understand that despite lofty goals, those of us who have been members of the academy for a reasonable time know that the "promise versus performance" quotient in the aforementioned scenarios can leave much to be desired. This is the case even at elite and prestigious private universities.

Admissions officials and campus tour guides are familiar with the refrain "Who will be teaching my son or daughter?" The answer depends on a variety of considerations but especially on the student's major and year in school. The likely answer at many schools, including the nation's research universities, is that graduate teaching assistants (TAs) conduct most of the instruction even though they are notoriously known to feel overworked and underpaid, and often have inadequate training and guidance.

One of the nation's leading public universities has attempted to address the almost universal concern of parents about the role of TAs in undergraduate instruction. At the University of North Carolina at Chapel Hill, graduate students are involved in well over half, nearly 56 percent, of classes in that university's General College during any given semester. On the Chapel Hill campus the more experienced teaching fellows handle 29 percent of those with enrollments of 30 students, and senior fellows with extensive classroom experience lead larger courses of 100 or more.

The University of Washington has a three-tiered training program for TAs. This graduated approach ensures that those responsible for instruction have had a more thorough grounding through tried-and-true exposure to classroom methods. In all, UNC most recently employed slightly more than 1,500 TAs in 2001, a figure comparable to the University of California, whereas the University of Michigan used more than 1,600 TAs in the fall of 2001.

Campus officials are quick to point out that these students are among the brightest and most advanced in their disciplines, but, as at most schools, the screening and training programs vary significantly across a campus, even one with a full complement of support programs. The balancing act of facing life simultaneously as student and teacher is central to challenging graduate assistants, and the issue of their overall effectiveness has been repeatedly raised. Studies funded by grants from the Pew Charitable Trusts and the Spencer Foundation under the leadership of Jody Nyquist of the University of Washington have investigated the stages of TA development. Dr. Nyquist has also looked at how the Ph.D. degree can be re-envisioned to meet the changing needs of our society.

In his book, *Imposters in the Temple* (1992), policy scholar Martin Anderson questioned whether institutions could reason the use of graduate students to oversee undergraduate instruction characterized as analogous to "children teaching children."

In a review of TA practices at UNC, journalism Professor Deb Alkat pointed out that the professor technically responsible for a large lecture course is often functioning as a figurehead while graduate students form the central core of instruction. In courses staffed by TAs the experience is similar. The effectiveness of the class is often dictated by the involvement of the graduate students in charge.

It has been well documented that external pressures to produce a higher education hierarchy resulted directly from the growth of public support, beginning with the baby-boomer generation and a large pool of graduate students during the post-Vietnam era (Hickson, 1999). This sudden growth is currently evidenced by the "echo" boomer phenomenon, with Vietnam era children and their siblings lining up for college coursework.

A *Chronicle of Higher Education* article, "College Enrollments Projected to Rise 15% by 2012 Washington," spelled out how, according to the U.S. Education Department annual report, enrollment in degree-granting postsecondary institutions is projected to increase to 17.7 million by 2011–2012 from 15.3 million in 1999–2000. The more than 15 percent jump includes the projection that the number of bachelor's degrees awarded is expected to rise to 1,437,000, a 16 percent increase. And the number of bachelor's degrees awarded to women is expected to rise a whopping 20 percent, to 850,000.

In his book *Making the Most of College: Students Speak Their Minds* (2001), Professor Richard J. Light found that students have an expressed need for assistance from their institutions and that they recognize the importance of a mentoring system. Light suggested that acquiring a mentor often seems to matter most in terms of mastering academic culture and that successful students use every form of initiative to get to know at least one professor each semester. He recommends that by the end of eight terms, even if the students succeed only half of the time, they would have at least four professors on whom to rely for recommendations when they begin their job search.

In practice, and despite the enhanced use of the term *mentor*, institutionalized mentoring programs are found less frequently than one might expect. While few would disagree that mentoring at the graduate level has intrinsic value, few schools have taken that next step in establishing a formal mentoring relationship. When a university hires a new faculty member, it makes a substantial financial commitment.

Even though experienced people are convinced that good teaching is too important to be left to chance, instruction in the craft of teaching is generally not a part of graduate education in mass communication. Mentoring is a step in the right direction even if perceived barriers include the fear that, for whatever reason, a less formal approach is the way to go, since graduate education has always placed great emphasis on research, independent thought and action.

So, to some extent, mentoring toward good teaching goes against the grain. And there is also a concern that some students might view this as a lack of confidence or an imposition on faculty. The lack of a mentoring tradition is underscored by there being little personal gain for mentoring amidst a culture that so heavily values the research component of what we do as academics.

It is accepted policy that the training of doctoral students in mass communication should concentrate almost exclusively on research and not prepare them to teach class. Graduate teaching assistants occasionally get a chance to lecture large classes, but this is usually done independently and often with little feedback. When graduate students are enrolled in a disproportionate number of small-enrollment seminars, this kind of added assignment can be fun and enlightening even if there is little opportunity for student interaction.

That kind of scenario may also produce a false sense of security for those planning to rely heavily on lecture notes, since there has been little discussion of styles of teaching. Different people learn in different ways, and the emphasis has shifted. Educators use a variety of approaches and technologies to develop courses.

Postgraduate expressions of the expectations and impressions that mentoring provided are almost uniformly positive, and most insist that it can be an important component of professional development. But even though *mentor* has become a buzzword in higher education, many of the biases against formal mentoring of advanced students and even junior faculty still exist. It seems as if some people feel that the kind of interpersonal assistance provided by a mentor must be based on mutual cooperation and a spontaneous, less structured agreement, beyond the sharing of a culture or apparent link to the field.

Mentoring may also be regarded as a safety net when it comes to addressing logistical concerns such as ordering textbooks, creation of syllabi, or the need for outside support and assistance. Others may view it as an attempt at damage control, particularly in instances when some preliminary, subpar performances are reported. Both of these concerns are legitimate and provide further evidence of the need for such a program. The synergism created when two individuals with similar goals engage in a dialogue of commitment to student learning is very likely too positive in an era in which attention is being shifted away from *learning* as a passive experience.

Of course, the ground rules on how mentors will function to create a synergistic dialogue in a formal context sometimes create confusion. When it comes to evaluating instruction, some senior faculty simply do not want to be placed in the uncomfortable position of making judgments on behalf of an entire department or college. Others are concerned about the confidentiality required in offering assessment and concerns that senior faculty may not be the best judges of effectiveness.

Some individuals who have participated in formal mentoring programs report that the relationship involved a far greater time commitment than initially anticipated. Discussions often centered on the approach to a particular topic or on a common understanding of an underlying principle. For a generation of senior professors weaned on the journalism of the '60s—the introduction of television into American society, the Space Race, Woodstock, Watergate, and the War in Vietnam—translating the lessons from those media-related events requires an expanded vocabulary and a great deal of time.

On the positive side of the ledger, this results in a sharing or pooling of information. Mentors who begin the relationship expecting to attend the lectures of their junior partners with the idea that they might provide feedback on the pace of a particular lecture report instead on the mutual sharing of ideas about content.

Another important aspect of mentoring is to avoid any attempt to impose ideas, noting that the ultimate decision on teaching a course rests with the person assigned to teach the course. An organizational scheme or a particular way of introducing a topic may be fair game. The right to follow one's instincts, to make mistakes, and to learn from them have to be a part of the give-and-take that mentors share with their protégés. All things being equal, mentors frequently report that their original expectations are greatly exceeded.

A great deal of bureaucracy is involved in administering and teaching a large lecture course, and the opportunity to observe TA meetings and participate in problem solving also contributes to the learning experience for a beginning instructor. Reviewing tests for clarity and accuracy, proctoring and grading tests, and handling the inevitable special circumstances that arise, as well as dealing with students who require some accommodation for test taking also play a significant role.

It is easy to become complacent after a number of years in the classroom in the absence of any challenge to one's teaching approach. The willingness to admit that one can still improve after two or three decades of teaching is a solid prerequisite for someone serving as a mentor and advisor to others. However, it is unrealistic to expect that mentoring will be successful in each and every case. Some people just do not work well together. Personal relationships can become strained and disparities in teaching style can make a relationship less positive. The prestige some professors hold can create mixed loyalties, and a lack of total confidentiality can also result in division within a unit.

We realize that entering a department at a major university can be daunting and intimidating. To have an experienced teacher standing by to offer assistance or just a sympathetic ear can help to allay some of the fears that teachers may face at the beginning of their careers. On the opposite end of the spectrum, we also bear testament that a mentoring assignment can actually help to rekindle enthusiasm for teaching on the part of a senior person who had waned under the pressure of other commitments.

Of course the mentoring model applies just as well to undergraduate students. Regular personal student contact is also recognized as being critical to success at that level. Richard Light suggests that connections with professors can best be made in small classes, the ones beginning students are least likely to take at the outset of their education. Although it often appears counterintuitive to parents, the starting of a college career with small, specialized courses can result in less anonymity for a student and increase the chances that professors will remember them or perhaps invite them to assist with a research project.

The preponderance of instruction in many fields, such as mass communication, occurs within the context of large state institutions of higher learning and often in specialized colleges of mass communication and journalism. At most of these schools the challenges for faculty to maintain solid research programs while offering quality instruction grow ever greater, even without a team of undergraduate researchers in tow. But this specialization increases the chances that students will link up with a professor in their field, and it also helps identify a potential career track.

Professor Light likewise advises student and their parents to recognize the importance of emphasizing extracurricular activities as a means of assuring additional contact with the real world. He maintains that students involved in such activities are the happiest and also the most successful because they are frequently making the connection between the academic world and the world of getting things accomplished. When education becomes connected to a life or life's work, it becomes much more meaningful.

Most of us in academia, who also function in that "real world," recognize that undergraduate instruction at most institutions is handled most often by assistant professors. In the words of one senior professor, instructors in these settings tend to be thrown into the water without a single, formal swimming lesson. In an era in which much lip service is paid to teaching quality, attention to that particular detail is not always as clearly demonstrated and certainly not evaluated as well as we would like it to be. But as this volume will attest, often it is. Indeed, a decade ago, one senior editor pointed to studies showing that only half of academic departments offered teacher training programs even though two-thirds of all TAs had assumed responsibility for classes by their second year. In a formal study of departments, only a quarter of the schools offered campuswide training for beginning teaching assignments, and even these were elective.

Further complicating the situation, recent assessments of mass media education continue to point to a "split personality" for a scholarly mission in which social science, liberal arts, theoretical and practical, as well as a dichotomy between academic and professional concerns compete for attention. In an environment in which all of the various areas require technological resources, university departments and colleges of mass communication and journalism can easily get caught in the bind of trying to be all things to all people.

Beyond all of these traditional concerns or the "usual suspects," a new but increasingly frequent call for *media literacy* training at the elementary school and secondary school levels, on a par with what is being done at some Canadian and European schools, places added pressure on mass communication programs. If you investigate some of the nation's biggest schools of communication, you discover a number of senior professors, many of whom have received considerable acclaim for their ability to work with undergraduates. While some of these senior people rely heavily on TAs, most function independently, imparting wisdom accumulated over long careers.

This book takes a careful look at coursework as it is being offered at a number of institutions around the country. Rather than having specialized instructors describe their course, the editors have asked some perceptive people to survey a number of courses to gauge the strategies being used and what teaching philosophy underpins instruction.

Some authors focused on a few key schools whereas others generalized from massive amounts of data accumulated through organizations such as the Association for Education in Journalism and Mass Communication, the Broadcast Education Association, the National Communication Association, and the Public Relations Society of America. Some of the authors have held office or served on the boards of these groups. Others are junior faculty relatively new to academe. All were selected on the basis of their passion for teaching.

Each chapter is self-contained, and there was no attempt to provide a scientifically sound sample of courses or instructors. In some instances, instructors chose institutions on the basis of size. For example, the first chapter reviews instructors at a variety of small, medium, and large universities. The instructors at most of those schools turned out to be, for the most part, experienced senior people with an average of 20 years in the classroom. Most have a record of achievement as scholar/teachers, with many teaching awards to their credit.

Also included are a number of essays relating mentoring experiences. The addition of the "Remembering a Mentor" essays was the result of initial discussions with contributing faculty in which *mentor* kept cropping up. Subsequent talks led to a rather large pool of people who were identified as not only having instilled knowledge but exuding a sense of enthusiasm, indeed passion, for teaching. We decided that it would be valuable to relate some of these stories and experiences.

We recognize that we live in an age in which professional athletes and entertainers command much attention, but we felt that it was time to pay tribute to some of the truly dedicated teachers among us. We chose individuals as mentor subjects whose names were consistently cited by others as having helped or inspired them. We sought out individuals who were qualified to comment on their effectiveness by virtue of their personal contact.

This particular exercise proved useful and fascinating. Although the essays are spread throughout the book, if read in tandem, a number of very positive patterns emerge. One of the most positive has been the evolution of the professorate from the standpoint of female leadership and mentoring. We note that women are represented among contributing authors but also more generally as significant mentors and leaders. Such people as Maurine Beasley (University of Maryland), Margaret Blanchard (University of North Carolina at Chapel Hill), Barbara Cloud (University of Nevada at Las Vegas), Bernell Tripp (University of Florida), and Betty Winfield (University of Missouri at Columbia) are influencing a new generation in the field. We are also encouraged that many of these individuals have held major leadership positions in professional organizations.

On the negative side of the ledger there are still comparatively few minority faculty members to serve as mentors for students wishing to enter the field. This leads to a reliance on others for counsel. A recently published interview with the recipient of the award for 2002 Outstanding Journalist of the National Association of Black Journalists reveals some interesting reasons why. In 2000, CBS News' Byron Pitts became the first African-American television correspondent to appear in the national study by the Center for Media and Public Affairs as one of the 10 most visible national network television correspondents. He covered the Elian Gonzalez story and the presidential vote recount in Florida, and was chosen to report on the execution of Oklahoma City bomber, Timothy McVeigh. Today Pitts is best known for having reported from the scene at Ground Zero on 9/11 and then shortly afterward from Afghanistan on the early war effort.

As a young reporter he had few professional role models or mentors, but some of the best advice he ever received came from his college professor at Ohio Wesleyan University, who remains a friend. He had been thinking about leaving his freshman year because of being discouraged by a professor who told him that he just was not college material, not cut out to be successful.

He was about to drop out of school when he met Dr. Ulle Lewes, who became his mentor throughout college. The advice of Dr. Lewes was to never reject an assignment and never let money be a motivation early on in a career. At some point it will be, she said, but not starting out. So for the first 17 years of his professional life, those were driving considerations, conveyed by a mentor.

Occasionally today Pitts plays the role of mentor himself, especially on occasions in which he is encouraged to help recruit people of color to work at CBS News. He gladly participates in that effort, often talking about his own career track and noting that in his first job in television he made $8,500 a year. In his second job in television he says that he made $12,000, adding there aren't a lot of young people, black or white, coming out of school who are willing to make less salary in a year than their parents paid for their college tuition for a year. But he insists that is the kind of commitment it takes.

He also notes that he has met a lot of young people who are more interested in being TV anchors than being reporters or correspondents. This bothers him because, if the institution of journalism does not embrace a person due to their background, the individuals have to work extra hard to make it happen.

On the other hand, according to Pitts, growing up in a poor community can help a reporter to better identify with people, also making him mentally tough and providing a more realistic appraisal of what hard work is and what sacrifice means. He was raised to believe his mother's philosophy: "Whatever doesn't kill you makes you stronger." And in fact, in his view, one of the things that he brings to CBS News as a correspondent is life experience. At any point on early assignments, he automatically assumed that he was one of the dumbest people on the case. But his background and experience also told him that he is one of the hardest workers—and as mentally tough as anybody due to life experience, his mother's strong influence, the things he's seen on the job, and his growing up as a member of a minority in America.

Today Pitts considers Dan Rather his mentor even though he worked in television journalism for 16 years before he met Rather. Pitts first worked at his university newspaper. After graduation he joined the staff of the *Carolinian* and held a part-time job as night editor at the ABC affiliate in Raleigh-Durham.

His first full-time position was at CBS in Greenville, N.C. He left to become a military reporter in Norfolk, Va., followed by an assignments in Orlando, Tampa and Boston, starting as a general assignment reporter and then investigative reporter. Pitts worked in Atlanta and this earned a spot at CBS News, based at bureaus in Miami, Washington, D.C., and New York City.

As a young person growing up in Baltimore he had always been a fan of CBS, and his first job was at a CBS affiliate that valued words and the ability to tell a story effectively. And he employs his own mentor's background as an index of hard work, noting that Dan Rather was the son of parents of modest means from Texas, the reason that he has such a tremendous work ethic. Raised in a household where people worked hard to survive, Pitts regards that as a key ingredient and views his background as an advantage competing against people who had an easier upbringing.

Noting that discrimination and racism are part of America, journalism is part of that mix, and in that sense like every other national corporation and institution. There is no excuse for exclusion, but it cuts both ways. Pitts felt good about his coverage from Afghanistan, and in being a member of a minority from America because he knows what it feels like for people to assume things based on appearance or on where someone thinks that you are from. That is a level of sensitivity and awareness that aids coverage of stories based on challenges and life. So those same kinds of issues that exist outside, exist inside. Minorities are underrepresented in academe but also in national journalism companies and especially in management and new media positions.

We selected Byron Pitts to discuss briefly here because of his recognition as the National Association of Black Journalists' top journalist of the past year, among the most visible correspondents on television. We were invigorated by examples of excellent work we uncovered for this book, such as the program at Trinity College in the nation's capital, discussed in the next chapter. But we recognize how his story plays out in mass communication classrooms across America when there are still few minority role models and mentors to point the way. This is a major oversight, one that must be addressed.

One of the other themes of this book is attention to *new media*. Since a good number of people are moving forward with an agenda to improve the use of integrated Internet material, this makes good sense. In the fall of 2000, Bruce Henderson of the University of Colorado at Boulder, then chair of the Teaching section of the Association for Education in Journalism and Mass Communication's Communication Theory Division, encouraged instructors and schools to move toward reconceptualizing and reorganizing coursework rather than continuing with a traditional media-specific curriculum.

This was part of a series of recommendations, including the need for updating technology infrastructure and content specialization rather than narrow concentrations. The recommendations were controversial because some journalism and mass communication schools have been wedded to separate sequences for many years, whereas many practitioners argue that this is no longer reflective of the way they work.

The Freedom Forum's Adam Clayton Powell III also issued a white paper at the 2000 AEJMC convention in Phoenix in which he argued for a convergence of pedagogy and practice, a movement toward integrated models away from the curriculum sequencing. At the same time, this movement raised some eyebrows because of arguments to integrate new media into all courses rather than segregating material in a few courses. A separate chapter on *convergence* addresses many of the questions these issues raise and provides examples of what some schools are doing.

As veteran educators we understand the culture of higher education in America. We know for example, that when many professors gather at professional meetings they are still more likely to discuss research, even office politics, than approaches to teaching. But the Internet and technological innovations have opened doors. The overall consideration of what we do and how we do it invites scrutiny at good schools today.

This book surveys approaches while acknowledging the central role new media will play in future media education. It is in no way a definitive account of educational excellence, merely a series of snapshots. It reports where some of us are now. It provides diverse illustrations that we hope will offer insight and encourage mentors for the next generation.

References

Christ, W. G., ed. 1997. *Media education assessment handbook.* Hillsdale, N.J.: Lawrence Erlbaum.

"College enrollments projected to rise 15% by 2012 Washington." 2002. *Chronicle of Higher Education,* 22 August. "Projections of education statistics to 2012."

Dickson, T. 2000. *Mass media education in transition: Preparing for the 21st century.* Hillsdale, N.Y.: Lawrence Erlbaum, 76.

Henderson, B. 2000. Media-specific JMC curriculum needs to be redesigned. *CT&P News* 3:4. www.newmedia.colorado.edu/aejmc.

Hickson III, M., D. Stacks, and J. Boden. 1999. The status of research productivity in communication, 1915–1995. *Communication Monographs* 66, no. 2 (June):178.

How to Ace College. 2001. *Newsweek*, 11 June, 62.

Jenkins, C. 2002. Tough Assignment. *Carolina Alumni Review*, May/June, 30–41.

Light, R. J. 2001. *Making the most of college: Students speak their minds.* Cambridge: Harvard University Press.

Murray, M. D., and A. J. Ferri, eds. 1992. *Teaching mass communication.* New York: Praeger.

National Communication Association. 1996. Speaking, listening, and media literacy standards for k through 12 education [On-line], June. www.natcom.org.

Nyquist, J. D., and D. H. Wulff. 1996. *Working effectively with graduate assistants.* Thousand Oaks, Calif.: Sage.

Remembering a Mentor:
Walter J. Ong, S.J.

Frank E. X. Dance

Memory has fallen on hard times. Most of us are not particularly anxious to exercise our own memories rigorously or to require memorization by others. This exercise, to remember my interaction with Walter (Jackson) Ong, S.J. (Society of Jesus), has proven a welcome occasion to recall, to relive, and to remember.

I first encountered Father Ong through his writings. In 1968 I read *The Presence of the Word* (1967) and experienced the thrill of a resonance of thought and approach to a subject with the book's author. It was for me an exciting book. By this time in my career I had decided on the question that was to guide research and writing throughout my professional life: "What difference does it make to the human condition that human beings speak?" The centrality of the spoken word was not a research focus much supported within the professional discipline. Ong's writings induced in me a feeling of intellectual kinship. Knowing that there were others, such as Ong, who shared a belief in the importance of the spoken word provided incentive and support to pursue studies on that subject.

Having found this kindred spirit I started to read Ong's other writings. I say "started" because, when I discovered the number of publications, I focused on his book-length works. For those wishing an encounter with authors who have read everything Ong has written, I suggest they turn to the writings of Professor Thomas J. Farrell and those of Professor Randolph F. Lumpp.

During the mid-1970s I put together a series of guest lectures hosted by my department at the University of Denver. I went for the best scholars I could attract and, since I had a minimal budget, relied on excessive flattery and shameless wheedling. The fact that so many of those invited came is a testimony to their professional commitment. I got Father Ong's phone number from his Jesuit brothers at Denver's Regis University and gave him a call. He was interested in the subject matter and the opportunity of revisiting the Denver Regis Jesuit community and accepted the invitation.

I met Walter in person for the first time when he arrived for the lecture series in May of 1976. Father Ong is a compact gentleman of average height. He gives the impression of frailty, but it is only an impression. Born in 1912, in his youth he was an Eagle Scout and as a youngster actively participated in all the sports typical of a boy's life in the middle America Kansas City, Missouri, of the 1930s. What I found distinctive was his habit of wearing clerical garb, including a Roman collar, clerical vest and black

13

suit on all occasions when he was in public. By 1976 in the history of the American Roman Catholic Church many priests, when not officiating as a priest, felt comfortable wearing relaxed civilian clothes—not so Father Ong.

Father Ong's lecture was given on May 3, 1976. Prior to the evening lecture he came to my home for dinner. My wife, Carol Zak-Dance, and I prepared a meal of Korean steaks and spent a wonderful hour chatting with him. He was an amiable conversationalist demonstrating a mind fully stocked, a wit accessible and fertile, and a warm respect for others. At the end of the meal he asked, "Is there somewhere in the house I could go to pray and meditate before my lecture?" Both Carol and I were taken aback by the question. Really, how often does a dinner guest make such a request? However we faked urbanity, calm, and sophistication and ushered Father Ong into the family room where he sequestered himself for about 45 minutes. His ensuing lecture, which demonstrated his typical thoughtfulness and incisiveness, was well received by an audience of faculty and students.

It was also in 1976 that I first started thinking, researching and writing about a possible acoustic trigger to conceptualization. Bill Work, then executive secretary of the Speech Communication Association (now the National Communication Association) asked that I represent the SCA at the 1977 meeting of American Association for the Advancement of Science. Dr. Work asked that I put together a program jointly sponsored by the AAAS and the SCA. This was the era of great popular and professional interest in the topic of signing apes, so I generated a program entitled "The Acoustic Mode: Man versus Ape."

The program speakers included Father Ong, Dr. Philip Lieberman, the renowned scholar from Brown University, Ralph Thompson, who was studying neologisms and cognition, and me. It took place February 16, 1978, in Washington, D.C. I think I went first with my acoustic trigger hypothesis, and then Father Ong, drawing upon years of study and writing, gave a talk emphasizing the importance of voice, sound and speech/spoken language. There were those in the audience of scholars who were so offended by the emphasis on sound and speech, which they seem to have interpreted as diminishing the value and importance of those who were hearing challenged, that they walked out in the middle. Father Ong's calm prevailed, and the very satisfying program continued.

In the 1980s and 1990s I kept in touch with Father Ong. He made a number of trips back to Denver. On one occasion he was speaking at Regis University, and I attended the presentation where he demonstrated once again the profundity of his conceptual skills. After the talk we spent some time together in conversation during which Father Ong touched on his concern with the "I" inside each one of us. Who exactly is that "I" and in what voice does that "I" speak? Self-reflection is an aspect of spirituality fostered by meditation. This is a theme to which he returns from time to time in his own writings. His 1986 book *Hopkins, the Self, and God* allows him to contemplate the "I" question, as Gerard Manly Hopkins also considers the identical theme.

In the early 1990s (1992, I think) I was teaching a graduate course on the speech theory of human communication and arranged for a telephone hookup that allowed Father Ong not only to talk to the class but with the class, including a question-and-answer discussion. The students had a ball, and the telephone lecture/discussion provided content for hours of conversation and reflection.

Ong's work has given me ideas and materials from which I have developed published essays, course orientations, convention presentations and a state of mind. It has also encouraged a spirit rooted in a belief in the centrality of the spoken word and the pre-eminence of speech, though not a medium, as primordial root of media. It is gratifying to see how Father Ong's scholarly works and presence have grown and continue to prosper within the academic community.

Since the mid-1990s I have had very few occasions to interact directly with Walter J. Ong, S.J., but I have continued to read his works, to apply his thoughts to my work and the subject matter that I teach, to use his books as texts, and to track his personal well-being. In addition to my role as John Evans Professor of Human Communication Studies I also teach a course in the Digital Media Studies program at the University of Denver. The DMS course, Digital Noesis, is in its evolution heavily dependent upon Ong's work on oral noetics. One of the required readings is Ong's *Orality and Literacy* (1982), a book treating in condensed manner some conceptual contributions. I love the book, and the students, though considering it a tough read, find it engaging and worthwhile. Each year when I teach the course I re-encounter Ong the scholar and Walter the friend. Each year when I read the book I find myself returning to others of his writings. Each year I find Father Ong restocking my imagination and reinvigorating my quest. Given the rhetorical purity of Ong's roots it is interesting to find how his work has exfoliated to popularity within the growing membership of the Media Ecology Association.

In June 2002, on a long air flight from Taipei to San Francisco, I took the opportunity of spending my time reading Ong's *Ramus, Method, and the Decay of Dialogue: From the Art of Discourse to the Art of Reason*, a book based on his 1955 doctoral dissertation at Harvard. This is a study characterized by painstaking research. Ong leaves no tempting path untrod. If a question is raised by circumstance in Peter Ramus' life or writing, Ong researches and answers or clarifies the question without consideration for time and energy. This is literary, historical and conceptual scholarship of the highest order.

Over the years of our acquaintance I became cognizant and appreciative of the degree to which Father Ong was not just a scholar but also a priest scholar. For Walter J. Ong, the initials S.J. (Society of Jesus, or Jesuits) that followed his family name were as much a part of personal identity as the rest of his name. He didn't seem to be just a scholar but a priest-scholar, a person whose scholarship is always viewed through his priestly character.

Mentor, a friend designated by Ulysses to counsel Ulysses' son Telemachus in Ulysses' absence, was a man and a warrior. In the *Odyssey* (Chapter 2) we learn that on occasion the goddess Athena/Minerva would take over the body of Mentor to give her own brand of wisdom to Telemachus. I don't think of Athena/Minerva as a mentor, a giver of counsel to Telemachus, but more of a Muse, source of inspiration rather than counsel. In mythology Muses were daughters of Zeus and Mnemosyne (memory). At the start of this remembrance I alluded to memory. We know that arts and sciences all depend on memory, their mother.

I went to Brooklyn Preparatory, a Jesuit High School, and from there to Fordham, a Jesuit University. In my Jesuit education both models and memory were very important.

There were occasions when we had to write an essay modeled after an author such as Cicero or memorize passages from Latin authors such as Caesar. Three of my sons have attended Regis Jesuit High School in Denver, and it has been through their Jesuit teachers that I have been able to track the path taken by Walter Ong in the Jesuit Community at St. Louis University. The Jesuits have a mystique.

The Jesuit educational tradition follows a 16th-century template called the *ratio studiorum* or schedule of studies. Included in that schedule is a commitment to *eloquentia perfecta* or the perfect use of spoken language. Father Ong was shaped by the *ratio studiorum*. The Jesuit tradition embodied in individuals has in a real manner served to give me lifelong counsel, to be my mentor. Ong's life has been one of dedication, one of following the discipline of his religious order and the discipline of his subject matter. To me the greatest gift of my Jesuit education is self-discipline, and it is in the fulfillment of self-discipline that Father Ong serves as my guide.

I am gratified to know Father Ong and honored to be among his disciplinary friends. His has been an exemplary scholarly life. His interests are universal and his reading all-embracing. His choice of subject matter includes the drum language of Africa and the scholastic meditations of Peter Ramus. On his quest for a total grasp of his chosen subject he does not give up. I can readily conceive of Minerva/Athena encouraging Walter with the Alfred Lord Tennyson words of Ulysses "To strive, to seek, to find, and not to yield." Father Ong has fulfilled each of these exhortations.

Reflecting on my long acquaintance with Walter J. Ong, S.J., I believe that rather than mentor Father Ong has served as model, inspiration, my Muse.

CHAPTER 2

Introduction to Mass Communication

Michael D. Murray

Introduction

In terms of mass communication coursework, one of the most consistent themes in examining successful introductory offerings is that the attitude of the instructor respects the importance of this course and its role in the curriculum. Of the half-dozen instructors surveyed for this chapter, all insisted on the role of the introductory course in helping students understand the parameters of the field and in getting them off to the proper start. For some this beginning included obligatory emphasis on business influences whereas others maintain that a lack of focus on ethics has resulted in the decline of media institutions.

For both of these reasons, some of the instructors take the position that they not only value the assignment, they virtually insist on it. Because of the position at the very start of a student's exposure to the field, they view themselves as the last line of defense against falling standards. They also realize that if students are deficient or have inflated expectation, the course instructor is a clear culprit or at least identified as a part of the problem.

The instructors selected for this informal survey are all experienced people. Those interviewed include senior faculty from some of the nation's largest schools, such as Donald Godfrey of the Walter Cronkite School of Journalism and Mass Communication at Arizona State University and Dr. Anthony Ferri of the Greenspun School at the University of Nevada at Las Vegas.

Also sought were representative faculty from departments located in the midrange in terms of size and within the typical context of Colleges of Arts and Sciences, such as Dr. John Ferré at the University of Louisville and Dr. Matt McAllister of Virginia Tech. Although the selection process was unscientific, an attempt was also made to achieve some kind of variance, to get senior people who hold administrative responsibilities as well as a few slightly less seasoned representatives, of a decade or more. Some are also known for work overseeing teaching assistants.

To those ends Dr. Douglas Ferguson of the College of Charleston, an experienced department chair who takes personal responsibility for this course, was interviewed. In addition, Dr. Elizabeth Perse of the University of Delaware, Dr. Raul Tovares of Trinity College, and Dr. David Domke of the University of Washington also discussed their courses.

Dr. Perse has taught the course for some time and chairs her department at Delaware. Dr. Tovares has been able to teach a relatively modest enrollment, 15 to 25 students per section of the course for the past two years at his school in Washington, D.C. Prior to that he taught for four years at the University of North Dakota, where the course ranged from 25 to 45 students. He also teaches news writing and serves as advisor to the school newspaper.

Dr. Domke oversees a large lecture course with multiple discussion sections and with as many as 500 students. He was recently recognized as the recipient of the distinguished teaching award for 2002 at the University of Washington in Seattle.

Position of the Course in the Curriculum

The Introduction to Mass Communication course typically serves as a gateway or overview, and a window to the field. At some institutions it is also regarded as a barrier course, that is, an obstacle for students, a means to ensure basic competency and minimal understanding. In this course students start to gain habits, good and bad, that remain for college and often careers.

One of the most consistent observations in surveying introductory courses is that enrollment can be quite large, even at relatively small schools, except in those special instances in which the course is limited by being offered through multiple sections or divided into discussion sections. A large lecture section of the course with one instructor tends to be the norm.

Because it is an upper-level, 300-level course status, at the University of Louisville, for example, it provides a rigorous introduction, communicating that this is a very serious-minded approach, one in which students have to work hard to do well. Only 100-level and 200-level courses can be used to fulfill General Education requirements at Louisville.

At the College of Charleston, the instructor, Doug Ferguson, taught previously at Bowling Green State University, where the class could enroll 200 students. The Communication program at Trinity College currently has 80 majors, drawn from the over 1,500 students enrolled at that private, Catholic institution for women in Washington, D.C. Communication 265 is required of all majors, as is public speaking and also writing. Nearly half of all students at Trinity are minorities, and a large number of them attend weekend classes. The orientation dovetails nicely with Tovares' research concerning how local television news covers minority issues.

His doctorate at the University of Texas at Austin included attention to these areas from his own graduate instructors, along with attention to ethnicity in media and mediated stereotypes. Tovares also completed a Radio-TV News' Directors Foundation

Fellowship focusing on local television with his book on that topic, *Manufacturing the Gang: Mexican American Youth Gangs on Local Television News* (Westport, Conn.: Greenwood, 2002).

Many of the students who attend Trinity College also work while they pursue their degrees, and a good number have traditionally been employed with government agencies. These positions sometimes provide opportunities to share experiences and insight gleaned from work in the nation's capital.

The course Communication 245 at the University of Delaware is offered in a traditional format with as many as 350 students. That department has nearly 600 majors. The course is targeted to fulfill the General Education requirement for many units, thus inviting even more interest for potential majors.

Dr. Elizabeth Perse has also taught it as one of a few courses required of majors, also an honors course with emphasis on in-class discussion and as a distance learning option. Dr. Perse has a background including both a doctorate from Kent State University and experience as a newspaper correspondent.

Communication majors at the University of Delaware have two areas of concentration—Interpersonal and Mass Communication—with 75 percent of students currently occupying the latter area. Journalism courses at Delaware are offered through the Department of English.

Students at the University of Nevada at Las Vegas are required to take two of three core courses, of which Introduction to Mass Communication is one. Anthony Ferri has been teaching this course for 17 years at UNLV and, before that, taught it for three years as a grad student at Wayne State University. Ferri has taught the course as a large lecture section with 50 to 120 students. For the first time recently it is also being taught over the Web, with an enrollment of nearly 140. It usually attracts less than a quarter from outside of the department. That curriculum takes a sequential approach, with broadcasting and public relations attracting a great deal of interest.

In enrollment a specialty in Corporate Communication currently attracts the largest number of students with Telecommunications and Human Communication following behind. Graduate teaching assistants (TAs) at UNLV are usually assigned to teach primarily Public Speaking or courses in TV Production.

The course instructor at Arizona State University, Dr. Don Godfrey, is also a very well known senior person in the field. A contributor to this book, he is the author or editor of a number of other works, including a biography of TV inventor, *Philo T. Farnsworth: Father of Television* (Salt Lake City: University of Utah Press, 2001). Dr. Godfrey appreciates that students who take this class at his school are mostly freshmen. As with some others he notes that, as a consequence, many of his students enter the course with a clean slate. In his role as course instructor he has the responsibility to explain realities and opportunities.

Another contributing instructor, John Ferré, has taught Introduction to Mass Communication since fall of 1985, when he joined the faculty of the University of Louisville. He has taught it every semester since being at that school, except occasions when he has been on academic leave. Because courses can become somewhat repetitious, the assumption is that some instructors dislike the year-in and year-out assignment of a basic course, but for Ferré there is no class that he enjoys teaching more.

Ferré looks forward to the course every semester, even though he tries to keep the numbers within reason to get to know students better. He notes that some students put it off until late in their program because it has a reputation for being information intensive and somewhat challenging.

In terms of class size, Ferré has systematically worked to decrease the class from over 100 students to a more workable number. As of the fall term 2002, the class stood at 60 students. It is a requirement for all majors at his school as well as for students who minor in a department of 475 majors.

Even the most junior professors of those seven surveyed for this chapter have taught the course for over a decade. Dr. David Domke of Washington taught previously at the University of Minnesota, where he completed his doctorate. He previously worked as a reporter for major newspapers. He stresses the importance of highlighting media influence in our culture and integrating research into the course.

The introductory mass media course at the University of Washington is large. It averages 450 students but can be as large as 550. It uses four to six TAs each term. Domke uses his background as a journalist to emphasize the importance of issues from his time in the field as well as relating issues to his scholarly work.

At Washington, the introductory course is both an elective for outsiders and a course for majors. A third of the students are usually interested in communication as a major, while another third have some interest and consider it as a potential major. The remaining third has a general interest in the course.

The department at the University of Washington offers a broad range of communications courses and a general major and is in transition from having held separate status as a School of Communication. Although they do offer a sequence in journalism, they do not offer specialized or advanced coursework in advertising and public relations per se, even though many students seem to have some career goals in mind through which they hope to produce messages in some format. A good number of students are also currently pursuing interests in International Communication.

Similar Courses

Many schools offer introductory courses in the various subfields whereas some rely on the Introduction to Mass Communication and break off into skills, theoretical and advanced courses. The context of this course at UNLV occurs through what the course instructor terms artificial bifurcation of Old and New Media.

That comparison appeals to those students totally absorbed with the mass media of the day in order to gain a better understanding and appreciation for what may have come before. The instructor for this course also encourages students to examine academic journals and, like others in this particular grouping, will also occasionally refer them to things that he has written. This stimulates interest and gives the students insight into what professors do outside of the classroom.

Ancillary/Related Courses

Closely related to the Introduction to Mass Communication are introductory classes in electronic media, advertising, public relations and film. Depending on the size of the institution, enrollments can be large, especially with schools accredited by the Association for Education in Journalism and Mass Communication (AEJMC), generally offering students a broader mix of courses in both theory and practice.

The larger schools can also accommodate additional courses with the support of more developed faculty resources. At Virginia Tech, beyond the Introduction to Mass Communication course, Matt McAllister teaches both a large lecture Introduction to Communication Studies course in which many areas are broached, but also oversees a course oriented more toward media institutions, in which more in-depth information can be covered. In those instances he tries to elicit written material and reaction papers as a means of stimulating interest.

Also playing into the mix is the status of courses as they fall within the parameters of fulfilling requirements. Doug Ferguson of the College of Charleston points out that there is often a feeling about a course that a student is required to take, that is, they may not want to embrace it quite as much.

As a result the instructor has to work a little harder to ensure that students understand the importance of covering all areas. Raul Tovares points to the fact that students seldom have a clear view of what they might want to do when they graduate, and the role of this course is to consistently provide a broad overview. Dr. Tovares takes advantage of his school's location in Washington, D.C., to take students on field trips to the Newseum, National Press Club, and Museum of American History. These opportunities help students to connect and keep current.

Comparative Features

Comparisons of approaches are often reflected in the textbook the instructor selects. A variety of books have been used by virtually all of those surveyed, and most expressed the view that while such books provide some structure and a topical outline of content, a textbook can also sometimes be a secondary consideration. They are always testing the effectiveness of books through off-and-on adoption and are not tied to a single book or a singular approach.

The typical rundown for a basic text includes a philosophical overview and information about media theory, a comparison of basic forms of media, and their history broken down by specialty. Most of the basic texts have a section concerning regulation and relation of the press to government, feedback mechanisms, and audience measurement, as well as attention to media effects research, media ethics, and convergence issues.

Some of the books in use, such as Ron Farrar's *Mass Communication: An Introduction* (St. Paul: West, 1998) include an extensive international section and glossary. It is not uncommon for a basic text to address career opportunities, education and professional development, but Farrar, the Reynolds-Faunt Professor at the University of South Carolina, also includes a section on Minorities and Media and Religious Media.

For the current textbook at Arizona State University, Don Godfrey, textbook author himself, has used the third edition of *Media Now: Communications Media in the Information Age* (Belmont, Calif.: Wadsworth-Thomson Learning, 2002), by Joseph D. Straubhaar and Robert Larose, known for its emphasis on telecommunications and interactive media. Online resources support new texts. In this case a learning tool entitled

WebTutor is offered. Access to the book's course center is at Wadsworth Communication Café with related material at http://communication.wadsworth.com/media_now.

Douglas Ferguson, author with Susan Tyler Eastman of *Broadcast/Cable/Web Programming*, now in a sixth edition (Belmont, Calif.: Wadsworth-Thomson Learning, 2002), has used two, one by Joseph R. Dominick, *The Dynamics of Mass Communication: Media in the Digital Age*, 7th edition (New York: McGraw-Hill, 2002), and one mentioned in the preceding paragraph, by Straubhaar and LaRose.

Dr. Raul Tovares also uses this text but frequently supplements it with some readings from trade publications such as *Broadcasting and Cable* as well as the work of broadcast historian Erik Barnouw. Also popular for its treatment of history, as well as women and minorities, is Shirley Biagi's *Media/Impact: An Introduction to Mass Media* (Belmont, Calif.: Wadsworth-Thomson Learning, 2003), now in its sixth edition. The Biagi text has been published in Canadian, Greek, Spanish and Chinese editions and includes a student CD-ROM with interactive outlines, key term quizzes and time lines.

In terms of organization, the course breakdown at the University of Washington is also fairly straightforward and consistent with the text, although the course instructor does not view the book as being the centerpiece of the course. Both Drs. Perse at the University of Delaware and Domke at the University of Washington have used the book by John Vivian, *The Media of Mass Communication*, 6th edition (Boston: Allyn and Bacon, 2002), known for its attention to cultural issues, mainstream and popular influences.

Other major texts in this area include Richard Campbell's *Media and Culture: An Introduction to Mass Communication*, 3rd edition (Boston: Bedford/St. Martin's, 2002), and Stanley Baran's *Introduction to Mass Communication: Media Literacy and Culture*, 2nd edition (Boston: McGraw-Hill, 2002). Besides the Vivian text, Domke has adopted other books, including the one by Melvin DeFleur, Everette Dennis, and Margaret Hanus, *Understanding Mass Communication*, 7th edition (Boston: Houghton Mifflin, 2002); and Dr. Perse has used the book by George Rodman, *Mass Media Issues: Analysis and Debate*, 4th edition (Dubuque, Iowa: Kendall/Hunt, 1993). Dr. Domke has also reviewed a number of basic textbooks and has considered Joseph Dominick's book as well as outside readings he has collected himself.

For a four- or five-year period, Tony Ferri has used a basic text by Jean Folkerts and Stephen Lacy, *Media in Your Life: An Introduction to Mass Communication*, 2nd edition (Boston: Allyn and Bacon, 2001). Ferri points out that this was one of the first basic texts in the field to go into some depth on *convergence*, which he views as critically important.

Dr. Ferguson currently uses the Dominick text because he has become very comfortable with it and notes that it follows the general format that he employs for the course. The course is structured in a traditional way: print, broadcast, advertising, public relations and film. He has also used the Straubhaar and LaRose book and is favorably disposed to these alternatives.

Preliminary to the overview, Godfrey includes publications: Radio-TV News Director's *Communicator* and weeklies *Broadcast & Cable* and *Editor & Publisher*. The Louisville course director also feels that it is important to introduce engaging material at the outset. As soon as he gets basic information passed out, he immediately moves into the work of Walter Lippmann. It sets a tone for the course and its content, to reinforce the idea that the topic is interesting but also important.

The reading list for Ferré's course is somewhat unique. He does not employ the use of a basic text but has a sequentially arranged reading list that examines the way journalism and journalists function in our society. In 2002 the course readings began with Barry Glassner's *Culture of Fear* (New York: Basic, 1999). This book forms something of an orientation to topics that will help students to understand research and other earlier work by people such as major mass communication scholars like George Gerbner.

Ferré's approach is to address topics specifically and topically, following Lippmann's writings about "the world outside and the pictures in our head." He challenges students to evaluate how their perspective is formed and altered by intense media coverage. In the same way the second major book on the list, *Committing Journalism: The Prison Writings of Red Hog*, by Dannie M. Martin and Peter Y. Sussman (New York: W. W. Norton, 1995), is one of Ferré's all-time favorite works about journalism. It is a First Amendment project concerning a federal prisoner who tries to rehabilitate himself by writing about what is going on around him.

As the story is told, this sometimes gets the incarcerated author into trouble because he starts sharing details about the warden of the prison in which he is situated. Of course, he gets soundly punished for doing that. So this represents an interesting and somewhat complex test case of the extent to which we should have freedom of expression in the country and for whom should this liberty be extended? Should a person who has committed a felony lose First Amendment rights in the same way that he or she would lose Second Amendment rights?

These are issues raised in this section of Ferré's course. To what extent is expression a fundamental human right and to what extent is it a by-product of living in a democracy in which freedom of expression is so valued? As a result of this particular reading, Ferré says, the class regularly gets into a good discussion of related issues. It is highly readable book, and the instructor's favorite testimony is that some students have regularly bought copies to give to friends and relatives.

The last book used in the Louisville course, *Deliberate Intent: A Lawyer Tells the True Story of Murder by the Book* (New York: Crown, 1999), was authored by Rod Smolla and is also on the libertarian theme. Smolla, a First Amendment attorney and law professor, joined a suit against Paladin Press, the publisher of *Hit Man: A Technical Manual for Independent Contractors* (Boulder, Colo., 1983), a step-by-step guide to assassination that was used in a grizzly triple murder. Analysis of Smolla's book again raises a basic question: How much do we really believe in the principles of the First Amendment? Should we permit the publication of a book that describes how to murder someone? The challenge of answering that question involves the publication of *Hit Man*. Again, the question Rod Smolla explores in his examination of that case is whether a book of that kind should be permitted since it was ultimately used as a training manual in a grizzly murder case. The lawsuit ended in 1999, when Paladin Press settled for a reported $5 million and the promise to cease distribution of *Hit Man*.

According to Ferré students usually agree that a line needs to be drawn somewhere regarding dangerous books. If someone commits a murder because of a book like *Hit Man*, is it a good idea to let the book be published? But, complicating things further, Ferré points out that *Hit Man* is now available over the Internet. This fact leads to a discussion of the phenomenon of free access by all to material available on the net.

The broader question the reading of this book raises is the relationship between the material and its direct influence. Given a careful reading, students tend to speculate on whether, as the availability of this material somehow increased, how it might have affected the murder rate. And since, as is often reported, the murder rate has actually gone down recently, how can the book's negative influence or consequences be interpreted as a result? There may in fact be no relation to this particular book, but it raises questions about the influence of the media and issues of access to information.

The criminal acts would probably have been committed whether or not the book was there, but again it lends itself to discussion. Ferré tries to have the students encounter material that makes them re-evaluate positions they have held and uses the last major reading, *The Victorian Internet: The Remarkable Story of the Telegraph and the Nineteenth Centuries On-line Pioneers*, by Tom Standage (New York: Walker and Co., 1998), as part of a developing section on new communication technologies. It argues that the telegraph functioned in much the same way in 19th-century society as the Internet does today.

Special Features

Along the same lines, Ferguson has recently returned to an emphasis on individual, in-class presentations, as a forum for requiring students to offer ideas on a subject. As a result, each student is required to give a presentation to the class, and recently this usually takes the form of a book report. Each student must present in summary form a five-minute overview of the content of a book but also explain her or his reasons for accepting or rejecting the import of what is covered.

Classes at the College of Charleston usually include 30 or 40 students, with all but a few being majors. Doug Ferguson deposits things in their mailboxes daily and uses a Web site at Boston University. In terms of support material, he regularly uses the summary of news from daily newspapers compiled and provided over the Web by Dean Brent Baker at Boston University at http://www.bu.edu/com/html/comnewstoday/html.

Dean Baker oversees the page and sees that stories are summarized regularly. It always ties in to a mass communication class. Ferguson taps the distillation of stories that can be shared with students. He tests by using unannounced quizzes about the world today. There is always something valuable in the news worth testing over regarding the Internet, privacy issues, or general media-related topics. He has also established a page of newspaper links that students consult and provides students with a study guide.

Dr. Perse has collected supplementary readings that are offered to students as a support tool to whatever basic texts are being used by her department. It is not unusual for the department to be using more than one. She has also published some books about the Internet that serve as reference works, including a student guide and *Communicat-*

ing Online (Mountain View, Calif.: Mayfield, 1998), both published with Delaware colleague, John Courtright.

Because of its location, students at Trinity College pay special attention to government regulation, and the instructor, Dr. Tovares, suggests that this is due to the coverage that particular news beat tends to receive in Washington, D.C.

Common Goals and Objectives

The course at Arizona State University begins with an emphasis, also as one might expect, with attention to theoretical considerations under the general heading of Human Communication and the Media, but by the end of the first week students are introduced as well to a media economic model. Week 2 addresses the media functions, including the role of government and the importance of news, with attention to writing.

The logical progression of emphasis, treating print (books, magazine and newspapers), film, music, broadcast media, cable, advertising, and public relations is followed. Each section has the expected historical background but includes an explanation of how this particular aspect functions, including business precedents and partnerships. The course also provides special attention to business concerns with issues like syndication, convergence, and research, as well as global media perspectives.

Doug Ferguson tries to use the Socratic method of getting students to contribute to the class, as a means of getting over what some students view as a social stigma of talking in class to get them to participate. He might challenge them, for example, with an outrageous statement to provoke thought and interaction—the kind of thing, he says, that a talk-radio host might do—to stimulate thought and reaction.

This assignment is evaluated on a written outline students must provide, as well as the content, and careful, thoughtful analysis of the value of the book. The style of the presentation to the class is also a factor. Less emphasis is placed on content than on student evaluation of the book itself. He wants them to take ownership of their ideas and make a statement about how they feel about the significance of a book related to the field. His background is in television, and his research in interactive TV is a thread of interest permeating this class.

Dr. Tovares tries to emphasize the role of alternative media in letting students know about its special importance as a potential source of information for the mainstream press. He also likes to reinforce cultural influences from the media that have become even more pronounced since the 9/11 attack.

Instructor Philosophy

The Walter Cronkite School of Journalism and Mass Communication at Arizona State University has more than 1,300 undergraduate majors and over 70 graduate students. This large-section course, including an emphasis for majors, takes a very realistic business-oriented/industry versus purely ivory-tower approach. It is designed especially for those students who think that they may want to pursue a career in the field.

Many students in the course at ASU say that they intend to pursue a career in broadcasting, and the school has a reputation for excellence in that field. These expressions of interest are closely followed by advertising/public relations and print as areas of possible professional pursuits. The testing approach is straightforward. Four tests are given. Students can gain extra credit on the final examination by memorizing the First Amendment and writing it out verbatim.

David Domke's approach at the University of Washington is to try to identify a concept and then illustrate it rather than showing the class something and then discussing it after the fact. He has found that students are much less interested in learning about the professional details of journalism practice. He tries to provide the bigger picture, to look at context, cultural trends and norms, then evaluate underlying motivation.

At the University of Delaware students have a four-course requirement overall that they must complete with a 2.75 grade-point average in those courses for admittance to the major. This introductory course is one of those four. So Elizabeth Perse tries to stay consistent in her approach, highlighting certain things while providing a good general overview. She credits the university culture at Delaware that allows for independence in organizing and structuring her course.

In the post-9/11 media culture, Tovares asks his students where they were when the World Trade Center was attacked, how they received that information, and what they now recall. He is also able to take advantage of the fact that many of his students are minorities. Although his course is smaller than some others it is not unusual for him to have a representation of Muslim students and some from foreign cultures in his classes.

He has relied on these students for special insights in terms of media coverage and cultural bias. He also tries to integrate current cultural examples. If a cell phone goes off in class, he is likely to point out how the pervasiveness of their use is very recent and how they are blurring the lines between public and private communication.

The Introduction to Communication Studies course at Virginia Tech enrolls in the hundreds of students, often as many as 500, with most in the fall-term section made up of majors and minors. Dr. Matt McAllister, who joined the Tech faculty in 1991, takes the position that the larger the class is, the greater the need is for the instructor to be well organized and enthusiastic. This applies to all facets, he says, in terms of giving students direction, helping them to learn.

At the College of Charleston, with as many as 980 majors (as of May 1, 2002), traditionally as many as half express an interest in advertising or public relations. When Doug Ferguson taught previously at Bowling Green State University, broadcasting was the most popular area of student interest, and that school had a reputation for excellence in that specialty. At the University of Delaware, a good number of students used to stress entertainment elements of broadcasting. Elizabeth Perse expects that this might change with a developing emphasis in broadcast news. Ferguson also faced the challenge of reinforcing the importance of good writing in the pre-Internet days.

At the University of Louisville, the more textbookish material is given in class in the form of lecture notes. So in the same way that a literature professor teaching about Shakespeare would expect students to read the works with the professor providing the background, that is the approach of this course. This professor has students read material about the relevant topics such as the First Amendment or the Internet outside of class and come to class prepared to discuss it.

He provides background material in lectures on such areas as libel or the topic of the day. According to Ferré, areas of student interest have varied. If a student in the course had been selected at random 10 years ago, the student would probably have selected advertising or public relations as a central interest.

Today students at the University of Louisville are more likely to be interested in broadcasting, even though there have been scarce offerings in that area. An extensive internship program exists, however, and after graduation some students find positions working in broadcast news as a result of this activity.

Ferré developed his curricular philosophy when first given the assignment at the University of Louisville, and he views it as something of a first course in media literacy. He wants students to have a critical understanding of the place of the media in society and, to a lesser extent, its role in world culture. The idea is that the better students understand the media, the better they will grasp the world around them.

The introductory course is especially rigorous at University of Louisville because there is a lot of lecture material and Ferré expects encyclopedic knowledge from students. Tests are a mix of identification and essay. He has never given true/false or multiple-choice questions because he wants to be confident that students know material very well and are not merely guessing. His easiest question usually consists of requiring students to write out the First Amendment to the Constitution verbatim.

His philosophy on retention of information from class is that if it is said as part of a lecture, then students are responsible for the material. A standard-issue reading list of four books provides background for discussion. Ferré points out that in the course of any term he is likely to get to know six to eight students very well, and these are individuals who will tend to drop by his office for counsel and to discuss issues involving the media. He may become well acquainted with as many as 25 students before the end of the term. On the first day Ferré encourages participation but points to demands.

Common Emphasis

Ferguson also insists that students enrolled in this course e-mail him the first day of class. He will not e-mail study guides, however, because he wants his students to use the library site. He also mails them quiz items via the net and sends them many things just to think about. In addition to quiz items, they also join a Listserve Internet group to see how those work. Although he admits that has not been done as much as he would like.

He says that these days he will usually get to know well as many as five to seven students. As to tests, he gives multiple-choice and true/false questions, many of which are derived from the teacher's manual, but he will also add some lecture material and an occasional current-event item. He also offers his students the option of taking short-answer essay tests as a means of addressing the needs of those who might have difficulty memorizing material in a so-called objective format. Few students pursue this option, but it offers some variety.

In such cases, students get the same essential material, with the same stem for each question, an approach that helps some students achieve partial credit. Again, a relatively small number of students elect to take this option. Ferguson points out that requests for that form of test usually appear with some remorse after the initial tests are complete in the sense that "hope springs eternal." There is not a significant difference in the tests. Only a handful of students pursue the option.

By the same token, Anthony Ferri of UNLV encourages attendance by giving students one test question during each lecture. These questions do not appear on the class Web site www.nevada.edu/~drums. By offering questions, he can sometimes gauge the effectiveness of teaching. This helps him to focus on important concepts that may be harder for students to grasp.

Ferri's philosophy is to teach students how the media manipulate time and space and to create an environment that engages students. He regards those as the two most important elements of what media mean in our lives today. To deliver this message he has to find ways to make the content challenging and interesting. If you are going to teach well you have to excite people. He dislikes the straight lecture format because it belies what we know about our students, so he tries to integrate outside resources whenever possible.

In this respect, Ferri was influenced by Marshall McLuhan and, in fact, was able to have limited contact with the media author on two different occasions while still a student in Canada. The use of McLuhan, he argues, makes sense in terms of what is going on with the Internet, since he wrote about media effects in a popular vein after Harold Adams Innis and discussed convergence of media well before there was any personal interest in the Internet.

Common Challenges/Solutions

In terms of interaction with the course instructor, there seems to be generally less participation today than there once was. As one strategy at Virginia Tech, the instructor has been employing a system in which he invites a couple of former students who have done really well in this particular course to serve as a mentor to others. They can meet in this way in small groups, and McAllister reports how he sometimes is able to use these students to get feedback when a particular issue seems to raise special interest. It helps him gauge his role when a controversial issue is raised. Student helpers receive course credit and appreciate especially the behind-the-scenes aspect.

At the University of Washington, students regularly meet with their TAs in discussion sessions and, as a result, develop a closer relationship with those graduate students. The professor is dealing less with day-to-day drudgery and has less contact overall unless he or she develops a mechanism to force students to stop by. As a result, professors tend to attract the really talented or motivated students who want to pick their brain, looking at the instructor as potential mentor.

By the same token, others who might seek out an instructor might be those really struggling with the course and looking for assistance. Serving as a TA for the introductory course is often considered the toughest teaching-assistant assignment because the workload can be substantially higher than others. It often means that they will have to attend the lecture section of the class when it meets twice during the week and then also oversee multiple discussion sections meeting on Fridays.

They often oversee as many as four sections of 25 students meeting back to back for discussion on Friday. There can also be considerable grading involved, plus office hours.

Teaching assistants are usually assigned 20 hours a week, including each of their discussion sections. For other course assignments they might not actually be burdened with quite so heavy a load, but for this class that is not the case.

On the other hand, they often welcome an opportunity to gain an acquaintance with a survey course when there might have been less concentration in one or two of the content areas covered in their educational preparation to date. So they want to cycle through this course as a means of gaining a further acquaintance and overview of the core ideas presented to all students, particularly those seeking a major in the department.

Every TA wants to teach this course but after one or two exposures are usually satisfied. At the University of Washington, in a previous designation as a School of Communication, 15 to 20 TAs would not be unusual with as many as four or five of those assigned to the introductory course. Typically teaching and research assistants will have three opportunities to discuss what is expected. They will usually receive some kind of university-wide orientation for teaching and research assistants, a few days in length. A Department of Communication orientation for new TAs lasts a few days during one week before the fall quarter.

A Professional Development Committee conducts meetings for TAs—for all new TAs, not just the ones in the introductory course. Any new TAs (some get assigned to other courses, for example) go through the pedagogy sequence during their first year at the University Washington. These programs include participation of the "lead" TAs, the senior graduate students in the department, including doctoral students.

In terms of student contact Matt McAllister claims the Internet and e-mail has, in some ways, actually become something of a detriment because fewer student seem to stop by the instructors offices these days but will instead send an e-mail message. While the instructor has received a great deal of teaching recognition he suggests that people in the field of communication have the advantage of being able to tie their research more easily to student and public interests.

McAllister insists that student focus on fields of public relations and advertising has been maintained over many years at Virginia Tech. This instructor has often used his own research projects on promotional issues such as TV news coverage of their own network entertainment programs as a means to get students thinking about business and ethical considerations. In terms of keeping things topical he uses an assortment of electronic resource materials kept up to date to keep attention.

David Domke of Washington takes a fairly conventional and chronological approach but attempts to employ media-analysis essays as a means of getting students to recognize the ability of the constructors of media messages to have an influence with their audience. He suggests that in his class students must evaluate the type of language and question who is behind it.

For some of his other classes Domke assumes a role and takes on the history of an individual, adopting the approach of major figures in the news. He had developed lectures that he wanted to deliver for courses addressing the intersection of politics and the press and had the material together. He decided that it might have more meaning to students if conveyed in the persona of a popular figure in politics and public affairs.

He could talk about the individuals in the context of this particular class and then explain why they are relevant. Instead he decided to "be them" in terms of their public positions and overall philosophy. He decided to interact with students as these figures might, answering questions from students as he believes the individuals might. This strategy has illuminated the public position of a variety of individuals on all sides of the political spectrum and helped students to understand the subtext of messages as they are presented through the mass media.

While the idea has stimulated some media attention on his campus, Domke suggests that this approach isn't a big deal except for the first 20 minutes of class. This is when he takes questions for about 10 minutes about issues and people in the news from the perspective of the particular person whose political positions he has assumed. It is generally worth 30 minutes of class time, followed by a lecture as that person.

Domke also incorporates a "stump the professor" quiz in which his initial motivation included trying to come up with an approach that would deviate from what he does in other classes. Eight of 10 weeks during the quarter, each student has a chance to develop a question about a problem related to journalism and politics. Each student also develops a prospective solution to this question. Students bring questions to class, typed, and the TA sifts among the questions to find the best one. The chosen question is then read aloud by the student author. Dr. Domke has 90 seconds to answer it. The student than gives their answer. The rest of the class joins in to buttress the student's answer. After a few minutes of students helping each other out, the TA is asked to decide who had the better answer, students or Domke. If students win, then they get participation points (all of them, not just those who talked in class).

This exercise humanizes the instructor within the context of a large class and lets students see that he is accessible and available to interact on important issues. It also again provides an excellent opportunity to show interconnections between the past and present, to incorporate important material from the daily news and place it in a broader context.

Outside Resources

At Arizona State University supplements to the course may include occasional films or segments of films, but they vary widely and are always used in conjunction with other things. These might include a portion of the documentary film about a key inventor such as Philo Farnsworth, entitled *Big Dreams, Small Screen* from the PBS "American Experience" series. This reflects the professor's interest as author of the book on Philo Farnsworth. Students also screen the National Film Board of Canada's classic *City of Gold*, segments from *Nightline* or *60 Minutes*, and parts of historic television broadcasts such as Walter Cronkite's (namesake of the ASU school) last day on air.

Of the audiovideo material John Ferré shows in his class, *Stranger with a Camera* is one of the strongest and most dynamic videos he screens. Employed near the end of the course and in conjunction with a discussion of the New World Information and Communication Order, it reinforces concepts from a section devoted to the protection of journalists. The underlying idea is that if a society is going to have a free press, reporters have to be safe to report their stories. And the track record in this regard in recent years has, of course, been pretty bad.

The film is about a Canadian filmmaker who was shot in the rural South in the late 1960s. The odd twist is that it presents a case study of a foreign journalist who comes to the United States to make a documentary. In the home area of the university in which students reside, he is working on his film about Appalachian stereotypes and is murdered. The film contains interviews, including one with his daughter. The award-winning filmmakers, Appalshop, included original material and dealt in detail with stereotypes of Appalachia.

The murderer assumed that the documentary and journalist, Hugh O'Connor, was in the region to ridicule local people, when in reality it was compassion toward their plight that drove the filmmaker's work. This film encourages consideration of the degree to which media images can be simultaneously helpful and harmful and can trigger extreme, sometimes unlawful behavior, leading to a broader discussion of media effects.

The literature on media effects is the focus of what many instructors in the field feel is very critical today, and an area in which students have a natural interest. Concerns about subliminal influence are always ripe for discussion. And while the solid research is lean, some logical ties between marketing and influence are dominant in student discussions on that topic.

Tovares often uses clips from the Ken Burns' documentary *Empire of the Air*, focusing on an important era and competitive issues from broadcast history. He has also used some selected material from Bill Moyers' series on press performance but is generally less likely to use contemporary off-air material concentrating on material unavailable elsewhere.

Ferguson has used examples from a Mediawave Video Library from 1997–98 and occasionally employs special segments of stories from *60 Minutes*, *Dateline NBC*, or *20/20*. He will also sometimes use parts of PBS productions from programs such as *Frontline*, and shortened accounts of news events from *The NewsHour with Jim Lehrer*, with coverage to reinforce reporting points or to help clarify topical issues.

While remaining flexible in this regard, Elizabeth Perse has employed tape, film and video emphasizing cultural issues about media topics. She often reviews George Carlin's *Seven Words You Can't Say* when discussing First Amendment topics and over-air restrictions. She has also used a segment from a TV program concerning advertisers' influence on news stories.

Perse shows segments of tapes such as *Killing Screens*, with George Gerbner talking about the effects of violent media content, as well as part of a Robert Townsend film spoof, *Hollywood Shuffle*, about how Hollywood treats black performers. John Ferré also sometimes employs the classic CBS episode of *See It Now* about Joseph R. McCarthy, narrated by Edward R. Murrow, which focuses on the important characters but also offers context from the anti-Communist era of the early 1950s.

Tony Ferri incorporates visuals in a PowerPoint presentation containing photos of key innovators to help to understand media culture. He also uses an *American Experience* PBS television documentary program on the life of Nelly Bly. Ferri enjoys emphasizing that this is a person that most beginning students have never heard of, yet, because of investigative reports, she turns out to be more exciting then any contemporary journalist.

Ferri sometimes screens the feature film *Easy Rider*, just to give students the sense of narrative and speed in terms of how things have changed in the way films are constructed. Considered a classic of the 1960s it serves as springboard for a discussion on how movies were made then versus how films are orchestrated in today's more fast-paced production environment.

David Domke uses short video and film clips to illustrate points. He employs a segment from *Nightline* when discussing TV news and race, and how people of color are reported. He shows a sort segment from features such as *Jerry McGuire* on the topic of product placement, noting use of athletic shoes in the film.

He also sometimes uses brief excerpts from popular television series such as *Law and Order* to underscore the complexities of issues related to reporting and the First Amendment. Here a journalist delivers a scandalous story. His murder is depicted as by-product of aggressive reporting.

This example raises issues regarding the nature of news and preoccupation with what is journalism about today. It invites questions concerning recent reporting scandals and acknowledges preoccupation with sensational stories and awareness that what is rumor today could develop into a major story. Domke also uses brief segments from entertainment programs such as *The Late Show* in which the rock singer, Madonna, appeared as a guest.

On that occasion, the parent television network extracted some of the rock star's language, and this has inevitably led to a class discussion about what is considered fair or offensive on the airwaves, and who decides? Short TV segments give students a chance to relax and reflect on the current environment and the realities of decision making. They help to focus attention on basic media concepts, challenges and basic production ideas.

Exposure to press coverage of the war on terrorism are available from sources such as Insight Media with up-to-date videos divided by interest: *Media and Society, Introduction to Mass Communication, Media Literacy, History of Communications, Journalism, Basic, Photography*, and others. The Insight Media list is available via www.insight-media.com.

Also useful are tapes available through Teacher's Video Company, including A&E's *Biography* series, classics like *Citizen Kane*, and TV documentaries such as *Mark Twain's America* from the NBC *Project XX* series. The Journalism segment of videos includes biographies of Joseph Pulitzer, David Brinkley, Barbara Walters, coverage of the *Great Debates, Tabloid: Inside the "New York Post"*, and *Shooting Stars: Paparazi*. Information regarding these videos is available by calling 1–800–262–8837 or at www.teachersvideo.com.

Use of media resources is consistent across institutional boundaries. A wide variety of resources are available, and a greater degree of specialization is on the rise. Faculty who regularly teach the introductory course are taking special steps to ensure that their students are not only getting a survey, but are also keeping up to date in terms of expectations, should they pursue some aspect of mass communications as a career.

Conclusions

Among the many observations gleaned from surveying faculty members responsible for teaching the Introduction to Mass Communication course is that the stereotype of the basic course taught by junior faculty members is not totally accurate. In many cases, senior faculty members, with years of experience, are teaching the course. Their commitment is clear, as is their concern that the growth in the use of technology is enhancing opportunities to connect with the professional mass media world.

A second stereotype, that these courses garner extremely large enrollments, is also not consistent with the evidence; that is, these courses typically, at even some larger schools, could average less than 100 students. And as instructors point out, once a lecture class exceeds a few dozen students, size becomes less important. In most instances in which enrolment exceeds a couple of hundred, the instructors are employing special strategies and support systems to enhance learning.

Faculty members responsible for this course are using what were once referred to as nontraditional sources, consistently recommending Web sites as a means of following important trends with respect to changes in the field and current news stories that may relate to their interests. This development has invited increased participation, with at least one of the instructors pointing out that his class Web site was completed a number of years ago with assistance of an student enrolled in that course.

By the same token, some of the instructors commented on how excessive use of new technology may also be hampering, to some degree, personal contact with students. For this reason, some of these individuals have taken special steps to stay in touch with student needs or incorporate strategies to get students to follow up on requests and queries. If you ask them about how many students they typically connect with on a personal basis, in the sense that students might stop by during office hours for a discussion to follow up on the reading or some point from class, they report that the number is down somewhat from the past.

While reasons are unclear, some professors attribute this to the rise of the Internet; that is, some of the students, even on a residential campus, appear to be more likely to query the course professor by e-mail rather than stopping by the office. The thinking is that because they have been using that medium to stay in touch with others, they feel less comfortable in contacting someone regarded as an authority figure in person. In big classes personal interaction might make it more daunting.

Ironically, some of the faculty members are insisting on e-mail interaction but putting some kind of parameters around the interaction to avoid having overly aggressive students trying to take advantage and overdo it with excessive messages. Some instructors are also attempting to integrate exercises into their class that will guarantee a certain level of additional contact without encouraging too much e-mail traffic.

At the bigger institutions in which graduate students are employed, a greater awareness of the role of personal contact and mentoring are being emphasized. A considerable number of instructors still employ daily quizzes over material, whereas others use current-event quizzes as a means of testing familiarity with daily events, also used as a strategy to check class attendance. E-mail has given instructors the option of giving students a chance to provide quiz items, a means of rewarding preparation.

Senior instructors are also well aware of the perceptual changes and practical concerns that have arisen recently and, in at least one instance, the instructor is switching from the use of a time-honored textbook to a packet of outside readings to encourage additional interaction. Instructors seem more active in incorporating their own work into the mix to ensure that the students appreciate how their interests tie to course material.

Sources

Edmundson, Mark. 2002. Soul training: Increased testing is another blow to the most vital aspect of education, great teachers. *New York Times Magazine*, 18 August, 9–10.

Fish, Stanley. 2002. You probably think this song is about you. *Chronicle of Higher Education*, 22 March, B-20.

Jenkins, Colleen. 2002. Tough assignments. *Carolina Alumni Review*, May/June, 30–41.

Perini, Jay. 2002. It happens every spring. *Chronicle of Higher Education*, 17 May, B-20.

Thompson, Brad. 2002. If I quiz them, they will come. *Chronicle of Higher Education*, 21 June, B5.

Remembering a Mentor:
Sam Becker

John A. Kline

In the spring of 1967 I visited the University of Iowa intent on entering graduate school. I knew of some of the most senior faculty: Drs. Orville Hitchcock, Donald C. Bryant, and Douglas Ehninger, nationally known for studies in rhetoric, as well as a couple of rising stars in the field. I hoped one of them would be my advisor. Then I met with the Chairman of the Department of Speech and Dramatic Art, Dr. Clay Harshbarger, who suggested Dr. Sam Becker would be a good advisor for me. I was surprised and had actually never heard of this Becker fellow. Wasn't I good enough to work with one of the more senior people in rhetoric at Iowa? Becker was an expert in the study of radio and television, Harshbarger said. He added that our discussion had convinced him that I should study with Dr. Becker in the emerging field of Communication Research.

I wasn't totally convinced, but Harshbarger was an imposing figure sitting there dressed in a white shirt and tie, behind his large antique desk, and possessing an admirable amount of snow-white hair. And when he talked it sounded like God speaking. So I headed off to the Television Center and a meeting with Sam Becker. There was Sam, with bow tie and suspenders, and with sleeves rolled up to his elbows. The books on his shelves were in ordered disarray, as if they had been pulled out often and not shoved quite back in place. On the bottom row of one shelf were dozens of books with various bindings—I later learned these were copies of doctoral dissertations and master's theses he had directed.

On one occasion when nominated for an award Sam was asked to supply his curriculum vitae. In response he submitted only one part: the list of students whose dissertations he had directed. That list, he believed, was the ultimate measure of his worth as a university professor. Sam has always taken mentoring seriously. As one of his colleagues and former National Communication Association president Bruce Gronbeck pointed out, Dr. Becker has, by example, shown a generation of scholars how to mentor, which is one reason why his influence has become pervasive. Doctoral students from all over the country credit his assistance because he is willing to accept inquiries from anywhere, any time or place, and respond to them as seriously as those from the University of Iowa.

Sam advised my master's and doctorate and directed both my thesis and dissertation. He advised me early that I should write every essay with my thesis in mind. Research courses should provide a theoretical rationale and a chance to review

35

relevant literature. Projects in research courses should serve as pilot studies for the thesis itself. He suggested that if I followed his advice I could finish the coursework and thesis in one year. I knew people who took more than two years to complete their degree, so I followed Sam's advice.

Ten months later I worked nearly nonstop on Chapter 1 of my thesis. Late one afternoon I handed it to Sam. The next morning it was back on my desk. The margins and spaces between lines on the double-spaced manuscript were nearly full of corrections, suggestions, and rewrites from Sam's pencil. I thought I had failed miserably. But on the last page were these words: "Great job, John. Make these little changes and return it to me with the next chapter." Encouraged I soon turned in Chapter 2 and a revised Chapter 1. The next morning both chapters were on my desk. Chapter 2 had been practically obliterated with black pencil markings. Chapter 1 had some marks as well, but on the last page were encouraging words from Sam. I finished the thesis on time. Two years later with Sam's advice and encouragement I completed my doctoral dissertation. Dennis Gouran, my office mate from our graduate-school days, and today a national figure in the field, said Sam's strengths in mentoring include "a consistently high level of encouragement" with a finely honed skill of criticism that is "accurate and perceptive, but never demeaning." I can attest to that.

Sam is a great teacher because he is a clear thinker and an outstanding communicator. His speaking, like his writing, is direct. Even tired graduate students stay awake in his classes. He is enthusiastic, motivating, and animated. Besides, students are afraid they might miss something. The first class I took from Sam was his well-known Communication Research Seminar. The first day he walked in and handed each of us 12 pages of single-spaced purple mimeographed notes and said, "Read these and come back next time ready to discuss what you read." Then he walked out of the room.

The next meeting he asked, "Any questions?" Nobody said anything. He said, "Good! Glad you understand them so well." He handed each of us 15 more pages of notes and said, "Read these for next time and we'll see if you have any questions." Then he was gone. We sat there and were speechless. Next time we were ready to discuss. And what discussions we had. Sam probed, challenged, questioned, and never let us get away with making unsupported discussions. Time passed rapidly. This is what graduate school was supposed to be. Inquisitive students sitting at the feet of the master, learning from him and one another, more than we ever thought possible. We eagerly awaited the next set of notes. Even more eagerly we anticipated our next meeting, as his personal attention and assistance intensified with our interest.

This was just a start but I still have the notes from that class. Over the next three years I learned a lot in classes from Sam, but I learned things outside class that have influenced my behavior, such as always having time for students or junior faculty members. And, above all, insisting on excellence from my students and from faculty members I led as provost of a large university. A mark of an outstanding teacher is the influence he has on his students. Few, if any, teachers have had as much positive influence on their students as Sam Becker.

As a counselor, Sam is one of the wisest people I have ever known, not just about communication studies or other academic subjects—as provost at the University of

Iowa he could converse with all faculty members about their disciplines. Sam is wise in his assessment of people and their potential. He sized me up and did it early. He saw a young man who had spent six years as a farmer in Iowa, gone off to college, and now three years later was in a graduate program. He saw beyond rough edges. He understood better than anyone else the possibilities in me.

Sam counseled me often. He guided me through my academic program but his counseling went much further. For example, Sam and I each have a handicapped child. He told me to never use that child as an excuse or a crutch for any failure of mine. Such thoughtful counsel stayed with me.

Perhaps his best counseling was done informally. Late each Friday afternoon Sam would join a group of his grad students at a local "watering hole." We looked forward to those gatherings. They provided a chance to observe how Sam, more than anybody else I've known, is a great respecter and defender of beliefs, attitudes and values of others, even if they differ from his. His openness, acceptance, candor and willingness to spend time shows people that he has their best interests at heart. For over half a century people have sought him out. That is why now Sam can't walk across a convention hotel lobby in less than half an hour because people seeking his wise counsel tend to mob him.

Sam becomes a trusted friend to those he mentors with teaching tips outside academia. Once while I was a graduate student we were playing racquetball. I caught one of his shots in the head and fell down. He shouted, "You okay?" I replied, "Yep." Before I could get up the ball whizzed by me and hit low and in the corner, resulting in a point for Sam. His only comment, "You said you were okay; you gotta be ready." He wouldn't cut slack and didn't expect any. A good friend brings out the best in you. Sam consistently brings out the best in those around him.

Sam never forgets those he mentors. When people try to discuss what Sam is doing, he cleverly turns the discussion to what is happening to them professionally and personally. He remains interested in what they are doing and continues to mentor. After five years of teaching and a respectable publishing record for a young scholar, I called Sam and told him I was thinking of leaving traditional academia. I expected him to be upset, since I was on my way to a strong academic career. I underestimated Sam. He had my well-being and that of my family in mind. He listened to my circumstances and said, "You know, John, I think that might be a very good move for you at this time." He was right!

Even today, over three decades after I completed my doctoral degree at Iowa, I still consult with Sam. I called him the other day to mention that I saw his picture in the *Iowa Alumni Review*. Before I knew it, he turned the conversation toward what I was doing. Sam focuses on others and is always there when those he mentors need him.

It's no wonder Sam has been recognized with a University of Iowa Distinguished Professorship and the Distinguished Service Award, as well as its Hancher-Finkbine Medallion. The Central States Communication Association honored him with its outstanding graduate student paper award, the Becker Prize. The National Communication Association bestowed both a Distinguished Service Award and a Distinguished Scholar Award (with the service award later named after him). He was also the recipient of the Fisher Distinguished Mentor Award and was named a Fellow of the International Communication Association.

He is a living legend at his school because he even has the Samuel L. Becker Communication Studies Building named after him. Of course he has received many other awards and distinctions, but I would be willing to bet that, besides the respect of the people he has helped, the recognition Sam is most proud of is being the named the first National Communication Association Mentor in 2000. Samuel Leo Becker is a trusted teacher, a counselor to hundreds of scholars, a critical mentor, and always available when you need him.

CHAPTER 3

Communication Theory

Lowndes F. Stephens

Introduction

The traditional stand-alone, required mass communication theory course is uncommon today in the undergraduate curriculum of journalism and mass communications programs, signaling not the lack of emphasis on understanding communication theory, but the integration of theory into many other required courses.

In a book of this kind it is valuable to explore some of the reasons the stand-alone theory course has become less common. Some of the vocabulary of traditional theory courses taught from a social science perspective (i.e., variance control, hypothesis testing, dependent and independent variables, and other concepts having to do with *testing* theory, or explaining media effects) is included in undergraduate research methods courses.[1] The content of scholarly reflection (theories evolving from systematic research based on communication science and critical, cultural studies) and lessons learned from practitioners (normative theories) are covered in other courses.

Similar Courses

This book includes a review of many core courses in the undergraduate curriculum that undoubtedly include a *theory* component. Many other factors may account for why communication theory instruction is integrated across the curriculum rather than being covered in a stand-alone, required core course. First, accreditation requirements are increasingly difficult to meet, and programs seeking accreditation must make trade-offs to meet these requirements. The Accrediting Council on Education in Journalism and Mass Communication (ACEJMC) is the accrediting body for professional journalism and mass communication programs in the United States. Only 108 programs in 39 states are accredited at this time; about 400 colleges and universities offer formal programs in the field, and 1,000 offer some courses in journalism and mass communication.

The ACEJMC's new curriculum standard (which applies to programs undergoing accreditation reviews beginning in 2003–2004) requires students in undergraduate programs to take a minimum of 80 semester hours or 116 quarter hours in courses outside the major. In addition, it requires no fewer than 65 semester hours or 94 quarter hours in the basic liberal arts and sciences. Journalism and mass communications courses may not be counted in the 65-hour requirement.

Most journalism and mass communications programs, while conferring only one degree (a bachelor's of art or science degree in journalism and mass communications), offer sequences or areas of specialization. These include news-editorial (newspapers, magazines, periodicals, management, and the like), electronic journalism (television and radio news and production), public relations, advertising, photojournalism and visual communications, and perhaps communication studies.

Ancillary/Related Courses

The increased specialization of undergraduate sequences in journalism and mass communications, increased needs to ensure that students are technologically and visually literate, and an emphasis on media convergence have made the curriculum more complex. The ACEJMC's standard calls for a balance between theoretical and conceptual courses and skills. It notes that a sound educational program "should provide broad exposure to the liberal arts and sciences . . . it should also provide up-to-date instruction in the skills and in the theories, history, functions, procedure, law, ethics and effects of journalism and mass communications" (www.ku.edu/~acejmc/BREAKING/newstd3.shtml).

The accrediting body also expects the curriculum to be responsive to the professional values and competencies specified in the ACEJMC's Principles of Accreditation of September 16, 2000. Among other things these values and competencies include to "demonstrate an understanding of the diversity of groups in a global society in relationship to communications, understand concepts, and apply theories in the use and presentation of images and information."

Second, despite the accrediting body's concern that a balance between conceptual courses and skills courses be maintained in the undergraduate curriculum, the communication industries that hire undergraduates from journalism and mass communications programs want students who are skilled practitioners, and the refrain is often "the more skills courses the better." Many journalism and mass communications programs have added capstone senior-semester programs and internships in an attempt to improve the skills of the students.

Experiential learning opportunities involve an intensive laboratory environment equating to a 35- to 40-hour week and 12-semester hours of course credit (often the case with a senior-semester capstone experience). The alternative is considerable time off campus in internships where students have fewer elective hours and fewer opportunities to take other conceptual courses.

A third factor has to do with the profile of faculty members teaching in journalism and mass communications programs and the positioning of these programs administratively within the university or college. The sentiment about whether a stand-alone, required communication theory course is necessary will likely differ depending on the faculty mix. Faculty members with an earned doctorate may be more likely to see the need for such a course while those who do not have the Ph.D. may not.

Academic tenure-track faculty members may be more inclined to emphasize conceptual courses, whereas those in a professional tenure track may be more likely to emphasize applied courses. Faculty members with an earned doctorate usually teach conceptual courses such as communication theory, while *practitioners* (those with extensive professional experience) teach the applied courses.

The *academics* in mass communication and journalism programs come from different disciplines and are hired to teach in various specializations. They may have different sentiments about where communication theory instruction should fit in undergraduate programs (as a stand-alone, required or elective; as something integrated across curriculum; or as both a stand-alone course, required or elective, and emphasized in other courses). The practitioners also come from different disciplines for varied sequences. They may feel pressure to make sure students know "How to?" and have less time to teach "Why do it that way?" or "What are the consequences of what you do or don't do?"

In stand-alone journalism and mass communications programs there is more likely to be a balance between "chi-squares" (academics) and "green eyeshades" (practitioners). It may be easier to strike a balance between conceptual and applied courses in these programs. It may be more difficult to strike a balance in programs within colleges of liberal arts and sciences, for example, where faculty members in journalism and mass communications programs are likely to have the earned doctorate and where there may be fewer practitioners on the faculty. In these programs there may be more pressure to offer conceptual courses and less to offer skills courses, even if the program is accredited.[2]

One final issue regarding the profile of faculty members in journalism and mass communications programs and the institutional setting in which the programs are situated has to do with tenure and promotion pressures. As in all disciplines, journalism and mass communications programs must justify their importance to the central mission of the university or college.

Many programs have a two-tiered tenure and promotion system: one for academic-track faculty and another for professional-track faculty. Academic-track faculty members are expected to be effective teachers and productive scholars and demonstrate a respect for the norm that a good academic citizen participates actively in faculty governance, committees, and the usual obligations associated with membership in learned societies and academic associations.

Academic-track faculty also serve on the graduate faculty in units that also offer graduate degrees and are actively involved in teaching graduate courses, including theory and methodology courses. They serve on thesis and dissertation committees and write and grade comprehensive exams. Scholarly contributions are often expected to go beyond contributing to the knowledge base from which they teach. Academics are also expected to generate external funding to support their research and the graduate and undergraduate students who work with them. Less attention is given to service contributions in tenure and promotion decisions for academic-track faculty members.

Professional-track faculty members are expected to be effective teachers and to contribute to the professional trade journals representing their areas of specialization. They, too, are expected to be good academic citizens and tend to the usual obligations associated with membership in professional associations. Practitioners also are expected to maintain ties to media outlets likely to hire students and carry a disproportionate burden in advising professional student groups.

They also serve as graduate faculty members in programs with professional master's programs. These duties involve serving on professional project committees and writing and grading comprehensive exams. Teaching loads are usually lighter, but student contact hours are greater because faculty members in comprehensive programs are spending more time supervising students in senior capstone courses, in internship programs, on thesis and dissertation committees, and during regular academic advisement periods.

Academic units are continually being challenged to defend their contributions to the central mission of their colleges and universities. Sixty-three research universities hold membership in the prestigious American Association of Universities (AAU), and 26 of these universities have accredited programs in journalism and mass communications.[3] Many other universities aspire to AAU membership, and they are designating certain programs as "cathedrals of excellence" and directing more resources into these academic units. Small professional schools have difficulty competing in this environment for scarce resources.

The central administrations in research universities often take tenured faculty slots back when faculty members leave or retire and reserve the right to reallocate faculty lines to other units. These universities are also experimenting with a value-centered management approach to budgeting, which ties an academic unit's funding not to a general allocation from the central administration but to its own tuition revenue, grants and gifts (donations). Designed to make academic units more efficient and responsive to students, the effect of value-centered management on curriculum may be to encourage some programs to emphasize high-enrollment courses. Arguably, the courses in communication theory ("too abstract") and research methods ("requires understanding of statistics") are among the least favorites for mass communication students, and so enrollments will likely be low in these courses unless they are required.

If enrollment increases are not realistic, academic units operating in a decentralized budgeting system will need to encourage faculty members to spend more time seeking research and training grants, resulting in less time that can be devoted to teaching. Adjunct faculty members, part-timers, and doctoral students help carry much of the load in these research universities, but full-time faculty members still do the "heavy lifting" when it comes to committee work, annual performance reviews, and the teaching of conceptual courses at the undergraduate and graduate levels.

These factors and others account for why undergraduate theory instruction in mass communications programs is rarely covered in a stand-alone, required communication theory course and instead is covered in other courses.

Comparative Features

Journalism and mass communications historians often compare and contrast the rationale behind theoretical models of journalism education represented by the two founding university-based programs at the University of Missouri and the University of Wisconsin. Walter Williams (1864–1935), a Missouri newspaperman who traveled widely but had little formal education, founded the journalism school at Missouri in 1908. Willard G. Bleyer (1873–1935), born into a prominent Milwaukee newspaper family, founded the Department of Journalism at Wisconsin in 1912, after earning three degrees from that institution.

These historical figures are associated with different orientations toward training and educating journalists: a professional-school tradition at Missouri versus a liberal arts tradition at Wisconsin.

Stephen D. Reese, G. B. Dealey Professor and Director of the School of Journalism in the College of Communications at the University of Texas at Austin, captures the essence of this in his 1999 essay, "The Progressive Potential of Journalism Education: Recasting the Academic versus Professional Debate," in the *Harvard International Journal of Press and Politics*. He offers an overview of the two competing historical models for journalism education that set the tone for debate over theory versus practice. The essay contrasts Willard Bleyer's approach at the University of Wisconsin (integrating journalism with liberal arts) with that of Walter Williams at the University of Missouri (establishing a free-standing professional school). The latter emphasizes hands-on training in a real-world environment. Reese points out that Bleyer did not make a strong distinction between theory and practice, with the thought that research would help improve practice (Reese, 1999, p. 72)

In *A Creed for My Profession: Walter Williams, Journalist to the World*, Ronald T. Farrar, now distinguished professor emeritus at the University of South Carolina, documents views of the founder of the School of Journalism at Missouri. According to Farrar, Williams was interested in both theory and practice, with journalism courses listed in the school's announcement during the inaugural year of 1908–1909, including the History and Principles of Journalism course taught by Williams and required of every student.

The university catalog description for this course was "Designed to present the main facts of the history of newspaper making, of journalism in various periods and conditions, the meaning and aims of journalism and its fundamental principles" (quoted in Farrar, 1998, p. 141) Other journalism courses listed include Newspaper Making, Newspaper Administration, Magazine and Class Journalism, Comparative Journalism, Newspaper Publishing, Newspaper Jurisprudence, News-Gathering, Correspondence, and Office Equipment. Williams taught the Comparative Journalism and Newspaper Administration courses.

Williams developed a code of ethics (*The Journalist's Creed*) in 1914 that the journalism students had to know by heart. The code was incorporated into the school's style manual for *The Missourian*, the newspaper published at the school by the students. His ethos stressed truth telling and social responsibility as part of a public trust in which journalism is regarded as a profession, with trustees accountable for clarity, accuracy and fairness. He indicated that journalists should convey only what in their heart they held to be true, with suppression of information as indefensible (Farrar, 1998, p. 203).

In their monograph "Willard G. Bleyer and the Relevance of Journalism Education," Carolyn Bronstein and Stephen Vaughn of the University of Wisconsin, explain Bleyer's philosophy (Bronstein and Vaughn, 1998). Bleyer believed critical thinking should be emphasized in all the courses that journalists take (including skills courses). He believed journalism students needed a broad, general education, and that they should take most courses in the liberal arts (two-thirds to three-quarters) rather than journalism (one-fourth to one-third). He was a pioneer in graduate education in the field, establishing the first graduate course in journalism in the United States.

Course offerings in journalism at the University of Wisconsin date to 1904. At first, students registered for two courses (spanning two semesters) covering basic reporting, copyediting, the history of the American press, and the organization and management of the modern newspaper. In 1905–1906, Bleyer organized an upper division (junior-senior) curriculum of preparatory courses combining classes in political science, economics, English and history, with the reporting sequences (Bronstein and Vaughn, 1998, p. 19).

Williams and Bleyer worked together to establish a national organization of journalism educators. Although a few journalism professors had previously met to think about such an organization in 1910 at the University of California, Williams invited professors from the 32 schools that in 1911 were offering some journalism instruction during Journalism Week at the University of Missouri in April of that year. The American Association of Teachers of Journalism (AATJ) was born out of this meeting, and Bleyer served as its first president.

Farrar, who authored a history of the association representing academic journalism administrators (Association of Schools of Journalism and Mass Communication), noted Walter Williams' role in promoting journalism education to the newspaper profession, gaining a "gratifying measure of acceptance for journalism education. This is what 'Daddy' Bleyer did for his discipline within the academic community" (Farrar, 1998, p. 181).

Even though it can be argued that these early pioneers in journalism education were of the same mind regarding the need for both theory and practice, those educators who believe journalism education should be patterned after the Missouri model probably listen more to professional journalists. Conversely, those educators who believe journalism education should follow the Wisconsin model probably listen more to their academic colleagues. As Reese notes, *theory* and *practice* are code words that suggest different approaches "with an emphasis on reason and experience, respectively, whereas the terms *academic* and *professional* are often used to describe institutional outlook, inward toward a discipline or outward toward practitioners" (Reese, 1999, p. 74).

The debate about whether journalism is something you experience and learn on the job or is a profession requiring an understanding of theory and practice (worthy of a place in higher education) goes back at least to the early 1870s. In 1872, Whitelaw Reid of the *New York Tribune* proposed that journalists be educated in the liberal arts and trained in the practice of journalism in institutions of higher education (Bronstein and Vaughn, 1998, p. 14). Joseph Pulitzer had to some extent contributed to this notion through his attention to Columbia University (Farrar, 1998, pp. 128–129).[4] Many academics, editors and journalists were skeptical about whether journalism education should be situated within institutions of higher education.

The debate goes on even as a record number of students enroll in undergraduate journalism and mass communication programs (168,254 undergraduates in the autumn of 2000).[5] Good reviews of various positions on this debate and recommendations for reform include the following:

- Cohen, Jeremy, ed. 2001. Symposium: Journalism and mass communication education at the crossroads. Special issue of *Journalism and Mass Communication Educator* 56, no. 3 (Autumn): 4–27. Columbia, S.C.: Association for Education in Journalism and Mass Communication.
- Reese, Stephen D. 1999. The progressive potential of journalism education. *Harvard International Journal of Press/Politics* 4, no. 4 (Fall):70–94.
- Betty Medsger. 1996. *Winds of change: Challenges confronting journalism education.* Arlington, Va.: Freedom Forum.
- Blanchard, Robert O., and William G. Christ. 1993. *Media education and the liberal arts: A blueprint for the new professionalism.* Hillsdale, N.J.: Lawrence Erlbaum.
- *Planning for curricular change in journalism education.* 1984. Oregon Report: Project on the Future of Journalism and Mass Communication Education. Eugene: School of Journalism, University of Oregon.

Special Features

The stand-alone course in communication theory and other courses that have a theory component provide a vocabulary for understanding journalism and mass communication. They offer explanations for the norms of journalistic practice, the functions and effects of mass media, and the expectations and concerns of stakeholders in our media systems.

Theory courses acquaint students with important philosophical questions and issues in the field. *Ontological* questions focus on the nature of what we seek to know about sources, communicators, messages, feedback processes, and audiences. *Epistemological* discussion focuses on how people know what they claim to know and various worldviews on how knowledge is, or should be, generated.

Journalism and mass communication students need to reflect upon epistemological questions as they sort out the conventional wisdom in their field and those of the fields of study or areas of specialization represented by the sources they will consult and the clients they will serve in the real world. *Axiological* issues focus attention on the values of the journalist, investigator, scholar and theorist: Do the values of the knower affect what she or he can know? Students need to appreciate how values may influence the nature and purpose of inquiry, and the basic theory course can sensitize them to these issues.[6]

G. Stuart Adam, a Canadian scholar/journalist, in "Notes Towards a Definition of Journalism: Understanding an Old Craft as an Art Form," defines journalism as "an invention or a form of expression used to report and comment in the public media on the events and ideas of the here and now" (Adam, 1993, p. 11). As poetics, journalism "is a creation—a product of the Imagination—in both an individual and a cultural sense. It is a form of expression in which the imaginative capacities both of the individuals and of a culture are revealed" (Adam, 1993, p. 13).

Adam argues that the journalist, in using imagination to "frame experience and form consciousness," uses culturally sanctioned methods to report and gather evidence: "Journalists are concerned with facts and information, and they follow, however crudely and randomly, an epistemological procedure . . . they construct a picture of fact and information" (Adam, 1993, p. 28). Journalists use various tools as rationales for defining the meaning of the evidence they gather—myths, metaphors, and explanatory methods.

Adam explains, "Like all storytellers, journalists inscribe meaning on the facts and events they describe." He describes how some of these depend on myth and/or metaphor while others rely on secular devices for explanation of social science, as is often true in journalism, even when practitioners are not fully aware of these techniques (Adam, 1993, p. 37). Adam identifies four theories that journalists use to explain human motives: rational individualism, sociological theory, nonrationalism and cultural theory (Adam, 1993, pp. 37–38). The basic communication theory course can introduce students to these various techniques/theories that journalists may use to frame consciousness.[7]

Pamela Bourland-Davis at Georgia Southern University uses metaphors in her undergraduate mass communication theory course to get students to understand better their relationships with mass media (Bourland-Davis, 1998). A number of scholars have emphasized the use of *precision journalism* techniques in reporting classes (Weaver and McCombs, 1980).

Communication theory is a logical course in which to teach argumentation skills, rules of evidence and inference, and other critical thinking skills. Students in these courses learn how to evaluate the claims of others, as they develop research questions and hypotheses to pursue on their own. A good theory course will touch on many of the critical and analytical reasoning skills recognized as requisite for any well-educated citizen. The Foundation for Critical Thinking identifies key elements of reasoning, and a basic communication theory course will address each of these elements (Paul and Elder, 2001):

1. All reasoning has a PURPOSE. What am I trying to accomplish? What are the central aims and my purpose?
2. All reasoning is an attempt to figure something out, to settle some QUESTION and solve some problem. What question am I raising? What questions am I addressing?
3. All reasoning is based on ASSUMPTIONS. What am I taking for granted? What assumption has led me to that conclusion?
4. All reasoning is done from some POINT OF VIEW. From what point of view am I looking at this issue? Is there another point of view I should consider?
5. All reasoning is based on data, INFORMATION and evidence. What information am I using in coming to that conclusion? What experience have I had to support this claim? What information do I need to settle the question?

6. All reasoning is expressed through, and shaped by CONCEPTS and IDEAS. What is the main idea here? Could I explain this idea?
7. All reasoning contains INFERENCES or interpretations by which we draw CONCLUSIONS and give meaning to data. How did I reach this conclusion? Is there another way to interpret the information? Infer only what the evidence implies. Check inferences for their consistency with each other. Identify assumptions that lead you to your inferences.
8. All reasoning leads somewhere or has IMPLICATIONS and CONSEQUENCES. How did I reach this conclusion? Is there another way to interpret the information? Trace the implications and consequences that follow from your reasoning. Search for negative as well as positive implications. Consider all possible consequences.

In *Communication Theory Instruction in the Professional School*, Donna Vocate interviewed eight leaders in mass communications education who explained why they believe communication theory instruction is essential in professional journalism and mass communications programs. She reported her results in *Journalism and Mass Communication Educator* (Vocate, 1997).[8] Topics discussed in these interviews included desirable theory course content, techniques and strategies for teaching theory, assignments, anticipated outcomes of theory study for students, and rationales for requiring theory study.

According to the administrators who were interviewed, historical information on mass communications is one content area that should be included in theory courses. Several administrators also pointed out that philosophy and science were included in their classes, though others said they focused mainly on paradigms and paradigm shifts. Overall, administrators felt that students need to learn about the relationship between theory and research.

Administrators admitted that students often entered research and theory classes with a negative attitude, and they concluded that it is the role of the faculty to show the usefulness of these subjects. Professors must demonstrate how theory will apply to professional work, how theory will help with problems and issues, and how theory serves as a predictor. Administrators said that theory education could be more effective when classes are conducted in discussion formats.

Administrators offered several different examples of assignments in communication theory classes. Most of these required extensive writing and application of theory. Assignments included case studies, term papers, research studies, and theory building. Exams were in essay form. Anticipated outcomes varied among the administrators. Whereas some prepared goals for student learning, others took a less strict approach to outcomes and focused on the development of better critical thinking skills.

The administrators were more likely to agree on the rationales for requiring theory study, including that study of communication theory provides a foundation of knowledge, an understanding of processes, and a framework of strategies. Grounding in theory improves media literacy skills and sensitizes students to the effects of their work. However, the respondents were divided on the issue of how theory should be presented. While some thought theory should be a separate course, others believed it should be included in all courses in the curriculum.

Overall, faculty both outside communication and within the field appreciate the value of theory. Additional support for theory education can be found in the fact that quickly changing technology in the field calls for better analytical skills and understanding of the basic concepts of communications. It is suggested that students be required to take a rigorous communication theory course to increase their *learning intelligence*, defined as an awareness of one's own mental strategies and the ability to transcend routine ways of thinking.

It is very important that theory concepts are not simply memorized, but applied in ways that will enable students to truly absorb the value of what they are learning. The practice of *metatheory* is suggested as a method of enabling students to understand communication as a discipline. Metatheory is compared to using the mind as a muscle; it must be exercised for it to develop. The final suggestion for a theory course component is an analysis and understanding of the symbolic process of human communication. If communication theory courses are presented with all of the necessary components just discussed, students will gain better overall knowledge of the field.

Common Goals and Objectives

The author examined the university Web sites and undergraduate bulletins of a variety of journalism and mass communications programs, and communication programs that include sequences that parallel those in professional journalism schools. Some of these programs are accredited professional programs. Others are not. The purpose of this scan was to demonstrate where theory courses are positioned in the undergraduate curriculum of some top schools.

College of Communication, Boston University (www.bu.edu/com/communication.html)

This highly regarded college has academic departments in film and television, journalism, mass communication, advertising, and public relations. Undergraduates need a minimum of 32 courses (128 credits) to graduate; students in the journalism department may take only 11 of these courses in the College of Communication; all other majors in the College of Communication are limited to no more than 15 courses offered by the college.

The freshman and sophomore core courses for all students are Perspectives on Communication and Introduction to Communication Writing. According to the description for the window-to-the-field course, Perspectives on Communication, it provides students with an overview of the information age and its significance in their lives. Students explore mass communication from the perspectives of the various subfields and learn about the latest multimedia and interactive technology. They are required to have a free university computer account. Assignments and other course information are exchanged by e-mail. The role of international communication in a global economy and information age is also introduced.

Film and television undergraduate majors are required to take the Television Revolution course, which usually occurs in the second semester of the freshman year. It is a requirement for all students in the Television Program. It provides a foundation of knowledge about the origins and development of television. Students examine turning points in the growth of the medium through its most significant programs, early radio, live drama, the first presidential debates, and recent innovative programs.

Boston University communication students must also take six other courses, which may be a mix of critical studies, production, writing, and management. Other film and television courses (500-level courses are open to undergraduate and graduate students) with the theory component include a Television, Culture, and Society course, which reviews the critical and research literature concerning the relationships between television and society, including the study of audiences. Issues are subject to change from semester to semester.

Using a seminar format and selected screenings, the course explores many of the topics that have given rise to debate about television, such as violence, sexuality, commercialism, stereotyping, children's programs, and specific controversial genres. Students contribute discussion papers and audiovisual materials. Also offered occasionally is an International Television course, which provides a survey of telecommunications in various nations and analysis of cultural, economic, demographic and political impact on internal and external operations, including the understanding between nations, especially for the United States.

A Film Theory and Criticism course introduces major styles of film criticism and theoretical positions, beginning with Eisenstein's *montage*, and includes screenings of films that have contributed to critical debate and those that challenge theoretical presuppositions.

The journalism department Web page at Boston University explains, "Out of the 32 courses required, the Department of Journalism requires that its students take no more than 11 courses within Communication." This encourages a broad liberal arts education so graduates have "the critical thinking skills and knowledge to be excellent journalists." Courses with a theory component include History and Principles of Journalism, surveying the evolution of the American press and broadcasting and their influence covering areas such as freedom of the press, ethics, professional goals, technical developments, social responsibilities, and literature.

The Advanced Reporting and Research Methods course provides a thorough grounding in more advanced reporting and writing methods, such as investigations, record searches, use of online databanks and other techniques. The Media Criticism course, taught by one of Boston's most popular talk-show hosts, covers current issues involving journalists and also stresses critical thinking and analysis. In the Columns and Editorials course, the role of the press as a shaper of society examines techniques and ethical problems of journalists who interpret and comment. Student's practice writing columns, editorials, news analyses, and essay reviews. The Critical Journalism course is aimed at developing critical sensibilities, teaching rudiments of critical theory and practice as it applies to practitioners, including students.

In describing the faculty in the Department of Mass Communication, Advertising and Public Relations the Web site notes, "Our professors are experts in theory, interactive communication, research, writing, media and more. Their years of experience in a variety of professional fields and in the classroom ensure that students will be able to directly apply what they learn to their future career development." Courses with a specific theory component include Mass Communication Research, introducing the philosophy and process of social scientific research and common methods used to study in the field, a variety of research methods, data-analysis procedures, and an analysis of mass communication issues.

Another course, Theory and Process of Communication, focuses on processes and consequences of both interpersonal and mass communication and how they differ. Class discussions revolve around the nature of verbal and nonverbal communication and the role of language in cognitive processing. Theories of the process and effects of mass communication and the relationship to the goals and activities of professional communicators are included.

In the Persuasion and Public Opinion course, the theories, strategy and techniques of persuasion are explored as a means of shaping public opinion and attitudes. Attention is given to how organizations and people shape messages to communicate through the press, advertising and public relations, ascertaining and understanding the beliefs, attitudes and values of groups and society.

The Principles of Persuasion course examines communication strategies to influence others through principles derived from social science and communication research used for influencing beliefs, attitudes and actions. It also includes source credibility, message structure, belief systems, emotional appeals, motivation, cultural influence, and evidence as foundations for designing campaigns and messages.

The Intercultural Communications course offers insight into communicative problems that arise between people from different cultural backgrounds in a variety of contexts. Using interdisciplinary approaches, students explore how a variety of factors, such as verbal and nonverbal presentation, affect communication. The course Communication Strategies in Negotiation and Conflict Resolution emphasizes skills necessary in business contexts, including labor management disputes, disputes between interest groups, and resolution of conflict between an organization and various stakeholders.

Cornell University Department of Communication (in the College of Agriculture and Life Sciences; www.comm.cornell.edu/undergraduate/index.html)

The curriculum is designed to introduce principles and theoretical ideas, with an objective to apply principles in particular contexts, including interactive multimedia, advertising, or public information. The program then strives to have students integrate principles and applications into a comprehensive understanding of communication. The goal at Cornell is to have the field presented as helping the student master communication as both a process and knowledge area.

During the freshman and sophomore years, students take eight core courses that deal with contemporary communication knowledge, theory and practice. During their junior and senior years, students choose one of four defined areas of focus or design one of their own. The defined areas of focus are Communication in the Life Sciences, Communication Systems and Technology, Communication Planning and Evaluation, and Communication as Social Science.

Syracuse University, S. I. Newhouse School of Public Communications (newhouse.syr.edu/)

At Syracuse, undergraduates can emphasize advertising, public relations, print journalism or broadcast journalism. The Syracuse Web site includes descriptions of the rationale for theory in the curriculum in these various sequences:

Advertising Program requirements: Encourage students to "look at some aspect of the media from a critical perspective," asking what are the key concerns related to advertising? How are various subgroups of consumers such as women and minorities portrayed? What differences exist between types of programs such as the classic *Gilligan's Island* and the current hit, *Survivor*, tell us about society?

Public Relations Program requirements: Specify the approach to the field as a communication science, a communication art but also a management function, requiring quantitative skills. Students apply research, theory and technical skills by working on a campaign for clients. With the science of PR, including a thorough grounding in theory, research methods, identification and analysis of issues, measurement, and evaluation, students conduct research, test findings, and apply them to solve their client's problems.

Newspaper Journalism Program requirements: This takes the emphasis off of theory and research, focusing instead on writing and practical skills. Syracuse emphasizes the practical background of its faculty. All of the members of its Newspaper Journalism faculty have practical, professional writing backgrounds, and they stress reporting basics to assist students in obtaining news clips by working for the award-winning student newspaper, the *Daily Orange*, Syracuse Online, or internships at Syracuse newspapers.

Requirements for the Syracuse Broadcast Journalism Program also emphasize basics of how broadcast news professionals reach their audience through both words and pictures. The overview goes beyond theory to focus on details of how the broadcast news industry functions and affects society.

University of North Carolina at Chapel Hill School of Journalism and Mass Communication (www.jomc.unc. edu/academicprograms/undergraduate/index.html)

The UNC Web page explains how students choose one of five sequences and take specialized courses in both theory and practice. These include advertising, electronic communication, news editorial, public relations, and visual communication. A sequence in this program represents a concentration in news-editorial journalism, electronic communication, advertising, public relations or visual communication that includes photojournalism, graphics or multimedia. Each sequence has specific course requirements; others are required for all majors.

Each student must take The World of Mass Communication, an overview of mass communication's role in society, media institutions, theories, practices, professional fields, and effects on all elements of society. Two other courses have an obvious theory component: (1) Process and Effects of Mass Communication, including journalism literature, social psychology, sociology, political science and history. It factors in message construction, dissemination and reception by audiences are also surveyed. (2) Advertising and Public Relations Research offers a critical understanding and application of both quantitative and qualitative methods used for strategic planning and evaluation of public relations and ad campaigns.

Trinity University at San Antonio (Communication Department; www.trinity.edu/departments/public_relations/Academic/ communication.htm)

Trinity's integrated curriculum acknowledges the new challenges and opportunities of the field and allows for flexibility. It reflects the rapid and revolutionary changes we face today. The curriculum is divided into three interrelated areas common to media and media-related systems.

Media Studies covers the history and theories of social and mass communication; public policy related to communication systems; and structure, organization, technology, ethics, criticism, and social and aesthetic functions of communication institutions and media. A second area, defined as Media Messages, includes writing and production skills as well as other procedures related to audio, print, video, and interactive multimedia message making. Media Management covers planning, research, management, and legal regulation in contemporary communication media and media-related organizations.

The department Web page explains how mastery of fundamentals, combined with a strong liberal arts and sciences background, enhance lifelong learning and the ability to adapt to change. Added to that emphasis is the caveat that this approach supports as well as prepares students for entry-level specialties, including broadcast, print, or electronic journalism; public relations; advertising; and production of audio, video, multimedia, and new media such as the Internet. The Mass Communication Research course is positioned in the media management core, and the theory courses in the media studies core include Media, Advertising, and Society; Arts Criticism; International Communication; Ethics and the Mass Media; History of Mass Media; and Media, Culture and Technology. Many special topic courses have a theory component (e.g., Women Journalists in Film and Novel, The Vietnam War in Film and Television, and Ethnography and Journalism).

University of Georgia (Grady College of Journalism and Mass Communications; www.gradyuga.edu/students/majors.asp)

The Grady School makes it clear that while students may emphasize a particular sequence, each student is awarded the same degree, a Bachelor of Arts in Journalism. Students are told that this is what will be written on "your diploma and the name of the degree recorded on your UGA transcripts." Advertising and public relations undergraduates are required to take the Advertising and Consumer Research course.

Public relations students at the University of Georgia are required to take a few courses in that specialty, such as Public Relations Research or another research course in political science, marketing, sociology, or speech communication. Broadcast news students are required to take Media Research and Theory. Print journalism students may take Social Effects of Mass Communication as an elective.

University of Iowa (School of Journalism and Mass Communications) (www.uiowa.edu/~journal/programs/undergraduate/curriculum.html)

Students at the University of Iowa School of Journalism and Mass Communications must take a premajor foundation course entitled Social Scientific Foundation of Communication. The course description makes it clear that it will include an examination of how mass communication theory relates to practical applications and issues, emphasizing the need for students to understand how research may be used to explain the role of media in society.

Requirements for the course include three exams, a mini-research project, and a presentation. Course materials include a course pack of research examples. The course is a prerequisite for admission to major status. Students must also complete Cultural and Historical Foundations of Communication. Professor Frank Durham's syllabus for this course expands on major objectives. He notes that students will understand the broader context of the field, pointing out especially that the history of journalism is "not made of a single 'truth,' but of many perspectives anchored in cultural contexts, meaning systems and representing different moments to recognize and understand many voices and perspectives."

University of Missouri School of Journalism (www.journalism.Missouri.edu/undergrad/graduate.htm)

Somewhat legendary as the early leader in the field, the School confers one undergraduate degree, Bachelor of Journalism (B.J.). Courses required of all students include a basic news course, plus Principles of American Journalism, either History of American Journalism or Solving Practical Problems in Journalism, Communications Law, and Cross Cultural Journalism.

The description of Solving Practical Problems in Journalism specifies the relationship between theory and practice: "Finding solutions to practical problems journalists face by applying insights from communication theory, using online secondary and syndicated research, and conducting original research. Hands-on experience conducting surveys, experiments and qualitative research."

University of Oregon (School of Journalism and Communication; jcomm.uoregon.edu/)

Undergraduates must take 45 journalism credits. Core courses at the lower division (freshman and sophomore years) include Grammar for Journalists, The Mass Media and Society, and Information Gathering, including a survey of methods and strategies for acquiring information of use to the various mass media. The examination of records, databases, sources, and interview methods are included, and the curriculum includes Writing for the Media as well as Visual Communication for Mass Media.

Upper-division (junior and senior) students at Oregon must take two breadth courses such as Communication Theory and Criticism. The description reads, "Survey of contemporary social, scientific, and humanistic theories focuses on the role of technology-mediated communication in modern society. Examines administrative and critical perspectives." The course is required of communication studies majors, and it is one of the upper-division breadth courses that may be taken by majors in advertising, electronic media, magazine journalism, news-editorial journalism, and public relations.

Communication studies majors are also required to take the Communication Economics course, which offers an analysis of economic relationships that exist in the communication system and how that system is integrated into both domestic and international economies. Other upper-division breadth courses from which students may choose are oriented toward Media and Law, History, International Communication, and Media Ethics.

University of Wisconsin (School of Journalism and Mass Communications; www.journalism.wisc.edu/undergrad/documents/ugrequire.html)

Wisconsin requires three four-credit courses from an advanced concept area: one from group B, one from group C, and one from group B or C. Group B courses include Effects of Mass Communications, Law of Mass Communication, History of Mass Communications, and Mass Communications and Society. Group C courses include Mass Media and the Consumer, Mass Media and Minorities, Literary Aspects of Journalism, Public Opinion, Mass Media and Youth, Health Communication, Mass Communications and Political Behavior, and International Communication.

Wichita State University (Elliott School of Communication; esc.wichita.edu/)

Students must take eight three-credit core courses in communication and a one-credit senior portfolio seminar. The core courses are Communication and Society, Writing for the Mass Audience, Visual Technologies, Speaking in Business and the Professions, Communication Research and Inquiry, Communication Analysis and Criticism, Communication Law and Responsibility, and Historical and Theoretical Issues in Communication.

Communication and Society looks at individuals and the mass media and the economic, social and governmental impact of mass communication and the communication industry. Communication Research and Inquiry takes the process of research into account across the discipline, helping students become better consumers of research and investigative inquiry, skilled at designing research projects and in information gathering, research design, and processing and reporting information.

Communication Analysis and Criticism offers an introduction to the methods used for the analysis and critique of various elements of communication for the purpose of becoming more discerning consumers of the various public and mass-mediated messages. Analysis includes linguistic, pictorial, and aural, advertisements, broadcast messages, newspaper accounts, and public talks.

Historical and Theoretical Issues in Communication examines the development of various issues in communication in historical context, including humanistic and scientific theories of communication as well as the historical development of mediated communication. Theories are employed to generate critiques of events.

Instructor Philosophy

Just as there is much variance in where theory courses are positioned in the undergraduate curriculum, professors' ideas vary considerably about teaching the undergraduate course in communication theory.

Bourland-Davis uses metaphors to teach her undergraduate course in mass communication theory. Students write journal entries in which they reflect on class discussions and talk about their personal observations of media. The last journal entry requires students to create a metaphor that represents their relationship with the media and that demonstrates a relationship to one of the theories discussed in the course.

Bourland-Davis has identified 11 key themes in journals maintained by students in several sections of this course over two years. Two major themes were basic needs and basic wants. Metaphors used by students in the basic *needs* category included comparing the media to Maslow's hierarchy of needs and to a refrigerator. In the basic *wants* category, students compared the media to objects they wanted but did not absolutely need, such as a car, chocolate, shoes and gum.

The remaining themes were libraries, powerful force, entertainment centers, "myself," reflections, water, objects, addiction, and metaphors that fit into the "other" category. Powerful force included natural disasters and strong athletes. Entertainment centers included Disney World and circuses. "Myself" metaphors involved students comparing themselves to a "radio head" and to a television. Students referred to mirrors and the subconscious form of dream makers in the reflection metaphors. Water metaphors included swimming pools and sponges. Objects that students used for metaphors were a "media tree" and the game of golf. The addiction metaphor involved a student comparing her relationship with the media to an addiction to drugs.

Bourland-Davis believes the use of metaphors allows professors to gain a better grasp of how students view mass communication theory (Bourland-Davis, 1998).

Common Emphasis

Cooper urges professors to read the discipline of communication as an important bridge to the liberal arts. He argues that communication is a bridge to the liberal arts at three levels. First, this bridge occurs at the universal level because communications is essential to all different types of study topics and disciplines.

Second, this bridge occurs at the academic level because communications research nearly always includes other fields involved with communications, except in conditions of extreme specialization. Last, this bridge occurs on the pragmatic level because all other academic fields rely on communication techniques for teaching and research (Cooper, 1993). An important implication of Cooper's essay is that the communication theory course should make connections to what students are learning in the liberal arts and sciences.

Durham's historical analysis of curricular changes at the University of Wisconsin School of Journalism and Mass Communications provides insights on how research-driven faculty members and practically oriented students can work together to meet different goals (Durham, 1992). A key implication of Durham's historical case-study analysis is that faculty members should engage undergraduate students in their research projects—courses in theory and research methods provide such opportunities.[9]

Goldman, who teachers an upper-division communication theory course, uses a dialectical teaching style to encourage students to learn theoretical perspectives that are different from the received views they may take as conventional wisdom or to which they are introduced in other courses. He introduces students to mainstream positivistic/scientific and critical humanistic paradigms. He uses a humanistic orientation that emphasizes critical theory perspectives and urges colleagues who teach theory to emphasize critical skills and humane values (Goldman, 1990).

Grunig uses attribution theory to teach students interviewing skills. She sensitizes students to the notion that interviewing is a dialogue, not a question-and-answer session. She also reinforces the notion that good or bad interviews can be as much the result of what the interviewer had done, or not done, as it is the result of actions on the part of the interviewee (Grunig, 1990).

Outside Resources

Jeffres and Atkin have used surveys of students' media-use habits to highlight associations among academic major and content preferences (Jeffres and Atkin, 1996). Kock, Kang and Allen have analyzed the broadcast curriculum at two- and four-year colleges and universities, and they conclude that not enough attention is given to instruction in communication theory and ethics (Kock et al., 1999). An important implication of their study is that faculty members who are teaching courses in broadcast journalism should examine these findings with their students and determine what opportunities might exist to integrate a theory and ethics component in the courses they are teaching.

Parisi argues that journalism students can learn to apprehend a different prism than traditional objectivity for framing their stories by being exposed to both critical and cultural studies. Critical studies scholars read *journalism* as a cultural institution with literary, historical, philosophical, political and economic dimensions. Thinking of objectivity as an active rhetorical strategy, as a *meta-editorial* viewpoint, could enrich news writing (Parisi, 1992).

Smith discusses how communication theories and concepts are emphasized in his mass media writing course. He argues that communication theory is important to journalism education because it offers ideas and vocabulary for discussions of writing. Various models of communication theory concentrate on process, meaning relationships, precision in meaning, general systems theory, audience theories, stereotypes, gatekeeping, and selection processes. Students were given one-page handouts outlining key concepts of communication theory as these concepts arose in student work (Smith, 1997).

Stocking discusses a senior seminar in journalism at Indiana University that focused on psychological blinders and the high degree of specialization that leaves scientists ignorant of important research outside of their limited expertise (Stocking, 1992).

In teaching communication theory, professors use a variety of materials, including examples of mass media content, trade journal and academic journal articles, instructional films, and textbooks. This final section examines the content of widely used and recently published theory textbooks, two other books, and a monograph.

These sources cover a variety of topics and include common themes about the need for teaching critical thinking and analytical reasoning skills. Some of these materials focus primary on mass communication theories; others focus mostly on human communication theories. A few of them are included because they represent good examples of explicating theory. These are the sources:

Anderson, Rob, and Veronica Ross. 2002. *Questions of communication: A practical introduction to theory.* 3rd ed. Boston: Bedford/St. Martin's.

Baran, Stanley J., and Dennis K. Davis. 2000. *Mass communication theory: Foundations, ferment, and future.* 2nd ed. Belmont, Calif.: Wadsworth/Thomson Learning.

Dayan, Daniel, and Elihu Katz. 1992. *Media events: The live broadcasting of history.* Cambridge: Harvard University Press.

Griffin, Emory A. 2002. *A first look at communication theory.* 5th ed. New York: McGraw-Hill, 576 pp.

Jeffres, Leo W., and Richard M. Perloff. *Mass media effects.* 2nd ed. Prospect Heights, Ill.: Waveland, 1997, 494 pp.

Littlejohn, Stephen W. 2002. *Theories of human communication.* 7th ed. Belmont, Calif.: Wadsworth/Thomson Learning, 378 pp.

Lowery, Shearon A., and Melvin L. DeFleur. 1995. *Milestones in mass communications research: Media effects.* 3rd ed. White Plains, N.Y.: Longman.

McQuail, Denis. 2000. *Mass communication theory.* 4th ed. London: Sage.

O'Keefe, Daniel J. 2002. *Persuasion theory and research.* 2nd ed. Thousand Oaks, Calif.: Sage.

Meyrowitz, Joshua. 1985. *No sense of place: The impact of electronic media on social behavior.* New York: Oxford University Press.

Rubin, Rebecca B., Alan M. Rubin, and Linda J. Piele. 2000. *Communication research: Strategies and sources.* 5th ed. Belmont, Calif.: Wadsworth/Thomson Learning.

Severin, Werner J., and James W. Tankard Jr. 2001. *Communication theories: Origins, methods and uses in the mass media.* 5th ed. New York: Longman.

Shoemaker, Pamela J, with Elizabeth Kay Mayfield 1987. Building a theory of news content: A synthesis of current approaches. *Journalism Monographs* 103 (June).

Sparks, Glenn G. 2002. *Media effects research: A basic overview.* Belmont, CA: Wadsworth/Thomson Learning.

Wood, Julia T. 2000. *Communication theories in action: An introduction.* 2nd ed. Belmont, Calif.: Wadsworth/Thomson Learning.

Conclusions

Though mass communication theory is seldom a required stand-alone course in the undergraduate curriculum in journalism and mass communication, theory instruction is essential for undergraduate majors, and a theory component is included in a large number of courses and curricular designs at major schools.

Theory instruction is important because it can provide students with frameworks for understanding why workers do what they do, how stakeholders in our media systems perceive what they do, and how stakeholders behave to ensure the media respond to democratic values and meet the needs of pluralistic societies. Theory courses emphasize not only the process of theorizing but content of theories explaining stages of growth, development, structure of media industries, and the effects of mass media.

Theory courses can serve as a bridge between the liberal arts and professional school curricula, teach and reinforce critical thinking and analytical reasoning skills, and improve media literacy skills. Mass communication theory is and surely will remain a staple in the curriculum of professional journalism and mass communication programs in American colleges and universities, a subject-matter area (among others) that differentiates a higher education experience from a strictly applied, trade school experience.

Notes

1. Twenty-five years ago (1976–1977), the author chaired the teaching-standards committee of the Theory and Methodology Division of the Association for Education in Journalism and Mass Communication. The committee analyzed the instructional approaches in theory and methodology courses reported in a survey of 84 members of the division. The course syllabi submitted by instructors represented 34 courses open only to undergraduate students and 47 courses open only to graduate students. While thousands of articles and texts were listed as required readings, only 55 texts and four articles received two or more mentions by at least two different instructors. In a report in *Journalism Educator*, I noted, "Judging by the types of course syllabi sent in by instructors, most journalism educators regard any course which involves the use of scientific knowledge or the application of the scientific method as a 'theory and methodology course' " (Stephens, 1979, p. 64).

2. Some journalism and mass-communications programs, such as the that at University of Wisconsin at Madison, decided years ago to no longer continue seeking accreditation by the ACEJMC. UW–Madison did not believe the curriculum balance recommended by the ACEJMC was possible or in the best interests of its students.

3. Twenty-six AAU institutions have accredited programs. See http://www.ku.edu/~acejmc/students/faqs.shtml for a list of ACEJMC-accredited journalism and mass-communication programs. *TheCenter* at the University of Florida tracks performance by research universities. TheCenter determines the Top American Research Universities by rank on nine different measures. See John V. Lombardi et al., *The Top American Research Universities* (TheCenter, University of Florida, PO Box 112012, Gainesville, FL 32611–2012, July 2001). Rankings are based on the number of measures in the top 25 nationally and number of measures in the top 26 to 50 nationally. This author has taken the center's list, allowed for ties, and assigned a ranking. Allowing for ties, Columbia University is the highest-ranking research university with an accredited program (rank, 6.5), followed by the University of California (rank, 9.5).

4. After his death Columbia accepted Pulitzer's offer to "commit millions not only toward building a distinguished school of journalism but also to create awards to honor exemplary journalistic performance." (Farrar, 1998, p. 129).

5. See Lee B. Becker et al., 2001, p. 31. These authors also note the growth rate for undergraduate enrollments should continue increasing, and exceed enrollment growth rate by field for graduate students.

6. See Stephen Littlejohn, *Theories of human communication*, 7th ed. (Belmont, Calif.: Wadsworth/Thomson Learning, 2002).

7. Adam is uneasy with both the "green-eye shades" and "chi-squares" on what should be taught in journalism schools.

8. I am grateful to Katie Smith, an undergraduate research fellow in our college and in the South Carolina Honors College, for reading and abstracting Vocate's article.

9. The Honors College at the University of South Carolina provides undergraduate research fellowships to work with faculty to propose a research project. In 2001–2002, Katie Smith studied economic literacy, business, and financial news.

References

Adam, G. Stuart. Notes towards a definition of journalism: Understanding an old craft as an art form. In *The Poynter Papers: No. 2*. St. Petersburg, Fla.: Poynter Institute for Media Studies, 1993.

Becker, Lee B., Tudor Vlad, Jisu Huh, and Joelle Prine. 2001. Annual enrollment report number of students studying journalism and mass communication at all-time high. *Journalism and Mass Communication Educator* 56, no. 3 (Autumn):28–60.

Bourland-Davis, Pamela G. 1998. Creating metaphors to analyze media and apply mass communication theory. *Journalism and Mass Communication Educator* 53, no. 2 (Summer):68–74.

Bronstein, Carolyn, and Stephen Vaughn. 1998. Willard G. Bleyer and the relevance of journalism education. *Journalism and Mass Communication Monographs* 166 (June):1–36.

Cooper, Thomas. 1993. Communication as corpus callosum: A reorganization of knowledge. *Journalism Educator* 48, no. 1 (Spring):84–87.

Durham, Frank. 1992. Cultural history of a curriculum: The search for salience. *Journalism Educator* 46, no. 4 (Winter):14–21.

Farrar, Ronald T. 1998. *A creed for my profession: Walter Williams, journalist to the world*. Columbia: University of Missouri Press.

Goldman, Irvin. 1990. Critical communication theory for undergraduate students. *Journalism Educator* 45, no. 1 (Spring):58–63.

Grunig, Larissa A. 1990. Applying attribution theory to teaching of interviewing. *Journalism and Mass Communication Educator* 45, no. 2:58–62.

Jeffres, Leo W., and David J. Atkin. 1996. Dimensions of student interest in reading newspapers. *Journalism and Mass Communication Educator* 51, no. 3:15–23.

Kock, Erin, Jong G. Kang, and David S. Allen. 1999. Broadcast education curricula in 2-year and 4-year colleges. *Journalism and Mass Communication Educator* 54, no. 1 (Spring):4–15.

Parisi, Peter. 1992. Critical studies, the liberal arts, and journalism education. *Journalism Educator* 46, no. 4 (Winter):4–13.

Paul, Richard, and Linda Elder. 2001. *The miniature guide to critical thinking concepts & tools.* Dillon Beach, Calif.: Foundation for Critical Thinking.

Reese, Stephen D. 1999. The progressive potential of journalism education. *Harvard International Journal of Press/Politics* 4, no. 4 (Fall):70–94.

Smith, Edward J. 1997. Professional and academic levels of a mass media writing course. *Journalism and Mass Communication Educator* 52, no. 1 (Spring):59–65.

Stephens, Lowndes F. 1979. Wide variety of texts, aids, employed in theory courses. *Journalism Educator* 34, no. 3 (October):64–69.

Stocking, S. Holly. 1992. Ignorance-based instruction in higher education. *Journalism Educator* 47, no. 3 (Autumn):43–53.

Vocate, Donna R. 1997. Teaching communication theory in the professional school. *Journalism and Mass Communication Educator* 52, no. 2 (Summer):4–14.

Weaver, David H., and Maxwell E. McCombs. 1980. Journalism and social science: A new relationship? *Public Opinion Quarterly* 44, no. 4 (Winter):477–494.

Remembering a Mentor: Steven H. Chaffee

Lowndes F. Stephens

One of the great mentors of all time, Steve Chaffee, died unexpectedly of cardiac arrest in May 2001, and countless numbers of us, whose dissertations he had chaired, or whose research ideas had grown out of a discourse with him, mourned his loss. His life was big enough to warrant significant obituaries in a number of outlets, including *the Los Angeles Times*. I understand why. Steve chaired my dissertation at Wisconsin in the early 1970s and so many other theses and dissertations at the University of Wisconsin and Stanford University.

Why was he so loved and admired, not only by those who studied under him personally, but also by many others who may have known him only through exchanges they had with him by snail mail or e-mail? I think it is because he loved ideas, he had many good ideas of his own, he was a master at developing new ways of exploring communication problems, and he stimulated us to think of different ways of framing questions. There was no hubris in Steve, even though he and Jack (McLeod) were already hot shots in the early 1970s. When I was at the University of Wisconsin, the work being done out of the Mass Communication Research Center on the Surgeon General's Report (on the social effects of television) was coming to a close, but more work was being done on family communication patterns, coorientation analysis, and political socialization. Steve was already a star, and Jack was too (as were so many other folks at Wisconsin). He was approachable and he had tremendous respect for his colleagues and students.

Steve was great at concept explication and he cared about real-world problems. My work at Wisconsin was in the Institute for Environmental Studies on a Lake Superior Project sponsored by the Rockefeller Foundation. I worried about how the work I was doing there could be the foundation for my dissertation, but Steve helped me understand how coorientation as a measurement model could be used as a basis for my applied studies in the institute and my dissertation.

Several of us gathered at the Association for Education in Journalism and Mass Communication (AEJMC) national convention in August 2001 in Washington, D.C., to remember Steve at a special session, and as we shared some formal and informal comments (while wearing our "I've Cited Steve Chaffee" buttons) about Steve's legacy, several thoughts went through my mind.

I thought about Steve as the ultimate collaborator, networker. He knew everybody and could always think of someone who was doing work that might help you do yours better. I remember working on my dissertation proposal late in 1973, and Steve said that Phil Tichenor and others at Minnesota were doing interesting work on community media systems and he encouraged me to drive up to Minnesota and talk with Phil. He was great friends with Dan Wackman and Jerry Kline at Minnesota and encouraged me to read their work as well.

I thought about what it means to do interdisciplinary, multidisciplinary research at a great university. When I was visiting schools and thinking about whether I would leave my job as an economist in a research institute to work on a doctorate, Steve gave me the orientation at Wisconsin. I will never forget what he said that made me decide to go to Wisconsin. He said, "Make your choice not simply based on whether the journalism/mass communication program is strong and a good fit, but because the supporting units in other disciplines are also first rate." He then proceeded to sell me on the Wisconsin Idea, the great programs like those at the Land Tenure Center and the Poverty Institute, and the great professors in political science (Dennis and Edelman), economics (Draper), and sociology (Elder and Wilkening).

Another thing I remember about Steve is his ability to put things in intellectual and historical context. It was fascinating to hear Steve talk about how he and Jack got the idea for coorientation analysis. Steve was influenced by his experiences with Wilbur Schramm, Dick Carter, and others at Stanford University, and he explained how that shaped his worldview. On the other hand, Jack had studied with Theodore Newcomb at the University of Michigan and hence leaned toward social psychological explanations. Chaffee and McLeod reflected on these influences but came up with a different paradigm. In the doctoral seminars that I now teach, I think it is important to put things in intellectual and historical perspective because Steve did that so well, perhaps without even knowing it.

I also thought about how Steve exemplified better than anyone else how first-rate scholarship can inform good teaching—he was a great teacher because he was constantly contributing to the knowledge base from which he taught!

Finally, I thought about how great a cheerleader he was for his colleagues and students. He wrote countless letters of recommendations for people. In my last year at Wisconsin, Steve developed a detailed *spreadsheet* (matrix) summarizing the skill sets (strengths) of those of us in the job market, matching the skills to available jobs. He used that matrix to target letters to several schools around the country, announcing that these students were ready to start their academic careers and should be looked at carefully. We got some nice job offers because Steve said we were ready and could do the job.

I do not believe there is a more important calling than being a university professor. We really do touch so many different people in our teaching, research, and service activities. Steve was a wonderful mentor to so many of us, and we have come to cherish what we do because he was among the best ever at this business and we cherish him.

CHAPTER 4

Race and Gender

Rebecca Ann Lind

Introduction

Interest in and awareness of race and gender issues in the media have been increasing for the past several years and, as a result, instructors have attempted to integrate material regarding these critical issues into their mass communication courses. In addition, many colleges and universities have begun offering at least one course that addresses such issues. Although the emphases of these courses vary across institutions, most notably, they differ on whether they incorporate race, gender or both (or even the inclusion of other socially constructed differences such as class, etc.)

This chapter provides some general material of interest to people who may teach courses addressing these issues. What you find here is based on syllabi submitted to a Broadcast Education Association (BEA) online syllabus project, and responses to an open-ended survey sent to members of the Gender Issues and Multicultural Studies Divisions. Contributors to my edited collection of readings about race and gender in the media played a role, as well as my own personal experience teaching this course.[1]

This chapter begins with a general discussion of the course, focusing on its goals and objectives and its place in the curriculum. I refer to *the course* and *this course* as if it is a singular entity, for the sake of convenience. That is followed by a consideration of instructors' teaching philosophies and the approaches teachers take in the course.

After that, I present an overview of the assignments that are often incorporated into the course, before moving on to some of the ups and downs of teaching the course, what people have noted as challenges, and special rewards. Finally, with the caveat that any such list is incomplete, I provide a list of resources that may be helpful to teachers and students in the course.

Position of Course in the Curriculum

The Race and Gender in the Media course is primarily offered at the advanced undergraduate level (juniors and seniors) or as a combined advanced undergraduate and graduate course. It also is taught at the lower division level (first-year and second-year students) and hence can fit into a junior college curriculum quite well.

The course is often an elective component of the Communication[2] major (meaning it is one of several courses a student may select to fulfill the major requirements), although it is a required major course in some Communication departments, and can even be treated as a capstone seminar. In some schools, the race and gender in the media course meets a *diversity* general education requirement, which frequently means that the course will enroll many students who aren't media or even communication majors.

Similar Courses

Referring to the race and gender in the media course as *the* course belies its variation. Some teachers focus on race, some on gender, and some on both. Some emphasize television, others film, and still others print media. Some address news and public affairs programming, whereas others look at entertainment content. However, the many common qualities in goals and objectives cut across focal points, making the courses fundamentally more similar than different. Generally, the objectives of the course revolve around encouraging students to understand race and/or gender as socially constructed phenomena.

We often discuss how the media act as one of several social institutions that teach us what it means to be of a certain race or gender, and perhaps to encourage student attempts to effect change when appropriate. If students are expected to undertake some form of research in the course, teachers may include an objective to that effect. The course always has as an underlying goal the desire to make students more active and critical media consumers, which may or may not be overtly linked to the concept of media literacy.

Ancillary/Related Courses

Most of the time, the course centers on issues of content and representation, but at times audiences and producers might be covered as they are in courses related to media history or criticism. Frequently, teachers find it important to include explicitly in the course goals the consideration of why issues of race and gender in the media are important.

Comparative Features

To Bradley Gorham of the S. I. Newhouse School of Public Communications, Syracuse University, an important underlying "goal of the course is to get students to see that the 'color-blindness' that is often thrown about in popular culture is not the same as 'color-irrelevance.' And that many Whites who see themselves as egalitarian and free from prejudice nonetheless act and think in ways that often support the dominant racial hierarchy. In other words, I try to problematize students' views of what 'color-blindness' means as a way of further sensitizing them to the perspectives of others."

Naomi Rockler of Colorado State University also spoke to this issue, saying, "So many Americans subscribe to post feminist and 'color-blind' mythologies that gender and race issues don't matter any more, and that we're all equal now. One thing I hope is that students learn in my class that this is not true."

Many instructors formally articulate their course goals; what follows is a small sample of how a few teachers conceptualize the goals of the race and gender in the media course. Debbie Owens of Murray State University said that after taking her race and gender in the media course students should "(1) demonstrate an understanding of why an awareness of diversity is important for communications and mass media practitioners, and develop a critical view regarding diversity in the media." Beyond that they should "(2) demonstrate a knowledge of the major contributions made by women and other groups to the media industry; and (3) recognize and evaluate stereotypes of racial/ethnic groups, women and others that appear in media products."

Cynthia Lont of George Mason University presented the following as the goals of her gender-focused course: "(1) To introduce students to the concepts of mass media influence and power." She also seeks to "(2) to help students see themselves as products of media influence; (3) to make students aware of themselves as purchasers of media products and perceive themselves as instruments of change." Finally, "(4) to give students a sense of women's role in the history of media as a force within the media as professionals as well as consumers; and (5) to develop experience in research using the library's resources in women's studies" (Lont, n.d., p. 1).

Another teacher said he had these four goals in his race-oriented course: "First, it aims to foster critical perspectives about race, culture, and representation. Second, this class seeks to acquaint students with the sociohistorical relationships central to prevailing stereotypes and recent efforts to alter them. Third, it strives to produce an environment in which sensitive and serious discussions about identity and difference can occur productively. Fourth, this course encourages students to think reflexively about their entanglements with prevailing understandings of self and other."

Fernando Delgado of Arizona State University–West said his course goals and objectives are to encourage students to "(1) develop an understanding of media construction; (2) develop an appreciation for the power of stereotypes; and (3) develop an ability to use media analysis techniques."

Finally, in her syllabus, Ann Savage of Butler University differentiates between her own objectives and the objectives for the students. She includes this in her statement of objectives: "In the interest of what I perceive as my social responsibility, I teach this course in a effort to effect change." She seeks "to play a role (regardless of how small it may appear) in helping the differences among all of us to not only be tolerated but supported, encouraged, valued and celebrated" (Savage, n.d., p. 1).

She follows this up with her student objectives: "Please bring an open spirit of inquiry to the material covered in this course. The objective of this course is to get students to recognize that 'the way things are' is not naturally occurring but are specific historical, societal and cultural constructs. Through the readings, assignments and discussions you will develop a critical eye and be able to not only recognize sites of oppression in the media but in society more generally. The objective of this course is to develop your critical skills as an independent thinker. Understanding the material and demonstrating that knowledge is the academic goal of this course. The choice of whether to engage this perspective outside of the class is entirely up to you" (Savage, n.d., p. 1).

As just noted, many schools combine the consideration of race and gender in the course, although some instructors who teach a combined course would like to see it separated. Amanda Lotz of Denison University said that her school began teaching the course "at an impressively early date," but she would prefer it *not* be a combined course. She said, "I oppose combining the topics for ideological and pedagogical reasons. Ideologically, it encourages a conflation that is problematic in the case of white women, many of whom are exceptionally privileged and have received the lion's share of Affirmative Action gains. . . . Pedagogically, there is too much to cover, and [race and gender] are distinct theoretical areas."

Lotz said that she covers a variety of media and content areas, and "there is barely time to get through those areas with just gender or race," although she emphasizes the importance of stressing the *intersections* of these socially constructed identities. She repeatedly brings gender issues into discussions of race and vice versa. On the other hand, some instructors might find that at times students are more comfortable discussing issues of gender than of race. So if gender is covered first in a combined course, this can lay a foundation to encourage active (and less defensive) participation in what for some students is the more difficult arena of race.

Still Lotz raised a key point that we should all keep in mind. Whether the class has just one focus, or several, teachers should emphasize intersectionality; as one instructor put it, we must help students understand that "all diversity issues are tied together. I don't believe you can adequately teach about 'race' without teaching about 'gender,' without teaching about 'class,' without teaching about 'disability,' etc."

Common Goals and Instructor Philosophy

Junior Bridge, an adjunct faculty member at George Mason University and media analyst, articulated the overall approach that seems to guide most people teaching the race and gender course: She emphasizes "hands-on, experiential learning. I do little lecturing; rather, I facilitate learning by engaging students in activities and discussion, then prodding them through questioning to think beyond their findings." Across the board, instructors teaching this course emphasize discussion, participation and active or experiential learning. As one teacher put it, "I strive to have a student-centered course in which reflection, self-discovery, and peer-directed conversations push individuals to question and rethink their ideas about media, race, culture, and power."

Some teachers actively try to allow students as much power in the classroom as possible. It can be pedagogically useful to acknowledge explicitly, in discussion of inequality, the power differences between teacher and students. This can fit in well when discussing temporary versus permanent inequality, perhaps rooted in a larger consideration of dominance and subordination, though teachers certainly aren't obligated to make this sort of theoretical linkage when offering power to their students.

In her syllabus, Ann Jabro of Robert Morris University includes this statement: "I support and implement a democratic teaching style whereby I will solicit your input on most matters that pertain to your graded performance and learning style" (Jabro, 2001, p. 2). Ann Savage, in her syllabus, says she'll give students the right to self-determination as they get deeper into the course: "The 'what' and 'how' of this part of the course is up to you! As a class (with some guidelines established by me), we will together make decisions about how to handle the second half of the semester and the group assignments/ presentations/discussions" (Savage, n.d., p. 3).

In my own classes, I let the students select which of the available readings will actually be required. I usually use a book with more chapters/readings than I wish to cover in one term, so after I assign a small set of chapters, I have the students decide which additional chapters we'll read. Depending on the number of students in the class and the number of readings available, each student picks one or two additional chapters, which become not only assigned readings but also the foundation for the student-led discussions.

In addition to these examples of instructors explicitly negotiating the power relationships with their students, the emphasis teachers of this course put on student presentations and student-led discussions (see the next section) also seems to reflect a significant sharing of power. At the very least, such assignments indicate the extent to which many of the instructors of the race and gender course actively strive to give their students an important and proactive voice in the classroom.

Common Emphasis

There is much overlap in the types of assignments that instructors offer in the race and gender in the media course. Most teachers emphasize written assignments, and this course easily lends itself to satisfying a school's particular specific writing requirements. For example, Susan Tyler Eastman's course (focusing on sports media) at Indiana University is formally designated as an Intensive Writing course (Eastman, 2000, p. 1), and when I taught the race and gender course as a visiting professor at the University of Minnesota, it could be used to satisfy the Senior Paper requirement.

Many instructors require some form of *reaction paper* to the readings, and most require a final paper incorporating course concepts into students' own analyses of media content.[3] Besides the written work, quite a few teachers have students lead class discussion of readings. All teachers emphasize discussion and class participation, and most incorporate screenings of media content. Most de-emphasize traditional examinations, though quizzes and exams are indeed given by some teachers. Below, I discuss the three most commonly used types of assignments: Reaction Papers, Student-Led Discussions, and Final Papers.

Some instructors use short reaction papers to encourage students to reflect critically on media texts encountered in their daily lives (and to apply course concepts in the process). But most reaction/response papers or journals (they have varying labels) seem designed to encourage students to engage in thoughtful and reflective readings of the assigned material. "Short" can be 1 to 2 pages, 3 to 5 pages, or even $1/2$ to 1 page of bulleted points. Some instructors require one reaction paper every day, some require one every week, and some require one per course unit. The length and format often depend on how many are required, the more that are required, the shorter and less formal they become.

The most important thing about the reaction papers is that students must reflect on the readings and cannot merely summarize or report on what the author said. Especially with lower-division classes, teachers may need to help students articulate and value their own opinions and responses to readings. If students find if difficult to avoid simple description, instructors can explicitly tell students something like "I already know what the author has to say; I want to know what you have to say. Don't tell me anything the author said unless you're reacting to it in some way and using the author's point to support your own opinion, evaluation, observation, or assessment of how it relates to a concept we've covered in class."

Besides ensuring that the students do the assigned readings, reaction papers have two important benefits. First, they can increase the quantity and enhance the quality of class discussion. If students have actively engaged with and reflected upon the readings in advance, they can have more to say, and they don't need to rely on spur-of-the-moment thoughts. I'm sure all of us who assign reaction papers have heard numerous classroom comments prefaced by something such as "I wrote about this in my reaction paper. . . ."

This type of preparation for class discussion can be especially helpful when the papers are about readings assigned for student-led discussions, because knowing one's classmates will be prepared can increase the confidence of the student leading the discussion. A second additional benefit of reaction papers is that they can allow students to explore relatively privately an issue they'd prefer not to address in class. According to Amanda Lotz, "The response papers allow a venue for response to issues that may seem too touchy to raise in class."

However, not all reaction papers or journals focus on the assigned readings, although the readings usually are expected to inform what is written. For example, Naomi Rockler assigns "journal entries where students have to find examples of media texts that reflect theories and ideas discussed in the course . . . to encourage students to look critically at the media outside the context of the course." Jody Roy of Ripon College has her students keep "weekly media consumer journals to raise awareness of their own behavior as viewers and also practice critical viewing." As with the other type of response papers, the emphasis is not on describing the media text but reacting to it, analyzing it, and linking it to course concepts.

As noted earlier, many instructors of the Race and Gender in the Media course seem to try to find a variety of creative ways to present information. Straight lecturing is rare, and students are often given the responsibility to impart information to the class. Sometimes teachers have the students lead discussions based on the readings, while at other times students conduct research and then teach the class about what they have learned. This latter type of discussion can focus on specific topics (such as temporary and permanent inequality, privilege, and the like) or important individuals (what are called *biographies* or *profiles* of women or people of color who have made contributions in the realm of media).

According to Amanda Lotz's syllabus, "Each student will be responsible for leading discussion on a class reading at least once. This presentation should include a concise summary of the reading and questions designed to provoke discussion. Creating additional materials (handouts, media clips, etc.) may be helpful in clarifying or illustrating key points from the readings" (Lotz, 2001a, p. 2).

Felicia Slattery, an adjunct faculty member at the University of Illinois at Chicago, requires "an in-depth group presentation about one issue I do not cover. . . . the group ultimately leads the class in a discussion of the issue." Michelle McCoy has her students work in groups to conduct research about various underrepresented groups and then present their findings to the class and lead discussions based on what they've learned.

Cynthia Lont's students teach the class what they learned in preparing a biography/profile of an important woman in the media, which was the topic of the students' first paper: "Your first paper is the basis for a 5-minute presentation to the class. Although you should include the highlights of her life, most of your presentation will revolve around her contribution to the media/society" (Lont, n.d., p. 2).

Many instructors have their students make presentations based on their papers, especially the final term paper (see below). In her class, Erika Engstrom of the University of Nevada—Las Vegas tells students, "You will present formally your research paper and research findings (up to that point) to the class. Your presentation will be graded on content and use of visual aids, including videos, posters, overhead transparencies, and the like" (Engstrom, 2000, p. 2). Susan Tyler Eastman handles presentations a bit differently; she has groups of students debate a relevant controversial topic. She requires students to "interview a real person and then role-play that person in the debate. A write-up of that interview is part of the assignment, but you should add examples and facts from the teacher's clippings and your own background research to bolster your [group's] arguments" (Eastman, 2000, p. 8).

As might be expected, final papers or term papers can be about almost anything. In the Race and Gender in the Media course, instructors assigning a final paper tend to require either some form of media analysis, whether textual analysis or content analysis. The emphasis on textual analysis or content analysis often reflects the extent to which the course emphasizes the social scientific or critical-cultural paradigm. An alternative to this is some type of biography/profile of an important and relevant organization or individual. Many instructors offer students a great deal of latitude in selecting the paper topic; as Lotz puts it in her syllabus, students are required to write "a critical analysis of a specific series, individual network, or industrial practice" (Lotz, 2001b, p. 2).

However, despite this latitude, nearly all teachers require their students to have their topics approved prior to beginning work on the paper, and most provide extensive (perhaps formalized) guidance to the students throughout the paper preparation process.

As an example of the biography/profile-type paper, Lont offers her students an option to "choose a media organization that deals primarily with women or is run primarily by women. . . . Detail their purpose, the organizational structure and their product, etc. You may find some information in the library but much of your research may come from personal interviews (phone or face to face), letters, etc." (Lont, n.d., p. 2).

Savage's syllabus includes examples of the types of person students may wish to study. Students may "focus on a particular actor's progression and challenging of or reinforcing current gender representation"; "a director who took risks in reference to gender, race & class in either TV or film"; or "a musical performer who challenges perceived gender roles or who buys into gender expectations" (Savage, n.d., p. 2).

The content analysis option that Jabro offers to students is "Select a form of media you wish to study. Focus on a specific content area (depictions of women in sports advertisements, sex and the soap, media portrayals of minorities during prime time newscasts, etc.). Devise a coding instrument to guide your analysis. (Some features may include number of characters in episode, gender, race and sexual preference, number of lines delivered, type of copy, etc.)" (Jabro, 2001, p. 6).

Savage's textual analysis option includes "a close examination of a specific TV program or film that garnered a great deal of attention because of challenges to the status quo in terms of gender, race and class." In addition, "a selection of three similar films that portray gender similarly or differently"; "a close examination of gender representation in a particular magazine genre, homemaking, sports, rock, news, etc." Savage, like many other instructors, stresses that the list of options she provides represents "only a small sample of possibilities you could focus your final paper on" (Savage, n.d., p. 2).

Common Challenges/Solutions

All of us who teach this course are bound to encounter a student who resists the subject matter or perhaps rejects the very idea of criticizing media content that is "only" entertainment. Additionally, as Naomi Rockler put it, "Teaching something this political and potentially uncomfortable to some students can make this class much more difficult to teach than something like public speaking." Several teachers mentioned the class can become "uncomfortable," and discussions can become "heated," which requires significant effort of the part of teachers—this can be quite draining.

As Bradley Gorham put it, such discussions are "not a bad thing, but it isn't easy, either." Michelle McCoy of Kent State University–Stark Campus noted that one way to help address these "sensitive" issues to make sure that multiple perspectives are covered, saying that it's "imperative" to weigh all sides of the issue. Debbie Owens said she expends a great deal of energy in reminding students to utilize the theoretical perspectives presented in class. This helps to guide their responses to media texts (rather than relying solely on their personal perspectives). She said she needs to keep a "constant watch over students' tendencies to resort to purely personal, often narrow-minded perspectives."

Fernando Delgado said the most typical challenge "is resistance to certain subject matters, particularly gay/lesbian issues and certain gender issues." One way he helps deal with this is to have the class "break down into smaller groups and discuss why we have the perceptions we have in order to challenge our own expectations."

Amanda Lotz noted that "countering assumptions that 'we're all equal now' " can be quite challenging, "especially in homogenous Midwestern classrooms." Slattery said, "I get many students from the dominant culture who don't believe what I'm teaching." Bradley Gorham finds it valuable to discuss "the psychology of race." He said, "I think that understanding the psychology of how we perceive ourselves and others (and the role the media play in that) helps students understand the complexity of the situation better."

Some student resistance might be due to the fact that, as one teacher put it, students "become defensive because they are taking the discussion too personally." Naomi Rockler noted that "sometimes male students do feel uncomfortable with some of the issues, especially because there tend to be so many more women in communication classes than men. I try to make them feel more comfortable simply by telling them that I'm sorry there aren't more men in the class, and that their opinions on the matters at hand are quite welcome. I also make sure I have some readings and discussion about 'men's issues' too."

Debbie Owens stresses "that the course is neither a gender-bashing nor a race-bashing course." Cynthia Lont encourages her students to take an active role in situations that might create tensions in the classrooms. She said that "when issues of race, gender, age, [etc.] come up I guide the discussion but usually there are several students who can help the rest of the class understand the issues."

Other teachers also spoke of the value of allowing students to help guide efforts to counteract defensive attitudes or other rejections of the concepts, though they noted that it takes skill, patience and energy to do so. And, as Rockler noted, "generally, even if students are uncomfortable with these kinds of topics, most [students] still seem to find these issues interesting."

Felicia Slattery said that students often claim that media critics are just "overanalyzing"—it's just entertainment, and "How DARE I pick on Disney?" However, most students eventually understand the value of critically examining even the most apparently benign or even beneficent content—including Disney films and *Sesame Street*.

Several teachers spoke of the importance of acknowledging their own racialized and gendered identity, because whether the teacher is a member of the dominant or minority cultural group, these cultural identities are always relevant to the course material. Bradley Gorham spoke of the need to overcome "student skepticism that a WASP like me has anything to offer about diversity. I confront this in the first class, head on, discussing frankly and openly about my own perspectives on these issues growing up and what changed. I'm a White, middle-class guy from the suburbs, and it is clear to me now how much that background privileged my understanding of what is right, normal, and desirable, but it wasn't always that way.

"By discussing my position in the social order, I try to establish how my views have been shaped and constructed by that social order and my interaction with it. That sparks a lot of conversation on that first day, but also helps establish that I have credibility in this area even though I'm hardly the definition of 'diverse'"

A different type of difficulty presents itself when instructors wish to incorporate films and videos into the course, which as most teachers agree is an important and valuable component of the Race and Gender in the Media course. According to Jody Roy, "It is really a time challenge."

She said that the benefit of in-class viewing is that "we can hit pause and discuss particular issues" and also noted that "it is difficult to manage 'outside' viewing." However, some teachers regularly require that students view texts outside of class. In such cases, the films or videos are usually available at a campus library or media center.

Finally, it's important to remember the profoundly political nature of this type of course and acknowledge its potential interaction with another political process, mentioned by one teacher: "To be honest, I worry almost every class about saying something the wrong way and having it misconstrued or misinterpreted. I share this fear with the class, to highlight to everyone that we all have this fear and that this is the class where saying things the wrong way is okay because we can and should talk about it in an environment of mutual trust. But that doesn't mean I still don't worry about it. As an assistant professor, the last thing I want is to have something happen in class that will come back to haunt me at tenure and review time."

Conclusions

Despite these challenges, this course is often a favorite of the instructors teaching it. Most of the teachers of the Race and Gender in the Media course have found teaching the course to be richly rewarding on a variety of levels. As Junior Bridge put it, this course "opens eyes, expands consciousness, and gives students a new method for thinking critically about this and other cultural topics." Another teacher said, "When students 'get it,' they really get it. It's a thrill to see their world views change." Most instructors echoed this sentiment; there is a strong reward for teachers in knowing that, as Gorham said, "I am helping do something to reduce prejudice."

Additionally, many teachers acknowledged the importance of (and took pleasure in) "helping students become critically literate about race and media." Some teachers spoke of the extent to which students become involved with the material and considered that a positive aspect of teaching this course. According to Jody Roy, "Students are intrigued and very open to learning more." Cynthia Lont said, "Students leave watching the media in a whole different light. The women often talk to their boyfriends about these issues."

On another level, Fernando Delgado and others noted how valuable it is to teach a course that is so closely linked with their programs of research. This is clearly an opportunity for us to take advantage of a wonderful synergy between our teaching and research. Some instructor's point out how much they can learn from their students, reinforcing the fact that, in the ideal classroom, we all learn from everybody else. Michelle McCoy noted that when her students make presentations about underrepresented groups, "I find new elements of diversity I hadn't considered before. For example, some students researched dwarfism. Other disabilities came up, too."

Finally, some teachers find that the student evaluations of the course are particularly rewarding. As Amanda Lotz said, student evaluations can show that "these are courses that students acknowledge really make a difference. That is as good as it gets." Besides the purely personal reward a teacher gets from receiving such an evaluation, it also provides hearty evidence of teaching effectiveness for an instructor's tenure and promotion file.

Notes

1. I thank everyone who participated in this project. In this chapter, direct quotations come either from the syllabi or from people's responses to the survey I e-mailed in the summer of 2002. Quotations from surveys returned by people who wished to be

identified are introduced in a manner such as "according to [name] from [university]." Quotations from surveys returned by people who preferred their responses remain confidential are introduced in a manner such as "according to one teacher." Quotations from syllabi are cited in the traditional manner. When given the opportunity, this chapter emphasizes survey responses because syllabi are relatively publicly available.

2. Here, feel free to insert Telecommunication, Radio/TV/Film, Media, Communication Studies, Speech Communication, or whatever other name has been given to the department offering the course.

3. One of the perhaps unanticipated advantages of emphasizing reaction papers, discussion leading, and content or textual analyses is that students cannot easily purchase ready-made papers, because such offerings rarely satisfy the course requirements. In addition, many teachers maintain close contact with students as they conduct their research, and often require a progress update that may be operationalized as drafts of sections of the final paper. Besides providing valuable support to the students (many of whom have never undertaken a project of this type before), this close contact makes it even less tempting for students to rely on a commercial paper-writing service.

References

Eastman, S. T. 2000. Sports & television, intensive writing. Syllabus available online: www.beaweb.org/syllabus/gender/Sports_and_Media.PDF. Accessed 16 September 2002.

Engstrom, E. 2000. Gender issues in the mass media. Syllabus available online: www.beaweb.org/syllabus/gender/Engstrom.PDF. Accessed 16 September 2002.

Jabro, A. D. 2001. Stereotypes and the media. Syllabus available online: www.beaweb.org/syllabus/gender/Stereotypes_and_Media.PDF. Accessed 16 September 2002.

Lont, C. n.d. Women and media. Syllabus available online: www.beaweb.org/syllabus/gender/women_and_media.pdf. Accessed 16 September 2002.

Lotz, A. 2001a. Women and American media culture. Syllabus obtained through personal communication, 10 July 2002.

———. 2001b. Race and ethnicity in American television. Syllabus obtained through personal communication, 10 July 2002.

Savage, A. M. n.d. Gendered media images. Syllabus available online: www.beaweb.org/syllabus/gender/Gendered_Media_Images.pdf. Accessed 16 September 2002.

Outside Resources

Books

Possible Textbooks

Biagi, S., and Kern-Foxworth, M., eds. 1997. *Facing Difference: Race, Gender and Mass Media.* Thousand Oaks, Calif.: Pine Forge Press.

Creedon, P. J., ed. 1993. *Women in mass communication.* 2nd ed. Newbury Park, Calif.: Sage.

Dines, G., and J. M. Humez, eds. 2002. *Gender, race and class in media: A text-reader.* 2nd ed. Thousand Oaks, Calif.: Sage.

Holtzman, L. 2000. *Media messages: What film, television, and popular music teach us about race, class, gender, and sexual orientation.* Armonk, N.Y.: M. E. Sharpe.

Kamalipour, Y. R., and T. Carilli, eds. 1998. *Cultural diversity and the U.S. media.* Albany: State University of New York Press.

Lester, P. M., ed. 1996. *Images that injure: Pictorial stereotypes in the media.* Westport, Conn.: Praeger.

Lind, R. A., ed. In press. *Race/gender/media: Considering diversity across audiences, content, and producers.* Boston: Allyn and Bacon.

Lont, C. M., ed. 1995. *Women and media: Content/careers/criticism.* Belmont, Calif.: Wadsworth.

Meyers, M., ed. 1999. *Mediated women: Representations in popular culture.* Creskill, N.J.: Hampton.

Wilson II, C. C., and F. Gutierrez. 1995. *Race, multiculturalism, and the media: From mass to class communication.* Thousand Oaks, Calif.: Sage.

Woodward, K., ed. 1997. *Identity and difference.* Thousand Oaks, Calif.: Sage.

Valdivia, A. N., ed. 1995. *Feminism, multiculturalism, and the media: Global diversities.* Thousand Oaks, Calif.: Sage.

Resource Books

Allport, G. 1954. *The nature of prejudice.* Cambridge, Mass.: Addison-Wesley.

Beasley, M. H., and S. J. Gibbons. 1993. *Taking their place: A documentary history of women and journalism.* Washington, D.C.: American University Press.

Campbell, C. P. 1995. *Race, myth, and the news.* Thousand Oaks, Calif.: Sage.

Carstarphen, M. G., and S. C. Zavoina. 1999. *Sexual rhetoric: Media perspectives on sexuality, gender and identity.* Westport, Conn.: Greenwood.

Entman, R. M., and A. Rojecki. 2000. *The Black image in the White mind: Media and race in America.* Chicago: University of Chicago Press.

Fiske, J. 1996. *Media matters.* Minneapolis: University of Minnesota Press.

Gray, H. 1995. *Watching race: Television and the struggle for "Blackness."* Minneapolis: University of Minnesota Press.

Jhally, S., and J. Lewis. 1992. *Enlightened racism: 'The Cosby Show,' audiences, and the myth of the American Dream.* Boulder, Colo.: Westview.

Lipsitz, G. 1998. *The possessive investment in whiteness: How white people profit from identity politics.* Philadelphia: Temple University Press.

Marlane, J. 1999. *Women in television news revisited: Into the twenty-first century.* Austin: University of Texas Press.

Means-Coleman, R. 2002. *Say it loud! African American audiences, identity and media.* New York: Routledge.

Nelson, J. 1994. *The disabled, the media and the information age.* Westport, Conn.: Greenwood.

Omi, M., and H. Winant. 1986. *Racial formation in the United States: From the 1960s to the 1980s.* New York: Routledge and Kegan Paul.

Peach, L. J., ed. 1998. *Women in culture: A women's studies anthology.* Malden, Mass.: Blackwell.

Roy, J. 2002. *Love to hate: America's obsession with hatred and violence.* New York: Columbia University Press.

Thorne, B., and N. Henley, eds. 1973. *Language and sex: Difference and dominance.* Rowley, Mass.: Newbury House.

Trotta, L. 1991. *Fighting for air: In the trenches with television news.* New York: Simon and Schuster.

Valdivia, A. N. 2000. *A Latina in the Land of Hollywood and other essays on media culture.* Tucson: University of Arizona Press.

Van Dijk, T. A. 1987. *Communicating racism: Ethnic prejudice in thought and talk.* Newbury Park, Calif.: Sage.

Zook, K. B. 1999. *Color by Fox: The Fox network and the revolution in Black television.* New York: Oxford University Press.

Journal Articles and Chapters in Edited Volumes

Bonnett, A. 1998. Who was white? The disappearance of non-European white identities and the formation of European racial whiteness. *Ethnic and Racial Studies* 21, no. 6:1029–1055.

Brown, J. D., and L. Schulze. 1990. The effects of race, gender, and fandom on audience interpretation of Madonna's music videos. *Journal of Communication* 40, no. 2:88–103.

Devine, P. G. 1989. Stereotypes and prejudice: Their automatic and controlled components. *Journal of Personality and Social Psychology* 56:5–18.

Dixon, T. L., and D. Linz. 2000. Race and misrepresentation of victimization on local television news. *Communication Research* 27:547–573.

Domke, D. 1997. Journalists, framing, and discourse about race relations. *Journalism and Mass Communication Monographs* 164:1–55.

Entman, R. M. 1990. Modern racism and the images of blacks in local television news. *Critical Studies in Mass Communication* 7:332–345.

Faber, R. J., T. C. O'Guinn, and T. P. Meyer. 1987. Televised portrayals of Hispanics: A comparison of ethnic perceptions. *International Journal of Intercultural Relations* 11:155–169.

Giroux, H. A. 1997. Rewriting the discourse of racial identity: Towards a pedagogy and politics of whiteness. *Harvard Educational Review* 67, no. 2:285–320.

Gorham, B. W. 1999. Stereotypes in the media: So what? *Howard Journal of Communication* 10, no. 2:229–247.

Harrison, K. 2000. The body electric: Thin-ideal media and eating disorders in adolescents. *Journal of Communization* 50, no. 3:119–143.

Hendriks, A. 2002. Examining the effects of female bodies on television: A call for theory and programmatic research. *Critical Studies in Mass Communication* 19, no. 1:106–123.

Lind, R. A. 1996. Diverse interpretations: The "relevance" of race in the construction of meaning in, and evaluation of, a television news story. *Howard Journal of Communications* 7:53–74.

————. 2002. Speaking of culture: The relevance of cultural identity as Afro-, Latin-, and Euro-American lay people plan a television newscast. *Journalism and Mass Communication Quarterly* 3:111–145.

Lind, R. A., and C. Salo. 2002. The framing of feminists and feminism in news and public affairs programs in U.S. electronic media. *Journal of Communication* 52:211–228.

McIntosh, P. 2002. White privilege, color, and crime: A personal account. In *Images of color, images of crime*. 2nd ed. Ed. C. Mann and M. Zatz. Los Angeles: Roxbury.

Oliver, M. B. 1999. Caucasian viewers' memory of Black and White criminal suspects. *Journal of Communication* 49, no. 3:46–60.

Peffley, M., T. Shields, and B. Williams. 1996. The intersection of race and crime in television news stories: An experimental study. *Political Communication* 13:309–327.

Reep, D. C., and F. H. Dambrot. 1989. Effects of frequent television viewing on stereotypes: 'Drip, drip' or 'drench'? *Journalism Quarterly* 66:542–550, 556.

————. 1994. TV parents: Fathers (and now mothers) know best. *Journal of Popular Culture* 28, no. 2:13–23.

Wong, W. 1994. Covering the invisible "model minority." *Media Studies Journal* 8:49–59.

Web Sites

Asian American Journalists Association. www.aaja.org.

Body Image Site. www.bodyimagesite.com.

Center for Media Literacy. www.medialit.org.

Citizens for Media Literacy. www.main.nc.us/cml/.

Directory of Media Literacy Sites Worldwide. www.chebucto.ns.ca/Community Support/AMLNS/internet.html

Fairness and Accuracy in Reporting. www.fair.org.

Jean Kilbourne (women and media). www.jeankilbourne.com.

Media Awareness Network. www.media-awareness.ca/eng/.

Media Education Foundation. www.mediaed.org.

Media Report to Women. www.mediareporttowomen.com.

Media Resources Center of the Library at the University of California at Berkeley (films by and about people of color). www.lib.berkeley.edu/MRC/EthnicImages Vid.html.

Media Resources Center of the Library at the University of California at Berkeley (films dealing with gender issues). www.lib.berkeley.edu/MRC/WomenVid.html.

Media Studies. www.mediastudies.com/.

Media Watch. www.mediawatch.com/.

Minorities and Media project at the London School of Economics. www.lse.ac.uk/Depts/Media/EMTEL/Minorities/.

Multicultural Skyscraper Online. www.multicultural.net.

NAACP (National Association for the Advancement of Colored People). www.naacp.org.

National Association of Black Journalists. www.nabj.org.

National Association of Hispanic Journalists. www.nahj.org.

National Lesbian and Gay Journalists Association. www.nlgja.org.

National Organization for Women. www.now.org/.

Native American Journalists Association. www.naja.org.

Selected women and gender resources on the world wide web: www.library.wisc. edu/libraries/WomensStudies/others.htm.

Southern Poverty Law Center. www.splcenter.org. Also see www.tolerance.org.

University of Iowa, Communication Studies Department (much information about gender, race, and the media). www.uiowa.edu/~commstud/resources/GenderMedia/.

Vernon Stone (race, gender, employment issues in broadcast news). www.missouri. edu/~jourvs/.

Films/Videos (distributors listed in parentheses)

bell hooks on video: Cultural criticism and transformation. (Media Education Foundation.)

Black is ... Black ain't: A personal journey through Black identity. Marlon Riggs.[Q15] (California Newsreel.)

Blue eyed. Jane Elliot. California Newsreel.

Campus culture wars, five stories about PC. (Direct Cinema Ltd.)

The celluloid closet. (Columbia TriStar Home Entertainment.)

Color adjustment. Marlon Riggs. (California Newsreel.)

Don't be a TV: Television Victim. (MediaWatch Videos.)

Dreamworlds II: Desire, sex, and power in music video. Sut Jhally. (Media Education Foundation.)

Ethnic notions. Marlon Riggs. (California Newsreel.)

Game over: Gender, race and violence in video games. (Media Education Foundation.)

Killing us softly 3: Advertising's image of women. Jean Kilbourne. (Media Education Foundation.)

Playing UnFair: The media image of the female athlete. (Media Education Foundation.)

Slaying the dragon. Deborah Gee. (Women Make Movies.)

Slim hopes: Advertising and the obsession with thinness. Jean Kilbourne. (Media Education Foundation.)

Tough guise: Media images and the crisis in masculinity. Jackson Katz. (Media Education Foundation.)

Warning: The media may be hazardous to your health. Ann J. Simonton. (MediaWatch Videos.)

Women in rock. (WEA.)

Remembering a Mentor:
Kathleen Hall Jamieson

Sean Aday

It is tempting in a volume such as this to describe one's mentor strictly in terms of how they provided a model for your own teaching. In the case of Kathleen Hall Jamieson, however, that would be telling only half the story. Kathleen belongs in a book on mass communication education not just for her legendary presence in front of a classroom, but at least as much for her rare ability to see, sculpt and support the total student.

At a recent conference, someone who had attended a different graduate school than I said she agreed with her professors that teaching is a necessary evil in the more noble pursuit of research. I doubt any student of Kathleen's former students would ever make such a statement. True to form for the author of *Beyond the Double Bind: Women and Leadership* (1997), Kathleen clearly views the alleged teaching/research dichotomy as a false one and rises above it every time she walks into a classroom. The unmistakable lesson for her students is that, by listening to their students, good teachers not only bring their best ideas to the classroom, but *from* it, as well.

Kathleen's dynamic, commanding, and of course entertaining approach to teaching has made her something of a celebrity among students wherever she has taught. Testimony to her reputation is that she is someone undergraduates consider a must-take even though they know they have little chance of getting an "A" from her. While some professors skate by on humor or charisma alone, Kathleen uses those gifts as any political advertising scholar knows they should be: to get an audience's attention before moving on to the more important business of making your point.

Due to her popularity, Kathleen's undergraduate classes are themselves something of an exercise in mass communication. Indeed, one semester her lectures were simulcast to half the students in another building because the university could not reserve a lecture hall large enough for her. In her smaller, graduate seminars, she is no less dynamic, but students are even more able to benefit from—and occasionally wither in the face of—her notoriously piercing intellect. As anyone who knows her would not be surprised to learn, she has a style that is best understood as Socrates on Speed. A typical first day of classes in her graduate seminar involves her walking in, playing a video of several political ads, and then going around the room in rapid succession asking each student for the most important insight into what they just saw. She then begins moving deeper and deeper into deconstruction and analysis. From this whirlwind, students quickly learn the ability not only to think on their feet, but to think well. Much of this, of course, is learned by example, as few possess Kathleen's alacrity of mind.

Kathleen's influence as a teaching mentor is not limited to her formidable ability to impart knowledge, however, but also in that she is that rarest of professors who truly cares about the well-being of her students professionally and personally. It is here that she has had the most influence on me as a teacher, and why so many of her legions of former students feel indebted to her. Ask any of her former students, particularly graduate students, and they will have their own story about what she did to help them get through graduate school. This includes working with them as co-authors rather than merely research assistants, helping prepare them for job interviews, or being there for them during personal crises. She has even been generous enough to fund dozens of students personally for summer research positions and even their own scholarly projects, an aspect of her benevolent commitment to students of which I am personally grateful.

The research we as academics do is important and, if we are asking the right questions and answering them carefully, can make a difference. Certainly Kathleen's does. But I have always felt that far and away the most important contribution we in the social sciences make is in nurturing young minds. I tell my students that my job, to borrow from Bernard Cohen, is not so much to teach them what to think, but how to think. We do this in the classroom by encouraging critical thought, but also outside of it by welcoming students into our office, taking an interest in their personal lives, and respecting them enough to listen genuinely to what they have to say and engaging them intellectually. As any of her former students will tell you, Kathleen does all this and more.

CHAPTER 5

Convergence

Max Utsler

Introduction

Blame it on the Internet. Without that particular invention, journalism and mass communication departments and schools could have just gone along their merry way. Keep the media-specific courses and majors such as television and newspaper. Keep the function-specific courses and majors such as advertising and public relations. Yes, they could have gone on like that forever. They certainly had the professors to perpetuate it. They had the copyediting teacher who had always taught copyediting. They had the TV production teacher who had always taught TV production. They had the advertising teacher who had always taught advertising. They were recruited because of their specific expertise, and those courses became required for a particular major. When one of those teachers retired, they set about to replace him or her with another equal expert in that area so the school could continue to offer those required classes. But what do we do about that pesky Internet?

We looked to our professional brethren for guidance. But they were having their own problems, such as what to do about that pesky Internet? Roger Fidler, then of Knight-Ridder, currently of Kent State University, developed a theory he called *Mediamorphosis*. He wrote a book on the subject in 1997 and outlined his theory for the coming changes in the digital world:

> Mediamorphosis is not such a theory as it is a unified way of thinking about the technological evolution of communication media. Instead of studying each form separately it encourages us to examine all forms as members of an interdependent system, and to note the similarities and relationships that exist among past, present, and emerging forms. (Fidler, Mediamorphosis, p. 23, 1997)

Fidler's concept along with significant changes in media ownership rules and increasing pressures for media profitability help explain the emergence of a practice called *convergence*. Companies that owned newspapers as well as broadcast outlets began exploring ways they could use information in more than one medium. Newspapers that did not own broadcast outlets began exploring partnerships with broadcasters.

But the roots of convergence go much deeper than that. In 1978, the Media Lab under the leadership of Nicholas Negroponte at the Massachusetts Institute of Technology began looking at all communication as a single subject. Negroponte would draw three slightly overlapping circles representing broadcasting, print and computers and talk about how each had a slight relationship to the other. Then he would draw the same three circles and have them almost overlap. He used that as an illustration of how broadcasting, print and computers were overlapping in such a way to suggest one future communication medium. The development of digital technology was guiding this evolution.

So while the term *convergence* was still a few years off, this change did not go unnoticed by mass communication educators. Schools began to discuss and then reorganize courses and curricula in an effort to keep up with what many assumed would be a demand for a new breed of multimedia journalist.

Integrated Marketing Communications (IMC) became one of the first displays of convergence. IMC advocates Don Schultz of Northwestern and Tom Duncan of the University of Colorado realized advertising, public relations, internal communications and promotions all fell under the same heading: marketing. Yet only a handful of schools have adopted the IMC approach. Most continue to teach advertising and public relations as separate entities, ignoring internal communications and promotions altogether.

Those schools that did examine and sought to change their curricula faced the usual dilemma of academic restructuring. They didn't want their students to graduate without the skills to work in the "brave, new digital world." But they also didn't want to be educating their students too far ahead of the industry curve: "We don't need people to shoot video. We need copy editors." This was the cry from a major newspaper managing editor while visiting the University of Kansas two years ago.

The issue was further complicated by the industry's inability to clearly define synergy or convergence. Disney and AOL/Time Warner were among the early standard bearers, promising to not only be bigger companies, but better able to serve a consumer in many different ways. As time went on, each of the individual pieces of their businesses seemed to be doing fine.

Together in an effort to create that "synergy," Disney and AOL/Time Warner were a mess. By 2002, Wall Street had taken those two companies into the alley for a good ol' fashion whuppin'. That prompted Rob Walker to write in a July 28, 2002, article for the *New York Times*, "Maybe we haven't heard the last of synergy or its close cousin 'convergence.' But if it ever returns, let's hope that it does in a form that has some tangible meaning, preferably one that's grounded in something consumers actually want." As it turned out, most people didn't care if the company that provided them with cable or TV also made movies, promoted a theme park, owned a baseball team, and provided them with merchandise tie-ins with a fast-food order.

That has always been one of the conundrums of convergence. Is it really grounded in something consumers want? If the issue is news, can a TV station partnered with a newspaper bring you *more* coverage? Do any consumers think we have a *shortage* of news today? No, quantity is not the issue, so what about quality?

Convergence has not changed one of the basic tenets of journalism. Some stories are best read in a newspaper. Some stories are best heard on the radio. Some stories are best shown on TV. By extension, some stories are best presented on the Internet. The place where combined resources would most likely show a visible effect would be in the areas of public affairs/investigative reporting, big stories of broad community interest or big breaking news stories such as natural disasters. That is where teams of reporters and editors would pool their resources to bring to light significant community problems and issues. Is there any evidence to suggest the converged media have devoted their resources to this cause?

Or could it be about the business of the mass media? Is it possible corporate America saw convergence as a way to get half the number of people to do twice the amount of work? The trail leads to that conclusion, but the evidence refutes it. "Do you ever remember a time of going into a newsroom, and the people on duty were not working or had idle time on their hands?" asked Bob Papper of Ball State (personal interview, August 2002). Just listen to the media cries of "We can't make any money on the Internet!" When the economic times got tough in post-9/11 America, the first place media companies targeted for cuts was the Internet. No, our professional brethren have not found the answer.

"It's not rocket science," wrote Wayne Roberts, an associate editor for *Editor and Publisher*. "Achieving this mixture, often referred to as Media Convergence, doesn't appear to be nearly as easy as rocket science."

If schools head down the convergence trail because of industry trends, they will find little guidance from the profession. That doesn't necessarily mean schools should avoid convergence. "I've sworn off the word convergence," said James K. Gentry, journalism dean at the University of Kansas. "We teach students to perform in a media world that demands multiple skills. Our students can work across platforms while developing skills that prepare them for careers in journalism" (personal interview, January 2001). But that assumes the outcome to be the most important part of the process. Perhaps the real educational benefit may come from what happens at the beginning of the curriculum rather than the end.

The old curriculum system was built around the concept of *majors*, sometimes called *sequences*. The sequence system owed its success (or lack of) to the ability of students to enter the right sequence at the beginning of their schooling. The students kept the faith, knowing that at the end of their course of study, they would possess the necessary skills to get a job. And, in the future, perhaps they would progress to a better job. That might have been an appropriate concept when the world of journalism and mass communication consisted of newspapers and magazines that led to only one choice—reporter or copyeditor.

As our mass media world added new technologies such as radio and TV, we added new sequences. As our mass media world added new functions such as advertising and public relations, we added more new sequences. The choice of "which sequence" was becoming more complicated. Pity the poor students who took the first two courses in sequence and then changed direction. They had the privilege of going back to the start of a sequence. What if all they had determined was "I know I don't want to be a (fill the blank)"—not the same as knowing what you want to do.

Schools kept adding new choices, new sequences. Then along came the Internet, and, for the most part, we could not even come up with a sequence for it, although some schools have created sequences with names like Multimedia and New Media.

But imagine what it would be like if students didn't have to declare their intent coming in the door. Imagine if a student could actually sample different media and different functions before making that career decision. Imagine if a curriculum was built on student need rather than faculty interest and expertise. But that is much easier said than done.

"You have to establish a common direction and focus among the faculty," said Gentry, one of the early proponents of a convergence curriculum. "It won't work if a sizable percentage of the faculty isn't on board. But you can do it with a couple of dissenters."

The beginning convergence courses described in this chapter come from schools and departments that have pursued the notion of convergence enough to turn up in scholarly papers, the popular press, or convention programs. All of the schools are either members of the Association for Education in Journalism and Mass Communication or Broadcast Education Association. They represent a cross section of schools that are close to teaching convergence, among others struggling with the concept.

University of Kansas graduate student Frances Gorman assisted in the research for this chapter. We compiled the information through a check of online materials about each course, a short phone or e-mail exchange, an examination of course syllabi, and a 30-minute phone interview with the course instructor. Schools include Arizona State, Brigham Young, Ball State, Emerson, Kent State, South Carolina, and Kansas.

Position of Convergence in the Curriculum

Critics have often chastised journalism and mass communication education for being too "trade school" oriented. Convergence would seemingly address some of that charge by encouraging less specialization and a broader approach. Convergence should, at least theoretically, enable students to make better-informed choices of which careers to enter.

For purposes of this book, we concentrated on the entry-level writing course in schools and departments that purported to be *converged* or at least, *converging*, teaching cross-platform skills. The word *news* occurred in all of the course names except Kent State (Media Writing) and Kansas (Introduction to Research and Writing). Prerequisites included some or all of the following: grade point average, a Survey of Mass Media course, an English requirement, or admission to the major.

Course syllabi listed goals and objectives for each course. Although the actual wording may vary, the following goals appeared in the syllabi for each of the courses studied here: (1) Prepare students to work in emerging fields. (2) Give students confidence in their skills and make them employable. (3) Learn to write news for different audiences. (4) Identify, find, and focus news.

All schools mentioned the *learning of style* but did not necessarily state it as a goal. Six schools listed something like *active multimedia participation in a lab framework* as a goal. Sources at only two schools, Kent State and Kansas, consider public relations and advertising as part of convergence. The University of South Carolina tried a fully converged beginning class but scrapped it. It also scuttled a common lecture to gain more lab time.

At least two of the schools have garnered outside financial support through gifts designed to prepare students better for the future. In 1996, Ball State combined their departments of journalism, communication studies, telecommunications, and the Center for Information and Communication Sciences into the College of Communication, Information and Media. The school has begun what they term a "bold new initiative" supported by the Lilly Endowment. The program "will build on the university's existing strengths in creating communication content, using communication and information technology, and cultivating global partners."

The Kent State School of Journalism and Mass Communication has opened the Carl E. Hirsch Media Convergence Lab. The Hirsch Lab is a "prototype classroom of the future where students and faculty can experiment with the latest technologies for news and information gathering, editing and production."

South Carolina set a goal in 2001 to create a "Newsplex, a beyond state-of-the-art studio for teaching mass media and journalism." Newsplex is a $1.5 million news center being developed in conjunction with Ifra, a German-based company that focuses on publishing strategies and technologies for the news media. Courses tied to the Newsplex will use its resources for "cross-media newsgathering and story presentation."

Arizona State presents new curriculum as being able to "better describe the emerging mass media fields that are developing through convergence and the evolution of new media." Brigham Young had the first newsroom in the country to physically merge all of its media outlets in 1997, but the curriculum so far is not completely converged.

Emerson revamped the department curriculum in the new millennium "to reflect rapid changes in the news industry and wed theory and practice." They require students to choose a specialty, either print, broadcast or online, but introduce all students to an integrated core curriculum to keep up with the rapid pace at which media are evolving.

Similar/Related Courses

Those who expect convergence to run through the entire curriculum will be disappointed in the results so far. All of the schools surveyed have at least some level of convergence somewhere in the curriculum. In the prerequisite or concurrent Introduction to Mass Media course, all schools cover convergence as a phenomenon in the field. However, none of the seven schools would qualify as fully converged.

Arizona State developed its entry-level course and is looking at other courses where convergence may come into play. South Carolina will be changing the way they teach some of the old courses. They are also considering a new course in the visual communication area that would be required for all journalism majors.

Ball State is using part of a grant from the Lilly Endowment to develop new ways of doing the news. Convergence is one of the centerpieces of their plan, and elements of their convergence curriculum preceded the grant. Emerson has a second-level class required by all students that includes Web, video, audio, and digital stills. Kansas is fully converged in the beginning of the curriculum, goes into specialties in the middle, and somewhat converges in the end. Kansas does not have one single newsroom but separate ones for the newspaper and the broadcast stations. Those media outlets occasionally provide stories for each other. Calling that convergence might be a stretch, but, as in some other instances, a level of cooperation is present that never existed before. On the strategic side, the capstone course, Strategic Campaigns, is fully converged both in medium and function.

Once again, we find schools with widely varying definitions of convergence throughout the curriculum. That is partly due to the varying definitions of courses in previous curricula. Several schools teach information gathering, audio and video production, and visual communication separate from writing. Some schools teach one or all three of those components in the beginning writing class. Clearly, the school's choice in this basic decision strongly influences what will take place in other classes. In any case, one would expect a beginning convergence course to help prepare the students to work in other convergence courses, labs, newsrooms and other parts of the curriculum.

In the case of convergence, *related courses* is a very relative term. Steve Doig of Arizona State University said his beginning writing course is currently the only convergence course in the curriculum and, with its heavy emphasis on print newswriting, one could question how converged it really is. ASU will be looking at other courses where convergence can come in.

Ernest Wiggins at South Carolina said his school will just tweak the existing courses. South Carolina offers a separate Senior Semester Practicum for print and broadcast students. Wiggins said those two courses offer "a limited cross-pollination of print news and broadcast with an on-line component based at the print Senior Semester's Web site."

"Our school has not gone into convergence as strongly as I had hoped," said Roger Fidler of Kent State. "We had a new curriculum six years ago. At its core was convergence." However, Fidler noted his school has the electronic media in a different building (the same as Ball State and Kansas), and they have not resolved all of their convergence issues.

Emerson, Ball State and Kansas are among the most converged programs. Emerson offers a second-level course called Images of News: Words, Pictures and Sound. The required class includes basic use of video, digital stills, audio and the Web. From there, a student would go into either a print or broadcast writing class. A planned capstone experience will take place in a convergence newsroom.

At Ball State, the second-level class takes everything from the first convergence writing class a step further. The students rotate through radio, TV and newspaper newsrooms at four-week intervals. The course then allows the students an option of four additional weeks of radio, TV or newspaper. The news/ed and broadcast news programs are 50 percent merged and 50 percent specialized in the new curriculum said Papper.

Kansas moves from its fully converged beginning course that includes advertising and public relations plus audio and video production. Students then opt for a second-level writing and production course: Multimedia Reporting (News) or Message Development (Business Writing, Public Relations, Advertising, Promotions), depending on interest. The News Track ends with two campus media experiences among six or seven alternatives in a choice of media and function. The Strategic Track ends with a Strategic Campaigns class that combines elements of advertising, public relations, promotions and marketing.

Comparative Features

The greatest differentiation among beginning convergence classes perhaps centers on print newswriting and how much the course will feature it. The second greatest differentiation relates to writing style. BYU, Emerson, Kent State and KU emphasize similarities between styles. South Carolina and ASU emphasize the differences. Ball State falls somewhere in the middle. Certainly, the choice of instructors for the class is a strong determining factor regarding what is in the class.

The best comparison of the courses comes from looking at four criteria: the instructor(s), class format (lab, lecture), class assignments, and emphasis put on writing style.

When you examine instructors, you find that three tenure-track faculty members and three adjuncts teach the beginning convergence course at Arizona State. All six instructors are very experienced and come from a print background. At South Carolina, one faculty member from broadcast and one from print had previously taught the course. Ernest Wiggins, whose professional background is print journalism, now is comfortable enough to teach both. Other sections are taught by adjuncts.

Joel Campbell of Brigham Young began his first year of teaching in 2002. He comes from a print background and was most recently a Webmaster for a newspaper. Of the six instructors who regularly teach the course at Brigham Young, one is a broadcaster, and the rest come from print. Roger Fidler came to Kent State in 1996 after a 34-year newspaper career, including 21 years with Knight-Ridder. He also came to Kent State with 16 years of New Media experience beginning in 1979 with Knight-Ridder's pioneering online service called Viewtron.

Emerson faculty member Janet Kolodzy has spent her professional career in both newspapers and television. Her school offers four to six sections of the first-level newsgathering class each semester. Each instructor develops his or her own syllabus. "But we keep scaling back that freedom," said Kolodzy. "We need to have a common syllabus with common exercises." Kansas has eight or nine different instructors teaching the beginning convergence class each semester. Two or three are adjuncts, the rest full-time faculty. They come from all of the schools' disciplines including print, broadcasting, advertising and business communications (PR).

Ball State's Bob Papper's professional experience covers both radio and TV news in markets such as Minneapolis and Washington, D.C. All the converged skills at Ball State involve PAIRS of instructors, one from print and one from broadcast. Rick Musser of Kansas spent his professional career in newspapers, but did a Radio-Television News Director's Association internship at WGN-TV, Chicago during summer, 2001.

In considering class format, ASU features one common lecture and one lab period. At South Carolina, the class features five weeks of print, five weeks of broadcast and three weeks of convergence. Wiggins teaches all three components in his section. Other instructors will develop their own syllabi so they may or may not include broadcast and convergence.

The BYU course includes "a lot" of reporting. Four of eight assignments include a 1,600-word news story. The class has 11 sections with all instructors teaching from the same syllabus. Ball State enrolls three pairs of sections with 32 students per section and two instructors, one print and one broadcast. Kent State has a central lecture and uses lab time for assignments. Emerson also offers a lecture/lab format designed to help students "think like journalists and act like journalists."

In terms of *class assignments*, most of the schools studied primarily focus on print writing. Arizona State's course includes one week of writing for radio, one week for the Web. "Eighty percent of the course is print newswriting," said Steve Doig. "The broadcast faculty wanted their students to have strong writing skills." South Carolina also places heavy emphasis on newswriting. "Ninety percent of the course is newswriting. We give them facts and scenarios so they can concentrate on style struc-ture and timing," said Wiggins. The class features no outside reporting, no audio, video or Web.

The focus at Brigham Young is on a midterm exam over class discussions, readings, and writing construction and style in addition to the regular writing assignments. The first four weeks of the class concentrate on print writing whereas the later sections of the course emphasize newsgathering, including public documents, databases, and spot news stories.

Each section of the class at Ball State has four weeks of common lectures and assignments with an emphasis on "What Is News?" The students then split into two groups to spend four weeks on print writing and then four weeks on broadcast writing or vice versa. The class comes back together for the final four weeks to work on Web assignments.

Emerson teaches its students, first, how to determine what is news. Then they con-centrate on interviewing and how to write for different media. Kent State students write press releases and ad copy for all media in addition to the early assignments of print news. The course also includes news quizzes and grammar, punctuation and spelling exercises. Students turn in a portfolio of their work at the end of the semester.

Kansas offers a beginning course similar to Kent State's but greatly different from the ones just outlined. In Introduction to Research and Writing, the students learn to edit audio and shoot and edit video as well as write for all media. Student assignments are split two-thirds news and one-third strategic (press releases, press kits, print ads, broadcast spots). As a result, students usually do one assignment in an area and then quickly move on to the next one.

In terms of writing style, Arizona State and South Carolina both cover AP and broadcast style. Campbell said BYU offers a first-level writing class that is a gateway to admission: "We teach the print journalism model. We're not converged here." Campbell also cited an advantage of teaching in a private university: "Students come in here with few English/grammar problems." At Kent State, the syllabus for Media Writing notes the fact that good writing is important to all media. At some schools, instructors emphasize movement and transition in line with good intentions, consistent with the rest in calling it convergence but acknowledging that their course has yet to address some of the key issues.

At Kent State, the students take an Introduction to Mass Media course concurrent with the writing course. In that course, the instructors expose the students more broadly to the history and future of media. Convergence is among those topics. Kent State also saves reporting, as well as audio and video production, for a separate semes-ter later.

In Kolodzy's course, students spend approximately 20 percent of their time writing news stories in different media. Most writing in the class involves journals and story memos. This course places a much stronger emphasis on reporting but offers no audio or video production or Web development.

Special Features

Most of the instructors interviewed for this chapter report heavy use of scenario-based writing, because, for the most part, the schools bill the introductory convergence course as a writing course, not a reporting course. The main difference comes in how the instructors operationally define convergence in these assignments. It ranges from discussing how different stories are handled in different media to actually producing the same story for different media.

Janet Kolodzy wants her Emerson students to learn to think visually in all stories, including print stories. She also teaches the similarity of editing sound bites and pulling quotes as well as reporter access issues. Joel Campbell of Brigham Young requires his students to get real facts for a real story. Campbell said that, by the end of that course, the students should be able to write for either broadcast or print.

In addition to the print newswriting, Ernest Wiggins at South Carolina teaches his students to produce the same story for different media. He teaches that Web-based stories should include video, still pictures and graphics, but students won't actually produce those stories until a later class. At Arizona State, the students write their news stories either in class or as homework. Two-thirds of the way through the course, they find and report a feature story.

In the first-level course at Ball State, students execute a group final project that includes print, radio and Web versions of the same story. The second-level course adds video to the mix. Kent State requires a final story, an in-depth feature that requires interviews. It accompanies a final exam that covers terminology and readings.

Common Goals and Objectives

Most of the common goals and objectives revolve around the notion of preparing students for careers in the mass media whether they seek to be specialists or well-rounded, multiskilled journalists. That is not surprising given that all of the schools mentioned here consider themselves professional schools. It is also not surprising that all of the instructors emphasized the need for strong writing skills regardless of career track. Despite all of the previously mentioned school-to-school variations in how to do it, all of the schools studied for this chapter include the word *writing* in the course name. "We sell writing as a vehicle to get you somewhere," said Joel Campbell of BYU.

The schools often use different language in their syllabi to make this point. But, as previously stated, the most common goals revolve around some combination of assignments to teach students writing for different audiences, identifying and finding news, learning different newswriting styles, and improving grammar, usage, punctuation and spelling.

Most schools also refer to the future by using terms such as emerging fields, convergence, New Media, and the digital world. "We must teach them to be flexible," said Steve Doig of Arizona State. "A common misconception is that digital technology is leading to one common medium that will eliminate radio, TV, and newspapers," said Roger Fidler of Kent State. "Will the reporter be a do-everything jack-of-all-trades? No! We should learn from our previous experiences (regarding development of new media)." Fidler also said the reporter of the future should be aware of all types of message delivery and know how to use them: "That's not the same as proficiency."

Ernest Wiggins of South Carolina offers a similar take: "We have all agreed that outcomes should not be weighted toward students who can master everything. But we should be able to expect minimum competency." Wiggins said students need a comprehensive experience in the curriculum that will give them skills in all areas of media.

Bob Papper of Ball State said his school recognizes that whatever replaces the Internet will involve a converged universe: "I'm teaching for what's beyond the Internet." Papper also discussed how their students will need a variety of skills but will likely enter one distinct career track.

All of the beginning courses provide some component of ethics and an exposure to current events, news in all different types of media. The Kent State syllabus offered the following advice to students: "To write for the mass media one must read it, view it and listen to it on a regular and frequent basis."

Instructor Philosophy

The schools surveyed for this chapter have set up many committees and spent many years trying to, first, figure out just what is convergence, and, second, how (or if) that should influence the curriculum. As a result, the instructors cited here have spent many thoughtful hours analyzing those same two things. Also, each of these instructors has spent significant time in various professional journalistic endeavors, so their philosophies are grounded in the real-world application of convergence.

Bob Papper said Ball State had been talking about convergence for four or five years. Papper had also overseen the merging of print and broadcast teaching at Ohio Wesleyan back in 1986, before the term convergence had even emerged as part of the journalistic vocabulary. "We did it because it was best for the students," said Papper. "It didn't offer us any operational savings." Papper said that is a myth of much of today's convergence thinking: "We're still handling X number of students. If they're not in Class A, they'll be in Class B." Papper said through workshops most of the Ball State faculty has at least modest multimedia skills.

He said the instructors in the beginning class sell convergence on the basis of shared values. "But if we're going to sell it," Papper said, "we'd better believe it ourselves." Papper said the faculty must sell it everyday in both skills and philosophy. He said most of the Ball State faculty members have developed convergence skills. They did that mainly through a series of workshops that guided them through Web-site development.

Rick Musser served as Executive Producer during the first two years of the introductory convergence course at Kansas. Musser, a former Indianapolis newspaperman, came up with the term *multimedia moment* to help define the similarities between media and various assignments. He used that term in comparing sound bites to quotes, the *Wall Street Journal* method of story organization in both print and broadcast, and the purpose of a Creative Work Plan (sometimes called Program Needs Analysis or Copy Platform) in looking at press releases versus ads.

Musser led the charge to a convergence curriculum from the print side. The executive producer meets weekly with the seven or eight lab instructors to go over the next week's assignments and grading criteria. All instructors work off a common syllabus, meet for common lectures, and follow the same assignment deadlines.

David Guth, head of the Strategic Track at Kansas, has been involved in the beginning course since its inception. He pointed to breaking down of artificial barriers among the faculty as a key to making the new course (and curriculum) work. "There has been unprecedented cooperation between print and broadcast, news and strategic, advertising and PR. It is like cats sleeping with dogs," said Guth. His professional experience includes stints in radio news and public relations.

Janet Kolodzy said Emerson hired a new dean and department chair with the charge "develop a program for the 21st Century." Convergence has become the centerpiece of that program. Kolodzy noted that most students who come to college from a high school were already grounded in one medium. "But I don't think they know what journalism really is," said Kolodzy. "We really have to sell convergence to the students."

Kolodzy said that is relatively easy for her. She divided her career between newspapers and television before joining the Emerson faculty: "We have a strong broadcast tradition here. Some have worried we might dilute what we have as our curriculum moves in another direction." She said her philosophy of convergence revolved around two key points: telling the same story in different media and thinking visually regardless of medium. Kolodzy considers herself 70 percent converged, but she is shooting for 100 percent.

Joel Campbell of Brigham Young is the newest faculty member of those interviewed. "I'm inheriting a lot from an old class, but I'm also developing a number of new things," he said. Campbell began his teaching career in the fall of 2002 after spending 15 years in Salt Lake City as a reporter, editor, and most recently, Webmaster.

Campbell's recent professional experience gives him a very strong understanding of the Web. He touts writing as the key to being successful in any journalistic career, and writing style is just a part of the discipline. "Good writing is good writing," said Campbell. His beginning convergence course used to have audio, video, and some advertising and public relations included, but he said, "We're going back to where we were three years ago." And that is back to more of an emphasis on writing. Campbell considers himself "pretty converged" but also admits to a blind spot in broadcasting. His goal is to fill in that blind spot.

Roger Fidler of Kent State has probably spent as much time as anyone thinking and also writing about convergence. Only he did not call it by that name. Fidler wrote the book *Mediamorphosis* in 1997. "Mediamorphosis is a term for convergence, but Mediamorphosis is also an evolutionary process, not an end product," he said. Fidler said nothing has really happened in the ensuing years to change his definition. In his book, Fidler outlines another part of his philosophy: "Established forms of communication media *must* change in response to the emergence of a new medium—their only other option is to die."

So, inherent in Fidler's philosophy is the assumption that journalism and mass communication programs must develop courses and curricula not only to meet the needs of New Media such as the Internet, but to meet the changing needs of existing media. "Digital technology has allowed us to borrow characteristics of other forms of media," said Fidler. He considers himself to be fully converged: "I use everything."

"I'm a pragmatist in this area (convergence)," said Ernest Wiggins of South Carolina. "When it comes to delivery, it's just another way of getting the news out." Wiggins said he doesn't have to spend much time selling convergence to his students: "I tell them, just look at a newspaper or TV Web site." Wiggins admitted he needed to do some retooling to get ready to teach convergence: "My colleagues helped, but I'm still a print person." Wiggins added, "I still think it's reasonable to expect the students to have minimum competencies in all areas."

Steven Doig taught the beginning convergence class at Arizona State for the first time in the fall of 2002. He spent 20 years at the *Miami Herald* before pursuing a teaching career. In those 20 years, he observed cameras being installed in newspaper newsrooms, partnerships developing with television stations, and print reporters appearing on radio talk shows, so he tells his students, "This is your future, like it or not."

"I realize there are lots of different feelings about what convergence is," said Doig. "But the target is moving so fast. There's going to be a different way of doing things in the future. Our students need flexibility." Doig said he is certain about one thing: "We all need to be able to recognize a good story."

Common Emphasis

One key theme stands out in the area of common emphasis: the importance placed on clear, concise and accurate writing. Although all of the schools make some mention of writing for different or all media, the actual course content does not always reflect that. The courses vary widely in the degree of convergence, including the introduction of technical skills. Here is a rundown of what the different schools put in their beginning convergence class.

At *Kent State University*, the syllabus for JMC (Journalism and Mass Communication) 20004 Media Writing includes eight assignments that would fall into the print newswriting category. Three of the assignments cover lead writing. Two assignments cover ad copy, and one covers press releases. They also have one assignment each in radio and television. Three other miscellaneous assignments make up the semester, including an in-depth feature, which is at least 12 paragraphs long with at least nine of the paragraphs longer than one sentence. The assignment begins with the submission of a story-proposal form. Other than the in-depth feature and a personality feature, the class contains no outside reporting or interviewing. Often, the instructor will act as a mock source.

Students are allowed to rewrite any assignment that receives a grade of B or lower. JMC 20004 also includes weekly news quizzes. The semester begins with print news topics such as summary leads, anecdotal leads, types of features, and story structure.

Ad copy comes in during the first half of the semester and lasts for one week, followed by one week each of public relations and electronic media. The class returns to a print orientation with topics such as nut graphs, query letters and AP style. The back quarter of the class also contains topics such as good writing for all media and Web fundamentals. Textbooks include *Reaching Audiences* by Jan Johnson Yopp and Katherine C. McAdams, *When Words Collide* by Lauren Kessler and Duncan McDonald, and *The Associated Press Stylebook*.

At *Ball State University* in the beginning convergence course News 201 Newswriting, the instructors break down their assignments into percentages with news-judgment exercises (10 percent), weekly quizzes (15 percent), critiques of print/broadcast/online stories (10 percent), and print/broadcast newswriting assignments (10 percent) such as a police-beat story, meeting, or speech coverage. There are also workshop assignments (10 percent), a community profile (final project, 25 percent), and instructor's evaluation (10 percent).

The final project is an in-depth story done by a team that explores economic, political or social issues affecting the university, the city or the county. The students produce a 1,000-word story for print plus a four-minute audio story, and an online story with text, audio clip, digital photos, and links.

As mentioned before, the students work four weeks in non-media-specific topics and assignments, and then they go for four weeks of print news with an instructor from a print background followed by four weeks of broadcast news with an instructor from a broadcast background (or the other way around). The semester ends with four weeks back together in multimedia/Web topics. Ball State is the only school surveyed that requires two hours each week outside of class in both print and broadcast campus media. Required textbooks for the course include *Telling the Story* by the Missouri Group, *Broadcast News Writing Stylebook* by Robert Papper, and *The Associated Press Stylebook*.

Emerson College's beginning course JR 102 The Newsgathering Process includes quizzes, in-class and homework assignments, weekly journal entries, and a final reporting project. The quizzes include questions on news terminology, current events, and assigned readings.

In-class and homework assignments cover news analyses, information gathering, interviewing, and ethical problems to help students develop news-judgment and reporting skills. The weekly journal entries include one section called Notes on News. Students find current stories in print, on the air, or on the Web and analyze them on the basis of what the instructor is covering in class at that particular time. They are encouraged to look at the outside world and see how the media present different stories in different forms. The Lessons Learned section requires each student to write a couple of paragraphs per week about what each has learned, does not understand, or needs to understand. The final reporting project is a team assignment relating to a topic provided by the instructor, such as the housing shortage in Boston.

Course topics in the syllabus are non-media-specific. They include such headings as the news business, where news comes from, interviewing, ethics, and documents, databases, and computer-assisted reporting. Required textbooks include *News in a*

New Century by Jerry Lanson and Barbara Croll Fought, and *Creative Interviewing* by Ken Metzler; a subscription to a daily Boston newspaper; and viewing a daily cable or broadcast newscast.

At *Brigham Young University*, Communications 311 Newswriting includes weekly quizzes, six in-class lab assignments, take home lab assignments, a midterm exam and a final project. The early part of the course covers fundamentals such as: what is news, story organization, quotes, attribution and interviewing. The second half of the course includes special event coverage such as speeches, press conferences, and disasters. One week is devoted to broadcast writing. Textbooks include *News Writing and Reporting for Today's Media* by Bruce Itule and Douglas Anderson, *Workbook for Use with News Writing* by Janet Soper, and *The Associated Press Stylebook*.

At the *University of South Carolina*, the Journalism 202 Newswriting syllabus begins with an emphasis on grammar and style, including AP style exercises. Other early lessons focus on print leads and then move to building the body of a print story. Many of the early stories have a police basis. The class contains no outside reporting or interviewing.

The writing-for-television exercises that come later in the semester also have a heavy police basis. All stories are written using given scenarios and information. The later assignments involve a time requirement, preparing students to work on a deadline. They are to prepare a news story from given information during a specified amount of time, from 10 to 25 minutes. Recommended textbooks include *The Elements of Style* by William Strunk and E. B. White and *The Associated Press Stylebook*.

Arizona State University's JMC 201 focuses on newswriting, with a follow-up course JMC 301 covering reporting. JMC 201 features lectures, online stylebook quizzes, a short weekly news quiz, a news clip "treasure hunt" where students gather 50 clips on specific topics throughout the semester, a dozen or so scenario-based newswriting exercises, and a couple of basic street-reporting assignments near the end of the semester. The midterm and final both have a short-answer component and a writing exercise.

Three weeks of the course are devoted to broadcast and web writing; the rest is basic newspaper writing. Half of the grade comes from the writing assignments, 15 percent each from the midterm and final, and the remaining 20 percent from a combination of the style quizzes, the clip collection, the news quizzes and attendance.

The central text is *News Writing and Reporting for Today's Media*, 6th edition, by Bruce Itule and Douglas Anderson. Students also buy a copy of the current *AP Stylebook* and a copy of the *AP Broadcast Handbook*.

At the *University of Kansas*, unlike the previously mentioned courses, Journalism 301 Introduction to Research and Writing begins with a broadcast writing assignment. The instructors do that to set a tone that the class will be multimedia in nature. Other assignments throughout the semester will include print newswriting, editing a 30-second voice-over from provided tape, press releases, a press kit, a magazine ad, a 30-second radio spot, and a one-minute TV commentary shot and edited. Textbooks include the *AP Stylebook* and a handbook of instructor-generated handouts copied for student distribution.

Common Challenges/Solutions

The most common challenges mentioned by those interviewed generally fall under the category of *change*, with subheadings of equipment, faculty and approach. The dean of the School of Journalism and Mass Communication at the University of Kansas, James K. Gentry, has studied change, written about change, and consulted several newspapers, TV stations, and Web companies in managing change. Through those experiences, Gentry has developed what he calls a number of his "convergence truisms."

First, convergence always takes longer, costs more, and is more difficult than the organization's management thinks it will be. Second, you should not do convergence because you think you will get serious staffing efficiencies. "Many of our students have a high level of anxiety about technological change," said Roger Fidler. But in some ways the equipment challenge may be the easiest to solve. It only takes money.

"If we increase the number of students working with all of the different technologies (convergence), then we have a technological gap of cameras, editing systems and computers," said Wiggins. Kansas certainly found that to be the case when it moved from 90 beginning students using cameras and editing systems to more than 220. A student per-credit-hour technology fee and some matching state money helped bridge that gap, but as the technology changes, the schools must replace outmoded systems. Where that money will come from is anyone's guess.

Several of those instructors interviewed for this chapter said that faculty change would have to come slowly, through attrition if not through retooling. "We're going to have to find people who can teach in this new curriculum," said Gentry. "That's especially true of adjuncts."

"We've got to think beyond our own experiences," said Doig. "But the ASU faculty has gone out of its way to learn more about convergence." A certain element of academic freedom also comes into play here. "I will teach my class the way I will teach it," said Kolodzy in referring to faculty attitudes.

"Part of the problem is a traditional faculty," said Fidler. "We have a great faculty, but change is intimidating. We want to teach the same way journalism faculties taught 20 years ago. We *talk* about doing it differently, but it's hard to break out of the mold."

The approach, the actual implementation of a convergence course or curriculum, has proven to be as dicey as all the philosophical discussions that led to the change. "We never realized how many organizational issues such as lab times, team teaching staffing, room assignments and other logistics there were," said Linda Davis, KU journalism associate dean. "But we do now." Partly because of lead times on schedules, it has taken Kansas two full years to get all the trains running on the proper track.

Ball State started its implementation of convergence in the fall of 2002. "We're still trying to figure out how to get breadth in the program without sacrificing depth," said Papper. Kansas has not found an answer to that question. Remember, its beginning convergence class includes writing for all media, audio and video production, as well as advertising and public relations. Faculty member David Guth has often referred to the course as a "a buffet line where everyone samples every selection. The second-level writing class represents a second trip to the buffet, where the students target the things they like."

Student evaluations from the first four semesters reinforced that. "We only got to do things once," said the students. When the students moved on to the second-level writing course, the evaluations came back a bit different: "We already did that in the first class." Throughout the first two years, the faculty members who teach the class have tweaked the assignments in an effort to find that correct balance between breadth and depth.

Janet Kolodzy of Emerson and Steve Doig of ASU have a similar problem, trying to put 10 pounds of potatoes into a 5-pound bag. "We've had to back off on some of the content," said Kolodzy. "The first two semesters I taught this, I got the worst student evaluations I'd ever had." Doig taught the class for the first time in the fall of 2002. "The difficulty is bringing in the proper weight of the other media," he said. "We must throw out a lot of the old stuff we used to teach."

David Guth of Kansas noted the same thing: "Everyone was dismayed to find none of our old lectures worked," he said. "Having to revamp lectures is not a bad thing— but it is a lot of work." This approach leads to another common challenge faced by the convergence instructors: time, or rather the lack of it. Many an instructor of beginning classes has been a victim of the "We have to teach them everything this semester" syndrome. But convergence didn't create that problem. The problem has faced every instructor who ever taught a beginning class. Convergence has just exacerbated the problem.

Conclusions

"If you don't know where you're going, most any direction will get you there." Richard Bolles offered that advice in his best-selling career counseling book, *What Color is Your Parachute?* He wrote his first edition of that book in the late 1970s, long before widespread, concentrated media ownership, long before media companies operated with both eyes on Wall Street, and long before anyone had heard the term convergence meaning anything other than "two things coming together."

But Bolles' phrase aptly describes early efforts to bring convergence into the courses and curricula in journalism and mass communication education. Granted, this chapter only includes case studies from seven schools. But if we expanded the study to 77 schools, we probably would have found 77 different ways of defining convergence instead of seven.

In many instances, schools appear to be making this up as they go along. The problem stems from several sources, including a lack of professional guidance. A cursory look at professional newspaper/broadcast partnerships offers only hints of how to make convergence work. Every model appears to be different. Some newspapers and their broadcast counterparts share most of their information and audiovisual materials. Others just talk about sharing. Most occupy a position somewhere in between.

In addition, there is little or no tradition to back up this development. When television news came into existence and schools decided to add a TV news program, they simply copied what had worked so well on the print side—Reporting I, II, III and a dose of Copyediting (shooting and editing to the TV folks). Another part of that tradition is that so many schools have earned a large part of the reputation through their print news teaching.

A number of schools have also mined that tradition into significant levels of donations, something that has, so far, been foreign to other media and other functions. As a result, the tradition-bound school can easily sound the bugle of "Don't fix it if it ain't broken." And they make a pretty convincing argument. Convincing, that is, if the industries all around us were not changing.

The existence of formal sequences and the tradition of sequencing coursework may be the biggest hurdle of all. The sequence (or major) is predicated on the notion that a freshman or sophomore college student can select the "correct" career track. If 40-something media persons can't figure out what to do with their life (note the number who become JMC professors), then how can they expect their young students to be so insightful. No, faculties created sequences because it assured a professional skill level of the instructor passed down to the students.

Sequences also provided a good structure for governance (i.e., the department chair). It gave the faculty member a group to belong to. It also enabled that group to wield significant power particularly if the sequence was a large one with numerous faculty members. Thus, when a member of the group changed jobs or retired, the schools replaced the old member of Sequence X with a new member of Sequence X. The schools had to. Students were already pre-enrolled in the *required* course of the sequence that the old professor taught. Schools seldom examined the real needs of the school, needs that should be defined by "What's best for the students?"

The structure of sequences also made it easy to provide advice to students. All they had to do was pick a sequence and follow the bouncing ball of requirements. No real advising was needed. If the schools had ever examined student needs, they would have found that the sequences did not serve the students very well. Take a look at your graduates from five years ago. See what careers they have pursued. Then see how it matches to their chosen sequence. Kansas did that recently and found some startling results. You could not tell the students' sequence by looking at their current job. In some instances, Broadcast News majors were selling college textbooks. Magazine majors were working for ad agencies. News-Editorial majors were working for Fortune 500 companies in internal communications. Advertising majors were writing for magazines. Business Communication majors were doing media sales.

Another obvious detriment is the clash of cultures as evidenced by the wide variation of assignments from the seven schools. The balance varies greatly between in-lab writing assignments and homework or outside assignments. That may be more of a result of the different cultures and backgrounds of the instructors than a rational-based, student-centered decision. Print teachers developed their writing courses in a lab environment, where part of the model required the instructor to walk around the room, peering over the young writers' shoulders, and offering advice for improvement.

Broadcast teachers, mostly because of film and video, often took more of the "outward bound" approach to learning. They would give students a camera, some film or tape, and say "Come back when you've got something." Each has its own advantages. The courses studied in this chapter lean heavily on in-class, writing experience, rather than assignments based on information gathering. Also note the books assigned. The only constant was the *AP Stylebook*. If you require students to buy the *AP Stylebook*, then you teach AP style. The lack of a widely accepted convergence textbook is one obstacle to any kind of consistency.

The era of faculty specialists and specialization also took its toll. Consider the plight of the poor old instructor who taught black-and-white photography with a darkroom component. Do we continue to teach that even though the industry has evolved to digital? Do we teach ad copy as only print ads? Do we teach copyediting as only a few words on paper? Do we teach public relations only as a function unto itself, unrelated to the company marketing organization?

The sequence system helped build faculty specialists and helps perpetuate it, but escaping that cycle is easier said than done. Several of the schools studied have shown that can be accomplished through open-mindedness, in-service training, faculty internships, and/or team teaching. The solutions always begin with the faculty members' willingness to retool and learn new things. That is easier for some than for others, particularly when you compare newspapers to television.

In earlier times, the newspaper reporter would write his or her story on a Royal typewriter and place it on a spike for the copy editor, who would make the necessary revisions and place it on another spike. The next morning, the reporter and copy editor would each pick up their morning paper on the front lawn. Neither had to go back to the pressroom, load paper or ink, run the press, or drive the delivery truck. By contrast, the TV reporter or producer had to learn new technologies from film to tape, from microwaves to satellites.

The TV person often would play another role to get the story on the air. From running the tape to master control or dialing in the coordinates for a satellite feed, the TV person had to deal with technology, and as a result change. When the TV instructor finds he or she also has to teach students how to develop a story for the Web, the typical reply would be, "Hey, could somebody show me how to open this program?"

We learned a key element at the University of Kansas when we tried just to tweak the curriculum. That did not work because, by definition, change does not take place in a static state. When you change one thing, the beginning course for example, you automatically change everything else that comes after it. When one person changes, it creates stress in the people around him or her.

Theodore Caplow of the University of Virginia wrote a book in 1976 entitled *How to Run Any Organization*. He built his theory from the premise that each organization must submit to demands of its environment, knowing that demands change as the environment changes. He looked at change from different perspectives: a growing organization, a stable organization, and a declining organization. Each of those has distinct managerial advantages and disadvantages. Some of his observations about those organizations seem appropriate.

In so-called growing organizations, expanding resources can pay for mistakes and offer protection against risks. But growth makes some people obsolete, even some who were originally responsible for the growth and, thus, diminishes the consensus of organizational values. In stable organizations (most colleges and universities), morale is often higher than in growing or declining organizations. But those stable systems tend to be inflexible and predictable. Also, because of a built-in resistance to change, they are vulnerable to crises. In declining organizations, we find low morale and some-times corruption. Low productivity is due to inability to keep up with progress or inability to recruit and retain competent personnel. Failure is not disgrace, since chances for success are enhanced.

Almost all schools of journalism and mass communication would probably *like* to fall into the first category but likely do fall into the second category. Caplow offers several ideas for managing change in that environment. Problem-solving efforts will be slow moving. Group members want to adhere to tradition, procedures such as democratic participation in decision making. They will want accessible records and a system for designation of successors (faculty and administrators) to prevent surprises. With the academy aging, reliance on adjuncts, and tight economic times, some schools may be moving or have already moved into the third category. That presents a differ-ent management challenge.

Convergence should have come about even without the changes taking place in industry. Teaching convergence gives students a chance to work in different media performing different functions *before* deciding on a career. We do see some schools operationally defining convergence by teaching print newswriting and adding one week of broadcast writing. If that constitutes convergence, some institutions were doing that back in 1971, the author's first year of graduate school. And, if that is the case, we have learned little from 30 years of curriculum development. Now at least schools are discussing doing things differently. Impetus from the industry assured it. Many schools are considering change even though real change is hard to come by.

References

Bolles, R. 2001. *What color is your parachute? A practical manual for job-hunters and career changers.* Berkeley: Ten Speed.

Cohen, J. 2001. Symposium: Journalism and mass communication education at the crossroads. *Journalism and Mass Communications Educator* 56:4–6.

Cragun, A. 1997. From competitors to cohorts: The convergence of print and broad-cast media. Unpublished honors thesis, Brigham Young University.

Egan, K., and S. Hammond. 1997. What about the worker? The search for identity in the converged newsroom. In *Manchester Broadcast Symposium,* University of Manchester, UK.

Fidler, R. 1997. *Mediamorphosis.* Thousand Oaks, Calif.: Pine Forge.

Goldstein, N., ed. 1996. *The Associated Press stylebook and libel manual.* 6th ed. Reading, Mass.: Addison-Wesley.

Hammond, S., D. Petersen, and S. Thomsen. 2000. Print, broadcast and online conver-gence in the newsroom. *Journalism and Mass Communication Educator* 55:16.

Irby, J. 2000. Journalism educators seeking partnerships. *American Editor* [Online]. www.asne.org/index.cfm?id=530.

Itule, B. D., and D. A. Anderson. 1999. *News writing and reporting for today's media.* New York: McGraw-Hill.

Kessler, L., and D. McDonald. 1999. *When words collide: A media writer's guide to grammar and style.* Belmont, Calif.: Wadsworth.

Lanson, J., and B. C. Fought. 1999. *News in a new century: Reporting in an age of convergence.* Thousand Oaks, Calif.: Pine Forge.

Metzler, K. 1996. *Creative interviewing: The writer's guide to gathering information by asking questions.* Boston: Allyn and Bacon.

The Missouri Group. 2001. *Telling the story: Writing for print, broadcast and online media.* Boston: Bedford/St. Martin's.

Outing, S. 1999. Preparing J-school students for New Media convergence. *Editor and Publisher* 132:49.

Papper, R. A. 1995. *Broadcast news writing stylebook.* Boston: Allyn and Bacon.

Porter, W., and S. Hammond. 1997. The coming of New Media organization: Organizational convergence and news content in integrated newsrooms in the United States. In *Manchester Broadcast Symposium,* University of Manchester, UK.

Sandeen, R. 2000. How much multimedia should students learn? *American Editor* [Online]. www.asne.org/kiosk/editor/00.march/sandeen1.htm.

Strunk, W., Jr. 1979. *The elements of style,* with revisions, an introduction, and a chapter on writing by E. B. White. New York: Macmillan.

Utsler, M. 2001. The convergence curriculum: We got it now what are we gonna do with it? *Feedback* 42, no. 3:1–5.

Utsler, M. 2002. The convergence curriculum: Lessons from year one. *Feedback* 43, no. 2:22–27.

Yopp, J. J., and K. C. McAdams. 2002. *Reaching audiences: A guide to media writing.* Boston: Allyn and Bacon.

Remembering a Mentor: Marshall McLuhan

Thomas L. McPhail

I had the good fortune of working with Marshall McLuhan, (1911–1980) the Canadian communication scholar who coined such terms as "the Medium is the Message" and "Global Village," for the last decade and a half of his life. I taught at Concordia University in Montreal, Quebec, when Marshall was a professor at the University of Toronto. We frequently found ourselves at the same conferences and on the same panels discussing aspects of communication. In addition, McLuhan ran a graduate seminar in Toronto to which I was frequently invited as a guest lecturer. Before relating some of the interesting and idiosyncratic interactions during this period, the mid-1960s to 1980s, I will provide some background which helps explain how McLuhan came to be what he was.

Born in Edmonton, Alberta, McLuhan studied English at the University of Manitoba and at Cambridge University. He did his doctoral dissertation on Irish poets and poetics, and he joined Saint Louis University in the late 1930s. He met his wife Elizabeth and was married in St. Louis. He converted from the Episcopalian Church to the Roman Catholic Church, and this would dominate a great deal of his outlook. He left St. Louis at the start of World War II and, as a Canadian, he became eligible for conscription as soon as Great Britain entered that war. He saw limited action in Europe and returned to the University of Toronto in 1946. His writings on the media made him popular with the press. Eventually, he would appear in the *New York Times*, as subject of feature stories and in the movie *Annie Hall*.

In 1962, he published his first book the *Gutenberg Galaxy*, followed by *Understanding Media* in 1964, and in 1967 the *Medium is the Massage*. Due to his increasing popularity, some colleagues were jealous. He was criticized badly by some peers whereas others thought he was among the greatest philosophers of communication to ever live. He commented extensively on popular culture issues during many radio and television interviews.

I recall having lunch with him one day at the University of Toronto faculty club. He detailed how some colleagues became somewhat mean spirited in terms of handling his scholarship, ridiculing his popular success. He was made Director for the Center of Culture and Technology as a way of focusing his energy and attention.

The center consisted of a small, two-story building in the middle of the campus. At the turn of the last century, the university used it to house a few horse-drawn fire trucks. By the 1960s, this small building became Marshall's Center. He had his office on the ground floor, and a large seminar room was on the second floor where various programs and lectures were held. It was here that a growing number of intellectual guests from both the mass media and academia came to participate in his musings.

One cannot discuss McLuhan without referring to his mentor, Harold Adams Innis (1894–1952). Innis was educated at McMaster University in Hamilton, Ontario, as well as the University of Chicago. He joined the economics faculty at the University of Toronto in 1920 and, at the time of his death at the age of 58, was Dean of Graduate Studies. His doctoral dissertation on the Canadian Pacific Railway looked at it as a transportation medium, but he shifted the paradigm to consider it as a communication corporation. This was based on the communication of mail, newspapers as well as the telegraph that the railway took with it as it traveled across Canada. Innis' two key books, *Empire and Communications* (1950) and *The Bias of Communication* (1951), served as McLuhan's bridge from traditional English professor to global communication philosopher. They corresponded but had limited interaction during the last few years of Innis' life.

McLuhan did his major intellectual work on the *Medium is the Message* while on sabbatical leave at the University of Wisconsin at Madison. It was there while teaching a graduate seminar, as he discussed how Canadian culture was influenced by America, that he came to understand that, because of the advent of new technologies such as cable and satellite, Canada would be even more dependent on U.S. mass media. His position was that the medium, regardless of content, determined that technology itself created expectations, mental processes, and messages, much like the introduction of the printing press by Gutenberg. He also expanded the concept of the shift from oral to print culture that was described initially by Innis.

I can recall a few interesting conversations with McLuhan. First, at a conference in Montreal, we were seated beside each other, and we discussed what he thought was a tragic error in terms of the Catholic Church dropping Latin from the mass. He was concerned about how faith and belief in God are mysterious and that the Latin language added to this mystery. He also pointed out that Latin helped define a universal Church with officials communicating with the Vatican in Latin. He commented how he had communicated his concerns to the Pope, warning him of a disastrous change. He even suggested that the Pope read Innis.

This was not the first time that he had discussed changes in the Church. It bothered him that young people were rebelling against a value system—his value system during that period. He related concerns about his young family and sometimes would take me aside to share ideas, since I was a younger person, about what could be done about the state of things. My response was basically that we could do nothing but tough it out, an answer that he did not want to hear.

Another interesting episode arose out of a seminar for a World Banking conference. In preparation, he discussed how money was a medium—not only a financial currency but an economic communication channel among powerful Western nations. I frequently filled in at the seminar when he was away and, in this instance, he stated that the World Bank officials did not understand that fundamental concept, nor the irony of explaining this phenomenon in exchange for a substantial speaking fee.

In 1980 following his death, the United Nations Educational, Scientific, and Cultural Organization (UNESCO), based in Paris, decided to award an annual McLuhan

Prize. Teleglobe Canada, a major telecommunication carrier, funded the award. I served as a member on the selection committee that was formed. We selected recipients, and an award ceremony was attended by the prime minister, media executives, and McLuhan's wife, Elizabeth.

She described their beginnings in St. Louis and how much they were like the graduate students he was teaching at the time. They had very little, but still he was always inviting students home to discuss communication issues for hours. I asked Elizabeth when she first knew he was bright. She said he startled her with insight and eloquence on their first date. When I returned home, I asked my wife when she first realized the same of me? She said that she was still waiting. I learned not to ask her such questions unless I knew the answers in advance.

Another McLuhan-inspired incident occurred in the late 1970s when Ottawa created a Federal Department of Communication. McLuhan was invited to discuss with the Canadian Cabinet and Prime Minister Pierre Trudeau what communication meant to countries situated geographically next to the United States, one of the greatest powers on earth. McLuhan got into a debate with the prime minister, an intellectual who once taught at the University of Montreal. The two went on for a time in front of the Cabinet, whose members seldom intellectually challenged that prime minister. At the end of the meeting, the ministers seemed to regard the visit as a waste, but Trudeau thanked McLuhan, saying it was one of the most interesting mornings he had spent in Ottawa.

McLuhan taught me many things as mentor. First, and perhaps most importantly, to think independently. Never a traditionalist, he would go to lengths to question theories of the day, moving beyond established ideas to create new knowledge. He was also convinced of the need for a thick skin.

He had critics, including some from his own institution and later outsiders, who denigrated his ideas, but he was confident that his ideas would prevail, adamant that the "global village" concept would evolve. Finally, he always took the global view, describing himself as an internationalist, seeing media technology as a common denominator among nations, with theories applied to remote villages as well as big cities. Location did not matter. What he had to say applied without regard to time or space.

PART II

Fundamentals

CHAPTER 6

Electronic Media

Dale Cressman and Donald G. Godfrey

Introduction

B roadcasting and telecommunications have revolutionized the heart of our nation's families, cultures, business and classrooms: "It is no accident that the rise of printed literature coincided with the Renaissance and Reformation" (Whetmore, 1982, p. 5). Likewise it is no accident that the information, entertainment, and popular cultural ages of today coincide with the rise of broadcasting and the electronic media. The impact of broadcasting and the new media make the *introduction to broadcasting* course one of the most exciting and challenging of today's curriculum.

The long-range goal of this introductory course is to elevate the standards of the industry and the consumer. Dr. Robert Guy, a former Program Director for KING-TV, Seattle, used to tell the story of a luncheon he attended with several university dignitaries, presidents, deans, and academic officers of the West. Dr. Guy earned a doctorate in marketing and had returned to work in commercial broadcasting. At the luncheon, each member at the table was asked to introduce themselves and tell a little bit about their work. Following Dr. Guy's introduction, everyone in the room sat silently. Finally one of the university presidents spoke, with some indignation: "You're the man responsible for that garbage we're seeing on our television!" Without any hesitation, Dr. Guy responded, "You folks in education have had a captive audience for over a hundred years and you've failed to elevate the states of the American public!" (personal communication). This is our consumer challenge! This is the challenge of those who will shortly enter and direct the industry.

The purpose for this course is twofold: professional preparation and consumer education. Those who teach the course bring a world of insight into the minds of those students eager to work in the media. As one colleague noted, "It is just fun to take the sex appeal out of the media." There is no denying the impact of radio, television and all the new media of communications. To teach this course is to uncover some of the mysteries of its history, law, impact, issues and business operations. For students desiring to work in the profession, the class establishes the foundations for understanding the varied careers in the field and serves as an important springboard for those upper-division and job-related courses. The instructor has the responsibility of basic consumer and professional education.

Looking at an overview of this course with an eye toward the broader process of mass communication education, the authors surveyed several schools to assess their learning about differing approaches to purpose, the nature, source materials and objectives. The schools responding to the survey were: Florida A & M University, Jacksonville State University, Oswego State University of New York, Southern Illinois University, Ohio University, the University of Oregon, Brigham Young University, and Arizona State University.

Position of the Course in the Curriculum

The course is primarily taught in a lecture format. Its position within the curriculum is always as an introductory 100- to 200-level course. The titles of the course vary. Ohio University's is titled A Mediated World and Florida A & M's is Telecommunication Environment. Most titles are less graphic and merely descriptive of content, such as Arizona State's Introduction to Broadcasting and Electronic Media, and Oswego State University of New York's Broadcasting, Cable, the Internet and Beyond. All were basically organized to examine the American broadcasting and electronic media systems, their historical basis and philosophical foundations, and the system patterns, functions, and problems of communication.

There's only one course similar to the Introduction to Broadcasting and Electronic Media. It is the Introduction to Mass Communication. The lines of distinction between these courses are often blurry. Oregon, for example, confines its teaching of broadcast history, policy and regulation to the Mass Communication survey course. Its other broadcast classes are skills based. As convergence and new technologies push educators to adjust the curriculum, there is debate about the relevancy of having the two different courses. The traditional broadcasters generally balk at such combinations, feeling there is too much electronic industry information to have it "shoehorned" into a single semester/quarter horizontal survey course. For example, in the one course scenario, media law may be limited to First Amendment, libel and privacy issues. If broadcast law is discussed at all, it is limited to election law. Where both introductory courses are offered, the broadcast curriculum is expanded and includes extensive discussions of Federal Communications Commission (FCC) law and operations.

In the broadcasting and electronic media class, as a separate entity from mass communication, the focus is clearly on radio, television, cable, satellite and the Internet, whereas the mass communications courses include discussions of newspapers, magazines, books, and media of a print editorial nature, as well as some discussion of electronic media. It's just too much information to squeeze into a quarter or a semester.

The broadcast electronic media course primarily serves four content objectives: acquainting students with the historical precedents as these precedents are related to past, present and future trends; providing students with an understanding of the basic business structures of the industries; acquainting students with the basic operations of key operations; and helping students understand and formulate critical judgment related to understanding the effects of electronic media on society. As one instructor put it, "My students will never watch television, listen to radio, or surf the Internet the same way again, but they'll enjoy it more!"

Updating the Broadcast Education Association's (BEA) published behavioral objectives for the introductory course, Val Limburg, of Washington State University, reports his objectives are (1) to identify significant contributions of selected individuals in the development of broadcasting and electronic media; (2) to identify significant elements in the structure and organization of the varying industries; (3) to explain the basic formulas used in sales and audience measurement; (4) to define or identify selected terminology related to the broadcasting and electronic media industries; (5) to explain the growth and formation of regulatory agencies, particularly the Federal Communications Commission; (6) to explain the organization and departmental functions of a broadcast station, cable system, satellite organization, and syndication firm, plus advertising and public relations as related to electronic media; (7) to explain the organization of trends and innovations; and (8) to outline various programming services in the local and national arenas (Limburg, 1984).

Note that one primary objective appears as both a content and behavioral objective: that is to acquaint the students with the elements and operational systems of the business. In other words, it is important once the basic operational systems are understood that students know how these components interrelate. Too lose sight of the fact that all media are businesses is to change the behavioral objectives to that of a popular culture course.

Common Goals and Objectives

Our survey suggests that individual philosophies and goals are as varied as the instructors themselves. Yet, the challenges of each are similar: maintaining currency and creating a learning atmosphere.

Ohio University's survey class A Mediated World (100-level), according to David Mould, is "not a traditional introduction to mass communication survey class" (electronic mail communication, Aug. 21, 2002). In fact, Ohio University has two (100-level) courses appearing to be a typical Introduction to Mass Communication: one for majors, the other reserved for those from outside the unit. The telecommunications majors are required to take A Mediated World. Mould, notes the breadth of that course, believing that it is "more important to engage students in contemporary media issues, than to try to cover the gamut of theory, history, economics, etcetera" (ibid.). Ohio uses A Mediated World to inculcate students into the major and familiarize them with career options, as well as the faculty with whom they will work.

Southern Illinois University at Carbondale and Arizona State University require broadcasting students to take the Introductory to Mass Communications course, plus Understanding Radio and Television and Introduction to Radio–TV (at the 200 level). Jake Podber and Fritz Leigh both teach radio–television electronic media majors, at SIU and ASU, respectively, in groups of 80 per semester.

SIU's Professor James Wall also teaches a second version of the class for a group of approximately 270 students from outside the unit. This version is, according to Wall, "a rather wicked student lecture that runs for only eight weeks, beginning at midterm" (electronic mail communication, Aug. 22, 2002). The course seeks to give students a basic understanding of the development and evolution of broadcasting, as well as its operations, including programming, advertising, and network affiliations. In addition to dealing with the history of broadcasting, the SIU course touches on current trends in electronic media, legal and regulatory issues, new technological issues, and future developments of the industry.

Florida A&M's Telecommunication Environment, a 300-level course offered by the Radio-Television department, is required of all broadcast journalism and public relations majors to "acquaint students with the history, structure, economics, methods of operation, technologies and issues related to the telecommunications industry" (course syllabus). As in most other schools, students take the course after having completed the Introduction to Mass Communication course. Professor Phillip Jeter strives to have students "explore the policy considerations" (electronic mail communication, Aug. 22, 2002) of such issues as spectrum allocation, programming, economics and management.

Despite the focus on broadcast-related telecommunications, Jeter used Joseph Straubhaar and Robert LaRose's *Media Now* (2002), a text also used in mass communication survey courses. Despite its wide scope, Jeter has his students "follow the money." To those ends, he also requires students to subscribe to *Broadcasting and Cable* and the *Wall Street Journal*, directing them to its Marketing and Media section.

Professor Fritz Messere at Oswego State University of New York and Professor Fritz Leigh at Arizona State University have unique situations in that they co-authored books written specifically for the Introduction to Broadcasting course: *Broadcast, Cable, The Internet* (2000) *and Beyond* and *Electronic Media* (2000), respectively. Broadcasting, Cable, the Internet and Beyond, which is offered at the 300 level, is required of Oswego's sophomores and juniors after they have taken an introductory skills class. Messere emphasizes convergence, the "changing nature of the field" as well as the "public service component" of the business—the notion that broadcasting is "more than just fooling around with equipment" (electronic mail communication, Aug. 22, 2002). The course enrolls about 60 students and is primarily lecture. Messere also teaches additional students in a distance-learning section.

Instructor Philosophy

Student engagement and interaction using new technology are part of the key to success for many instructors. Of the schools surveyed, three make extensive use of online material. Professor Messere has developed ancillary online material for his students, including chapter outlines, summaries, glossaries, links and quizzes. His website also facilitates online chats. At Ohio University, Professor David Mould relies on Blackboard, a Web-based classroom management system, to distribute learning materials and encourages interaction between students. Mould emphasizes active learning, student engagement, and writing, so he finds Blackboard helpful for managing large sections. Mould meets with his class twice a week for one hour and 50 minutes.

Group assignments are also among the common methods of instruction. To keep 180 freshman interested, Mould breaks the class time period down into "four or five different learning activities (electronic mail communication, Aug. 21, 2002)," each about 20 or 30 minutes long. The sessions involve discussions of readings, class team exercises, and media examples. Although some of his students don't like it, Mould prefers to have them work on projects in teams, as he feels it prepares them for the working world. The groups are encouraged to come up with a creative name and way to introduce themselves to their colleagues and then are charged with producing profiles of faculty members and descriptions of a sequence, program, or student organization, as well as a research paper and presentation.

Messere also has his Oswego students working in small group settings. For one assignment, student groups are charged with finding a format "hole" in the market or developing a counterprogramming strategy for a local radio station. When studying television, the students are required to develop a pilot idea for a specific television network and a specific time period and then, as a television production company, present it to the class.

The term paper assignment appears to disappear as the enrollment grows. Messere's students write research papers, usually on an assigned historical topic. For example, a paper on key inventor Guglielmo Marconi would require that students find newspaper accounts of Marconi from the turn of the century. For his distance-learning students, Messere requires field surveys of media usage in the students' community: "It provides an interesting perspective and students begin to see family media usage differently as a result of talking with families about the role media plays in their lives" (electronic mail communication, Aug. 22, 2002). Although writing is a critical part of our discipline, many budgets simply are not sufficient for providing faculty support for such assignments, so especially for the larger classes a term paper becomes prohibitive.

Traditional sophistry remains at the foundation in the approach to the introductory course. Professor Jake Podber echoes the sentiment of this approach as meeting the challenge of keeping a large class of freshman engaged in the material: "I find that the Phil Donahue approach, where I constantly run around the room, asking questions, appears to keep students more alert" (electronic mail communication, Aug. 27, 2002). Podber says he finds this method adds a degree of intimacy, "which allows students to feel less intimidated" (ibid.). Phillip Jeter uses lectures and assignments to get students thinking critically about media: "I frequently put them in the position of trying to defend commercially successful programs" (electronic mail communication, Aug. 22, 2002).

Professor Jeter has his students write book reviews, typically biographies, "of significant figures in the development of the telecommunications industry." He assigns research papers on topics such as "African Americans and the Information Superhighway." Professor Jeter's students develop profiles and presentations on media companies. These assignments require students to provide the names and titles of company executives, cite revenues and stock values, identify competitors, and analyze the company's weaknesses and strengths.

The University of Oregon's Professor Alan Stavitsky says he is challenged by the broadly diverse objectives of his Mass Media and Society course, into which Oregon has combined editorial print and broadcast materials. He seeks to resolve the challenge by "offering students a theoretical framework for studying media that emphasizes common issues across media, as opposed to spending blocks of time lecturing on the varying industries." Those common issues include such things as ownership concentration, convergence, and fragmentation of the audience (electronic mail communication, Aug. 27, 2002).

Outside Resources

One of the most commonly used outside resources is *Broadcast and Cable Magazine*. This is the weekly major trade publication of the profession. There are other trade journals such as the Radio-Television News Directors Association *Communicator* (www.rtnda.org), with a focus on radio and television news, and *Electronic Media* (www.emonline.com), with attention to television programming and management. *Broadcast and Cable Magazine* (www.broadcastingcable.com) sets the industry standard with the broadest emphasis on management, law, technology and programming. *Editor and Publisher* (www.mediainfo.com), traditionally a print trade source, often contains information on electronic distribution and the new media. *The Hollywood Reporter* (www.hollywoodreporter.com), with its emphasis on film and entertainment, helps students who are unfamiliar with the terminology, business, and current issues of the industry. Students may be initially frustrated by the depth of some of these professional journals; however, they present an opportunity to facilitate discussion, define the terminology in its operational context, and relate current developments to the course content. Students should be encouraged to start reading in magazine sections reflecting their own personal interests, commonly programming, and then, as the course proceeds, their interest will naturally expand to other areas.

Each of the publications has online offerings, so students can save time and money. Several of the journal's circulation departments have student discounts. To take advantage of these discounts, however, the instructor has to order in bulk, and subscriptions are delivered to the department. The flaw in this system is obviously that by the time the moneys are collected from the class and subscription has started, most professors are well into their course. Then when the quarter/semester is over, the magazine is still coming until the bulk subscription runs its course. Only those most hardy students will continue to come in and ask for their subscriptions. Nevertheless, it is a valuable supplementary tool reflecting a wide variety of issues faced by the industry today.

Other valuable supplements include national and local newspapers. As noted, the marketing section, the programming, television critic columns, etc., all present opportunities for discussion. *USA Today*'s Life and Technology sections are available online (www.usatoday.com), and free subscriptions can produce daily updates on the latest technology and so on. Today more and more papers have a broadcast critic on staff. These columns can be invaluable for localizing your course materials. Some of these critics are going to be merely program reviewers and, though that does serve a readership purpose, your interest will be primarily with those critics who are watching the media within your community, localizing national media trends, and functioning as a consumer information reporter/critic as well as review national programs. Other periodicals important to broadcasting include

- *Advertising Age*, www.adage.com/
- *TV Guide*, www.tvguide.com/
- *BillBoard*, www.billboard.com/billboard/index.jsp
- *Rolling Stone*, www.rollingstone.com/
- *Hollywood Reporter*, www.hollywoodreporter.com/hollywoodreporter/index.jsp
- *Journal of Broadcasting and Electronic Media*, www.beaweb.org/jobem.html
- *Journalism and Mass Communications Quarterly*, www.aejmc.org/pubs/
- *American Journalism*, www.elon.edu/dcopeland/ajha/ajha1.htm
- *Journal of Communication*, joc.oupjournals.org/
- *Canadian Journal of Communication*, www.cjc-online.ca/
- *Columbia Journalism Review*, www.cjr.org/
- *Critical Studies in Mass Communication*, www.natcom.org/pubs/CSMC/critical_studies.htm
- *Journal of Mass Media Ethics*, jmme.byu.edu/

These are professional and academic journals you may find in most broadcast stations, production houses, media creators and academic institutions. Many are popular on the shelves of most public libraries. *TV Guide* is included among this group because of its critical essays. Relate any articles that interest students, and you have instant discussion material. The Broadcast Education Association's Research Clearing House Web site at www.beaweb.org also lists many professional links where current materials and research can be found. Journalist Jim Romenesko maintains a log, updated every weekday, which provides links to many useful media-related stories published on newspaper and magazine Web sites. It can be found at www.poynter.org/medianews.

The listing of any group of periodicals as outside sources is necessarily abbreviated. A quick check of the Internet under almost any relevant topic can produce additional materials, information on specific broadcast and cable corporations, and a wealth of pop culture information. These supplementary publications complement content, stimulate interest, keep the instructor current, and let students know where they can go in the future as questions arise.

Every one of the schools responding to the survey, in addition to the use of periodicals, used guest speakers, and media clips as outside sources of information. Speakers are not only available locally, but opportunities have increased the number of media and mediated celebrities who visit campus or through satellite feed, as available through the Museum of TV and Radio. Speaker options are varied and abundant enough that a professor has to be selective. One of the most important supplementary resources is your local broadcast community. Local chapters of the National Academy of Television Arts and Sciences (NATAS) often support academic endeavors, including student scholarships. It is an opportunity for both the students and instructors.

This course is enhanced by carefully selecting guest speakers. Speakers learn about learning in the academic setting: Don't be afraid to ask anyone, even those people at the top of the notoriety list. Most will enjoy the experience. Opportunities can be as simple as inviting the local station manager, to organizing a group of international students to offer their perspectives on American media as well as that in their own country. Preparing the class for the speaker and the speaker for the class is critical.

At Arizona State University, Walter Cronkite visits once a year, and Dr. Leigh has to prepare the students by providing the background, since today's students do not know Mr. Cronkite. The challenge with an outside speaker is simply avoiding the soapboxed ego, and getting the individual who can truly have input into the topic under discussion within the class. It is pleasantly surprising to have the guest speaker address the subject of the previous lecture and watch as suddenly the students seem to "get it," like they had never heard it before. Speakers, television programs, video clips, interactive multimedia, and the Web all provide classroom source materials.

Supplementary films and audio materials are available through the audiovisual department or films you can use through an exchange service with other universities. The following represents these authors' favorites. There's a classic called *Television-land*, by Braverman Productions. It is a composite film of the history, giving the students a good laugh as well as an understanding of the early programming. For those who struggle to maintain student enthusiasm within your history section, use this film to enrich this content.

Braverman Productions also has an old classic called *The Making of Live Television*. This is a dated look, with Johnny Carson, at the behind-the-scenes Emmy Awards from a production viewpoint. It is almost a cinema verité look at the production of the Emmys. The film is old and thus requires some environmental explanation to establish its import within the setting, but professionally oriented students find it exciting.

The Clio Award Films are simply reels of award-winning commercials from all over the world. They are available from the Clio organization (www.dailydigest.net/clioawards.html) or can be purchased cooperatively with the local advertising community. The Associated Press has produced films for classroom utilization. These are dated but available with just a phone call. For the discussion on program ratings, there's a classic clip from *WKRP*, where the ratings come to the station in "plain brown paper wrapping." No one dares open them. It is a good discussion starter. Other films include *Empire of the Air*, by Tom Lewis, which is long but provides a good historical narrative.

At Arizona State University, Professor Godfrey uses a part of the Farnsworth documentary, produced by PBS, *Big Dream Small Screen*. It has a graphical demonstration of *scanning*, which is helpful in discussing technology and digitization; it has obvious historical reflections, and, surprisingly, the author reinforces how students relate to the film because here's this young person, 19, 20, 21 years old and he's doing something that has changed the world. He is their age!

Entertainment classics are available in video stores everywhere. Mentioned in our survey were the films *Mr. Rock'n Roll*, distributed by NBC Home video; *The History of Rock'n Roll*, by Time Life; *Nanook of the North*, by Kino Video; *Citizen Kane*, by Turner Classic Movies; and *The Hindenburg*, by Goodtimes. Old radio programs are available almost everywhere, including the video story. Play those programs you enjoy and relate your enthusiasm to the class. Many instructors use the Orson Welles *Mercury Theatre of the Air*'s "War of the Worlds." This is a good piece to illustrate societal effects, but even better examples of Orson Welles' work are available and better programs from radio's golden age! Check out Orson

Welles' "Hitchhiker" (an episode of the *Suspense* radio series) for a premier radio production.

Several directories have been published that list institutional collections where professors can acquire examples of radio's golden age (Godfrey, 1992). A visit to the local library or museum can produce surprising results. Marvin Bensman of the University of Memphis has one of the most extensive collections available at www.people.memphis.edu/~mbensman/welcome.html.

Two words of caution in using anything that's not yours, such as films, audio, videotape, off-the-air, or Internet material. These two words are *copyright clearances*. Be careful. Teach your students how to observe this law, not how to break it. This is not difficult, just stay within the realms of honesty and common sense. If something is recorded off the air, the law allows a limited use.

Educators cannot library and/or distribute these materials for public showings. When recording off the air, a good rule of thumb is to record it, use it, and then erase it. Although you might be tempted to library your materials because its seems like that will make it easier the next time you teach, there are always good examples of programming, past, present, and future. Use what is current and obey the copyright law.

Common Emphasis

The survey produced some interesting similar features for the introductory class. Professor Mould of Ohio University requires his students to use the technology as all assignments are posted to the Blackboard database. This enables everyone to read and comment on the work of other students. Professor Messere from Oswego State University also makes extensive use of the Internet, such as having students develop Web sites of media issues. His students work extensively developing ideas for new programs. A new program requires a treatment using demographics analysis, characters, and a first-season plot analysis.

The industry is calling for improved writing skills from our graduates, so many schools are requiring some form of writing assignment in almost every class. In the introductory electronic media class, this can take on several forms. The first is the traditional term paper. The second is to have your students write critical essays on specific topics of discussion. A third exercise used periodically by an author as a writing option is an oral history paper. This is a bit unusual, but with the proper preparation can provide a very successful exercise.

The stated purpose of the final oral history paper option is to record the historical insight of people who "have enchanted us with accounts of their lives in another era" [from Gary L. Shumway and William G. Hartley's *An Oral History Primer* (1980)]. The development of this project requires the students to do many of the same things a term paper would accomplish. They must demonstrate a review of appropriate periodical literature, as well as organizational skills and editing and writing abilities. Students begin by selecting an interview subject, a person who is at least 65 or older. Ideally the person would have had some professional involvement with the mass media; however, some of the most successful student interviews can come from members of the student's own family. Begin with a general historical reading.

Readings should reinforce the social, political and cultural environment of historical eras. For example, when reading about the Roaring '20s, according to Frederick Lewis Allen, "Radio was the youngest rider on the Coolidge prosperity bandwagon" (Allen, 1931). Have the student survey the appropriate journals and periodical literature for events and biographical information. Once the student has a flavor for the era, and the broadcast historical events within that era, then open-ended questions for the interview subject can be formulated and the interview conducted efficiently.

The success of the interview depends on preparation. During the interview, the most important thing the student can do is be quiet and listen carefully. Let the mind of the subject tell the story as the interviewer listens and develops open-ended and follow-up questions. In this regard, it is a good strategy to consult the pamphlet *An Oral History Primer* (1980), by Gary Shumway and William Harley, in which they discuss the interview process and even suggest general questions that are appropriate to almost any interview. Once the interview is complete, the student transcribes it verbatim. It is then edited to conform to written speech. This is an excellent editing exercise for the student.

There are some differences between editing an oral history and editing a piece of news copy. In the oral history, editing is not to correct grammar or to conform to written standards of English. Editing an oral history is transposing the spoken word to the words others will read. The personality of the subject must remain intact. This is not as simple as it sounds, and it provides an excellent editing exercise. There are obvious differences between a good oral history and a good term paper.

One difference the authors have noted is that those students who opt to undertake an oral history and successfully complete it return with a far greater appreciation for the historical foundations of our industry and an excitement for history. An example of how this occurs is when a student interviews a grandparent. Rapport is already established, so they might discuss the Depression, how the family came through it, and their feelings toward Herbert Hoover and Franklin Roosevelt. The student asks, "Can you tell me about Roosevelt's speeches on the radio? Where were you on the day the Japanese attacked Pearl Harbor? There was a radio program that described an invasion from Mars. Do you remember it? How did it make you feel?" The average interview subject is not going to know anything about the history of broadcasting; however, if the student weaves broadcast-related topics carefully into the fabric of the overall interview, facts and feelings will surface.

Conclusions

Broadcasting, telecommunications and the new media have revolutionized our world. Those who teach the introductory course are elevating the fundamental consumer's understanding of today's modern media and at the same time providing the foundation for those who wish to pursue careers in the field. Begin course preparation by carefully examining personal and departmental objectives. There are a number of appropriate texts, but remember that the text is secondary to your planning. Begin planning your curriculum outline one week at a time, one day at a time: divide lectures, readings, discussions, guests, films and exams, and pace them accordingly. The outline becomes your syllabus: it balances subject material and manages time planning for the total semester.

This can be one of the most exciting courses. These authors have taught it periodically for 30 years, and each course is different. There are different personalities to every class, and you've heard it before: "The only constant in the industry is change." It is exciting to see students change and to assist them in understanding systems and information flow operations and developing their own standards. It is exciting to watch the lights go on and the glamour disappear from a student's eyes.

A greater understanding of our industry results in the education of the consumers and, as they progress, it produces uplifted practitioners. Teaching is far more than the relation of old war stories. Stories can enrich, but the essential components of teaching are to guide the students through an experiential learning process, relate principles to them, exchange dialogue with them, and challenge their own and the industry thought processes. In other words, as a teacher, the challenge in the introductory course is, as the late Fred Friendly noted, to make learning so intense that students can escape only by thinking.

References

Allen, Frederick Lewis. 1931. *Only yesterday.* New York: Harper and Row.

Godfrey Donald G. 1992. *ReRuns on file: A guide to electronic media archives.* Hillsdale, N.J.: Lawrence Erlbaum.

Limburg, Val. 1984. Course outlines: Introduction to broadcasting. *Feedback* 25 (Summer):40–41.

Shumway, Gary L., and William G. Harley. 1980. *An oral history primer.* Fullerton, Calif.: Shumway and Hartley.

Straubhaar, J., and R. LaRose. 2002. *Media now: Communications media in the information age.* 3rd ed. Belmont, Calif.: Wadsworth.

Whetmore, Edward Jay. 1982. *Mediamerica.* 2nd ed. Belmont, Calif.: Wadsworth.

Further Reading

Abramson, A. 1987. *The history of television, 1880 to 1941.* Jefferson, N.C.: McFarland, 1987.

Abramson, A. 1985. *Zworykin: Pioneer of television.* Chicago: University of Illinois Press, 1995.

Abramson, A. 2002. *The history of television, 1942 to 2000.* Jefferson, N.C.: McFarland, 2002.

Alexander, A., J. Owners, and R. Carveth. 1998. *Media economics: Theory and practice.* Mahwah, N.J.: Lawrence Erlbaum.

Benjamin, L. 2002. *Freedom of the air and the public interest: First Amendment rights in broadcasting to 1935.* Carbondale: Southern Illinois University Press, 2001.

Blumenthal, H., and O. Goodenough. 1998. *The business of television: A practical guide to the TV/video industries for producers, directors, writers, performers, agents, and executives.* New York: Billboard, 1998.

Craft, J., F. Leigh, and D. Godfrey. 2000. *Electronic media.* Belmont, Calif.: Wadsworth, 2000.

Dominick, J., A. Sherman, and F. Messere. 2000. *Broadcast cable, the Internet and beyond.* 4th ed. Boston: McGraw-Hill.

Donaldson, M. 1996. *Clearance and copyright: Everything the independent filmmaker needs to know.* Los Angeles: Silman-James.

Godfrey, D. 2001. *Philo T. Farnsworth: Father of television.* Salt Lake City: University of Utah Press.

Godfrey, D., and F. Leigh, eds. 1998. *Historical dictionary of American radio.* Westport, Conn.: Greenwood, 1998.

Head, Sydney W., Thomas Spann, and Michael McGregor. 2001. *Broadcasting in America.* 9th ed. Boston: Houghton Mifflin.

Lewis, T. 1991. *Empire of the air: The men who made radio.* New York: Harper Collins.

Newcomb, H., ed. 1997. *Encyclopedia of television.* Chicago: Fitzroy Dearborn.

Sterling, C., and J. Kittross. 2002. *Stay tuned.* 3rd ed. Mahwah, N.J.: Lawrence Erlbaum.

Zettl, H. 1998. *Sight, sound, motion: Applied media aesthetics.* Belmont, Calif.: Wadsworth.

Remembering a Mentor: Hanno Hardt

Bonnie Brennen

As a doctoral student at the University of Iowa, I often envisioned the Ph.D. program as a series of hoops. I felt that my success in the program would be measured by ability to navigate those hoops successfully. While some seemed straightforward and realizable, others, such as the dreaded comprehensive exams, were daunting. At our first official meeting as doctoral students, the director of graduate studies told us that while we might get "A"s in our classes and do well with our research and teaching fellowships and assistantships, that it would take "something more" to complete the program successfully. Being the somewhat naïve Los Angeleno that I was, I raised my hand and asked, "What is that something more?" With an exasperated glare, he replied, "That's for us to know and you to find out." Great, I thought, more hoops, and I don't even know what they are. I quickly decided that I could not do it alone. I needed a mentor.

And so I did my homework. I read at least one article by each faculty member, tried to engage each in conversation, elicited opinions about professors from other graduate students, observed their interactions with others, and of course I listened to gossip in the halls. And soon, a clear choice emerged: Professor Hanno Hardt. I asked other students and faculty about him and was told, "He's retiring," "He's not taking on any new students," "He's too busy," "He's too demanding," "He's too difficult," "Choose someone else." Although no one seemed to agree with my choice, I was undeterred. I set up a meeting and in preparation outlined a strategy to convince him to work with me. I would focus on how his work related to my own interests, express my interest in becoming a *serious* researcher, and hope that my current work in one of his classes might help to persuade him. On the appointed day and time, I sat down and began my pitch. Not wanting to bury the lead, I asked him straight away to be my mentor and explained that I would proceed to explain why he should take my request seriously. He interrupted my script and simply said, "Sure, I'd be happy to work with you." And of course, at that moment, I knew that I had picked the best possible mentor for me.

Hanno Hardt is a serious intellectual who truly believes in the revolutionary power of knowledge. A committed academic, he works extremely hard and attempts to instill that work ethic in his students. He challenges them to question their assumptions, to think deeply, and to try and make connections between theories and concepts and issues in contemporary society. He is also the most giving teacher that I have ever encountered. He has always made me feel like my work is important and, no matter how busy he was, he has always made time for me. To this day his encouragement remains unwavering, his guidance consistent; he has continually encouraged (and sometimes prodded) me to do my best.

I learned very quickly that Hanno would always give me an honest evaluation of my research—and that usually that meant that there was more work to be done. I once heard him assess a colleague's research as "rather pedestrian" and vowed to myself that I would do my best so that he would never be forced to dismiss my work that way. So far, so good. Not lavish with a compliment, his assessment of the final draft of my dissertation was, "Well, this will have to do." Yet, his criticisms are well focused, on target, and always include concrete ways to improve the research. I've learned that when my work meets Hanno's standards, then I've actually done something meaningful.

Throughout his career, Hanno has taught by example. His philosophy of teaching suggests that it is through research that a professor actually becomes a better teacher. He's taught me that when you are engaged with your work, you bring an excitement to your teaching, and it is that excitement and engagement that are contagious. As a professor, Hanno is always up on the current research and incorporates it in each of his classes. His courses evolve over time and often respond to and interact with contemporary arguments in the field. When I visited his Social Theory course a couple years after I initially took the class, I was surprised by how much of the content had changed, and I took the opportunity to sit in on the class the rest of the semester. In all of his graduate courses, he shares his own current research and encourages students to critique his work. I doubt that any of his students have ever been at a loss for an appropriate research topic. Virtually every class session, Hanno would mention at least one interesting and important research project that needed to be done. One semester I decided to write down all of his ideas; revisiting my class notes, a few years later, I found 30 viable research ideas that he had outlined. Hanno has an uncanny ability to encourage classroom discussion on a myriad of topics but not to let the conversation dissolve into chaos. He has a knack for getting reticent students to talk and always makes the classroom environment feel safe and at the same time exciting.

Throughout my doctoral program, Hanno simply made the academic hoops fall away. His guidance on all the specifics of the program was excellent, and he helped to make my graduate experience a great one. But he didn't relinquish his duties as a mentor once I had successfully completed the program. His critical eye continues to shape my research, and he repeatedly challenges me to keep going with my work. His advice and guidance on research as well as employment-related issues is unwavering. His research strategies helped me to survive the tenure process with a minimum of stress. Over the years, I've been fortunate to work with him on a variety of research projects and, each time, I have learned more about the nature of research in media studies. Ten years after successfully defending my dissertation and officially joining the club, Hanno Hardt remains my mentor and friend. And I remain convinced that choosing the right mentor is one of the most important things that a doctoral student can do.

CHAPTER 7

Introduction to Advertising

Donald Jung and Karie Hollerbach

Introduction

The generally accepted objectives of advertising education involve both theoretical and practical goals. These include, but are not limited to, appreciation of the field of advertising, instruction in the latest advertising approaches, training and judgment in problem solving, and preparation for both a first job and a long-term career in the field. The first course in a communication-based advertising curriculum is most often referred to as Introduction to Advertising or Principles of Advertising. Although there is significant variation in how this course is taught, it generally revolves around certain basic principles and content.

Generally, the introductory advertising course seeks to provide students with an understanding of advertising principles and practices, including creative, communicative and managerial aspects of advertising. This is accomplished by examining advertising as a marketing tool and advertising history and principles, as well as understanding the use of demographics and psychographics in advertising. Students are introduced to SWOT (strength, weakness, opportunity, threats) analysis, market segmentations, target audiences, unique selling propositions, strategy statements, and creative concepts and execution using a variety of media. Finally, this introductory advertising course usually seeks to expand the individual student's capacity to critically analyze and constructively critique both successful and unsuccessful advertising communication.

Additionally, this course at times is also used to explore advertising as an institution in society, both as a marketing tool and as a communication process. When this is the case, the course is designed as a comprehensive view of the subject, including such topics as advertising history, regulation, communication theory and practice, and the nature and impact advertising has on society.

Often, the Introduction to Advertising course is designed to foster a sense of professionalism and visual ethics seeking to utilize the student's liberal arts and communication background in a new way. And, based on what is taught in this introductory course, students are expected to understand the nature of visual as well as written/spoken language, and gain an increased critical awareness of advertising strategies and techniques.

The ultimate goal is to provide students a practical understanding of the practices and techniques used in the advertising world today by both agencies and clients. This includes issues currently facing the business side of advertising: the environment that advertising operates in today, career and employment opportunities, strategy development, writing advertising plans, and understanding media and the creative aspects of the field, as well as integration of other communications.

This chapter surveys a variety of approaches used to teach an Introduction to Advertising course. Described are the basic elements of introduction to advertising/advertising principles, including a variety of course approaches, assignments, requirements and projects. Also discussed is a variety of course philosophies regarding teaching this type of course, technical problems encountered, and the place of such a course in the communication/advertising curriculum. Also provided are advertising-related resources, including Web sites, and suggested readings, including books and articles.

Advertising instructors at a variety of institutions around the country teach the specific courses described in this chapter. While many of the results reported here are from detailed material from four institutions, over 35 course syllabi were reviewed, as well as course Web sites where available. Participating instructors answered 13 open-ended survey questions about the place of the introductory advertising course in the particular institutions and departmental curriculum, similar or ancillary courses, common features of the course, individual goals and objectives, instructor philosophy, overall emphasis in the course, challenges to teaching such a course, and suggestions for outside and Web-based resources. The survey can be accessed at cstl-cla.semo.edu/hollerbach/adinterviews/advertising.htm.

Position of the Course in the Curriculum

It seems obvious based on both the response of course instructors and from reviewing a variety of courses with resources posted online that the Introduction to Advertising course is usually a junior- or senior-level introduction to a specific advertising track in the curriculum. Although in some institutions it may be listed as either a specific course found within a general mass communication degree or a specific course found within the advertising option of a mass communication or journalism degree, it is most often a specific first course found within a degree or concentration in advertising.

As such, most students take this course either as a required departmental course because advertising is their primary field of study or as a departmental course within the department because advertising may or may not be their primary field of study. There are also a smattering of students who take the course as a general/university course or elective.

As an introductory-track course, it shares a similar place with a variety of other introductory course, including introductions to public relations, journalism, and telecommunications. As such, it generally serves as the first advertising course in a sequence. It is the first advertising course taken before any other advertising courses and is a prerequisite for taking any other courses in the advertising major. The survey nature of the course provides a general overview, touching on topics covered in detail in more specific courses to follow (e.g., advertising techniques, copywriting, media planning, account planning, and advertising campaigns).

Common Goals and Objectives

The stated goals and objectives of the Introduction to Advertising course vary. They range from very short and specific statements such as University of Louisville Professor of Advertising Stuart Esrock's "a broad overview of the advertising industry," to more elaborate statements such as University of Georgia Professor of Advertising Jay Hamilton's "an attempt to provide students with an historical and conceptual understanding of advertising in society; an attempt to merge this with a procedural overview of how the advertising process is organized." He continues with his objectives for the course, providing "a theoretical, historical, and practical overview of advertising primarily in the United States. Stress is placed on conceptual understanding of theory and philosophy, and applications through specific tools and techniques."

Professor Esrock's objectives, though similar in some ways to Professor Hamilton's, are also somewhat unique: "Understand what advertising is and how it functions as part of the economy. Know the important role of research in development of advertising campaigns. Realize the importance of delineating and speaking to specific target audiences." He goes on to describe the importance of having students understand available media options with advertisers aware of "unique strengths and weaknesses, and how advertising messages are tailored for a specific medium. Know how advertising materials and campaigns are created. Understand why ads or campaigns succeed and fail."

Other goals and objectives from a variety of other institutions include exploration of advertising's institutional role, referring to how advertising campaigns are organized and conducted and how they function as a part of the economy (Boston College). Others offer a basis for conceptual understanding, examining the philosophy and theory of advertising along with applications in the marketplace.

As one might expect, the practical considerations regarding the roles that advertising agencies play and the ways they interact to serve their clients occupy a great deal of attention. Some courses take a special look at the role of research at agencies that provide applications both in America and internationally (Rutgers University). Some syllabi use terms such as *commercial persuasion* or *social interaction* to describe strategy and decision making in both external and internal environments (Purdue University). They note that advertising occurs in a variety of contexts and try to give students an overview of both how and where that happens. Both the beginning and end of the advertising process are considered, with strategic thinking playing a central role in informing consumer choices (San Jose State University).

Some of the courses take the next step and encourage consideration of the principles of basic advertising copy writing and layout. The use of case studies, particularly those geared to college students, demonstrate targeted ads as a commonplace approach. National events such as the Super Bowl and World Series invite scrutiny, and sponsors are evaluated for effectiveness and creativity as a means of gaining insight and getting the big picture in the most competitive of environments. In recent years, due to growing corporate concerns, an emphasis on ethical decision making and regulatory considerations has become a key issue for examination in even introductory courses.

Just as there is some variation in the goals for teaching an Introduction to Advertising course, there are also some variations in the objectives that instructors have for students who complete such a course. In programs where Introduction to Advertising is the first course in a sequence, these goals go beyond a general knowledge of the field. For example, for Professor Janice Bukovac at Michigan State University, other goals include understanding the field as a marketing tool as well as its history and principles.

This is part of a course plan to develop and "build a base of understanding on the use of demographics and psychographics in advertising; develop familiarity with SWOT analysis, market segmentation(s), target audience(s), unique selling proposition." This professor also includes strategy statements, creative concepts with attention to execution using various media "to expand individual student's capacity to critically analyze and constructively critique both successful and unsuccessful advertising communication."

Additional goals identified at other institutions include identifying major players in the industry, usually by looking at the creative process and the various steps along the way. The courses tend to examine the process step by step to provide a better understanding of the important roles that advertisers, agencies, vendors and various media play. The historical background reinforces the many successes that the advertising industry has enjoyed as well as the factors contributing to its growth.

An overview of regulatory considerations in terms of the roles of the Federal Trade Commission and the Federal Communications Commission helps to put development in perspective in terms of appropriate behavior. An analysis of the structure and function of various advertising departments gives students a preliminary idea of who does what and helps them to begin forming ideas about the areas in which they may have the most interest.

Examination of salient issues concerning what methods agencies employ through their research to determine whether a campaign has achieved its goal is a common theme in such courses, as well as research-based efforts to improve a brand. An examination of the creative process is viewed as being worthwhile, and analysis of how media buying is conducted also helps student learning in most commercial contexts. Attempts to monitor various media outlets, evaluating effective and failed strategy, thus making observations on the probable formulation of a plan of action and decisions leading to ad placement, contribute to the learning process.

Special Features

To achieve the specific unique goals and objectives, individual professors apply a wide range of approaches. When asked specifically about what features they believe their Introduction to Advertising course has that are unique or special relative to other such courses at other schools, there were a variety of responses.

For instance, Professor Bukovac at Michigan State University reports that since her particular introductory course is so large, her reliance on the use of online resources may make it unique. She uses LON CAPA for online testing and has homework assignments and submissions set up online as well. The students still do work in class but, with 600 students involved in the online option, this provides efficiency and enables better communication and feedback. This multipronged approach is viewed as the wave of the future at many institutions.

Professor Esrock at the University of Louisville believes a unique characteristic of his particular course is the use of a team project in which students research and report about an existing advertising campaign. A number of smaller to midsized enrollment courses seem to use some aspect of a final team assignment to simulate the use of teams in the agency culture. The approach is effective because it simulates real-world experience by forcing students to acknowledge what decisions were made and to what end.

Professor Hamilton at the University of Georgia states that he spends a fair amount of time introducing various conceptual tools from cultural/critical studies to help students in the analysis of advertising and its larger role in society. Professor Hamilton uses extensive examples of ads culled from the Internet in video files and presents them in a PowerPoint presentation.

Instructor Philosophy

Obviously, understanding the instructors' individual philosophy is imperative to understanding what goals and objectives need to be met. For instance, Professor Bukovac at Michigan State responded to the instructor-philosophy question by stating, "I hope that students come away from the course with a better understanding of the industry as well as with the desire to learn more." She continues, "I think in part the job of the introductory course is to excite students and promote the advertising major."

Professor Hamilton at the University of Georgia stated, "It is imperative to provide students with both a conceptual/critical understanding of advertising in society, as well as a procedural introduction to the process." For him, neither one is sufficient by itself, either for aspiring practitioners or for college graduates in other majors.

Professor Esrock of the University of Louisville summed up his course philosophy by stating, "I think this is a course that should be of interest to students, whether or not they are thinking about a career in advertising, because the industry has such a broad impact on all of our daily lives." He continues, "So, while I teach the course thinking that some of the students in the class may consider the industry for a career, I also teach the course so that hopefully everyone who takes it will understand the impact of advertising in our society and how ad campaigns are put together so that they will become better-educated consumers."

Common Emphasis

Given the range of classroom contexts (from 600+ lecture/survey student sections at Michigan State University to 15 to 20 laboratory-style student sections), obviously the major emphasis in an Introduction to Advertising course varies, as does the means of achieving this emphasis. For instance, Professor Bukovac said, "We don't have any heavy emphasis. We try to take a broad approach, looking at all topics from all angles."

For Professor Bukovac, this emphasis involves online testing where students can log in from any location and take the test. The course involves homework assignments posted at the beginning of the week, and students have the week to complete and return their submissions. To address the need for generating elements of critical and creative thinking, the course requires some in-class strategic and creative exercises (like brainstorming) and the production of at least one hard-copy advertisement.

A more moderate-sized class (30 to 40) such as Professor Esrock's at the University of Louisville emphasizes marketing overview, history, functions of advertising in society, ethics, regulation, advertising agencies, consumer behavior and decision making, target audiences, ad planning, strategy, creativity, how ads are put together (production), media planning, media options, sales promotion, direct marketing, and public relations overview. This is generally identical to the emphasis of the aforementioned large lecture class. To achieve this emphasis, Professor Esrock uses exams combining multiple-choice and essay questions, as well as a variety of team projects.

Finally, another course similar in size at the University of Georgia emphasizes four conceptual areas: (1) definitions, history, and development; (2) strategy and media; (3) creative development and execution; and (4) understanding as well as practical overview. To achieve this emphasis, Professor Hamilton uses lectures and exam questions. In addition, he uses an optional group project, providing a chance for the students to put pieces together while analyzing specific campaigns.

Common Challenges/Solutions

When it comes to teaching any course, any professor can identify what are to them barriers to being able to bring across the subject effectively to the students. A course such as Introduction to Advertising is no exception. For the large-lecture professor, such as Professor Bukovac at Michigan State University, the biggest challenge is standing in front of 600+ students and challenging and exciting them.

She uses stories, guest speakers, and videos to help keep up the student interest level. She believes that another challenge is to provide assignments that are reasonable for the instructor to grade and interesting for such a large group. On the plus side, Professor Bukovac believes that the online option has made this much more reasonable, allowing more assignments to keep student interest high with quick turnaround rates.

For a midsized class such as that taught by Professor Esrock at the University of Louisville, the challenge is trying to cram all of the information into a 15-week course. This forces him to touch too briefly on various topics in a survey-course manner. Even for a midsized course, he thinks the number is still too large to have students working with development of actual advertising materials. His solution is to use the team project approach to reporting about an existing ad campaign.

Finally, for Professor Hamilton at the University of Georgia, the major challenge is engaging a broad array of student interests (from casual for those taking it as an elective to intensive for those hoping to major in advertising). He addresses this by including material appropriate to both and explaining the relevance of all material to all interests. Another challenge that he identifies is providing sufficient examples of ads to illustrate points. To address this, he uses extensive examples (print, audio, and video) from Internet sources and merges them using PowerPoint into multimedia presentations.

Outside Resources

No consensus emerges on the use of textbooks for readings. Some professors use only one traditional Introduction to Advertising textbook, some use a combination of text and readings, and some use only selected readings. A list of suggested readings appears later in this chapter. Web resources such as company sites, agency sites, regulatory sites, Hoovers, Ad Critic, Ad Forum, and Ad Graveyard were also mentioned. A list of advertising links, categorized and based on a heuristically driven super ego, is included later in this chapter and also available at http://cstl-cla.semo.edu/Jung/ADVERTISINGLINKS/AdvertisingHotLinks.htm. Of course, this list may be totally antiquated by the time this book reaches print, but the point is that there are many good linked advertising sites.

Also, the professional organizations associated with advertising (AAF, AEF, AAAA, AEJMC, NCA, etc.) all have well-developed Web sites designed to help students and faculty locate information and resources.

In addition to a wealth of online research materials, the local university library probably has electronic resources, which can be useful to any Introduction to Advertising student or professor. As is key in the information age, knowing where information resides can help move us toward knowledge.

Conclusions

Final thoughts from some professors of the Introduction to Advertising course are in order. For instance, Professor Bukovac at Michigan State University notes that introductory courses are often neglected as simply large survey courses, which in part they are. She observes that what many people tend to forget is that the introductory course is where you identify and encourage future advertising majors. So considering this, the introductory class is really the first and most important course in any curriculum.

She also notes that online resources are invaluable because the technology for large courses is lacking or difficult to navigate. For her, it takes considerable individual effort to identify and implement reliable online tools.

The final insight from Professor Esrock at the University of Louisville about teaching the Introduction to Advertising course is that it is a fun class to teach. He enjoys the challenge to work everything in and continually seeks better ways to group the presentation of material. He does this by thinking of this course as "one of those courses where you can see the tumblers clicking for some students as they think to themselves, 'You mean, I can make a living doing this? Cool!' That is the best thing about this course."

And for Professor Hamilton at the University of Georgia, it is "a continual challenge to bring together students of a wide variety of levels of interest. Yet, it is also a crucial course for the university as a whole, in that advertising plays such a central role today." It's hard to say more.

Advertising Book and Article Links

Suggested readings from the University of Texas Advertising Department: advertising.utexas.edu/research/books/index.html.

Must-read advertising list from the University of Wisconsin: www.aded.org/channel.asp?ChannelID=5&DocID=33&location=Must-Read%20Lists.

Readings from Steve Norcia's Principles of Advertising class at Fordham College: www.aded.org/channel.asp?ChannelID=5&DocID=1109&location=Must-Read%20Lists.

Readings from AEF must-read list: www.aded.org/channel.asp?ChannelID=5&sp=sp_FrontPage_List&F_P=9&O_D=0&location=Must-Read%20Lists.

Remembering a Mentor:
Michael Schudson

Elliot King

Like many others, I made my way to the academic world after spending some time as a working journalist. In my own experience, there has always been a somewhat uneasy relationship between practitioners and the professorate, and consequently the road from the media industry to the university is not always a comfortable one. In any case, I was very unsure if I really wanted to walk it.

Nonetheless, as I increasingly became aware that I was more interested in understanding the big picture about the media than in cranking out stories about the personal computer industry, which is what I was doing at the time, I began to investigate graduate programs. Eventually I found an obscure, offbeat offering in sociology at the University of California at San Diego. The program focused on what was described as the sociology of culture. In addition to fairly standard fare in social thought and research methods, I would be able to take courses in subjects like the sociology of knowledge and *sociolinguistics*, whatever that may be. Although I had never taken a sociology courses in my long and sordid college career, this program sounded intriguing. I could see myself addressing what I thought were core questions: How do people know things? Why do they believe what they do and act on those beliefs? What makes something interesting to large numbers of people?

I applied and was accepted. Still unsure about attending, I talked to Richard T. Baker, my advisor at Columbia University, where I had received a master's degree in journalism. After assuring me that I was not committing some grave heresy, he told me that one of the brightest young minds writing about the media was at UCSD, and if I could study with him, it would be worthwhile going. That person was Michael Schudson.

So I made an appointment to visit Michael Schudson. As I made my way to his office in the Department of Communication, I was struck by how shabby, dark and quiet the building was. There was nobody around. Painted in state-school cinderblock yellow, it didn't look like a place where people would like to hang around much. About 15 minutes after the appointed time, just long enough for me to wonder if I had gotten the appointment time wrong and to question if I would feel comfortable back on campus, a fairly slight guy not much older than me and dressed in an old, oversized green sweater approached. Michael let me into his office, which looked not unlike my own; that is, as if a bombshell hit it. We cleared a place on a couch probably salvaged from a rummage sale and we sat down to chat. After a few minutes of uneasy small talk, he finally asked, "What do you want me to tell you? I don't know if you should come here or not but it is a good program. It will be interesting."

He seemed like a nice, friendly guy. He certainly wasn't intimidating. That weekend, I was reading the book review section of the *Los Angeles Times* and saw a review of Michael's book *Advertising: The Uneasy Persuasion*. I turned to my wife and said, "That is the kind of book I would like to write." Reading the review and notification that I had won a Regents Scholarship cinched the deal. I decided to attend.

I arrived on campus that fall eager to enroll in a class with Michael Schudson, my mentor to be. I surveyed the course offerings and, sure enough, Michael was on a leave of absence that quarter. (That proved to be a not uncommon occurrence during my seven years in graduate school.) I looked at the winter quarter offerings and saw that Michael was scheduled to teach a graduate seminar in social psychology. Perfect. I had anticipated that social psychology would be one of my primary areas of interest.

When I went to enroll in the seminar, however, there was one small snafu. I had misread the catalog. Michael was not teaching social psychology. He was teaching a seminar in something called *collective memory*. I had no clue what that might be about, but it sounded *tres* icky—a course about memory in the Soviet Union perhaps. So I was faced with a Faustian choice. Should I enroll in the course in which I was interested, or should I cravenly opt for the course taught by an instructor to whom I wanted to suck up?

I decided that social psychology would be offered again in the future. (It was—four years later. It wasn't that interesting.) I enrolled in Michael's Collective Memory course. And it was in that course I learned how I wanted to conduct myself as a teacher.

In student evaluations for a course that I taught about media culture and society, I received the following comment: "This is a course where the entire class is challenged everyday to formulate and voice observations and opinions. During these daily discussions, Dr. King was a part of the student body rather than the omniscient teacher. I thoroughly enjoyed those class discussions."

I see my role as a teacher as creating learning experiences in which I participate with my students. That was exactly how Michael structured that seminar on collective memory. On the first day, he shared his observation that there were several ways to conduct graduate seminars. There were seminars in which professors knew a lot about the subject matter, and the goal was to impart the material, along with professor's accumulated wisdom and deep insight, to the students. Alternatively, he said, there were classes in which the professor did not know all that much about the subject but was interested in exploring it with others. The seminar in collective memory, he added, fell into the latter group.

As it turns out, I think collective memory is a powerful conceptual framework. Over the years, I have presented several papers applying those ideas to the history of journalism. As importantly as the content, however, in that class, I had found somebody who could guide my learning experience through graduate school. Following that seminar, Michael invited me to be his research assistant, and we embarked on a project to understand the image of Ronald Reagan as a "great communicator." Articles based on that work are still being recycled in various collections and anthologies.

Then Michael agreed to serve as the chair of my thesis committee. As many people know, he had burst onto the academic scene with the publication of his book *Discovering the News* (1978) which looked at the rise of objectivity as a value among journalists in the 19th and early 20th centuries. For my thesis, I chose to investigate the political activities—i.e., the antiobjectivity—of journalists during the same period. That could have been a foolhardy choice. As Michael observed, I focused on everything that he had ignored in his own research. But instead of demonstrating to me the errors in my thinking, as a MacArthur Foundation-certified genius might be tempted to do, he listened to me and, at the end of process, professed to modify his own views. One of his most critical comments on the final draft of my dissertation was "You didn't rake Schudson over the coals harshly enough."

Over the years, I have relished basking in Michael's reflected glory. At one academic conference, as I read the name tags of attendees at a poster session, mentally assigning faces to names that were famous to me, a leading luminary approached me and asked, "Are you *the* Elliot King who works with Michael Schudson?" Another time, I introduced myself to a well-known speaker at Loyola, who replied, "I was hoping to meet you. I use your article about Reagan all the time." He was hoping to meet me? In 2001, I was invited to give a talk about Michael's work at the American Journalism Historians Association, with Michael responding to my remarks. He allowed that I understood his work, thank goodness.

Of course, that a thesis advisor would have a profound intellectual influence on a graduate student perhaps is to be expected. That a graduate student would have an intellectual influence on the advisor is, I believe, more unusual. That is a result of Michael's readiness to enter into authentic learning relationships with his students.

Creating an environment in which the teacher is an active learner works for both the students and the instructor. I have taught a class in free speech almost 25 times, and it remains fresh and interesting for me. Almost every semester, a couple of students will complain that they didn't know where I stood on any of the issues. That is because each semester I am forced to rethink my positions based on what I learn from my students.

I routinely close each semester with a farewell speech. I summarize what I hoped the students learned in the class and then leave them with this thought: I became a teacher because I love to learn. In my opinion, one of the dirty, little secrets of higher education is that the teacher gets to do about 70 percent of all the learning that takes place in the classroom. I finish by thanking them for being my students and joining me in the learning adventure. And I sincerely mean it.

I believe that there is no more exhilarating experience than people learning together. I try to create that experience in every class in every semester. I came to understand how powerful learning together can be from Michael Schudson.

CHAPTER 8

Introduction to Public Relations

Liese L. Hutchinson

Introduction

pproximately 80 years ago, Edward Bernays, one of the founders of modern
public relations, taught the first university course on the fledgling field.
Since that historic moment in 1923 at New York University, the teaching
and practicing of public relations have flourished. Today, more than 200,000 practitioners claim public relations as their career of choice. Approximately 200 universities and colleges offer public relations (PR) degrees and/or majors. Untold others
offer sequences, minors, or emphases in public relations. In 1999 alone, over 4,500
undergraduate students graduated from PR degree programs, eager to join the profession (Johnson and Ross, 2000). And what an expanding field they have chosen.
According to the U.S. Department of Labor, employment of PR specialists is
expected to "increase much faster than average for all occupations through 2010"
(stats.bls.gov/oco/ocos086.htm). This means an expected growth rate of 36 percent
and higher over the next few years. From the internationalization of trade to an
explosion of mergers and acquisitions to the increasing democratization of nations,
organizations are realizing more than ever the need for effective public relations.

To achieve effective public relations, effective practitioners are needed. The education
of future practitioners has shifted beyond journalism-style programs to a liberal arts
focus that incorporates communication theory and research along with intercultural,
international and organizational communication. Business courses in management,
accounting and marketing are also often part of a PR student's academic experience.
Public relations defines itself differently from other mass-communication majors or programs because of this integrated approach. No longer are students expected to become
practitioners by being journalism or marketing majors taking just one course in public
relations. The breadth and depth of courses have exploded over the last few decades.

Who teaches these courses? A survey conducted by Sallot and colleagues (1997) on professional standards in public relations used the 1995 membership directory of the Educators Academy of the Public Relations Society of America (PRSA). Of the 291 members, 127 responded. In terms of degrees in hand, nearly 53 percent of the educators had doctorates, with 40 percent possessing a master's. In terms of professional experience, 30 percent of the educators reported five to 10 years of professional experience, 24 percent with 11 to 20 years and 25 percent with 21 to 45 years. Because of the call for educators to have professional PR experience, they belong to professional organizations such as PRSA, the Arthur Page Society, the International Public Relations Association (IPRA), and the International Association of Business Communicators. In addition, PR educators play active roles in various academic groups, such as the Association for Education in Journalism and Mass Communication (AEJMC) and the National Communication Association (NCA). These educators teach in a variety of programs from specialized degrees with focused majors, to minors, to sequences with emphasis areas. Few programs in public relations are accredited by an academic body. For example, the Accrediting Council of AEJMC accredits 15 U.S. university programs in public relations (www.ukans.edu/~acejmc/STUDENT/PROGLIST.SHTML). PRSA, the prevalent association for the profession, recognizes more than 200 student chapters across the country that meet several criteria, including the college or university's accreditation by a national association, the program or department offering PR courses and opportunities in six broad areas, a full-time faculty advisor, and a professional advisor (www.prssa.org/about/establish.asp). Only 10 of these universities, however, have been certified in Education for Public Relations by the Educational Affairs committee of PRSA (http://www.prsa.org/_About/overview/certification_info.asp?ident=over5).

To prepare this chapter to highlight common practices in teaching the introductory PR course, dozens of syllabi from programs across the United States (via the AEJMC PR division Listserve, online syllabi and personal requests) were gathered, recent pedagogical research reviewed, and the author's own experiences reflected upon. It is the hope that this chapter will assist PR educators in teaching the introductory PR course by discussing three broad areas: what the course is and where it fits within the PR curricula; the features, goals, philosophies and challenges outlined in syllabi; and the outside resources available to educators.

Position of the Course in the Curriculum

The common names for the introductory PR course are Principles of Public Relations (or Public Relations Principles), Introduction to Public Relations, and Public Relations Principles and Practices. This course is a requirement in a program with a degree or major. In a program without a major, but with multiple PR courses available, the students must take this course first before any other PR course such as Public Relations Writing, Cases in Public Relations, Public Relations Campaigns, Public Relations Research, and Public Relations Ethics. The introductory course is also a typical requirement for a PR internship.

Though there are numerous schools or colleges of communication where public relations would be housed in its own department or program, the majority of PR classes are taught within a department of communication, mass communication, speech communication, or journalism. Students from these programs tend to receive bachelor's degrees in communication with an emphasis in public relations, for example.

The course is mainly labeled as a 300-level course, with a 200-level course being the second most common moniker. This means students typically don't take the introductory PR course until they've declared their major in their sophomore or junior year.

The number of students varies dramatically in the introductory course from approximately 250 students at the University of Florida to 30 students at Saint Louis University. The difference can by explained in that the University of Florida's College of Journalism and Communication has several departments and programs, with the PR department alone serving more than 1,000 undergraduates with a dozen full-time PR faculty. On the other end of the spectrum is Saint Louis University's Department of Communication, which has approximately 300 communication majors who can take a variety of PR courses as electives to create a self-designated PR emphasis with one full-time PR faculty member teaching them all.

Similar and Ancillary Courses

Similar courses are available to students interested in public relations, such as Introduction to Mass Communication, Introduction to Integrated Marketing Communication, Principles of Advertising, and Introduction to Marketing. Organizational Communication can be compared with the introductory PR course to the extent the organizational course focuses on internal communication issues similar to those faced by an employee-relations specialist. Ancillary courses such as those offered in film, media studies, advertising, marketing, management, broadcasting and journalism help round out the degrees of students interested in pursuing careers in public relations.

Comparative Features

Several areas will be compared on how educators teach the introductory PR course. The next few pages highlight the textbooks used, outside resources, areas covered, teaching techniques, assessment tools, and use of technology.

Textbooks Used

The four most common textbooks cited by educators in their syllabi are, in alphabetical order by first author, Cutlip's *Effective Public Relations*, Newsom's *This is PR: The Realities of Public Relations*, Seitel's *The Practice of Public Relations*, and Wilcox's *Essentials of Public Relations*. To a lesser extent, Grunig's *Managing Public Relations*, Guth and Marsh's *Public Relations: A Value-Driven Approach* and Baskin and colleagues' *Public Relations: The Profession and the Practice* are cited as well. Several of these texts offer videos of case studies, video news releases, public service announcements, and media clips; PowerPoint class discussions; sample tests; and online access to other teaching and learning materials, such as supplemental readings, chat rooms, and useful links.

Outside Sources

Numerous educators required or encouraged students to read the largest daily newspaper in their area to facilitate class discussion on current events. Public relations professional periodicals such as *PR Tactics*, *PR Week*, *and PR Strategist* were also mentioned. The two main academic journals, *Public Relations Review* and *Journal of Public Relations Research*, were cited as useful outside resources for research papers and presentations. Other suggested materials include *The Associated Press Stylebook and Libel Manual* (Goldstein, 1999) and *The Elements of Style* (Strunk, 2000).

Areas Covered

Typical topic areas that educators emphasized covered the spectrum of the field:

Definition of public relations. Where did the term come from? What are its connotations? Whose definition is the most accurate?

History and development of public relations. Instructors outline the profession's ancient beginnings through the era of modern public relations adopted in the United States. From Socrates to P. T. Barnum to Ivy Lee, the history and PR's growth in the 20th century is taught.

Definition of publics and public opinion. What is a public? How do we shape public opinion? Discussed are the communication field's work on the importance of public opinion and how organizations realized its relevance to survival.

Public relations' role in management. A technician or a manager? A strategist or an implementer? What a practitioner's role is in an organization exemplifies the importance that organization pays to PR counsel.

Research and evaluation. Before a PR campaign is introduced, what research must be conducted to determine the problem/opportunity, massage key messages, and target the right audience? After the effort, evaluation determines PR successes and failures.

Ethics and codes of standard. Public relations practitioners are faced with numerous ethical choices and dilemmas in their careers. What guidelines, frameworks or standards help steer practitioners through ethical quagmires?

Legal issues. From copyright infringement to privacy laws to insider trading and SEC regulations, students must understand the legal issues they will face.

Theory. Systems, two-way symmetrical, social-interpretive, communication models and effects are a few of persuasive, communication, and PR theories covered.

Public relations' roles. Public relations practitioners are involved in numerous areas: community relations, investor relations, government relations, employee relations, media relations, consumer relations, etc.

Crisis communication. From syringes in Diet Pepsi's to the Exxon Valdez crash to Enron's collapse, communicating in a crisis combines all of a practitioner's skills.

Teaching Techniques Used

To enhance these topic areas and to encourage active learning, educators across the country use a variety of techniques:

Lectures. Highlighting textbook examples and content, encouraging discussion of current situations, and showcasing examples of good and bad public relations all enhance an educator's lecturing style.

Media writing. From the simple press release to an entire press kit, teaching students basic media writing, following AP Style, provides them with the writing skills that practitioners demand and portfolio materials for internship and job interviews.

Research papers. Topics range from how to handle ethical decisions based on accepted principles to monitoring legal changes in the field to technology's implications on the profession. Other paper ideas include interviewing a practitioner on a typical day, and what skills he or she thinks are necessary for students to have in order to succeed.

Presentations. Students are asked to present everything from information on leaders in public relations to examining real-life situations. Critiquing organizations' handling of various PR scenarios enhances critical thinking skills.

Group activities. Preparing mini-PR campaigns in a team environment mimics a department or agency's method of analyzing a situation and developing a communication solution.

Web-site critiques. Communicating using the Internet is a favorite tool among PR practitioners. Which organizations use the tool effectively and which do not?

Case study critiques. How could the organization have handled the case differently? Did the students come up with the same solution? What implications does the case have on other practitioners?

Guest lecturers. Bringing in a practitioner from the trenches offers students the opportunity to inquire about the real world.

Agency tours. What's a typical day in PR agency or in-house department? Offering the students a chance to witness public relations in action can be a valuable learning tool.

Chat rooms. Many educators have created chat rooms for the students to discuss current events, ethics and assignments, among other topics. This offers students access to technology and easy access to others with similar interests in learning about public relations.

Assessment

Assessing student skills and knowledge base involves assigning research papers, media writing assignments, presentations, and group projects. Other assessment tools include essay tests, in-class participation, chat-room participation, and peer reviews.

Use of Technology

Technology and public relations are forever linked. Practitioners use technology to e-mail news releases, simulcast news conferences on their organization's Web site, post investor-relations materials, and communicate with colleagues around the world. Students in the introductory PR course are encouraged to use technology as well by joining class chat rooms, visiting textbook publisher's Web sites offering supplemental class materials, downloading professor's assignments via their Web sites, e-mailing assignments to their professors, writing for the department's Web site, presenting case studies on PowerPoint to their classmates, and working on virtual assignments with students in the same course across the country.

Common Goal and Objectives

The overall course goal seems to be universal: Combine theoretical knowledge with practical experience. Educators point out to students that, by the end of the course, the students should be able to

- Define public relations
- Understand the history of the field
- Understand the need for and basics of research
- Conduct and evaluate research
- Understand PR roles and functions
- Identify key theories
- Prioritize and understand publics
- Demonstrate clear writing abilities
- Understand ethical, social responsibility, and legal issues
- Decide if they want to pursue PR as a profession

These objectives, naturally, coincide with the areas covered by educators in an early section of this chapter.

Instructor Philosophy and Common Emphasis

To support the universal goal of combining theoretical knowledge with practical experience, the overarching philosophy of PR educators is to provide students with information on the history of the profession, definitions, functions and roles. It also covers prevalent theories to assist students in the practice of public relations through real-world readings, assignments and activities. This course is the gateway to other PR courses and to the practice of public relations, and is taught as such.

Common Challenges

Public relations educators face challenges. The most common are that there aren't enough instructors and that they're teaching too many students. Another challenge is the educator's need to keep up with the latest developments in the profession while contributing to the academic body of knowledge through participation on panels, presentation of research papers, and publication in academic journals and books—hence, their commitment to at least one professional organization and one academic association.

In terms of teaching the introductory course, not all of the teaching activities outlined earlier can be incorporated into this one class, especially if the institution offering the course does not have access to PR professionals and agencies. But what these activities help do is develop the skills and knowledge base encouraged by the 1999 Commission on Public Relations Education (see below). What these activities and class discussions also do is prepare students for PR situations they may face in the future. As interpreters for organizations, practitioners often find themselves in the middle—caught between one public's demands and expectations and the organization's goals and objectives. How should situations be framed? What ethical and legal considerations are at play? What are the short-term and long-term effects on the bottom line? These are just a few of the questions educators must teach soon-to-be practitioners to ask and answer.

Outside Resources

The main source for information on suggestions for PR curricula is the report from the 1999 Commission on Public Relations Education. The Educational Affairs Committee of PRSA sponsored the two-year review of PR programs across the United States. For students enrolled in PR majors, a minimum of five courses comprised of the following were recommended: introduction to public relations; case studies in public relations; PR law and ethics; PR writing and production; PR planning and management; PR campaigns; and a PR internship (Kruckeberg and Paluszek, 1999). These course recommendations are an expansion of the 1987 Design for Undergraduate Public Relations report that recommended principles, practices and theory of public relations; PR techniques such as writing; PR research; PR strategy and implementation; and a PR internship (Ehling and Plank, 1987). The five courses outlined by the 1987 report are the standard by which PRSA certifies Public Relations Student Society of America (PRSSA) chapters at universities and colleges. As mentioned earlier, only 10 such programs have earned this certification.

Why did the 1999 commission feel that more courses should be offered to undergraduate students studying public relations? According to the almost 50-member panel, undergraduate education in public relations should instill knowledge in several areas and this can only be accomplished through several courses. These areas are

- Communication and persuasion
- Relationships and relationship building
- Communication and PR theory
- Societal trends
- Ethical and legal issues
- Management, finance and marketing
- Research and forecasting
- Public relations history
- Multicultural and global issues
- Organizational change

While knowledge of these areas is important, a strong skill set, consisting of the following, should also be taught:

- Informative and persuasive writing
- Research methods and analysis
- Management of information
- Technological proficiency
- Ethical decision making
- Oral communication

The 1999 commission also made recommendations for topics that needed to be covered in a theory, origin, principles and professional practice of PR course:

Content in this area specifically pertains to the nature and role of public relations, the history of public relations, the societal forces affecting the profession and its practice and theories of public relations. Also included are practitioner qualifications (including education and training), responsibilities and duties, functioning of public relations departments and counseling firms, and career-long professional development. Addressed here as well are specializations in public relations such as community relations, employee relations, consumer relations, financial and investor relations, governmental relations, public affairs and lobbying, fund raising and membership development, international public relations, and publicity and media relations.

According to a study conducted by Schwartz and colleagues in 1992 of PR practitioners, the number-one skill practitioners look for from recent graduates is writing proficiency. Then comes an internship, followed by problem-solving skills, media-relations abilities, and presentation skills. These recommendations from the 1999 commission and the 1992 study are, of course, for students taking multiple classes over their undergraduate career.

To support and provide data for the 1999 commission's work, the National Communication Association hosted the Summer Conference on Public Relations Education in July 1998. At the conference, PR educators from across the United States divided into four work groups (outcomes, assessment, curriculum and pedagogy) within four models (undergraduate journalism-based programs, undergraduate communication-based programs, professional master's programs, and theory-based master's and doctoral programs). This four-day conference resulted in recommendations from educators, curriculum models, and a special issue of *Public Relations Review* devoted solely to the results of the four work groups (*Public Relations Review*, 1999). In addition, each spring, *Public Relations Review* offers a special issuing focusing on PR pedagogy. From the pedagogy team's work at the summer conference comes a basic recommendation: Use instructional deliver techniques (IDTs) that emphasis active learning. The top techniques preferred by practitioners and educators are dialogue/class discussion, exercises/application of concepts, lecture, small group discussion, and group work. Four of these top five emphasize active learning. Assignments that reflect these techniques include individual speeches/presentations, group presentations, publicity materials, case studies, and written exercises (Coombs and Rybacki, 1999). Public relations educators are clearly using IDT as outlined in the earlier section on teaching techniques.

The Educators Academy of PRSA published another valuable resource for educators. *Learning to Teach: What You Need to Know to Develop a Successful Career as a Public Relations Educator* offers 28 chapters written by the educators on subjects such as how to prepare course syllabi, organizing lectures, and teaching ethics (Sallot, 1998).

Other outside resources are offered as a list of common textbooks, journals, professional publications, associations and Web sites at the end of this chapter.

Conclusions

An educator should encourage students to continue exploring the PR field beyond the introductory course. Even if no other PR courses are taught, students can acquire a solid knowledge base and skill level from joining a PR club or Public Relations Student Society of America chapter at the college or university. They should also consider volunteering at a nonprofit organization that needs their PR skills; writing for the university newspaper; serving as the PR chair of their student organization; attending local PRSA chapter events and luncheons; and attending the PRSA/PRSSA conference every fall. Last, but definitely not least, a student can learn from the second most requested skill or experience practitioners cited, beyond writing, and that is an internship. This is an area that an educator can play a critical role in helping the student develop beyond the introductory course in public relations by encouraging and facilitating internship opportunities. Whether in a large metropolitan area or in a rural environment, institutions such as the university itself, an area hospital, police department, or city or county government agency all need and are typically willing to hire a student interested in public relations. In metropolitan areas, the internship opportunities expand considerably, but if there is one addendum or outside activity encouraged by PRSA and other associations, practitioners and academicians alike, it is the internship.

The professor can also encourage students to read seminal books such as the *Handbook of Public Relations* (Heath, 2001) and *Managing Public Relations* (Grunig and Hunt, 1984), professional publications such as *PR Week, PR Strategist,* and *PR Tactics,* among others, and academic journals such as *Public Relations Review* and *Journal of Public Relations Research.*

The foundation that the educator builds in the introductory course enables the student to explore the field in more advanced courses and in practical experiences. Students experience different courses and different requirements at different universities. This is no cause for alarm. The breadth of educators, from Ph.D.s to experienced practitioners with master's degrees, the breadth of knowledge compiled of the field, diverse resources from the academic and professional associations, and PR activity ongoing in the world allow instructors to tailor their courses, within reasonable frameworks, to students' needs. No two introductory courses in public relations look alike and nor should they, for no two solutions to a PR problem or opportunity look alike, and that's what makes this field such an exciting one.

Works Cited

Coombs, W. T., and K. Rybacki. 1999. Public relations education: Where is pedagogy? *Public Relations Review* 25, no. 1:55–63.

Ehling, W. P., and B. Plank. 1987. *The design for undergraduate public relations education* (Report of the Commission on Undergraduate Public Relations Education). New York: PRSA.

Goldstein, N., ed. 1999. *The Associated Press stylebook and libel manual.* New York: Addison-Wesley.

Grunig, J., and T. Hunt. 1984. *Managing public relations.* New York: Holt, Rinehart and Winston.

Heath, R., ed. 2001. *Handbook of public relations.* Thousand Oaks, Calif.: Sage.

Johnson, K. F., and B. I. Ross. 2000. Advertising and public relations education: A five-year review. *Journalism and Mass Communication Educator* 55, no. 1:66–78.

Kruckeberg, D., and J. Paluszek. 1999. *A point of entry: Public relations education for the 21st century* (Report of the 1999 Commission on Public Relations Educations). New York: PRSA (1999). *Public Relations Review* 25, no. 1:1–122.

Public Relations Review. 1999. 25, no. 1 (Spring):1–100.

Sallot, L. M., ed. 1998. *Learning to teach: What you need to know to develop a successful career as a public relations educator.* New York: PRSA.

Sallott, L. M., G. T. Cameron, and R. A. Lariscy. 1997. Professional standards in public relations: A survey of educators. *Public Relations Review* 23, no. 3:197–216.

Schwartz, D. F., J. P. Yorbrough, and M. T. Shakra. 1992. Does public relations education make the grade? *Public Relations Journal* 48, no. 9:18–25.

Strunk, W. 2000. *The elements of style.* Boston: Allyn and Bacon.

Other Resources

Public Relations Textbooks

Baskin, Otis W., Craig E. Aronoff, and Dan Lattimore. 1997. *Public relations: The profession and the practice.* 4th ed. Boulder: West.

Cutlip, Scott M., Allen H. Center, and Glen M. Broom. 2000. *Effective public relations.* 8th ed. Englewood Cliffs, N.J.: Prentice-Hall.

Guth, David W., and Charles Marsh. 2003. *Public relations: A values-driven approach.* 2nd ed. Boston: Allyn and Bacon.

Newsom, Doug, Judy VanSlyke Turk, and Dean Krukeberg. 2000. *This is PR: The realities of public relations.* 7th ed. Belmont, Calif.: Wadsworth.

Seitel, Fraser P. 2000. *The practice of public relations.* 8th ed. Englewood Cliffs, N.J.: Prentice-Hall.

Wilcox, Dennis L., Philip H. Ault, and Warren K. Agee. 2000. *Public relations strategies and tactics.* 6th ed. New York: Harper Collins.

Academic Journals and Public Relations Publications

Journal of Public Relations Research. An academic journal published quarterly by Lawrence Erlbaum.

Public Relations Review. An academic journal published quarterly by Elsevier Science.

Journalism and Mass Communication Educator. An academic journal published quarterly by AEJMC.

PR Quarterly. A blend of professional and academic pieces published quarterly by PRSA.

The PR Strategist. A quarterly professional publication sent to PRSA members.
PR Tactics. A monthly professional publication sent to PRSA members.
PR Week. The PR industry's version of *Ad Age* is published weekly.

Public Relations Associations

Arthur Page Society. www.awpage.society.
Association for Education in Journalism and Mass Communication PR Division. www.lamar.colostate.edu/~aejmcpr.
Association for Women in Communications. www.womcom.org.
Council of PR Firms. www.prfirms.org.
Direct Marketing Association. www.the-dma.org.
Health Care Public Relations Association. www.hcpra.org.
International Association of Business Communicators. www.iabc.com.
International Public Relations Association. www.ipra.org.
National Association of Government Communicators. www.nagc.com.
National Communication Association PR Division. www.pr.grady.uga.edu/pride.
National Investor Relations Institute. www.niri.org.
National School Public Relations Association. www.nspra.org.
Public Affairs Council. www.pac.org.
Public Relations Society of America. www.prsa.org.

Useful Web Sites

About.com. www.publicrelations.about.com
   This is a free PR Internet resource complete with more than 1,500 links to PR resources, articles, and Web sites for PR consultants, corporate communicators, and PR students or researchers.

Boston College Center for Corporate Community Relations. nfoeagle.bc.edu/bc_org/avp/csom/cccr/
   This site provides research, executive education, consultation, and convenings on issues of corporate citizenship.

Institute for Public Relations. www.instituteforpr.com
   Through publications, lectures, awards, symposia, professional development forums, and other programs, the institute has been at the leading edge of efforts to promote and encourage academic and professional excellence.

Investor Relations Network Services. www.irnetserve.com
   This site houses annual reports and educational resources for PR professionals in investor relations.

Lexis Nexis. www.lexisnexis.com
   The lexis-Nexis service contains more than 1.4 billion documents in more than 8,692 databases. It adds 4.6 million documents each week.

Online Public Relations. www.online-pr.com
   This is an online catalogue of public relations, media and marketing sources.

PR Cybermall. www.prgenius.com

This is a marketplace of PR ideas, publications and research.

PR Education. www.pr-education.org

This is the most comprehensive Web site devoted totally to PR educators and students, and is complete with links to dozens of other sites.

PR Place. www.prplace.com

This site features a free guide to 700 major U.S. media, and hot-linked lists of PR publications and PR organizations, news sources and news services, and media and journalism interest groups.

Remembering a Mentor: Sidney Kobre

Alf Pratte

Although its been more than seven years since the death of Sidney Kobre in 1995, traces of the old-school newsroom, professionalism, teaching techniques, and the passionate love of history that animated his life are still imbedded in my journalistic gene pool.

Along with the impact of my own parents, the chair of my doctoral committee, Stuart Gerry Brown, church associates, and a handful of other reporters, professional teachers, and colleagues, Sidney's influence has been a crucial factor in my professional and academic life.

During the 13 years after we first met in Dallas in 1982 at the founding meeting of the American Journalism Historians Association (AJHA), we collaborated on a revision of his classic *Development of American Journalism* (1969) as well as other academic and professional projects.

In addition to our letters and phone calls, we regularly met when I drove the 160-mile round trip from Shippensburg University in Pennsylvania to his home in Pikesville, Maryland. The visits, as well as overnight stays at his home, are my version of *Tuesdays with Morrie*. (The politically correct word today would probably be *Mentoring with Morrie*.)

For me it was *Mentoring with Sidney*, *Saturdays with Sidney*, or *Collaborating with Kobre*. The venerable, old scholar was passing on his heritage, experience, wisdom, attitudes, values and loyalties to me and to those I would teach.

In the process I found myself further immersed in the sociological approach he had identified at Columbia University, where his doctoral thesis on the development of the Colonial Press described the interaction of the media with the changing American social forces.

But equally as important as weaning me beyond chronology to a more cultural approach to history, we had the opportunity to reflect and commiserate over the disappearance of real-world journalism in converged communications departments in academe coupling with antithetical, some would say, more commercial disciplines of advertising and public relations.

A number of the schizophrenic departments dominated by corporations and academe were growing soft on journalism history. Some teachers were ignorant of the world about which they hazarded to teach. If they had never practiced journalism, how could they presume to teach with passion and sincerity? How could they sincerely understand its history, its professional standards or ethics?

Although I argued that teaching journalism and media history without practical experience was a form of fraud, Sidney had a kindlier approach to such imposture. His feeling was that some of the Ph.D.'s who had never darkened the door of a newsroom nor met a deadline might learn the journalism craft, traditions and ideals through osmosis. Sadly, as documented by Betty Medsger in her 1996 arraignment of journalism education, *Winds of Change*, our murmuring had a basis in national surveys.

A former reporter and editorial writer for the *Newark Star-Eagle*, the *Newark Ledger*, as well as a weekly newspaper chain, Sidney never let go of his roots in real journalism. He continued to freelance for newspapers in Florida and Maryland as well as professional publications such as *Editor & Publisher* and *Media History Digest*, always connecting the nuts and the bolts of the vocation with its history.

In addition to updating *Development of American Journalism* (1969 and 1972), he was equally concerned to have other colleagues help revise versions of reporting and editing texts such as *Reporting News In-Depth* (1981). As noted by his friend Maurine Beasley, Sidney originated the term *backgrounding* the news, the concept of telling not only what happened but why.

It was a thrill and honor to assist, because I had used his texts and workbooks as an undergraduate student at Brigham Young University. I also used them when I taught at the University of Hawaii and Hawaii Pacific College while working at the *Honolulu Star-Bulletin* and the Hawaii State Senate.

Even though I was only teaching on a part-time basis in Hawaii, I adopted some of the instructional techniques that he was recognized for at Florida State University and the Community College of Baltimore. These included having students become "experts" by serving on various committees related to their historical interests and selecting from among three major projects: a biographical study, a regional community history, or a specialized history.

I still require all of my undergraduate history students to write a full-fledged history paper or video project, based on primary sources. The secret Sidney taught me was, like a good reporter, find out what the students are interested in, point them to original sources or methodology, and let them go. Some of them get so self-motivated you didn't have to crack a whip.

The results of implementing Sidney's approaches in my classes have been a number of above-average papers and a handful that are exceptional. One of the papers written for my history class this year was named the best university paper for a junior student. Another, from three years ago, was judged the best student paper of our college. Ten other undergraduate and graduate student research papers, or works in progress on historical or professional topics, have been accepted at AEJMC regional meetings or at AJHA national or regional conferences.

Because of his identification with the profession, it was no surprise when he did not present a pedantic discussion on the methodology and current trends of journalism history after the AJHA presented him with the Sidney Kobre Award for distinguished service in media history in St. Louis in 1986. It was the highest award journalism historians have to offer. Instead Sidney chose to describe how a good reporter has much in common with a good media historian. To be a good journalism historian you have to be a good reporter, he emphasized.

In covering a news story, the reporter seeks to reconstruct the event, determining just what happened. Finally the newsman or newswoman tries to package the news for the reader, selecting the most interesting or significant points for the lead to capture attention. Then the journalist unravels the story in some logical form. The media historian is faced with similar problems.

Looking on were his son Ken, a professor of photojournalism, and his wife, who was always at his side at the professional conferences that were always a major part of his life. Reva also edited much of Sidney's work pecked out on a typewriter. The last of his 16 books was co-authored with Reva: *A Gallery of Black Journalists Who Advanced Their Race* (1993).

Sadly, our joint project never quite made it back to the classroom before Sidney succumbed to cancer. We spent too much time and energy contending over how to treat modern journalism, which I believed had morphed beyond its historical roots and purposes to embrace the crony capitalism justified under the umbrella of giving the people what they want.

In place of our project, I turned most of my energy into a five-year study of the American Society of Newspaper Editors (ASNE), in which Sidney strongly supported and coached me. It was published shortly after he died. What I found in the minutes and through interviews was not a pretty picture. That book, *Gods Within the Machine* (1995), described lost leadership and pandering to the wants of the publishers and readers rather than to the needs of the greater community.

Rather than his more accepting view, what I saw were the footprints of modern economics, another form of cancer that had castrated the historic journalism that Sidney reported on, documented and celebrated. His approach to the softer reporting was less desperate than my shrill warnings and more benign.

Perhaps it is in my roots in the bleak prairies of Saskatchewan that makes me more skeptical and distrustful than my sparkling and ebullient friend and mentor. Of course, I am inclined to believe that I was and am more correct than he was about the tumor of corporations and convergence emasculating journalism and journalism education.

The Kobre genes Sidney inoculated me with, however, whisper that I need to be more genial. I just wish he were still around to remind me.

CHAPTER 9

Introduction to Film

Gretchen Bisplinghoff

> When strangers strike up a conversation in a bus, bar, or supermarket, chances
> are they talk about the movies, not politics or Proust, because in the United
> States movies are the cultural vernacular, the demotic language of democratic
> culture.
>
> —CLARK (1997, p. 138)

Introduction

Each of the emerging media technologies of the 20th century—radio, television, film, and the Internet—arrived amid promises of great opportunities for education and enlightenment. Each now adds its voice and visuals to the modern, media-saturated environment. As an art form of the 20th century (Bywater and Sobchack, 1989) as well as a popular entertainment medium, film has played a vital role in the culture since its inception at the end of the 19th century. In the last decades of the century, educators began addressing the need to understand these powerful new languages of the culture.

Thus, the serious study of film as an academic discipline is relatively recent: "Film departments were first established in five universities: USC in 1932, and UCLA, New York University, City College of New York, and Boston University by the end of the 1940s" (Clark, 1997, p. 139). The professional Society of Cinematologists founded in 1959 as the Society for Cinema Studies (currently considering a name change to Society for Cinema and Media Studies to reflect the impact of the Internet age) has over 1,300 members today (*ibid.*). Film scholars note, "Cinemaliteracy is long overdue in American education, and not just at the college level" (Giannetti, 2002, p. xi).

Unlike some chapters, the source for this discussion did not evolve from efforts to collect syllabi. This chapter is based on responses from professors and their syllabi. These include examples, both historical and contemporary, of the introductory film courses at Auburn University (Dr. Emmett Winn), Georgia Institute of Technology (Dr. Robert Kolker and Dr. Jay Telotte), Minnesota State University (Dr. Donald Larsson),

New York University (Dr. Anna McCarthy), and Northern Illinois University (Dr. Jeffrey Chown). Also included were examples from Northwestern University (Dr. Scott Curtis), Old Dominion University (Dr. Gary Edgerton), Towson University (Dr. Peter Lev), the University of Illinois at Urbana (Dr. Ramona Curry), and the University of Wisconsin at Madison (Dr. David Bordwell), also gathered by the author (with my thanks to all for their participation in the project).

Instructors responded to a questionnaire concerning their background teaching the course, their goals and objectives for the course, their teaching methods, and approach to the course, as well as other pertinent information. The chapter uses their responses and their syllabi (and others consulted) as well as the author's experiences teaching the course. The respondents represent a great deal of experience teaching this introductory course from a few to 30 years of offering/designing the course. Their commentary provides a historical perspective on the evolution of the course in addition to teaching methods and insights gained over the years. Quoted material throughout the chapter come from the responses on the participants' questionnaires or from their course syllabi, unless otherwise indicated.

The general outline of the chapter, however, does follow the overall framework used in the other course discussions of the book. The opening introduction discusses the current need for media literacy, with special emphasis on the key importance of the Introduction to Film course and its positioning in the curriculum. This chapter then gives an orientation to the unique characteristics of the film form as they relate to issues of teaching, and discusses the specific pedagogical choices and philosophies represented in the sample syllabi. This discussion covers the textbooks and topics that structure these courses, the course objectives (addressing the attitudes and assumptions shaping student perceptions), responses to the unique challenges of this course, and specific examples of assignments and outside resources.

Position of the Course in the Curriculum

In some ways, the Introduction to Film course is also unique in its position in the curriculum. The mass popularity of the medium (a double-edged sword) makes this course very attractive. It often draws large enrollments and interest across disciplines from students and administrators alike. A search on the Internet will quickly turn up many sites for Introduction to Film courses being offered at colleges and universities. Sometimes these courses offer students their first and only exposure to media literacy, and in other programs they are the introduction to the rest of the media curriculum. In either case, these courses are critically important in providing students with the analytical tools necessary for building the foundation structures of visual literacy.

According to a majority of the respondents, their class is required for majors and often operates as a gateway prerequisite. In some cases, students may take it for General Education credit or as an elective. Dr. Donald Larsson has taught English 114, Introduction to Film, at least once a year since 1981, although he will be teaching it much less now as the department chair. It is a General Education course, not required, but the largest class that the department offers (two to four sections per term, with a class size limit of 200 students). Only a small percentage of the freshmen and sophomores taking the course are majors.

At Northwestern University it is a required course for all freshman majors but is also offered for non-majors in a separate quarter. Thus, the class may range in composition from a class of majors only to one consisting entirely of students outside the major, with many configurations in between. Students taking the course may be freshmen majors or sophomores taking it for General Education credit or seniors taking an elective.

Typically the class size splits between being offered as a smaller class of 30 to 35 students (sometimes with a production component) or as a mass lecture of 100 to 300 students [usually with a screening lab and sometimes with teaching assistant (TA) support and separate discussion sections]. At the University of Illinois at Urbana, English 104, Introduction to Film, is offered as multiple stand-alone sections of 10 sections of 36 students each (per semester) taught by TAs and postdoctoral students plus a Discovery section for freshmen only of 22 students taught by full-time faculty. The class meets twice a week for 75 minutes per each session plus a film screening in a lab. At Northern Illinois University, Critical Interpretation of Film/TV currently enrolls 270 students. The class meets in mass lecture twice a week, with an evening screening, and has three half-time TAs, primarily for grading support.

Film is a composite art, a collective creation of multiple artists and art forms. Its hybrid and evolving nature, as well as the variety of approaches to the study of film, can lead to the placement of Introduction to Film courses in a wide-ranging number of curricula, including English, theater, art, communication, and languages. Syllabi of the sample group reflect its position in such areas as communication arts; English; radio-TV-film; communication and theater arts; literature, communication and culture; and mass communication and cinema studies. In the fall of 2000 the Introduction to Film course at Towson University became titled Principles of Film and Media Production within the newly designed Department of Electronic Media and Film.

Comparative/Special Features

Film represents a business commodity and an entertainment industry as well as a technologically based art form; it is "simultaneously an art form, an economic institution, a cultural product, and a technology" (Tomasulo, 2001, p. 112). And for the instructor of an Introduction to Film course all of these areas raise issues relevant to pedagogical decisions, "where teachers face the very practical questions of what to emphasize, what to gesture toward, and what to pass over altogether. The rich variety that enables film scholars to range from close textual readings to psychological studies of fandom to economic analyses of the entertainment industry and so on becomes a challenge to those who must represent the field to students taking their first and perhaps only film course" (Bates, 2001, p. 109). Such decisions concerning course structure and emphasis often rest upon curricular placement (particularly if offered as part of a production-oriented curriculum) as well as text choice.

Thus one demarcation within approaches to the Introduction to Film courses involves the inclusion or exclusion of production elements. In fact some syllabi make a point of noting that their Introduction course will not provide hands-on experience in making films. In a few cases, however, the description of the course points out the benefit of combining theory and practice in the learning practice. Assignments that address these goals typically include creation of a storyboard or working as a group to produce a short film that demonstrates the students' understanding of the film techniques under study. Dr. Ramona Curry, faculty course administrator of English 104, Introduction to Film, includes a group storyboard section to stress theory/practice connections in her Discovery Section.

Dr. Peter Lev taught the Introduction to Film course at Towson University from 1983 until the late 1990s. At first it was taught in small sections primarily as a production course using Super 8 film. When Dr. Lev began teaching it in 1983 he noted that he tried to make it "a more equal blend of theory and practice, since this course was a prerequisite for history/theory as well as production courses." The course continued to use filmmaking exercises that Dr. Lev felt were "in fact a way to learn a lot about film in a hurry." Then, because of the expense (it was required in a large Mass Communication major) and difficulty with Super 8 stock and equipment it was eventually offered as production and nonproduction sections. The nonproduction sections began to grow into large sections of 100 students, with one or two smaller production sections also offered.

As part of integrating the areas of the new Department of Electronic Media and Film, the Introduction to Film course became transformed into Principles of Film and Media Production, a lecture/discussion/screening class about both production and aesthetics. The technical aspect has always been a component of the class for Dr. Lev and, even when sections of the class went nonproduction, he had each student make a drawn or photographed storyboard. During the unit on animation he reported that he "talked about the techniques of animation, showed a wide variety of animation (cartoon, claymation, experimental, etc.), and then the students made a short flip-book." The evolution of this course in the curriculum at Towson also according to Dr. Lev addresses the reality that "film is merging with other media."

Dr. Scott Curtis teaches Analyzing Media Texts, which is required for all freshman majors in the Radio/TV/Film Department at Northwestern and is also offered in a section for non-majors. The course provides concepts and critical tools for analysis of film, video and digital media. He reports that most students in the program want to be filmmakers. He tries "to address that by getting them to think about style as a series of choices that they must make. And that the well-made film demonstrates a lot of thought about the relation between form and content." As one of his many strategies to engage the class he has one of the TAs play a tape on which he has prerecorded part of his lecture on film sound—"at that point I start lip-synching my lecture on the ideological relation between sound and image."

Film grew out of developments in technology in highly industrialized nations. This technological basis determined the art's unique properties in the areas of photography, editing, sound, etc., and continues to be affected by the technical evolution of the form (the digital revolution). Thus the instructor encounters the impact of technology as it shapes teaching the art form (and class assignments) and class interaction, as well as in the selection of the differing formats available for viewing films with their corresponding text issues. It can also affect more mundane matters in the process of screening material that sometimes depends on technological expertise and friendly equipment.

Decisions surrounding the choice of screening format often depend on the budget for purchase or rental of films or other formats, or available archival resources. However, the use of differing formats raises serious issues about changing the composition and perception of the text. The fundamental nature of the text changes dramatically from film to the video version in size, shape, running time, etc., and more importantly students may be unaware of such changes. [For a thorough introduction to this problem, see Chapter 1 in Bordwell and Thompson (2001).] There are as well different versions released on video, laser, etc., that have footage edited out or added, are a director's cut version, or contain other important changes from the original film. This, in addition to the inaccessibility of much material (due to lack of preservation, etc.), makes these decisions more complicated than it would appear.

The sample syllabi reflect a wide range of options concerning format. Some of the instructors stress the centrality of the projected film experience. For example, Dr. Curry draws upon an archive of 35mm films as well as rentals and warns in the syllabus, "BE SURE to attend your assigned film screening lab in 101 Armory. We have arranged for you to see each film (for 'free') on the BIG SCREEN; *Do take advantage of that opportunity*. While videotapes and DVDs of films are acceptable for close study or quick review, they have often been modified for TV viewing (cutting off part of the image or changing the original film movement) and otherwise cannot usually offer the quality (or the joint viewing experience) of the projected film." A couple of other instructors mention the use of 16mm, whereas Dr. Gary Edgerton specifically mentioned moving away from the availability, distribution and projection problems of 16mm to DVDs. He said that he interprets film liberally not as just celluloid, as most students are watching films on television or online.

Several instructors use a mixture of formats, primarily DVDs. As Dr. Donald Larsson points out, the format choice is also of course affected by the technology available to the instructor. He notes, "We have been helped over the years by technological upgrades to the auditorium where we usually teach. We now have touch-screen controls for VHS, DVD, CDs and laser discs—all with overhead projection—as well as 16mm projectors. In the last couple of years, we also have had computer (PC and Mac) and Internet access." Interestingly, Dr. Jeff Chown notes that "one of the problems with using something like *Pulp Fiction* or films by Spike Lee or Kevin Smith is that the students would prefer renting the video to coming to our arranged screenings. I feel some of the sense of audience for film is being lost."

Online courses and telecourses such as the American Cinema Television Course (which uses the text *American Cinema/American Culture* by John Belton), which may be licensed or bought on video, are a recent development with ramifications for this issue. Dr. J. Emmett Winn teaches Introduction to Film Studies both on campus and as a distance learning class offered through the Distance Learning/Outreach Technology Department at Auburn University. The on-campus class has a movie lab, whereas students in the distance learning class choose films available in a variety of formats on television, in theaters or through rental. Regarding the impact of all new technologies, one of the participants in a workshop on the Introductory Film Course at the 1995

Society for Cinema Studies conference asked, "Is There a Film in This Film Class? (Policies and Practices of Presentation Technologies in the Introductory Film Course)" (Costanza, 1995, p. 81).

Common Goals/Philosophies

As this cross section of syllabi shows, the main issue that introductory courses in film address is that while students may be familiar with lots of movies as mass entertainment, they may feel that they are experts, even though they have often been exposed only to a narrow range of the art and are often unable to articulate their understanding of the moviegoing experience beyond a subjective evaluative response ("thumbs up or thumbs down"). So, in all of the syllabi, the goal of cinematic literacy provides the basic structure underlying the course. Learning how to read a film depends on the students acquiring a unique language system with a specific grammar and terminology as the basis of building their analytical skills.

Dr. David Bordwell (Jacques Ledoux Professor of Film Studies) and Dr. Robert Kolker (Chair of the School of Literature, Communication and Culture) are both authors of popular textbooks for the introductory course. Both base their texts on years of teaching the course; their books continue to affect countless courses although they no longer teach it personally. Of the sample syllabi consulted, the text adopted by the majority of the respondents was *Film Art: An Introduction* (2001) by David Bordwell and Kristin Thompson, now in its sixth edition. The stated goal of the Bordwell and Thompson text is "to introduce the reader to the fundamental aspects of cinema as an art form" (p. xv).

In their approach, Bordwell and Thompson stress the acquisition of conceptual skills, "an approach that leads the reader in logical steps through the techniques and structures that make up *the whole film*" (*ibid.*). They focus on helping students master general principles of film form that they can then use on their own to analyze specific films. They cover specific topic areas of different types of filmmaking and films, film forms (both narrative and nonnarrative), elements of film style (mise-en-scène, cinematography, editing, sound), and the historical development of film, as well as examples of critical analyses of individual films. The latest edition of the text includes a Filmgoer's Guide and Online Learning Center as well as other Web services and support for instructors and students.

According to the Web site for the second edition of his book *Film, Form and Culture* (2002), Dr. Kolker's goal in teaching and writing about film is "about getting control of the image and handing that control over to students" (www.mhhe.com/soc-science/art-film/kolker2/author.html). This goal led to the development of the textbook with its accompanying interactive CD-ROM introducing and analyzing key film elements and techniques. The text is an introduction to film and new media that "discusses not only the basic issues of film construction but the way film is constructed for and by the culture in which it is made. It thinks about film as part of the world it inhabits" (Kolker, 2002, p. viii). The final chapter discusses the impact of digitization on the future of the film image; resulting in the death of celluloid-based film, with its technological, economic, artistic and cultural ramifications.

Some other texts mentioned by the respondents include *Understanding Movies* (2002) by Louis Giannetti, *An Introduction to Film* (1998) by Sobchack and Sobchack, and *Movies and Meaning* (2001) by Stephen Prince (see the end of the chapter for further listings of introductory texts). Selection of a textbook guides course structure and topics as well as film selection.

All of the syllabi stressed that the films under consideration were a set of visual texts to be critically analyzed. One syllabus states that they are in fact the "most important" texts for the course. As with any art, the choice of these texts raises important questions regarding the canon: which films to teach, which representative films and filmmakers to study, and whose perspectives and vision to explore.

A common theme especially from instructors using the Bordwell and Thompson text was the need for a wide diversity of films, including classic Hollywood and foreign films, documentary and experimental, narrative and nonnarrative. Also considered are black-and-white silent films as well as color, films by women and people of color, shorts and features. Dr. Kolker reports using a broad range from "Eisenstein to Fincher, including (always) *Vertigo* or *Psycho*." Dr. Larsson also said that he shows a "fairly wide range. I almost always show at least one silent film (Buster Keaton, usually) and at least one foreign film . . . I try to vary the titles and order from term to term, while choosing films that relate to that week's topic . . . I use many film clips and short films. One or more of the films shown will usually have been made within the last 10 years (although I have to keep reminding myself that my students don't always think of 'new' films in the same way I do!)." Dr. Curry includes at least three international films as well as films by women and people of color. Many of the instructors mentioned using many clips throughout.

Another commonly stated goal involved using the screenings to stretch the students' experience and taste. Both Dr. Bordwell and Dr. Edgerton noted that students' taste has narrowed from the more adventurous 1970s. Dr. Edgerton recalled that back then students were far more open and sought out different types of films such as foreign films, but felt that now they aren't as curious. So he reports that his goal in this regard is to "give alternatives to the multiplexes." Dr. Lev says that he "would look for films that illustrated a section of the syllabus and would engage the students. Films that were off the beaten track were a plus, because I wanted to show students that film was a tremendously varied art and communication form."

Thus, the instructors' philosophies concerning the course focus on introducing the students to concepts of film analysis and interpretation, teaching them critical thinking approaches, and ways of understanding the techniques of the medium, as well as exposing them to different types of films and educating their tastes. Dr. Chown's "goal is to expose the students to things they haven't considered or seen—be it documentaries, foreign films, experimental film, or classic Hollywood cinema that they've never seen in a theater (e.g. *Citizen Kane*). I want them to be more critical in their viewing experiences and to have a better understanding of film art and its effect on culture."

Dr. Kolker stressed the goal of teaching the students "how to distance themselves from a film in order to understand its form and structure, its cultural significance, etc." And Dr. Larsson summed up: "My main purpose is to get the students to think of watching film as an active process that will allow them to get more out of films and also to think more critically about them. One purpose also is to expose them to some films and film types (including black-and-white movies!) that they might otherwise never watch on their own."

Course Objectives/Common Emphases

Objectives for the Introduction to Film course fall generally into four categories: overall goals (focusing on critical thinking and interpretation), and specific goals concerning introduction to film language and vocabulary, to film history and development, and to film theory and criticism. (Below are selected examples.)

The overall objectives for students are to gain a better understanding of movies, to develop the student's ability to view films critically, to deepen students' understanding of the film experience, and to help students articulate what they understand in films.

In terms of film language and vocabulary, the objectives are to develop and use knowledge of basic film terms and concepts, to learn the technical film terminology necessary for discussing and criticizing the basic film system, to learn to use film terminology properly, and to identify technical components of film production and narrative aspects of cinematic storytelling.

With regard to film history and development, the goals are to understand the basic history of film, especially the "classical Hollywood style" and various alternative responses to that style, and to identify major historical and technical developments in film, film movements, film genres and film theories.

With regard to film theory and criticism, the goals are to see beyond films as entertainment by grasping how formal systems such as editing, lighting and sound create style, effects and meaning; to use a variety of critical "lenses" to recognize and articulate how films contain underlying meanings; to recognize the creative contributions of the artists who make films; to use critical thinking skills to understand how a film serves as a reflection of the values and concerns of the era during which it was produced; and to learn to examine critically how films depict characters of various ethnicities, nationalities and sexual orientations.

To address these goals, syllabi topics focus on providing students with critical tools of analysis to use in understanding how a film creates meaning as an aesthetic form. In the syllabi, basic analysis of film form typically covers elements of cinematography, mise-en-scène, and image composition, as well as narrative and story. A few courses begin with an introductory lecture, handout, or films specifically on the language and grammar of film. Dr. Jay Telotte initially emphasizes "cinematic structure, i.e., the basics of shot, scene, and sequence. I then move on to the varieties of shot, i.e., the shot in terms of its content (e.g., long shot), in terms of the technique involved (e.g., tracking shot), and in terms of specific functions (e.g., establishing shot). We then discuss editing, soundtrack, and overall style. With that basis we discuss a variety of film types: documentary, experimental/avant-garde, and genre."

Topics covering film styles/types typically focus on examining the development of the narrative fiction feature film as the standard for discussion. As the most influential form (and the one that the students are most familiar with), the Hollywood fiction feature film is often the basis for stylistic analysis in introductory courses. The evolution of the art of storytelling in film as well as its expression through the various film-language techniques are sometimes presented in the context of developments in film history. Initial segments cover the contributions of early filmmakers such as D. W. Griffith to continuity editing and narrative construction. This lays the groundwork for discussion of the conventions of classical narrative style, the norm (as well as for discussion of divergence from that norm).

Other topics regularly appearing as part of introducing students to the study of film cover critical methods or the theories developed to analyze film. Most often these include examination of two basic approaches: the genre approach to categories or types of films, such as gangster films, musicals, etc., and the authorship approach to films of a director such as Hitchcock or Scorsese. Instructors also include emphasis on film as a reflection of and influence on culture throughout the course in various contexts, sometimes covered explicitly in a section on ideology. Often this discussion focuses on stereotyping and representation in film of images of race, class and gender. Another topic covered is examination of the characteristics of film as an institution of big business.

The four examples that follow demonstrate specific statements of course objectives and organization of course structure/topics as presented in individual course syllabi.

Analyzing Media Texts (Dr. Scott Curtis)

"This course is an introduction to the study and structure of film and other media. We will define and examine the expressive and aesthetic power of the basic elements of the moving image. Specifically, the course will investigate, across a variety of different media, modes, and historical periods, the fundamentals of cinematography, especially the shot and its composition; editing; set design and acting styles; sound and control of space, time and imagery. We will also discuss narrative, genre and media specificity. The goal of the course is to acquaint students with a vocabulary specific to film and other media, and to provide students with the critical tools required for formal analysis of the moving image."

Course Outline and Screenings: Introduction (*Singin' in the Rain*, 1952); Pattern Recognition 101; Mise-en-scène/Color and Character (*Written on the Wind*, 1956); Widescreen Aesthetics, Camera Movement, and Off-screen Space (*Yojimbo*, 1961); Cinematography; Editing/Montage (*Battleship Potemkin*, 1925); Sound/The Function of Film Sound (*The Conversation*, 1974); Narrative (*Citizen Kane*, 1941); Introduction to Classical Hollywood Cinema Narrative and Narration; Analyzing Film Style (*La Jetee*, 1962); Postclassical Hollywood Cinema (*She's Gotta Have It*, 1986); Alternatives to Classical Hollywood Narrative; Television News and Other Documentary Forms (*No Lies*, 1972); Nonnarrative Forms (*A Movie*, 1958); Animation and CGI; Digital Cinema; and Digitality and Media Specificity.

Film as Communication (Dr. Gary Edgerton)

"This course is an introduction to the mechanics, aesthetics, and social dimensions of film as art and cinema as an institution. The class examines how film communicates as a visual medium. The composition and sequencing of images are treated as complex message systems that interact with an audience's ability to decode them. This course also presents the basic concepts on how films are made, how they are evaluated, and what relationship they have to their society and culture."

Course Outline and Screenings: Introduction and Orientation (*Casablanca*, 1942); Beginnings of Film Narrative: Early Melodrama (*First Programs*, 1895–96; *A Trip to the Moon*, 1902; *The Great Train Robbery*, 1903); The Melodrama/Drama Continuum (*Tender Mercies*, 1982); Visual Language and Culture; Classical Hollywood Cinema: Narration; Storytelling and Plot Structure; and Five Principles of Film Form (*Citizen Kane*, 1941).

Also included are topics and films such as Mise-en-scène; Classical Hollywood Cinema: Style; Space in the Cinema (*Rear Window*, 1954); The Shot; Camera Movement; Building Characterizations; Contemporary Noir; Personal Visions and the Detective Formula (*Chinatown*, 1974); Time in the Cinema; Understanding Genre (*Witness*, 1985); Editing/Continuity Style and Montage; The Relationship Between Genres and Society; The Multigeneric Film; The Western (*The Last of the Mohicans*, 1992); Editing/Building Scenes and Sequences; Screen Stereotyping: The Hollywood Indian; Generic Transformations in Cultural Context; The Animated Film (*Pocahontas*, 1995); The Postmodernist Western (*Lone Star*, 1996); and Sound in the Cinema.

Additional attention is paid to Modes: Narrative, Experimental and Documentary (*The Civil War: 1861, The Cause*, 1989); The Experimental Mode (*Frank Film*, 1973, and *Crac!* 1982); Understanding the Nature of the Filmmaking Process (*Day for Night*, 1973); Beyond Genre; The International Art Film (*Amelie*, 2001); and Hollywood versus "Foreign Films." Also considered are Motion Picture Production, Distribution and Exhibition; Majors, Mini-Majors, and Independents (*The Crying Game*, 1992); The Studio System; A Business and Industry in Transition; Movies in the Digital Era; The Ascendancy of Science Fiction: Conventions and Inventions (*The Matrix*, 1999); The Global Film Industry (*Crouching Tiger, Hidden Dragon*, 2000); and The Future.

Introduction to Cinema Studies (Dr. Anna McCarthy)

"This is a lecture/discussion course for new cinema studies majors. It has two basic goals. The first is to help students develop skills in film analysis. By the end of the semester you should be fluent in the vocabulary of film form, familiar with basic questions of film culture and politics, and be able to construct an argument about a film's meaning. The second goal of the course is to introduce the field of cinema studies. The readings illustrate a variety of approaches to film, from formalism to feminism, and the screenings raise issues central to various kinds of film production (narrative, documentary, avant-garde)."

Course Outline and Screenings: Introduction (*Citizen Kane*, 1941); Form and Meaning (*Exterminating Angel*, 1962; and outside screening, *North by Northwest*, 1959); Narrative Patterns (*Rashomon*, 1950); Mise-en-scène (*Our Hospitality*, 1923; and outside screening, *The Young Girls of Rochefort*, 1967); and Mise-en-scène and Cinematography (*Lola Montes*, 1955).

Also addressed are topics and films such as Cinematography and Form (*The Good, the Bad, and the Ugly*, 1966); Editing (*Meeting 2 Queens*, 1991, and *At Land*, 1944;

and outside screening, *Notorious*, 1946); Sound (*Nashville*, 1975, and *The Conversation*, 1974); Genre (*A Woman Is a Woman*, 1961; and outside screening, *An American in Paris*, 1951); Avant Garde and Experimental Filmmaking (*Meshes of the Afternoon*, 1943; *Wavelength*, 1967; *Mayhem*, 1987; and *Maxell*, 1990); Documentary (*London Can Take It*, 1940, and *Titicut Follies*, 1967; and outside screening; *Letter from Siberia*, 1957); and Mixed Modes and New Directions (*Close Up*, 1990).

Introduction to Film (Dr. J. P. Telotte)

"This course serves to introduce students to film studies by focusing on various film types and techniques. It begins with a brief historical context, establishes a rhetoric keyed to the various techniques and technologies involved in film production, and applies that rhetoric to a variety of film forms, including the documentary, experimental film, and genre films. This introduction to film should provide students with a foundation for additional film study, as well as one useful for investigating various other media categories, including television and digital arts."

Course Outline and Screenings: Introduction; Historical Context (*Battleship Potemkin*, 1925); Film Structure (*The General*, 1927); Film Realism; Shot Techniques (*Grand Illusion*, 1937); Problems of Realism (*The Pirate*, 1948); Film Reflexivity; Screen Shape (*The Searchers*, 1956); Editing /Montage (*The Third Man*, 1949); Sound (*Kiss Me Deadly*, 1955); Film Style (*The Killer*, 1989); Other Film Types (*The Plow That Broke the Plains*, 1936); Experimental Films (*Un Chien Andalou*, 1928); Animated Film (*The Clowns*, 1970); Color in Film (*Robocop*, 1987); Science Fiction Themes; Classification Problems (*My Darling Clementine*, 1946); Nature of the Western Character in Genres (*Dark City*, 1998); and Shape of Film Production.

Common Challenges/Solutions

Initially, early inventors like Edison and the Lumiere brothers conceived, developed and presented their work as a commercial enterprise for mass consumption, not as an artistic creation. Today more than ever in the current era of multi-million dollar blockbusters and media mergers, budget considerations drive decisions central to the production, distribution and exhibition of films. Money affects the art form from preproduction to the merchandising tie-ins with every fast-food franchise promotion. The commercially driven, entertainment basis of the art form is a strong force shaping cultural attitudes toward movies within students as well as administrators.

Students often bring assumptions and attitudes into the Introduction to Film course that are based on their familiarity with the subject matter as entertainment. They may often feel that they already possess sufficient knowledge of film for this to be an "easy" course. They have grown up watching movies, reading reviews, seeing "behind the scenes" specials on television as well as programs such as *Access Hollywood*, and discussing the merits of the latest Oscar contender with friends. But often this will be the first serious study of film for the majority of the class. Some secondary schools are recognizing the importance of media literacy by including the study of the media as part of their curriculum. However, in many classrooms before college, the announcement of films or other audiovisual material is still often received as a welcome relief from "real" learning.

Clearly, instructors of an introductory course need to consider the implications of such attitudes and how to address them effectively. Many instructors address this issue directly at the outset in their syllabus. This sets the academic tone and establishes parameters for behavior for the coming semester: "Almost everyone enjoys going to the movies but few, in comparison, ever learn much about the art of film-making or the critical approaches to explaining films. For the general public the study of film is primarily learning trivia about their favorite motion pictures, entertainers and directors. However, the serious study of how movies make meaning is a challenging and interesting endeavor. We are constantly exposed to information about the latest movies and their budgets, stars, directors and reviewers' evaluations of the films. But the most exciting and interesting aspects of film are left to those of us who are willing to commit to film studies on a more rigorous (and in this case academic) level" (Dr. Winn).

Dr. Larsson also notes in his syllabus: "We tend to think of watching film as a passive activity—we kick off our shoes, put up our feet and just let the images and sound wash over us. Sometimes after a hard day, that kind of 'passive' viewing is necessary. But unless we are asleep, we always take part in what we watch—we catch clues and cues, anticipate events, react to characters, and notice themes and meanings. Much of the time, we aren't aware of this participation. But when we do notice it, our active involvement in watching the film can reward us. And as we learn more about how to look and listen and what to look and listen for, we can find more rewards: more to think about, more to appreciate, and even more to enjoy."

The instructors of the sample syllabi have taken pains to address this situation immediately and often. They explain at length the seriousness of their approach to the subject and the class assignments, and the importance of a serious attitude toward the films as texts. This involves proper viewing etiquette and the importance of learning to take notes during screenings in order to assist in learning this new language system. One syllabus reiterates "Take this course very seriously" twice. Dr. Curry notes, "Students in this class should be prepared to work hard," and that they should "Always come to class, be on time, and be prepared to discuss the films and the readings!"

As discussed earlier, one of the common goals of this course was to stretch the experience of film types encountered by the students. Based on attitudes gained from limited viewing experience and personal tastes, students may be resistant. According to Jay Telotte, "Students want to re-see current films and to have their preferences in current films validated." Dr. Chown concurs: "Every year it seems to get more difficult to screen black and white films or subtitled films. Students see them as inferior to big budget, color, special effect Hollywood cinema and have little curiosity about what was done in the past."

Several instructors prepare the students by explaining in the syllabi that examination of a variety of film styles was being covered to expose the students to alternate film styles and to challenge their ideas of the film aesthetic. Deciding how far to go in challenging students in their experience with the medium can also present a difficult balance for a new instructor. Dr. Larsson offers this caution: "Contemporary films shown in this class sometimes include strong language, nudity and 'sexual situations,' and/or scenes of violence. As adults, you are expected to approach these films with the same seriousness that you would approach any object of study in college. However, if you have genuine objections to watching such material, let me know."

Typical assignments thus focused on the overall goal of increasing the students' cinematic literacy, thus increasing their analytical abilities and their understanding of the cinema experience. Instructors often use essay assignments to engage students with the films as serious texts for critical study, introducing them to different film texts for scrutiny using analytical tools to understand and interpret the cinematic experience. Dr. Curry's assignments include short-response papers (one written on a film made before the student was born, with extra credit available if it was also made outside the United States in a language other than English or a silent film or a feature documentary or made before Dr. Curry was born).

Dr. Curry also assigns critical analysis papers on elements such as cinematography, mise-en-scène, editing and sound. Dr. Chown uses four one-page papers that each cover technical aspects (lighting, composition, editing, sound and camera movement) of a screened film and its relation to the thematic/aesthetic aspects of the film. A final paper applies a more comprehensive, extended analysis of all of the techniques to a film playing in the theaters. Dr. Edgerton uses two analysis papers: one in-depth critical analysis based on Bordwell and one analysis of the sociocultural milieu of a film.

Other selected examples of assignments from various syllabi include the following:

■ Students do a segmentation paper (an outline of a film's narrative organization and structure based on Bordwell and Thompson's discussion and examples) on a film screened in class or a film of their choice.

■ Students write an analytical paper based on segmentation work as their starting point. They also use segmentation outlines to write analyses of techniques (mise-en-scène, sound, etc.).

■ Students prepare an essay explaining how a film's form (editing, sound, cinematography, etc.) develops its meaning. They analyze different techniques in each paper or all of the techniques in one film or a sequence from one film.

■ Students collaborate as a critical collective to go through a film sequence by sequence to analyze the interaction of film style and ideology, and each person is assigned to write a portion of the analysis.

■ Students conduct a shot-by-shot analysis of an assigned film. They compose an argumentative essay to demonstrate mastery of narrative film form or compose an argument based on reaction to a film by using critical analysis skills and knowledge of film construction.

■ Students conduct an ideological analysis of a contemporary film. They investigate, do research on the Web, and complete a study of an individual filmmaker or a specific film genre, or of a theory, technique or theme related to a group of films or historical issue related to film such as the Hollywood Code.

■ Students keep journals or write response papers recording their reactions to films graded on completion on time. They hand in screening notes done according to note-taking guidelines.

■ Students create a Web site or maintain a Web board for discussion of films, links to reviews, and study guides. Students respond to readings, films and assignments via conferencing software when the instructor calls on them, or they are required to post responses to films or class issues and discussions via a class Listserve.

■ Students work in groups to give presentations and movie talks where they teach the whole class how the ideas in one of the chapters relates to a particular film, including a detailed description of one or more scenes or shots. They work as part of groups to prepare handouts and present research on the context and historical background of particular films.

■ Students present a final research project on a film, including showing and discussing film clips and their significance. They explore various film resources on the Web and build a simple Web page with annotations for the sites.

Examinations in the form of quizzes, midterms and finals often stress the importance of concepts and terminology forming the basic vocabulary of the course. Quizzes usually focus on comprehension of the readings, including pop quizzes to keep them on their toes in keeping up with the reading assignments. Examinations include objective questions and identification of terms, as well as application of concepts in essay questions. The final exam often includes an essay asking the students to analyze a film or portion of a film screened in class. Take-home exams based on film analysis questions were an option in two cases.

Recognizing that for many of the students this is new critical territory, most of the instructors establish very precise expectations for all coursework, especially analysis assignments. Several instructors include very detailed instructions for papers or indicate that there will be forthcoming guideline sheets. Some instructors indicate that there are sample papers or course packets of material available for examination (often online at a course Web site), and some include tutorials, workshops, or revision sessions to guide students in their preparation of assignments. One syllabus takes three full pages to describe the analytical writing assignments in detail.

Because of the centrality of the films as serious texts, as well as other factors, instructors often stressed the importance of class attendance and participation (some said that it was mandatory) in the grading. Those instructors who emphasized the film experience as film stressed the necessity for attendance at screenings that was based on the inadvisability of seeing the films in other formats except as backup to the initial wide-screen experience or as necessary for the multiple screenings needed to do writing assignments. Others noted the unavailability of many films outside of class screening time (silent film, experimental, etc.). One syllabus indicates that the "films and slides are texts that cannot be read at any other time than class meeting."

Instructors also adopt ancillary materials for the courses, including texts specifically addressing the issues involved in writing about film, such as *A Short Guide to Writing About Film* (2001) by Timothy Corrigan. Three syllabi use film theory texts in addition to the main introductory text, and two include a case-study book on the making of a particular film like *Psycho* or *The Wizard of Oz*. Several courses include course packets of additional readings. Some instructors post readings, study guides, course notes, handouts, and other course materials on the Web and use e-mail and chat rooms to answer questions. And many textbooks have accompanying Web sites for research, as well as other digital resources for the student and instructor.

Outside Resources

As previously mentioned, many factors, including the nature of film as an art form, lead to the inclusion of film studies in a variety of curricula. Thus, an English instructor might have been (and might still be) asked to teach a class entitled Introduction to Literature and Film. The recognition of film studies as a separate discipline, and the rapid rise in film schools since the 1950s, provide the opportunity for rigorous training for professionals in the field in all areas of theory and practice. However, the recent increase in interest in media literacy (as well as the popularity of this course) might still lead school administrators to ask someone already on staff (perhaps in an area seen as "related") to work up an Introduction to Film course.

For instructors new to the introductory course, as well as seasoned veterans of many semesters, quite a few resources are available. Individual scholars from many schools, such as the University of Illinois at Urbana, have made their course syllabi readily available by placing them online. ScreenSite (www.tcf.ua.edu/screensite/), an especially valuable educational resource on the Web, established by Jeremy Butler at the University of Alabama, contains a collection of sample media course syllabi covering many topics, including the introductory course to film.

Sites associated with the American Film Institute and the British Film Institute, as well as those for professional organizations such as the Society for Cinema Studies and the University Film and Video Association, offer educational services and connections to explore extensive teaching resources. For example, the American Film Institute and the British Film Institute list various seminars and workshops on film education offered through their departments. Both the Society for Cinema Studies and the University Film and Video Association have been active in collecting and disseminating teaching materials on film.

The University Film and Video Association has regularly published "Course Files" in the *Journal of Film and Video* that cover a variety of film course syllabi. Many have been reprinted in a collection edited by Patricia Erens and Marian Henley (*College Course Files*, University Film and Video Association Monograph 5). The monograph is available from the editor of the *Journal of Film and Video*, currently Suzanne Reagan (Department of Communication Studies, California State University, 5151 State University Drive, Los Angeles, CA 90032; sregan@calstatela.edu). Also useful in this regard is a book edited by Erik Lunde and Douglas Noverr on *Film Studies* (1989) that includes information on the study of cinema and examples of sample syllabi from film scholars.

The Society for Cinema Studies has a Standing Committee on Teaching focused on sharing pedagogical tools in the organization's publication *Cinema Journal* and at conferences by sponsoring panels and workshops (including those on teaching the Introduction to Film course). Important pieces on the teaching of film have appeared in the journal and are available on the SCS site (www.cinemastudies.org/). These articles include "Resources for Teaching Film and Video Courses," by Frank Tomasulo (1995), "Statement on the Use of Video in the Classroom," by John Belton and committee (1991), "Teaching Film with Laserdiscs," by William Costanzo (1995) and "Hypermedia as a Scholarly Tool," by Ben Singer (1995).

The fall 2001 issue of *Cinema Journal* devoted an entire section to "Introducing Students to Film," which "looks at issues that arise in planning and teaching these introductory classes" (Bates, 2001, p. 109). Articles include "Teaching an Introductory Cinema Class to Production-Oriented Students," by Doreen Bartoni; and "Cinema in the English Department Introductory Course or How to Make Film an 'Element of Literature,' " by Peter Mascuch.

Also available are pieces on how to approach film history in a survey course, how to promote deep learning through the use of effective film textbooks, and how to address the attitudes reflected in the perennial question of "Aren't we reading too much into this? After all, it's just a movie." And the *Journal of Popular Film and Television* published a special issue on "Media Literacy and Education: The Teacher-Scholar in Film and Television" (2002) examining issues of literacy in a visual age.

Powerful images pervade our daily life—images that are consumed uncritically and then dismissed as only entertainment. Media technologies continue to evolve and converge at a rapid rate, while critical understanding of their power and influence lags behind: "Cultural historians generally acknowledge that a time lag occurs between the moment when a new medium is invented and the age when a literate community finally emerges to create a more complete understanding of that technology's full potential (Edgerton, 2002, p. 2). The evolution of film spans a century from the Industrial Revolution to the Internet age; instructors of the basic film course face the challenges of developing "cinemaliteracy" for the new century.

Works Cited

Bates, Robin. 2001. Introducing students to film. *Cinema Journal* 41, no. 1:109–110.
Bordwell, David, and Kristin Thompson. 2001. *Film art: An introduction.* New York: McGraw-Hill.
Bywater, Tim, and Thomas Sobchack. 1989. *Introduction to film criticism.* New York: Longman.
Clark, Robert. 1997. *The real guide to grad school.* New York: Lingua Franca.
Costanza, William. 1995. Teaching film with laserdiscs. *Cinema Journal* 34, no. 4:78–83.
Edgerton, Gary. 2002. Introduction: Media literacy and education: The teacher-scholar in film and television. *Journal of Popular Film and Television* 30, no. 1:2–6.
Giannetti, Louis. 2002. *Understanding movies.* Upper Saddle River, N.J.: Prentice Hall.
Kolker, Robert. 2002. *Film, form and culture.* New York: McGraw-Hill.
Tomasulo, Frank. 2001. What kind of film history do we teach? The introductory survey as a pedagogical opportunity. *Cinema Journal* 41, no. 1:110–114.

Further Resources

Selected Introductory Film Textbooks

Belton, John. 1994. *American cinema/American culture.* New York: McGraw-Hill.
Boggs, Joseph. 2000. *The art of watching films.* New York: McGraw-Hill.
Corrigan, Timothy. 2001. *A short guide to writing about film.* New York: Longman.

Dick, Bernard. 2002. *Anatomy of film.* New York: St. Martin's.

Gollin, Richard. 1992. *Guide to film: Arts, artifices, and issues.* New York: McGraw-Hill.

Kasdan, Margo. 1998. *The critical eye: An introduction to looking at movies.* Dubuque: Kendall-Hunt.

Kawin, Bruce. 1992. *How movies work.* New York: Macmillan.

Lehman, Peter, and William Luhr. 2002. *Thinking about movies: Watching, questioning, enjoying.* Orlando, Fl.: Harcourt Brace.

Lunde, Erik, and Douglas Noverr. 1989. *Film studies.* New York: Wiener.

Phillips, William. 1985. *Analyzing films: A practical guide.* New York: Holt, Rinehart and Winston.

Phillips, William. 1999. *Film: An introduction.* Boston: Bedford/St. Martin's.

Prince, Stephen. 2001. *Movies and meaning: An introduction to film.* Boston: Allyn and Bacon.

Roberts, Graham, and Heather Wallis. 2001. *Introducing film.* New York: Oxford University Press.

Sobchack, Thomas, and Vivian Sobchack. 1998. *An introduction to film.* Boston: Little, Brown.

Wead, George, and George Lellis. 1981. *Film: Form and function.* Boston: Houghton Mifflin.

Periodicals and Journals

Camera Obscura: A Journal of Feminism and Film Theory. "Innovative feminist perspectives on film, television and visual media." Published three times per year by Duke University Press.

Cineaction! Interest in radical film criticism and theory, attention to foreign film. Published three times per year by Cineaction, a collective in Toronto.

Cineaste: The Art and Politics of the Cinema. Articles on film genres, film personalities, and specific films with emphasis on foreign and independent cinema. Published quarterly by G. Crowdus, New York. www.cineaste.com

Cinema Journal: Journal of the Society for Cinema Studies. Scholarly articles from historical and theoretical perspectives. Issues contain a "Notes" section, announcements, and reviews. Published quarterly by the University of Texas Press. www.cinemastudies.org/cj.htm

Film and History. Articles from historical as well as contemporary perspectives. Published quarterly by the Film Committee of American Historical Association. www.h-net2.msu.edu/~filmhis/.

Film Comment. Nonscholarly journal covering popular, foreign and avant-garde films. Published bimonthly by the Film Society of Lincoln Center.

Film Criticism. Scholarly articles on historical and contemporary issues. Published three times per year at Allegheny College.

Film Quarterly. Scholarly articles and interviews. Published quarterly by the University of California Press.

Films in Review. Articles aimed at the general public that concern film, video, and laser disc, as well as interviews with actors and directors. Published bimonthly by the National Board of Review of Motion Pictures of New York.

Journal of Film and Video. Scholarly articles with special interest in film theory and practice. Published quarterly by the University Film and Video Association.

Journal of Popular Film and Television. "Concentration is upon commercial cinema and TV: stars, directors, producers, studios, networks, genres, series, the audience, etc. Articles on film and TV theory . . . as well as interviews, filmographics, and bibliographies." Published quarterly by Heldref Publications.

Jump Cut: A Review of Contemporary Media. Articles on film, TV/video within "radical analysis of mass culture and oppositional media." Published annually by Jump Cut Assoc.

Literature/Film Quarterly. Scholarly articles concerning the relationship between literature and film. Published quarterly by Salisbury State College.

Millennium Film Journal. Articles on independent, experimental, avant-garde cinema, video and new technologies. www.sva.edu/MFJ.

Post Script: Essays in Film and the Humanities. Articles on the relation of film to many other fields such as photography, history, and American studies. Published three times per year at Texas A&M University at Commerce.

Quarterly Review of Film and Video. Scholarly pieces on both theoretical and practical issues concerning film with special issues on genres, theories and topics. Published quarterly by Harwood Academic Publishing.

Screen. British journal contains scholarly articles on film theory and criticism. Features a special column on "Reports and Debates" covering current topics and film festival reports. Published quarterly by the Society for Education in Film and Television. www.oup.co.uk/screen/contents

Sight and Sound. Film criticism, interviews and film reviews for the general reader on film and television. Published monthly by the British Film Institute.

Wide Angle. Each issue takes a theme on a "variety of topics from international cinema to history and aesthetics of film." Published quarterly by Johns Hopkins University Press.

Professional Organizations

Society for Cinema Studies. The oldest professional film society founded to promote university study. Its Committee on Teaching sponsors ongoing work on teaching resources as well as panels at the yearly conference specifically on the Introductory Film Course. www.cinemastudies.org/

Popular Culture Association. Founded in 1970 to "study thoroughly and seriously all aspects of everyday culture world-wide." Its annual conference is held with the American Culture Association. www2.h-net.msu.edu/~pcaaca/pop.html.

University Film and Video Association. The UFVA is "an organization where film and video production meet the history, theory and criticism of the media . . . an international association of image makers and artists, teachers and students, archivists and distributors, college departments, libraries." www.ufva.org/

Selected Useful Web Sites

Academic Info. Excellent independent educational directory to "Quality Educational Resources." Click on Humanities to get Film. www.academicinfo.net/.

Cinemania. Features reviews of films, film fests, books and videos as well as special features such as special tributes to movies and directors and the Cinemania Collection, a library of essays about "movies you must see before you die." www.cinemania.com

CineMedia. "The Internet's largest film and media directory," with over 25,000 links to categories of Cinema, Film. American Film Institute. www.cinemedia.org

Digital Librarian. "A librarian's choice of the best of the Web." A section on movies includes general sites, studio sites, film festival coverage, and film institutions. servtech.com/public/mvail/movies.html

Flicker. Information on "films and videos that transgress the boundaries of the traditional viewing experience, challenge notions of physical perception and provide cutting edge alternatives to the media information technocracy." www.sirius.com/~sstark/

Greatest Films. Specializes in classic Hollywood films. References include decade-by-decade cinematic history, genres, and extensive sources. www.filmsite.org

Internet Movie Database. "The IMDb is the ultimate movie reference source." Fully hyperlinked within the database and to thousands of external sites. Extensive, valuable as quick reference for facts. us.imbd.com

Library of Congress Motion Picture Collection. Searchable database of the L of C film collection. lcweb2.loc.gov/papr/mpixhome.html

Media Resources Center. Based at the University of California, this site contains a Research and Reference Service: indexes, guides, filmographies and bibliographies, an online database of distributor information, and several online film studies databases, such as the American Film Institute Catalog. www.lib.berkeley.edu/MRC/Film-BibMenu.html

Pacific Film Archive. Center for exhibition and study of film. www.uampfa.berkeley.edu/pfa/

SCREENsite. Scholarly, stressing teaching and research, this site offers very useful information on film and television studies, including bibliographies, references, course offerings, and syllabi. www.tcf.ua.edu/screensite/

Sofia: study of film as internet application. Resource for the study of film, and teaching film theory on the Web. www.imperica.com

UCLA Film & Television Archive. Holds listings on the archive's collection of over 220,000 films and television programs: "largest university held moving-image archive in the world." www.cinema.ucla.edu

The Wheel: Media, Music, Film, TV, and Theater. Includes a movie database, film and video resources, and links to newspapers and magazines. www.unn.ac.uk/~isu8/media.html

Distributors Online

Facets Multimedia. This organization maintains a selection of hard-to-find film releases such as classics and foreign films in video format. www.facets.org.

Frameline Distribution. This nonprofit media organization is the only national distributor "solely dedicated to the promotion, distribution and exhibition of lesbian and gay film and video." www.frameline.org.

Ken Crane's (Laserdiscs & DVDs). Distributor of the Criterion Collection of laserdiscs. www.kencranes.com.

Kino Online. This company, which is devoted to classic and overlooked silent films, distributes in 16mm, 35mm, video and DVD formats. www.kino.com/.

Kit Parker. This is a longtime distributor of a film collection that "covers the whole spectrum of the film makers' art." It distributes in 16mm, 35mm, and video formats. www.kitparker.com/.

National Film Board of Canada. This is government run and famous for documentaries, shorts and animation. www.nfb.ca/.

New Day Films. This cooperative of independent producers and filmmakers distributes in 16mm format "high in quality and social consciousness." www.newday.com.

New Yorker Films. This important distributor of foreign and independent films handles 16mm, 35mm, and video formats. www.newyorkerfilms.com.

October Films. This company, which specializes in American independent and contemporary foreign film, distributes in 16mm and 35mm formats. www.october-films.com/.

Women Make Movies. This distributor carries the world's largest collection of films and videotapes by and about women. www.wmm.com.

Related Useful Guides to Web Sites

Deivert, Bert, and Dan Harries. 1996. *Film & video on the internet: The top 500 sites.* Michael Wiese Productions. Describes and evaluates sites in categories.

Murphy, Kathleen. 1997. Frames: Breaking the waves. *Film Comment* 33, no. 1:84–87. Web sites of interest to movie fans and critics.

Remembering a Mentor: Maurine Beasley

Kimberly Wilmot Voss

The first time I spoke to my mentor and dissertation advisor, Dr. Maurine Beasley, I was standing in my Maryland kitchen. It was late afternoon on a fall day when the phone rang. I was to begin my doctoral classes in a few weeks.

When she introduced herself I was speechless because on the other end of the line was the woman whose work I had read and whose words I had cited many times. It was her research that had inspired me to go to the University of Maryland when I was an undergraduate in Milwaukee.

A specialist in the subject of women's portrayal and participation in journalism, Dr. Beasley's particular focus is Washington women journalists, including their coverage of First Ladies. Her work inspired me to look at the history of journalism from a perspective beyond a few big names. I had read many of her eight books, which had led to a long reading list of women's role in journalism.

As I attempted to hide my excitement, she asked me some general questions and I rattled off information about my educational background and my research interests. As I spoke, Dr. Beasley politely stopped me—she said she wanted to know more about *me*.

She wanted to know why I was interested in studying women and journalism. She wanted to know my interests. She wanted to know what I did when I wasn't studying.

For the next three years, Dr. Beasley approached our interactions the same way. She cared about her students as more than scholars/teachers. She cared about them as people. She realized the need for balancing family, work and school. Last-meeting-of-the-semester graduate classes took place at her home. Conferences with her students took place over a comfortable table in her office, face to face. Her inquiries were thoughtful and caring.

Dr. Beasley quickly earned my—and my classmates'—respect and trust. She was kind and honest, explaining the politics of the college without alienating anyone. She thoroughly read every student's paper, adding her comments next to each paragraph.

I was thrilled to have Dr. Beasley as my advisor, but I hadn't imagined her becoming my mentor. Too shy as an undergraduate and too busy working full time while in graduate school, I never really connected with any professors. Few were supportive of my research. During my first semester of classes at the University of Maryland, I was envious of other doctoral students who spoke glowingly of their experiences with their advisors.

169

Dr. Beasley encouraged my research interests. Her questions led me to a topic that I'm still curious about after three years. She taught me how to be a better teacher. Her teaching methods inspired me to try new things and raise my students' standards for themselves.

Now, when I hear colleagues discuss their graduate-school mentors, I have my own stories to tell.

Dr. Beasley is the kind of professor who everyone wants as his or her advisor. I was lucky enough to be a graduate assistant in her Women and Media class. Dr. Beasley, with her many years of journalism and teaching experience, could have easily rested on her laurels in the classroom full of restless-to-graduate students. Instead, she pushed the students to contribute and shared with them valuable firsthand accounts of a changing time in journalism.

Her stories about her tenure at the *Washington Post* (1963–1973) made the dry textbook points come alive and pierced the drowsiness of the students. She had witnessed the changing role of women in journalism. An effective teacher, Dr. Beasley was able to translate her experiences—positive and negative—into teachable lessons about who has the power to make change. The students and I were often in awe as Dr. Beasley shared her journalism experiences.

Dr. Beasley used current teaching methods, assigning group presentations and reaction journals. Several times during the semester Dr. Beasley would gather up piles of notebooks and return them a few days later full of notes. There was no sitting back for the students in her class. Students were required to be active learners—Dr. Beasley was willing to wait those uncomfortable extra seconds for students to answer questions. Yet, she was also sensitive to students' thoughts and opinions and recognized that different people required different types of direction and instruction. She required students to e-mail her about their learning styles. As a result of their answers, she adjusted her teaching methods.

When the students in that class fought her efforts to encourage participation, she looked for ways to reach them and often asked for my ideas. I was thrilled to be asked and was impressed that she was always looking for feedback. In the end, it was Dr. Beasley's passion for the topic that made the class successful. Even the most jaded students paid attention when she spoke about her favorite research topic—Eleanor Roosevelt. Three years later, I regularly repeat the anecdotes she shared. The stories hold my students' interest every time.

From Dr. Beasley, I learned to view teaching as a constant learning process. I regularly read about new teaching methods and make sure to share my experiences from the newsroom. I try to follow her example of guiding students through the learning process.

I work to make my students accountable in the way I watched Dr. Beasley hold her students to high standards. I've waited for three long minutes for quiet students to respond. I've spent long nights responding in detail to reaction journal entries. My first days of class begin with a discussion of learning styles and mandatory introductory e-mails. After all, I've seen the success of these methods.

Dr. Beasley has equally impacted my research. She has inspired me to ask questions I wouldn't have otherwise. I now put more of a focus on representation and ethical issues. I work to give a voice to those who have been only a footnote in journalism history. And when I oversaw my first graduate student at the University of Wisconsin–Stout, during a break I made sure to call that student. I began by asking the student to tell me about herself. She, like I had, began telling me about her past classes and her planned thesis. I stopped her and said I wanted to hear about her, without realizing how well I had learned Dr. Beasley's lessons.

PART III

The Practice
of the Field

CHAPTER 10

Writing and Reporting

Dave Bennett

Introduction

S ome of today's college students approach reporting, interviewing and writing with a near-phobic reluctance.[1] They really want to learn to do it right but do not always see the value of mastering the intricacies of the journalist's craft. They are simply scared. For some students, the thought of writing is intimidating enough because, after all, they may have spent years dodging writing assignments. Now they learn that to pass your reporting class they must do such scary things as talk, face to face, with *real* people about *real* problems and issues; figure out what it all means; and then somehow get the resulting story written by deadline.

Simply put, the issue is one of confidence, not competence. Build some trust first, and the second will emerge with practice. That, of course, is much easier to say than to do. In this chapter some approaches are highlighted to building confidence and tackling other problems that seem inherent in the fine art of coaching students to become reporters.[2] Many observations are rooted in my own experience as a longtime reporting instructor and in that of other teachers, most particularly the 20+ educators selected for an American Society of Newspaper Editors' Excellence in Journalism fellowships.[3]

Position of the Course in the Curriculum

If you have been tagged to teach a reporting or writing course at your school it is probably because of your interest and background in the subject. Perhaps you did some reporting at a newspaper or television station in an earlier professional incarnation before you returned to the classroom. Ideally, having worked as a reporter is the best preparation for teaching reporting. Maybe you still do some reporting as an adjunct to your role as instructor. This places you in a particularly enviable position.

Sometimes academic situations are far from ideal. If you do not have professional experience, or if your days in the newsroom are only a distant memory, contemplate possible remedies. Consider freelancing for a local newspaper, magazine, business publication, or television station. Editors and news directors are usually short on staff and may view you as a valuable resource, especially if you walk in with interesting ideas for stories they have not yet done. Work part time at a local newspaper or television station on holidays or during the summer. Again, management is often interested in filling gaps, particularly when regular staff is on vacation.

You may also apply for a full-time summer reporting internship, either in your own community or somewhere you would like to spend a season away from the classroom. You will find some editors are intrigued by the idea of having a college professor in their newsroom and are interested in strengthening ties between the journalism you teach and the profession they practice.

Apply for a formal program such as the Excellence in Journalism fellowship, in which the American Society of Newspaper Editors (ASNE) matches college professors with newspapers for a summer's work as a journalist. Most, but not all, ASNE fellows have previous professional experience; for some it's their first time in the newsroom.[4] Work for your university's public affairs office during the summer writing news and feature stories for release to the news media.

Similar/Related Courses

Reporting students should at minimum have successfully completed freshman composition, a course that is required at most universities. At some schools passing a language competence exam (usually a grammar test) is also a prerequisite. This is probably a good idea since a reporting course is not where students should be learning, or brushing up on, English basics. Students can remedy inadequacies through work at the campus writing center (most have tutors available) or by taking a grammar class in the English Department.

Ideally, reporting should be a second or third journalism class, taken after the survey course in mass communication and a course in newswriting. The strength of this progressive and developmental pattern of instruction is that students enter the reporting class with an understanding of how the news media operate and what news is. They will also have some experience with the basic forms of journalistic writing. If you must teach these things in your course, your students will not get nearly as much reporting done.

Comparative Features

Early on in the class and long before you start lecturing about leads, quotes, sources and interviewing techniques, consider having an informal roundtable discussion with your would-be reporters. The goal of this session is to get students talking about any reluctance or misgivings they have regarding interviewing, reporting and writing. Those with a real "fear of flying" need to hear that they are not alone, that many and perhaps most journalists have to overcome similar concerns. If you are like most of us, you probably were scared the first time that *you* had to quiz someone important on a touchy subject.

Do not be reluctant to recount the times that you had the reporter's equivalent of stage fright. Remember to emphasize how much easier interviewing became with a little practice and self-confidence. Encourage students to talk about other things they have done that were frightening or intimidating at first, but turned out to be not only doable but sometimes even fun. I mean the first roller-coaster rides, learning to swim, driving a car, acting in a play—those kinds of really scary things.

You may also want to invite a student from last semester's reporting class to the session to tell about the bad case of jitters she may have had before her first story. Today perhaps she works on the campus newspaper and thinks nothing of interviewing fellow students, faculty, or even the college president when they are part of a story. Relating to her trials and tribulations may be easier for students than relating to your experience, which is probably somewhat outdated anyway. Talk a little about *why* reporters report and the important role that they play in our society.[5] Some students are reluctant to interview because they fear they are being nosy, or believe they are invading someone's privacy even by asking legitimate questions. Reinforce the fact that a reporter is a stand-in, a proxy, for readers who cannot be there to question public officials and others whose answers they deserve to hear.

Special Features

As the reporting class develops you will probably want students to generate their own story ideas (more about that later). But initially you can help them break the ice by making the first actual story assignment fairly structured and as unthreatening as possible. Stay away from complex issues and the major campus controversies. Instead, consider a short personality profile that combines a single-source, face-to-face interview and a little background research.

One assignment that works on any campus is to have each student reporter locate, interview and profile a different international student. Before their interviews, each reporter must research the government, culture and demographics of their story subject's home country. This assignment has several strengths. Students are forced to look outside their usual peer group for the story.

The preparatory work underscores the value of doing background research *before* walking into an interview. Many international students seem to enjoy that someone is interested in them and thus are quite cooperative. And since it focuses on a campus group whose activities are often underreported, editors at the student newspaper or magazine are often quite willing to publish the resulting profiles, often with accompanying mug shots for art.

You can get the project off to a good start with a written assignment sheet, or story memo, that builds in structure and is very specific about your expectations for the basic story. Here's an example of a memo for the international profile:

Reporting the first story, internationals

Your first reporting assignment is a profile of an international student of your choice. Your completed first draft (2 to 3 pages, double-spaced) is due during your lab on the week of XXX. Have your story on disk and print it out, then we'll critique it and you can fix any problems. In the story you might consider exploring these, among other things: Why they choose to attend college in the United States and how they ended up at this university. How they find the United States different (customs, food, etc.) from their homeland.

Other considerations might include what they expected America to be like before they arrived, with the prospect that these were formed based largely on images from the American mass media. You may want to have them consider how well those expectations squared up with reality. Ask what they expected college to be like before they arrived and how well those preconceptions played out. Consider some sensitive questions, such as what they miss most from home. What do they like most about the United States and the university? What are their goals, ambitions, and long-term career plans? Your lead should capture something so *interesting* about the person that your readers won't want to put the story down.

Good direct quotes *are always essential*, and can be a strong link between the interview subject and the reader. Provide incentive for them to look for a logical theme to organize a story around. Lack of a strong theme often results in a story simply being an unrelated series of facts rather than a *meaningful look* at a person that offers us some insight about them. The theme should be inherent in your lead. Before your interview, do some library or Internet research on your profile subject's country. Knowing a little about their homeland can provide you with a platform from which to launch key questions.

Background on a country in a story as context for your readers may offer insight to be used as a demographic sidebar if the story is published. At the end of the story, they can list demographic facts in the following format. Source: (*list your source of demographic info here*) concerning population, climate, languages spoken, major religions, form of government, major industries, popular national cuisine, and significant historical fact. The political climate may provide additional insights into challenges the students must face.

Common Goals and Objectives

A roundtable discussion after students have finished the international student profile allows class members to share any problems encountered either in interviewing or in writing. This is also a good time to invite student reporters to talk about insights the assignment provided and speculate on what they might do differently on their next story.

Invariably, a student or two will have discovered that their initial interview didn't yield either enough information or perhaps not the "right stuff," so they had to do a second session with their international student. This, too, is a good lesson, and usually a point that emerges is that the second interview was much more relaxed and productive.

Some students will have used tape recorders to capture their interview; others will have taken notes. This may be an appropriate time to talk about the strengths and weaknesses of each approach and how combining good note taking with tape recording is superior to either alone. One tip for new reporters is not to depend solely on the interview tape (retrieving taped conversation is slow and subject to technical malfunctions), but instead to use it to verify important quotes from their notes. A direct quote or two from student stories can be a good segue into a later discussion of how direct speech can—and should—be used to capture the flavor of the interview subject's speech or to underscore interesting or important points in a story.

An alternative starting assignment, one that is both effective and publishable, is a similar short profile, but this time with graduating seniors as the central topic. Seniors' postgraduation employment plans can provide a "news peg" that can make the stories more than just feature pieces. The resulting stories may be quite appealing to student editors during the spring semester who are planning special graduation editions.

Consider an example of a memo for the graduating senior, the profile of a senior of their choice. Your completed first draft (2 to 3 pages, double-spaced) is due during your lab on the week of XXX. Have your story on disk and print it out; then we'll discuss it.

In the story you might explore these, among other things: Why did they attend this university? What did they expect college to be like before they arrived at school? How well did those expectations square up with reality? What was the most difficult aspect of college life as a freshman? How did they cope? As a senior, what advice do they have for new students? What was the most significant thing that happened while at college? What is it like to be nearly through with college? Where do they hope to live after graduation? Why? What do they expect to do after graduation? Have they begun their job search? What are they doing to prepare? Do they expect a career in their field of study? Why/why not? What are their career goals and short-term goals today and five years from now?

Your lead should capture something so interesting about the person that your readers won't want to put the story down. Good direct quotes are essential and can be a strong link between the interview subject and the reader. Look for a logical theme to organize your story around. Lack of a strong theme often results in a story being an unrelated series of facts rather than a meaningful look at a person that offers us some insight into his or her life and aspirations. The theme should be inherent in your lead.

You will also need background in your story as context for your readers. The information will be used as a demographic sidebar if the story is published. At the end of your story, list demographic facts in order: hometown, high school, college major/minor, activities at college, a favorite class, most demanding class, or fondest college memory.

Instructor Philosophy

One of an editor's most effective tools can be the story memo, a short, specific note that encourages "noodling" or basic preparation before much reporting has been done. At some newspapers, reporters must "sell" their editor on any story they want to tackle that is to be more than just a hard news response to events. The story memo and discussions it begins can be the negotiations for that "sale." It can be a good technique—one that is easily adaptable to the classroom.

Having to crank out a typed memo as a prereporting strategy means that students must think further than an initial idea and go on to speculate, in writing, about possible story angles and appropriate sources for information. It also reinforces the coaching approach to teaching reporting and writing, in that it provides a framework for discussing possible approaches to a story early in the reporting process—before much investment of time, energy and ego.

Initial story ideas from young reporters often have one of two flaws: either they are too narrow and need to be placed in a broader context or are overly general and thus need a more limited, deeper focus. Think of a story memo as an entry point into the thinking of the student reporter—one that provides you the opportunity to help them frame the story into an interesting, relevant and doable project that will likely result in a good read. Like most planning tools, story memos can reduce actual task time by heading off false starts.

A danger is that student reporters, armed with approved memos, may not respond flexibly enough in field situations that differ from their original expectations. They should understand that the best of plans often change as more becomes known about a situation.

A story memo example you can use before asking students to come up with several of their own each week involves the cost of cold weather. This story will detail how expensive winters are for the university. Explore the cost of winter in terms of hours of labor and money expended. Include such things as snow removal, rock salt, fuel for heat, and preparing vehicles for cold weather. Among other things, find out the average money and man-hours spent each winter on such things. Compare the costs for mild winters and severe winters. What was spent last winter? How much money is budgeted for this winter?

Which winter was the worst in recent years, and what did it cost the university? What was the mildest? What sort of winter is forecast for this year? What sort of impact, in overtime pay for example, might a major storm have? How many miles of sidewalks and roads does a work crew shovel and plow? (Get a few good quotes from the folks who do the shoveling and plowing.) What other building or maintenance challenges does winter weather pose?

Possible sources include such things as office of planning and budgets, facilities management, or the university engineer. Sometimes my response on a story memo is "Sounds good. Go for it!" This is either jotted in the margin or in a quick conversation with the student reporter. On others where more focus seems appropriate, I'll respond in more detail, give the student some specific suggestions, or ask the student to see me for a longer discussion of the story's possibilities.

Consider setting aside a little class time each week to discuss story ideas that your students submit. Not only does this help folks stay abreast of stories classmates are reporting, it also gets the creative juices flowing and promotes group brainstorming on story possibilities. The class will often have ideas for sources on a proposed story that you and the reporter have overlooked.[6]

Common Emphasis

Kevin McGrath of *The Times* of Munster, Indiana, put it well when he wrote, "The worst writers deny the awful truth that nobody produces perfection on the first try; the best writers embrace it. The best writers revise, then revise some more, then revise again."[7] Editors lament that, because of deadlines, revision is often a neglected part of journalistic writing. Even the most talented writers, when backed into a corner, will admit that their work, too, sometimes needs more than just another comma or two. McGrath, a writing coach for *The Times*, suggests that the answers to these four basic questions about a first-draft story can provide the framework for effective revision by asking basic questions such as: What works? What needs additional work? What's there? What's missing?

The fact that the most polished pros rewrite, often extensively when time allows, is an essential lesson for student reporters. They need to buy into the idea of revision from day 1 in reporting class. One way to underscore this is to invite the best reporter from your local newspaper into class to talk about a recent front-page story she wrote and how rewriting improved it. If possible, ask her to bring the first draft *and* the final published story; then you can make overheads for easy comparison in class.

A reasonable standard for reporting classes is that student stories aren't finished until they reach publication quality. That yardstick may force a story through several major rewrites plus a series of minor revisions, especially if the "What needs work? What is there? What is missing?" kind of questions reveal flawed reporting *and* poor writing.

Some students may initially balk at having to do their work more than once because they've become accustomed to simply turning assignments in and receiving a grade. Positive feedback on effective parts of their first draft, coupled with earned compliments for revision improvements, will help overcome the reluctance to rewrite. But the best inducement by far is to see a story on which they toiled published under their byline—and then have it praised by their peers.

Common Challenges/Solutions

Reporting and writing without publication is much like cooking a gourmet meal that is unlikely to be consumed. Who cares if there are a few inaccuracies in the story or too much salt in soufflé? This is a challenge that any student chef or reporter can face. But when there is at least the *possibility* that your cooking will be enjoyed or your story will be published, cooks and writers alike pay more attention to details.

It is important to recognize that we owe it to our students to make a reporting class as realistic as possible, within the limits of the classroom and the campus. That means finding avenues of publication, at least for the best work done by students. Here are some ideas employed on many campuses to making that happen: Work out an arrangement with the editor of the university campus newspaper or student magazine for submitting publishable news stories and features done in class. Editors can treat such work as freelance material to supplement staff coverage. Offer the stories for free, but insist they be bylined if used.

It is also important to encourage reporters to be on the lookout for stories about students whose families live in nearby communities with small daily or weekly newspapers. Hometown newspapers are usually quite receptive to timely stories about students from their area who are involved in newsworthy activities on campus. You may also wish to approach your university's Public Affairs Office about the possibility of using student work in the school's alumni magazine or newsletter. Set up a Web site where stories and photos from journalism classes can be published.

Another major selling point well worth consideration is that students can build up *clip files* of competently reported well-written published stories. Those will come in quite handy when they seek summer internships or part-time jobs at newspapers, magazines, and television stations as well as public relations agencies.

Outside Resources

Once a story is complete, you might have the student fill out a simple, boilerplate form that briefly recaps their reporting activities and pinpoints any problems they encountered and how they solved them. Completing the form forces students to consider what went right and what went wrong, while reinforcing the lesson that good journalists, above all, are problem solvers.

Instructors, who use story memos and then coach students as they report, write and rewrite their stories, can expect valuable feedback throughout the process. You quickly discover what is working for each student, as well as get a better sense of individual strengths and weaknesses. For more about coaching, see *Coaching Writers: Editors and Reporters Working Together* (New York: Bedford/St. Martin's, 1991), by Roy Peter Clark and Don Fry. Other material on coaching is available from the Poynter Institute (www.poynter.org/), including a 30-minute videotape by Clark and Fry titled *Coaching Writers: The Human Side of Editing* (St. Petersburg, Fla.: Poynter Institute for Media Studies, 1993).

Here are basics you might want a poststory form to include: Number of days to complete the story; approximate number of hours to complete the story; summary of their reporting activities, any obstacles encountered, and how they were overcome; and lessons the story taught them about reporting.

The completed form, clipped to first and final drafts of the story and placed in a student's *writing file*, is an effective way to document individual progress. Another major confidence builder occurs at the end of the semester, when students look through the body of work in their writing files and discover how much how their reporting and writing have matured.

We sometimes hear the blanket indictment of today's students, or perhaps even voiced it ourselves, that they just do not read enough, even those who say they are serious about becoming reporters and writers. It is as true today as when we were undergraduates. That being a given, the question becomes "What do we do about that?"

Consider the reporting class a starting point. Take every opportunity to underscore the value of being widely read and inquisitive by strongly labeling those personal attributes as predictors of success as a journalist. When students ask, "But where can I find story ideas?" one response is to suggest that they become more aware of things going on around them.

Ask them to listen to the topics of discussion in the dorms or the campus commons and tune into what their friends talking about. What is happening in the area of campus organizations? Pay attention to things changing on campus that might affect the university community. Pocketbook issues are always of interest, especially to students who are often on tight budgets.

Most of all insist that reporting students read. Basic reading fare for would-be reporters certainly includes newspapers and magazines—these keep students abreast of trends and issues.[8] Most of us build such requirements into our class reading list and give news quizzes to ensure those students keep up on the day's news. In addition you might urge students to use the Internet to browse online campus publications from other schools to see what student reporters elsewhere are writing about.

Also be sure to scan memos put out by the university administration for story ideas, noting that at many schools those are available online, as are such documents as the meeting minutes of the Faculty Senate and the Student Government Association. Pay attention to flyers posted in common campus areas and peruse the classifieds in the campus newspaper. Students will be amazed at the things being advertised there.[9]

Use World Wide Web searches to track down articles and information about topics and issues that interest them. Introduce students to Northern Light Search http://northernlight.com/, a tool they will appreciate for its ease of use and the way it organizes information into handy folders. Read at least one biography each semester about a contemporary "mover and shaker." Not only will the students learn about the person but also the times in which we live.

Conclusions

Arranging a reporting course so there is a high probability of quality reporting and writing being published goes far toward making the experience much different and more relevant than things students do in most other college classes. Real reporters in the real world write for real readers. And therefore it is best if your students do, as well.

Bringing local reporters in as guest speakers, or simply to sit down informally and talk to your students, can expose them to some lifelong information-gathering strategies. This can add a touch of the newsroom to your classroom. Reporters are garrulous by profession, and most are happy to talk about their jobs. Many are flattered by the interest. Some of the best sessions are with younger reporters who can say to students, "You know, two years ago I was sitting where you are wondering what it would be like." Students can relate to that.

Guest reporters can be prompted to focus on whatever you are covering in class at the time. Good topics for visitors include such things as handling reluctant sources, listening for good quotes, whether to interview in person or by telephone, and why accuracy is so critically important. Students quickly conclude that the pros face the same problems with which they have been wrestling. Leave plenty of time for informal questions and answers, and you will likely be both surprised and pleased at the things students want to know about life in the fast lane.

You can turn to those same colleagues in the news business to set up a *shadow day*, during which reporting students are paired up with working journalists. Spending a shift observing a reporter at work can be important to college students; most will never before have been past the reception desk of a newspaper, magazine or television station. That afternoon or evening in the newsroom and out on a beat may be the unique experience that firms up career goals.

Whatever you do to add realism to your classroom will pay off in enthusiasm from your students, for journalism in general and reporting in particular. That enthusiasm alone is a great remedy for "fear of flying." Coupled with opportunities to succeed, it will build what we all look for in our reporting students: confidence that grows into competence.

Notes

1. Such phobias are represented in literary works such as *Fear of Flying* (Holt, Rinehart, and Winston, 1973). Novelist and poet Erica Jong's heroine is consumed by flight phobia but forces herself to travel by airplane in her search for adventure. In this sense (not of course in peccadilloes) it is a model for reluctant reporters.

2. The coaching approach to working with writers and reporters is popular in newsrooms; academically, it represents a very effective model for teaching reporting.

3. ASNE Excellence in Journalism fellows spend a week in intensive workshops in Reston, Virginia, discussing and examining the problems of journalism and journalism education, and then work for the remainder of the summer at host newspapers throughout the country as reporters, editors, photographers and graphic artists before returning to the classroom. As an ASNE fellow I had the opportunity to participate in both formal and informal discussions of the problems we share as journalism teachers.

4. I had been a longtime reporter and newspaper editor—but not for nearly two decades. As an ASNE fellow, I found that working as a metro reporter for the *Journal-News*, a large Gannett daily newspaper in Westchester County, New York, gave me a fresh perspective on the problems and rewards of contemporary journalism. The fellowship includes transportation and lodging. The organization and the host newspaper pay the educator's salary. For information on the program, contact Diana Mitsu Klos, senior project director (703–453–1125 or dmk@asne.org).

5. For an interesting nontheoretical and up-to-date explanation of why reporters report and the importance of news gathering in America, see "Our Role as Journalists Searching for the Truth Should Never Change," an address by Helen Thomas of United Press International (Freedom Forum World Center, Arlington, Va., Sept. 23, 1999). Her speech, the 22nd Annual Frank E. Gannett Lecture, can be read online at www.freedomforum.org/professional/1999/9/27hthomasremarks.asp.

6. A student reporter working on a story about eating disorders had all the statistics and had interviewed local medical experts. But she hadn't been able to find someone who actually suffered from an eating disorder. In class, another student said she had bulimia and offered to talk—on the record—about it. She was able to provide names of several others on campus with eating disorders, one of whom also agreed to be a source for the story.

7. Kevin McGrath, "Remember: Good writing is rewriting," *American Editor*, April 1998. His article can also be read online at www.asne.org/kiosk/editor/98.april/mcgrath1.htm).

8. Students in my reporting class must read, at minimum, the campus newspaper, a weekly newsmagazine and a daily local newspaper. To reinforce the habit of read-

ing news, I use these as the basis for a short, weekly quiz over major news events. I also recommend *USA Today* for its coverage of national trends and issues that can be localized.

9. A Planned Parenthood ad in the campus newspaper tipped one student reporter to the fact that abortions, although legal, were not being performed at local hospitals or clinics and were not available anywhere in the community.

Remembering a Mentor: John Merrill

Fred Blevens

Several years ago, a community newspaper editor in Texas asked what I was doing to relax in the summer "off season." "Teaching," I said, "and writing." "Writing what?" he asked. "I'm helping John Merrill write a book about the history and effects of 'communitarianism' in the civic journalism movement," I replied. "So, I guess I can assume you are against civic journalism," he said with an exasperated tone of resignation.

"No, I don't think that's a safe assumption," I said, asking him if he could tell me how he defined the movement. "Well, I think it's about listening to my readers," he said. "And I hope you're not writing a book that tells me *not* to listen to my readers."

In a phone conversation a few weeks later, I related the story to Merrill, who, along with Peter Gade and myself, had been thinking and rethinking such a book since I finished my dissertation in 1995. "Makes you wonder whom he's been listening to all these years," Merrill said, I'm sure with the devious twinkle that lights his eyes in moments of levity and/or incredulity.

Studying under John Merrill was not the sole reason for pursing a doctorate at the University of Missouri, but he quickly became the influence that kept me hurtling, sometimes head over heels, toward the finish. Having known Merrill only through repeated readings of *The Imperative of Freedom* and *Existential Journalism*, I knew we had much to talk about. After all, he had written two books that I had revisited time and again as a newspaper journalist, often seeking direction or solace in what can only be described as a profession of obsession and its related neuroses.

That opportunity came in my first few days on campus in the fall of 1992. Merrill had an office in what was known affectionately as "the pit," a small, sunken bullpen for doctoral students that once served as the composing room for the *Missourian*, the daily newspaper published by the Missouri School of Journalism.

Merrill had a teach-and-write work ethic that started early and ended late. If not in class or reading or losing himself in the library stacks, he was writing, often ripping out halves of chapters before lunch, which often consisted of a bowl of soup and grilled cheese sandwich. Several times a day, he would summon a doctoral student into his office, sharing an article or quip that had jumped to mind from the conversations that often erupted just outside his door.

When he summoned me that first day, I quickly took a seat. To my surprise, Merrill knew almost everything he needed to know about my professional and academic background. That left a series of questions. Why did I want to teach? Why would I select Missouri? Did I have any children? Had I found a place to live? What courses was I taking? And, most important, what was I reading? He was brief, sincere, sagely, and, in more than one instance, hilarious. He wished me well, handed me a recent article on media ethics, and then gently dismissed me with a pledge that his door always would be open.

A few days later, I started meeting with my undergraduate students in one-on-one sessions in my office. I used his questions and stated his pledge, even though I still did not believe Merrill (much less I) would keep the promise. Perhaps my doubts emerged from the daunting thought that if Merrill *really* kept his door open all day, every day, I, too, would be compelled to do the same.

He did and I did, even on days when diversion or distraction tempted our resolve. In three years at Missouri, I never saw John Merrill's door closed. On command, his or mine, he would listen and talk, often pulling things from the shelf and going on-point from dozens of pages marked with yellow sticky notes.

Merrill teaches from the heart and mind. Questions and answers are ways to get at thinking about the world. As an ethicist, Merrill knows the range of answers cannot be recorded on a Scantron or inserted in a question with a blank spot. He pushes students to think about the question on the notion that all of the best answers integrate the thoughts of others into new, coherent and important combinations. During a class, for instance, he asked me to explain the *differences* in philosophy between Louis Brandeis and Oliver Wendell Holmes. Relearning the obvious and common is not in the Merrill playbook.

That is why teaching has become a much bigger challenge in my post-Merrill academic career. Recently I was asked to talk about a few people who had an influence my teaching life. There was an eighth-grade teacher who related Shakespeare to Mencken; a master's adviser who taught the importance of reaching out to students; a doctoral adviser who opined correctly that those who teach college best are those who can best suffer fools.

Then, I said, "John Merrill taught me how to walk into a classroom, set off incendiary rhetorical bombs in each corner, and conduct a controlled burn for 50 minutes." Long ago, Merrill acknowledged and adjusted to the simple and painful fact that few of us can lecture effectively. More important, he became a master of the alternative seminar theory that if you can make them think you can make them talk.

Merrill's best teaching, however, occurs when he invites students to think and write with him. If you are enrolled in one of his classes and *if* you let him nudge and prod you to do your very best thinking, your thoughts and words are likely to be somewhere in one of his books. There simply may not be a better validation of learning, or a better way of learning from students. I am quite sure that during his five decades of teaching and writing, former students and colleagues have attempted to divine Merrill's secrets to success. I have not and will not, mostly because such an exercise would be counterintuitive to thinking about the question.

Instead, I will think about the question, not the answer. By example, I will set higher and higher expectations for my students. I will teach the uncommon even to community editors who may not get it the first time. Each time the opportunity presents itself, I will invite my students to voice and write their best thinking by becoming important parts of my own.

And, the door always will be open.

CHAPTER 11

Broadcast Newswriting

William R. Davie and Philip J. Auter

Introduction

Few subjects generate as much heat and as little light as academic discussions about the quality of broadcast newswriting. Famous network anchors have scoffed at the very notion of a college major in journalism or mass communication, while their producers plead in exasperation for better writing from our "J-school grads." A few former professionals, who have found refuge behind ivy-covered walls, have drafted their own strategies to improve broadcast newswriting. One former network news executive made his point clear the first day of class each semester. Former NBC and ABC News president Elmer Lower hoisted a bold sign in front of the class simply declaring, GOOD WRITING. By the end of the semester, Lower's students knew what he meant. They would need good writing skills not only for success in his class but in their career as well.

Our colleagues have cataloged a variety of symptoms that can be attributed to bad broadcast journalism. In their introduction to the classic textbook *Writing News for Broadcast*, Ed Bliss and James Hoyt sadly shook their heads over "too many clunking phrases and illiterate sentences. Too many bromides . . . " Vernon Stone's dire verdict was "literacy may be eroding in the medium that holds such potential for education by example." Mervin Block reviewed CBS radio news and TV news scripts for years before entering the college classroom. He wryly discovered he was wincing so much from broadcast newswriting his friends said he suffered from a tic.

If news audiences are enduring what Block described as the "rain of error," then those of us at the front of college classrooms ought to be worried. After all, where will the future generation of anchors and reporters learn their fundamental principles in broadcast journalism? If we combine our wisdom and attempt to learn from one another, then perhaps we can improve the quality of broadcast newswriting instruction. 189

With that aim in mind, we addressed five questions pertinent to this problem: First, where does the class fit in the curriculum as whole, and how is it shaped in terms of its size and enrollment? What philosophy do professors bring to bear in terms of teaching materials and textbooks? What learning goals guide their instruction, and how are they expressed in media activities? Finally, how is the student's knowledge and performance evaluated at semester's end? To supply some useful answers, we drew data from two groups of broadcast professors by using both questionnaires and e-mail interview techniques.

Our goal was to shed light on the means for effective instruction in broadcast journalism by collecting syllabi and interviews from faculty at private and public institutions of higher education. In aggregate data, we tallied responses from 43 broadcast educators. Those participants in our survey were drawn randomly from the Broadcast Education Association's directory and responded to a telephone questionnaire administered by our students. They also submitted their syllabi outlining their course plans. After analyzing those data, we selected colleagues for open-ended questions sent via e-mail.

The criteria for selecting schools was based on leadership in national groups dedicated to broadcast journalism education, as well as our desire to represent a diverse sample in size and location of campuses. Even though the schools differed in particular ways, their broadcast newswriting curriculum reflected a strong emphasis on journalism. At the time of this research, participating faculty taught at Arizona State University (Bill Silcock), the University of Colorado (Lee Hood), Florida A&M University (Phil Jeter), the University of Montana (Denise Dowling), Southern Illinois University at Carbondale (Ken Fischer), and Syracuse University (John Nicholson), and the authors added their responses as well. We began by locating this particular course in the degree program.

Position of the Course in the Curriculum

In the middle-college years between a student's foundation courses and their senior capstone, broadcast newswriting is usually taught. Of the faculty surveyed, 67 percent said juniors were enrolled in this course; 51 percent offered this class to sophomores, and a few schools allowed freshmen or seniors to enroll in this course.

From both our survey respondents and e-mail interviews, we discerned at least one prerequisite, although the number and nature of those preliminary classes varied. Since the broadcast newswriting class is a midlevel experience marking the passage of sophomores and juniors, it capitalizes on lower-division surveys of mass communication and/or basic writing courses.

Similar, Ancillary, and Related Courses

Prerequisites in media writing generally fall into one of two categories. Students were introduced to journalism writing as part of a news-editorial class aimed at the print side of the mass media, or they were enrolled in a media writing class featuring advertising, public relations, and other non-news formats. Survey courses focus broadly on mass communication or more specifically on electronic media. Subsequent to broadcast newswriting, students opened the door to advanced classes in television production or took upper-level offerings in media law, management and research.

Not all of the antecedent courses focused on news production techniques, but students eventually gained exposure on a local or campus radio station, TV station or cable system. Some schools ushered broadcasting students to internships in the local media, while others contributed content for the university's cable system and occasionally its Web site.

At varying points, students enhance their understanding of broadcast newswriting through complementary courses. Some of the skills for producing broadcast news are peppered throughout other classes in writing, production and aesthetics. The less frequently offered performance class—broadcast announcing or one of its cousins—may give students additional opportunity to practice radio and TV news exercises. Complementary courses also may cover basic radio skills, TV studio production, and video-editing techniques. Media Web-design classes offered by a few schools give students a chance to construct Web pages incorporating broadcast newswriting.

This raises the question of just how much can be accomplished in one semester. A class focused on perfecting the fundamentals of gathering news and story construction is a time-consuming affair for both teacher and student.

Most of the basic broadcast newswriting classes limit enrollments in order to facilitate the remedial work that has to be done. Writing classes pose a special challenge when enrollment exceeds 20 students. Twenty or less was the number most often specified by our survey, which would give the professor enough time to organize class projects creatively while carefully reviewing the student's writing. Nearly half of the sample (48 percent) reported class numbers ranging from 16 to 20 students. Slightly more than a third (35 percent) estimated their class size ranged from 10 to 15 students.

Comparative Features

This essential course raises an interesting array of questions. Should the teacher impart the basics of both radio and television journalism? Should she or he assign stories with the potential for broadcast exposure, or limit student assignments to only class exposure instead? Should professors include field production with camcorders and microphones or refine the work to script writing instead? These questions generated interesting responses reflecting the demands of both facilities and academic curricula. We begin with our general observations.

Most broadcast newswriting courses opted for a combined radio and television approach to instill the basics of broadcast nomenclature, scripting formats, reporting procedures, and interviewing techniques. In that way, students would learn to recognize the tools of radio and television as well as the contrasting elements in conversational writing. Both media appreciate the importance of simple, declarative sentences; both construct narratives with a beginning, middle and end, though television more so than radio. The ultimate goal in both forms of broadcast news instruction is ensuring that students can calmly produce quality writing under deadline pressure. Most programs offered students at least a taste of the production activities to complement the writing exercises. Students sponge up these aesthetics as much as possible before honing their talents for what usually follows: a TV news production course. To place these media activities properly in their context, we looked more closely at the material covered.

Common Goals and Objectives

Despite contrasting perspectives, facilities, departmental structures, and regional differences, different schools had in common certain learning objectives. Of the 43 instructors surveyed, the majority felt that teaching the students scripting style for television (65 percent) and radio (61 percent) was a worthy aim of the broadcast newswriting class. Faculty also taught students how to report for radio (65 percent) and/or television (58 percent). About a third of our sample had their students learn how to produce radio (37 percent) and television newscasts (37 percent). Nearly a third of the professors considered announcing to be a component (TV, 33 percent; radio, 30 percent). Announcing also was cited by six of the eight programs selected. It was followed by the use of recording equipment in the field (audio, 28 percent; video, 21 percent) and post-production editing techniques (audio, 26 percent; video, 16 percent).

These learning objectives received comments in our e-mail interviews. Faculty from selected programs identified conversational newswriting to be the primary goal, followed by developing sound news judgment for radio and television. There was nearly unanimous agreement students should learn how to conduct interviews in this class. From the personal interviews and syllabi, we learned how important it was to teachers that students understand the aesthetic elements of radio and TV production, though not necessarily in that class. Denise Dowling at the University of Montana, for example, veers away from TV news production. In most instances, the learning concepts centered on writing and reporting assignments, but equipment-based exercises were more common to radio news than to TV news assignments overall.

Production of a radio newscast for practice was part of the requirements in six of the selected programs; three schools asked students to work at an entry-level capacity at the university radio station. While teaching at the University of West Florida, however, Phil Auter had his students complete a practice TV newscast and, at Arizona State, Bill Silcock made university TV news or radio news production a significant portion (50 percent) of their grade.

The faculty interviewed noted certain inevitable trade-offs when determining what material could be mastered by semester's end in this class. For example, should greater emphasis be given to reporting and writing assignments, or should the class become a broad overview experience? From the telephone survey, we discerned a variety of answers to this question, but one finding stood out as significant. Professors emphasized solid reporting, which usually meant accuracy and strong writing skills, including meeting deadlines, as the most important objects. Learning through practice was mentioned frequently, and several professors indicated that practice would help students understand how important teamwork was to the process.

For most, it was a step-by-step process in the early stages. By the end of the semester, however, students were to have a clear understanding of the whole process in terms of reporting and writing stories, and putting together newscasts. In applying various hands-on approaches, faculty aimed to develop a strong sense of news judgment among their students so they might become discerning about what stories to cover and how to present them. Several professors underscored the necessity for critical thinking, which would have a direct bearing on the student's future success.

A clear majority of our sample observed students had unformed habits in terms of reading newspapers and paying attention to newscasts. Faculty had long passed the point of surprise in recognizing even journalism majors tend to be unaware of local, regional and even world events. To correct their complacency, most felt it's necessary to test students on their knowledge of daily headlines. Sixty-five percent of the classes added news material to the midterm and final exams, while nearly the same number (63 percent) gave periodic quizzes on current events.

Common Emphasis

We observed from our telephone survey and e-mail interviews that a majority of the faculty agreed broadcast newswriting should emphasize accurate reporting skills and strong storytelling technique. Deadline pressures and conformity to broadcast writing style were considered key elements. A number of instructors felt it was important to offer practical, hands-on experience to students. In addition, most agreed testing was important, especially over current events.

Faculty in our sample made an effort to see their students became professionally acquainted either by inviting broadcasters to visit the class or by sending out students to take internships. Eight selected programs covered in this chapter emphasized writing and reporting broadcast news under deadline pressure. Even though responding faculty took different approaches to teaching this class, they all insisted students must develop a clear understanding of collecting and presenting broadcast news.

Instructor Philosophy

Instructors preferred personalized approaches to the challenge of training broadcast journalists. Some focused exclusively on writing styles, whereas others looked toward basic or advanced production projects. To sort through different preferences, we asked six colleagues to describe their semester in the broadcast newswriting class.

None of the faculty responding limited their activities to strictly reporting and writing exercises but took the time necessary to engage some elements of production. Variations on this theme appeared to be a product of the school's equipment and facilities more than the professor's philosophy. By examining the syllabi and explanations from this assortment of professors, we ascertained how individual schools differed in their approach to broadcast newswriting.

At Arizona State University, Bill Silcock teaches a course designed to build upon basic communication skills and prepare students better for advanced TV production work. His class serves as gate through which broadcast news majors pass in order to take higher-level skills and content courses. Before students may enroll in Silcock's class, they first have to gain admission to the Walter Cronkite School, pass an English writing exam, and complete the introduction to mass communication course.

Students who successfully finish this broadcast newswriting course advance to other reporting classes, including one where they produce a cable news program. Consequently, Silcock also focuses on newscast producing. He tries to achieve a balance between lecture and learning by doing. Taught two days a week, the first day is almost always devoted to lecture learning, whereas the second class teaches principles needed for skills-based labs, giving students their hands-on experience.

For a textbook, Silcock supplements James Redmond, Fred Shook, and Dan Lattimore's *The Broadcast News Process* (2001) with John Hewitt's *Air Words* (2001). In addition to exams on the text and current events, his course provides in-class and homework writing assignments, as well as lab work with on-campus broadcast media. Before the semester is over, each student must complete a report on a book relating to the broadcast news industry.

At the University of Colorado at Boulder, Lee Hood teaches broadcast journalism with a strong emphasis on clear writing. She devotes an equal amount of time to radio and television journalism. Although her class is situated between beginning and advanced courses, it serves as the introduction to broadcast newswriting techniques.

Students taking the Radio and Television News course first complete an introductory survey of mass communication, Contemporary Mass Media, as well as a class in Critical Thinking and Writing. Students often take a course in basic production skills simultaneously with her writing class. Both the broadcast newswriting and production courses are demanded of students before they can advance to work in TV reporting and news production.

Critical discussions of broadcast news coverage are encouraged and conducted via the class e-mail Listserve. In addition to writing assignments and class discussions, Hood divides her students into small groups to produce one practice radio newscast around the midpoint of each semester. Students are not assigned advanced audio production work, but instead learn rudimentary editing skills for this exercise.

Current-event quizzes and a final project covering the semester give Hood the evaluation scores she needs to assess each student's progress. Hood prefers Robert A. Papper's *Broadcast News Writing Stylebook* (2002) and also recommends supplementary material on TV newswriting by local news anchor Ed Sardella.

Florida A&M students gain initial experience in broadcast news by reporting, writing and producing for radio *and* television. Philip Jeter's class is a prerequisite for the advanced TV news and radio news practica, where students work in news teams to produce TV programs for air. The lessons encompassed in the broadcast newswriting class include conversational style writing, story selection based on news values, and conceptual aspects of audio and video production.

Jeter emphasizes conceptual learning so students may understand how to gather, produce and deliver content. He explains technology is constantly changing and a solid knowledge of broadcast newsgathering and story production techniques is more useful than simply teaching the nuts and bolts of one particular set of media tools.

At FAMU, Jeter also delves into the history of, and current issues related to, broadcast news. He uses contemporary examples of news stories and industry issues to generate discussion. Students also are required to review a book or video related to the broadcast journalism industry in order to fulfill the class requirements.

Homework writing assignments are not graded but critiqued. Students soon learn they may lose points, however, if they choose not to turn in their written homework. In addition to writing and reporting exercises, Jeter tests students on current events and the material covered in the textbooks by *Air Words* by Hewitt and *A Broadcast News Manual of Style* (1994) by MacDonald.

At the University of Louisiana at Lafayette, Bill Davie teaches a course that trains students in writing and production skills while concentrating on radio journalism. Even though both radio news and TV news reporting techniques are covered, class production centers on a weekly radio show, *Louisiana Focus*, broadcast by the university's National Public Radio (NPR) affiliate, KRVS-FM. Students work individually and in teams on a series of hands-on projects featuring news interviews, natural sound recordings, creating packages, story rewrites, and rundowns. Davie's class serves as the gateway to more advanced courses in television news and production.

He also prefers Papper's *Broadcast News Writing Stylebook*, which he initially supplemented with M. D. Rosenbaum and J. Dinges' *Sound Reporting: The National Public Radio Guide to Radio Journalism and Production* (1992) until it became outdated. Grading is computed by a combination of tests and quizzes covering lecture and class discussions, readings and current events.

At the University of Montana, Denise Dowling places a strong emphasis on reporting and writing techniques. Her Reporting for Broadcast course prepares students for advanced production and broadcast journalism classes by making them familiar with recording and editing techniques while practicing basic reporting skills. This class precedes three classes in the broadcast journalism track: Advanced Broadcast Reporting, Newscast Production, and Broadcast Newsroom. It also comes in advance of two general television production classes: TV Production I and TV Production II.

Dowling guides her students in the proper technique for interviewing news makers, collecting relevant facts and details, and answering questions to engage and inform the audience. In class, she holds discussions about theory, ethics and audience concerns. In addition to writing news reports, students spend a good deal of time discussing and critiquing real-world coverage.

Drill and repetition are the cornerstones of Dowling's approach. Students are asked to write practically every day, and learn how to prepare reports for radio. Radio production exercises establish the foundation for students' use of natural sound, actualities and other effects. They write and produce two radio packages during the semester that often feature actualities and natural sound. Dowling's students need not have those stories aired to achieve a passing grade, but superior work is rewarded with broadcast time on the student radio station. She also uses Papper's *Broadcast News Writing Stylebook* as the primary text for the class.

The Broadcast Newswriting course at Southern Illinois University at Carbondale offers students an overview of broadcast journalism but focuses predominantly on radio news. Students learn about the basics of newsgathering—reporting and writing techniques, career opportunities—but Ken Fischer emphasizes writing above all else. He says that, by keeping students engaged in the writing process, they ultimately learn how to correctly apply the principals needed for professional success. On-air deadlines are critical, and Fischer encourages his students to become more adept at coping with other realities they will encounter after graduation in radio and TV newsrooms. He teaches his students how to handle feedback from classmates and the professor in order to help them improve their writing, while at the same time developing a thick professional skin needed to withstand future criticisms from the audience, professional peers, and news directors.

SIU–Carbondale's program offers students considerable opportunities for hands-on experience in class and out, but the bulk of the learning in Fischer's class is focused on critical thinking and creative writing. During the semester, Southern Illinois students write radio news, work on audio projects, and take exams over class materials and the textbook, as well as quizzes on current events. Broadcast Newswriting is a basic course at SIU, and it has no production or journalism writing prerequisites. Students, however, have to take two introductory overview classes prior to this course. The broadcast newswriting class is taken before students advance to reporting classes in either radio or television news. Fischer supplements Papper's *Broadcast News Writing Stylebook* with Jerry Lanson and Barbara Fought's *News in a New Century* (1999).

The teaching of Broadcast News Writing at Syracuse University provides realistic instruction and training. John Nicholson and his fellow broadcast journalism professors teach interviewing, production, and field exercises, but the majority of this class is devoted to writing.

It builds on the student's experience in a prerequisite print journalism course or Discovering the News—a broadcast, print and Web writing course, which combines on-site briefings from representatives of such groups as police, fire, local government, education, and the courts. Students then report on real events in those areas and others.

Broadcast News Writing serves as a prerequisite to classes in radio and TV reporting as well as TV news production. Developing strong writing skills is a key learning objective in the Syracuse program, and this class is designed to drill students on collecting information, writing and rewriting it under deadline pressure.

Nicholson and the other broadcast journalism faculty supplement the textbook material covered by Peter Mayeux in *Broadcast News Writing & Reporting* (2000) with additional assignments drawn from local and national news publications and wire services.

There are regular current-events discussions in class, and the textbook material comes into play when students write their assignments. Cognitive learning and hands-on skills are closely interwoven in everything the broadcast journalist does, and Nicholson says a professor should not try to teach one without the other. The Broadcast News Writing course at Syracuse encourages students to soak up information and clearly communicate it. Nicholson summed up his philosophy with one piece of advice that he gives hundreds of times each semester: "Just tell me the story."

The class offers opportunities for students to conduct interviews and to work with some equipment, but it concentrates almost exclusively on writing. Nicholson does assign one production project where students learn how to produce a five-minute newscast, put together a rundown and then write all of the stories in one 80-minute class period. A key feature of this class involves the work students do with their in-class assignments on actual newsroom software. A professional newsroom system, AP NewsCenter, integrates script writing, timing, and show production.

Students in the broadcast journalism class once taught at the University of West Florida by Phil Auter capitalized on skills acquired in prior production and writing classes. Auter refined their knowledge gained from prerequisite courses in studio production, electronic field production, and writing (print journalism and broadcast script writing). By the end of the term, students were expected to have a solid foundation in newscast production, with the necessary reporting and writing experience for advancing in the program. He prepared sophomores and juniors for a capstone production class where they produced a weekly TV newscast and provided material for a companion Web site.

Auter's students at West Florida created a TV newscast step by step. This cumulative learning project was designed to supply content for the college newscast, *Nautilus News*, and gave students valuable experience in crew assignments. A typical class of 20 students would be divided into five teams (producer, associate producer, director, and assistant director). The rest of the students served as cast and crew. As an incentive, Auter encouraged friendly competition among crews, with producers of the best newscast gaining bonus points.

By two-thirds of the way through the semester, each student had produced a news package from scratch, edited video from a CNN news feed, and prepared a list of prospective stories for the semester. The final third of the course was devoted to newscast rehearsals, and actual live-to-tape shooting of the newscasts.

The Broadcast News Process, by Redmond et al., served as the foundation for this course. Auter gave two written tests over textbook material and equipment/facility usage, including how-to manuals that comprised 20 percent of the grade. The remaining 80 percent was calculated by incremental learning projects, newscast production, and peer reviews.

Common Challenges/Solutions

What are the common challenges to teaching the broadcast newswriting class, and how do we solve them? Solutions vary, but the majority of our sample cited three broad areas of concern: curriculum, facilities, and student motivation. Curricular issues centered on essential prerequisites and subsequent course work designed to prepare students for entry-level jobs. Equipment concerns weighed heavily on finding up-to-date facilities and opportunities for teaching students how to meet technical challenges they would face later. Holding the enrollment to the appropriate size for such a writing class was a chief concern for some broadcast news faculty. As noted earlier, 20 students or less was considered manageable.

Student-centered issues focused on the question of motivation. Some professors found students' desire to be waning for broadcast journalism. For example, professors found broadcast journalism majors who just wanted "to be on TV" but became disenchanted after realistically assessing the unglamorous nature of behind-the-scenes work necessary to achieve success in this business. Students who enroll in broadcast journalism for frivolous reasons eventually awaken to reality in this class and usually respond by either buckling down or changing majors.

Some programs encounter a greater challenge with motivation chiefly because the same classes in broadcast journalism are required for a diverse group of journalism and nonjournalism majors. One professor claimed his solution was to retain the focus on broadcast journalism but to look for ways to relate concepts to other areas of video production. Others motivated student interest by provoking class discussions on current events and later quizzing them over that material.

Apathy was a common complaint that cropped up in our survey. One professor said simply that it is difficult to convince today's students that news matters. He met this challenge by generating class discussions on news relevant to the students' lives, and encouraging them to follow the news through the media of their choice and comment on what they learned in class.

A related problem involved students' motivation to work harder on their writing and realize the importance of *rewriting* copy and *re-editing* tapes to achieve air quality. His solution was to *not* grade the writing until students corrected its flaws and presented their best possible work. Another instructor suggested the solution to the motivation challenge was to emphasize competition among students working individually or in teams throughout the semester.

Writing problems abound. One professor said she struggled with her students' limited grasp of the English language and in particular their ability to write effectively in conversational style. Those with severe language problems were directed to remedial classes in English composition at one campus.

Helping students discern what is a "good story" was another challenge cited by our collection of professors. Here the goal was to get students to look beyond their personal interests and develop a feel for the general audience, which translated into professional news judgment.

The students' lack of understanding regarding how news figures in the business of electronic media concerned some faculty. One professor said he assigns students a book or video review to relieve the deficit in that regard, along with conducting class discussions about the industry. By stimulating and guiding students to thinking critically about the news, he felt he could better prepare his students to compete in the industry.

Professors also wrestled with grading issues, and how best to give students constructive criticism to correct their performance without injuring their confidence. Writing takes time to perfect, and there never seemed to be enough time. One solution suggested was peer coaching and editing, where students critique and edit one another's work in addition to the professor providing feedback.

Outside Resources

Traditional teaching resources found in the broadcast newswriting class include one or two textbooks, computer lab facilities (for timed, in-class writing assignments), and access to departmental (or student-supplied) audio and (less often) video facilities. In addition, the majority of professors ask students to inform themselves by subscribing to a newspaper or through online and broadcast news media.

Several professors recommended playing audio and videotapes of award-winning stories and newscasts as a way to impress students with model examples of work. Award winners also underscored for students how important it is to be competitive to secure their niche in the business. Some teachers apply the fundamentals of broadcast journalism by inviting students to critique and deconstruct quality stories, such as news from NPR (www.npr.org). Most professors assemble personal archives of videotapes to play in class, while also relying on feeds from CNN Newsource, and other network programs.

Another faculty member found videos from PBS (www.pbs.org) to be useful, including *Newswriting* and an *American Masters* profile of Edward R. Murrow. He also recommended the HBO (www.hbo.com) film *Murrow* and the Educational Video Network (www.edvidnet.com) programs on producing TV news.

Several professors cited CNN Newsource (newsource.cnn.com/) as a tool not only for filling student-produced newscasts but for supplying video and scripts to be used in story exercises, including voice-overs and sound bites. Access to the CNN Newsource Web site is free to educational institutions in addition to their satellite feed. For the latter, schools must only purchase and calibrate an appropriate satellite dish.

Broadcast journalism faculty recommended students be allowed to experience the computing side of production in radio and TV newsrooms as an important learning experience. Scripts, rundowns, prompter copy, and closed captioning are all integrated into a number of interactive programs. Several schools recommended EZ News (www.autodatasys.com) as a package of newsroom software. Syracuse University, on the other hand, chose AP News Center (www.enps.com/).

Broadcast news faculty also recommended a variety of Web sites to their students. These include professional online guides of conduct such as the Radio-Television News Directors Association (RTNDA) and Society of Professional Journalists (SPJ) codes of ethics (www.rtnda.org/ethics/coe.shtml and www.spj.org/ethics_code.asp), and academic or personal Web pages that were more narrowly focused. Ken Fischer at Southern Illinois University at Carbondale supplements his course materials with Ohio University's producer Web page (www.scripps.ohiou.edu) that he says serves as a valuable supplement to the class textbook. The University of Colorado's Lee Hood directs students to Abe Rosenberg's Newswriting.com (www.newswriting.com). His *100 Worst Groaners* are a particular favorite among the students.

Conclusions

Becker et al. (2001) counted more than 168,000 undergraduate students majoring in journalism and mass communications at four-year institutions in the fall of 2000, and a large number of those students were enrolled in broadcast newswriting classes. A broadcast newswriting course usually follows media-survey and introductory classes and builds upon those subjects as one of the skills-oriented classes. It comes midway in a mass communication major's program of work that often culminates in a capstone course during the senior year. Broadcast news is a pivotal course in the curriculum, and the professors interviewed take special pains to see that certain fundamental principles are acquired.

We found through the reports of more than 50 different broadcast newswriting programs that teachers expect their sophomores and juniors to develop the discipline and skills necessary to succeed in preparing a newscast on time with clear and informative content. Though our telephone and e-mail interviews, we found that, by the end of the semester, college professors expected their students would be capable of writing and reporting stories for air independently.

Most of the professors emphasized reporting, writing, script preparation, current events, and producing newscasts under pressure. Production techniques for either radio or television were usually involved, with students performing duties as anchor, reporter and producer during the semester. Tests and graded assignments assessed each student's performance.

The decision concerning where to put broadcast newswriting in the curriculum related both to content covered in other classes as well as the overall scope of the program. Recognizing that students must sharpen their skills in writing and performance, as well as in editing portfolio tapes and drafting their first résumés, it was clear that one class could not do it all. This subject tended to focus on the foundation writing skills and information gathering through interviews, while relying on other classes for more advanced training.

Generally a graduating mass communication major is asked to demonstrate familiarity with basic radio and television technology, the aesthetics of production in audio/video, and legal and ethical principles, but most importantly to demonstrate an ability to shape prose into meaningful narratives of daily events.

This class in broadcast newswriting is the essential building block for a highly competitive industry that ultimately will test the quality of each student's instruction. The news media continue to evolve and challenge instructors not only to keep relevant in their course plans, but also to properly instruct the skills necessary for the next generation of electronic journalists.

In the past, reporters, videographers, editors, anchors and producers divided duties in the newsroom. Today, fewer workers are involved in the process, and they often are asked to perform multiple duties and measure up to the increasing competition of an expanding array of media choices.

Digital convergence and consolidation of huge media corporations have brought attendant pressures on profit margins and contributed to a rise in the "one-man band" solution. Broadcast journeymen and women working independently for TV stations were once the hallmark of small-to-medium markets. Now they are employed throughout the industry, and new hires are expected to be just as self-sufficient in gathering, shooting, and reporting news. Further complicating the broadcast journalist's task is the demand to "re-purpose" stories for multiple channels—radio, television, cable, print, and Internet-based services. In a real sense, then, these pressures have forced news managers and editors to ask more from entry-level employees. They must know not only how the write and produce the daily radio or television newscast but also how various departments (sales and promotions, engineering and management) relate to each other to form a profitable enterprise.

Should academics then expect future broadcast journalists to become "jacks of all trades and masters of none" in this competitive realm? We contend not; any broadcast journalist hoping to ascend the career ladder must excel in either shooting, reporting, producing, or anchoring, though certainly not in all of them. Naturally, basic broadcast newswriting classes cannot, and should not, address all of the issues; professors must discern which ones are most relevant to their students' personal and professional goals.

References

Books

Alten, S. R. 2001. *Audio in media.* 6th ed. Belmont, Calif.: Wadsworth.

Biagi, S. 1992. *Interviews that work: A practical guide for journalists.* 2nd ed. Belmont, Calif.: Wadsworth.

Blanchard, R. O., and W. G. Christ. 1993. *Media education and the liberals arts: A blueprint for the new professionalism.* Hillsdale, N.J.: Lawrence Erlbaum.

Bliss, E., Jr., and J. L. Hoyt. 1993. *Writing news for broadcast.* Irvington, N.Y.: Columbia University Press.

Block, M., and J. Durso Jr. 1999. *Writing news for TV and radio.* Chicago: Bonus.

Block, M. 1990. *Rewriting network news.* Chicago: Bonus.

———. 1994. *Broadcast newswriting: The RTNDA reference guide.* Chicago: Bonus.

———. 1997. *Writing broadcast news: Shorter, sharper, stronger.* Chicago: Bonus.

Boyd, A. 1997. *Broadcast journalism: Techniques of radio and TV news.* 4th ed. Boston: Focal.

Carroll, V. 1997. *Writing news for television.* Ames: Iowa State University Press.

Chantler, P., and S. Harris. 1997. *Local radio journalism.* Boston: Focal.

Cohler, D. K. 1994. *Broadcast journalism: A guide for the presentation of radio and television news.* 2nd ed. Boston: Allyn and Bacon.

Cremer, C. F., et al. 1995. *ENG: Television news.* 3rd ed. New York: McGraw-Hill.

Hausman, C. 1999. *Crafting the news for the electronic media: Writing, reporting, and producing.* Belmont, Calif.: Wadsworth.

Hewitt, J. 2002. *Airwords: Writing for broadcast news.* 3rd ed. Mountain View, Calif.: Mayfield.

———. 1992. *Sequences: Strategies for shooting news in the real world.* Mountain View, Calif.: Mayfield.

Kalbfeld, B. 2000. *The Associated Press broadcast news handbook.* New York: McGraw-Hill.

Kessler, L., and D. McDonald. 2000. *When words collide: A media writer's guide to grammar and style.* 5th ed. Belmont, Calif.: Wadsworth.

Looker, T. 1995. *The sound and the story: NPR and the art of radio.* Boston: Houghton Mifflin.

MacDonald, R. 1994. *A broadcast news manual of style.* 2nd ed. White Plains, N.Y.: Longman.

Mayeux, P. E. 1994. *Writing for the electronic media.* 2nd ed. Dubuque, Iowa: Brown and Benchmark.

NPR Staff. 1992. *Sound reporting: National Public Radio's guide to radio journalism and production.* Dubuque, Iowa: Kendall-Hunt.

Papper, R. A. 2002. *Broadcast news writing stylebook.* 2nd ed. Boston: Allyn and Bacon.

Shook, F. 1994. *Television newswriting: Captivating an audience.* White Plains, N.Y.: Longman.

———. 1996. *Television field production and reporting.* 2nd ed. White Plains, N.Y.: Longman.

Shook, F., and D. Lattimore. 2001. *The broadcast news process.* 6th ed. Englewood, Colo.: Morton.

Stephens, M. 1993. *Broadcast news.* 3rd ed. Fort Worth: Harcourt Brace Jovanovich.

Strunk, W., and E. B. White. 1979. *The elements of style.* 3rd ed. New York: Macmillan.

Tuggle, C. A., F. Carr, and S. Huffman. 2001. *Broadcast news handbook: Writing, reporting, and producing.* New York: McGraw-Hill.

Ward, P. 1994. *Basic betacam camerawork.* Stoneham, Mass.: Focal.

Wendland, M. 1999. *Wired journalist: Newsroom guide to the Internet.* 3rd ed. Washington, D.C.: RTNDA.

White, T. 2001. *Broadcast news writing, reporting, and producing.* 3rd ed. Boston: Focal.

Wulfemeyer, K. T. 1993. *Beginning broadcast newswriting: A self-instructional learning experience.* 3rd ed. Ames: Iowa State Press.

———. 1995. *Radio-TV newswriting: A workbook.* 2nd ed. Ames: Iowa State Press.

Trade Magazines

American Journalism Review. Journalism in print, television, radio, and online media is covered. Offers controversial opinions and profiles. News and industry issues are evaluated through in-depth reporting and analysis.

Columbia Journalism Review. This watchdog of the press, which was founded by Columbia University's graduate school of journalism, lends analysis with reporting directed at improving the practice of journalism in a free society.

RTNDA Communicator. This monthly magazine, which is directed at radio and television news directors, producers, anchors and reporters, provides information on newsroom management, industry issues, and technical updates. It offers research surveys of the broadcast stations newsroom.

Web Sites

ajr.org. Online presence for *American Journalism Review* (see above).

newslink.org. Links to newspapers, magazines, radio and television stations, listed by state, nation and continents.

www.current.org. A Web service about public broadcasting, with selected content from *Current*, the biweekly newspaper that covers public TV and public radio in the United States.

www.journalism.org/publ_research/local-tv. Web site for the Project for Excellence in Journalism, an initiative by journalists concerned about the standards of the news media.

www.journaliststoolbox.com. The *Journalist's Toolbox* features more than 13,000 Web sites helpful to the media and anyone doing research, and includes information from a variety of beats and news-industry-related topics.

www.mervinblock.com/tips.html. The *Television Newswriting Workshop* site includes a number of writing tips from Mervin Block.

www.missouri.edu/~jourvs/index.html. Behind the scenes of local news broadcasts; a systematic look at the people and institutions that produce television and radio news in the United States. It includes such topics as newsroom profitability, salaries, staff diversity, careers and internships.

www.NewsLab.org. *NewsLab* is a nonprofit resource for television newsrooms, focused on research and training. It serves local stations by helping them find better ways of telling important stories that are often difficult to convey on television.

www.nppa.org. The National Press Photographers Association is dedicated to the advancement of photojournalism, its creation, editing, and distribution, in all news media.

www.npr.org/inside/styleguide/stylmain.htm. The *Public Radio Ethics and Style Guidebook* is an online style guide compiled from guides in use in public radio news organizations.

www.prndi.org. Public Radio News Directors Incorporated, a nonprofit, national service organization, encourages the professional development and training of public radio journalists.

www2.drury.edu/rtvj. *RTVJ Online*, the Radio-Television Journalism Division of the Association for Education in Journalism and Mass Communication, focuses on the teaching, practice, and study of broadcast news as a profession. The division maintains ties with professionals through the Radio-Television News Directors Association (RTNDA). Members also individually maintain ties with broadcast journalists as they train students to work in local newsrooms around the country.

www.rtnda.com. The Radio-Television News Directors Association is the world's largest professional organization devoted exclusively to electronic journalism. The RTNDA represents local and network news executives in broadcasting, cable and other electronic media in more than 30 countries.

www.rtndf.org. The Radio and Television News Directors Foundation promotes excellence in electronic journalism through research, education and training for news professionals and journalism students. The RTNDF's work is supported by contributions from foundations, corporations and individuals.

www.scripps.ohiou.edu/producer. The *Producer Page* is freely available to TV news producers and broadcast journalism students. Its main purpose is to provide a convenient source of information and advice to help producers improve the quality of the news programs they produce.

www.scripps.ohiou.edu/producer/thebook. An archive of the *Producer Page* (see above).

www.spj.org/quill_list.asp. Online presence for *Quill*, the Society of Professional Journalists' national magazine. For more than 85 years, *Quill* has been a respected and sought-after resource for journalists, industry leaders, students and educators on issues central to journalism.

www.tvnewz.com. *TVNewz* is the first "webzine" exclusively for television news professionals.

www.tvrundown.com. *The Rundown* reports to television executives on local television news, programming, and community service projects.

www.tvspy.com/shoptalk.htm. *TVSpy* is a Web site for broadcast professionals that provides job seekers, professionals, and employers with insider content, community and business services. With its daily *ShopTalk* newsletter and its *Watercooler*, it unites network presidents, station executives, broadcasters, technicians, journalism professors, and students in a unique forum.

Journal Articles

Becker, L. B., T. Vlad, J. Hu, and J. Prine. 2001. Annual enrollment report: Number of students studying journalism and mass communication at all-time high. *Journalism and Mass Communication Educator* 56(3):28–60 [also online]. www.grady.uga.edu/annualsurveys/Enrollment00/educatorsummary.htm.

Blaney, J., and G. Donnelly. 2000. Relationships between academic broadcast facilities and pedagogical outcomes. *Feedback* 41(1):1–8.

Duhé, S. F., and L. A. Zukowski. 1997. Radio-TV journalism curriculum: First jobs and career preparation. *Journalism and Mass Communication Educator* 52(1):4–15.

Fisher, H. A. 1978. Broadcast journalists' perceptions of appropriate career preparation. *Journalism Quarterly* 55(1):140–144.

Gotfredson, D., and E. Engstrom. 1996. Video essay: Teaching and learning with alternative news presentations. *Journalism and Mass Communication Educator* 51(2):55–62.

Remembering a Mentor: David Sloan

Bernell E. Tripp

One of the things I remember most about David Sloan as my professor was his "magical box" of index cards. The box was the source of numerous miracles for me, or any other bewildered graduate student who would finally succumb to frustration and slink into his office for guidance on a research project.

David would sit behind his neatly organized desk, barely concealing a smile as he listened to the borderline hysterical pleas for help. Then he would calmly get up and walk to his bookcase to remove "the box." After briefly thumbing through its contents, he would pull out a fistful of cards, hand them to me, and remark, "Why don't you look through these and see if some of them might be helpful?" Neither David nor his cards ever failed to provide the answers or at least clues to the solution for whatever problem I had.

His media history seminar was one of the first classes I experienced in my first semester as a master's student at the University of Alabama. Having been away from the classroom for several years, I was overwhelmed by the reading list and his expectations for the course, and I seriously questioned the wisdom of abandoning my job as a sports writer to return to college. His impressive reputation as a top-notch media historian only added to my feelings of inadequacy, especially when I botched our first assignment.

As the other students' discussion of the assignment swirled around me that night in class, I became more and more dejected, realizing just how far off track I had been, and I dreaded handing in my papers at the end of the three-hour session. The next morning, I vowed to go to his office, admit my incompetence, and beg for his mercy. Yet his response was amusement rather than disappointment in my predicament. Unperturbed by my confession, he explained that I was probably not the only one in the class who had erred, and he assured me that he had intended the first few assignments to be part of the learning process (and not graded work). He then provided detailed instructions on completing future assignments and on conducting historical research. Satisfied that I now fully understood what was expected of me, he sent me off to the library with renewed enthusiasm for the seminar and a newfound passion for the study of media history.

I learned so much from David's seminar that semester, and I kept all the readings, as well as my assignments, to use with my own students at the University of Florida. Many of the articles, papers, and book chapters he assigned have been required readings in my seminars. But my old assignment papers serve as a reminder of how much a student can accomplish under the tutelage of the right professor. Plus, they allow me to listen sympathetically when befuddled graduate students come to my office to confess misgivings about their own abilities in conducting historical research.

David's official obligations to me as an advisor and mentor ended the day he placed the doctoral hood on my shoulders and escorted me off the stage during the University of Alabama commencement ceremonies. Yet, not a week or, sometimes, not a day, goes by that I don't mention his name or something he taught me 10 or more years ago.

My "Sloan stories" have become legendary among my students as I try to pass on some of the many lessons I learned as his student. He placed no restrictions on topics, and he encouraged his students to find and develop their own media history interests. Because of David's open-mindedness, this well-known colonial press researcher ended up as advisor to a student whose fascination for the 19th-century black press continued even after I became a faculty member at Florida. And as a result of his influence, I have found myself advising students interested in such topics as military public relations practices in World War II, civic journalism, techniques of 1960s broadcasting, children's television regulation, the 19th-century black press of Kansas, and the use of film in modern political campaigns.

Similarly, his classroom techniques have become an integral part of my own teaching methods. Rather than formal lectures during the entire class period, he emphasized student participation and encouraged students to express their own interpretations about issues and events in media history. However, he was a stickler for rigorous research practices. Too often I catch myself responding to a student's question with one of David's remarks: "Ask yourself if that's the absolute best source you can find for this information." "If you're not convinced that your work is significant, how do you intend to convince anyone else?" "What does it add to the current pool of historical knowledge?" "You need support for this information from a primary source." "Use a variety of primary sources to make your point, instead of relying on one type of source."

Now, at conferences, my students always ask me to introduce them to David, too awestruck to approach him on their own. Invariably, their interaction with him at the conference is the thing they remember most. They brag to fellow graduate students that "I had dinner with David Sloan," or "I talked with David Sloan about my research," or "David Sloan is *so* nice and so approachable," or "David Sloan said I could contact him if I needed help on a project." The initial remark is always uttered with pride and the appropriate smirk that never fails to elicit just the right amount of admiration and envy from the listener. My graduate students have now started referring to themselves as his "grandchildren" of media history research.

Although I no longer have access to David's magical box of index cards, his published works still provide me with starting points that I can pass on to students who need direction in their research. If I don't automatically know the answer to a question, I can usually find it in one of his books or draw from my own experiences to give them clues on where to look.

Several months ago, I heard that the contents of the box were being transferred to computer files. For some reason, I became sad. I'll miss that box. I guess all students need to believe that their advisors can do magic and perform miracles.

CHAPTER 12

Advanced Reporting

Sonny Rhodes and David Davies

Introduction

Teaching the 5 W's and the H is one thing. With repetition, an instructor can teach most students to include routinely in their stories the Who, What, When, Where and How, and, when it can be determined, the Why. It's quite another thing, though, to teach students to go beyond good note taking and accurate reporting and to delve into the deeper issues behind an event or matter of public concern, to put facts in context and show readers why an issue is important.

To do this, students need to be instructed to answer more probing questions. Such questions include Who cares? So what? What does it mean?[1] To ask such questions requires research, which means, among other things, instruction in how to use various library resources and the Internet, and how to ferret through and interpret public documents. This preparation can lead to a student's formulating thoughtful questions and refusing to accept pat answers from sometimes-reluctant sources. Then comes the organization of the material, the writing, rewriting, and the student's ultimate reward: publication.

Beyond the satisfaction of publication, students may find self-confidence in knowing they have survived the rigors of a sort of journalistic boot camp. Further, students may find satisfaction in feeling that they have contributed to helping readers better understand the world around them.

Instructors may feel some sense of accomplishment in knowing they have helped produce hardworking, conscientious journalists who are capable of providing more than routine coverage of city hall, cops and courts.

The instruction that can produce such students can be found in advanced reporting classes. This chapter takes a look at upper-level reporting classes taught by six instructors whose course titles include Advanced Reporting and Writing, Depth Reporting, and Public Affairs Reporting. The programs that offer these courses range from relatively small to large state universities and private institutions. Regardless of their institutions' sizes or locations, all of the instructors emphasize the vital nature of the course in an aspiring journalist's training and the need for the student to develop professionalism.

The instructors serve not only as lecturers, but as meticulous and sometimes hard-nosed editors. In most cases, the courses are capstone courses or offer a *capstone experience*, being the last writing course a student may take before entering the world of professional journalism.

These capstone courses trace their historical roots to the increasing popularity of interpretive reporting during the 20th century. A milestone in the teaching of interpretive reporting was Curtis D. MacDougall's early and influential book, *Interpretative Reporting*, first published in 1938. MacDougall, a Northwestern University journalism professor, was part of a chorus of educators calling for a greater emphasis on the teaching of explanatory journalism in the nation's journalism programs early in the last century. The Commission on the Freedom of the Press, the so-called Hutchins Commission, reinforced the need in its 1947 report, *A Free and Responsible Press*, which criticized the nation's press for shallow reporting and called instead for reporters to produce "a truthful, comprehensive, and intelligent account of the day's events in a context which gives them meaning."

Advanced and public affairs reporting courses aim to teach young reporters to meet such a standard. The serious purpose of such courses can be seen in the statement Earnest Perry of Texas Christian University includes in his syllabus: "If you intend to go into reporting this is one of the most important classes you could ever take. It will be challenging and rewarding. If you spend most of your time worrying about your grade instead of whether or not you understand the concepts of advanced writing and reporting, then you might want to drop this class. . . . Professionalism and ethical standards will be practiced in this course. In this class you are reporters and will be treated as such."

These sentiments are echoed by Doug Anderson at Pennsylvania State University, who says the goal of his Depth Reporting class is straightforward: "Students are to develop the best-researched, most-comprehensive, well-written stories they ever have produced."

And, Edmund Lawler, who teaches Advanced Reporting at DePaul University, adds, "I want to convey to the students that a thoroughly researched, well-written story can have an impact on the public agenda. That is done, of course, by turning over as many stones as possible on an issue and writing about it in a compelling manner. It's hard work. Those interested in addressing an issue only superficially won't get far."

Fred Blevens, who taught Advanced Reporting and Writing at Southwest Texas State University, believes courses such as these should be taught as a hands-on experience for students: "The philosophy is that students nearing the end of their print journalism curriculum need to be able to function as working journalists who can meet at least the minimum standards of employment at entry-level newspapers."

Unlike courses discussed elsewhere in this book—such as Advanced Television Production—the courses examined in this chapter require the students to work individually. Very often, a print journalist's first job requires starting at the bottom rung of the newsroom ladder—as a general assignment reporter for large publications or possibly a beat reporter for small publications. In any case, the new reporter is expected to be enterprising, not just taking assignments from editors but keeping his or her eyes open for story ideas, pitching the ideas to an editor and then developing them into articles. Later, the reporter may become part of an investigative reporting team or work with specialists from other areas of the newsroom, such as copy editors, photographers and designers. In this way, they can produce news packages, but initially a reporter's work can be solitary, so it is important for a student to learn to work on his or her own.

Position of the Course in the Curriculum

The courses described in this section are upper-level offerings. All involve student work that requires extensive planning, research and interviews. Beyond such elements, Penn State's Anderson, who teaches Depth Reporting, observes this age-old axiom in saying that stories for his course require writing, rewriting and more rewriting.

The courses have at least one basic newswriting course as a prerequisite. The following are specifics on where some of the courses fit into their programs' curricula:

Anderson says that because of the various interests of students in his program's journalism major (print, broadcast, photography), there is no single capstone course. But, he said, "I would certainly label Depth Reporting as a 'capstone experience' for students interested in reporting. ... Virtually all students who take the course are seniors."

"We offer a handful of courses beyond basic newswriting and advanced reporting: editorial writing, feature writing, magazine writing and sports writing. What makes Depth Reporting a bit different, I suspect, is that long-form writing is required." By long-form, Anderson means a final project of 4,000 words is involved.

The course is the only one Anderson teaches because he also is dean of Penn State's College of Communications. The course is offered each fall and is limited to 10 students. Normally, seven to 10 enroll. Anderson says, "I interview students who are considering enrolling. This session gives me an opportunity to tell the prospective student what the course entails, which may or may not be what the student had in mind. It just gives the student an opportunity to tell me about his or her background, the courses he or she has taken and the expectations he or she might have of the course. Sometimes the student decides not to enroll. Sometimes I decide it would be best for the student if he or she did not enroll—or that the student delay enrollment until the next year."

Similar to the case at Penn State, Advanced Writing and Reporting is offered each fall in the Department of Mass Communication at Southwest Texas State University. Usually, 15 to 20 students are enrolled in the course. Fred Blevens, who teaches the class, does not interview the students: "By the time they take this course, I pretty much know what they can do."

To take the class, students must have completed a lower core of courses: Introduction to Mass Communication, Information Gathering and Analysis, Writing for the Mass Media, and Visual Communication. Advanced Reporting and Writing is the capstone writing course for print journalism majors.

Ancillary, Related, and Required Courses

Public Affairs Reporting is the capstone journalism course in the School of Mass Communication at the University of Arkansas at Little Rock and is offered each spring semester. Enrollment is capped at 15; normally 10 to 12 students take the class each year. It has two prerequisites: the sophomore-level course Introduction to Mass Communication Writing and the junior-level course Reporting Principles, for which students generate stories for the campus newspaper.

Like Blevens, course instructor and chapter co-author Sonny Rhodes has usually had students take other classes under his tutelage before they reach Public Affairs Reporting: "We have a relatively small program, so I've had most students in an editing or feature-writing class by the time they take Public Affairs Reporting, and I have a pretty good idea of their abilities. Likewise, they know pretty well what to expect from me."

At the University of Southern Mississippi, Advanced Reporting is the capstone journalism course, the fourth writing course that news-editorial students must complete. The prerequisite to the course, Investigative Strategies, introduces students to detailed information gathering using in-depth interviews and government documents, and prepares them to meet the two primary challenges of the advanced course.

First, students gain valuable practice in reporting public affairs. Second, students gain experience in writing long-form articles that are far lengthier than what they have written in previous reporting classes or for the student newspaper. "The course gives students both the practice and the clips they need to get their first permanent reporting job after graduation," said course instructor David R. Davies. "The emphasis on the course is for students to do the types of stories that would be demanded of them in their very first jobs."

Common Goals and Objectives

Penn State's Anderson introduces students to strategies for writing in-depth newspaper or magazine articles by emphasizing information gathering through interviews, library sources, electronic databases, and surveys.

The nature of the works can vary. They may be news or sports articles on a single topic; profiles; investigative pieces that reveal wrongdoing by a person or agency; or research-based editorials or opinion columns. A student must publish at least 4,000 words in a final project that could be a single story, a mainbar and sidebar, two separate stories, or a series.

Anderson says, "We spend the first few weeks of the semester discussing the qualities of good writing; organizing long-form stories; use of quotations and attribution; the importance of smooth transitions; characteristics of well-researched stories. They review good writing by others (students are routinely asked to bring to class long-form stories from newspapers or magazines that they admire. They distribute copies of the stories to all class members and lead a discussion of what makes the story and the writing so good). ... Each student is expected to develop his or her story fully. We allocate time in virtually each class to allow each student to give an update on the progress he or she is making—the obstacles, the good things, etc. Students sometimes are frustrated at their inability to locate sources or reference material; during these discussions, their classmates often have helpful suggestions. And I frequently refer students working on particular stories to other faculty members who might have more expertise than I on the topic. That way, they are able to consider sources and story approaches that might not have been apparent to me."

Once the stories are completed, students sometimes are able to place their stories in the campus daily, community newspapers, or magazines. The Penn State College of Communications provides an additional outlet for students by periodically publishing *The Lion's Roar*, a tabloid-sized newspaper.

Instructor Philosophy

Anderson does not require a textbook for the course, although "we make repeated references to the text most used for newswriting and/or advanced reporting. And students bring their stylebooks to each class. I also expect them to read three or four different newspapers each week, and I'll often go around the table asking each of them to detail for the rest of the class some interesting stories they recently read."

Fred Blevens teaches Advanced Reporting and Writing "as an experiential learning process." Although he, too, does not require a textbook, he holds scheduled lecture periods covering advanced concepts in information gathering, interviewing, story structure and style, ethics, and law.

In his syllabus, Blevens writes, "The course integrates writing and reporting skills to produce in-depth stories using multiple sources of information. Techniques might include investigative reporting, social science reporting, and feature reporting."

According to the syllabus, upon completing the course, students will be able to report fully developed in-depth issue stories, write fully developed in-depth issue stories, produce well-honed copy for publication, analyze a story assignment, and develop a reporting strategy. They must also analyze a story assignment and develop a writing strategy, and refine work through a process of story drafts.

Blevens' syllabus tells students that the course requires a great deal of outside work, and, to get an A, students must publish at least two bylined articles—in-depth (news or feature), investigative, or issue pieces—and submit a portfolio that is current and in good order. A deficient portfolio could lower a grade by one letter.

Students have several options by which they can meet the course performance requirement. The options vary from year to year, but Blevens offered an example of what he planned for the fall 2002 semester before joining the University of Oklahoma—one that preceded the biennial meeting of the Texas legislature:

1. Publish no more than six such stories in the campus newspaper.
2. Publish as many stories as possible in an Accrediting Council on Education in Journalism and Mass Communications partnership project with the *Houston Chronicle* Capitol bureau in Austin.
3. Publish as many stories as possible in the Central Texas Reporting Project.

The Central Texas Reporting Project is an informal association of six local newspapers, daily and weekly, that regularly publishes work by students enrolled in the class. Students often graduate with good clips from four or five papers, in addition to those they might collect in formal, paid internships.

Among other things, the course attempts to identify good venues for student work. "Assignments come from all the papers involved," Blevens said, "but students are encouraged to enterprise their own under the age-old industry admonition that if you develop your own ideas, you'll be a lot happier doing the work."

Blevens limits the number of stories in the campus newspaper to push students into the professional world for at least half of their experiential learning. The partnership project with the *Houston Chronicle* was undertaken to allow students to report and write advance issue stories leading up to the biennial legislative session the following January. Those stories may be published in the *Chronicle* or the campus's *University Star* or both.

Blevens edits the stories like an independent editor working in a freelance capacity for the client newspapers. Students often have to re-report or rewrite all or parts of their stories before he releases them to the newspapers. The papers seldom seek additional work, but they have that option in the process. Any major reworking of the stories must be cleared through the student and Blevens, however.

"Most of our newspaper clients actually pay for the stories—from $25 to $50, depending on the scope of the story," Blevens said.

Blevens, at the time of this writing, had been teaching the course for four years. The course has undergone dramatic change in those four years. "It once was a fairly easy course that had no publication requirements," Blevens said. "[Requiring students to get their stories published] was the primary change and, of course, the one that really makes it work."

Common Emphasis

Earnest Perry, who teaches Public Affairs Reporting in Texas Christian University's Department of Journalism, writes in his syllabus, "This course is designed to enhance your reporting and writing skills at public affairs and investigative reporting. In this course you will report and write about government and other public institutions. This class will show you how to go beyond many of the superficial stories you read in newspapers or watch on television news programs. We will not only explore the who, what, when and where, but also the why, the how and the 'so what.' Your stories will be more in-depth than stories you have done in previous classes."

The course's objective is to help students develop advanced reporting skills that go beyond surface answers to questions.

As part of this, students are taught how to use the Internet and library sources for background material to help formulate the questions necessary for in-depth reporting and writing. Further, students are instructed how to conduct public record searches. Perry requires *The Reporter's Handbook*, 3rd edition (1995), by Steve Weinberg.

Perry tells students that the class's writing objective is to go beyond the straightforward stories by "reporting, writing and rewriting until your story is acceptable to me. In-depth reporting requires more complex writing and doing that will require you to do more self-editing." The course also is intended to help students develop analytical skills to help separate important facts from the extraneous.

Students are required to write six stories during a semester and all of them are approved by Perry: "The deadlines will be set . . . to give you plenty of time to complete the assignment. The semester will start off slow and end in a flurry, so don't get behind. Try to start on the next as you are completing the other."

Each story is worth 100 points, 50 for writing and 50 for reporting. A grading sheet is attached to each story that explains what elements went into a grade. Of the final grade, stories are worth 50 percent, rewrites 20 percent, a public record project 20 percent, and tests 10 percent. Of the six required stories, three are for TCU publications and three for off-campus publication.

Common Challenges/Solutions

Perry cautions students that there are few perfect stories: "Rewrites are important and should be taken seriously. You may be required to rewrite a story several times so give yourself time to do it." He comments on the stories themselves, but goes beyond that by recording comments on a cassette tape that each student provides when he or she turns in a story.

Perry requires that he see every story so that he may comment on it before it is published. If a student publishes a story without getting Perry's comments first, the student will not get credit for the work.

Perry emphasizes the need for meeting deadlines in a deadline-driven business. He deducts 20 points a day for a story turned in after the deadline, and will not accept a story after the second day.

"Meeting deadlines is very important," Perry writes in the syllabus. "If you stay ahead of the deadline and turn your stories in early that will leave you more time for any additional reporting and/or rewriting."

Perry also places a high premium on accuracy: "Accuracy is essential. A misspelled name or other major fact error that gets into print will result in a zero for that story and will require two additional stories to make it up. You will also be required to write a letter of apology to the person who was wronged."

A second misspelled name or other major factual error that gets into print will result in a zero and will require a student to write three additional stories to make it up and to send a letter of apology to the person wronged. A third misspelled name or other major factual error in print will cause the student's final grade to be dropped by two letter grades.

Throughout the semester, Perry also gives tests on news events and other matters discussed in class.

Chapter co-author Sonny Rhodes at the University of Arkansas at Little Rock has similar requirements of students in his Public Affairs Reporting class. Students must first submit a story proposal, worth 10 points. Besides requiring a summary of what the story is to be about, the proposal asks a student to identify what market he or she is writing for and to provide a list of sources. Six stories are required, five of them 1,000 to 1,500 words long, worth 100 points each; the final must be 1,500 to 2,000 words long, worth 150 points. A story turned in late will be penalized 10 percent for each day it is late and will not be accepted if turned in a week late.

Rhodes tries to return all stories at the first class period after the due date. In the past, the class has been held on Tuesdays and Thursdays, so ordinarily Rhodes would have the stories come due on a Thursday so he could have the weekend to give the stories a thorough evaluation. (The meeting time for the class has since been changed, which will be explained later in this chapter.)

Rewrites of the shorter articles are worth 20 points each; and the rewrite of the longer story would be worth 30 points. Rewrites are due a week after they are returned.

Outside Resources

The stories cover the actions of public boards, agencies or other organizations. These may include legislative committees, city councils, school boards, police departments, and courts. Rhodes requires students to read *Public Affairs Reporting* (1992) by George Killenberg and the *Associated Press Stylebook and Libel Manual.*

In addition to the grades for the stories and story proposals, Rhodes gives quizzes on Associated Press style, tests on current events, and periodic exams on the lectures. These are based on the Killenberg text and on handouts taken from such sources as a handbook on the Arkansas Freedom of Information Act and a booklet on state and municipal government published by the state branch of the League of Women Voters. Like education in general, Rhodes says, knowledge of Associated Press style should be an ongoing learning process if one is to be a good journalist, so he thinks the style quizzes are essential.

He has known students who have gone on to work in a variety of jobs, from in-house hospital publications to daily newspapers, and all use the *AP Stylebook* as their bible. As for the current-event quizzes, Rhodes feels these force students to read more news than they might otherwise. It is a cliché, perhaps, that good writers are good readers, Rhodes says, but it is amazing how many students who aspire to write do not have a habit of reading a daily newspaper or otherwise keeping up with current events.

Included as part of the exams is a scavenger hunt, given early in the semester, that requires the students to exercise some of their research skills in sifting through library resources and Internet sites. The hunt requires students to find information ranging from the address of city hall, the form of municipal government, and the circulation of the daily newspaper of a small town in Arkansas, to the population density, largest newspaper in, and religious and ethnic makeup of Austria.

Students are required to document where they obtained the information and, if from a Web site, to provide a printout of the site. The sources must be found in libraries or on the Internet; a telephone call to a source is unacceptable. Ultimately, the final grade is broken down this way: Stories are worth 50 percent, the editing exercises 20 percent, and the exams 30 percent.

Stories written for the course are offered regularly to more than 100 daily and weekly newspapers in Arkansas through the UALR Journalism News Service. The stories are distributed via mass e-mailings to the newspapers. The newspapers are asked to include student bylines on any stories they decide to publish. If a story is published, a clipping service returns a copy to the Journalism Program, and the copy is given to the student for his or her portfolio.

Rhodes recommends, but does not require, the students to attend city-council and school-board meetings to get a firsthand look at how such bodies conduct business and to meet the public officials. (Getting students to attend such meetings can be a problem, though, an issue addressed in this chapter under the "Challenges" heading.)

Attendance at such meetings can generate story ideas that might not occur to someone whose only knowledge of an event has been filtered through a newspaper or broadcast report, given that space and time limitations often force reporters to focus on the more topical or controversial aspects of public meetings.

At the University of Southern Mississippi, the Advanced Reporting course is structured around a beat system. Students are required to cover three different beats during the semester, covering one 600-word story a week for each of the 15 weeks of the semester. In addition, students write three 600-word spot stories, three 1,000-word news features, and one 1,500-word final project during the course. "This practice gives students training in both day-to-day beat coverage as well as issue stories," according to chapter co-author David R. Davies. Beats cover police, courts, local government, health, religion, and other routine sources of news.

All stories written in the class are published in an online newspaper called the *Hub City News*. Area newspapers are supplied the Web address of the publication (www.usm.edu/hubcitynews) with the understanding that they may reprint any article so long as students are given bylines and are supplied a tear sheet of the published story. Articles are heavily edited and rewritten before they are placed online. Students must learn the basics of coding documents for the World Wide Web as part of the course. "The online publication is an incredible advantage," Davies said. "Students may use printouts from the online publication for their clips, with the added benefit of getting tear sheets if their article is picked up by a local publication."

All students attend city-council and school-board meetings in outlying towns as part of their beats, but the entire class attends Hattiesburg City Council meetings every other week. The class was scheduled to coincide with council meetings. "The continuity of attending the local council meetings month after month is tremendously beneficial to learning the ins and outs of city government," Davies said. Guest speakers, such as the *Hattiesburg American*'s city reporter, visit the class to explain politics of the council.

The Southern Mississippi advanced reporting course has evolved over the years. In some years, Davies has partnered with a local publication, usually the *Hattiesburg American*, to produce an investigative series in cooperation with the newspaper's editors. In 1998 students did a story package on the investigation of a missing teen-ager from nearby Petal, Mississippi. Reaction to the students' work, from readers and editors of the *American*, was positive.

Conclusions

Penn State's Doug Anderson says that because his Depth Reporting generally is the first writing course students take that does not have shorter stories due during each class period, "students have a tendency to wait too long into the semester to dig diligently into their stories. Because complete drafts are not due until the semester is more than half over, many students have a tendency to sit back, thinking they have ample time to develop their stories. That is why I ask for progress reports each week; drafts of lead blocks early on, etc."

Blevens said one challenge is getting all the stories in shape for publication without any teaching assistants. For the fall 2002 semester, the program planned to experiment with bringing in a graduate teaching assistant and a full-time professor who coordinates the beginning writing course. As Blevens notes, "I believe this is going to cut down on the 30-hour weekly load that historically has faced the teacher of record."

Rhodes noted that his institution is an urban university with a large number of non-traditional students. One of the challenges of teaching at an urban university is that many of the students have families and work at full-time jobs, often at night, so the students' schedules may not be as flexible as those of students at traditional institutions.

Rhodes believes it is important for students to have the experience of attending city-council and school-board meetings, but since many of these bodies convene at night, some students' schedules are not flexible enough to enable them to attend such meetings. If students are unable to attend night meetings, Rhodes recommends they attend meetings such as those of the water or planning commissions, which often meet during the day. To ensure that students get a taste of local government in action, Rhodes videotapes local-access channel broadcasts of city-council meetings and shows portions of the meetings in class. Sometimes, for practice, he will have students write stories based on what they see on the tapes and then compare their stories to how the local news media covered the meetings.

Being at a university in the center of state government has advantages, Rhodes notes. UALR is only a few miles from the state Capitol, so it is easy to take field trips to the state Capitol, and it can be fairly easy to contact state officials and legislators for stories. On a field trip to the Capitol one semester, one of Rhodes' students saw a legislator she had been trying repeatedly to reach by telephone for a story she was working on for the class. The elusive legislator was speaking on the floor of the state Senate at the time. At Rhodes' recommendation, the student sent a note to the senator via the sergeant at arms, asking to speak with him. The student waited nearly an hour outside the Senate chambers, but finally the legislator emerged and the student got her interview.

After offering Public Affairs Reporting on Tuesday and Thursday afternoons for many years, the UALR Journalism Program decided to shift the class time to Tuesday nights, beginning with the spring 2003 semester. This way, attendance at night meetings of public bodies could be built into the class schedule, Rhodes said.

Another key challenge to the advanced reporting/public affairs reporting course is adjusting the students to the tremendous workload required in the class and in the news business generally. "In my experience, students have great difficulty adjusting to the amount of time and writing involved," said chapter co-author David Davies of the University of Southern Mississippi. "By the end of the semester, they adjust, of course, but it's a slow process." Davies said he must often remind students that the writing load in the course, if anything, is less demanding than what would be required in a typical newsroom. Ironically enough, working professionals who have taken the class nearly always agree with him on the workload question.

For the students, these courses provide a taste of the real world through deadlines and writing stories that go beyond the walls of academe. Students also get some satisfaction of meeting the challenges of digging deeper and writing potentially more meaningful stories. "I think students enjoy—in the final analysis—seeing their long-form work in print," Penn State's Doug Anderson says.

Fred Blevens says his students consistently remark that the coursework pushes them to heights they never believed possible. Most of the students are not confident reporters when they come to the class. Blevens says, "Almost all leave with reasonable assurance that they can, in fact, function as working journalists, even if it's as a beginning staff on an 8,000-circulation daily. Fundamentally, they see all their curriculum come together into tangible results and practical application."

The courses also provide satisfaction for the instructors.

Anderson said, "As an administrator, I sometimes don't have as much positive interaction as I would like with students. Even though this class is small, it gives me the opportunity to end my day—at least once a week—with a positive experience."

Blevens says teaching the course allows him "to experience the joys I knew in 20 years of journalism without suffering the vagaries of the daily newsroom grind. And, most important, it allows me to see student work come to fruition almost immediately."

Davies sees his course in similar terms. "Working with advanced reporting students is almost like being in the newsroom again. You get to see the students develop over the course of the semester and develop confidence," he said. "The satisfaction of working with the students is palpable."

Rhodes, who was a newspaper reporter and editor for 25 years before becoming a professor, has similar sentiments: "Newspaper work can get to be so specialized that it's easy to get caught up in producing just one piece of the pie. And, if you're a news editor, as I was for 10 years, you're often seeing stories that have been pretty well polished by the time they get to you, and there's little, if any, interaction with the person who produced the story. In a course such as Public Affairs Reporting, you see a story from conceptualization to publication, and, most importantly, you have the satisfaction of seeing an aspiring reporter go from someone with basic reporting skills to someone who knows what it takes to write meaningful articles."

In terms of advice he would offer someone new to teaching such a course, Blevens said, "Get [students] out of the building. Get them hooked up with as many publication opportunities as possible. Make the contacts to create the opportunities. Get a lot of help."

Note

1. The three key questions—Who cares? So what? What does it mean?—These are among six questions that editors, especially copy editors, should ask themselves every time they handle a story, writes Doug Fisher, who teaches journalism at the University of South Carolina. The other three questions are: Do I understand what this means, what the writer is saying? How do I/we know this? Does this make sense? These questions were included in an installment of Fisher's column "Common Sense Journalism," originally appearing Feb. 18, 2002, in the *South Carolina Press Association Bulletin*. Fisher's column is published in a number of press association newsletters in the Southeast. He wrote that if the question "Does this make sense?" had been asked. "Then perhaps a newspaper would not recently have told us about a '12-year-old' sudden infant death syndrome victim. Was it 12 months? But then why not say 1 year?"

Maybe it was 12 weeks?" Fisher further wrote regarding press deceptions and outcomes: "If we can avoid one Janet Cooke, one confused reader, one needless correction, then it's worth taking time to go beyond the five W's and H and always ask these six questions."

References

Books

Brooks, Brian S. 1999. *Working with words: A handbook for media writers and editors.* New York: Bedford/St. Martin's.

Goldstein, Norm. 2000. *The Associated Press stylebook and briefing on media law.* New York: Associated Press.

Kessler, Lauren, and Duncan McDonald. 2000. *When words collide or working with words.* 5th ed. Belmont, Calif.: Wadsworth/Thomson Learning.

Mencher, Melvin. 2000. *News reporting and writing.* 8th ed. New York: McGraw-Hill.

Killenberg, George M. 1992. *Public affairs reporting: Covering the news in the information age.* New York: St. Martin's.

Izard, Ralph, and Marilyn S. Greenwald. 1991. *Public affairs reporting: The Citizen's News.* 2nd ed. Dubuque, Iowa: Wm. C. Brown.

Itule, Bruce D., and Douglas A. Anderson. 2000. *News writing and reporting for today's media.* 5th ed. New York: McGraw-Hill.

O'Conner, Patricia T. 1998. *Woe is I: The grammarphobe's guide to better English in plain English.* New York: Riverhead.

Walsh, Bill. 2000. *Lapsing into a comma: A curmudgeon's guide to the many things that go wrong in print—and how to avoid them.* Lincolnwood, Ill.: Contemporary.

Weinberg, Steve. 1995. *The reporter's handbook: an investigator's guide to documents and techniques.* 3rd ed. St. Martin's.

Wickham, Kathleen Woodruff. 2002. *Math tools for journalists.* Oak Park, Ill.: Marion Street.

Web Sites

American Copy Editors Society. www.copydesk.org
Investigative Reporters and Editors Inc. www.ire.org
The Poynter Institute. www.poynter.org
The Reporters Committee for Freedom of the Press. www.rcfp.org
The Society of Professional Journalists. www.spj.org

Other

A state pocketbook on libel and open records/meetings is essential to teaching this course. Check with area chapters of the Society of Professional Journalists, local press associations, and state attorney general offices for copies.

Remembering a Mentor: Ed Lambeth

Walt Harrington

He was a long, lanky, gentle man who always seemed to be pausing just an extra few seconds to decide how he was going to tell me my story was awful without saying exactly that. Sitting behind his desk in the University of Missouri's Washington Reporting Program office in the National Press Building more than 25 years ago, he paused even longer than usual, his head bent and nodding over my story. He looked up, still nodding, spun in his chair to face his typewriter, rolled in a sheet of blank paper, and, finally, spoke in his languid Southern drawl.

"You've got a good lead here, Walt." He clacked away at the keys for two or three minutes and then, in a sweeping theatrical motion, tossed up the typewriter's bar, spun the wheel with is right hand, yanked the page out with his left, turned back to me and dropped it on the desk between us. "And this is what I think you're trying to say." I read the new lead. It was what I was trying to say. As Rick told Louis in Casablanca: It was the beginning of a beautiful friendship.

Over the many following years, I would work with brilliant reporters and editors, from daily deadline hounds to crusty investigative reporters to gentle wordsmiths. In my years at the *Washington Post*, I worked every day with men and women whose deep competence made me better.

Yet no single person had a greater influence on my career—on what I think of as my outlook on the doing of journalism—than the long, lanky, gentle Edmund B. Lambeth.

Ed was the first journalist I knew who was also an intellectual. He liked big ideas. He liked theories and concepts and strong opinions. I had come out of graduate school in sociology and knew plenty of teachers with big ideas and opinions. But Ed was an intellectual who was also a journalist. Grand thinking was fine but to turn that thinking into stories, every detail and nuance had to be grounded in documentation. That meant hard, gritty work way beyond what the big thinkers ever imagined.

After a semester with Ed, I understood the implications of the work I so admired: that of David Halberstam, Robert Caro, and John McPhee—journalists with big ideas grounded in rock-breaking journalistic craft. Ed's unspoken message: Don't pretend to memorable work if you can't commit the attention, effort and labor. Ed's was a journalistic version of tough love: Do your best. Your best is never enough. Live with it. Be better next time.

I was among a generation of reporters influenced by the New Journalism of the era. Unlike many journalists his age, Ed wasn't hostile toward a journalism that valued the evoking of human experience as much as the reporting of facts. He recognized a big idea when he saw it and realized, as always, that for journalism it was a challenge of craft: Can the work be done without violating the sacred rule of documentary evidence?

After my semester in Washington, a member of my master's committee said of my work, "This is all good but where in the world are you going to get a job?" Ed Lambeth found me a job—at a little shopper's guide in Harrisburg, Pa., where a single editor was hiring a single reporter to do investigative reporting. "A shopper's guide?" I asked. "It'll round you out as a reporter," Ed drawled. I trusted him, and he was right.

I was at the age of spit and vinegar. I called Ed regularly to ask advice on everything from reporting techniques to writing to my next career move. I always talked about me. Looking back, I realize it never dawned on me that dozens of Ed's other students were also calling him. Ed came to feel to me like a friend long before I was mature enough to be a friend to Ed. As I got older, he began to remind me that my wife and children, my parents, faith and community, my life away from work were all profoundly important. We probably saw each other once a year for the next 20 years. I came to realize that Ed was old enough to be like a father to me, young enough to be like a brother, and confident enough to be not only a mentor but a friend.

Along the way, I grew up enough to ask Ed about his own life, to realize that he had his own insecurities, that he was human. But he never lost the fire. I saw many colleagues become embittered toward their work. I believe they weren't as well armed as I to fight day-in, day-out against the real limits of doing good journalism. They hadn't had Ed Lambeth as a teacher: Do your best. Your best is never enough. Live with it. Be better next time.

Today, I'm a teacher of journalism. Indeed, I am a teacher because half-a-dozen years ago Ed called me and said he'd seen an ad in the *Chronicle of Higher Education* that seemed as if it had been written just for me. Was I interested? No, I said. Ed, gently persisting, said he would send the ad to me anyway. He did. I took the job.

These days, not a week goes by that I don't notice myself telling a kid something Ed told me decades ago. Now I get calls from former students, each of whom thinks he or she is the only person who calls me. I think of my teaching as a debt to be repaid. And I will think myself a failure if someday some kid who has finally grown up doesn't feel the same debt to me.

CHAPTER 13

Advertising Campaigns

Yorgo Pasadeos and W. Glenn Griffin

Introduction

The conventional wisdom among educators in our field appears to be that "the most important function of capstone courses in journalism and mass communication is to prepare students for the real world" (Benigni and Cameron, 1999, p. 50). The Advertising Campaigns course, perhaps more than any other in an advertising program or sequence, provides this experience. As the pedagogical arm of a professional field, the advertising curriculum was initially designed to prepare students for jobs in advertising agencies, the advertising departments of large corporate or mass media organizations, or in support capacities (research, consulting, production, and the like).

Advertising programs are located in a variety of college and departmental environments. Advertising sequences or majors are most commonly housed in communication or business administration units on campus. In the former case, advertising is taught in departments of Journalism, Communication, Mass Communication, Advertising and Public Relations, or Advertising. In business schools, advertising is typically taught as a separate sequence or in the form of limited coursework within a marketing department. In this chapter we discuss the Advertising Campaigns course as it is typically taught in communication units, for three reasons.

First, Communication units house the majority (as much as 80 percent) of all advertising sequences or majors in the United States. Second, while business units tend to emphasize the *marketing strategy* and *management* aspects of advertising—there the campaigns course is typically titled Promotional Strategy—communication units often place considerable emphasis on the *creative* and *messaging* components of the business in concert with marketing concerns. Third, the present book is directed to teachers and teachers-in-training of Mass Communication, who are more likely to teach the Advertising Campaigns course within a communication curriculum.

This chapter was prepared based on a review of the advertising education literature. Insights from a 1996 American Academy of Advertising panel on teaching the Advertising Campaigns course were incorporated into the discussion, including a survey of Advertising Campaigns teachers (Applegate and Parente, 1996). Although the bulk of the discussion reflects the authors' preferences for and experiences with the Advertising Campaigns course, several educators with experience teaching the course also offered their insights to supplement the discussion.

Common Goals and Objectives

As a capstone course, the Advertising Campaigns course is meant to provide students with an opportunity to synthesize everything that they learned in previous courses. Mike Little, instructor of advertising at the University of Alabama, hopes that his students get "the widest possible range of experiences" through the planning and execution of an advertising campaign, and sets up his course with an eye toward that goal. Whereas earlier courses are designed to give students specific skills, the campaigns course aims at training them in integrating those skills, which requires strategic and tactical thinking. At the University of Texas at Austin, advertising professor John Murphy lists the following items as important lessons the students should take away from the course: "critical thinking, time management, presentation, writing, teamwork, listening, resiliency in the face of adversity, and how to work hard and enjoy it."

Another objective of the course is to aid in the development of students as advertising professionals. As Jim Avery, professor of advertising at the University of Oklahoma and author of *Advertising Campaign Planning* counsels students, "The objective of [the course] is to provide you with an environment wherein you can gain a working professional knowledge of advertising. The emphasis here is on *professional knowledge*. You have spent considerable time learning the theory of advertising; this class will allow you to implement that theory. We will assume the setting of an advertising agency." Indeed, the ideal course setting is one in which the students assume the roles of individual members of an advertising agency team.

Changing with the Times

The Advertising Campaigns course was initially conceptualized and implemented in a manner that would resemble, as closely as possible, the development of a real advertising campaign. As clients have grown to demand more from their agencies and the advertising that they produce, the integrated marketing communications (IMC) approach has updated the traditional definition of an advertising campaign by incorporating sales promotion, direct marketing and public relations as synergistic promotional activities (Schultz et al. 1993). In turn, most advertising campaigns courses have adapted to this phenomenon (Griffin and Pasadeos, 1998). At Pennsylvania State University, advertising instructor Wayne Hilinski sees the primary objective of the ad campaigns course as helping students "understand what an IMC campaign is and how it collaboratively comes together." In general, most of these courses being taught across the country track the industry model for campaign development and offer students a sense of how things work in the real world.

Expectations for Student Performance

Drawing upon everything they have learned about advertising in their other classes, ad campaign students are expected to research, conceptualize, plan and propose a complete advertising program, typically for a real client. Most campaign courses require the development of a detailed written proposal or *plans book* that summarizes research and articulates strategy. Students also prepare complete media plans and produce creative executions based on the strategies that they recommend for the client. Such artifacts often wind up in students' portfolios as evidence of their experience with campaign development and potential as researchers, media planners, strategic thinkers, or "creatives." In short, this most "applied" course within the advertising curriculum is also considered by students to be one of the most valuable in helping them get their first job.

Position of the Course in the Curriculum

Most advertising programs offer an Advertising Campaigns course. Typical class size is 20, and it is offered as a capstone course to be taken only after all or most other advertising requirements have been completed; consequently the vast majority of students enrolled in the course are seniors (Applegate and Parente, 1996).

Typically, advertising students begin their major coursework with an Introduction to Advertising course, which is usually followed, at the very least, by courses in creativity (graphics and copywriting), media planning, and sometimes by electives such as retail advertising or advertising management. Traditionally located at the end of the advertising sequence, most courses offer students the opportunity to apply all that they have learned in their previous coursework—to "put it all together." The campaigns course usually differs from most of the advertising student's previous coursework in several important ways. First, it is, at its core, a course that is more about application of relevant knowledge and skills than simply their acquisition. Second, the course traditionally requires students to hone and develop key communication skills, both interpersonal and presentation related. Third, the course challenges students to take more responsibility for their own learning and performance than any other course in the advertising curriculum. Although all of these factors demand a great deal of maturity and motivation from students, designing a course that will challenge students to do their best work requires a great deal of consideration and planning on the part of the advertising educator.

Approaches to the Course

The first step in planning an Advertising Campaigns course is determining the overall template that the course will follow. Most instructors adopt one of two commonly used approaches to teaching advertising campaigns. Some require their students to develop an advertising (or IMC) campaign for a selected real-world client (local, regional or national), whereas others have their classes participate in one of the national campaigns-based student competitions. A few instructors have even designed their courses to incorporate elements of both these strategies.

The 1996 survey of Advertising Campaigns teachers revealed that 56 percent had employed an actual product or service after contacting the advertiser, 50 percent had used the American Advertising Federation campaign competition case, 30 percent had employed an actual product or service without contacting the advertiser, and 18 percent had used a fictitious product or service (Applegate and Parente, 1996).

The Client-Based Campaigns Class

The mechanics of the client-based course are simple: A local, regional or national advertiser is identified who wants (or simply needs, in someone's opinion) a new advertising campaign. Students are faced with the challenge of solving problems that face their client by achieving specific objectives. Working in competing teams during the semester, students develop an advertising (or IMC) campaign for the client. At the end of the semester, the client (or designated surrogates) listens to each team's presentation (or "pitch") and selects one team's proposal as the best or most appropriate solution. In short, student teams operate as advertising agencies in competition for a single client's account, and only one team will "win the account."

Arranging a Client for the Class

Instructors can find interesting, challenging clients for their campaigns courses in a number of different ways. Experienced campaigns instructors cite a number of unique, successful methods for selecting a client. Wayne Hilinski, senior lecturer at the Pennsylvania State University, reports using the Accounts In Review lists from *Advertising Age* and *Adweek* as choices for his students to consider. This method also allows students to "track trade news about their client and often know where the account wound up at the end of the semester." It is more common, however, for instructors to make final client decisions because of concerns about how closely the students' work for a particular client will mesh with their own educational objectives. Sometimes, working on a client's campaign gives students the opportunity to explore sectors of the business world that they have not encountered in earlier courses. Advertising education is full of examples of the promotion of packaged goods and services.

The class client, on the other hand, could be in need of a business-to-business campaign, an opportunity Michael Little at the University of Alabama pursues actively because he sees it as "something brand new" for the student to deal with. "A business-to-business campaign also gives the student an opportunity to plan the buying of space in business magazines, a large and important medium that's largely invisible in earlier coursework," Little says. Alabama assistant professor Tom Reichert's approach to client selection also results in a relatively novel experience for students. He arranges for his class to work on a government-sponsored "social marketing campaign." Examples include an HIV/AIDS-awareness campaign sponsored by the state health department and an organ-donation campaign sponsored by a division of the U.S. Department of Health and Human Services.

The larger the geographic scope of the client's operations is, the greater are the opportunities for the students to learn. Obviously, national advertisers have larger budgets with which they can reach vaster audiences than local advertisers. Don Parente, an advertising professor at Middle Tennessee State University and author of *Advertising Campaign Strategy: A Guide to Marketing Communication Plans*, prefers "clients that offer multiple media." A larger client often means a larger and more varied allocation of the media budget.

Jim Avery's first preference is that the "client . . . be national so that students can learn media allocation. Only national clients afford the decision making process of national versus local allocations. Second, they cannot appeal only to a student age group. Students need to learn to get outside themselves. Third, they must be willing to make a contribution to the student's learning. They must come to [the campus] to judge the work."

The first consideration in choosing a client correlates significantly with the amount of control that the instructor wishes to have over the students' overall learning experience. If students are going to work for an actual client and take an active, cooperative role (meeting with the students and evaluating their work), then the instructor should understand that this level of involvement would have a dramatic influence on the potential quality and success of the course. Such a *cooperating* client can offer students unmatched insight for what it is really like to create a campaign that meets a client's specifications. A cooperating client may also decide to implement the students' ideas or even hire a member of the class.

These clients can also be unreasonable, unavailable or downright *un*cooperative when both the instructor and the students rely on them so heavily to make the class work. Also, since many clients who agree to cooperate with campaigns courses are local or regional advertisers with relatively small promotional budgets, this factor may prohibit students from even considering some traditional campaign elements, such as broadcast television commercials, sweepstakes or direct-marketing strategies. Nevertheless, working with a cooperating client lends the greatest level of authenticity to the students' experience. But choosing a client involves more than just finding a local business eager to get some free marketing advice. Some potential clients (particularly nonprofit organizations) are actually looking for help with publicity only, which is a task better suited for the public relations campaigns class.

If an instructor wants to retain more personal control with regard to the student-client relationship, a written client case study can provide students with an overview of the same kinds of information they would likely receive during face-to-face client meetings. Instructors may engage a cooperating client's help in drafting such a document, or choose a client and create the case study independently. This approach has obvious advantages, the greatest among them being that the course cannot effectively collapse due to an uncooperative or difficult client's involvement. A case study can also be "engineered" by the instructor to incorporate specific challenges for the students. The downside to this approach is that students will not have the experience of regular, face-to-face interactions with their client. However, an instructor may enlist faculty or industry professionals as client representatives charged with evaluating the students' work at the end of the semester and choosing a "winning" campaign from the class. Case studies often work best with national clients for logistical reasons. Also, a national client with a hefty advertising budget will enable students to "go all out" with their recommendations.

Initial Lectures

Even though the campaigns course is primarily designed to give students the opportunity to draw upon all of their previous coursework and put it into practice, it is a good idea to provide the class with an overview of campaign development and the unique issues relating to this kind of work.

Placing Students in Teams

Most campaigns courses organize the students into teams for two primary reasons. First, since course sections often accommodate 20 students or more, it is usually impractical for that many students to work as a group on the campaign project because there are "too many cooks in the kitchen." Second, dividing the class into smaller teams or *agency groups* sets up the in-class competition for the client's account. While some may quibble about the potentially negative aspects of competition in the classroom, most teachers of campaigns courses seem to believe that the competitive element creates excitement and helps motivate students to do their best work. It also offers students a more realistic sense for how things work in the real world. The in-class competition does not, however, amount to the winner-takes-all scenario typical to industry. More discussion on this point will come later.

In selecting teams, it is important to ensure that different student interest, expertise and talents (e.g., media planning, copywriting, editing, graphics, production, research, people skills, organizational abilities) are equally represented in each team. The first day of class is typically a get-to-know-each-other session during which students are asked about the various work functions of advertising they most like to perform and what particular talents they think they have. Some instructors ask students to indicate their preferences regarding which people in the class they would like to have as teammates, while others make these assignments independently. The teacher can spend a few days confirming students' interests and talents (e.g., by checking students' grades in earlier skills courses or by asking colleagues) and assigning students to teams using diversity of team members' talents and interests. A word of warning: Sometimes close friends do not make the best teammates. John Murphy, professor of advertising at the University of Texas at Austin, cites team-member conflicts as perhaps the "biggest challenge" in teaching the Advertising Campaigns course, but he encourages his students "to solve their own problems" in that regard. He encourages his students to understand how different personalities interact in group work and reports that most of his students "respond appropriately" once the issue is addressed. So it seems prudent for the instructor to focus primarily on balancing teams in terms of skill and expertise rather than trying to accommodate students' personal preferences.

Organizing the teams is easiest when the course enrollment figure is easily divisible into same-sized groups. For example, a class of 20 students can have four five-student teams or five four-student teams. On the other hand, a class of 17 or 19 students will necessarily have teams of different sizes. There is no magic number for team membership, although four-member or five-member teams are most common. Teams of more than five members will inevitably lead to an inordinate amount of "social loafing" by one or more students. Teams of fewer than four works only if all team members are drawn from among the most motivated and most talented students.

Some instructors designate a *leader* or *account executive* for each classroom team. Account executives can help the instructor by monitoring attendance and participation by all members of the team and keeping the instructor apprised of each team's progress during the semester. The instructor should describe the account executive's role as organizational, not dictatorial. An account executive's position is not necessarily secure, and an ineffective executive may be "fired" by the teacher or by the team. In asking students whether they would like to be considered for the account executive position, Middle Tennessee State University's Don Parente also notes that the position's extra workload may earn extra credit toward an "A." Still, he says, many students opt out of volunteering for the position. Once he has picked account executives for teams, Parente gives them information on class members' self-reported past experience and preferences for specific positions on the team; then the account executives select their teams following the time-honored method of a "football draft."

Within their own teams, students may wish to give themselves agency titles corresponding to their areas of personal expertise, such as *media planner*, *creative director* or *account executive*. There is nothing inherently wrong with this as long as the students understand that everyone should be willing (and able) to help with all parts of the campaign.

Meeting with the Client

If the class is working with a cooperating client, client representatives should be brought in at the beginning of the semester to talk to the students. Before making a presentation to the class, the client is normally briefed by the instructor regarding the kinds of information the students will need to get started on the campaign project. First, the client is expected to communicate the problem to the class in specific terms. For example, is there an awareness problem? Is there a specific competitive problem? Is there a problem with the current media being used? Or does the client want a totally different, but very broadly defined, approach to speaking to consumers? Second, the client should provide the students with a specific budget (e.g., the total amount of money they want to spend on implementing any campaign) and the length of time they want a campaign to run (e.g., 12 months or 6 months). Third, a client representative should be designated as a contact person for the students. This person should be willing to meet with students at scheduled intervals during the semester and able to provide answers to their questions.

The class should also be briefed about the client's visit beforehand. Students should be made aware that clients have busy schedules and that they can communicate with students only with advance notice. It is generally a good idea to have students prepare their own lists of questions for the client prior to this initial meeting. Each team should also designate a client liaison who will make all contacts with the client representative throughout the semester. This helps to reduce the likelihood that the client will feel harassed by too many student inquiries.

After the client makes a presentation (delivers the "brief"), the instructor should review the client's presentation with the class and discuss any lingering questions or concerns. Following the initial client meeting, some teachers end meetings with the class as a whole and move to a schedule of weekly meetings with individual teams. Others may continue to meet with the whole class for a few more weeks.

At any rate, there comes a point where the teams have their work cut out for them: prepare a marketing plan, develop a creative strategy, come up with a media plan, allocate the budget, finalize the creative executions, and rehearse the presentation (or "pitch") to the client. Other than those required by the instructor, student teams schedule their own meetings.

Campaign Research

A great deal of primary and secondary research is to be expected in the development of any campaign. In the campaigns course, some instructors allow the entire class to collaborate on the primary research effort (e.g., a consumer survey or focus groups); each team then gets a copy of the findings and uses the information separately. Other instructors require each team to do its own research. Since research plays such an important role in understanding the client and developing strategy, it can be argued that team-based research should be part of the competitive experience. However it is conducted, students should be given a specific time frame in which to complete their primary and secondary research. Generally, research should be completed within the first six weeks of the semester to use the results to plan strategy and tactics. If team assignments are made by the first or second class meeting, research can begin immediately, even as the initial lectures are being delivered.

The research conducted by students may be of particular interest to the client, more so than the campaign itself. Middle Tennessee State University's Parente often uses the potential findings of effort to be undertaken by the class to "sell the client on the idea." Alabama's Michael Little agrees that even if the clients don't use the campaign's media plans and creative executions, they often find great value in the consumer or market research information collected by the students. Sometimes the value of such research is in confirming a client's hunch about customers or in gaining insight into a neglected segment of the market.

Compensation

Some schools receive a monetary donation from the client in exchange for the students' (and the instructor's) time and effort on their behalf. This honorarium may be presented to the student ad club or directly to the academic department. The client might also agree to cover any reasonable expenses that the students incur during work on their campaigns. Eighteen percent of teachers surveyed by Applegate and Parente (1996, p. 235) indicated that the client had compensated their ad campaigns class. Such compensation can range from $500 to $1,000 contributions to a development/ scholarship fund, as is the case at Middle Tennessee State University (reported by Don Parente of the MTSU advertising faculty), to a few thousand dollars, as is the case at the University of Florida (Pisani, 1996, p. 228).

The Competition-Based Campaigns Course

Some students are given the opportunity to participate in a national advertising competition for a big-name national client. The competition format is beneficial to clients, who can obtain fresh ideas presented by dozens of teams made up of some of the brightest advertising students. It is also beneficial to students, particularly those teams winning or placing in the competitions.

Typically, a few months before a competition starts, advertising faculty members are sent competition details and are provided with information on how to participate and how to order the competition cases. Each competition has set rules that need to be followed for student teams to be eligible. These range in importance from the required color of the plan's bookbinder to the types of media placements that are acceptable.

We will not present an outline for a competition-based class, because the basic components of a competition-based campaign are not very different from what has just been described. Typically, these contests require submission of a bound document that includes a marketing plan, a creative strategy, a media plan and budget, and samples of creative executions. In a competition-based class, greater demands are often made of the teacher's time by comparison to the level of involvement required in a client-based course. In this scenario, the amount of time students are given to develop a campaign may be significantly compressed, requiring lots of extracurricular meetings and effectively turning the instructor into a "coach."

The American Advertising Federation's National Student Advertising Competition

Many advertising, mass communication, journalism and marketing departments around the country reserve a special section of their Advertising Campaigns course for students who want to participate in the American Advertising Federation's (AAF's) National Student Advertising Competition (NSAC). Called the College World Series of Advertising, the NSAC format invites students across the country to prepare a national campaign for a national client. Past clients have included such well-known national brands as American Airlines, Folger's Coffee, Burger King, Levi's, Hallmark Cards, Kodak, Toyota, and the *New York Times*.

To compete in the NSAC, students need to be members of the local college chapter of the AAF. Case studies are distributed to participating schools early in the fall semester, and some student teams begin working on the project immediately. Most participating colleges and universities, however, organize teams in the fall and offer a special campaigns course section in the spring that is devoted to the competition. Written campaign proposals or *plans books* are usually due in March, giving most teams a great deal of work to do in a very short time.

Because the development of an NSAC campaign can be so intensive and time-consuming, most schools select relatively small teams (eight to 15 members) based on competitive interviews. Consequently, most NSAC team members represent the brightest students from a particular program. Although most of these students are undergraduates with no prior experience in developing a campaign, some may have already taken a regular campaigns course and be selected for the NSAC team as well. In these cases, the academic department may enroll students in an independent study or special topics course as a means for giving them course credit. Graduate students are also allowed to participate in the NSAC in limited roles. Approximately 200 teams compete in the NSAC in an average year (Marra et al., 1997, p. 21).

When selecting an NSAC team competitively, it is advisable to establish some objective criteria for the selection process (e.g., individual interviews, evidence of prior work in the form of class projects or portfolios, recommendations from colleagues, and grades in skills courses). Students should also fully understand the extensive time and effort that will be required of them. John Murphy, advisor to the NSAC team at the University of Texas at Austin, admits that the competition "is a killer" but also calls the NSAC "the best situation" for teaching the campaigns course. Despite the endless hours of work and the heated competition involved, Murphy insists that "out of the blood come important lessons."

Once the students have prepared and submitted a written campaign proposal to the AAF, they then have two to four weeks to prepare a client presentation for the regional competition held in their home "district." Competition winners from each of the AAF's 15 districts send one student team to the AAF national conference in June.

We should note that, although the NSAC is an opportunity for a select number of students to gain good preparation for the real world, sometimes "faculty believe that too much focus is placed on too few students" (Vanden Bergh, 1996, p. 227). The five students who participate in the presentation portion of the competition are perceived as receiving a lot of attention. The matter of fairness then comes up, since the NSAC team tends to receive greater advisor time than other campaign classes, and the presenting members of the team tend to receive more attention than other members. Further pros and cons of using the NSAC are discussed by Cogan (1996), Jordan (1996), Parente (1996), Pisani (1996) and Stutts (1996).

Still, the competition is viewed by many as an excellent instructional device, and both communication and business schools enter teams in the NSAC each year. In some cases, the competition is a campuswide effort. For example, at Southwest Texas State University (twice national winners and often in the top three in the regional competition) "approximately 20 students are selected from the following majors: Marketing, Technology, Advertising, Art, Public Relations, and Photography" (Stutts, 1996, p. 229). The rationale is that an interdisciplinary team is well suited for the recent integrated marketing communication plans required of the campaign. Clearly, then, even liberal arts students can participate in the NSAC. Music students can compose and record jingles, art students can help with visuals, and theater students can help with makeup and sets when shooting commercials. Such diversity in the composition of the NSAC team is exemplary of the kind of interdisciplinary efforts prized by college and university administrators and typical of the divergent areas that unite to create all advertising campaigns.

The Leonard J. Raymond Collegiate Echo Competition

The Direct Marketing Association (DMA, based in New York City), through its Direct Marketing Educational Foundation (DMEF), sponsors the annual Leonard J. Raymond Collegiate Echo competition. *Echo* is the name of the direct-marketing industry's annual "Oscars", and the collegiate-level competition gives college students yet another opportunity to prepare a national campaign for a national client. Although the emphasis is on direct-response efforts, most campaigns prepared for this competition include a significant component of media-based advertising as well.

Past clients have included HBO/Cinemax, American Express, the United States Postal Service, Pitney Bowes, and Publishers Clearinghouse. Students can work on this competition project in the fall term (due date in December) or in the spring term (due date in April). Undergraduate and graduate teams are evaluated together, but awards may be given in separate undergraduate and graduate categories. There is no limit to the number of teams a university may enter, but team size is limited to four students. In a first round of judging, the top 10 percent of all teams are selected as semifinalists. A second round determines the ultimate winners, who are announced in late June of each year. First-place (Gold Echo), second-place (Silver Echo), and third-place (Bronze Echo) awards are given each year, together with awards for Best Marketing Strategy, Best Creative Strategy, Best Media Plan, and Best Budget. In recent years, honorable mentions have also been awarded. More than 150 teams have participated in the competition annually, so even being named among the semifinalists (approximately the top 16 to 18 teams) is a considerable achievement worthy of listing on a student's résumé.

At the University of Florida, "using the Echo competition as a campaigns course has evolved from offering a course called 'Direct Response and Sales Promotion Writing.' This course was originally created as a professional elective," says Lisa Duke, whose teams have won the Echo competition. "Given the extensive nature of the competition and the growing demand for our campaigns class, we decided to allow students to take the course as a substitute for campaigns. Students have the opportunity to take the class as a professional elective or as a campaigns' course.

"This means our Echo Competition class helps the department achieve two goals . . . (1) to give students the opportunity to synthesize and apply their class knowledge to the development of an advertising campaign and (2) to give students the opportunity to broaden their learning experience beyond traditional advertising. In short, the course . . . helps us add breadth and depth to our students' learning experiences."

Other Competitions

Other student competitions have been sponsored by a variety of companies and industry groups. However, most of these are more limited in scope than the AAF's NSAC or the Collegiate Echo competition, so they are better suited as supplementary projects to advertising campaigns classes that are not built around a single major campaign project. Past examples of such projects have included the Yellow Pages Student Creative Competition, sponsored by the Yellow Pages Publishers' Association based in Troy, Michigan, and the Promotional Products National Collegiate Competition, sponsored by Promotional Products Association International based in Dallas (Parker, 2000).

The Halo Effect of Success in Competitions

Sometimes a program's success in national competitions has an additional positive effect on programs that use the competition in one section of campaigns and local or regional clients in others. At the University of Alabama, Mike Little used to have to work at soliciting local and regional clients for his section of the Advertising Campaigns course. "Then Alabama won the NSAC nationals," Little said, "and I didn't have to go look for clients any more. Now companies contact me and ask if they could become clients for the class."

Variants of the Two Methods

Some teachers adopt a teaching method for the Advertising Campaigns course that combines some of the items just discussed. For example, a campaign for a local client could be supplemented with readings from case studies, or participation in the Collegiate Echo competition could be combined with a series of lectures on Integrated Marketing Communications.

Special Features

Sections of a Traditional Plans Book

Since the written campaign proposal or plans book constitutes the major assignment for most advertising campaigns courses, we offer an overview of the major sections of a campaign plans book here with brief commentary on how to present these sections to students.

Marketing Plan

This section typically includes a situation analysis, including a SWOT (strengths, weaknesses, opportunities, threats) analysis, identification and description of target audience(s), and campaign objectives. The marketing plan should also describe the research done by the team and offer detailed findings. It is very helpful to explain to students that the situation analysis is based on a thorough examination of the *client* (i.e., the company and the brand), the *competition* (i.e., competing companies, competing brands, and competing products) and the *consumer* (i.e., markets and consumer segments).

Creative Strategy and Tactics

Immediately following the completion of the marketing plan, students develop and articulate the campaign's creative strategy. Not surprisingly, many students attempt to jump to this stage of the campaign process from day one. For this reason, it is useful to explain early on the importance of setting objectives before developing the creative strategy. It is important to define good creative work as *smart* creative work—work that is based on an in-depth understanding of the product, the client and the consumer. Students should be reminded that their research findings should also be reflected in their creative strategy.

Media Strategy and Tactics

Once the creative strategy has been determined, students need to plan the media mix that will deliver that strategy. Again, some students attempt to jump to this stage of the campaign process from day one. For this reason, it is useful to explain the importance of determining the target audience(s) before developing the media strategy. Additionally, creative strategy may significantly influence media selection. This section of the written plan should not only indicate vehicle selection but also provide a time line for when various media will run and how media and other promotional activities may overlap. Rationale should be provided for all strategic and tactical decisions. For most IMC campaigns, other promotional activities (sales promotion, database marketing, publicity, personal selling, etc.) are also articulated within the media plan.

Budget

It is important for the students to remember (and they do need to be reminded) that their expenditures must stay within the budget limits set by the client. The instructor should provide students with a list of the specific line items that need to be represented in the budget. Students should understand the level of detail and accuracy (Do we round up to the nearest dollar? A hundred dollars? A thousand?) that the instructor expects. Also, since students do not have access to some specific media pricing information, they should be advised regarding when it is appropriate to estimate costs.

Creative Executions

Students should have ample lab time to complete their creative executions. At schools that routinely teach some advertising classes in computer labs, it is useful to reserve at least some laboratory hours for campaign students. To give students an idea of the level of "finish" expected in the course, it is helpful to show them examples of student work from previous campaigns classes. Students should also be reminded that they will be expected to show samples of their creative work both in their written proposal and in their client presentation.

Evaluation

A good campaign plan should include some reference to how the students intend to measure whether their campaign objectives were met. It is important for the students (and sometimes for the client) to understand that they will be proposing ways to evaluate the success of the campaign in terms of the advertising objectives (not the marketing objectives) set at the end of the marketing plan.

The Book Itself

The marketing plan, creative strategy, media plan, budget, and evaluation are collected in a bound *plans book*. Two things need to be communicated to students in this context. First, the report must have a professional appearance and be free of grammatical, syntactical and factual errors. Second, the report should be more than just a collection of sections written by different team members. Different students may have different articulation styles, which may make the report difficult to read. At least one student should edit the report thoroughly before it is submitted, ensuring uniformity of language and continuity from one section to the next. In fact, students should be admonished from the first day of class that a team project is a team responsibility and that applies to the campaign report, to the creative executions, and to the final presentation.

The Presentation

Once the written plan is completed and submitted, students should immediately begin planning their presentations to the client. Students should be cautioned not to start working on their presentation before finishing their written plan, since that document usually constitutes a much larger percentage of their course grade and needs to be as good as it can be. One thing that cannot be stressed enough toward the end of the campaign: Students must rehearse their presentation and should rehearse repeatedly!

The instructor should pace the course so that they have a week or so to do that. An unrehearsed presentation is the kiss of death for student teams.

Before the teams deliver their proposals (and ideally before they begin planning them), the client and the students should be briefed separately about how student presentations are structured. Clients may need to be told that they have to select only one team after the presentations are completed (although some campaigns teachers prefer to not let the client pick one campaign as the best). Clients and students need also to be reminded about a college's or university's policy regarding the ownership of the students' work. If no other arrangements have been made, team members are collective owners of the campaign, and they are free to give it or part of it to the client in exchange for an agreed-upon remuneration.

It is a good idea to provide students with a sample outline that they can use to structure their presentation. In many cases, students try to include too much information (i.e., present every detail of their campaign) in the brief presentation time frame. If available, it is also a good idea for the instructor to show students a tape of a well-executed client presentation. Students should be briefed about the mechanics of a presentation, such as the importance of incorporating visual aids (e.g., storyboards, slides, charts, overheads, and PowerPoint) into their presentation.

Some students feel uncomfortable if other teams are present when they make their presentation to the client. For that reason, it is sometimes (but not always) advisable to have each presentation with only the client representative(s), the presenting team, and the teacher present. The class can meet at a later time for the teams to present their work to each other. Normally, all of the team members are expected to participate in the presentation. Some instructors set a time limit for presentations (e.g., 20 to 30 minutes), followed by question-and-answer session with the client (e.g., 10 to 20 minutes). MTSU's Parente allows about an hour for each team's presentation and encourages the client's representative(s) to interrupt and ask questions during the presentation. Whatever the format, it is important that two-way communication take place between the student teams and the client.

After the last presentation, the client takes some time to make a decision, after which the class is assembled and the client announces the winning team. This is the most difficult part for the client. Even the most hard-nosed business people sometimes find it hard to disappoint students who have invested so much time and effort on their behalf.

Evaluation in the Advertising Campaigns Course

Often, grades earned by students in the course reflect the evaluation of team effort to a much greater extent than they reflect individual effort. Due to the nature of the course, this is to be expected and, given the importance of teamwork in the advertising business, it is not necessarily a bad thing. However, for instructors who wish to do so, there are methods for making individual performance a greater part of students' final grades. The most commonly used strategy is the incorporation of a *peer evaluation* component to the grading criteria. Using this method, instructors can require each team member to provide assessments of their colleagues' performance at the end of the term. It is recommended that the instructor develop specific criteria, including such things as attendance, preparedness, quality of work, level of participation, and willingness to cooperate and compromise. This provides a guide for their assessments.

Some instructors use peer evaluation to determine as much as 10 percent of the students' final course grades in an effort to emphasize the importance of cooperation and collaboration. Students also appreciate that their own hard work (or lack thereof) will be recognized apart from group evaluation.

Some teachers (e.g., Wardrip, 1996) assign individual grades as each part of the campaign process is completed (creative strategy, media plan, budget, etc.). "Admittedly, this slows the campaign development process somewhat, but that's what this course is all about: learning the process and not just completing the plans book" (Wardrip, 1996, p. 43). One way to avoid this slowdown is to have the students complete short individual assignments during the initial lectures that address the material being reviewed. For example, on a day when the instructor plans to teach how to write clear and concise campaign objectives, students might be given a homework assignment requiring them to rewrite some poorly written ones.

On the syllabus, students expect to see a breakdown for how their final course grade will be determined. Here's a sample from one campaigns course at the University of Alabama:

Individual assignments	25 percent
Class participation	15 percent
Peer evaluation	10 percent
Agency campaign	50 percent*
(Written plan, 40 percent; oral presentation, 10 percent)	
Total	100 percent

*The winning team receives perfect score automatically.

In this scenario, a full 40 percent of each student's grade is determined by individual performance. Peer evaluation, an accountability measure, is assessed equivalent to a full letter grade. The agency campaign, which incorporates both the written plan (40 percent) and the presentation to the client (10 percent), constitutes half of the overall grade. In this particular course, the instructor awarded a perfect score to the "winning" team automatically. Other teams received a grade calculated from both instructor and client evaluations. The *perfect score* technique is a great way to motivate all of the teams to do their best work. Of course, the instructor still grades all plans and provides each team with feedback on its work, regardless of whichever team wins.

We should note that awarding more points or a better grade to a student campaign solely because the client picked it as the best is not a universal practice. "What if the client picks a poor campaign?" MTSU's Parente asks, a question echoed by other colleagues. Indeed, especially at the local level, the students' potential ability to psych and dazzle an unsophisticated client with a mediocre (or worse) effort must not be discounted. "The day I stopped having the client pick the best campaign, the students started feeling better about the course," Parente says.

In addition to this breakdown of their overall course grade, campaigns students should also be provided with a detailed list of the grading criteria to be used in evaluating their written plans and presentations. Criteria for a plans book and a presentation include evaluation of the mechanics of the plan itself—*grammar, spelling, punctuation, adherence to plan outline, and the overall neatness of presentation*—as well as the level of research *and* objectives, the creative strategy, and the advertising media plan. Important items would include a budget summary, and direct response would be evaluated along with public relations and promotional plan and the creative executions. For the presentation, we would consider items such as *mechanics of the pitch, overall sales effectiveness, creativity, the use of the proper format, audiovisual presentation, familiarity and comfort with the material, and the quality of responses during the question-and-answer period.*

Timetable for the Advertising Campaigns Class

Below is a simple week-by-week suggested timetable for the Advertising Campaigns course, based on a 15-week semester. It is not necessarily typical but provided as a general guide for planning:

Week 1   Get-acquainted class. Ascertain the students' strengths and weaknesses. Secure the client.

Week 2   Review weak areas. Brief the client. Brief the students about the client. Make team assignments.

Week 3   Client presentation to class; question-and-answer session afterward.

Week 4   Go over the client's brief with the entire class; start research effort.

Week 5   Start meeting with individual teams.

Week 6   Discuss the marketing plan.

Week 7   Individual marketing plans are due.

Week 8   Return the individual marketing plans. Discuss weaknesses in individual plans.

Week 9   Teams' marketing plans are due. Go over creative strategy.

Week 10 Creative strategy is due. Go over the media plan and the budget.

Week 11 Media plan and budget are due. Go over the final ideas for creative executions.

Week 12 Preliminary creative executions are due.

Week 13 Campaign report and final versions of creative executions are due. Teams rehearse presentation. Brief the client about next week's presentation.

Week 14 Presentations to the client; the client's decision; distribute peer evaluation forms.

Week 15 Meet as a class for teams to show each other their work; collect completed peer evaluation forms.

Final Comments About Clients

There is a lot to be gained from reading about how allied disciplines handle problems similar to those encountered in the advertising campaigns course. Here we give two examples:

1. Kelly (1997) discusses how marketing students at Colorado State University not only plan and propose but also *implement* (i.e., run the ads in the media) *and evaluate* a campaign for a paying client.

2. Aldoory and Wrigley's (2000) discussion of using real clients in the Public Relations Campaigns course is useful reading for the Advertising Campaigns teacher as well.

Comparative Features

Assessing Student Preparation

As previously discussed, the campaigns course gives students the opportunity to integrate subject matter they learned in their other advertising classes. Their cumulative understanding for the business and how its different areas interrelate is usually demonstrated via their development of a single major campaign project. In large part, the success of campaigns course depends on the prior knowledge that the students bring into the classroom. There is simply not enough time for the instructor to reteach all of the advertising material relevant to campaign work.

In many cases, however, instructors find that students do need to brush up in particular subject areas before feeling prepared to tackle a campaign. It is not unusual, and perhaps even advisable, for instructors of campaigns courses to offer some review of key content and skills of particular importance to campaign planning and implementation. For maximum efficiency, the instructor might require students to provide suggestions of areas where they feel least competent as a guide for planning "refresher" lectures. In any case, it is important for the instructor to try to ascertain the students' level of preparation for work that they will be doing over the rest of the semester.

Methods for Reviewing Key Information

To provide students with a review of key concepts, some teachers include a discussion of case studies as part of the Advertising Campaigns course, usually during the first half of the semester. This may be particularly helpful in programs that do not offer a separate Cases in Advertising or an Advertising Management course. Whether delivered in the form of cases or topic-driven lectures, most campaign students will benefit greatly from in-class exercises on issues like selecting target audiences or writing campaign objectives. Too often, students want to rush into working on creative executions or selecting media vehicles, so emphasizing the importance of some of the crucial front-end activities can prevent neglect of these important steps in campaign development.

Another method for giving students trial-run experiences in the campaigns course is through the assignment of a minicampaign early in the course (Pasadeos, 1987). This allows students to make—and correct—some typical mistakes (e.g., mistargeting or misbudgeting) with less disastrous consequences for their final course grades. Instructors who use this method report that the kinds of errors made in these initial plans are seldom repeated on the major campaign project.

Common Challenges/Solutions

In addition to synthesizing previous coursework and offering students a real-world simulation, the Advertising Campaigns course has two other important pedagogical objectives: campaigns students will come to understand the highs and lows associated with (a) *competition* and (b) *cooperation*. Often, students enter the campaigns course with little appreciation for how challenging these aspects of campaign work can be. After all, every student has heard these terms before, and each has been involved in some kind of competition or taken part in some cooperative effort in their past.

So what makes the competitive and cooperative elements of the campaigns course different? Why do some students experience a sort of culture shock when faced with developing a campaign with their peers? The simple fact is that, as young adults, most students have been more passively than actively involved as competitors or participants in cooperative experiences. The stakes are higher here. There are grades involved, and many of the students are in their last semesters and must pass the course to graduate. Many students are anxious when they learn that their fate is in many ways tied to the performance of others.

Few are sufficiently aware of the zero-sum nature of the competition among advertising agencies, nor do they really appreciate the *systems* approach and teamwork involved in preparing an advertising campaign. In their previous coursework (e.g., media planning or copywriting), they have been given mostly individual assignments, which are evaluated on their strategic and/or creative merits. For many of the students, this experience will constitute one of their first opportunities to self-organize, self-motivate, and self-monitor their work. Instead of relying on an instructor to designate roles, specify plans, and coordinate meetings, these functions are now their responsibility. Along with the real-world nature of the course come higher expectations for self-regulated student performance.

According to Lisa Duke, assistant professor of advertising at the University of Florida, "One of the biggest challenges has been putting together the right teams. On the first day of class, I pass out an info sheet for students to complete, noting their work schedules, coursework completed, desired team positions; fairly standard information. In addition, I ask them to write a paragraph on their work style and strengths/weaknesses and to describe the work styles and strengths of the kinds of people with whom they might be most successfully teamed. Then, finally, I have them answer three questions regarding the most frequently occurring problems in team-oriented endeavors.

"All this information is collected, along with student résumés, and placed in a book. Students have one week to read through the book and pick their 'dream team' of three other people, along with backups for each team position. In the second week of class, we devote one class period to 'interviewing.' Students wear name tags. They interview people they saw in the book that most interested them as teammates. They submit their choices to me, and I team people as closely as I can with their choices."

Don Parente, of Middle Tennessee State University, sees four unique challenges associated with the course: (1) evaluation of students' work (by teacher and peers), (2) forming balanced teams, (3) monitoring students' progress throughout the semester, and (4) coaching them to do better work. "It is important to ensure that the students' work proceeds at an acceptable pace," he says. To monitor the quality of students' contribution to the plan book, Parente asks each student to initial the pages he or she has written and evaluates the work accordingly. He, like other campaigns teachers, requires weekly reports (some call them *memos* or *briefs*) of what the team and each member has been doing.

Outside Resources

A recent survey of advertising educators found that *comprehensive information* was the chief criterion for selecting an advertising campaign's textbook (mentioned by 45 percent of respondents). They found that 38 percent of teachers were dissatisfied with the advertising campaigns textbook they had adopted, and that "lack of teaching aids" (48 percent) and "inadequate information" (40 percent) were primary causes of dissatisfaction with the textbooks (Ha, 1999, pp. 39–41). These figures reveal two peculiarities of the course and of those teaching it. First, it makes sense that instructors want more comprehensive content in advertising campaigns textbooks, because campaigns involve just about everything related to the practice of advertising. The question is whether any textbook can deliver it all. Second, the fact that so many educators feel that teaching aids are inadequate reveals that the course may, too often, be assigned to junior faculty members. Senior faculty know that intuition, more than any teaching aid, is the most important attribute in dealing successfully with student teams and motivating individual students. In more ways than one, the Advertising Campaigns course may ultimately be less about teaching and more about coaching. In fact, in the best of all possible worlds, where students have understood and digested all the material in their earlier courses, a textbook might not even be necessary for the Advertising Campaigns course. Indeed, one educator survey found that many teachers did not assign a textbook (Applegate and Parente, 1996).

Still, most teachers find it necessary to assign a textbook, and for them three excellent textbooks are available, written by seasoned advertising educators: Avery's *Advertising Campaign Planning* (2000), Parente's *Advertising Campaign Strategy* (1999), or Schultz and Barnes' *Strategic Brand Communication Campaigns* (1999). After consecutive editions, all three now go far toward satisfying educational needs articulated by teachers. But do students read their textbook in the campaigns class? Not unless they are quizzed on it, according to MTSU's Parente and Alabama's Little. Both educators ensure the book is read by giving written quizzes on assigned chapters.

The most widely used resource other than a textbook is *Standard Rate and Data Service*, used by 92 percent of programs surveyed by Applegate and Parente (1996, p. 235).

Conclusions

The Advertising Campaigns course will likely continue to evolve in an effort to keep pace with a rapidly changing industry. It continues to offer educators great opportunities to innovate, challenge students, and serve the advertising community. Perhaps more than any other course in the curriculum, the campaigns course gives students a taste of the real world. Those who teach the course and those who take it all agree that it is different from anything else they have done before.

Teaching the Advertising Campaigns course requires a great deal of advanced planning and careful monitoring once the course is under way. This chapter sought to provide some suggestions to instructors based on the insights and advice of educators with significant experience in teaching this class. The course offers students the chance to prove their mettle as young advertising professionals. Most relish the chance to make their own decisions and work with less direct supervision. They also enjoy having the opportunity to present their campaigns at the end of a semester filled with work. As University of Texas at Austin's John Murphy puts it, "Students learn best in this course by doing. The professor sets up the projects and lets the students, working in groups, run with it."

References

Aldoory, L., and B. Wrigley. 2000. Exploring the use of real clients in the PR campaigns course. *Journalism and Mass Communication Educator* 54, no. 4:47–58.

Applegate, E., and D. Parente. 1996. Highlights of a survey on approaches to teaching campaigns. In *The proceedings of the 1996 Conference of the American Academy of Advertising*. Ed. G. B. Wilcox. Austin: University of Texas, 234–236.

Avery, J. 2000. *Advertising campaign planning*. 3rd ed. Chicago: Copy Workshop.

Benigni, V., and G. T. Cameron. 1999. Teaching PR campaigns: The current state of the art. *Journalism and Mass Communication Educator* 54, no. 2 (Summer):50–60.

Cogan, H. 1996. Small program—AAF winner. In *The proceedings of the 1996 Conference of the American Academy of Advertising*. Ed. G. B. Wilcox. Austin: University of Texas, 233–234.

Griffin, G., and Y. Pasadeos. 1998. The impact of integrated marketing communications on advertising and public relations education. *Journalism and Mass Communication Educator* 53, no. 2:4–18.

Ha, L. 1999. Advertising educators' textbook adoption practices. *Journal of Advertising Education* 3, no. 1 (Spring):35–43.

Jordan, T. 1996. Large program: National clients, AAF winner. In *The proceedings of the 1996 Conference of the American Academy of Advertising*. Ed. G. B. Wilcox. Austin: University of Texas, 232–233.

Kelly, K. 1997. Taking promotional campaigns beyond the planning stages. *Journal of Advertising Education* 2, no. 1 (Fall):85–87.

Marra, J., J. Avery, and M. A. Grabe. 1997. Student advertising competitions: Faculty advisor beliefs concerning the AAF national student advertising competition. *Journal of Advertising Education* 2, no. 1:21–33.

Moriarty, S., and T. Duncan. 1989. *How to create and deliver award winning advertising presentations*. Lincolnwood, Ill.: NTC Business.

Parente, D. 1996. The course or the competition? Teaching campaigns in a mid-sized program. In *The proceedings of the 1996 Conference of then American Academy of Advertising*. Ed. G. B. Wilcox. Austin: University of Texas, 230–231.

Parente, D. 1999. *Advertising campaign strategy*. Fort Worth, Texas: Harcourt.

Parker, B. J. 2000. Putting it all together: Effective participation in advertising competitions. *Journal of Advertising Education* 4, no. 1 (Spring):19–29.

Pasadeos, Y. 1987. Mini campaign smoothes bumps for advertising campaigns. *Journalism Educator* 42, no. 3 (Autumn):39–40.

Pisani, J. R. 1996. Large program with multiple sections and national clients. In *The proceedings of the 1996 Conference of then American Academy of Advertising.* Ed. G. B. Wilcox. Austin: University of Texas, 228–229.

Schultz, D. E., and B. E. Barnes. 1999. *Strategic brand communication campaigns.* Lincolnwood, Ill.: NTC Business.

Schultz, D. E., S. I. Tannenbaum, and R. F. Lauterborn. 1993. *Integrated marketing communications.* Lincolnwood, Ill.: NTC Business.

Stutts, M. A. 1996. Interdisciplinary AAF course—AAF winner. In *The proceedings of the 1996 Conference of the American Academy of Advertising.* Ed. G. B. Wilcox. Austin: University of Texas, 229–230.

Vanden Bergh, B. G. 1996. Running the AAF competition in an environment that doesn't really support it. In *The proceedings of the 1996 Conference of then American Academy of Advertising.* Ed. G. B. Wilcox. Austin: University of Texas, 227–228.

Wardrip, J. P. 1996. Ensuring individual student understanding in advertising campaign term projects. *Journal of Advertising Education* 1, no. 1 (Summer):43–45.

Selected Internet and Other Research Sources for Advertising Campaigns Students

Resources marked with an asterisk (*) are subscription- or membership-based and may be available to students if their college or university provides access.

Advertising

Advertising Age. www.adage.com.

The American Advertising Federation. The leading advertising trade association representing 50,000 professionals in the advertising industry. Operates a national network of 210 advertising clubs and connects the industry with an academic base through its 210 college chapters. Sponsors the National Student Advertising Competition (NSAC) annually. www.aaf.org.

*AdWeek.** www.adweek.com.

Advertising World. The largest clearinghouse for advertising and related sites on the internet. Maintained by the Department of Advertising at the University of Texas at Austin. advertising.utexas.edu/advertisingworld/index.asp.

Branding

Brandchannel.com. Online information exchange about branding, from Interbrand. www.brandchannel.com.

*Brandweek.** Coverage of America's top brands and marketing executives. www.brandweek.com.

Companies

Hoover's Online. Comprehensive database of information on both public and private companies as well as industry and market intelligence. www.hoovers.com.

PR Newswire. Searchable database of press releases from 40,000 organizations worldwide. www.prnewswire.com.

Consumers

KnowThis. Source for market research, marketing plans, and internet marketing. www.knowthis.com.

U.S. Census Bureau. Detailed demographic, geographic and other forms of information derived from the most recent U.S. Census. www.census.gov.

Direct Marketing

American List Counsel. Database of available mailing lists for direct marketers, with cost estimates. www.amlist.com.

Direct Marketing Educational Foundation. Academic program of the Direct Marketing Foundation and sponsor of the Collegiate ECHO Awards. www.the-dma.org/dmef.

Library Databases

ABI/INFORM

Dow Jones Interactive: Publications Library/Company & Industry Center

Lexis/Nexis Academic Universe

Media

Arbitron. Information on network and local market radio audiences, their retail, media and product patterns. Also measures audiences for webcasts, outdoor and cable. www.arbitron.com/home/content.stm.

Mediamark. Source for demographic, lifestyle, product usage and media information. www.mediamark.com.

Mediapost. Free tools, news and directories for media planning. www.mediapost.com.

Mediaweek.* Latest breaking news in the media business with analysis and commentary. www.mediaweek.com.

Simmons Market Research Bureau.* Market research covering more than 8,000 brands, 400 product categories, and all media venues. www.smrb.com.

Products

Epinions.com. Millions of products reviewed by real consumers. www.epinions.com.

The J.D. Power Consumer Center. Quality and customer satisfaction ratings from seven product categories, collected by J.D. Power & Associates. www.jdpower.com.

Planet Feedback. What consumers are saying about products, brands, companies and issues online. www.planetfeedback.com.

Remembering a Mentor:
Clifford G. Christians

John P. Ferré

I met Cliff Christians on a steamy summer Saturday in Champaign, Illinois. I had driven down from Chicago to attend a wedding with the woman I was seeing at the time. She and her friends were discussing dresses and shoes and such, and I was bored senseless. Looking for a reason to leave, I remembered that Clifford G. Christians, who had written the most penetrating article I'd read for my recent survey of media ethics, taught at the University of Illinois. The article, "Fifty Years of Scholarship in Media Ethics," which appeared in the *Journal of Communication*, is a classic. So in the off-chance that he could meet with me on such short notice, I called him at home, and he graciously invited me over. We spent the next two hours on his porch, sipping tea and deep in discussion about ethics and religion and media institutions, standards, and practices. By the time I left Cliff's house, it was clear to me that there was so much more to learn, and by the time I got back to Chicago, clear that I needed to return to Champaign to study with Cliff at the Institute of Communications Research. That's precisely what I did.

I took four of Cliff's courses: Proseminar in Communications, Qualitative Research Methods in Communications, Values and Communications Technologies, and Popular Culture. Each course was enlightening and engrossing, but the true gift that Cliff gave to me was his time, not just in the classroom, but also in the office and the coffee shop. During my first year, Cliff would meet me on Fridays at the Newman Center cafeteria for coffee and intense discussions about media ethics. These were absorbing one-on-one experiences that both challenged and encouraged me. How he found the time for these meetings I'll never know. In addition to his teaching and committee responsibilities, Cliff is always engaged in several scholarly projects and he travels frequently to attend conferences and to give invited papers. He is also a devoted husband and father—he used to deliver newspapers with one of his sons every morning at four—and an active member of his church. But he found the time somehow, and when we were deep in discussion, that was all that mattered. Cliff never seemed rushed or distracted. Those conversations eventually became the basis of an Oxford University Press book, *Good News: Social Ethics and the Press* (1993), which Cliff wrote with Mark Fackler and me after we had finished our dissertations and had taken academic positions elsewhere.

When Cliff, Mark, and I were writing *Good News*, we would periodically rendezvous at Cliff's house. We'd eat dinner and then clear the table and work late into

243

the night. By two or so in the morning, I would be bleary, so we'd call it a night—or rather, Mark and I would call it a night.

"What time should I wake you up?" Cliff would ask, putting a couple of thick accordion files onto the table "to get just a little more work done." At 7 a.m., Cliff would rouse us, ready for breakfast and a full day of work.

I've never ceased marveling at Cliff's graciousness or at his energy, discipline, and drive. In 2001, Cliff stepped down as Director of the Institute of Communications Research, a position he had held for 14 years, because the administrative duties had prevented him from concentrating enough on research and writing. "I'm involved in four different book projects and 10 different book chapters and essays, articles that are, in fact, behind deadline," he said apologetically.

Cliff wrote his dissertation on Jacques Ellul, a French philosopher who found in Western societies' idealization of efficiency the seeds of much inhumanity. Cliff found tremendous resonance in the observation that faith, love and joy distinguish us as human beings from the technologies that we create, that our humanity is antithetical to efficiency. Ask anyone who has studied with Cliff and you'll hear similar accounts of the hours he devotes to his students individually, of his love of learning, his modesty, his smile, his warmth, and his wise counsel. He is a model and an inspiration.

CHAPTER 14

Television Reporting and Producing

B. William Silcock

Introduction

Edwin O. Haroldsen, who taught newspaper reporting at Brigham Young University, once asked longtime CBS News anchorman Walter Cronkite what were the most important qualities that a reporter should have. Cronkite responded with three keys to success: "First, the young journalist must really want to be a journalist, and nothing more ... Second, he must be gifted with an insatiable curiosity about people ... Third, he must be ever skeptical, without becoming cynical."

"Cynicism," wrote Cronkite, "deadens the enthusiasm with which any good journalist approaches a story." Following Haroldsen, today's broadcast news instructors would do well to not only instill these three keys in their students, but also remain committed to the principles in teaching. Teachers of this course must want to teach for the purity of the profession's sake and not for ego aggrandizement or because they failed to make it in the business. Second, teachers must remain curious about the different ways that students learn, function and relate to the material. Third, teachers must watch out for cynicism, because the burnout factor in teaching can be just as real as those experienced grinding away in a newsroom.

The two prime goals for this chapter are (1) to help the beginning broadcast news teacher design a news course and (2) offer the veteran broadcast journalism professor new ways to improve an existing class. Insights offered by professors from six schools, detailed herein, help achieve these goals. Schools selected in consultation with the editors represent a wide geographic diversity, a mix of state and private institutions, and, most importantly, a variety of broadcast news curriculum models that allows for the student broadcast journalist to experience a near real-world newsroom setting.

The schools include the University of Missouri, the University of Texas at Austin, Brigham Young University, the University of Oregon, the University of Montana, and

Southern Illinois University at Carbondale. Instructors from these schools provided syllabi and answered questionnaires to explain their pedagogy. My own experiences teaching broadcast news since 1984 at Brigham Young, the University of Missouri, and the Cronkite School at Arizona State served as data-sifting process.

At first glance, combining this chapter's two subject topics—television reporting and producing—might seem as common as a breakfast of bacon and eggs. How can you have one without the other? In practice, broadcast journalism professors serve up television reporting and producing courses in a variety of ways, some distinctly different, some blended, in colleges and universities across America and overseas. Think of the many ways eggs can be cooked, scrambled, hard-boiled, or over easy, and one begins to understand the variety of creative ways and the complexity of teaching television reporting. To push the metaphor further, if bacon is akin to the producing course, a vast majority of schools eliminate this item altogether from the students' diet, citing it as too expensive. The producing course requires a lab experience duplicating as nearly as possible the decision-making pressure of a daily 30-minute, live newscast. The infrastructure necessary for this model is cost prohibitive.

For the stand-alone reporting course, a sophisticated menu appears at many schools. For instance, the School of Journalism at the University of Missouri offers a beginning broadcast reporting course, without an on-air lab component; a basic TV reporting course, including an eight-hour weekly lab shift as a reporter for KOMU-TV (NBC); and an advanced reporting course. In this final, elective course, Missouri students produce in-depth investigations, sometimes using hidden cameras, or develop a series of stories for sweeps' periods that are promoted and aired on Channel 8 newscasts. In the past, these series have included civic journalism projects that combined the resources of both broadcast and print reporters to cover such complex topics as health care and race.

Only a handful of schools offer a stand-alone producing course. Missouri's affiliation with NBC enables students in the producing class to have a multiweekly lab experience producing under deadline pressure in a variety of time periods. Working side by side with a teaching assistant and under faculty supervision, students in the class typically produce three newscasts a week: early morning, 6 p.m. and 10 p.m. Other schools also offering a separate and distinct producing class include, among others, Syracuse University, Ohio University, Brigham Young University, and Louisiana State University.

A challenge faced in teaching the producing class separately and distinctly from reporting is having a media outlet that provides a deadline-driven, "live" experience. Schools, such as Ohio University's E. W. Scripps School of Journalism, Southern Illinois University at Carbondale, Brigham Young, and New Mexico State, use their PBS channel to create a daily, live newscast that provides producers with this real-world experience. A third model, exemplified by Syracuse University and the University of Texas at Austin, uses a cable channel as a publishing outlet. Finally, a larger group of schools produce a weekly newscast that is taped rather than live and distributed over a public access channel. This is the model for the Walter Cronkite School of Journalism and Mass Communication at Arizona State University.

Many TV news directors cite that finding newscast producers is their most critical employment gap. If this is the case, then why are not more schools producing producers? According to Ken Fischer of Southern Illinois University at Carbondale, who has also taught at Ohio University, the University of Florida, and New Mexico State, "Part of the problem is twofold. Either the program is not as well developed or does not have enough resources."

By resources, Fischer means not only sufficient funds to sustain a broadcast media outlet with all of its expensive television equipment but also enough professional staffing to carry the workload in the local PBS newsrooms. He makes the distinction that newsroom operations with student-produced daily newscasts on PBS stations, and the University of Missouri's commercial operation, rely on professional staff to run the day-to-day newsroom activities. The faculties at these schools teach related classes and have lesser roles in the day-to-day operation.

For an academic department to launch a daily student newscast on a broadcast station, close attention must be paid to staffing and equipment. Beyond financial pressures, Fischer identified curriculum demands impacting the potential producing course: "One reason bigger programs do not have a separate producing class is because of accreditation. This limits the students' ability to have only so many classes within a major."

Whether the school combines reporting and producing or teaches the subjects separately, the broadcast news instructor faces three audiences: other faculty who are sometimes prejudiced against TV news; working news directors who offer a mixed chorus of opinions as to how the course should be taught; and the students themselves.

The first critical audience, the print faculty, too often either does not understand the nuances of reporting for the electronic media or harbors some prejudice against it. In the 21st century, as economic pressures force media to converge, issues surrounding this old fissure between print and broadcast have been exposed. There are many hopeful signs that the gap is beginning to close. Whereas it's beyond the scope of this chapter to deal fully with the issue (whose roots can be traced back to the radio–press wars of the 1930s), an earlier chapter in this volume focuses on convergence. Broadcast professors recognize that many valuable techniques can be learned from their print counterparts. Dale Cressman of Brigham Young University is a former newspaper reporter and television news producer who helped pioneer the school's converged student newsroom operation, Newsnet. It puts the student radio, television, newspaper and Web operation all in the same room.

Typically, TV news directors fall into two camps. The first is made up those who often work in small markets where they are eager to hire students for low salaries who can hit the ground running with basic skills needed to produce news packages to fill up newscasts. The second camp is comprised of those, often from larger markets, who speak more philosophically about the need for reporters not only to possess basic skills but also to bring sound knowledge to the newsroom. This enables reporters to confront tough subjects such as economics and politics. Thus, what is referred to as the *nomadic system* is perpetuated wherein students typically start in a small market, continually improving basic skills while gaining broad knowledge and ultimately migrating to a medium or larger market.

Progressing from the small to medium to large markets corresponds directly to an increase in salary. Students taught by broadcast news teachers know this migration system very well. Each student hopes she can launch her career in the lowest-numbered market to obtain a higher salary in a larger market as quickly as possible. As students secure jobs and become loyal alumni, a critical feedback loop is created for the broadcast news teacher. A source of fresh reporting examples by the alumni becomes an important instruction resource in any television reporting and producing course. The classroom student in turn sees the connection between the instructor and alumni and develops a sense of confidence and hope that, if the teacher helped forge the alumni's skills necessary to succeed in the business, then she likewise can achieve the same.

It is important that the current classroom students, who make up the third audience faced by teachers, remain the prime focus for the teachers. Students enter the classroom with high expectations, and within 14 weeks come to believe that the teacher can transform them into reporters. This happens as the teacher helps students catch a vision of the future, focusing their attention beyond the classroom, into their first television newsroom, be it on campus, at an internship, or in first their job at a small market station.

All the instructors interviewed recognized the importance of building on a series of basic skills that enables the student reporter to take her place among the professionals. The interviews, coupled with a content analysis of their syllabi, helped to clarify what these common skills are. Collectively, they are named *master skills* for teaching television reporting. (From this point forward, the prime focus of the chapter is the reporting portion of this course. Producing elements of the course are discussed and identified as warranted.)

The traditional pattern to teach television news followed a linear one of instruction in writing, sound and pictures. This often corresponded to the print, radio and television formats dictating the style of reporting, which frequently meant students took their first writing courses, and sometimes a second or third, with print students. Then, at some point, "writing for the ear" in broadcast style would be introduced and distinguished from the print style of "writing for the eye." The next skill to master was sound. The easiest way to teach this was through a radio news course. Despite a lagging industry demand for radio news journalists, many schools, among them the University of Florida, SIU at Carbondale, and the University of Texas at Austin, continue to teach the course. Finally, in the traditional pedagogy, the most complicated technical skill set was taught last. This is the ability to shoot and edit tape and to manipulate pictures to create television news stories.

The American teaching method for television news reporting, following the British pattern, calls for the written words to come first (Stephens, 1980; Fang, 1985; Shook, 2000). Reporters then record the audio track, and then the pictures are match-edited to the copy. This does not mean that Americans downplay the importance of visuals in television news. On the contrary, as NBC's Bob Dotson pointed out in workshops before America's National Press Photographers Association, when Americans conceptualize a news story, the most powerful pictures come at the beginning and the end of the news package (NBC News, 1996, quoted in Dotson, 2000). Therefore, Dotson instructs reporters to ask themselves *before* they write, "What is my most powerful picture?" and then to begin the story with words that will complement it. Rather than describing the video that the audience can see for itself, Dotson suggests writing what the audience cannot see, a technique he calls "writing to the corners of the screen."

Dotson's picture-driven formula brings a cinematic sense to a television story, possessing a distinct beginning, middle and end. Hence, words must always be composed with pictures in mind. As the late CBS reporter Charles Kuralt noted, "Every single sentence I ever write when I'm doing a television story is to a picture I know is there." Despite technological changes impacting television reporting and producing, faculty interviewed stressed the importance of not letting such advancements overpower the words in a news script.

In the 21st century, many curriculum models have discarded the old linear curriculum pattern of teaching in sequential order writing, sound and pictures. Enriched by high school experiences using relatively inexpensive cameras and computer editing, entering college freshmen come to the classroom with many of these technical skills partially mastered. Forcing students to go back through the linear pattern of first working in radio with sound, and not focusing on their chosen television career until nearly their junior year of college, became a source of frustration. Technology changes allowed for simplification of understanding of television cameras and editing systems.

These technological innovations paralleled a movement toward convergence evident in the business world of news media. Media chains like Media General, Gannett, and Belo began to share newspaper and television reporting resources at the beginning of the new century. These two elements—the fading of radio news in the curriculum and the industry adaptation of a convergent model—have had an impact on how television reporting and producing is taught and where it fits in the curriculum.

Every broadcast news instructor knows that even quick-study students must pay the price to learn important principles of writing, sound and pictures, even as they test or refine their skills in the laboratory newsroom. To achieve the perfect marriage between words and pictures, students must develop competency with a series of what we shall call *master skills*. Master skills are identified as being necessary to teach television reporting successfully and are divided into three categories: story selection, fieldwork and field production.

Master skills related to the story selection process include recognition of a story, data collection, fact sifting and selection, and source identification. The Web and the telephone become indispensable tools in the practice and development of these master skills. Acquisition of the next skill set requires reporters to leave the newsroom for fieldwork. At this stage, where technical skills involving camera operation are required, the reporters travel in a buddy system, helping with equipment and shooting for each other.

Journalistic skills need to be added, such as interviewing; elements of visualization, including shooting cover video; and the performance of stand-ups. Once back at the station, further technical skills will be used to edit the videotape. Journalistic master skills required at the editing stage include the ability to select sound bites, write to pictures, creatively select graphics and artwork, and voice the narrative audio track. This last stage is best described as the post-field production process.

But, hey, what about the writing? Overgirding and underarching the master-skills development process is the broadcast news teachers need to emphasize good writing.

These two words are the first placed on classroom blackboards when Elmer W. Lower lectures around the country. Lower, the former ABC news director who discovered Peter Jennings, Sam Donaldson, and Ted Koppel, will write those words and turn to the students and declare, "If you remember nothing else about me or what I say, remember these two words."

The writing process begins when the story is first assigned, notes are taken, and initial fact-based sentences are composed. The process progresses from this prescripting stage to composing words for the on-camera stand-up in the field. Once back at the station, the art of the visual poet takes over. Words must be carefully chosen to link facts and sound bites. At the same time, student reporters must be taught to keep in constant focus the pictures that will match the words. Finally, a critical master skill, which is frequently and unwisely left to the last, is writing the anchor lead to the news package and, if the station format dictates, composing an on-camera tag.

The remainder of this chapter focuses on the various curricular models that allow for these master skills to be taught. The challenges that teachers face in this course and the innovating ideas used to best prepare the students will be discussed. These instructors are committed to the notion that that TV reporting and producing lead to some of the most rewarding career opportunities available to young people today.

Position of the Course in the Curriculum

Schools offering this television reporting and producing course typically fall into what can be called the *J-School* or *Communications School* model, the prime differences being that J-School models often do not include the production courses that are typically found in Communications School models. For instance, at Missouri, a traditional journalism school, there is no stand-alone production course that focuses solely on camera and editing operations offered to the broadcast news student. Instead, these skill subjects are folded into a series of three required courses.

As a faculty member and the news director of KOMU-TV, Missouri's lab outlet for student work, Stacey Woelfel orchestrates the interplay of these courses so that students maximize their opportunity to test skills taught in the classroom in a real live newsroom environment. He teaches the third required television reporting course. He explains that this course is where students' stories actually appear on the local NBC affiliate, Channel 8. "Broadcast News Three is seen as an intermediate television reporting course," Woelfel noted. "Students in this course have taken two previous courses specifically designed to introduce them to the art and science of television reporting. In this course, students have their first semester-long chance to do general assignment reporting. The main goal is to take those laboratory skills they've mastered, and use and improve them to meet daily newsroom deadlines."

Beyond this course, students in the senior year then choose between advanced reporting, producing, or some other specialty courses, including producing for the Web. Professor Mike McKean pioneered Missouri's Web course. At Missouri, the television producing course is taught separately from television reporting and fits into the curriculum as an elective. To qualify, students must have already completed the triple series of television reporting courses. They can choose producing, Web producing, or advance reporting.

Like the Missouri model, producing is taught as a separate and distinct course at the University of Texas at Austin. Rather than a commercial TV channel outlet for the student journalism, Texas follows a more typical pattern of taking advantage of access to local cable channels. Students at Texas produce a weekly cable newscast with material coming from two courses: one reporting and one producing. Don Heider explained the model, beginning with the television reporting course: "The first few weeks of the course are a video boot camp. Students learn and practice shooting and editing. The rest of the semester is spent learning how to report and produce packages."

In contrast to the Missouri and Texas broadcast news models, students at the Walter Cronkite School of Journalism and Mass Communication at Arizona State University do not provide technical support. Instead, students in the broadcast production emphasis direct in the control room, run audio boards, and serve as camera operators in the studio. This pattern follows more closely that of a Communications School model, where production courses are taught under same academic umbrella as the journalism courses.

Prompted by industry trends toward convergence, a revised curriculum at the Cronkite School keeps print and broadcast students together in their first two newswriting courses. In the first course, at the 200 level, the basics of how to discern what is news and how to interview, take notes, and write in journalistic style (although not specifically broadcast style) are taught. Further, during a semester of meeting twice weekly, only two lectures are devoted solely to broadcast news. The 300-level reporting course continues to combine broadcast students with their print counterparts, with all students striving to perfect the print writing method. Interestingly, revitalizing efforts are under way to balance this course, whereby a more equal approach to writing for both print and broadcast styles is taken.

After completion of these two courses, broadcast news students begin to specialize by taking an advanced broadcast writing course where both television and radio news, distinct and separate from print, are taught. Lab components include radio news writing, producing a live weekly campus station newscast, and contributing news copy to weekly student newscasts on campus cable. Finally, the students enroll in the TV reporting course, which includes assignments to shoot with field cameras.

There is no separate producing course at the Cronkite School. Instead, seniors can elect to enroll in a course that produces a weekly, taped, 30-minute newscast broadcast on public and commercial cable systems in the 16th largest market. The course, named after the *Newswatch* broadcast, allows one or two students to produce while the rest hone their television reporting skills. Competitive auditions determine who anchors the weekly semester newscast.

This same senior-level class that becomes a working newsroom model is used at the University of Oregon. A weekly cable newscast that is the outlet for the students' work falls under the direction of veteran NBC reporter Jim Upshaw, the KEZI distinguished professor of broadcast journalism. He explained the capstone course: "J434 is a capstone course in which most newsroom jobs rotate every week, with at least eight (of the total of about 16) students doing field packages and the rest handling producing tasks and filling in on tech jobs as needed. We do live half-hour newscasts on six Fridays of a 10-week term, airing on the metro area's AT&T cable system. A TA (teaching assistant) and I critique every element, with reporting efforts, shooting/editing, and producing approaches and execution all receiving close attention."

Currently Oregon offers no stand-alone producing course, but Professor Upshaw says that is changing: "We're developing a separate producing course, and meanwhile are using weekend immersion workshops (for only 1 to 2 credits) to provide extra producing, training and education, focusing on matters such as 'producing with purpose' (not just show-stacking) and story management." Upshaw believes it is important for students to recognize the unique aspects of producing and that the best reporters are those who fully understand the producing functions: "Producing is a separate orientation and in most cases needs a separate course envelope, which we're preparing now. It certainly requires separate treatment in the early to middle phases of a broadcast news curriculum. It also needs extra development in workshops and other experiences."

Oregon's currently combined 400-level course, Reporting/Producing for the Electronic Media, focuses on critical newsgathering skills. Upshaw takes full advantage of the configuration to cross-train his students, pairing them together to critique each other's writing and reporting. Upshaw charges up the classroom by swapping reporter-producer roles and spinning "reporting assignments into dialogues about producing by midway in the term to teach basic show construction and thematic principles."

One assignment in Upshaw's course exposes all students to producing. Students use their own reports in the construction of mininewscasts. He requires each student to use his or her own favorite news package in a five-minute wire-copy show much like NBC's *Today Show* local cut-ins. The student anchors it in the studio for taping and assessment. Evaluations of this assignment are based on comprehensiveness, coupled with timing and flow.

In each step of the Oregon model, visual elements are strongly emphasized. Premajors must complete a course in visual communication. Prior to taking the aforementioned main television reporting and producing course, students must take two production classes that introduce them to video aesthetics and visual storytelling. The first course introduces students to the electronic media and includes lab exercises in writing for nonfiction TV, whereas the second course focuses tightly on field production where students work in small teams to learn shooting and editing techniques. Equipment includes VHS/S-VHS cameras, with some introduction to digital equipment. The Oregon faculty believes students, armed with this production background, can then find success in the television reporting and producing course.

While Upshaw, with 22 years of experience as a local and network correspondent, leads the broadcast news program at the University of Oregon, another network veteran, Bill Knowles, formerly of ABC, has revitalized the broadcast news curriculum at the University of Montana. Knowles spent 22 years as a television news producer and executive managing ABC News bureaus in Los Angeles, Washington, D.C., and Atlanta. He recruited Denise Dowling from KHQ-TV in Spokane to bring her medium-market anchoring, producing and reporting experience from that NBC newsroom into the University of Montana classrooms.

Twenty students each year are admitted into the Montana program. The selection criteria include GPA, prerequisites, and samples of previous work. Prerequisites to enter the program and begin the year-long, junior-level reporting course include an introduction to mass media, broadcast writing, and a television production course.

The Montana program requires juniors to spend a full year reporting for both radio and television in an intensive, hands-on, advanced broadcast reporting class. They report for the campus radio station, Montana Public Radio. For television, juniors produce "Nat Sound" packages for a program called *Business: Made in Montana*. Junior-level students' final television project also airs as part of two half-hour shows produced for Montana's PBS system.

Montana seniors spend one semester reporting in television for a trio of media outlets: *PBS Newsbrief*, *UM News*, and the *Montana Journal*. Seniors produce three half-hour programs called *Montana Journal* that air on Montana's PBS outlet.

Montana has a unique model for the advanced producing course, which provides a multiple platform experience for students in both PBS and commercial news environments, as Dowling explains: "After completing the year-long junior course, and the first semester senior reporting course, students can then specialize into advanced reporting or advanced producing. Seniors produce a nightly PBS update (90 seconds), a weekly segment (3 minutes 30 seconds) called *UM News* that airs on the local NBC affiliate's morning show."

A parallel to the advanced producing experience just described is offered to those students electing to focus on pure reporting their senior year. Dowling added, "Seniors produce three half-hour programs called *Montana Journal* that air on the Montana PBS system. The students pick a topic (education, environment, etc.) and produce five- to six-reporter pieces, which are produced into the half-hour program. These shows are also offered to the local CBS affiliate. They sometimes air the shows, depending on timeliness and scheduling factors."

While Montana uses a variety of media outlets for its student work, Oregon, Arizona State, and Texas use cable access, and Missouri takes full advantage of its network affiliate. Each of these schools displays student reporting and producing through different outlets. Two schools exemplify yet another model.

The PBS channel model, for airing student news product, is used by a score of programs across the country, including the University of Florida, Ohio University, and New Mexico State University. Discussed in this chapter will be those models practiced by the state-run Southern Illinois University at Carbondale and the privately run Brigham Young University. Together they illustrate how the broadcast reporting and producing course can fit into the curriculum, yet at the same time feed the local news needs of the campus PBS-affiliated station.

The methods used to teach this course, and especially the various news-operation models, do allow for different schools to offer unique features. Ken Fischer, assistant professor at Southern Illinois University at Carbondale, brings the unique perspective of working at four universities with recognized broadcast news programs: New Mexico State University, the University of Florida, Ohio University, and Southern Illinois University at Carbondale. Each of these schools, and many others, take advantage of their campus PBS stations to become a vital partner in the students' broadcast news education.

In some cases, the television reporting course feeds directly into the nightly newscast on the PBS station. In other models, a separate student news staff was hired to

254   Mass Communication Education

produce the news. Fischer, who was WOUB-TV/FM news director at the E. W. Scripps School of Journalism at Ohio University and the assistant news director at WUFT-TV at the University of Florida, observed, "I did not teach reporting classes at Ohio or Florida. But as an observer I saw the same problems as at SIU. The classes sometimes conflict with the needs of the newsroom. But Ohio and Florida had an advantage. Both schools have a beginning TV reporting class outside of the day-to-day show operations. That means the students know more about the equipment and reporting before they start working on the shows."

Fischer has particularly keen insight into the different models of media outlets that can harmonize with the reporting and producing course to maximize the experience. Fischer became introduced to newsroom management and student curriculum development as a master's student at Brigham Young University in the 1980s.

The current model at BYU encompasses combined print and broadcast students in the early stages of the curriculum and then a sharp focus in two broadcast reporting classes. The first broadcast reporting class is preceded by a print reporting class and producing class. In the broadcast reporting course, students concentrate on learning visual storytelling and the mechanics of television and radio reporting. An advanced reporting course is designed to polish the technical skills but also give great concentration to content. The lead faculty member for BYU's broadcast news program, Dale Cressman, spoke of efforts to converge print and broadcast students in classes both in the early and later stages of the curriculum: "We also want them to think about journalism philosophy. Our capstone class is a multimedia class in which we use 'teams' of broadcast and print reporters to work on in-depth projects. Ideally, we would like a capstone producing class, but with limited hours we end up offering it early and using it as a broadcast writing and anchoring course, also."

The television and reporting course takes a different position in the curriculum of each of the schools just discussed. Common to all of them is the belief that, prior to enrolling in this course, students have joined with print students in a basic newswriting course. Some models placed a heavier emphasis on separate courses in technical production skills. In some cases, these were requirements to be completed before students took the television reporting course. For others, technical skills in shooting and editing become integrated parts of various advancing levels of instruction as students progress through different courses. One conclusion that can be reached is that the traditional radio news course is no longer the fundamental gateway into instruction in TV news.

Similar Courses

Interviewing broadcast instructors revealed far more commonality than originality in the various ways this course is taught across the country. This is not to disparage the uniqueness of the instructors. Rather, it quickly became apparent, because of the unique professional background of each instructor, that added dimensions came into the classroom. Since much course material, the master skills described earlier, seems to be common to nearly all, the approach and passion demonstrated by these instructors, and many others not mentioned, surely contributed to the success of their school's programs. As Oregon's Jim Upshaw noted, "I suspect that most of the features of our courses are common around the country. We do have strong relationships with public agencies, schools, etc., and with stations here in market #121, so the students have a good launching pad for internships. Many of those involve producing concurrent with class work."

Although the schools shared many similar courses such as basic writing and, in some cases, basic production as prerequisites, schools varied widely on the requirement of an internship. But every faculty member spoke to the value of a professional internship in preparing students for future job opportunities. At the Cronkite School, tapping into the numerous internships available in the 16th-largest market with seven stations doing local news, including two in Spanish, some faculty felt the internship was just as valuable as student campus newsroom experience. Nearly all faculties consulted for this chapter joined in the chorus of frustration that so few broadcast news internships are paid. But both faculty and students seemed resigned to the tremendous value of the internship.

Ancillary/Related Courses

Across the curricula, students were encouraged to take a wide variety of related courses. Accredited programs often were designed to minimize the required courses to maximize the student opportunity to design their own unique programs to match student aspirations and interests. This enables students at the Cronkite School who are interested in becoming foreign correspondents to take a course in international communications or Missouri journalism students to tap into investigative reporting techniques taught in conjunction with the national headquarters for Investigative Reporters and Editors (IRE) located at that school.

Faculty who focused on grooming newscast producers often encouraged these students to take courses in graphic design, art history, and even musicology in order to bring the maximum number of creative, communicative elements into their future roles as critical gatekeepers of local news across America. Balancing out the need to have some elements of show biz, producers were pushed to enroll in the courses to provide them with a heavy dose of history, politics and economics. Faculty seemed to feel these courses help balance the scales between entertainment and the journalism knowledge required for students to become successful newscast producers.

Comparative Features

In common with these schools and others are the vital elements in teaching principles of journalism to future broadcast reporters and producers that go beyond the master skills discussed earlier. These include issues such as diversity, fundamentals of ethical reporting, and new trends in journalism impacting both broadcast and print. Public journalism is an example of such a new trend.

Another shared value of the broadcast news faculty seems to be the notion of as near as possible duplicating a real-world experience in the student news operation. Often the students' learning takes place not in the classroom but in the deadline pressure-driven atmosphere of the student newsroom. As Don Heider from the University of

Texas at Austin observed, "In the reporting course, a lot of learning takes place in our story meetings and in our story critique sessions." The University of Missouri's Stacey Woelfel emphasized strongly how the teacher must move beyond the classroom into the newsroom to be truly effective: "The common element of this course, as would be found anywhere, is a lecture component that addresses concerns any reporter would face: ethics, diversity, writing, interviewing, etc. What is different about the approach here is that the lecture component takes a subservient role to the laboratory portion of the course; the newsroom reporting shifts. They are the centerpieces of the course. And it is during those shifts that the bulk of the real teaching takes place."

Missouri's reporters and producers spend a minimum of 12 hours a week in a newsroom shift. Across America, as this course is taught, instructors emphasized the need for hands-on, side-by-side learning. At the University of Montana, instructor Denise Dowling emphasized the importance of the hands-on approach: "Every student learns to gather and edit sound for radio. They learn how to shoot, write and edit for television. They learn what it takes to be a successful on-camera reporter and/or anchor. They practice interviewing with live and taped segments."

Special Features

Missouri's School of Journalism upholds its national reputation as a producer of producers in part because TV news directors know Missouri producing-oriented graduates have produced multiple newscasts, under deadline pressure, for at least one semester. The NBC network affiliation of KOMU-TV, the newsroom lab, avails Missouri students of the resources of NBC NewsChannel. Manipulating incoming video feeds, both domestic and foreign, the producers can input the latest pictures into their newscast rundowns. In a similar way, many schools use CNN News Source to provide producing students with experience working with video feeds. But, in addition to NBC's NewsChannel, Missouri students receive "on-air booth training" in handling live satellite feeds from the network and three live trucks of the local station.

Television reporting taught at Missouri includes lectures and practical experience in doing "live shots." Other schools, such as Brigham Young University and Ohio University, insert live reports from campus into their newscast, and Syracuse University's innovative training room "live lab" is a special feature that school offers students learning to become television reporters.

Syracuse University also provides multilevel experiences for newscast producers. Both undergraduate and graduate students are required to take a producing class. Part of this course includes producing two 30-minute newscasts in a six-hour lab. Each week, students rotate positions parallel to those that are found in the industry, including, producer, associate producer, anchor, co-anchor, sports reporter, weather reporter, live reporter, and tape editor.

An elective course enables producing-oriented students to gain insight also into the field of broadcast management. Syracuse offers a three-hour lecture/discussion class with a field lab. For the lab portion of the course, the student is paired with a producer/show at a local TV station and works that shift once a week. Working alongside the professional as a writer or associate producer, the student's goal is to produce by himself or herself. Syracuse University's growing national reputation in educating future newscast producers is augmented by the success of faculty member Dow Smith's best-selling textbook *Power Producer: A Practical Guide to Televison News Producing* (2000), published in sponsorship with the Radio–Television News Directors Association.

Finally, a special feature offered to broadcast news students at the University of Texas at Austin teaches them a skill not widely used in local television news: on-air editorials. Professor Don Heider articulated the merits of including this type of writing in the course: "Our students write and produce commentaries, something that is a lost art in broadcast news. We have been very pleased with the quality of student editorials, and like the fact it gives students an opportunity to wrestle with issues and their own stand is on a particular story or event."

Common Goals and Objectives

"Writing, writing, writing" became the most common goal emphasized in this course among broadcast news instructors. A second goal shared by all broadcast teachers is to help students quickly obtain a professional edge to their reporting and producing work demonstrated through an audition tape.

Evidence of the students' transformation to news professional is manifest in the TV news "audition tape," which in some courses, including advanced TV reporting at Missouri, replaces a final exam. This tape shows samples of a student's TV news stories in the same way a print reporter has a clip book of published articles to entice a future editor into hiring her. Often, state universities send examples of student work via these audition tapes for evaluation by news consultants and news directors. This fulfills an outside, professional assessment requirement mandated by many state legislatures and funding bodies. Thus, the teacher, as well as the student, recognizes a manifest example of successful student work not just as a classroom grade but also as a tangible media product represented by the audition tape.

The third common objective for instructors of television broadcast news can be labeled the *weeding out* factor. It is not a secret that television news attracts students with various motivations. Far too many young students select this course because they see it as a ticket to instant fame and fortune. As Montana's Denise Dowling explained, "There are students who seem to have no real interest in news. They are not informed about what's happening in the world, the country, Montana or Missoula. I try to force them to stay current with current events quizzes, but that's just treating the symptom, not the problem."

The problem faced by many faculty is a certain group of students entering this major and hence this class for the wrong reason. Faculties teaching this course concentrate on helping the students catch a heavy dose of reality regarding the competitive nature of the business. Teachers lecture students about the small number of people who remain in business after five years due to low salary levels. Mechanisms are often in place to help differentiate serious students from those merely attracted to television's fame and fortune. These include passing an English proficiency exam and a current-event test, and meeting minimal GPA levels. Some faculty were quick to caution that not every good journalist is a straight-A student. Therefore, some leeway was allowed for students who showed the spark or the spunk to be admitted into the program and thus were allowed to take this course.

Instructor Philosophy

Teaching television reporting and producing takes the energy of a coach and patience of a mother. Having found a vision and comfort level with their own teaching style, these six faculties were able to speak freely about their craft. Oregon's Jim Upshaw sees his job as an engineer of sorts, helping student's breakthrough into professionalism: "Reporting done well is more than just one of the surface features, packaging, presentation, live performance, that our students see on TV. Strong skills and civic knowledge combined with youth's normal altruism and idealism can change society. I work to pull the strands together, giving students power and confidence to lead."

Building self-confidence is a common philosophical approach to the teaching of this course. Small classes allow the teacher-student relationship to flourish. The better a teacher knows the individual backgrounds of the students, the more adept the teacher becomes at motivating and challenging them. For Dale Cressman at BYU, this type of learning takes place best in a newsroom where "we want to make it 'real world' so they can survive and thrive, but also get them to question the status quo and strive to produce better journalism." Ken Fischer at SIU emphasizes the well-rounded nature of students and often gathers the newsroom together for a softball game or other activity so that the pressure of the newsroom can be balanced with the zest and fun needed for this career.

Feeling strongly the need to not graduate more prima donnas, Fischer's philosophy is to help each student prioritize by becoming "a good writer and news junky first; next understand the tools (production elements), work on performance aspects and then the student is truly ready to start telling stories." Denise Dowling at Montana echoes her other broadcast reporter colleagues in her approach: "You must learn by doing. Lessons in theory, ethics and philosophy all come with the practical experience."

For Don Heider at Texas, that practical experience includes knowing when to stand back as a teacher and let students make a mistake or two. Heider observes, "One of the constant things I think we have to be vigilant of is to not have the instructors and TA's take over the newscast. The goal here isn't to produce the best-quality student newscast possible. The goal is to teach the students to produce the best-quality newscast they are capable of, but also to allow them to exercise judgment, make mistakes (short of something we could get sued for), and use the newscast as a learning experience."

Finally, Stacey Woelfel at Missouri concurs with Heider that sometimes the teacher simply has to let a student falter in order for true learning to occur. He believes he approaches the teaching of television reporting and producing with a bit of a split personality and explains, "In the newsroom, as students come to report and produce our news, I treat them very much like employees working in the field. As soon as their work shifts are done, or in the classroom, I quickly revert to treating them like students and trying to figure out what worked best and what did not. I teach with a very positive sense and try to dwell on success, not failures."

Each of these six broadcast news teachers shares a common bond of dedication with their students, a loyalty that remains even when obstacles block the path to quality instruction.

Common Challenges/Solutions

Teachers of this course face a host of old challenges, such as dealing with outdated equipment, and a list of new ones, especially those driven by curriculum changes toward a convergence model. BYU's transformation into a convergent curriculum presented faculty member Dale Cressman a combination of both equipment and curriculum headaches, as he articulated: "Probably our biggest challenge is balancing convergence with the students' need to specialize. BYU's lab is fully converged, that is to say that television, radio, newspaper, and Web all operate out of the same newsroom. While I find that a useful experience for the student, I worry about watering down the students' broadcast journalism experience."

For those schools not yet faced with convergent curriculum pressures or those choosing a different path, keeping up with ever-changing equipment remains a constant challenge. Deans and directors must be educated to the importance, for instance, of converting to digital editing systems. Often alumni can be very valuable in this process. As Denise Dowling explained, "We have a problem with outdated equipment. Juniors are still shooting and editing on 3/4-inch tape. While we believe tape-to-tape editing skills are important to teach, we have trouble finding replacement parts and keeping the gear working. We hope to replace the aged gear soon, but we will continue to teach tape-to-tape editing with the digital format." At Montana and elsewhere, production majors in the same school demanding access to the latest equipment can limit the type of course requirement for this class.

Beyond curriculum and equipment, motivating the students to take full advantage of all aspects of the program challenges many faculties. When a school such as Southern Illinois at Carbondale has a solid daily newscast feed by material from the reporting course, the demands of this operation can sometimes inhibit learning. Ken Fischer observed, "Having to feed the daily newscast can sometimes get in the way of learning. In particular, this applies to the students who never volunteer for the newsroom in their early years. They are usually overwhelmed by the operation and the veterans blow by them in class."

In an era of tight budgets, when reductions in numbers of newscasts are even being considered, discussion of the need for more courses can fall on deaf ears. Yet many teachers spoke of the desire to offer specialized courses in computer-assisted reporting or web producing but felt encumbered by accreditation concerns that would not allow them to expand the course selections. Innovative ways have been found to meet this challenge, such as the availability of short-term minicourses running for four or five weeks or even weekend workshops. When these can be partnered with existing professional organizations, such as the local chapter of Radio–Television News Directors Association (RTNDA) or Society of Professional Journalists (SPJ), not only do they bring professionals back into college to improve their skills and meet and mingle with current students, but they can be a small source of revenue streams that can please a budget-strapped department chair.

Interestingly, often students offer the best challenges to the obstacles encountered. Their energy, ideas, and willingness to stay to the midnight hour to build sets, produce news, and open and run database searches often reignite the sometimes weary broadcast news instructor. Sometimes the challenge is convincing young students that time invested is actually a dividend. "Every year students complain that this course is too much work for the number of credits they earn," Denise Dowling observed. "I tell them it will be the hardest year of their college careers, but it will be worth it in the end. They always agree after they've made it through the year!"

Enticing students to try various roles and accept those needed for the greater good of the entire broadcast can be a challenge, as Dowling points out: "Every student must fill every role, even if they have no particular interest in that part of the business. For example, we have students who know they never want to anchor. But they must sit in the anchor chair and anchor a show to better understand what that person faces. It will only make them better producers, reporters, etc."

Seeing the students as a helpful solution to the obstacles faced in this course, rather than the obstacle itself, enables teachers to enter into the student world and recapture for themselves what it is like to be young, less cynical, and idealistic. Once in their world, some additional teaching can take place, whether out in the field helping them set up a live shot, a frequent teaching spot for Missouri's Stacey Woelfel, or in another setting where other lessons can be taught. Oregon's Jim Upshaw believes one key is understanding their culture. Once there, inside their culture, real learning can take place: "Youth culture's perspective on media's role can be a drag on progress; we have to do a lot of basic civics education. One challenge is to tie the effort to journalism's historical value, opening eyes to the differences it makes, not just TV's glamour."

Outside Resources

This course naturally lends itself to outside guest speakers, generally from local area television stations. Once on campus, these working reporters not only share their own stories but also provide valuable feedback in one-on-one critique sessions with the students. This brings an added dimension of credibility to the instructor, as often the same feedback the instructor has given the students is repeated in this session with the working professional. A host of excellent tape examples from around the country become available to faculty as they keep in close contact with alumni. Faculty also identified the value of closely monitoring the Web sites of RTNDA and the Poynter Institute for new trends in TV reporting and producing. The Newslab led by Deborah Potter in Washington, D.C., is a valuable link between the best practices in local news, because the articulation of the methods explain how "best practices" work.

At least two schools, Oregon and Arizona State University, took advantage of the Association of Schools of Journalism and Mass Communication (ASJMC)/Knight's Broadcasters-in-Residence Projects to bring in professionals from the trenches of local American newsrooms, or, in the case of ASU, England's ITN.

Conclusions

Teaching television reporting and producing can be a tough assignment requiring a major time commitment on the part of the instructor. Keeping abreast of the changes in technology and trends in news coverage are minimal requirements. Learning to work with news directors, fellow faculty, and students remains a challenge. Walter Cronkite's maxim for new journalists, cited at the beginning of this chapter, affords a powerful lesson. To be successful, a broadcast news teacher must want to be a journalism teacher and nothing else. She or he must encourage diversity among students who will enter the classroom and newsroom. Finally, the instructor must be alert to the warning signs of cynicism that can deaden any teacher's approach.

References

Dotson, B. 2000. *Make it memorable: Writing and packaging TV news with style.* Chicago: Bonus.

Fang, I. 1985. *Television news, radio news.* St. Paul, Minn.: Rada.

Shook, F. 2000. *Television field production and reporting.* 3rd ed. New York: Longman.

Stephens, M. 1980. *Broadcast news.* New York: Holt, Rinehart and Winston.

Remembering a Mentor: Louis Day

Val E. Limburg

Maybe *mentor* isn't the term to use in relating my long association with Lou Day of the Manship School of Mass Communication at Louisiana State University. He has been more of a colleague, someone with whom I share the same vision of the absolute necessity of a course in media ethics in the communication curriculum. But he is very much a mentor to me because he has demonstrated his enthusiasm and energy through his perspective and his work in his textbook, *Ethics of Media Communications*, now in its fourth edition (2003).

For many years, I have associated with Lou Day at the annual meetings of the Broadcast Education Association, often being on panels with him. Always he is concerned about doing a thorough job, even on informal panels; always sharp, always articulate. And there is something of his character that makes him a good media ethics instructor of genuine character, a person of integrity, sincerity and humility. In his modesty, he might reject such descriptions, but such are my observations and reflections on this distinguished mentor.

Simply stated, I believe that it takes an honest and ethical person to teach ethics. Lou Day is such a teacher. His concern for the teaching of media ethics is reflected in his feel for the need for a textbook that initially grew out of a sense of frustration and a sense of optimism, like others who have thought about the place of an ethics course and those who have become cynical concerning the value of ethics instruction within the public academy. Day notes, somewhat prophetically, before the Enron and other big business scandals, that "skepticism about the moral education produces skepticism about moral responsibility, and this in turn produces leaders who lack a moral vision" (p. ix). He then goes on to discuss the values of ethics education and the principles of moral virtue right from the onset, in his first chapter.

While some just shake their heads in wonderment at today's ethical messes, many of which are related to the media, Day tries in his own way of doing something about it by executing his sharp teaching skills apparent in his text. In questioning Day about this, it is apparent that he pulls his students into discussion by relying heavily upon interesting case studies, bringing the vagaries of ethics into everyday dilemmas. Using the hypothetical cases from his text, he requires his students to do a lot of original thinking, providing a basis for some interesting class discussion. He also provides in-class cases and sometimes has the students work in groups before providing the team solution to the class.

A look at this recently released fourth edition reveals 66 cases of media ethics in 12 chapters. He says he does not stay strictly within professional areas of interest (e.g., journalism, advertising, and public relations). The chapters and course modules are integrated with a variety of media subjects. For example, in the chapter on truth and honesty, he deals with journalism, advertising, and public relations. Similarly, in the chapter on privacy, he deals with journalism and advertising, etc.

Day insists that other pedagogical requirements also be in place: that small sections include no more than 40 students, that teaching assistants aren't used for the course, that the course be required of all mass communication majors, and that students demonstrate critical thinking in their assignments and on essay exams. It's a large order in the teaching workload; it's not an easy course to teach, nor one sought after by those seeking an easy road in teaching.

Since student interaction is important, Day sees to it that the opportunity for such contact is there. He makes himself readily available in such a way that he can connect with those who seek consultation. When a small percentage of the class takes advantage of such an opportunity, he allows those who feel more comfortable communicating by e-mail to keep in touch that way.

Although the course may deal with ancient issues of ethics, morality, and the search for truth, Day integrates the new media in his teaching and uses them as objects for his subject matter. I tell my students it is easy to become infatuated with technology without understanding its ethical implications. In my judgment, new technology (like the Web) does not present new ethical problems. What it does is to make the resolution of these issues more difficult (e.g., the case of Napster was about intellectual property). This doesn't really change regardless of whether piracy is done through conventional or high-tech means. Similarly, digital technology makes it easier to alter news photos without detection. But deception is still deception regardless of whether it involves new or old technology.

Many media ethics instructors probably have not been groomed to be such. Day indicated to me that "there was a long break between my graduate work and teaching of media ethics. But the most influential course in my doctoral work was one in media philosophy." I am not sure who taught that course, or who might have been Day's mentor, but it is certain that Louis Day has been and continues to be a mentor, not only for his students, but for many of us who share common teaching interests.

PART IV

The Applied Curriculum

CHAPTER 15

Audio Production

Robert Musburger

Introduction

R adio production was the first hands-on course taught in the early days of broadcast higher education. Since then the field has evolved to include television/video audio, motion picture sound, and more recently the audio portion of multimedia production. The basic techniques of the course as it is now taught have not changed, but today the course must recognize the new technologies in video/film sound, multimedia audio, and digital production and editing techniques.

Audio/sound production remains a mainstay of electronic media/film departments as both an introduction to the basic philosophy and techniques of media production as well as an education in audio-specific production techniques. The relatively low cost of audio equipment and facilities continues to make audio production a practical means of giving students some skills coupled with production theory. In some cases colleges and universities also couple audio production with the operation of a student radio station. That operation may broadcast on cable, the Internet, or if a frequency and finances are available, on the air.

Position of the Course in the Curriculum

Digital audio production techniques appeared on the academic scene earlier than digital video production. Lower cost of equipment, simpler operating procedures, lower demands for extensive compression, and more easily obtained memory requirements made digital audio recording, processing and editing accessible to academic units.

Digital audio workstations (DAWs) combine nearly all of the functions normally found in an audio control room. Most DAWs include input mixing, a variety of processing actions, recording, editing, and providing output in either analogue or digital formats. DAWs combine the techniques of operating a standard audio mixing board with digital entering, cutting, pasting and filing techniques similar to those found on digital word processors.

By the turn of the century, over 19 different manufacturers were producing DAWs. The workstations ranged from simple hard-drive recorders with some mixing capabilities to complex systems offering every technique and tool available on the largest analogue multitrack systems.

The part rewritable CD-ROMs will assume in replacing tape recorders, either analogue or digital, is yet to be determined. But there is no doubt that disk and eventually solid-state recording will make all tape operations obsolete. Students need to be taught to operate both analogue and digital tape decks, as well as CR and DVD burners. As rapidly as technology is changing, our responsibility to our students must include the possibility of mastering all recording formats, regardless of their shape or size.

At the time of this writing, the final outcome of Internet audio production and streaming is in a state of legal and standards flux. Streaming for either or both audio and video requires the signal be digitized and then fed down the Internet on a Web site. The actual production of a streaming station is no different than any radio broadcast except the signal must be digitized and compressed for distribution. Listeners must have on their computer a matching system to download a streamed signal and that is one area that has not been standardized. There is little doubt that a quality audio production course needs to include the teaching of both analogue and digital equipment operations and techniques. Analogue, like film, will not disappear, especially in small markets and studios, where students are most likely to find their first employment.

Similar Courses

To determine how audio production is now taught, a survey was completed that addressed the techniques used by the instructors and the variations in the methods of introducing hands-on experiences to the students in a variety of schools ranging from high school to four-year research institutions.

The survey was obtained by requesting syllabi from members of the Broadcast Education Association (BEA) Listserve and the Production, Aesthetics, and Criticism Division members of that organization. A total of 20 syllabi were collected describing courses ranging from secondary schools to graduate programs. Reading syllabi reveals that not all of the information needed to make a critical analysis of the field appears in the printed form.

Often information that is critical to such judgments are not listed on individual syllabi, since the information is common knowledge among students in the academic unit, or the faculty member verbally provides the information during introductory lectures. Typical of such information is whether the course is taught as a semester or quarter-length course. The actual number of hours available for laboratory, either open or supervised, are seldom listed.

Ancillary Courses

The academic level—lower, upper, or graduate course—may be indicated by a course number, but no uniformity exists between schools on their numbering systems. Another missing link is that the name of the college of university is seldom indicated on a syllabus. Because all of the syllabi were obtained through e-mail, additional research was required to ferret out the location of the response. The respondent received an additional message requesting the details that could not be determined directly from the syllabi provided. In most cases the missing information was collected and included in the analysis.

Because of the rapid changes in technology in media production, the survey did not include a specific request for a listing and types of equipment used. A careful reading of some syllabi indicated how schools use unusual or advanced equipment for the laboratory projects required to be completed by students.

The goal of this chapter is to assist faculty new to the field of teaching audio production, regardless of the level of the course offered or the size of the unit. The basic goal of all audio production courses remains the same—to apply introductory media production theory to audio production projects in order for students to realize the value of a systematic process of producing a creative work.

A number of schools responded to the initial request and provided necessary information, including Cerritos College, North Greenville College, Friends of Baltimore, Harding University, East Carolina University, University of Wisconsin at Eau Claire, University of Houston, Oklahoma University, Evangel University, and John Carroll University. In addition, SUNY at Albany, University of South Carolina, Oklahoma State University, Elizabethtown College, California State Polytechnic, University of Wisconsin at Whitewater, Towson University, Regent University, Rice University, and University of Wisconsin at Stevens Point also answered the call. Not all schools teaching audio production are listed; only those that responded to the request for a syllabus. The schools indicating a Web site for the course are listed at the end of this chapter.

Comparative Features

Interestingly the course designators may indicate a shift toward the utilization of a common designator of Communication. Nine of the 20 used COM, COMB, MCOM, and CTT, and we may probably assume the "C" stands for Communication in most cases. Of all of the other designators, only JOUR and JMC had a common designator. The titles of the courses also had a common thread of Audio Production (12 courses) and Radio Production (three courses), the only courses with more than one common title. Eight courses were offered on the semester system, and two were offered on the quarter system. Eleven were undetermined.

A secondary school provided one syllabus: colleges and universities offered one for freshman, seven each at the sophomore and junior levels, and two for seniors. Two graduate-level courses and two undetermined-level syllabi were among those indicated in the response.

Common Goals and Objectives

Nearly all of the syllabi listed some type of objectives or goals. They ranged from brief ("To familiarize the student with technical equipment utilized in the audio production studios and radio stations, and to develop the skills needed to produce quality audio programming") to lengthy page-long lists. Some of the interesting objectives were "To challenge to THINK and to PERFORM UNDER PRESSURE while gaining skills in organization and time management." These goals are frequently shown in bold, underlined, with italic included for even more emphasis on the original syllabi.

In addition to the skill portion of operating equipment, some syllabi listed listening, writing, interviewing and performance skills. Several indicated the need to explore new technologies. The goals consistently referred to gaining *professional* level of competence. The units located in journalism departments also included a variety of additional specific journalism skills: awareness of current events, understanding story balance, applying ethics to stories, and editing writing and editing news copy.

Special Features

A limited follow-up survey of other select schools teaching audio production revealed a wide discrepancy in available equipment, yet a common set of objectives regardless of the student academic level or size of the school's enrollment. The units surveyed included a private K-12 school, Friends School of Baltimore enrolling over 1,000 students; a small private university, Harding University in Searcy, Arkansas, with 5,000 students; and a midsized state university, Stephen F. Austin State University in Nacogdoches, Texas, enrolling 10,000 students. Also included was a large state research institution, the University of Houston, with over 34,000 students.

The Friends School teaches audio production to 30 students in two sections once a year. Sophomores, juniors and seniors are allowed into the course without any prerequisites. David Heath has been teaching this course for the last four years. Professor Dutch Hoggatt at Harding University offers the course to a 30-student section every other year. He has taught this course for well over twenty years.

At Stephen F. Austin State University, Professor Sherry Williford offers their course to sophomores and above, with three prerequisites, including Introduction to Broadcasting, Basic Speech, and Mass Communication. Students must earn at least a "C" grade in each of the prerequisites to continue with Radio–TV courses. Audio production is offered three times a year to 22 students in each section. Sherry has been teaching audio production for 12 years.

At The University of Houston, instructor Toni Lambert, who has been teaching for four years, offers the course to 20 students each semester after they have completed four core courses: Media and Society, Theory of Communication, Communication Research Methods, and at least a "C" grade in Introduction to Media Production. The range in experience of the faculty interviewed did not appear to affect their attitudes or differences in purpose or basic methods of teaching audio production.

Equipment varied from several Avid suites plus the latest computer editing applications, to a mixture of analogue equipment and some digital equipment. Despite the variations, all of the schools' objectives comprise a fairly tight-knit set of goals. Each attempt to introduce the students to basic concepts of audio production, and appreciation for the knowledge and skills are required to use the equipment in a creative and positive manner. Some emphasize radio more than other audio uses, usually because the school operates a student radio station or cable/streaming service as part of their curriculum.

Teaching techniques varied from an emphasis on learning production processes to as much hands-on as possible within the available laboratory schedules. One school concentrates on music production, following the interests of the students in that school. Working as a DJ or news reporter leads the interest of students at the other schools.

In all of the schools, the instructors wished for more time and newer, better and more equipment. The greatest frustration comes from not being able to give every student as much time on equipment for them to develop to their maximum creative level. In several cases a second semester might solve some of those problems if additional equipment and facilities were made available.

At the high school, students work with especially high energy to learn and apply new techniques for the pure pleasure of learning, whereas, at the higher education level, students' motivations have moved to a job preparation attitude where many have lost the passion of their earlier school days. The attitude often degenerates to a level of "just tell me what I have to know to get a job so I get out of school and on my way." This is a difficult attitude for faculty to deal with when audio production offers so much more in the way of experimenting and learning how to use each student's individual creativity.

The departments that responded varied from Communication to Journalism to Broadcasting. That variation was evident in the method of teaching audio production. In journalism units, the emphasis was on interviewing and on editing stories for a newscast or documentary programs. Broadcast and Communication units emphasized commercial, music, dramatic and experimental productions. Those schools operating a broadcast channel emphasized board operating and production of specific programs for the station. In most cases students were expected to produce both individual and group projects. It was apparent that the three-step production process of preproduction, production and postproduction is emphasized in most cases, especially in the Communication units.

In some cases it also was apparent that some amount of time was spent on the theory of communication, including lectures, text-reading assignments, and written examinations over theoretical material. In addition to limited written examinations, the majority of the evaluation of students came from their production operational skills, techniques, and finished laboratory productions (including air checks). Due to the subjective manner of grading productions, few of the syllabi indicated in any detail how the grading was accomplished.

It is assumed that the instructor possessed some professional background enabling a rational and systematic evaluation within the confines of the subjective nature of media production. In some cases students were allowed to rewrite scripts and/or rerecord projects if found unsatisfactory on the first grading round. The value of this method is to provide a means for students to learn by correcting their mistakes and improving their work. In the long run this also provided a more suitable addition to a résumé tape for future employment applications.

Assignments ranged from short quizzes, longer exams, spot production, mini-documentaries, and short programs, to working shifts on student radio stations. The thrust of the course was to teach students to transform a concept into a viable, professional level, audio production. Some schools combine audio and video production into a single class. Some assume audio production skills may be acquired as part of the experience gained in a visual production course. It is disappointing that more programs do not appreciate the value of a solid education in audio production.

Instructor Philosophy

As is true with most production courses, the contact hours per week for audio production courses far surpasses that of a typical lecture course. In this survey the majority (six) of the respondents required three schedule class hours followed by four hours (four reports) and 2.5 (three reports, probably quarter-session), and as few as two and as many as six hours a week of scheduled class time.

In each case the short class was compensated for by longer scheduled or open lab times, and the converse for the long classes probably included lab times. Open lab times varied from 20 to 120 hours a week. At least 12 respondents did not indicate open lab times or allowed totally open labs at any time. Some set limits per student, from four to five hours each week.

Written exams and quizzes covered the spectrum from one per semester/quarter to 10. In most cases written testing consisted of a combination of short quizzes and longer exams (midterm and final). At least one school required a research paper on an audio topic. No consensus exists between the reports on the method of written evaluation.

Studio and field projects also ran the gamut from three to 11 per semester/quarter. Seven of the 20 required from four to six projects completed per student per session. Some included a final major project, either a documentary or a drama. Several required scheduled hours of board shifts on the radio station as part of the class requirement.

Common Emphasis

Instructors often agree on much of what is available to form a centerpiece for the course, and the most popular textbook was Stanley Alten's *Audio in Media* (2002) the most comprehensive audio production textbook written for university classes. The book includes enough material for at least two semesters, including multitrack and digital technology and techniques. If not used as a textbook, it may serve an excellent resource for faculty. Four schools use Alten as their primary required text.

Lewis O'Donnell et al.'s *Modern Radio Production* (2000) and David Reese and Lynne Gross' *Radio Production Worktext: Studio Equipment* (2001) shared honors as the second most popular text. Each of those texts is a requirement of three different schools. The O'Donnell text is one of the best texts for strictly radio production. Like Alten it is continuously updated with new editions. Reese and Gross' popular text is also useful for teaching radio production techniques. It includes self-study exercises and an accompanying CD. Michael Keith's *The Radio Station* text (2000) concentrates on the basics radio/audio programming as opposed to production. Three syllabi indicated no required text, and the remaining schools each required a unique text from the rest of the respondents. A listing of those and other possible textbooks are given at the end of the chapter.

Michael Adams and Kimberly Massey's *Introduction to Radio: Production and Programming* (1995) combines coverage of both programming and production for radio. Stanley Alten's *Audio in Media* (2002), is useful, as is Tim Aymes' *Audio Post-Production in Video and Film* (1999). The latter is an especially good overview of postproduction history, equipment and techniques, including digital and nonlinear information.

For some British terms and spelling check out Chuck Crouse's *Reporting for Radio* (1998), a radio news textbook; and Tominson Holman's *Sound for Film and Television* (1997). These offer much on film and television sound technology. Fairly advanced technically, but a valuable reference and excellent for an advanced course in audio production, is O'Donnell et al.'s *Modern Radio Production*.

Geoffrey Hull's *The Recording Industry* (1998) covers both the business and production sides of the recording industry. Joseph Johnson and Kenneth Jones' *Modern Radio Station Practices* (1978), now dated and out of print, was the best source for information on the management of a radio station. It covered programming, sales, promotion, operation, law and on-air production.

Keith's *The Radio Station* (2000), mentioned earlier, and Gorham Kindem and Robert Musburger's *Introduction to Media Production: From Analog to Digital*, 2nd edition (2001), cover all media production: audio, video, film and graphics.

Vincent LoBrutto's *Sound-on-Film: Interviews with Creators of Film Sound* (1994) provides personal insight, just as the title suggests.

Reese and Gross' *Radio Production Worktext* and David Huber and Robert Runstein's *Modern Recording Techniques* (2001) concentrate on the recording industry and multitrack recording techniques. Sam Sauls' *The Culture of College Radio* (2000) is the best source for information on how to run a college radio station along with the culture, social and institutional information on such an operation.

Michael Talbot-Smith's *Sound Assistance* (1999) is a training text designed to be used by British students working toward certification in the U.K. media market. It is more technically oriented than most audio texts but provides good background electronic technology that all production personnel should possess within their knowledge base.

John Watkins' *The Art of Digital Audio* (2000) is considered one of the best overall digital audio books. Herbert Zettl's *Video Basics* (2001) is primarily a video text, but as with the rest of Zettl's books, an excellent source for audio production.

Within the realm of periodicals and journals a thoughtful instructor would want to consult *Communication Booknotes Quarterly*, published by Lawrence Erlbaum and Associates, as a bibliographic source for publications in all forms of communication. They would also want to take a look at the *Communicator*, a monthly publication of the Radio–Television News Directors Association. For a more academic orientation *Critical Studies in Mass Communication*, published quarterly by the Mass Communication Division of the National Communication Association, sometimes includes articles on audio production, as does *Feedback* and the *Journal of Broadcasting and Electronic Media*, both published quarterly by the Broadcast Education Association.

Other scholarly publications include the *Journal of Communication*, published quarterly by the International Communication Association; the *Journal of Film and*

Video, published quarterly by the University Film and Video Association; and the *Journal of Radio Studies*, published twice a year by the Broadcast Education Association. In addition, the *Mass Communication Review* is published quarterly by the Mass Communication and Society Division of the Association for Education in Journalism and Mass Communication.

Outside Resources

The most valuable links may offer shared information between instructors. In addition, all major manufacturers of audio equipment maintain detailed sites describing the latest equipment and production techniques. Professional production publications also maintain sites offering insight into the direction in which the industry is moving. Industry links are listed here.

Inside Radio. www.insideradio.com.

Federal Communications Commission. www.fcc.gov.

Media Communications Association. www.itva.org.

Museum of Television and Radio. www.mtr.org.

National Association of College Broadcasters. www.hofstra.edu/~nacb.

National Broadcasting Society/Alpha Epsilon Rho. www.onu.edu/org/nbs/irts-aerho-alphaepslonrho.

National Public Radio. www.npr.org/.

Radio Advertising Bureau. www.rab.com/.

Radio Archive. www.oldradio.com.

Radio Television News Directors Association. www.rtnda.org/.

Society of Broadcast Engineers. www.sbe.org/.

Society of Motion Picture and Television Engineers. www.smpte.org/.

Marvin Bensman Collection, University of Memphis. www.people.memphis.edu/~bensmanm/.

University of Missouri School of Journalism. web.missouri.edu/~jourvs/ginterns.html.

Yahoo! Entertainment. www.yahoo.com/entertainment/.

Remembering a Mentor: Lynne Gross

Susan Plumb Salas

My mentor, Lynne Gross, has mentored many students through her research and textbook publications, her national and international classrooms, and as a producer of several hundred television programs. It was indeed my good fortune to meet Lynne my first day as a new faculty member at Pepperdine University, and she soon became my teacher, friend and mentor.

I had returned to the classroom after twenty 20 years in production and was excited to share the knowledge I had gained with my students, but challenged as to where to begin. Lynne, as I'm quite sure she has done many times over the years, reached out to me with not only advice, but also shared examples of her teaching methods. Implementing her pedagogy into my classroom helped to make a smooth career transition into teaching. That day also marked the beginning of a valued friendship.

Lynne's reaching out to me is a quality that makes her such a stand out among educators. Not only does she reach out to colleagues, but also to staff and especially to students. Always there is a line at her door, and it does not matter what students' needs are or if they are graduate students or a freshmen in a theory class. She always makes time; students never feel they are inconveniencing her, even if she has to run to her next class. The students' issues at hand are always her foremost priority.

This teacher, who is always available for students, is also a prolific researcher. Lynne's work has been published in the most distinguished journals of her discipline, and she has published 11 textbooks. The time and effort her publishing takes never diminish the time she makes available for her students.

Lynne's teaching and mentoring go beyond the classroom and out into the world. She has done consulting work for Children's Broadcasting Corporation, KCET, CBS, and the Olympics, to name a few, and she has taken her knowledge and expertise to classrooms in Malaysia, Swaziland, Estonia, Australia and Guyana. A wonderful ambassador for the telecommunications field, Lynne has been recognized for her service to professional organizations, serving as governor of the Academy of Television Arts and Sciences and president of the Broadcast Education Association (BEA).

Lynne's wide-ranging contributions and teaching have been recognized with numerous awards, including the Frank Stanton Fellow for Distinguished Contribution to Electronic Media Education from the International Radio and Television Society and the Distinguished Education Service Award from the BEA.

Lynne's synergistic approach to teaching constantly challenges the students and herself to learn and grow with the knowledge she provides in her classroom. She also listens to students' suggestions and implements change in her syllabi, assignments and lectures based on student feedback.

In addition to all of this, she shares her wealth of contacts from her production experience and professional organizations with her students by bringing these contacts into the classroom to broaden the students' understanding of what possibilities await them. Overall, Lynne guides her students to make intelligent decisions about their future roles in the telecommunications industry and provides them with an understanding of the ethical responsibilities that come with the job.

Lynne has impacted my life and teaching on many levels. I have modeled my syllabus and assignments after her proven successes. She has inspired my teaching style to always have high expectations for myself and for the students, to listen more closely, and to always keep my office door open.

I describe myself to my students as their teacher, coach, facilitator, collaborator and advisor. This is what my mentor, Lynne Gross, gave and showed me. Overall, Lynne's teaching approach has enriched my teaching experience, and I'm proud to say that my friendship with Lynne has enriched my life.

CHAPTER 16

Broadcast Programming

Dom Caristi

Introduction

One of the challenges facing a programming instructor is that our students enter our classes having watched years of television and listened to a lifetime of radio. For many of them, programming is something that just *is*, not something that needs to be studied. What's more, for those who have listened to one radio format all of their lives, they naturally assume that all radio stations program that way. Since most of our students belong to a circle of friends that closely match their own demographic characteristics, they often believe that *everyone* listens to the same station. They are astonished to find that a station they've never even heard of (heaven forbid, an AM station) tops the ratings in the market. Without question, the first role of a programming class must be to provide our students with an awareness of radio, television and cable programming that is much broader than their limited experience has been.

The task, however, is much greater than awareness. Just a few hours with a programming textbook or an online search of radio and television station Web sites can provide students with some of that. There is no shortage of pedagogical research that tells us we must engage our students in the process to a much greater extent than just as listeners to lectures. They must be asked to do more than just darken the bubble corresponding to the correct answer on a computer-scanned test sheet.

The broadcast programming instructor's job is made more difficult because we are unable to provide students with the formula for success. Throughout their years in school, students have been taught to find the "right" answer from multiple alternatives and then to provide that answer when presented with a problem. Unfortunately in programming there is no formula for success. Students need to know that the most successful programmers in history have also had their flops. The late, great, Brandon Tartikoff, who resuscitated a flailing NBC in the 1980s and revived the situation comedy genre with *The Cosby Show* is the same person responsible for *Manimal*, an absolutely awful show that was promptly canceled.[1] Just when a genre like westerns or reality programming seems to be all the rage, the audience tires of it in favor of something else.

To a certain extent, then, a programming class must examine history. So much of what students see and hear today is the result of innovation in the past. The top-40 concept in radio, late-night TV talk shows and all-news cable TV channels, staples for our students, were radical departures from the norm in their day.

This chapter examines the elements of a successful course in Broadcast Programming, including the sorts of assignments that will engage students in learning and the historical framework they need to understand the context into which they hope to enter.

Position of the Course in the Curriculum

A student enrolled in broadcast programming needs to have at least a general understanding of the electronic media industry. Virtually every college and university currently offering a broadcast programming class has the introductory survey course as a prerequisite at the very least. For that reason, few institutions offer the course at the freshman level.[2] Precisely where it falls in the curriculum, however, varies considerably. University of the Sacred Heart has a series of four successive courses that must be taken before reaching the programming class.

Broadcast programming classes can be found at every level of the curriculum, but the preponderance of universities offer the class at the junior (or 300) level, with senior-level offerings coming in a close second.[3] A few universities offer the class strictly at the graduate level, whereas some dual list the course as an offering for either undergraduate or graduate students.

Just as the level at which the course is offered varies, the titles of the departments that offer the course vary. Faculty and students searching college catalogs for comparable courses must check departments of broadcasting, communications, journalism, mass communication, radio-TV, telecommunications and even English.[4]

Perhaps in part because of the variety of departments, the centrality of a broadcast programming class varies. Few departments require broadcast programming of all their majors, although some require it for specific subsets of students. For example, Ball State University requires programming for the students in the management and sales track but not for any of the other three sequences in the broadcast curriculum. Similarly, Middle Tennessee State University requires its Electronic Media Management students to take the Electronic Media Programming class, but does not require students in Electronic Media Journalism or Electronic Media Production to take the class. At the University of Alabama, it is not even a requirement for students in the management sequence in the Department of Telecommunication and Film. Instead, students in the management sequence must take either the Telecommunication Programming class or a Telecommunication Audience Analysis class. The class is much more likely to be within a department's electives or may be found as an optional choice from among two or three offerings.

Similar Courses

Despite the variation in broadcast programming's position within the curriculum, there is very little variety in the types of courses offered in place of a programming class. There is a slight variation in the name of the course, often related to the difference in aforementioned department names. An examination of the 10 largest programs[5] showed courses named Broadcast Programming and Audience Effects, Broadcast and Cable Programming, Telecommunication Programming, Electronic Media Programming, Radio and TV Programming, Television Programming, and Programs: Evaluation and Analysis. An examination of the course descriptions shows that the titles may not be a perfect fit. Syracuse University and Boston University both offer a course titled Television Programming. Syracuse, however, offers a separate course in Radio Station Operation (which includes programming), whereas Boston University's course description includes radio in the television programming class. Most of these courses combine industry overviews with practical application of the principles learned.[6]

Ancillary/Related Courses

Not every university with a broadcast or mass communication curriculum offers a course dedicated to programming. In such institutions, programming is usually offered as part of a course in broadcast or media management. Even within those curricula where a specific course in broadcast programming can be found, elements of the course are included as units in other classes. In addition to a programming segment in the introductory class, programming content is covered in the law/regulation class, promotions class, and media research methods. The University of Florida, which offers Telecommunication Programming, also offers Telecommunication Research, which covers analysis of audience attitudes and characteristics, often included by other institutions as part of the programming class. The University of Texas teaches Broadcast Programming and Audience Effects, combining the study of programming with an analysis of the cognitive and behavioral impact of that programming—something that many other universities offer as a separate course.

Comparative Features

Creating assignments for broadcast programming classes can be somewhat challenging. Unlike video production classes having a natural connection to project-based learning, faculty teaching programming classes must devise creative ways to move beyond the standard lecture/exam fare. Fortunately, there are many faculty members who have already devised creative projects that achieve several educational objectives of a broadcast programming class.

The importance of projects to the broadcast programming class cannot be overemphasized. The courses at the universities listed below all put a premium on projects as a way of engaging the students in the subject. This is obvious in the weight assigned to the grades. Exams and quizzes made up less than half of a student's grade in the majority of the programming classes, whereas projects were the preponderance of the grade.[7]

Before students can begin understanding the complexities of programming, faculty must be certain they are familiar with the diversity of programs and formats that currently exist. Like most media consumers, students are likely to listen to radio stations or watch cable channels that match their specific demographic group and be virtually unaware of other formats or channels. For this reason, Misericordia College has projects that require students to survey the existing media landscape. A radio assignment requires students to listen to three different commercial radio stations in the market (at least one of which must be AM) for at least one hour in each of three different dayparts. Students must then provide a comparison of each station's programming across different dayparts as well as a comparison across the stations. A cable programming assignment requires each student to program 60 channels of a hypothetical cable system. Although students may be able to identify a number of cable channels with little or no research, the project requires the students to provide justification for their selections, as well as their channel placement on the system. This assignment helps reinforce the differences in demographic groups and how programming is targeted to each. Students are required to provide their reports orally and in writing.

One aspect of the class that faculty want to convey to students is the process of developing a television program idea and attempting to get it on the air. California State University at Fullerton has an assignment to engage students in the process. Pitch Project requires students working in a group to present a mock pitch session. Some students act as members of a programming company while others portray network executives. Students must work together to create an idea, determine an appropriate network (pitches to public television are permissible), and create the presentation and accompanying supporting materials. The pitches are performed in front of the class, take 15 to 30 minutes each, and end with an exchange between the students doing the pitch and the students observing the process. Students pitching programs are required to provide written information about the following required elements in their presentations: a precise program concept (referred to as the "*TV Guide* blurb"), and a treatment for the idea. If a series is pitched, ideas are presented about what will happen in episodes following the pilot; the program genre; the target audience; some of the creative people who will be involved in the project; program traits (such as conflict, durability, innovation); and an approximate budget for a single episode. Students are further encouraged to address the time slot where the program would work best and why the network should want it, advertisers that might be interested in the program, promotion techniques, and any benefits that might result from ancillary products or awards. To enhance their presentations, students are advised that they may use charts, play a brief tape, or use other techniques to add sizzle to the presentation.

At Oklahoma State University, programming students are required to create proposals for local television programs. Early in the semester, student groups conduct focus-group research to learn about the attitudes and opinions of "their viewers." They learn about the realities of focus-group research, what it can and cannot do. The students then apply some of what they learn by developing five separate proposals for local programs. The proposals must account for the production methods as well as the budget requirements. Like the California State assignment, the Oklahoma State project requires both a written outcome and a class presentation.

Instead of pitching new programs, students at the University of Tennessee are required to evaluate existing programs. They are provided with specific criteria to use in evaluating the show's opening, its theme, the plot, the characters, the dialogue, the ending and the production elements. Students are also expected to explain how the episode they've evaluated could have been improved. The project does not require students to work in groups and can be completed in much less time. It also does not require that class time be committed to presentations, although certainly they can be incorporated by those faculty who would like to do so.

The University of Oklahoma programming class requires students to write memos to the instructor, who acts as general manager of the station. The writing assignments are not intended to be research papers and are limited to one single-spaced typed page. One of the purposes of the assignment is for students to boil an issue down to its essential elements and succinctly state their case for action. As with the program-evaluation assignment, these exercises help students practice their critical thinking skills while not requiring them to work in groups or make class presentations. One assignment calls on students to respond to a program of questionable taste on their station. In some ways, this assignment includes some of the lessons of the program-evaluation assignment in that students must provide some critical analysis. The memo assignment requires that they also suggest a specific change in the program for improvement. Students must provide realistic solutions based on market conditions. For example, if a student chooses to address the taste of *The Jerry Springer Show*, the solution cannot be to replace the program with *Oprah* if in fact *Oprah* is currently licensed by a competing station in the market.

Two of the assigned memos require students to make programming changes. One of the memos deals specifically with syndicated programming, and the other is a radio station assignment. In each case, the student must briefly address the problem in a concise memo and be persuasive in providing a tangible solution. The University of Alabama has an assignment requiring students to analyze the existing radio stations in the market and propose the format for a new station in town, providing all the requisite background information in their reports.

The fourth of the memo assignments requires students to suggest a campaign that a station or local cable system might develop to promote community involvement. Students not only think about the promotional aspects of a campaign, but they also learn the value of community involvement for a broadcaster.

At the University of Alabama, students are required to examine the World Wide Web critically as a tool for programmers. Each student is required to provide a critique of three different station Web sites, including at least one radio station and one television station. Students then write brief papers (two pages each) outlining what they have found. They are encouraged to look for specific items, such as how the stations promote themselves using the Web, and whether any online content is available exclusively online. Not only does this exercise involve students in critical thinking, but it also gets them to think about the Web from a business perspective. When the Internet was new, the assignment may have served a much more basic purpose of simply making students aware of the variety of stations that use Web sites. Now that the Internet has matured and most students come to college with a fair amount of Internet competency,[8] the web programming assignment encourages students to apply business models to the Internet. While they may intuitively realize that a Web site constitutes a cost to a station, they have not likely looked at it from that perspective before. When examined from a cost-efficiency basis, students may begin to question why stations have chosen to include the elements they have.[9]

While the aforementioned universities use multiple projects with shorter deadlines, Ball State University has created a semester-long project that involves students in a programming game.[10] The class is divided into eight groups. Half of the groups serve as local television stations, while the other half begin the semester as syndication companies. In the first half of the semester, each station must purchase approximately four hours of programming each day. Stations are given a programming budget they may not exceed. Syndicators are given a minimum price they must receive for each program they sell. Students on both sides are encouraged to negotiate the best deal possible since profitability is one of the grading criteria. For the second half of the semester, the groups that had served as syndication companies become advertising agencies. Each agency must now purchase advertising time during programs that were purchased by the stations in the first half of the game. At the end of the semester, each group provides extensive records, including the contracts they have signed, a breakdown of cost per ratings point for each of the advertisers, and profit/loss statements for each of the shows they purchased. Although many of the realities of television programming have to be modified for the simulation (for example, there are no barter programs available, and all budgets use straight-line amortization rather than a more realistic declining-value amortization), students are introduced to many of the principles of programming a station. Most importantly, they are able to see the direct connection between a specific program's success and its desirability to advertisers. Perhaps the greatest indication that the students are learning these lessons comes from the many students who have been through the simulation and profess that they know they would do a much better job if they were to go through the process a second time.

Special Features

Beyond the projects just discussed, a broadcast programming class has other unique attributes. Students may be introduced to the concept of ratings and shares in introductory courses, but it is unlikely they will have had to actually apply that knowledge. Except for those universities that provide a separate course for broadcast research,[11] broadcast programming classes require their students to compute ratings and shares. Whether on exams, in quizzes, or on take-home worksheets, students are often required to calculate the ratings and shares for programs, given just the raw data of total households and households watching each station in the market. Realistically, industry professionals are not often required to calculate ratings and shares, being provided with the numbers by agencies, buyers, or ratings services. Learning to compute ratings, however, helps the students to understand what the numbers *mean*. Students are well served when they learn to interpret ratings and not merely to plug numbers into some memorized formula to come up with an answer. Faculty who choose to require students to compute ratings and shares must be certain to vary the questions enough to discourage students from memorizing nondescriptive formulas and instead to encourage an understanding of the relationships between the variables.

In addition to the understanding that comes from computing ratings, students need to learn to be comfortable with the presentation of ratings. Students who may have read news reports about ratings or seen top-10 listings of stations and programs have not been prepared for the shock that is a ratings book. Students given a ratings book for the first time are overwhelmed by the pages of numbers and are generally unable to make sense of them without some tutelage. Programming classes must introduce students to these tools of the trade and help them to understand the appropriate situations in which to use metro ratings versus the Designated Market Areas (DMA) ratings, the difference between the columns with percentages versus the columns with audience expressed in thousands, and the usefulness of the demographic break-outs.

As is the case with all courses in the broadcast curriculum, current realities must be accounted for in the class. The consolidation of the broadcast industry has had an impact on the programming industry, and the course must certainly reflect this. Concepts of vertical integration, repurposing, and international syndication must be included in the course. The individual faculty member's tastes and syllabus best determine whether these concepts are introduced separately as current realities or integrated into the existing course framework. Most likely, the concepts will be presented more than once throughout the term, as are many of the other recurring themes. It is impossible to introduce the concept of ratings and then never again to revisit ratings during the course, and so it is with the concept of vertical integration. A faculty member may introduce the concept early in the semester when discussing the structure of the industry, but vertical integration will reappear as soon as the class turns its attention to off-network syndication, or licensing fees paid by networks to production companies, or getting cable systems to carry a new cable channel.

Common Goals and Objectives

Barbara Moore of the University of Tennessee provides her students with a thorough list of course objectives. The 12 goals below are taken from her syllabus,[12] with my own commentary provided:

1. *Understand and use the concepts and vocabulary of programming.* Most programming classes make it a point to emphasize the vocabulary of the industry. To understand the subject, one must have a thorough understanding of the language.[13]

2. *Trace major trends in programming from the past to the present and project those trends into the future.* Students cannot be taught to be effective programmers. Because there is no formula for success, we must help them understand what has and has not worked in the past and help them extrapolate the lessons for the future.

3. *Describe the steps in the creation and sale of a TV program, including the economic, social, institutional and other pressures that affect the end product.* One of the lessons of a programming class must be an understanding of how an idea eventually

becomes a program. Students need to be aware how this happens for local television, broadcast networks, and cable channels. While there are some similarities, there are also important differences. Students must also appreciate the multitude of external pressures that bear on programming decisions.

4. *Analyze a TV program from an aesthetic and cultural viewpoint.* Part of understanding programming is an appreciation of content. Some universities offer courses in media appreciation and analysis (akin to music appreciation), so this course objective might only be reviewed rather than introduced in those institutions. Still, programming students need a cultural and aesthetic context with which to evaluate program quality.

5. *Describe how decisions about buying programs are made at a TV station.* This is the other side of the program creation and sale process. Although these decisions may have shifted from local hands to corporate headquarters and some of the priorities may be different, critical analysis is still required to make a rational decision.

6. *Summarize the types of qualitative research now being done and the effect research has on programming decisions.* With all due respect to Fred Silverman, who was known as the "man with the golden gut" for his knack for being able to choose successful television programs allegedly based only on gut reactions, broadcasters spend millions of dollars each year on research. Students need to learn not only about the quantitative world of ratings, but also about the qualitative tools such as TvQs, focus-group research, and pilot testing.

7. *Summarize major regulations and laws governing broadcast programming and the Federal Communication Commission's attitude toward program regulation.* Deregulation has certainly reduced the number of program regulations but has not eliminated them. Students need to know the laws regarding children's television, hoaxes by radio personalities, and ownership/cross-ownership limitations. Even some of the laws that no longer exist help students to understand the industry. The growth of magazine-format TV shows can be traced to the existence of the prime-time access rule.

8. *Describe and apply to broadcast programming the various strategies of scheduling.* As stressed earlier, students must learn not just the theories but also their application. Because broadcasting must be programmed with attention to profitability,[14] students have to learn the techniques to be successful. Not all strategies are successful in every situation, so students must learn the array of possibilities.

9. *Describe the system for choosing programs in public broadcasting.* Without the commercials that fund the programming, public stations operate somewhat differently from commercial stations. Expectations of underwriters are not the same as those of advertisers. Programming pressures are every bit as real, and students need to be aware of the similarities and differences.

10. *Outline the types of radio formats and the duties of a program director at a radio station.* Students have grown up with radio, but it's likely that they are unaware of the diversity of radio formats that exist. A programming class must introduce them to these differences and explain the ways in which formats are created. Program directors' tasks differ based on format, market size, and corporate structure, and students need to know what these duties are.

11. *Discuss the differences between programming in the United States and other countries.* More than ever, programming is an international industry. Program pitches made in Hollywood for syndicated programming always consider the potential *after-market* of international distribution. Even students who have no interest in anything outside the United States need an awareness of programming in other countries. The structure of the international programming industry impacts the domestic program market.

12. *Offer a vision of the future of programming and justify the logic behind the vision.* Looking back on what has happened in programming is important, but it is essential that students be able to look forward to the future. No one can predict with certainty what will happen, but our students should be able to use what they have learned to make educated forecasts about future trends and conditions.

Instructor Philosophy

The majority of students who take a class in broadcast programming will not make a career as programmers. If a faculty member develops a broadcast programming class strictly as training for future broadcast programmers, the majority of students in the class will not be well served. Instead, the purpose of the course must be broader.

Broadcast programming is one of a series of courses that help to orient students to the business of broadcasting. Programming, promotion, sales and marketing are all interconnected; therefore, faculty ought to approach the course as one that helps future professionals understand the realities of the broadcast industry. Faculty ought to recognize that some of our students have been attracted to this discipline because of their perception (real or mistaken) that broadcasting is glamorous, its employees are well compensated, and the work is relatively easy. It is the responsibility of faculty teaching broadcast programming to introduce students to the real world of broadcasting.

One effective means of inculcating students to the industry is the use of guest speakers from industry. Industry guests are appreciated by students and are much more likely to have their undivided attention. Some faculty may be reluctant to contact industry professionals, believing that programmers are far too busy and uninterested to spend time with college students. In fact, most industry professionals look forward to telling college students about the real world and actually look forward to an occasional visit.

Universities that find themselves near New York City, Chicago and Los Angeles are able to call on professionals from the broadcast networks. It might be difficult to get Les Moonves of Viacom/CBS to speak to a class, but many others actively involved in programming are happy to make an occasional classroom appearance. Universities not located near those three metropolises can also find representatives from major media companies. Major cable Multiple System Owners are headquartered in Philadelphia, St. Louis, Denver and Atlanta.

There are broadcast station groups with offices across the country, with major groups in San Antonio, Dallas, Cincinnati, Washington, D.C., Tampa, West Palm Beach, Des Moines and even the relatively small town of Davenport, Iowa (market size, 92). Although the largest cable networks may be in the biggest markets, some smaller cable nets have their operations in Knoxville, Louisville, Miami, Las Vegas and Nashville. These are but a small sampling of the many media companies that may be able to provide prospective guests.

If located close enough to your university and the logistics are not too complicated, it might be worth taking the class to the media company. If located so distant from any of these companies that even getting a guest to come to your class is out of the question, consider having a video or telephone conference. Even the busiest media executive can make time for a 20-minute phone call. Faculty can make the conference more interesting by providing visuals (especially a picture of the guest) from the company's Web site while the guest speaks. Finally, don't overlook local talent. Small stations and cable systems still have people who are knowledgeable about the business, although they may not have the star power that some from larger media companies will have.

One philosophy that broadcast instructors must adopt is the concept of active learning.[15] The research on pedagogy provides overwhelming evidence that students learn more and retain it better when actively engaged in the learning process, rather than sitting passively listening to a lecture. The projects mentioned in this chapter are just a few examples of ways of engaging students. Students will learn best when the class involves them. Broadcast programming classes should incorporate a mix of class discussion, writing and projects.[16]

Common Emphasis

Several of the courses examined required students to keep abreast of current industry issues and developments. In light of the changes occurring in the industry, this appears to be a meaningful way to engage students in discussions about the current application of programming techniques. Evaluation techniques vary. In some cases students are quizzed regularly,[17] whereas in others class discussion of current events is assessed. Current events content is available from a multitude of sources. *Broadcasting & Cable* offers a classroom discount for student subscriptions.

Many Web sites with news of broadcast programming are available (see the list at the end of this chapter). Television columnists at the major American newspapers provide a wealth of both news and analysis about current programming trends. Rather than photocopying each of these articles, students can be e-mailed the URLs (Web-site addresses) of articles that faculty want them to read.

The majority of broadcast programming classes seem to stress the importance of good communication skills, both in writing and in oral presentation. Syllabi emphasize that written work must be flawless, and that class presentations should be ripe with visuals or multimedia. Perhaps because the course is often an upper-division offering, the faculty expectations for this class appear to be high. It can also be attributed to the this course dealing with an aspect of media management, and, as such, students are expected to perform as management personnel—much more so that they might in courses dealing with video or audio production.

Perhaps it is self-evident, but it is worth reiterating. College courses should prepare students to be lifelong learners.[18] Broadcast programming must contribute to that goal.

Throughout all the curricula that offer broadcast programming, and despite the diversity in the way in which the class may be taught, it is not an overstatement to say that every different programming class attempts to teach its students critical thinking skills. Whether this is accomplished by program critiques, or building a hypothetical cable lineup, or pitching a program, students engage in activities that help them develop the skills of critical analysis and assessment needed not only in broadcast programming, or even in broadcasting, but in all of their adult life.

Critical thinking is one of those skills developed over time, with repeated challenges and exercises from a variety of perspectives. Critical thinking is not the exclusive purview of broadcast programming, nor should it be only general education classes that develop this skill. In broadcast programming, students expand upon their critical thinking skills and apply them to industry-specific situations. It is the connection between theory and application that makes critical thinking most real for students.[19]

Reasoning in the professions ... combines characteristics of both problem solving and critical thinking. In professional practice, problems are ill defined, but solutions can often be tested, although without scientific or mathematical precision. Faced with complex problems, professionals conduct informal but rigorous "action experiments," evaluate the results of their experiments, and modify their approaches based on the results. Action experiments allow practitioners to act with some assurance even when problems are ill defined. Their hypothesis-testing quality allows the practitioner to learn from the outcomes.[20]

Common Challenges/Solutions

One of the greatest challenges facing a broadcast programming class is the same faced by most university courses: keeping enrollment manageable. Unfortunately the economics of most universities is such that some courses must be large in order to allow enrollments in other courses to be kept low. While administrators can understand the need to cap enrollments on writing and production courses, they are less aware of the need to limit the size of a programming class. In most broadcast curricula, therefore, enrollment in the programming class can grow to a size that makes writing, presentation and projects more difficult to manage. Certainly the problem is not as pronounced as one finds in introductory survey classes. Fortunately, because programming often is not a required course and because it is usually offered to upper-division students, enrollment generally does not exceed 40 students. Although a manageable number, classes of that size make requiring extensive writing assignments or project-based learning difficult.

Short of convincing the university that the broadcast programming enrollment should be capped at 20, or providing a teaching assistant whose time is devoted to grading (requiring additional resources), other techniques are available to faculty who want to provide active learning for large classes.[21] Group activity can still occur even in large classes, although there may have to be some modifications made, and the amount of time provided for each group to report may have to be limited.

Faculty who would like to require individual student presentations can schedule them at alternate times, with only a portion of the class attending each session. It increases the amount of time the faculty member spends watching presentations, but also increases the amount of time available for class presentations. In terms of writing, broadcast faculty need to learn the lessons that our colleagues in rhetoric have known for years: not every writing assignment must be graded, and those that are do not all have to be graded equally extensively. While a faculty member might spend a great deal of time reading and commenting on a student's term paper, that professor should not spend nearly as much time on brief writing assignments. Some papers can be peer reviewed either as a supplement to or in place of faculty evaluation.

Professionalism can also be promoted by making certain that students are held accountable. Faculty members are well practiced in this art, yet sometimes standards are less rigorous, especially when group projects are involved. Every faculty member who has ever assigned a group project has been approached by a student who claims that a group member is not pulling his weight or a member is dominating a group. Faculty can spend an undue amount of time attempting to arbitrate these disagreements. Instead, there are two effective techniques to assist in-group (or internal group) management.

First, any class involving group projects ought to incorporate a peer evaluation as a portion of the grade. Faculty members ought to provide students with clearly stated evaluation criteria before the project begins, so students are aware of how they will be evaluated by one another[22] Knowing in advance that there will be peer evaluation motivates students, regardless of whether the actual percentage of the grade determined by peer evaluation is relatively low. In addition, peer evaluation provides an additional exercise in thinking critically. Some students are extremely uncomfortable providing evaluations of their peers and may even resort to giving every student a perfect score. To counteract this tendency, faculty should incorporate some means of forcing students to evaluate more realistically. Students can be required to rank all group members from highest to lowest (with no ties allowed) regardless of points assigned.

Faculty can meet personally with any student who gives all group members the same score and require an explanation. If this is stated in advance, it greatly reduces the number of students who will give everyone the same score. Students should be required to provide comments in addition to just a score or grade, and every student should receive these qualitative assessments in some form. To protect anonymity and save myself from having to transcribe all of the comments, I simply invite students to come to my office to hear what was said about them, but not to know by whom.

Another method for ensuring student accountability is to institute rules for "firing" a group member. Before a project begins, faculty should explain that a group may remove an unproductive group member based on clearly stated criteria.[23] Removal of a student from a group ought not to be easy but should be available. To experience some of the realities of personnel decisions, removal of a group member ought to require a face-to-face confrontation with the offender.

Conclusions

As pervasive as radio, television and cable may be, broadcast programming is unlikely to be viewed as a course critical for a student's general education. Mass communication departments never think to require the course of their diverse majors. In fact, even within broadcast curricula, the course is likely to be an elective. Because of its humble position in the university curriculum, one might mistakenly conclude that the course is not especially valuable.

The course can be of such value to broadcast curricula that it can serve as the capstone course for students in a broadcast management or media industry sequence. The University of Idaho states, "The primary objective of a capstone course is to provide an opportunity for students to integrate the general knowledge and skills gained in their undergraduate curriculum with the specialized knowledge they have developed in their major" (see note 2). Montana State University's catalog provides a working definition of capstone course criteria:

A capstone experience requires seniors to integrate principles, theories, and methods learned in courses required throughout the major. Students creatively analyze, synthesize, and evaluate learned knowledge in a project having a professional focus and communicate the results of the project effectively at a professional entry level by a method appropriate to the discipline (see note 2).

Broadcast programming integrates elements of sales, research, management and promotion into one course. Course content includes history, law and economics. Through active, project-based learning, students apply what they have learned and develop their critical thinking abilities.

Faculty must make certain that the class serves the students well by involving students in active learning, especially projects; introducing students to the business realities of the industry by including industry guests and enforcing real-world expectations; and requiring students to think critically.

While broadcast programming may not achieve the status of a capstone course at universities where it is offered, it can still achieve key objectives, provided faculty members are mindful of the greater educational goal. They must not focus on creating a class full of students who have memorized a set of content for exams without ever having engaged the material.

Notes

1. Tartikoff himself described *Manimal* as a show "about a scientist who could transform himself into any species of animal; unfortunately, the show was stuck on 'dog' " [Brandon Tartikoff, *The Last Great Ride* (New York: Random House, 1992), p. 171].

2. A few community colleges, including Hillsborough Community College (Fla.), offer Broadcast Programming at the 100 (freshman) level, but still have at least one prerequisite course. When offered at the community college, Broadcast Programming is more likely to be a 200-level class, as is the case at Isothermal (N.C.) and Volunteer

State (Tenn.). Five Towns (N.Y.) and Menlo College (Calif.) were the only four-year schools offering the course at the 100 level, but also had prerequisite courses. Catalog information is available from CollegeSource online at www.collegecatalogs.org/.

3. The majority of colleges and universities code their courses with three- or four-digit numbers, where the first digit indicates the presumed class level (i.e., 1 = freshman, 2 = sophomore, etc). The precise assignment is more rigid in some cases than in others. Not everything can be discerned from these course numbers, however. Freshmen often take 200- and 300-level courses. What's more, universities may change numbers without significantly altering the content. California State University at Fullerton changed its Radio and TV Programming course from a designation of 477 to 360.

4. Although the variety of names of departments is not a new problem, it has only gotten worse in recent years. It is beyond the scope of this chapter (or this book) to examine the diversity of names given to our academic departments.

5. The largest programs are taken from Becker, Vlad, Huh and Prine, "Annual Enrollment Report: Number of Students Studying Journalism-Mass Communication at All-Time High," *Journalism Educator* 56 (Autumn 2001):28. The 10 largest undergraduate enrollments were at the University of Texas, Penn State University, the University of Florida, Middle Tennessee State University, California State University at Fullerton, the University of the Sacred Heart (Puerto Rico), Ball State University, Syracuse University, and the University of Alabama.

6. The University of Texas offers its Broadcast Programming and Audience Effects course as part of its media studies sequence. As such, the catalog emphasizes analysis and criticism over an industry perspective. This dichotomy is rare. In the majority of universities, analysis and application are combined.

7. Only one syllabus was found that assigned more than half of the total grade to examinations and quizzes (67 percent). All the rest ranged between 25 and 50 percent of the grade determined by exams and quizzes. The mean of the exam and quiz weight in a student's grade was 43 percent.

8. Like computer knowledge in general, there is wide disagreement whether students should be competent, literate or proficient on the Internet. The definition for these terms is also questionable. Certainly proficiency is considered to mean a higher level of knowledge and skill than competency, but exactly how those categories are put into practice is not universally accepted. Without engaging in a lengthy discussion of this issue, it can be safely asserted that familiarity with the World Wide Web and basic ability to *surf* (i.e., find sites of interest) would be necessary for competency, literacy and proficiency.

9. Oklahoma State University's programming class includes the World Wide Web as part of its overall Station Promotion assignment. Students at Oklahoma State design an overall station promotion, of which the Web is just one aspect. They also have a Web analysis assignment similar to Alabama's, but it requires students to critique only one radio station site. The Alabama project is highlighted here because of its focus on the Internet as a promotion tool.

10. A detailed explanation of the game is at David L. Smith and Dom Caristi, "A Television Programming Simulation that Engages Students," *Feedback* 42 (Spring 2001):19–23.

11. Broadcast research classes also vary in content. Some broadcast departments offer a broad course that covers the spectrum of social scientific research methodology, whereas others offer a more applied course that deals with survey and ratings methodology used by the broadcast industry.

12. See the Broadcast Education Association's Syllabus Project at www.beaweb.org.

13. Eastman and Ferguson's textbook on Broadcast Programming contains more than 600 terms in the 25-page glossary.

14. Even public radio and television stations must be concerned with the bottom line. Although the stations are not for profit, they still must make their budgets by attracting enough funds from underwriting, grants and memberships. The economic incentives may be less direct but they are nonetheless real.

15. Active learning is an educational movement that began in K-12 schools and has finally found its way to higher education. Sage publishes the journal *Active Learning in Higher Education.* See also David Lempert, *Escape from the Ivory Tower: Student Adventures in Democratic Experiential Education* (San Francisco: Jossey Bass, 1996).

16. For a truly unique view of project-based learning in this discipline, see Kim Schroeder, "Communication Studies with a Difference: A Project-Based Approach," *Feedback* 43 (May 2002):1.

17. *Quizzed* is used generically to mean "tested." In some cases there are specific current events quizzes, whereas in others the material is incorporated into the regular exams.

18. A description of the university of the future is located in Frank Rhodes, "The New University" in *Challenges Facing Higher Education at the Millennium,* ed. Werner Hirsch and Luc Weber (Phoenix: Oryx, 1999).

19. An excellent reference on combining the theory and practice of critical thinking is Marcia Mentkowski, *Learning that Lasts: Integrating Learning, Development and Performance in College and Beyond* (San Francisco: Jossey Bass, 2000).

20. Joanne G. Kurfiss, *Critical Thinking: Theory, Research, Practice and Possibilities,* ASHE-ERIC Higher Education Report, vol. 17, no. 2. Citations omitted.

21. See Wilbert J. McKeachie, "Why Classes Should Be Small, But How to Help Your Students Be Active Learners Even in Large Classes" and "Large Classes: Morale, Discipline, and Order," in *Teaching Tips,* 9th ed. (Lexington, Mass.: D. C. Heath, 1994), pp. 197–221.

22. Faculty should adopt a rubric that suits the particular group project. Dozens of samples can be located online by entering the search term *peer evaluation rubric* into any Internet search engine such as Google. See also Judith Arter, *Scoring Rubrics in the Classroom* (Thousand Oaks, Calif.: Corwin, 2001).

23. Here are the rules I have established for firing a group member. These are provided only as a sample. "Rules for Firing a Group Member" apply in some rare instances in which group members may become so frustrated with one of their own that they would rather have the member removed from their group. This is a choice to work with one fewer group member than to continue to have a group member who is not contributing or, worse yet, is disruptive of the group's progress. In those cases, the members of the group can vote to fire the particular group member, following the rules below. Group members can only be fired for more than one unexcused absence from a

group meeting; more than one attendance at a group meeting without having completed an assignment; or repeated unwillingness to contribute to group decisions. In addition, disruptive behavior at group meetings, including reading unrelated materials during discussions or being unwilling to revise work when found unacceptable, would qualify for ouster. Before firing, the group member must be confronted, face to face, with the complaints against him or her and allowed to respond to those complaints. The instructor must be present for this meeting. The instructor will *not* serve as arbiter. After having been previously confronted and if group members are still dissatisfied with the offender's behavior, the instructor must be present for a vote of the group. The vote to remove a member must be unanimous. Any group member who is removed from a group becomes a group of one. The same output is expected from this individual as would be from the other groups in the class. Similarly, the group that voted to remove the member is still expected to produce the same output despite working with one fewer member.

Suggested Resources

Brown, James, and Ward Quall. 1998. *Radio-television-cable management*. New York: McGraw-Hill.
Covington, William. 1999. *Creativity in TV and cable managing and producing*. New York: McGraw-Hill.
Eastman, S., and D. Ferguson. 2002. *Broadcast/cable/web programming*. 6th ed. Belmont, Calif.: Wadsworth.
Fishman, Mark. 1998. *Entertaining crime: Television reality programs*. New York: Aldine de Gruyter.
Frantzich, Stephen. 1998. *The C-span revolution*. Norman: University of Oklahoma Press.
Gross, L., and E. Vane. 1994. *Programming for TV, radio and cable*. Boston: Focal.
Hollis, Tim. 2001. *Hi there, boys and girls! America's local children's TV programs*. Jackson: University Press of Mississippi.
Howard, H., M. Kievman, and B. Moore. 1994. *Radio, TV and cable programming*. 2nd ed. Ames: Iowa State University Press.
Keith, Michael. 1996. *The radio station*. 4th ed. Boston: Focal.
Seagrave, Kerry. 1998. *American television abroad*. Jefferson, N.C.: McFarland.
Webster, James, Patricia Phalen, and Lawrence Lichty. 2000. *Ratings analysis: The theory and practice of audience research*. Mawhaw, N.J.: Lawrence Erlbaum.

Biographies and Autobiographies

Books are especially useful to faculty members who want to provide extra credit or independent assignments. A small sample of the hundreds of books available.
Cavett, Dick. 1974. *Cavett*. New York: Harcourt Brace Jovanovich.
Donahue, Phil. 1979. *My own story*. New York: Simon and Schuster.
Gelbart, Larry. 1998. *Laughing matters*. New York: Random House.
Leamer, Laurence. 1989. *King of the night: The life of Johnny Carson*. New York: Murrow.

Mair, George. 1994. *Oprah Winfrey: The real story.* Secaucus, N.J.: Carol.

Oppenheimer, Jess. 1996. *Laughs, luck and Lucy.* New York: Syracuse University Press.

Shanks, Bob. 1976. *The cool fire.* New York: Norton.

Tartikoff, Brandon. 1992. *The last great ride.* New York: Random House.

Tinker, Grant. 1994. *Tinker in television.* New York: Simon and Schuster.

Weaver, Pat. 1994. *The best seat in the house.* New York: Alfred A. Knopf.

Electronic Newsletters

Everyone complains about getting too much e-mail, but there are a few newsletters that are essential. Subscription is free, and each can be scanned in less than five minutes. Each of these newsletters could be listed under Web sites that follow, but are separated here because they also provide the unique attribute of a newsletter.

Cynthia Turner's Cynopsis. Subscribe by e-mailing cynopsis@optonline.com. A tremendous source of the latest news in TV programming. Also provides ratings info.

The Lost Remote. A weekly newsletter. You can register at www.lostremote.com. The Web site also has a thorough collection of news stories, updated daily.

Radioink.com. The trade journal's Web site with a free daily newsletter available. Register at the Web site.

ShopTalk. This weekday newsletter deals mostly with the world of television news but has expanded to include pieces about programming as well. Subscribe by registering online at www.tvspy.com.

TVInsite.com. Reed's home page for its online sites for *Broadcasting & Cable, Cablevision,* and *Multichannel News.* There are searchable archives and links to other news sources. Free daily e-mail news updates are available.

Web Sites

The relevant trade association Web sites are listed first. In addition to the online resources they provide, they offer a number of useful publications. Their annual conventions are great learning and networking opportunities. Most offer discounted memberships for academics.

www.Cabletvadbureau.com. Cabletelevision Advertising Bureau.

www.NAB.org. National Association of Broadcasters.

www.NATPE.org. National Association of Television Program Executives.

www.NCTA.com. National Cable & Telecommunications Association.

www.RAB.com. Radio Advertising Bureau.

www.Arbiton.com. While the site won't give you local market ratings, it is a valuable source of information, and even has training available.

www.Epguides.com. A fun site with episode guides for thousands of television shows, new and old.

www.Katz-media.com. This programming group's television newsletter provides a wealth of information, including sweep results and program rankings.

www.Nielsenmedia.com. Worth a visit by students just so they can see the company they've read so much about. While the site won't give you the overnights, it does provide a wealth of basic information and a current listing of DMA rankings.

www.Radioandrecords.com. A trade journal's Web page that has dozens of resources, including formats, music charts, and even the latest freely available radio ratings by market.

www.Radiojock.com. Used mostly by DJs, this site keeps an extensive list of links to music charts (though some are outdated).

www.TVBarn.com. Maintained by the *Kansas City Star*'s TV critic, this site links hundreds of television reviews. Free daily e-mail updates are available.

www.TV-Pilot.com. Not a free service. For a monthly fee, you can view TV pilots from your computer.

Remembering a Mentor:
Joe Foley

Doug Ferguson

Graduate schools socialize their students into the world of scholarship in many ways, but none more so than through the influence of faculty mentors. My own experiences in the early 1970s at Ohio State were guided by such minds as Don LeDuc and Len Hawes. My most influential mentor, however, was Joe Foley, and this essay is about him.

Joe Foley was my undergraduate adviser, who suggested that I should get my master's degree. I was very reluctant, despite my strong aptitude, because I was weary of school. At the time, however, Ohio State University had a combined undergraduate and master's degree by which students with high GPAs could double-count their senior courses if taken at the graduate level and if they planned to complete a master's thesis. Only a handful of students undertook this enterprise, maybe because so few administrative clerks even knew it existed. I am grateful that I was even told about it. Dr. Foley told me that I would be crazy not to take advantage of the program. That extra nudge was what I needed. He would later provide many more extra nudges to help me realize my potential.

The technology was different in those days. We used punch cards for computer programs, and I recollect an old manual calculator in Derby Hall that did long division by rapid subtraction, which was accomplished on a noisy, mechanical carriage return. We had some kind of early CRT terminal for running Q-sorts. Journals and books were the only scholarly media. I remember many long nights with Pike and Fisher at the law library.

That I remember Joe Foley as a mentor is not unusual. I have since encountered many colleagues who have fond memories of his piercing gaze and dry wit. We had immense respect for him, even if we sometimes pronounced his name as if he were Chinese, Jo Fo Li, though never to his face. His humor made him approachable, much more so than with my other professors, but he kept enough distance to keep us respectful.

His most memorable habit was his amiable badgering about some assignment. Whenever he encountered my fellow students and me having a good time, he'd ask, "Have you finished that paper?" or "Are you done with your thesis yet?" I think his half-friendly/half-serious nagging kept me focused, and it also made me more likely to do the same with my own graduate and undergraduate students. He let us know we could enjoy our pursuit of knowledge as long as we treated it (and him) with respect.

In the classroom, Foley was particularly adept at providing thought-provoking questions. Sometime I would share my mastery of media law gleaned from Walter Emery's class, and Dr. Foley would stop me in my tracks with the questions "Why are the media regulated at all? Is there really scarcity of spectrum, when each city has far more broadcast voices than print publications?" It was the kind of lesson that continues to influence the way I talk to my students, challenging their willingness to accept the status quo.

Outside the classroom, Joe Foley was a gracious host. I remember his inviting a group of us to his apartment for a celebration of the end of a quarter. I recall being impressed with his lifestyle and warm camaraderie. In later years, I had an opportunity to see him as a good father to his children at an academic convention.

What I remember most fondly is that he cared enough to encourage me to do more. Getting my master's degree was really his idea. Although he also advised me to stay for my doctorate, I never quite saw in myself the potential that he saw, and I spent many years working professionally in the mass media. Later I changed my mind, which led me to spend three years getting a doctorate in the 1980s that would have taken no more than two years in the 1970s. He had correctly predicted that I would regret not having entered a life of teaching much earlier.

Having good teachers and helpful mentors has proven invaluable to develop my own style of instructing and advising students. I owe a very large measure of gratitude to Dr. Foley.

CHAPTER 17

Advanced Television Production

Erika Engstrom and Gary Larson

Introduction

Advanced television production here refers to courses at the level above the introductory or beginning production classes offered by university broadcasting programs. These courses build on students' previous training in the basic production techniques of camera work, directing, switching, audio, and graphics. Production exercises at the advanced level involve more length, intricacy, or field production.

Many advanced production courses require students to produce program-length projects, such as dramatic or entertainment shows, documentaries, in-depth news packages, newscasts, or magazine shows. Of all the college-level courses in broadcasting, the advanced television production genre requires perhaps the greatest time, effort and commitment by both students and instructors.

Oftentimes students must put in inordinate hours outside the classroom or laboratory to plan, write, shoot video, and edit projects. Instructors must not only teach students about the detailed how-to of broadcast production but also need to instill in students the concepts of teamwork and professionalism; only a combination of the two leads to successful and rewarding experiences for both constituents.

Unlike lecture-style or beginning broadcast production courses, in which students can do well working independently, the advanced production course depends on students to work in teams, reflecting the process of production in the broadcasting industry. In turn, successful teamwork demands that students develop professional and positive attitudes when working together, despite time constraints and setbacks due to technical difficulties and unexpected challenges, similar to those encountered by broadcasting professionals, who must cope with such obstacles on an everyday basis.

While instructors and students might perceive the demands of the advanced television production course as daunting, time consuming and, at times, frustrating, the results of hard work, patience, and diligence can prove incredibly rewarding. When the final product, whether a three-minute studio interview exercise, a 30-minute newscast, or an hour-long documentary, realizes a script in the allotted time with few technical errors, the "high" experienced by the students reflects esprit de corps instilled in the class by the instructor. This banding together is accomplished either explicitly or implicitly. Thus, the advanced television production course requires not only an educational aspect but also aspects of leadership on the part of the instructor.

In this chapter, we describe the rudimentary elements of the advanced television production course, including course approaches, assignments, requirements, and end product. We also discuss instructors' philosophy regarding advanced television production, recurrent themes, common problems encountered and how they overcome them, and what instructors and students enjoy most about such courses. Additionally, we provide production-related resources, including books, articles, and Web sites, for current and future instructors who seek to expand or initiate courses in advanced television production.

The courses described in this chapter are taught by television production instructors who responded to a nationwide e-mail call, distributed by the Broadcast Education Association's Listserve, asking for their syllabi in their advanced production classes, with some follow-up. A total of 12 course syllabi, obtained through the e-mail call and from instructors known by one of the authors, were compiled and included as part of the original BEA Syllabus Project Web site.

The participating instructors also answered an open-ended questionnaire that asked them about their approach, philosophy, goals, common problems, and positive and negative aspects of teaching their advanced TV production courses. Syllabi and questionnaire answers, as well as the experiences of the authors as instructors in the field, serve as the basis for this chapter.

Position of the Course in the Curriculum

Perhaps surprisingly, most of the instructors whose courses we describe here do not list the advanced production course as a capstone course for their television students. In all cases, however, the courses serve as second- or third-tier courses; those courses following basic studio or field production courses, or both. In a few cases, however, the advanced production courses fills the role of capstone courses, albeit rarely, if ever, under that name as a degree requirement.

While many broadcasting programs appear to suggest broadcasting students take advanced television production courses as a recommended option in their programs of study, most programs apparently do not require advanced production students take an advanced production course.

Television production courses at the advanced level offer a variety of approaches and goals. Based on the individual instructor's course objectives, these courses fall into four general categories:

■ Studio Production: Courses of this type generally combine video production theory with application in the studio setting and in the field.

- Field Production and Editing, with the focus on editing: These courses hone students' electronic newsgathering (ENG) skills with linear and nonlinear editing techniques.
- Television News and Magazine Programs: Students sharpen their journalistic skills while improving shooting and editing ability. Students in these courses might serve as members of newscast team, producing regular newscasts or public affairs programs.
- Entertainment Programming: Students in this type of course serve as the production crew for a variety of non-news formats that combine studio and field production.

Similar Courses

With course titles such as Advanced Television Production, Television Studio Operations, and Television Studio Production, this type of course emphasizes those skills needed to work in the studio setting. Students work in two-person or multiperson teams on class projects, which can range from a simple interview or "how to" demonstration to the creation of a drama, documentary, or experimental program. Content of such courses usually combines a theoretical aspect with practical application in the production of various media products.

Frank Barnas, instructor of Television Studio Production II at Valdosta State University, incorporates video projects and text material into the course; students produce and direct three single-camera studio projects. Students must first take Television Studio Production I, as Barnas expects students to have a working familiarity with studio equipment and production concepts. Successful completion of the course depends on students' mastery of directing, producing, audio production, technical directing, camera work, and graphics.

Barnas takes a straightforward approach in instructing students in the advanced fundamentals of studio production, and uses the classic text *Sight, Sound, and Motion— Applied Media Aesthetics* (1990) by Herbert Zettl.

Assignments directly correlate to the course objectives: Students, working on their own and in groups, complete four projects, each three to five minutes long, using a multiple-camera format that tests their skills in all production areas—three "aesthetic" projects and one individual narrative project. The aesthetic projects require students to adhere to the classic production parameters of scripting and blocking while tailoring their production designs to the various aesthetic elements emphasized in each.

In the first aesthetic project, students, working in groups of three, direct and produce a three- to five-minute segment in which they demonstrate understanding of lighting and color techniques. To show their mastery of lighting techniques, students vary the lighting by using low light, heavy gels, or other techniques. Students create settings such as jail cells, campsites, or other "spooky" situations. For their second aesthetic project, Barnas requires students to demonstrate understanding of manipulating picture composition by using camera placement to emphasize, or de-emphasize, area, volume, and depth. Examples include putting small objects in the extreme foreground of a shot, shooting through a gobo, or experimenting with the speed and duration of pans and zooms. Barnas designed the third aesthetic project so students demonstrate understanding of the elements of time, motion, and sound.

Students typically emphasize the sound component of this project, using off-camera sounds, mood music, exaggerated sound effects or Foley, and other techniques that allow audio directors more creativity and input. "Think of [Edgar Allan] Poe's 'Tell-Tale Heart,' and you'll get the idea," says Barnas. Finally, students complete an individual narrative project four to six minutes long, in which they use the techniques mastered in the three aesthetic group projects.

In addition to the four production projects, student grades include a final written exam, nonproducer work, and lecture participation. Beyond teaching television production as a skill-oriented course, Barnas aims to instill in students the mind-set that viewers at home expect a product, despite the technical problems that can stymie a production: "My ideal goal is to teach students not to panic. Your job is to find a solution, not belabor the problem."

Seminar and Practicum in Television III, taught by Nikos Metallinos at Concordia University, serves as a six-credit, "third-tier," capstone production course. Students' daily involvement in the courses revolves around scriptwriting and production of various projects, with possible options dependent on the synthesis of the class in any one-year (two-semester) period.

These can include experimental television programs, documentaries, or television dramas. Students must earn a grade of B+ or better in the lower-level prerequisite course and obtain departmental approval before enrolling. Metallinos reports that students typically wait three years to get into the course and undergo an interview process before they can enroll, with an acceptance rate of eight students per 50 that apply not atypical.

Metallinos designs his advanced course to appeal to students in three ways: academically, for those students interested in media research; artistically, for those interested in television as an art form; and professionally, for those pursuing careers in the industry. Metallinos combines theory and practice by having students complete a series of studio exercises on lighting, staging, editing, sound, and directing. These exercises, plus lectures, prepare students for their final productions (documentary, drama, or experimental). Primarily an independent study course, students work without the constant, watchful eye of the instructor. Rather, they design and execute their own productions. Course grades are based on (1) studio exercises, (2) production research and development, (3) completed productions, which count for half of the final grade, (4) quizzes on the textbook, Herbert Zettl's *Television Production Handbook* (1999), and (5) student's performance—a combination of attendance, participation, creativity, professional attitude, and growth.

In the syllabus, Metallinos explicitly states as one of the course's objectives: "To encourage the student to utilize the television medium not simply as a mere vehicle which carries a message, but as a creative medium capable of producing and presenting art forms with an aesthetic merit." Metallinos' approach to advanced television production not only involves the acquisition of the knowledge and skill needed to research, plan, produce, and postproduce a finished program, but also stresses creativity, in terms of exploring the medium's potential and challenging its limits.

Advanced Television Production taught by Lorene Wales[1] at Regent University serves as a graduate-level course in which students are expected to have prior knowledge of single-camera film and video and multiple-camera remote and studio production. They explore the gamut of television genres—drama, sitcom, game shows, talk shows, magazine, and sports shows—and produce a program based on their own research and development. After studying past television seasons and analyzing what made some series more successful than others, students develop, pitch, and write their own television series and prospectus.

Wales emphasizes students' development of critical viewing skills and analytical abilities to help them better evaluate the content, aesthetic elements, and the effectiveness of television programs, and provides them with practical experience in designing, writing, directing, and producing. The course's structure models the process used in the television entertainment industry, in which program creators develop treatments for a new series and present them to TV executives.

As part of the course requirements, students must submit a one-page treatment for an original series and write critiques of a past TV season using Alex McNeil's *Total Television* (1996). Wales administers a final exam, testing students on the glossaries of television terms in Zettl's *Television Production Handbook* (1999) and Hickman's *Television Directing* (1991).

Wales incorporates a public speaking component into the class as well. Students formally, and in professional attire, present their series idea individually to the class in the form of a pitch, using feedback from their one-page treatments. They then write a show script and make another class presentation in the form of a full prospectus. Wales grades the show treatment and script on originality, timeliness, creativity, and format; she bases grades for the pitch and prospectus on the students' physical presentation and the interest generated among their classmates. This approach serves as one of the most appealing aspects of the course; Wales finds that students especially enjoy "the creative process of brainstorming ideas and critiquing different proposals for new series."

To foster a competitive atmosphere similar to that found in the industry, the class produces one or two shows as pilots, depending on budget. Wales then grades students not on the actual product, but on their performance during the preproduction and production stages on the pilot shoot. Additional performance factors include the ability to work with others, punctuality, meeting deadlines, behavior on the production set, and crew position preparation and performance.

These three examples of the studio-based television production course all incorporate testing students on lecture or textbook material and evaluating their work in terms of a series of projects. Because television production does not rely on a "one-man band" but on teamwork, these instructors also ensure that students' performance on the set comprises part of the final course grade. In essence, although the technical aspects of a produced work may not earn high marks, production instructors reward students who exhibit professionalism and a positive attitude toward the course and their fellow students.

Ancillary/Related Courses

Advanced courses in electronic field production take students outside the traditional studio setting. Instead of having control over elements such as lighting and sound, students must learn to work with the conditions of the "outside world" to produce a variety of television formats.

Not only do students learn to shoot videotape and gather sound in the field, they also learn how to edit most effectively what they have "harvested" on tape. Course projects common to this genre of instruction include television news stories, public service announcements, video montages, and short documentaries.

Janice Tanaka's Electronic Field Production course at the University of Florida mirrored the theory-plus-practice formula. Students learned about the theoretical foundations of composition and form, color, sound, and lighting. Tanaka, who has since returned to the industry, focused on single-camera shooting an industry staple.[2] Students must have taken two lower-level broadcast courses, Writing for Electronic Media and Introduction to Telecommunication, in order to enroll. Additionally, Tanaka encouraged students take both Fundamentals of Production and Advanced Writing prior to the course.

Among the course objectives listed in her syllabus, Tanaka included the development of critical viewing skills so students learned to appreciate both the content and aesthetic considerations of television programs. To prepare them for the course's major projects, students took a series of three skills tests, one each on basic editing, three-point lighting and camera placement, and nonlinear editing. For the basic editing exercise, students were required to take video footage of one scene from their choice of two popular television shows, *Knot's Landing* and *Highlander*, and edit that scene within a one-hour period. The lighting and camera setup exercise required students to set up an interview with a volunteer subject of their choice.

Students were required to show proficiency to set up three-point lighting, a white balance level, camera position, and sound, all within 30 minutes. The nonlinear editing skills exercise tested students on their ability to digitize, open a project file, identify media files and clips, and edit within a one-hour time frame. Tanaka designed all three exercises to emphasize to students the importance of working within a deadline, with proficiency and efficiency.

In addition to deadline-based skills exercises, the course emphasized that students take what they learn about the basic concepts of single-camera production and use them as they design, write, direct, and produce short video programs. These short programs made up the major projects in the course, which students completed in teams: (1) "montage-with-simple-story" project, basically a video essay edited to music; (2) music video or commercial; and (3) documentary/final project, a "student's choice" project that included a re-edit based on the instructor's feedback. As students completed these projects as teams, so, too, grading occurred by a team composed of the instructor, advanced editing students, and the graduate and teaching assistants assigned to the course.

Tanaka noted in the syllabus that the grading team took into account factors not related to the content, editing, and aesthetic aspects of the projects themselves. He also suggested examining the issue of attitude in response to feedback, sharing with teams, and helpfulness to fellow classmates.

At Washington State University, Marvin Marcelo, who also serves as assistant station manager at KWSU/KTNW-TV, the campus PBS affiliate, integrates his advanced production course assignments with the station, Cable 8. His course in Advanced Television Production: Electronic Field Production and Editing serves as a third-tier course for broadcast production students, who usually take it as their last production course before graduating. Some broadcast news students also take it to enhance their electronic field production and newsgathering skills.

Students learn advanced skills in studio and field directing and lighting, producing, directing, and editing as they complete a series of video projects while getting practical experience in ENG and postproduction editing. As part of the course requirements, students serve as production crewmembers for the station's newscast, *Cable 8 News*. They also must serve as the newscast's director at least twice during the semester and submit a critique of their performance for each show they direct.

Marcelo also has each student complete two writing assignments: a critique of a newscast and a public service announcement or promo, and a résumé writing project. He includes a midterm exam based on class lecture material, course assignments, and readings from the course text, *Video Field Production and Editing* (4th edition, 1997) by Ronald Compesi and Ronald Sheriffs. Marcelo lists *Non-linear Editing Basics: Electronic Film and Video Editing* (1998) by Steven Browne as an optional text.

Students complete two of the course's editing projects in pairs; projects include a written portion, which, depending on type, consists of detailed production books composed of instructor-approved proposal, script, log sheets, location scout report, storyboard, and self and crew evaluations. Four major video projects include (1) a public service announcement or promo for Cable 8, (2) an on-location, "interesting person" interview, (3) a news package or commercial, done in tandem with a Cable 8 reporter or upper-division advertising student, and (4) a seven- to eight-minute final project, either a minidocumentary or "how to" video. Marcelo also details in the syllabus requirements that students must meet for each project. They must submit projects on a SVHS blacked tape and include (1) 30 seconds of bars and tone; (2) slate including title of project, producer and director names, date, and total running time; (3) countdown from 10; and (4) audio or video starting at zero.

Marcelo screens all projects for the class to create a sense of competition. The campus TV station serves as a venue for outstanding projects, which air as part of the program *Best of 455* (after the course's number, Broadcast 455). Others might air as part of various student programs. As students in Marcelo's course collaborate with students in other courses and those working at the student station, so too does he work with another instructor on a project to incorporate computer technology. Both video-editing courses described here again reflect the theory-practice combination in which students take knowledge from lecture and readings and incorporate those principles of high production values into their projects.

Instructors of editing courses specify in exact terms their expectations for video submissions, describing in detail each requirement students must meet to master field production and editing skills successfully. As with studio production, students work in teams, though smaller groups that demand they work in a cooperative and positive atmosphere. This aspect of video production, no matter what focus a course takes, differentiates broadcast production courses from others in the communication field.

Comparative Features

The demanding and highly competitive broadcast news industry calls for an even greater level of professionalism and team spirit to achieve success, either on an individual basis or for a TV news operation as a whole. Advanced production courses with a focus on news typically require students to have taken classes in broadcast newswriting and reporting, and basic television production. The finished product for these classes can include entire 30-minute newscasts, complete with weather and sports segments, short "cut-ins" similar to news updates broadcast on local stations or networks, or newsmagazine-style programs. Schools with television broadcast or cable stations may air these shows as regular programming live or live-to-tape.

At the University of Nevada, Las Vegas, students in Gary Larson's Television News Production produce ten 30-minute newsmagazine shows each semester. Recorded live-to-tape in a three-hour period in the middle of the week, *Studio 70* airs three times the following weekend on the campus cable channel. Students must take both basic studio production and electronic newsgathering and editing as prerequisites. Students who have current or past internships at local network affiliate stations become the de facto leadership in the course by virtue of their experience outside the classroom.

Studio 70 follows the magazine format, which allows students a wider range of production styles and topics than would the standard news block. Larson grades students on the number and quality of the stories they produce, along with the degree of involvement they demonstrate during the production days. He expects them to produce between 10 and 15 stories during the semester and to work actively in the production of each of the shows. While Larson guides students in their work, he allows them a great deal of show "ownership," believing that ownership of the program instills more interest in their work and more pride in their accomplishments. Students meet for one class period on a separate day for critique.

Though he does not dictate program content, Larson urges students to take on "franchise" assignments along with enterprise reporting. Las Vegas's reputation as "entertainment capital of the world" leads to franchise topics that often include entertainment, and even off-Strip happenings to remind audiences that Las Vegas is more than the two-mile stretch of asphalt bathed in neon. Students use digital camcorders for acquisition and edit to Beta SP for their masters.

Though not state of the art, the school's equipment does give upper-division students a chance to practice on equipment similar to that they may find themselves using during internships or even on their first jobs. Larson has no textbook for the class; he distributes a self-authored production manual based on years of teaching production at the collegiate level.

As Fayetteville State University's resident journalism professor, Debbie Owens incorporates components of Advanced TV News, which she developed at another school, into her current courses, News and Public Affairs, Media Internships, and

Video Production II. These courses build on concepts learned in lower-level courses. "Students should already have a basic knowledge of interviewing, reporting, video-tape recording and editing, and production techniques for the broadcast media," she reports. Owens integrates journalism elements and television production into the assignments, which include field production and editing projects, anchoring, current event quizzes, and a research paper.

Regarding field production and editing, typical assignments in Owens' television news courses include edited news stories, including tapes and scripts for voice-over (VO), voice-over sound-on-tape (VOSOT), "short" packages, and conventional packages. A short "cut-in" news program (about five minutes), which includes segments on news, weather, and sports, serves as a production exercise. It includes a "news capsule" practice exercise, consisting of a one-minute script based on at least four front-page newspaper stories. Students also get practice on camera, with an anchoring exercise in which they serve as the on-air announcer for a five-minute news cut-in.

Owens incorporates an analytical side to her courses, such as requiring students to critique other classmates' packages and directing them to include constructive thoughts and observations in their peer evaluations. Students also complete short research papers on a topic of their choice—one that examines an issue salient to broadcast journalists. Owens encourages students to conduct ethnographic research by interviewing broadcast professionals, such as reporters, media analysts, and news-room managers. Suggested topics include issues such as the role of newsroom consultants ("friend or foe of the broadcast journalist?"), cameras in the courtroom, tabloid journalism, news event staging, and women's nontraditional news roles. Thus, students who want to pursue careers in the industry not only engage in the production and reporting of news, but also must investigate their chosen field and reflect on issues they may face once on the job.

At Humboldt State University, students enrolled in HSU TV News and in HSU-TV (both under the title Journalism 490) provided programming for the campus television station, Channel 12. Instructor Leanne Kozak[3] aimed to give students hands-on experience in producing "news/public affairs programming with professional production values and high quality content."

Students in Kozak's TV news course, HSU TV News, served as newsroom and studio personnel, producing twelve 30-minute newscasts during a semester. Students attended class twice a week: one day for newscast productions and the other for lectures, evaluation, and story planning (called "desk days"). On the news production side, students worked in all editorial facets: reporter/photojournalist/editor, producer, associate producer/"scripts whip," editor, videotape coordinator, archivist, sports director, news anchor, graphics coordinator, character generator (CG) operator, weather producer/anchor, director, and assignment editor. Studio jobs included technical director, audio, floor director/studio chief, VTR operator, and camera operators. Students kept a diary for the semester, in which they noted their progress and accomplishments, stories they covered, and jobs they performed. The instructor collected the diaries at certain points during the course and when the course ended.

Kozak assigned course grades based on letter-grade categories in which students fulfilled a list of minimum requirements. An "A," for example, included the submission of seven news stories (three packages, four VOSOTs or VOs), 18 on-camera reader stories, and perfect attendance for all class sessions. In addition, the successful completion of assigned production or studio jobs, positive evaluations from other classmates, no missed deadlines, and an 80 percent average for work completed on "desk" days must be present. Lower grades resulted when students contributed fewer stories, did "OK" work in their new production and studio positions, missed class, or received mixed evaluations from classmates.

In Kozak's other advanced course, offered under the same course title, students produced a TV newsmagazine program modeled after the famed *60 Minutes* format under the name *HSU TV*. Similar to the TV newscast course, students served in all production jobs and submitted stories in package form in two-person teams. The instructor approved all stories for air—scripts received approval before editing, and the instructor considered no story until she cleared it for broadcast. To meet course requirements, students submitted two stories, on SVHS tape, during the semester, each accompanied by voice-track script with suggested lead-in, cut sheet, CG list, and graphics list. For full credit, stories must have met show deadlines and contain no significant production defects or errors.

Kozak's grading criteria for stories included story newsworthiness and originality, writing (including style and mechanics), content (appropriate sound bites, organization, balance, accuracy), photojournalism (framing, audio and color quality, camera steadiness), and editing quality (such as effectiveness of edits, sequencing, and technical quality). The instructor encouraged students to use and rewarded "postproduction enhancements" such as graphics, wipes, dissolves, and other special effects.

The *60 Minutes* format also serves as a model for Stacey Irwin's Producing for Television course, formerly titled Television Studio Operations, at Towson University. Recorded live-to-tape for air on the university television station, students produce four to five episodes of the 30-minute magazine *8000 York* each semester. The program, which airs three times a week, focuses on issues of interest to three levels of audience: first, students living on campus and in the surrounding community; second, communities in northern Baltimore and the university vicinity; and third, faculty and staff viewers of the station. The show features single-camera ENG or film-style segments related to a weekly show theme. Prerequisites for the course include the TV Studio Production course and Electronic Field Production.

As with similar courses mentioned previously, students serve in all production staff and above-the-line (editorial) positions. Students' course grades come from tests, assigned readings in Frederick Shook's *Television Field Production and Reporting* (1996), performance as a co-producer or director of one episode, two five-minute segments done individually and as part of a team, and course participation and performance as a production crew member. Irwin assigns grades on a tiered scale, with an "A" reserved for excellence in both aesthetic and technical aspects of stories.

In order that students understand Irwin's expectations regarding their performance at the onset of the course, they sign a class contract. By signing, students acknowledge that they understand the skills needed to participate (such as videography, linear editing, and scriptwriting), that failure to meet deadlines results in a failing grade, that they must work well with others on the production crew, and that the nature of grading is subjective.

With the acquisition of new, updated equipment and editing software, Irwin added two additional assignments: an individual editing piece based on found footage, and an individual shooting exercise in which students use Canon XL1 cameras. The addition of more equipment allows Irwin to ensure each student knows how to use it; in the course's prerequisite, students worked in small groups.

Students at Towson use the same equipment, honing their editing and shooting skills in another production course, Corporate Video. Based on the same production principles learned in Producing for Television, students in Corporate Video work with a nonprofit organization for a semester, with the goal of creating a nine-minute video for use by their organization.

Because of the intricacies involved in the production of television news, such as the details required in scripts, videotape, and the "organized chaos" of the television newsroom, instructors of this type of course often include a set of newsroom rules, similar to news policies found in professional stations. Instructors might include in these rules anchor and reporter on-camera dress codes, script format elements, videotape and editing standards, and newscast rundown format. Having these very specific rules included in the course syllabus prevents misunderstandings and potential problems.

Instructors of television newscast courses stress the importance of dependability, punctuality, professionalism, and the recurrent theme in production courses, teamwork. As they prepare students for careers in the news business, they clearly intend future newscasters to learn both technical skills, such as writing, shooting, and editing, and "people" skills. Perhaps more importantly, students who get a taste of the "real world" process of television news can find out if they've made a wise career choice. As Debbie Owens notes, "Ideally, I hope that students come away with a full appreciation for what it takes to not just perform but also to succeed in the industry." Adds Stacey Irwin, "I want them to be confident and passionate about the fact that they want to do this kind of job or know by the end that they definitely know they don't."

Special Features

College-level broadcast production programs typically offer an entertainment category of programming course as a practicum—usually as the highest-tier course students can take aside from an internship. As described here, the practicum basically represents a production house in which students serve as crew, talent, and producers of regular scheduled programming distributed through a media outlet, such as campus television station, cable channel, or public television affiliated with the school. Programming includes all television genres: soap operas, game shows, sports shows, or comedy/variety. At this point in a broadcast production program, students should have all the necessary skills to work in television. Course grades rely mainly on student performance and participation, rather than on tests, projects, or research papers.

Offered each semester, Broadcast Practicum at the University of Nevada, Las Vegas, serves as the venue in which students create programming for the university's cable channel, UNLV-TV. Although not a capstone course, students can enroll after taking the basic studio production class. Past incarnations of the course have included a movie review show (*The Movie Show*, modeled after the Siskel and Ebert, or now,

Ebert and Roeper, format), a sports-magazine show (*Season Ticket*), and a human-interest-magazine program (*Rebel Report*).

Here we describe three recent incarnations of the course, supervised by instructor Laurel Fruth. These exemplify the entertainment programming approach to advanced television production: *This Ain't No Buffet*, a cooking show featuring chefs from acclaimed Las Vegas restaurants; *You Oughta Know*, a game show; and *Totally Band in Las Vegas*, an MTV-style program featuring up-and-coming local musical groups.

This Ain't No Buffet, whose title plays on the Las Vegas reputation for offering myriad, low-cost buffets to tourists, serves as a collaboration between the broadcast production program and UNLV's College of Hotel Administration. In each of the six 30-minute episodes produced each semester, a local chef prepares a signature dish with the assistance of a student host and a chef/professor from UNLV. Students serve as production crew and produce several food-related stories that they edit into the program during postproduction.

Fruth, who also serves as UNLV-TV's manager, grades students on their performance in completing preproduction and postproduction tasks. All class members complete some tasks, while Fruth assigns others on an individual basis. For example, all students must submit an analysis of a cooking show and serve on the on-site production crew. Individual assignments include preproduction tasks (such as creating a schedule, episode rundown, or publicity) and production duties (such as shooting, editing, or writing/voicing story packages). Students spend most of the semester shooting and editing packages, and planning the shoot for each of the episodes. The class then shoots the episodes in the cooking studio of the College of Hotel Administration during a three-day period at the end of the semester.

Fruth takes the same pedagogical approach to another show produced by Broadcast Practicum students called *You Oughta Know*, a 30-minute game show produced well before a similarly formatted syndicated program titled *Street Smarts*, produced by Dawn Syndicated Productions. University students, faculty, and staff members who appear as contestants guess whether "people on the street" (or university campus, in this case) know the answers to general knowledge questions. For each correct guess they make, contestants win a number of points. At the end of the program, the contestant with the most points goes on to the "lightning round," in which he or she answers a series of questions within a one-minute period.

Besides serving as members of the production crew, students take on semester-long positions, including writers, the head writer, contestant coordinator, field photographers and editors, publicity coordinator, prize coordinator, graphic designer, host, announcer, and postproduction editor. Fruth requires students to attend class every taping day; absences result in lower course grades. In addition to serving as production crew and in semester-long positions, all students must secure at least one consolation or grand prize.

Totally Band in Las Vegas serves as the latest iteration of Broadcast Practicum at UNLV. The program, developed by students, began with instructor Laurie Fruth's directive that students create a show that combined in-studio musical performances with on-location footage. The students decided to focus the show on local, unsigned rock 'n' roll bands and came up with the title, format, and show elements. Each hour-long show features three bands and airs twice weekly.

Students serve as the production crew, except for audio. Students work on the show in three stages including preproduction, production, and postproduction. Preproduction involves researching, selecting, and contacting bands, and then taping a live performance by the selected band at a local club. Students also develop interview questions and create portfolios for each band, which include stage plots, biographies of band members, and recorded music, such as CDs or audio recording.

During the production stage, students work in the studio over a weekend, taping the bands as they perform in the studio. Only those students who have completed a course in nonlinear editing can direct a band performance. Last, they produce show segments by deciding which sound bites to use from band interviews, editing field footage and taping wraparounds. They then critique the completed show, and each band receives a show tape and thank-you letter.

Totally Band in Las Vegas found success on the Las Vegas music scene after its first run. During the show's first semester, "we had to beg bands to appear on the show," reports Fruth. "Now bands are begging us to put them on. In addition, the students learn very quickly just how complicated a show like this can be to produce." Unlike other student-produced programs at UNLV, *Totally Band* forces students to work within a budget. As a learning experience, Fruth notes that students look for new ways to improve the program, while learning about audio mixing and directing shoots using five cameras.

This Ain't No Buffet, *You Oughta Know*, and *Totally Band in Las Vegas* meet Fruth's definition of "professional television show": they both (1) have a deadline, (2) go on the air, and (3) meet broadcast standards. With these requirements, Fruth aims to teach students about the amount of effort that goes into producing an airable program. In achieving this goal, Fruth stresses the importance of preproduction and writing, as opposed to postproduction: "All of the fancy editing in the world won't save a program that is badly written." All programs produced in Fruth's Broadcast Practicum courses, regardless of format or semester, air on the university cable channel, with *This Ain't No Buffet* airing on the PBS affiliate as well.

Common Goals and Objectives

As most people who teach advanced television production would agree, the expectations at the end of the course more closely resemble a graduate seminar than an undergraduate class. Faculty expect students to generate a tangible output good enough to enter into regional, national or even international competition. Students expect that output to demonstrate a high enough quality to include in their demo reels or résumé tapes. Administrators count on some, if not all, the output to serve an "outreach" in the community, showing a public face of the university or college through the work of students and faculty. This latter expectation often subsumes the former; students tend to include "airable" programs on their demo reels and, just as often, instructors submit them to various competitions.

Regarding postcourse success, several instructors report that their student-produced work has won media competitions. For example, some of the programs produced by Frank Barnas' students at Valdosta State University have been submitted to regional competitions and have fared well. Nikos Metallinos' students at Concordia University have found success in high-profile competitions, such as the Montreal Film Festival and the Toronto Film Festival. Several of Marvin Marcelo's students at Washington State also have experienced success stories from their projects, becoming finalists in local and national AERho (Alpha Epsilon Rho), SPJ (Society of Professional Journalists), and NATAS (National Association of Television Arts and Sciences) competitions, and winning national and regional Emmy awards.

Of the remaining respondents, Janice Tanaka at the University of Florida submitted outstanding programming to competitions if budget permitted, and Lorene Wales at Regent University reports that a half-hour sitcom pilot produced by her students is being posted for submission to competition. Debbie Owens at Fayetteville State looks forward to productions from her course to air on the closed-circuit campus channel: "Not only will this practice allow students to share their accomplishments with a broad audience," she says, "but it will also help us to recruit new students into the telecommunication program."

Several instructors mention making productions available via emerging media. Marvin Marcelo at Washington State says that faculty teaching advanced production courses need to address new media and convergence. With an eye to the future of media technologies, Marcelo works to teach students Web-site construction so they can stream out their video projects onto the Internet. He notes, "If this digital convergence comes through, I want them all to be ready for it," he says, adding, "It is a very exciting and new technology that some, but not all, are willing to embrace." Debbie Owens at Fayetteville State includes an online component in her advanced TV news courses. "While we have yet to launch any broadcast news Web sites, the classroom assignments incorporate many production and writing skills that students need in order to appreciate the various technologies required in a Web-based newsroom," she reports.

In terms of the form that end products might take, such as tape or live, both chapter authors have taught advanced news/magazine courses that have gone live on the air at a regularly scheduled time. During his time at Wichita State University, Gary Larson, now at the UNLV, took his advanced television production course on the air. The program at Wichita State produces 12 half-hour newsmagazine shows each semester; each airs live and then repeats on tape during the following week.

When Erika Engstrom of UNLV taught Broadcast News Production, her student-produced newscast went live on the air often just minutes after a full run-through of the show. Such an approach gives students the highly valuable experience of working in a live, "the show must go on" atmosphere, which Engstrom and Larson hope gives them the edge when they enter the fast-paced, high-pressure world of television news.

Because channel time has become a premium at UNLV-TV, which shares its programming time with other local entities, going live with the student-produced newscast has become problematic. Live-to-tape works, Larson says, as long as the instructor treats it as a live newscast, allowing no retakes or postproduction. Competition-wise, Larson notes that the Wichita State productions submitted both as entire shows and as individual segments to the Kansas Association of Broadcasters won a number of first- and second-place awards.

Instructor Philosophy

Virtually all of the instructors we talked to express the philosophy of treating students as working professionals. For most of them, this means an expectation of timely production that meets standards for broadcast. This concept is best expressed by Frank Barnas, who relates that hard "call" times and deadlines help his students at Valdosta State understand that he does not train them to work in a "college environment" because it is not the environment they will work in later.

Some instructors use production meetings with their students to actually demonstrate proper editing form or discuss the finer points of producing television. Stacey Irwin at Towson University says that while the pedagogical concerns in an advanced production course place demands on the instructor, she finds teaching students advanced technical skills and appreciation for aesthetics well worth the time and effort.

In her advanced TV course, postmortem sessions serve as what she terms "lesson time" in which grading is completed for their 30-minute show and their packages. This also reflects several pages of constructive suggestions, significant points off for major mistakes, and a lot of encouragement for going out on a limb with montages and creative shots. Students are also credited for including heavy-hitting interviews, great interview setups, good lighting with depth and warmth, and good storytelling. No verbal grade is ever given in this context, but this process pulls out elements and seems to work really well for this instructor to explain visually how a package on a feature/light news show is built. She also indicated that the class is encouraged to sit around a conference table to take the team approach: "power-with-situation rather than power-over-pedagogy."

Treating students as professionals sometimes calls for instructors to forgo "by the book" production methods. For example, Marvin Marcelo at Washington State makes the point that production in practice often contradicts what students have learned in some of their texts, noting that "oftentimes I have to erase some of the 'book' knowledge they get from others and re-train them for my class." Though she treats her students as pros, Laurie Fruth at UNLV tells her students that she will not penalize them for making mistakes, because mistakes are inevitable; they are penalized only for making the same mistake twice. Most instructors we talked to report that meeting schedules and deadlines and taking responsibility for the production of stories serve as important tenets of their teaching philosophies.

Not unexpectedly, all the instructors we include in this discussion express goals for their courses and their students in terms of preparing them for the exigencies of journalism—all the situations that they can never teach in a college class or laboratory setting—or as Irwin puts it, "making the leap from the 'basics according to Zettl' " to being an artist, a producer, a person with an eye for the visual and an ear for the sound. Making the point this way, Owens echoes the other instructors: "Hopefully, they gain all the skills necessary to succeed in any industry, not just the technical skills, but critical thinking skills that will allow them to recognize, assess and overcome new challenges in this ever-changing field. Also, they should understand the importance of teamwork and that team effort is a significant component to the function and organizational structures of broadcast media."

While instructors of the advanced television production course aim to give students preparation needed for industry careers, the skills and understanding required for success beyond the local level can come only from job experience. This holds especially true at the network and studio levels, where good writing, while always valued, depends on knowing how to construct show scripts with correctly placed breaks and understanding how each show in a series relates to the next. "I don't think any class can teach these things—you need to invest time coming up through the ranks if you really want to work in TV on this level," Janice Tanaka notes.

In short, instructors take a double-barreled approach to their pedagogy. On one hand, they treat students as professionals, with all that entails, such as adherence to deadlines, teamwork, and responsibility for all aspects of production. On the other, they maintain consistent goals of preparation for professional life as working journalists. This means preparing students to deal with the unexpected situations that may surface during any working day in the context of a television station or production house.

Common Emphases

Regardless of course approach, advanced production instructors make clear in their syllabi certain expectations of students that relate to three major themes: (1) time, (2) teamwork, and (3) professionalism. Concerning time, instructors let students know at the very start of the course that advanced television production demands a high level of commitment in terms of how much time students will spend in the studio and completing out-of-class projects. For example, Janice Tanaka told students in her electronic field production course that they should expect to spend at least 10 hours a week shooting and editing their projects, reading assignments, writing scripts and reports, and practicing for skills tests.

Students also learn of the importance of deadlines through the enforcement of them, especially in television newscast courses. Missed deadlines lead to lowered grades or even failure in the course. Debbie Owens includes a warning to students in her Advanced Television News course: "Broadcast news is a business where deadlines are essential to the success of the industry. These deadlines are set in stone: *if you miss a deadline, your story doesn't air*." Consequently, Owens lets students know that she does not accept late projects.

Broadcast production instructors also emphasize time in terms of planning; they warn procrastinators not to leave projects to the last minute. Though virtually all college students end up cramming at one time or another, because of the limited number of editing labs at most schools, waiting to complete a project may result in a missed deadline. Janice Tanaka of the University of Florida included this caveat in her electronic field production syllabus: "Don't wait until the last moment to edit your projects. Start projects early! Plan ahead! Do not wait until it is too late!" Stacey Irwin, in her Advanced Studio Operations syllabus, includes a slightly more philosophical statement: "If you plan ahead, any problem that may befall you can be corrected. People don't plan to fail—they fail to plan."

Teamwork crops up again and again in these instructors' syllabi, and they mention it often when discussing their ideal goals for their production courses. Demonstrating a cooperative spirit, contributing to the final product of the courses, and sharing the workload figures into students' final course grades for nearly every advanced production course, and certainly for the ones discussed in this chapter. Leanne Kozak's syllabi for her television news and magazine courses include a statement encouraging students who have taken production courses to show leadership to their classmates, as follows: "Veterans, those who have experience will be expected to help the newcomers. Please do so willingly and cheerfully, remembering that you, too, once benefited from a helping hand."

Instructors of these highly demanding courses stress professionalism in terms of independence, personal enterprise, responsibility, and dependability, and specifically make note of these issues in their syllabi. Student commitment to doing their best and producing quality work also falls in this category. Indeed, in addition to serving as part of a student's grade in the course, demonstration of this commitment can have longer-lasting effects, and some instructors make this clear from the onset. For example, when students apply for their first jobs, their advanced production instructors often serve as references. Stacey Irwin of Towson University makes students aware of this in the course syllabus: "Many of you will use me as reference after graduation and I like to be able to give you a positive letter. Conduct yourself professionally and I'll be happy to recommend you." In college broadcasting programs where the advanced production course serves as the capstone, instructors expect students to perceive the course as preparing them for industry careers after graduation.

Common Problems/Solutions

Common problems faced by advanced TV production instructors include lack of space, inadequate equipment, and equipment maintenance. For example, Frank Barnas at Valdosta State, sees the lack of studio space as his biggest problem. He says that even if his department doubled the amount of studio space, the large number of productions shot every year would still result in overcrowding. Barnas handles the problem through creative scheduling, offering night classes as well as juggling faculty schedules around the availability of the studios. Conversely, Lorene Wales at Regent University reports that enough studio space exists, but in her case, scheduling large blocks of time for production leads to problems. To alleviate some of that pressure, Wales says she shoots her productions in smaller time frames, about four to five hours.

Besides space, instructors must cope with not having enough hardware to served the production demands adequately in their course. Debbie Owens at Fayetteville State speaks for a number of the respondents with her take on the equipment *un*availability issue: "Sometimes it's due to equipment malfunctions. At other times it's due to the fact that the portable equipment is shared with other units throughout the campus, which means that it is not always available for students to use for field assignments." Often the technical support staff works the 9-to-5 schedule, leaving students who commute or want to cover sporting events without a means to shoot their stories. In this regard, Owens voices the same problem reported by most other instructors we surveyed.

Overcoming the problem of no or substandard equipment forces faculty to use their creativity in handling the course, as well as in dealing with the budget and even other faculty. As Nikos Metallinos from Concordia University reports, his problem of theory-oriented faculty failing to understand, support, assist, or buy equipment for "video people" results in a lack of up-to-date equipment and technology. Metallinos handles the problem at his school with "great patience, political maneuvers, iron-fisted attitude at faculty meetings, and being firm to what I think is right." Marvin Marcelo at Washington State reports he finds preemptive communication in this regard helpful: "I try to come up with a five-year plan to keep up with the technology. I also try and communicate with others about our needs, so that there isn't a surprise about cost of replacement equipment. I work with industry professionals on our board so that they know what we are doing and see if they have any suggestions for us."

Stacey Irwin at Towson University reports that funding for equipment at her school has been good. She says, however, that all of that choice equipment carries a hidden cost: "We get to use great equipment, and it is tough keeping other students in our program off our equipment. Even the beginners want the best stuff right away." The program at Wichita State, relates Gary Larson, dealt with the problem of continuing costs associated with maintaining equipment and studio facilities by striking an alliance with university media services, giving it access to the equipment and getting maintenance from its engineers in return.

Some schools provide all the accoutrements needed for the advanced production course: studio equipment, certainly. But what about non-studio-centered courses? For classes in ENG and field production, or those that require edited projects, if instructors have students purchase equipment, they usually require that students provide their own videotapes. At institutions where student demand exceeds the equipment supply, students might have to purchase their own equipment as well.

Janice Tanaka at the University of Florida included in her editing course syllabus a list of basic supplies students must buy, as well as the stores that supply them. These include eight to 10 "hi-grade, high quality" VHS tapes, an ultraminiature tie-clip microphone, a clip light and a halogen bulb, a pair of leather gloves, and a two- by three-foot white foam board. Due to the high student-to-camera ratio (about 120 students for about six cameras), Tanaka tells students they can use their own camera— and if they consider purchasing one, what features it should have (such as mic input, manual focus, and override on the iris). If students own a Hi-8, the university has facilities to dub from film to tape. However, because of the high demand, Tanaka writes in the syllabus that (in a section specifically explaining to students the state of equipment there) future policy might require broadcasting students to have "access" to a camera (similar to a policy on required access to computers).

Besides problems with equipment, inventory or maintenance-wise, production instructors also mention other day-to-day challenges. Janice Tanaka at the University of Florida voices a concern for consistency in teaching across labs, especially when graduate assistants might assign less stringent, more forgiving grading. To deal with such inconsistencies, she has constructed a unique evaluation system to try to establish higher levels of consistency. She brings together her best students from an advanced editing course to act as audience reviewers, along with graduate assistants and herself to form a grading team: "The final project grades are based upon an average grade from at least ten reviewers. Students receive the comments and grades so they can see where they are good and where they need work. This is to avoid the pressure of one person's opinion being the sole measure of a grade." This addresses fairness and "it is easier for the lab instructors because they cannot be challenged individually on a grade. We are in a medium that is audience driven, so an audience of peers is the fairest way to go."

Related to the teamwork concept so vital to the instruction of these types of courses, Laurel Fruth at UNLV reports that she sometimes sees students handing off responsibilities to others. "Invariably," she says, "there are some students who are willing to take on more than their share. I have to insure that everyone is pulling his or her weight." Fruth constantly monitors so students share the workload.

Instructor Resources

Advanced production faculty usually supplement textbooks with demonstrations, instructional videos and, most importantly, outside speakers. Laurie Fruth at UNLV says she brings in professionals regularly to lecture or conduct demonstrations. Stacy Irwin at Towson University brings in professionals close to her students' age and pushes students to use Web resources and trade magazines. Marvin Marcelo also brings former students to talk about their experiences in the "real world" in his class at Washington State. He occasionally takes students on field trips to different broadcast facilities.

Regarding video and script sources for advanced production courses in TV news, Gary Larson at UNLV finds CNN Newsource invaluable in teaching his news-magazine class. Students download scripts and rundowns from the CNN Web site and tape raw footage from the campus station's satellite downlink for use in their program. The best part of the arrangement: CNN Newsource costs the university nothing, other than the price of the downlink dish.

Appropriately, instructional videos serve as useful tools in the teaching of television production. Frank Barnas of Valdosta State suggests instructors use the companion video to *Sequences: Strategies and Shooting News in the Real World* by John Hewitt (1991), especially useful in field production courses. Films for the Humanities and Sciences offers a series of videos on television production.

Instructors might find "behind the scenes" videotapes useful in providing students with a look at actual working environments. For example, the National Association of Television Programming Executives (NATPE) produces videos such as *Inside TV: Careers in Broadcasting* and other titles. Additionally, the Museum of Television and Radio's university satellite seminar series features programs on different aspects of the broadcast industry, such as production, news, and sports, reports Barnas. "We air it on our educational access channel, VSU-TV, as well as air the feed in our studio for students for a live viewing," he says. "We also tape it for classroom use."

Digital videodiscs (DVDs) now include a director's commentary track, which can aid production instructors in teaching students how theory relates to film and video making. Barnas frequently uses this widely available technology: "This helps a great deal when we discuss automatic dialogue replacement, visual effects, and other advanced production techniques." Barnas uses recent DVD releases that include director's tracks, such as

1999's *The Mummy* (Universal). Popular contemporary films available on DVD that feature a director's track include *Air Force One* (1997, Columbia TriStar), *Good Will Hunting* (1997, Miramax), and *The Perfect Storm* (2000, Warner Bros.), among others.

Instructors might rely heavily on their own experiences and scholarship. Janice Tanaka, who kept active in the industry while teaching at the University of Florida, used her own work in teaching her editing and field production class: "I was always worried about being one of those people who 'can't do it, so they teach.' I try to continue quality producing during the summers, and so far it has worked." Nikos Metallinos at Concordia University uses material from production texts he has written, along with bibliographies he has created on television production, telecommunications, and aesthetics. Instructors might create their own instructional videos for specific classroom projects as well. For example, when teaching principles of sound effects, Frank Barnas at Valdosta State will shoot a silent scene and assign it to students for sound-effect placement as part of a specific Foley exercise.

Most instructors mentioned Web-site resources. Not surprisingly, however, Web sites often fall short in their usefulness as the resources, other than for information from networks, affiliates, trade organizations, and equipment manufacturers. Most instructors agree that no substitution exists for experiential learning in advanced television production courses: the real learning happens only when students put their hands on the equipment. We include a list of suggested resources at the end of this chapter.

Conclusions

For instructors, the benefits of teaching advanced production center around seeing their students immerse themselves totally in the course to bring ideas to reality. Many people who teach this type of course find joy in watching the creative process become tangible output for students. Laurel Fruth of UNLV sums up this sentiment: "I enjoy seeing the students progress through the semester. I like it when they take charge, get their creative juices flowing and reach a point where they begin to ask . . . what if we did this?" Other instructors find great satisfaction in teaching this kind of course by seeing teams of students come together and act as peers. Stacey Irwin at Towson University perceives the best part about teaching advanced production as the "spirit of camaraderie and spirit in the class." She adds, "We're a class of learners; I am just the head learner."

Of course, instructors of advanced TV production regard as the ultimate benefit of teaching their ability to provide experiential learning that helps students bridge the gap between collegiate and professional life. Janice Tanaka at the University of Florida says she enjoyed it when students came back after graduation to tell her how valuable they found her course. Marvin Marcelo at Washington State echoes many of the instructors: "The most satisfying part is seeing some of the students excel in their jobs after they leave here. I often keep up with most of my students to see where they are and what they are doing. It is very gratifying to hear from them, and hear from them that I wasn't really feeding them a line when they were in class."

On the other side of the lectern, instructors report their students most often mention they like the hands-on experience of working with the equipment and in quasi real-world situations. Many student evaluations also reflect satisfaction with such courses because students and instructors often act as peers, blurring the student-teacher hierarchies the students are accustomed to in other, less experiential, classes. As UNLV's Gary Larson has found in teaching production courses over the years, students enjoy "the chance to strip away some of the 'student-teacher' constructions and to act like responsible adults in charge of something important."

Outside Resources

Armer, A. A. 1986. *Directing television and film.* Belmont, Calif.: Wadsworth.

Browne, S. E. 1998. *Non-linear editing basics: Electronic film and video editing.* Boston: Focal.

Compesi, R. J., and R. E. Sheriffs. 1997. *Video field production and editing.* Needham Heights, Mass.: Allyn and Bacon.

Fairweather, R. 1998. *Basic studio directing.* Boston: Focal.

Farris, L. 1995. *Television careers: A guide to breaking and entering.* Fairfax, Calif.: Buy the Book Enterprises.

Feschbach, N. P., A. H. Katz, H. Fairchild, and E. Donnerstein. 1992. *Big world, small screen: The role of television in American society.* Lincoln: University of Nebraska Press.

Hart, C. 1999. *Television program making: Everything you need to know to get started.* Boston: Focal.

Hewitt, J. 1991. *Sequences: Strategies for shooting news in the real world.* Mountain View, Calif.: Mayfield.

Hickman, H. 1991. *Television directing.* New York: McGraw-Hill.

McNeil, A. 1996. *Total television: The comprehensive guide to programming from 1948 to the present.* 4th ed. New York: Penguin.

Metallinos, N. 1996. *Television aesthetics: Perceptual, cognitive, and compositional bases.* Mahwah, N.J.: Lawrence Erlbaum.

Millerson, G. 1999. *Television production.* 13th ed. Boston: Focal.

Papper, R. A. 1994. *Broadcast news writing stylebook.* Needham Heights, Mass.: Allyn and Bacon.

Patz, D. 1998. *Surviving production: The art of production management for film and television.* Studio City, Calif.: Michael Wiese.

Rabiger, M. P. 1996. *Directing: Film techniques and aesthetics.* 2nd ed. Boston: Focal.

Rose, B. G. 1999. *Directing for television: Conversations with American TV directors.* Lanham, Md.: Scarecrow.

Silbergleid, M., and M. J. Pescatore. 1999. *The guide to digital television.* 2nd ed. San Francisco, Calif.: Miller Freeman.

Shook, F. 1996. *Television field production and reporting.* 2nd ed. White Plains, N.Y.: Longman.

Van Tassel, J. 1996. *Advanced television systems: Brave new TV.* Boston: Focal.

Wurtzel, A. 1983. *Television production.* 2nd ed. New York: McGraw-Hill.

Zettl, H. 1999. *Television production handbook.* 7th ed. Belmont, Calif.: Wadsworth.

———. 1990. *Sight, sound, and motion: Applied media aesthetics.* 2nd ed. Belmont, Calif.: Wadsworth.

Web Sites

www.beaweb.org/syll1.html. BEA's Syllabus Project. Downloadable versions of syllabi described in this chapter.

www.cybercollege.com/tvp_ind.htm. A "cyber textbook." Ron Whittaker offers instruction presented in modules, from basic production concepts to detailed "how-tos" of shooting and editing with the latest equipment used in the industry.

www.films.com. Web site for Films for the Humanities and Sciences, featuring instructional videos in film, audiovisual production, and broadcasting.

www.mtr.org. The Museum of Television and Radio offers information on satellite seminar series and other resources.

www.natpe.org. The National Association of Television Programming Executives offers videos about the industry.

Notes

1. Wales currently teaches courses in location sound, audio postproduction and producing, and management.

2. Tanaka returned to the industry after 10 years of teaching, first serving as talent-show coordinator in the diversity development at Fox Network, now as a freelance producer for the Japanese American National Museum in Los Angeles.

3. Kozak has since returned to television news, first as managing editor at KGUN-TV in Tucson and then as managing editor at KPIX-TV in San Francisco. She currently serves as the public information officer for the California Superior Court in San Joaquin County, California.

Remembering a Mentor: Doug Anderson

Frederic Leigh

I met Doug Anderson in 1977 at the University of Nebraska at Omaha, where we were on the faculty of the Department of Communication. Doug had just taken a journalism faculty position, and I had been managing the public radio station on campus and teaching broadcasting since 1970.

Doug and I had little contact at UNO, as he was teaching journalism courses on one side of the campus and I spent most of my time at the station on the other side. We did see each other at faculty meetings and at the day-care center that our children attended. But I began to hear good things about the new faculty member who was a promising teacher and scholar.

Both of us had grown up in small towns on the plains of the Midwest so we had that background in common. Neither knew at that time, though, that the other was thinking about a move to a warmer climate. Doug's opportunity came first when he took a position with Arizona State University in the spring of 1979. I was not surprised when I heard that Doug was leaving. While the journalism program at UNO is a good one, it is not one of the very top-ranked programs in the country. I knew Doug would rise rapidly in journalism education, and the program at ASU had the potential to emerge as a premiere one.

I had no idea at the time that within a few months I, too, would be on my way to Arizona State University. During the summer of 1979, a new position with the Journalism Department at ASU was advertised. They were searching for someone to put a campus radio station on the air and teach broadcasting courses. The position seemed ideally suited for me, and it offered a new challenge in a warmer climate. I applied and was offered the position late in the summer.

The move to a new position in a different area of the country was daunting, but I had a contact at ASU: Doug Anderson. He had just made the move and was settled so I turned to him for guidance and support. It was then that I believe Doug's mentoring began, although I don't think either of us knew it at the time. As fellow refugees from Nebraska's cold winters, Doug and I became good friends and colleagues.

At ASU, our offices were just across the hall from each other so we had regular contact. Doug continued to build his already impressive scholarly record while I worked to put a radio station on the air. But I was also on the tenure track so I needed to pursue research and creative activities myself. Initially, Doug's mentoring involved direction in scholarly publication. The result of that direction was my first publication in

319

Feedback in 1984. It was not a refereed journal, but it was a publication. I thought that was pretty good at the time for a radio station manager.

Over the next decade, Doug and I partnered on research that resulted in four publications. I learned a great deal from Doug during that time about research and the publication process, but it was as an administrative mentor that he was to have the most profound effect on my career.

I think Doug recognized my administrative potential before I did, but I was thinking about a change in career direction by 1984. I had come to ASU with a master's degree, but I knew that if I were to pursue an administrative position in higher education, I would need a doctorate. With Doug's encouragement, I began work on a doctorate in Higher Education Administration.

That same year, the Journalism Department at ASU became the Walter Cronkite School of Journalism and Telecommunication. When the director of the School stepped down in 1987, a national search for a new director was conducted. While many good candidates applied, we knew we had the ideal candidate on the faculty: Doug Anderson. By then, Doug had emerged as a national leader in journalism education and was poised to assume the directorship of a nationally ranked academic unit. Indeed, Doug was named the new director of the Walter Cronkite School.

To my surprise and delight, Doug asked me to be the first associate director of the School. He told the faculty that he felt I would complement his administration, as my background was in broadcasting while his was in print. At that time, the School offered two undergraduate degrees: one in broadcasting and one in print. My responsibilities would include oversight of the broadcasting curriculum, student affairs, and supervision of the campus radio station. Doug encouraged me to take the position while continuing to work on my doctorate. I was a bit hesitant about the workload, but I knew that it was a great opportunity. With Doug's continuing support, I finished the doctorate in 1989.

Doug and I were administrative partners at ASU for 12 years until he left to take over as dean of the College of Communications at Penn State. I learned a great deal from our partnership. As an administrator, Doug has many talents. One of the most prominent is his ability to recognize the strengths of others and utilize them to the advantage of the unit. I saw this time and time again in his teaching, committee and project assignments. He regularly assigned leadership roles when he saw that another person could do the job better than he could.

At the same time, Doug led by example. His record spoke for itself. He was a nationally recognized teacher and scholar who became a nationally recognized journalism administrator. But, while he was a very effective manager, he did not hesitate to delegate authority and duties. In my case, he left student affairs, the broadcasting curriculum, and the radio station to my management and only asked for regular updates. We worked together on course schedules and teaching assignments. Again, he provided leadership and guidance but always valued my input and experience.

Another example of Doug's administrative mentoring was in the accreditation area. I had the opportunity to work with Doug on the preparation of two re-accreditation reports for the Cronkite School. Doug was active in national accreditation leadership at the time and provided excellent guidance in the process. He also recommended me for service on site-visit teams that led to my assignment to a number of those accreditation visits at other institutions. The experience was invaluable as I continued to build my administrative career.

Under Doug Anderson's leadership, the Cronkite School emerged as one of the top journalism schools in the country. I am pleased to have had the opportunity to contribute to that development. I was very fortunate to have a nationally recognized journalism administrator as a mentor. Doug always had faith in my administrative abilities and that faith was evident in 1999 when he recommended me as interim director of the Cronkite School. Although I did not seek the permanent directorship, I felt I was prepared to take the helm, if only on an interim basis.

My administrative partnership with Doug Anderson ended in 1999 when he left for Penn Sate. But his mentoring continues. I regularly seek Doug's advice on a number of administrative issues. I believe it was fate that Doug and I came to ASU at the same time from the same place. Through our partnership, I recognized that my future is in academic administration. His leadership was invaluable as I developed my administrative skills and experience. Today, I continue to serve as associate director of the Cronkite School. I believe I am a more effective administrator because of my mentor, Doug Anderson.

CHAPTER 18

Media Criticism

Michael J. Porter

Introduction

Television has become a dominant force or, some might say, *the* dominant force in our society. Criticism of the medium is a formal course that should be taught in every department of communication or mass communication, but it is not. Courses in television criticism are rarely treated as required courses; for most programs they are considered electives or optional courses. Nonetheless, courses in television criticism are very popular among students, and, for many programs, only majors are allowed to enroll because the demand for the course is so great.

A course in television criticism should be designed to provide the students with the tools needed to help them to become critical consumers of television texts. It does us little good to simply bash television and say it's unworthy of our time or efforts. Instead, we should try to recognize the information conveyed by television, so we can watch these stories with a critical eye.

The objective of a course in television criticism focuses on increasing awareness and application of the major approaches to television criticism. The course is designed to introduce the students to the concepts and theoretical foundation so they can begin to have the language to evaluate the television text critically. The goal is to help students to become more conscious, alert, critical viewers of television.

Taking a course in television criticism will change the way students watch television. Many of my students facetiously complain throughout the semester that I have ruined their television-viewing experience. They tell me that, as they try to assume the couch-potato position, they simply can't any more. Instead, they analyze the narrative, examine the visual codes, and look for ideological overtones and question whether they are the ideal audience.

Students sometime relate that their roommates refuse to watch television with them because they won't stop talking about it. Of course it is pleasing to know that what we are doing in class is having an impact on their lives, specifically how they are reading the television text. Such anecdotes could be repeated over and over from every instructor of a course in television criticism.

Position of the Course in the Curriculum

The majority of courses in television criticism are typically upper-level courses designed primarily for undergraduate majors. In some programs the course may serve as meeting the requirements of a humanities elective for non-majors. The problem is that the course is typically quite popular among majors and therefore non-majors are unable to enroll. Enrollment is usually small (20 to 30 students), but the course could be taught to a larger number with some modifications.

For most programs, courses in television criticism are considered an *add-on*; that is, they are not required courses within the program's curriculum. In fact, in a recent survey of broadcast education curricula, television criticism was not listed as one of the top-10 core courses of either two-year or four-year schools (Kock et al., 1999).

Nonetheless, those who teach courses in television criticism feel very strongly about the importance of the course and the need to include it in the curriculum. A course in television criticism provides a critical component missing in curricula that focus primarily on production skills or industry issues: programming, management and mass communication history.

Similar Courses

Courses in television criticism come with various titles: television criticism, media criticism and analysis, mass media criticism, television program analysis and criticism, media arts content and culture, critical frameworks, visual literacy, and media aesthetics, to name a few. For a complete discussion of critical approaches, be sure to consult *Critical Approaches to Television* (1998) by Vande Berg et al., especially Chapter 2 about "The Nature of Television Criticism" (pp. 16–36).

The material presented in this book is an amalgamation from a number of sources, including my own 25 years of experience teaching this course. Several colleagues shared their syllabi, and I have integrated some of their strategies in the material presented here. This chapter is designed to explore some approaches to teaching television criticism. A review of the compiled syllabi indicates that there is no uniform approach for teaching television criticism. Instead, the various syllabi examined reflect the interests and expertise of the course instructors.

Many instructors rely on the specific chapters from the texts they use (see below for a short list of possible textbooks for this course) to help organize their course. Others seem to pick and choose among selected essays and critical studies. Despite the differences among the syllabi, some fundamental concepts were universally recognized as valid objectives for the course.

Comparative Features

For a course in television criticism to work, students need to be aware of the special underlying assumptions that serve as its foundation. These assumptions can be used as a way to set the tone for the course and to introduce the students to the central issues surrounding the field of television criticism. Each of the following could be discussed at length to help the students recognize these assumptions.

We must begin with the assumption that television is an integral part of American life; it serves as the basis for much of what we consider the shared culture of America. Watching television is a dominant leisure activity of many viewers. In the average household, the television set is on for over seven hours a day. This does not mean that everyone watches seven hours a day, but it means that TV's influence is ubiquitous. Even if you don't watch television you are surrounded by others who do.

Special Features

Most of today's college students have not experienced life without television. Most consider watching television as a means of harmless entertainment and escape. Television is an immensely powerful expressive medium with profound cultural implications. The television program is a text that is to be examined and studied, as one reads a short story or novel. This text provides insight into our contemporary culture and ourselves.

We also tend to be largely unaware of how television programs are created and, more importantly, are unconscious of the processes we use to read a television text. We are active interpreters of television and not merely passive victims of it. There is no single correct reading of a television text. In fact, media texts are open to more than one interpretation. Television programs tend to naturalize the dominant ideology as *common sense*.

Each of the foregoing assumptions will become key to the construction of the course. They influence the readings selected, the focus of the discussions, the writing assignments and the lecture material. It is imperative that the students begin the course with an open mind and are willing to have their perspectives challenged. It is therefore important to create an atmosphere of trust and understanding in the classroom. The instructor needs to let the students know that they are about to begin to look at television from a new perspective, as an archaeologist may look at a finding from a dig of an ancient village. Television becomes an "artifact" reflecting the values of the culture. Given such a framework, the students appear to be more willing to move outside of their own comfort zone.

There are few criticism courses that students consider easy. The readings in the field are challenging and oftentimes difficult to read. The expectations on students are also demanding, usually because of the quantity of assigned readings and the amount of required writing. In other words, this is not a fluff course, where all students do is sit around and watch TV, although it is one of the few courses where we can require our students to watch TV!

For this course, it is important that you create an atmosphere of trust and mutual respect in the classroom. Everyone's opinions must be considered valuable contributions to the class discussion. Of course you accomplish this by remaining open to all opinions, but you should also feel free to challenge students who seem to be speaking from a very narrow, uninformed perspective. The issue here is not how someone else is interpreting the text, but is whether a student is arguing from a valid position and reviewing the aforementioned assumptions for the course.

Common Goals and Objectives

None of the instructors consulted for this chapter focused their course on developing writing skills as a television critic; instead, all subscribed to the broader humanities perspective presented here.

What follows is a distillation of common theoretical approaches to television criticism. These could be considered units of the course. A solid introduction sets the stage for the entire course. Here students are exposed to the aforementioned underlying assumptions of the course and develop an approach to television criticism.

Outlined below is a list of statements used in my course to begin a discussion of the relationship between readers of the text and the text itself. This provides for a rich discussion and helps to highlight the underlying assumptions that students bring with them to the course.

Viewers are passive recipients of mediated messages. TV programs are texts that are read by active viewers. There is only one correct reading of a television text. TV content focuses on the interests of the dominant elite. Television is nothing more than entertainment. Mass-mediated messages are innocuous, fairly harmless forms of entertainment. Media texts are open to more than one interpretation; they are open to criticism. We are free to read the text any way we want.

It is also valuable to discuss what criticism is, what it is not, and what standards we can use to evaluate serious TV criticism essays. According to Vande Berg et al., "The *primary goals* of criticism are understanding, explanation, and appreciation. They are not theory building" (1998, p. 31).

These same authors provide standards we can use to evaluate a serious TV criticism essay. Does it possess internal consistency? Does it provide sufficient, appropriate evidence for the claims implied by the thesis and advanced in the essay? Does it offer a plausible rationale for its cultural, critical, theoretical or practical significance? Does it cause astute readers to accept the critical interpretation or explanation argued for in the essay as a reasonable one?

In other words, it is important to discuss what we mean by *criticism*, and how we can recognize good criticism when we see it. This is new material and a new approach for most of the students in the class. It is important to provide a solid foundation before moving on to specifics of critical approaches.

A number of different critical approaches are used to examine television texts. Each approach should be analyzed in terms of the assumptions it brings to a media work, its main principles, and the major arguments it facilitates. Many instructors rely on the text to help determine which theoretical approaches to use in the course.

Semiotics, or the study of signs, offers the opportunity to consider how all forms of communication are broken down into discrete units of meaning. This form of textual analysis demands close analysis of the visual, verbal, and acoustic codes of television. This essential component of a criticism course provides the foundation for critical analysis of the text. It is important to help students understand that the text can be divided into discrete codes, each of which has meaning. For some, semiotics seems highly complex, but it need not be.

For many students, this may be the first time they will have been asked to examine how meaning occurs, and what the role of signs is in the creation of meaning. From that standpoint, it can be (and should be) a head-turning experience. The premise of semiotics is that meaning is socially constructed. The implications of that premise, alone, are enough to raise a multitude of questions. Be sure to help your students understand and appreciate the richness of this field. Once you have identified the basics, you can then move on to apply semiotics to the study of television.

A study of semiotics will often lead naturally into a presentation of the visual style, which focuses on the production values of a television text, including camera shots, lighting, editing and sound. These are the production building blocks of television narratives and may be covered within the discussion of semiotics. If we are asking our students to analyze a television text, we need to help them understand the language of that text. It is important to provide language to describe and discuss the visual elements found with the text.

The following terms represent a short list of the language that students should learn: These terms are commonly found in television production courses. It is likely that not all students have a production background, and they need to become familiar with the language of the visual and terms such as close-up, cross-shooting, depth of field, exterior shot, field of view, flat lighting, headroom, matched cut, and montage. Other terms should be presented, such as over-the-shoulder shot, point of view, reaction shots, scene, vectors and z-axis.

In many regards, we can consider these terms the building blocks of the critical eye. If we are not familiar with the language, we cannot begin to see the visual elements. I suggest providing a glossary of terms for describing the visual. Take one class period to review the terms, give students a short visual text to practice on, and let them at it. The students will quickly pick up on the language and begin to use it appropriately for the duration of the course. Later in this chapter I discuss a writing exercise commonly used to help students develop visual language skills.

Narrative theory can help to explain how a television text is put together—how stories are told. Basic narrative theory can help students understand what drives the story from the beginning to the end, and can help them to discriminate between a focus on character, setting and plot. A basis for understanding narrative theory is an essay that examines the narrative structure of the television text; see Porter et al. (2002) for a complete description of a method for analyzing the narrative structure. The essay provides additional language and analytical instruments for describing the narratives in television programs.

Genre theory has its roots in literary studies and is a means of classifying, by type or kind, different forms of television programs based on narrative structure, content and style. The more common genres include situation comedies, commercials, hour-long dramas, and news programs. Other possibilities are talk shows, game shows, sports, soap operas, children's programs, and music television. Some instructors focus their course around different genres and then examine a particular critical approach within that genre.

Ideological analysis examines how TV programs present a perspective about social reality. *Ideology* refers to a set of beliefs, assumptions and ideas. Issues of power, class, gender and race are often the focus of these studies. An examination of the different *discourses* found within the narrative can be compared with broader social perspectives. For many instructors ideological analysis provides the "meat" of the course. This type of analysis asks the students to step back to look at a broader perspective, the inherent messages buried in the texts.

Feminist criticism, which is sometimes seen as a subset of ideological analysis, foregrounds gender as an important part of our social identity and examines the representation of women in television texts. Meanwhile *reception theory* focuses on the readers of the text and how they negotiate meaning from that reading. Reception theory also examines how the text tries to control the reading act. Technically, reception theory is not a critical approach to reading a television text, for now the focus is on the readers of the text, the audience. Nonetheless, an examination of readers of texts has become a part of many courses in TV criticism.

Instructor Philosophy

All of the course syllabi examined for this chapter rely on a combination of readings, lectures, in-class discussions, and in-class viewing of specific texts. Class lectures, discussions and viewing are usually organized around assigned reading material. Some instructor's take a predominantly genre approach to organize the course, although there is no agreement as to which specific genres must be covered in a television criticism course. It is important to recognize from the start that no single course has time to cover all of the various genres that may be of interest.

In some ways, it does not really matter which genre you use. The instructor should cover the genres he or she feels most comfortable with. Most instructors seemed to opt for thematic organization of the course based primarily on presentation of different critical perspectives. Most combine the two in some way. For example, applying semiotic analysis to television commercials, discussing situation comedies to examine genre theory, applying narrative theory to hour-long dramas, exploring ideological criticism by examining both narratives and nonfiction programming (such as talk shows and wrestling), and visual codes of daytime dramas are examined. All of these can provide considerable insight.

It is difficult to provide a single formula to offer a description of what happens during class time. In smaller classes (25 or fewer), meetings will combine the presentation of new material with class discussions. Instructors often include video clips as specific examples of the perspective being discussed. For the sake of variety and to ensure that everyone participates in the discussions, it is useful to divide the class into smaller groups of three to four students to have them develop a concept or share their understanding of a theoretical framework. Several instructors reserve the final five or six class periods for individual presentations of the students' final research paper.

Expect class discussions to be lively in this course. The instructor's role is to make sure all perspectives are shared and heard by all. The instructor should always moderate these discussions and intersperse his or her observations when a teachable moment arises. Feel free to challenge your students to consider the validity of their perspective. Note that these discussions are never about how one interprets the text; you should always assume and expect a divergence of opinions about that. Again, the atmosphere in the classroom must be one of openness, embracing all perspectives. It is the instructor's responsibility to be a role model for such openness.

Common Emphasis

All of the instructors for this course ask their students to write. If asked, most all instructors would agree that writing is a pedagogically sound way for students to learn about their own critical perspectives and a valid means to help them integrate new ideas and critical perspectives into their own frame of mind.

Most instructors require two major papers in the course and several shorter papers of less magnitude and scope. Below are a few selected writing assignments in some detail to demonstrate the level of specificity required. It is always interesting to see how others structure their writing assignments. Below are four different assignments.

For what is termed the "Ethnography of a Television Fan," the student interviews a television fan of their choosing. The fan should be different from the student in terms of gender, race, social class, education or age so they have a personal point of comparison. The students are also urged to find a *real* TV fan so they will have much to write about. They audio record the interview running 20 minutes or more, and if they can not talk about television for 20 minutes, they probably are not asking good questions or perhaps have a really boring fan.

Proposed questions are included below. These are only suggested as a jumping-off point. The paper is to present the results of the interview. The students will not be able to share all of the information learned; instead they must select the more interesting areas from the interview to include in the paper. The paper must include quotations from the interviewee to support the perspective presented, another a good reason to record.

The following are suggested as starting points for the interview: How much TV do they watch? How do they watch? Do they do other things while watching? What are their favorite programs and favorite genres? Who controls the remote control? Do they talk about what they are watching or do they prefer to watch in silence? What type of talk would be appropriate in such a situation? How much of their viewing is planned or unplanned?

Beyond this, do they ever talk about what they see on TV? With whom? When? How do they use the VCR? What are their favorite cable channels? Do they consider TV beneficial or detrimental to their relationships? Do they think that TV plays a major role in society? Get them to talk specifically about one of their favorite television programs. How do they watch it? What do they like about it? Do they consider the characters as their friends? Do they ever use TV to facilitate social interaction?

This is typically seen as an eye-opening assignment. The students begin to detect how others view television, and they are always amazed. Most of us assume that all others watch television the same way we do, which simply is not true. I spend an entire class period having each student share the stories of their interviewees with the rest of us. We look for areas of commonality and uniqueness. This assignment raises some fundamental questions regarding the application of reception theory to television criticism. For what is termed a "Scene Analysis" paper students are asked to select a television program they are familiar with and do a visual analysis of three scenes from a single episode. A *scene* is defined as the smallest unit of narrative action.

A listing of possible questions should be included to help students focus the analysis. How does the camera frame characters? Are most shots medium shots (MS)? Are there any extreme close-ups (XCU)? When are they used? Is there any camera movement or character movement? How do shots help us to understand a character's emotional state? How is dialogue shot? Are two-shots or over-the-shoulder shots used? What about point-of-view and reaction shots?

Is there any consistency between scenes? When is one style used? Why? How are the characters blocked? Is there a focus on x-axis or z-axis blocking? What does blocking tell the viewer about the relationship between characters? Which characters in the foreground (if any) are the lead characters? Are they shot differently from the secondary characters? What type of light is used? How does this set the tone for the action? How does this help to define the genre?

Is there a color motif? Is it neutral, natural or bold? Who wears color? Who wears light-colored clothing? What do the costumes tell us about character? Is focus or depth of field manipulated to draw attention to one character or object over others? Describe the pace of the editing. Is it quick? Is the camera allowed to linger? How does this enhance the story? How and why are point-of-view shots used? Describe the set. What does it tell you about character? Do they use the fourth-wall convention? Do you miss the fourth wall?

Why is camera movement used? How are performers blocked along the x-axis or the z-axis? Does the director emphasize one approach or the other? Is the viewer treated as a voyeur? Are women presented as objects of voyeuristic pleasure (as spectacles seen from a male viewpoint as sexual objects)? Are men presented as objects of voyeuristic pleasure? Through what formal and technical strategies is this point of view communicated?

The focus here is not simply to answer all of the aforementioned questions. That is unnecessary. Instead, the focus is to help students to begin to analyze the visual text from a new perspective. I also provide a listing of elements for the paper, including an introduction explaining the focus of the paper and the name of the series, why they selected this series, and the questions they hope to answer by this analysis.

They must also present a series description with a brief, one-paragraph description of the series as well as scene descriptions, explaining why they selected these two to three scenes instead of others and tell the readers something about what happens in the scenes. These scenes should be selected for a reason besides being representative of the series. There should be something that happens that captures your attention and excites you—something that speaks to you in a visual manner.

The body of the paper is the description of the visual elements. Here students explain how the visual techniques they have chosen to analyze help to convey the action, meaning, mood and emotion of the narrative. It is imperative that students are reminded that production techniques are not an end in and of themselves. They are tools used to present the narrative. Therefore, only those production techniques helping to reveal character and story elements of the scene should be examined. After the body of the paper they should present a conclusion providing a summary of findings; put conclusions into perspective for the readers.

"Audience-Oriented Criticism" begins with a text the student is concerned about. The focus will be on how the text characterizes its audience and attempts to control the reading act; in other words, how readers make meaning from their experience with the text. This can be accomplished by either focusing specifically on elements within the text that help to control the reading act, or the student can conduct a small focus group to ask fans of the series (or novices to it) how they read the text.

Questions must guide this line of research. What gap filling must be done with this text? Is the mode of address cinematic or rhetorical? Discuss the semiotic excess of the series that allows for divergent and multiple readings of the same text. Where is the excess found? What is the preferred reading of the text? How does a different audience negotiate the reading of the text? How does the text project an ideological perspective, and how is the reader positioned relative to that perspective? Discuss the interpretive communities for a specific television series.

An "Ideological Analysis" assignment is used to study the relationship between the television text and the underlying ideological roots for the text. Such an analysis can begin by examining the pattern of binary oppositions in the text. Identify the topic that organizes the ideological relationship between these oppositions, and explore the relationship between the discourses out of which the text is constructed and the social discourses that viewers may use to create meanings from the text. What social order is being naturalized in the text, and how does it appear natural, i.e., invisible, inevitable, or eternal (e.g., legal authority, consumerism, free-market economics, paternalism)?

What are the text's representations of (1) power, (2) authenticity and (3) value, and how do they change during the program? How does the text illustrate some form of social control? What power relations between groups are expressed or implied? Which dominant groups are portrayed, and how is subservience depicted between instances of groups such as officials and citizens, Caucasians and Hispanics, males and females, and how do these relations play out in the text? Which larger social contexts are implied beyond the text?

Which surrounding events and relations are glimpsed at or implied, such as urban-rural conflict, class differences, and cross-cultural misunderstandings? What institutions are presented and in what light? What are the text's cultural, educational and technical institutions, such as marriage and government, and what does the text suggest about their value and meaning. How are events and relations presented?

Which individuals, groups and categories are silenced, placed at the margins, or decentered? Which groups are absent, which groups are presented only in a two-dimensional category, which are present but without influence, or which relegated to the text's sidelines: for example, women in action programs, minorities in a talk show, the poor in a situation comedy? What is the cultural/political bottom line or main point of this text? What are the ultimate, underlying meanings in terms of power, influence and centrality of groups and interactions?

Not all of these papers are required in a course. Instead, both the paper on the visual analysis and then one of the other three are examined. They are presented here only as representative of the type of writing that is done in this course, and so that others may borrow freely from these directions. Most instructors of TV criticism offer lengthy guidelines, as provided here, probably because we believe the students need more guidance as they prepare their drafts.

It is critical to reiterate the importance that virtually all instructors of television criticism place on writing in this course. We all firmly believe that it is in the process of writing that students begin to learn. Our goal here is to provide for substantive writing projects that stretch our students to new levels of understanding. Listed at the end of the chapter are textbooks used by those who shared course information.

Conclusions

Television serves as a significant transmitter of information, entertainment, and cultural values. As we prepare our students for careers in the broadcast and cable industries, it is imperative that they are aware of some of the central issues that make up this course. A degree in mass communication, or a related field, should be about so much more than learning the tools of the trade.

The field of mass communication plays a vital role in the reproduction of our culture, and our students need to look at all of television's texts with a critical eye. They must learn to ask questions about the cultural messages contained within the programs and not merely continue to be enamored by the flash and razzle-dazzle of many television programs. A course in television criticism should force students to look at television with a new set of lenses—a critical set of lenses that asks them to become cognizant of the cultural messages within entertainment and informational texts.

Those who teach courses in television criticism tend to do so with passion and energy. Some possess almost a missionary zeal to convert the nonbelievers. They recognize the importance of what they are doing, and take great delight and satisfaction in seeing their students evolve over a semester. There is no better reward for teachers than to see their students grasp at and eventually recognize a difficult concept, a nuance to a theoretical model.

Although courses in media criticism tend not to be required within a major, they are nonetheless an important addition to any curriculum in mass communication. Students with a more critical orientation often delight in the questions raised in this course. This is one of the courses within the curriculum that makes mass communication so much more than merely a skills-oriented program. As more young professors enter the academy with backgrounds in criticism, the field will be recognized as central to curriculum in communication.

As a concluding remark the author thanks all of those schools that responded to a request for course syllabi, including the University of Alabama, the University of Arizona, Boston College, Eastern Illinois University, Marquette University, Michigan State University, Montana State University, the University of Nevada at Las Vegas, and Salisbury State University. The author thanks the many instructors for their willingness to share syllabi and views: Gretchen Barbatsis, Ann Marie Barry, Jeremy Butler, Caren Deming, Frances Kendall, Fern Logan, Paul Traudt, Nikos Metallinos, Walter Metz, Larry Mullen, Frank Oglesbee and Gregory Porter.

Sources

General References

Allen, Robert C., ed. 1992. *Channels of discourse, reassembled.* 2nd ed. Chapel Hill: University of North Carolina Press.

Butler, Jeremy G. 1994. *Television: Critical methods and applications:* Belmont, Calif.: Wadsworth.

Casey, Bernadette, Neil Casey, Ben Calvert, Liam French, and Justin Lewis. 2002. *Television studies: The key concepts.* London: Routledge.

Kock, E., et al. 1999. Broadcast education curricula in 2-year and 4-year colleges. *Journalism and Mass Communication Educator,* Spring, pp. 4–15.

Newcomb, Horace, ed. 2000. *Television: The critical view.* 6th ed. New York: Oxford University Press.

Porter, M. J., D. L. Larson, A. Harthcock, and K. Berg Nellis. 2002. Re-(de)fining narrative events: Examining television narrative structure. *Journal of Popular Film and Television* 30, no. 1 (Spring):23–30.

Vande Berg, L., L. Wenner, and B. Gronbeck, eds. 1998. *Critical approaches to television.* Boston: Houghton-Mifflin.

Zettl, H. 1990. *Sight, sound, motion: Applied media aesthetics.* Belmont, Calif.: Wadsworth.

Books Exploring Critical Approaches

Barry, A. M. 1997. *Visual intelligence: Perception, image and manipulation in visual communication.* Albany: State University of New York Press.

Burton, G. 2000. *Talking television: An introduction to the study of television.* New York: Oxford University Press.

Butler, J. 2001. *Television: Critical methods and applications.* Mahwah, N.J.: Lawrence Erlbaum.

Dondis, D. A. 1973. *A primer of visual literacy.* Cambridge: MIT Press.

Durham, M. G., and D. M. Kellner, eds. 2001. *Media and cultural studies: KeyWorks.* Malden, Mass.: Blackwell.

Fox, R. F. 1996. *Harvesting minds: How TV commercials control kids.* Westport, Conn.: Praeger.

Geraghty, C., and D. Lusted. 1998. *The television studies book.* London: Arnold.

Gitlin, T. 1986. *Watching television.* New York: Pantheon.

Grossberg, L., E. Wartella, and D. C. Whitney. 1998. *MediaMaking: Mass media in a popular culture.* Thousand Oaks, Calif.: Sage.

Hartley, J. 1999. *Uses of television.* London: Routledge.

Himmelstein, H. 1994. *Television myth and the American mind.* Westport, Conn.: Praeger.

Lacey, N. 1998. *Image and representation: Key concepts in media study.* New York: St. Martin's.

Lester, P. M. 1998. *Visual Communication images with messages.* Belmont, Calif.: Wadsworth.

Messaris, P. 1994. *Visual literacy: Image, mind & reality.* Boulder, Colo.: Westview.

Metallinos, N. 1996. *Television aesthetics: Perceptual, cognitive, and compositional bases.* Mahwah, N.J.: Lawrence Erlbaum.

Potter, W. J. 1998. *Media literacy.* Thousand Oaks, Calif.: Sage.

Pungente, J. J., and M. O'Malley. 1999. *More than meets the eye: Watching television watching us.* Toronto: McClelland and Stewart.

Sillars, M. O. 1991. *Messages, meanings, and culture: Approaches to communication criticism.* New York: HarperCollins.

Silverblatt, A., J. Ferry, and B. Finan. 1999. *Approaches to media literacy: A handbook.* New York: M. E. Sharpe.

Internet Sources

Few instructors of television criticism rely on the Internet as a primary source of information. In fact, few of those citations are central to the course on TV criticism. Instructors provide Internet locations as a beginning point for student projects.

lcweb.loc.gov/rr/mopic. This is the Web page for the Library of Congress, providing a resource for their movie and television museum and research center.

www.cinema.ucla.edu. The UCLA film and TV Archives has over 220,000 films and television programs is the largest university-held moving-image archive.

www.medialit.org. This is the Center for Media Literacy's home page. The center, which is an advocate in media literacy education, focuses mostly on K-12 classroom and family.

www.ccnmtl.columbia.edu/. The Center for New Media at the Columbia Graduate School of Journalism is a teaching and research center dedicated to the enhancement of "teaching and learning through the purposeful use of new media."

www.criticism.com/md/. This site provided by Steve Hoenisch, technical writer/Web designer, includes two analyses of Stephen Kellner's Theory of Media Culture, and an introduction to Saussure's structuralism.

www.journalismnet.com/media/criticism.htm#us. This is a very rich source compiling numerous Web pages devoted to television criticism, with a strong focus on news.

www.robertmcchesney.com/FavoriteActivistGroups.html. The author's compilation of many media books.

www.epguides.com/. This contains episode lists for almost 2,000 TV, shows along with titles and air dates.

Remembering a Mentor: James Carey

John J. Pauly

T he most obvious thing I can say about my debt to Jim Carey is this: No other intellectual has influenced my own thought about communication and culture more powerfully or persistently. The voices that echo in my own work—Kenneth Burke, Clifford Geertz, Robert Darnton, Hugh Duncan, John Dewey—I first heard in Carey's lectures and essays. Less obvious but more important is this: Carey has taught me how to value university life.

I have never heard Carey use the term *mentor*. Truth told, his influence tends to be oblique. My formal studies with him, for example, were minimal. Even though I spent nearly seven years in the College of Communications at the University of Illinois, from bachelor's degree through doctorate, I took just one of his courses: his seminar on Communication Systems during my master's program. I sat in on that seminar again as a doctoral student, in order to take notes (the first time around, I had just sat marveling at the show). I attended Carey's lectures in the team-taught pro-seminar, a course I had taken with the late Al Kreiling. Carey chaired my dissertation committee, though he moved on to the Gallup chair at Iowa three years before I finished, leaving Kreiling to handle much of the day-to-day advising.

Nor can I honestly say that Carey taught me how to teach. He is a dazzling, nearly unparalleled performer. A student course evaluation guide published in the early 1970s advised that if you happened to miss William Jennings Bryan's "cross of gold" speech, a Carey lecture was the next best thing. What novice would dare imitate that? Tom Guback influenced my teaching style more deeply, and I have subsequently learned much from exemplary colleagues such as Earl Grow, Bob Doolittle, Joli Jensen, Jack Lule, Avis Meyer, and Rob Anderson. The craft of such teachers is more transparent, more easily emulated. A Carey lecture resembles a grand magic show, bursting with fireworks, sleight of hand, dramatic flourishes, and the occasional personal aside. Afterward, it is hard to explain to others what just happened.

Nor can one easily imitate Carey's style of research and writing. He works systematically but eschews method. Indeed, his commitment to cultural studies began, in part, as a critique of the methodolatry of empirical social science. For him, technical proficiency does not guarantee wisdom. Carey proposes no research program in the usual sense—no hypotheses, datasets, or methodologies to which graduate students can attach their careers. His essays are as likely to cite a historian, literary critic, legal scholar, or philosopher as a communication specialist. His writing luxuriates

335

in theoretical, historical and literary allusion. He is one of a kind, the field's truest essayist.

By now, you may think me a dense and intractable student. What sort of person learns so little from so renowned a teacher? Like many others, I could list the opportunities Carey has offered me over the years—recommendations for department chair and a National Endowment for the Humanities fellowship, a review essay in *Communication Research*, a chapter in a book he edited. But the most important lessons Carey taught me were about being a professor. It took me a couple of decades to understand those lessons, but I offer them to you now, gratis.

Be serious about your work. Carey is unfailingly polite, but when it comes to scholarship he has little patience for the frivolous. He would never haze a doctoral student in the way some professors do, but you do have to earn your way with him (it took a few years for the "Jim" in that opening sentence to feel comfortable). Carey believes that intellectual work is intrinsically worth doing. He considers scholarship a more disciplined version of the symbolic work by which all humans make their way in the world. And he considers his own writing and speaking a form of political action—not an ideological expression, as others would have it, but an enacted commitment to public life.

This is why Carey discourages premature professionalization. At no time in graduate school did he urge me to present a convention paper or author an article. (I once heard him ask, "Do we like the tenure system so much that we would drive it down into graduate school?") Carey thinks of graduate education as a time of self-discovery, an unparalleled opportunity to read and think deeply. Because he believes that genuine work must always be the product of personal struggle, he often seems indifferent to status anxieties that torture colleagues.

After all these years, he still finds himself embarrassed by others' flattery and perplexed by their envy (which I have too often seen). Indifferent to academic fashions, Carey has built a career on his own terms. We too easily forget that the cultural approach he advocated was, for many years, considered marginal to the field. His earliest works appeared in magazines like *Antioch Review*, *American Scholar* and *Commonweal* that appealed to a more general intellectual audience.

Honor the university tradition. Carey thinks about the university tradition in a way that others sometimes find romantic, even implausible. In his November 2000 Carroll Arnold Lecture to the National Communication Association, he said that being a professor has offered him worldly opportunities far beyond anything he could have imagined growing up as a working-class child in Providence. But he values the university most of all because it helps sustain a democratic politics.

His work constitutes "a plea for the university tradition," to borrow the title of an essay by the Canadian economist Harold Adams Innis that Carey much admires. He would never call the university an ivory tower; that is far too effete an image. But he does want the university to stand apart from the rest of society, as a place of critical scrutiny, ethical reflection, and study.

Thus Carey has always resisted plans to place universities in the ideological service of the Right or Left. In the 1960s Carey condemned universities' tragic involvement in the Vietnam War, and for over a decade now he has protested the corporatization of its curriculum and administration. But he also opposes the politicization of the university in the name of social activism. Asked to deliver the Arnold Lecture on communication as an "engaged discipline," Carey brilliantly argued for disengagement. I personally encountered his protective attitude when I led a group trying to unionize graduate assistants at Illinois. Carey thought graduate-student unions a bad idea. I have known conservative colleagues who oppose unions on capitalist principles, as well as radical colleagues who consider themselves too avant-garde to identify with other workers. Carey's reasons are more complex. He thinks unions would further bureaucratize university life and create yet another occasion for administrative power. Carey imagines the university as a self-governing republic, in which faculty jealously protect the institution's traditions of free thought and expression.

Look for the human. Carey's students have wondered for years what he sees in Harold Innis, a man whose work can seem to them obscure and apocryphal. The short answer is that he sees the man behind the work. This is the greatest intellectual gift Carey bequeaths to his students. He shows them how to discern the human moving beneath the surfaces of a text. We academic readers can be terribly literal-minded; we spend inordinate effort categorizing one another's work.

Carey, by contrast, constantly tries to ground abstract argument in personal and public history. I attribute this habit, in part, to his streetwise upbringing—a long period of interaction with working adults before his formal schooling began (a wonderful tale recounted in Eve Munson and Catherine Warren's introduction to his second collection of essays). For all their literate elegance, Carey's essays often feel conversational. They honor the oral as well as the literary traditions of public life.

Leave the door open. Professors in the humanities and social sciences often use citations and bibliographies to signal their politics. Carey refuses to play this game. He talks to everyone. He is as likely to quote Michael Oakeshott as Raymond Williams, as appreciative of the gifts of Stuart Hall as of those of his late friend Julian Simon.

I have never discovered a single moment in his entire corpus that I would call faddish or fawning. Carey rejects binary talk and the obsession with power that dominates current styles of cultural studies. For him, culture cannot be reduced to an underlying system of explanatory differences. It constitutes our very mode of being in the world. Culture, as Carey understands it, always admits the possibility of a "we."

That is why he leaves the door open. Carey's students learn that there is always room for one more chair at the table, for one more spoon in the pot.

CHAPTER 19

The Internship Program

S. Scott Whitlow

Introduction

*B*reaking into the business. That's the promise of internships to most students. Not surprisingly, this contributes to internships being hotly sought after by students eager for a roll-up-the-sleeves slice of education. For them, internships are no-risk investments they undertake on either a curricular or extracurricular basis.

Legions of industry practitioners share students' enthusiasm for internships. It's a venture with diverse, immediate rewards. Interns can increase productivity, inject enthusiasm, and give their supervisors the chance to pass on seasoned knowledge, skills and perspectives. All in all, the symbiotic nature of internships assures their ongoing popularity.

As a consequence, an internship support mechanism exists in virtually every undergraduate mass communication program. Of course, an internship course is quite a different entity from a regular classroom course. Its experiential, out-of-classroom nature liberates it from traditional concepts of structure and content. By extension, internship instructors are not instructors in the classical sense. Consequently, they don't bring an individual philosophy or mission to the internship course. More typically, the approach to the handling of internships reflects a collective faculty philosophy.

As with the prototype internship programs to be visited in this chapter, that collective philosophy is grounded in the belief that genuine experience is an invaluable learning tactic. Across the board, the goal is for each intern to *be* a working professional. The consistent view is that this translates into students being assigned appropriate, meaningful tasks and being accountable for the successful completion of them. This is fundamental regardless of where the student interns.

So here we examine and compare the way some well-known and well-respected internship programs implement this philosophy at these institutions:

- The University of Alabama College of Communication
- Syracuse University S. I. Newhouse School of Public Communications
- Arizona State University Walter Cronkite School of Journalism and Mass Communication
- University of Illinois Journalism Department
- University of Georgia Henry W. Grady College of Journalism and Mass Communication
- University of Kentucky School of Journalism and Telecommunications

Details and commentary about the handling of internships at each program came from the faculty or staff member who coordinated or had oversight of the program. Each responded to a range of questions about their handling of internships and their commentary is incorporated or quoted directly in this chapter. Many generously offered examples of some of the tools (forms) they've developed to aid them in their work—as well as to aid students and intern sponsors. Each also explained his or her role in the handling of internships.

Position of the Course in the Curriculum

By intent and design, the internship course occupies a unique position in the curriculum. Because it's outside the conventional course framework, it prompts faculty to wrestle with a question that's not at issue with other courses: *Should students receive academic credit for interning?* Of all the decisions to make in designing or reworking an internship program, this one is pivotal. The decision on this point has a ripple effect, influencing the direction of a host of other aspects of the internship program.

Surprising to some, but true, is that academic credit for internship work appeals to some students but not to others. It's not unusual to hear students ask, "I can get credit for it, can't I?" Others are just as likely to ask, "I don't have to do this for credit, do I?" To students, it all depends on perspective and money.

An internship typically calls for a sizable chunk of student time and energy. For many, it's a worthwhile investment in their future. Just the chance to do the internship is reward enough. Others take a more pragmatic view. Their time and energy as an intern merit compensation, and academic credit is welcome pay. For these students, credit, as *pay*, is all the more important when the sponsoring company provides no intern salary. Consequently, signing up for internship credit is simply part of the students' package of tuition-based courses during the fall through spring terms.

Many companies require that interns be enrolled for credit as a condition of interning with them. Two reasons are frequently at play here. Many companies want the commitment from their interns that a for-credit approach encourages. To them, for-credit equates with interns being more responsible about honoring their work hours and their assigned tasks. The other reason stems from the legal requirement that interns must be compensated for their work—salary or credit. Companies that can not, or will not, pay interns insist on credit being available.

These concerns and preferences are taken into consideration as mass communication programs wrestle with the credit versus no-credit issue. Illinois offers an internship course "mainly to address the problem of unpaid internships where the employer requires that a student earn credit to qualify for the internship." A similar practice exists at Syracuse: "The majority of students will opt to take internships for no credit unless credit is a requirement of the company. Certain communications fields almost always require credit and students often don't have the option of choosing whether they wish to receive credit."

Summer tuition fees coexist with a summer for-credit internship in many units. Syracuse students must pay for any summer credits on a per credit basis so "It's no surprise the majority of students choose *not* to take internships for credit." At Kentucky, students must be enrolled concurrently for the term in which they intern and, thus, pay a summer tuition fee. Nonetheless, summer is a popular time among Kentucky students for doing a for-credit internship.

Illinois links internship credit to the completion of tasks associated with a fall course that is connected to the summer internship. As explained by the internship coordinator, this approach strives to ease students' financial load:

It (credit) is awarded upon completion of work assigned for the course and not just for completing the internship. We feel strongly that students shouldn't have to pay us so that they can work for free for an employer. Because of that, the credit is awarded in the fall so that students don't have to sign up and pay separately for a one-credit class during the summer. A one-credit class fits easily into the full-time load on a student's fall schedule.

Credit Limit

The standards of the Accrediting Council on Education in Journalism and Mass Communications affect the philosophy as well as the practice of awarding academic credit for internship activity at units nationwide. The guidelines note,

Standard 7. Internships/Work Experience

Quality experience in journalism and mass communication should be encouraged. Academic credit may be awarded only for carefully monitored and supervised experience in fields relating to journalism and mass communication. Academic credit may be awarded for internships in fields related to journalism and mass communication, but should not exceed one semester course (or its equivalent) if the internship is away from the institution and, for the most part, supervised by media professionals rather than academics.

Schools may have up to two semester courses (or their equivalent) at an appropriate professional organization where the institution can show ongoing and extensive dual supervision by the institution's faculty and professionals. Schools may have up to three semester courses (or their equivalent) at a professional media outlet owned and operated by the school where full-time faculty are in charge and where the primary function of the media is to instruct students.

Units should advise students that employers are required to conform to applicable federal, state and local laws relating to employment.

Most of the programs examined for this chapter have similar standards about the number of intern credits they permit students to count toward their degree requirements.

The limit may be presented to students in terms of the number of internships. At Alabama, for example, students can receive academic credit for only one internship. Or the limit may be presented in terms of the number of credits. Syracuse students who opt to take an internship for credit are allowed to apply one to three credits toward their degree. This is also the practice at Arizona, Georgia, and Kentucky.

Comparative Features

Across the universities being examined here, the approach to the handling of internships reflects their view of the course's position in the curriculum. In a comparative sense, each tailors features of its internship course in line with its decision about whether credit will be awarded. Here, we'll compare views on the required versus elective status of the course, as well as views on prerequisites, students' preparation for an internship, and securing an internship.

Required versus Elective

Requiring an internship makes a singular statement to students. It confirms, in absolute fashion, the importance of their getting practical experience as an integral part of their education. But it also introduces a seismic shift to the building and maintenance of an internship program, for it involves a commitment to ensure that relevant internship opportunities are available to each student. Consequently, before a unit makes such a commitment, it must realistically assess the intern placement opportunities it has.

Geography plays a pivotal role in opportunities for intern placements especially if students are expected to intern during the traditional fall through spring terms. Media-lean locales may not be capable of offering the range or number of placements needed. Not just one unit's students pursue media-related internships; students from other majors that may have a logical media connection pursue such internships, as well. It's also not uncommon to find high school students competing for intern positions through a site-based learning program. Competition gets stiff. And the fact that the university-level internship program offers a better-prepared worker may not be the ruling factor in the intern hiring decision.

In a media-lean area, it's tempting to imagine that students can land an internship *elsewhere* during the summer break. After all, one can rationalize, with all the intern positions available nationwide, there's a position somewhere for each student. Common sense offers several reasons why this scenario can collapse. An *elsewhere* internship can be difficult, if not impossible, for a student to snare, for it often means long-distance pursuit through layers of hurdles: inquiries about possible positions, an application process, and interviews (maybe even a request that the student interview on site). If the student does land the internship, the unknown of lodging *elsewhere* has to be tackled. That unknown is often tied to how much the internship pays (if it indeed does). The ultimate stumbling block to this scenario is that many students *must* work during the summer to pay for their education. Requiring an internship and expecting it in summer could be an unmanageable burden for many students.

Conversely, a media-rich locale aids the practice of requiring internships as an integral part of major coursework. During the recent retooling of the Telecommunications major at the University of Kentucky, the program's faculty added the requirement that all its majors complete an internship. It is a doable requirement. Located in a midsized city, Lexington, with a bustling media-related community, the university is also only an hour's drive from two large cities, Louisville and Cincinnati. Similarly, at Syracuse, with its media-rich locale, the master's program in Public Relations requires a three-credit internship experience to complete the program.

Internship-as-elective works best for many units. In fact, it is the norm for the programs reviewed here. Quite simply, the flexibility of the approach appeals both to students and to those overseeing internships. It also reflects an expectation that's both realistic and reasonable: Students who are serious about prepping for their career will *want* to intern.

Following that perspective, the University of Illinois doesn't require internships. However, it advocates them, counseling students on the importance of getting practical experience. Likewise at Syracuse, students heed encouragement that includes the view that "it is a fact that outside experience is the single most important hiring criterion in the communications industry." Undergraduates at Syracuse take that view to heart and typically complete two to four internships even though internships aren't required.

Prerequisites

Internship prerequisites most commonly involve grade point average (GPA), the completion of specified courses, and/or the completion of a minimum number of academic credits (junior standing is a common expectation). Although many units link prerequisites to enrolling for internship credit, the implementation of that varies across units. At the units being examined here, for example,

- Juniors at Alabama can intern for credit once they've completed the first three courses in the major and carry a grade point average of 2.5 or higher. Students complete an Internship Eligibility Form (Exhibit A) so their compliance with prerequisites can be checked.
- At Syracuse, aspiring interns must have completed the 60 credits needed to reach junior standing before they can intern for credit.
- Arizona students complete a combination of courses [Introduction to Mass Communication, Fundamentals for Radio/TV, Radio/TV Writing (Basic), Production Techniques (Basic), News Writing (Advanced), Broadcast Reporting (Radio), and Broadcast Reporting (Advanced TV)] to ensure their readiness to intern.
- Students seeking for-credit internships at Illinois must be juniors or seniors. However, sophomores who are admitted for the following fall are eligible to undertake a summer internship, since the course through which credit is awarded is in the fall term. Such students will have taken a couple of the program's required courses—Introduction to Journalism and Beginning Reporting—before beginning an internship.
- At Georgia, students in each department complete a Request for Approval of Internship form (Exhibit B) that must be submitted before the internship begins.

Course requirements, unique to each department, are noted on the form. Students sign this form with a clear and specific acknowledgment of their responsibilities.

- Internship prerequisites vary from major to major at Kentucky. Each of the three majors—Integrated Strategic Communication (ISC), Journalism, and Telecommunications—requires the completion of specified courses. Both the ISC and Journalism majors require a cumulative GPA of 2.6, with a 3.0 in major coursework. Students document their preparation on an application form checked by the intern coordinator.

Preparing for an Internship

A gearing-up period invariably precedes the start of an internship. The need for this is fairly critical where units provide academic credit, since registration for the credit hinges on proof of readiness to intern. At most of the units being examined here, students step into the readiness pipeline by completing and submitting an internship application form. Although the format and content of this form varies, each form is highly specific in terms of the prerequisites and expectations established by their respective unit. As the application examples from Alabama (Exhibit A) and Georgia (Exhibit B) suggest, it's prudent to lay out all application-related particulars. It leaves nothing to chance or misunderstanding in a process where students shoulder far more responsibility than is the case with other courses they take.

Gearing up typically begins the term before the actual internship. The exact timing of this varies from unit to unit, depending on the amount of lead time preferred by intern coordinators before registration for the upcoming term.

Simply applying and being approved for internship credit isn't sufficient to be permitted to register at some units. At Alabama, "all paperwork must be complete before the student enrolls for the internship." Similarly at Arizona and Kentucky, the internship contract must be set before students can enroll for credit.

Students at Georgia who are approved can register for intern credit only when they've submitted their Request for Approval of Internship *and* the internship confirmation letter from their employer has been received by the unit. The students are responsible for ensuring that their employer sends the confirmation letter by deadline on company letterhead.

Preparing for an internship takes on a much different meaning at Syracuse, where internships are completely student initiated. The school's Career Development Center (CDC) offers an information-rich seminar twice a month aptly titled "How to Find an Internship." Seminar topics range from defining internship needs and goals to using resources for identifying internship opportunities to details associated with academic credit. Separate seminars tackle résumé/letter writing and interviewing. Seminar attendance by students is voluntary. Staff members of the CDC will also meet with students individually to offer direction and advice.

Securing the Internship

Search is the operative word in the securing of internships. And primarily, it's up to the student to launch, manage, and finalize the search. It's standard practice at many

Exhibit A

College of Communication
The University of Alabama
Field Services Office
P.O. Box 870172
Tuscaloosa, AL 35487-0172

Got Contract:_____
Letter to Employer:_____
Registration letter sent:_____
Copies to Department:_____
Evaluation Sent:_____

INTERNSHIP ELIGIBILITY FORM

NAME: _____ SOCIAL SECURITY # _____   DATE: _____

MAJOR: _____ MINOR: _____

QUALITY POINT AVERAGE:
Overall _____
Communication _____

HOURS COMPLETED AT THE END OF LAST SEMESTER: _____

LOCAL ADDRESS_____
            (Street/P.O. Box)   (City)   (State)   (Zip)

HOME ADDRESS_____
            (Street/P.O. Box)   (City)   (State)   (Zip)

LOCAL TELEPHONE: _____   HOME TELEPHONE: _____

PERIOD OF INTERNSHIP (Circle One)   FALL   SPRING   SUMMER

TYPE OF INTERNSHIP: (Circle One)
  Advertising   Broadcast/Film   Journalism   Public Relations

COURSES YOU HAVE COMPLETED RELATED TO THE POTENTIAL INTERNSHIP:

COURSE NUMBER   COURSE TITLE   GRADE
_____
_____
_____
_____
_____
_____

List two references who can support your qualifications for this internship

(1) _____

(2) _____

_____
Signature of Student

Exhibit B

TELECOMMUNICATIONS AND BROADCAST NEWS
Request for Approval of Internship Application

Name: _____   Date: _____

Social Security #: _____   Semester desired: _____

Athens Address: _____   Phone/Athens: _____

_____   Phone/Home: _____

Major: (Check one) _____ Telecommunications   _____ Broadcast News

Email Address: _____

Number of hours of credit requested: (Circle One)   1   2   3

I understand that in order to receive 1 to 3 variable hours of academic credit in the College of Journalism and Mass Communication Internship for Credit Program, I must concurrently register for TELE 5010, and further that I must meet the following requirements:

- ➡ I am a student enrolled in the Telecommunications Department.
- ➡ I have successfully completed TELE 3010, TELE 3210, and one other TELE course.
  The following items are needed to receive credit for my internship.
- ➡ A letter verifying the offer of an internship from the employer (see attachment B).
- ➡ A 3-5 page typed final report on my internship activities.
- ➡ My employer's evaluation of my internship activities.

Name of your supervisor(s), company, address, and phone number:
_____

_____

I understand the responsibilities placed on me in order that I may receive credit for the requested internship. My failure to carry out these responsibilities outlined above by the dates indicated will result in my receiving an unsatisfactory grade in TELE 5010 and loss of credit for the internship.

Student's Signature: _____   Date: _____

Advisor's Signature: _____   Date: _____

Submit this completed form for consideration by your department head who will let you know whether credit for the internship has been approved or disapproved. This request must be submitted **BEFORE** the internship begins. May be faxed to 706-542-2183.

FOR DEPARTMENT HEAD USE ONLY: _____ Approved _____ Disapproved

Department Head's Signature: _____   Date: _____

Exhibit C

Category	Superior	Good	Average	Fair	Poor
Level or preparation/skill at beginning of job					
Ability to work with others					
Capacity to follow instructions					
Willingness to take initiative					
Degree of enthusiasm					
Use of grammar					
Spelling ability					
Accuracy of information					
General writing ability					
Outside relationships -- clients, sources, etc.					
Quality of work produced					
Overall assessment of performance:					

*Grade equivalent: A   B   C   D   F units, including those examined here. To underscore the initiative expected of students in seeking and securing their own internships, the coordinator at Syracuse notes, "We avoid the 'placement' term as it implies we find internships and/or jobs, which we don't."

Arizona's approach differs somewhat. There, paid internships and unpaid ones call for different handling of the process. The decision about *who* will intern *where* for paid internships is based on how employer and students rank each other. For unpaid internships, employers simply select their intern from among those who apply for the position.

A range of support efforts exists across the units to aid students in their internship search. Leads come from posted notices from firms seeking interns—unit-produced publications targeted at industry organizations that identify students prepared for internships (or jobs).

Also important are

- Posted notices from firms seeking interns
- Unit-produced publications targeted at industry organizations that identify students prepared for internships (or jobs)
- Industry directories
- Commercial guides for internships
- Word of mouth from other students
- Database listings
- Alumni contacts

The *Employment Prospectus* is Georgia's annual booklet to help students locate internships and permanent jobs and to help employers find capable employees. Featuring short biographies of students, it highlights their skills and goals. Georgia's Placement Office staff mails copies nationwide, with the highest percent targeting the Southeast.

Syracuse's CDC points students to two ways to search for an internship.

- Students focus on posted internship announcements: "These can be current listings or listings that go back to a previous year (chances are the names may have changed but the internship still exists.)"
- Preferably, students set their own criteria, such as geographic market, and then locate opportunities meeting their criteria.

Syracuse students' *search* gets outstanding support from the database managed by the school's CDC. Readily accessible there are all internships that have come to the CDC's attention in the past three years. Armed with the criteria they've set, students can search the database by various categories such as field and city: "A student looking for a film internship in California can plug those two criteria in and come up with a list of all California film internships that have come through our office."

Notable Features

For all the programs being examined here, one feature that distinguishes each is its oversight of interns, the actual day-to-day supervision of the internship program. A key influence here, obviously, is the status of monetary resources. Other factors at play include the decision as to whether students should receive course credit and, if so, whether the course counts as a requirement or an elective.

Each participant in our examination of internship programs offers a glimpse, below, into just how their program is supervised. Whereas some intern directors are faculty members, others work in administrative positions.

Jim Oakley, Placement Director, University of Alabama

Oakley notes that his function is to ensure that all students who want an internship find one. Once students are situated in internships, each of the departments (Journalism, Advertising/Public Relations, and Broadcast) has one faculty supervisor monitor internships. Oakley is assisted by a student worker 20 hours a week.

Karen McGee, Director, Career Development Center, S. I. Newhouse School, Syracuse University

McGee oversees a range of career development efforts for students of the S. I. Newhouse School, including internships. Internships aren't a primary responsibility, however, since the School doesn't require that students participate in an internship. Internship-related tasks focus on posting information about internships, adding the information to an ongoing database, and aiding students in finding internships on their own. This assistance comes in the form of seminars and one-on-one counseling. McGee notes, "Once the student secures the internship, the credit issue determines the next step. If the company does not require credit and the student does not want to receive it, the School's involvement ends. If the students wish to or must do the internship for credit, they work through our faculty for sponsorship and the SUIP (a university-wide office) for registration. The Newhouse CDC is not involved with the credit process."

Mike Wong, Walter Cronkite School of Journalism and Mass Communication, Arizona State University

Wong coordinates news, sports, and production internships for majors once advisers have screened them their qualifications for eligibility to intern. He handles his responsibilities as coordinator without staff assistance or release time.

Dana Ewell, Instructor and Placement Director, University of Illinois' Journalism Department

Ewell balances instructional responsibilities with running the Journalism Placement Office, where she advises students about internships and handles the course through which majors earn academic credit associated with their internship. She is provided with one student helper for about 10 hours a week "who helps mainly with the flood of information about jobs and internships."

Emily P. Smith, Placement Office, University of Georgia

At Georgia, much of the work in managing internships is handled by the Placement Office. However, each department head is responsible for determining the approval of academic credit and for evaluation of the internship experience.

Scott Whitlow, University of Kentucky School of Journalism and Telecommunications

The School's internship program is coordinated by a full-time faculty member without staff or student assistance, but with a one-course release.

Common Tasks/Activities

For many interns, there's more to an internship than just *doing* it. Many units require additional effort, often in the form of journals and/or reports on the internship experience. Tasks such as these help intern coordinators monitor the internship as well as evaluate the intern's efforts and accomplishments. The tasks also push the students to engage in a bit of thought about the work they're doing and its fit into their education and career plans.

Although these tasks are typical at each of the units being examined, the implementation varies from unit to unit. At Alabama, students keep a daily journal of their internship activities and provide copies of all the work they participate in during the internship. At the end of the internship, they write a detailed final report.

Syracuse students seeking credit for their internship may enroll in the newspaper or public relations internship course. The course format requires a weekly meeting along with an activity journal and a final paper that recounts their work and accomplishments. Students whose internship thrust is outside the focus of the courses (either newspaper or public relations) enroll for credit under the auspices of a direct faculty adviser. These students determine a set of tasks in consultation with the faculty adviser.

Interns at Arizona State also attend a class once a week. In addition, they submit a midterm and a final report about their internship work. Illinois students register for a fall seminar class that's taken in connection with a summer news internship. Students are told specifically that the credit they earn is for the work associated with the class, not with the internship itself. Class work includes

- Meeting for pre-internship sessions late in the spring
- Meeting for three post-internship sessions early in the fall
- Writing journal entries during the internship
- Reading a book in a related field
- Writing a final paper that relates classroom and book lessons to observations during the internship

Students register for the course and the credit in the fall once the internship-based summer assignments are complete. However, students must receive approval to do so the previous spring. To secure approval, the proposed internship has to parallel the mission of the department:

> Our only stipulation in all cases is that the internship relate to the course of study offered in this department. We do not have a public relations sequence or an entertainment/programming emphasis within this department so intern-

ships in these areas don't qualify for Journ 293 credit. Internships that stretch the traditional definition of news are considered on a case-by-case basis.

Georgia and Kentucky don't require a formal class for interns. At Georgia, the head of each department defines tasks beyond the internship itself. Its Advertising Department, for example, requires that interns submit "a typed week-by-week final report of the internship activities" and augment the report with samples of work from the internship.

Kentucky students are also required to keep a weekly journal. Since students aren't always clear on what they should be writing in their journal, these suggestions are offered to them:

- Record the tasks you work on. Also, identify skills you're developing or perfecting. Specify how these tasks and skills are contributing to your learning objectives.
- State the comments, suggestions, and/or criticisms made by your primary supervisor and others and explain how these can benefit you. Make note of people you meet, the role they play in the firm's business, and what you've learned from them.
- Relate what you've learned in class to what you're experiencing on the job. As they become apparent to you, jot down skills and procedures you need to learn *more* about—on the job or in class.
- List questions you need to ask—and make sure you ask them. (It's a good idea to collect your questions into a list and keep the list with you at the internship. Then, you're prepared for formal and informal talks with your primary supervisor and others at the firm.)
- Set a "goal for the coming week" throughout your internship. For example, your goal might be to discuss with your supervisor how he or she responds to industry criticisms, or to use equipment that's new to you, or to complete a routine task more efficiently. Record in your journal how and when you accomplished the goal(s).

As their internship draws to an end, Kentucky students are also required to write a letter of appreciation to their primary supervisor and/or the president of the firm where they worked. They're reminded that the opportunity to serve alongside working professionals is a privilege that merits the courtesy of formal words of thanks. The task helps students realize that courtesy in business relationships is both appropriate and beneficial.

Common Challenges/Solutions

Internship directors agree that the challenges they encounter stem largely from working with two very distinct publics: students and intern employers. Trying to mesh their differing interests and desires about the internship experience introduces a collection of predictable challenges. These common challenges are associated with the intern employer's perception of internships, placement of students in intern positions, the salary issue, monitoring intern performance, and evaluating that performance. The challenges are common; so, too, are some of the solutions practiced by these internship directors.

Employer Perception

The tales students tell intern coordinators about their internship search paint two distinct images of employers. Not surprisingly, these images reflect polar-opposite views with regard to employers' approaches to the *hiring* of an intern. Some employers operate on an all-warm-bodies-welcome basis. Others choose to screen applicants carefully and prefer to interview several before making a selection. Of course, student applicants are rarely in a position to know the employer's orientation to internships or the motives behind it. It adds an element of luck to the internship search for students who jump at the first, quick offer.

It is likely that every intern coordinator has encountered the type of employer who simply desires a warm body. Such employers readily call and state, or insist, that they must have an intern. Often, these are work sites where interns are looked to purely for clerical and gofer tasks. Often, also, securing interns (plural) means one less regular employee needs to be on the payroll. Rarely is it a site where the intern engages in meaningful tasks that push his or her learning curve.

Savvy students, who are prepared to interview the employer as well as to be interviewed, steer clear of this type of setting. Across the board, interviewing the prospective employer is a tactic intern directors urge students to take.

A marginal note from one of the intern directors observed,

> One of our students had barely seated herself at an interview when the employer announced, "We'll take you. Deal done." The student saw that the employer had no interest in her skills and goals or in what she could do or learn at the site. She thanked the employer for seeing her, declined the offer, and left. Several days later, she accepted another offer where the interview had convinced her she could both learn and contribute.

Our intern directors agree that the ideal employer for interns is one who's eager to don the mantle of teacher and mentor. In a very real sense, by involving a student in what they do on a daily basis, they touch the future.

Placement

Announcements of national-level internships pepper the mail almost daily at most units. At some mass communication programs, these are often posted on bulletin boards for student perusal. Alternately, they're added to a binder of similar announcements and housed where students can scan them. Or, in the case of Syracuse, they're entered into a database for ease of search and retrieval.

The regular arrival of announcements linked to the array of mainstream and industry internship guides precludes the need to solicit information about nationally competitive internships.

At the local and regional internship levels, however, most intern directors find it a challenge to identify new internship opportunities. The solution is obvious: Many units consider actively seeking internship openings for their students to be one of an intern director's key responsibilities. Arizona State University keeps its students' statewide internship opportunities varied by working to constantly seek new companies.

Units regularly turn to standbys to learn of new businesses and changes in existing ones:

- Chamber of Commerce
- Networking via industry organizations (e.g., Public Relations Society of America and Sigma Delta Chi/Society of Professional Journalists)
- City magazines
- Newspapers/news shows
- Leads from current and former interns

Syracuse has innovated an outreach approach to build its internship base in a way that makes efficient use of technology. A marketing kit first works to sell employers on the advantages of recruiting and selecting Syracuse students as interns. The kit then eases the process for employers by telling them how to post their intern openings with the Newhouse CDC.

Kentucky invites input from each semester's crop of students who hold local or regional internships. For one of their regular log submissions, interns are told,

> With your two-plus months on the job, you're in a good position to identify people in your firm—and/or people your supervisor interacts with outside the firm—who might offer students a good internship.

> For your next log, please give me the name, title, firm and phone number of two or three people *you* think would offer a good internship and who (to the best of your knowledge) haven't used interns before.

Salary

The salary aspect of internships interests interns and employers alike. Employers hold a range of perspectives on the question. Some see it as the right and equitable thing to do or as symbolic of the student being accepted as a junior professional. Others employ workers whose union contracts affect how salary is handled. Still others feel that the opportunity they are offering the intern is its own reward.

The bottom line is that federal law requires that interns receive either pay or credit in exchange for their work. In fact, many employers speak of *giving credit*. It's an illusion, for, as Syracuse observes, "it is the University that actually grants the credit."

Savvy employers realize the value of offering an internship salary. Quite simply, it attracts a larger pool of applicants. Consequently, the employer can be more selective and bring on board the student who shows most promise as an intern. It's also reasonable to expect that a salaried intern will be able to work more hours than one who receives credit only and, thus, must work a salaried job also. More on-the-job hours result in an intern who learns the ropes faster and tends to be more productive.

For some students, the decision about interning with a specific company, or interning at all, pivots on salary. These are students who need income to continue with their education. They don't have the option of cutting back on work hours to squeeze in an internship on top of class hours and study hours.

Students think of pay strictly as money. It can be far more varied than that. It may come as use of a company credit card tied to business-related travel or eating. Or it may come as perks provided other company employees—use of a health club, tickets to sporting or entertainment events, etc. Some companies pay their students with an end-of-internship scholarship applied to student tuition.

Dealing with the salary issue is a challenge to all intern directors. It's often a sensitive issue to broach with intern employers and can tax the diplomatic skills of intern directors. And, not surprisingly, the units studied here differ markedly on their position and approach to the salary question. Alabama does not involve itself in pay arrangements.

Syracuse "encourages companies to pay (at least minimally) their interns but cannot force them to do so." Arizona expects employers to pay at least minimum wage, a scholarship, or a stipend. At Georgia, "some interns are paid and some are not. Some departments (print journalism and public relations) require compensation in order for the student to receive academic credit."

Monitoring

The Accrediting Council on Education in Journalism and Mass Communication makes no bones about it. Its to-the-point directive says, "Academic credit may be awarded only for carefully monitored and supervised experience in fields relating to journalism and mass communications."

The directive challenges intern directors to view monitoring as an integral part of each student's internship experience. Though it can be an arduous task, intern directors value monitoring for it serves basic and commonsense purposes, and it

- Provides updates on student learning and productivity as it bears on the student's internship goals
- Helps keep track of the number of internship hours worked by the student
- Conveys to employers (and students) the unit's interest in a valuable experience for the student
- Strengthens the connection between the employer and the unit
- Reminds students of their accountability toward earning academic credit

Most of the units examined here favor similar solutions to the challenge of monitoring. These range from phone calls to e-mail checks to site visits. They may be done on a periodic basis or on an appointment basis, or may be strictly impromptu. And they may be with the student, the site supervisor, or both.

At Georgia, advertising majors receive this announcement from the head of their department: "I may visit those of you who are located within reasonable traveling range and, in some cases, some of you who may be quite distant from us. Those whom I cannot visit personally, will be contacted by telephone."

The necessity for close monitoring ceases where credit is based on the coursework the students complete rather than the internship itself. For that reason, Illinois notes that "we have limited contact with the employers on the subject of how they run their internship programs."

Evaluation

Internship performance is notably difficult to evaluate, for obvious reasons. Each student functions in a separate, unique sphere with individualized goals and tasks. The immediate supervisor at the internship site rarely has experience in setting grade criteria. And then there are the extraneous factors making the challenge of evaluation even more difficult. Leading these are two factors that can profoundly affect performance:

- The supervisor changes jobs during the internship and the replacement envisions the intern's role differently from the original supervisor
- The intern feels the type of on-site activities promised are replaced by more menial ones and becomes frustrated

The difficulty of evaluating internship performance can be a logical reason not to offer internships on a for-credit basis. Commonly, the solution is for units to offer them on a for-credit but pass-fail basis. That's the case, for example, at Illinois, Georgia, and Kentucky.

At Syracuse and Alabama, however, credit is letter grade. With careful thought, evaluations can be designed to help with grade discrimination. Supervisors of Alabama's student interns, for example, complete a Supervisor's Evaluation of Student's Work Activities. On it, supervisors rate interns across a range of abilities using assessment scales with anchors of "Superior" and "Poor." The assessment options are keyed to letter-grade equivalents. This provides the unit's intern coordinator with diverse and specific gauges of the intern's work performance, thus facilitating grade assignment.

Resources for Perspective Interns
Books, Directories, and Reference Guides
America's Top Internships. Mark Oldham.
Directory of International Internships. Career Development and Placement Services/Michigan State University.
Directory of Internships. Ready Reference Press.
The Internship Bible. Mark Oldham.
Internships: On-the-Job Training Opportunities for All Types of Careers. Peterson's Guides, Inc.
Internships in Communications. James P. Alexander.
Internships and Job Opportunities in New York City & Washington D.C. The Graduate Group.
Internships Leading to Careers: Paid and Voluntary Internships That Can Lead to Professional Opportunities. The Graduate Group.

Jobs in Arts and Media Management. American Council for the Arts.
National Directory of Internships. National Society for Internships and Experiential Education.
Student Guide to Mass Media Internships. 1999. The Intern Research Group.
Society of Newspaper Design Internship Project. Graphic Design.
SNPA Internship Directory. Internships for Southern Newspaper Publishers Assoc.
Student Internship Guide. National Press Photographers Assoc.

Internship Opportunities at Online Sites
www.rsinternships.com. Rising Star Internships.
www.internships.com. National Internships.
www.idealist.org. Idealist-nonprofit groups.

Having site supervisors evaluate their intern is standard practice, whether grades are reported as letter or pass-fail. For this, many units opt for a standardized form. At Georgia, however, the unique nature of an internship is acknowledged by the evaluation tactic used there. Each intern's supervisor writes a letter to the department head at the end of the internship. Students in the Advertising Department are told, for example,

> Your employer must submit to my office, also no later than the last day of the semester (classes end), a separate letter evaluating your performance. The letter must include a recommendation as to whether you do or do not deserve credit for the course and it must be addressed to . . .
>
> Because I expect your employer to be completely candid about your performance, this letter will be considered a confidential communication with the college. Should the employer authorize us to release it to you, however, we will do so.
>
> If I do not receive all of the above materials by that date, you will be given an "Incomplete."

Students themselves are either required or requested to provide an assessment of their internship. Arizona State requires that students include the evaluation in their final report, as do Alabama and Kentucky. At Syracuse, even students who are not receiving credit are able to comment on their experience. The students enter their comments into the unit's internship database by using a dedicated screen.

Outside Resources

A range of internship self-help publications assists students and internship coordinators alike. Industry directories, many of them annual, enumerate internship openings and provide details on application requirements. Another group of guides offers leads to internships in a range of communications areas. Internships in both the industry directories and the more general guides draw applications nationwide.

Competition for internships can be intense. Intern coordinators at the programs examined here noted that they caution students of this and urge students to assemble a polished and compelling application package. They also advise students not to pin their hopes on one or two prize sites: *name* firms in *name* locales (Los Angeles, New York). They urge students to apply for a range of positions to include diamonds in the rough among those they apply for.

Remembering a Mentor:
Margaret A. Blanchard

David A. Copeland

I did not realize it, but Dr. Margaret Blanchard of the University of North Carolina's School of Journalism and Mass Communication began teaching me how an instructor should interact with students both inside and outside a classroom the first time I met her. This was before I was ever enrolled as her student in mass communication research. Looking for the proper program in which to pursue doctoral work, I visited the University of North Carolina.

When I met with Professor Blanchard and explained my interests, she informed me that she had similar interests in a slightly different field but found what I wanted to study fascinating. She explained to me how the program worked and encouraged me to apply. She said she looked forward to working with me. That day I wrote the obligatory essay explaining what I wanted to study and why, filling out the application information, and sending all on its way.

About two years into the UNC program, I realized the significance of that original meeting and what Professor Blanchard was trying to instill in me even before she knew for certain that I would be studying with her: That was taking an interest in what interests your students builds rapport and opens the door to more effective teaching. But this approach taught me more. Professor Blanchard used each of her students' ideas as an opportunity to broaden her own knowledge. "I have to learn something about what each of my graduate students is studying so that I can understand the topic and guide them," is how she described the process to me a few years after my graduation.

Though she had a good basic understanding of the relationships between media and religion already—my original proposal for study—I switched foci to colonial newspapers, and Professor Blanchard told me she had little overall knowledge on that subject. But she learned, probably faster than I did and taught me a second important lesson for the classroom: Instructors constantly need to learn and update their knowledge. New information may come from any source.

Following the interests and research of students is an ideal way to broaden one's knowledge base. Since most graduate students are looking for areas that have had little or no research done in them, having been understudied or misrepresented in the literature, working with them on projects, theses and dissertations allows instructors to be a part of information gathering that can be transferred to classroom lectures. This provides all students with cutting-edge information.

358

In my first class with Professor Blanchard—a seminar on free expression during my first year of doctoral study—I was able to combine my original interest in media and religion with my undergraduate and master's background in history. The class covered a massive amount of information. In this seminar, Professor Blanchard taught her students how valuable research was and is to improving what goes on in the classroom.

She was working on completion of a book, *Revolutionary Sparks* (1992), a history of free expression in America. Nominated for the Pulitzer Prize, *Revolutionary Sparks* detailed the intricacy of expression rights in America and the anomaly of the speech rights legally given Americans and the urge of many to censor anything that offends them or goes against their basic beliefs. In class she used this premise from her research to direct her students' understanding of the development of free expression in the United States.

For research in the free-expression class, Professor Blanchard directed her students toward applying this concept to our areas of interests. For me the relationship between ideology and action—essential parts of Professor Blanchard's approach to free expression—was applied to religion, specifically to Mormons, polygamy, and the Supreme Court case *Reynolds v. United States*. With this approach, Professor Blanchard taught another lesson: Research questions and methods may be applied in different subjects, in different areas, or in different disciplines to produce quality results.

Writing research papers and dissertation chapters for Professor Blanchard may have been the most instructive part of her teaching tutelage, however. If something was worth researching and writing, then it was worth close scrutiny by her. Professor Blanchard's readings and comments on what her students produce were and are thorough, and incorporate all that she teaches in other ways. The paper on Mormons, polygamy, and national reaction to *Reynolds v. United States* in newspapers underwent Professor Blanchard's careful reading. She filled the margins with comments on how to make the paper better, and she urged—actually demanded—that I submit it to a national conference. I had done the research and the writing, but Professor Blanchard honed it with her careful reading and suggestions.

The paper won the top student award and one of the top paper awards at the American Journalism Historians Convention in Philadelphia. Since it was my first convention and presentation, Professor Blanchard attended, more in support of me, I think, than for any other reason, since she did not have a paper or panel presentation at the conference. The experience confirmed all that I had been taught by her—take an interest in students, update your knowledge base (through research, conventions, etc.), apply sound methodology to research, and something good will be produced.

Professor Blanchard insists that each graduate class should produce research worthy of presentation and possibly publication, but she believes strongly that graduate students need to make their mark by themselves rather than in collaboration with their mentors. She told me as I was finishing my dissertation that she had considered working in collaboration with her students but felt that students doing research in media history have specific interests. Those interests, she said, are best served through research specific to individual and topic.

Her approach works because of the intense critiques she gives to everything her students write and her willingness to become an "expert" on whatever subject her students select for theses and dissertations. She will not approve a chapter until it is free of all grammatical, punctuation and style errors and is a thoughtful, well-arranged, and complete discussion of a subject. So, in a way, she is a collaborator with her students; she simply takes no credit in the byline for the results.

The information that Professor Blanchard imparts and the presentation methods she uses in her classes are worthy of discussion, too, but I believe that her more subtle teaching lessons have meant the most to me. She told me that she felt an obligation to give each of her students the best that she was capable of giving. Because I received that attention, I have felt impelled to provide the same for my students. My successes, therefore, are a reflection on the lessons I learned. Teaching, in the Margaret Blanchard scheme, is an intensely personal activity that demands interaction between mentor and student. Her former students who understood this have become good instructors and researchers, and that is exactly what she intends for each of them.

PART V
Advanced Curriculum

CHAPTER 20

Media Ethics

Val E. Limburg

At a time when society depends for its values as much on the media as on the
traditional pillars of family, church and school, we ought to care as much about
how journalists are educated as we do about how public schools and police officers are educated.

—John Seigenthaler, Chairman, Freedom Forum

Introduction

There are courses that often seem to have so much importance in our curricula
that we eagerly take hold to improve, polish and defend their place in the educational process. So is it with courses in Media Ethics. Many who teach such
courses do so with pride and with confidence that what they are doing will make a difference in the future direction of our society. It is with such an outlook that this chapter is prepared.

After a look at the place of ethics in the curriculum of mass media, a description of
a survey of course syllabi in media ethics is analyzed, revealing similar courses and
different approaches. Courses are a reflection of an instructor's personal philosophy
together with factors such as class size and available resources to determine
approaches. Pedagogy or teaching style also has a lot to do with how well the students
learn, as well as the substance of such a course. This course description does not contain detailed information about the course content, but enough information about common emphases reveals what the course really is. Also, a sampling of subjects can be
found in any of the many course texts cited at the end of this chapter. However, the
focus here is on the strategies of the *teaching* of this subject matter, which seems especially critical in the teaching of this course.

Although much of the information is merely descriptive, the great passion for this
subject cannot be hidden by many of the course's contributors. This chapter's objective is that the readers will have a good idea of what comprises courses in Media
Ethics, and why such courses are vital in today's communication education.

Position of the Course in the Curriculum

Perhaps the most ancient of all the subjects that is taught in the communication curriculum is that of ethics. Applying ethics to media or press performance pulls the course into the contemporary scene. It may well be that, in much of higher education with its emphasis on empirical analysis, instruction may have lost perspective and appreciation for values. In the 19th century, an ethics course was a keystone in the typical college curriculum. It was the course taken to put into perspective the place of all the courses from liberal arts and professional training. Here students would learn how to think about the information they had studied. Some might believe that this is where knowledge begins to turn into wisdom. Emphasized were historical thinkers such as Socrates, who indicated that knowledge is virtue and expressed such sentiments that the love of wisdom determines the *better* person, one who derives wisdom from being morally strong. As if to emphasize the importance of the ethics course, it was often taught by the dean or the college president back in the days when even administrators were expected to be *teaching* faculty.

Ethics has been, for many centuries, a branch of *philosophy* (literally "love of wisdom") and is an idea to which much attention is given, but whose subject matter is diminishing on college campuses. Stephen Covey (1997) observes that socially much of the literature describing success 100 years ago focused on what could be called the *character ethic*. However, after this country moved into the industrial age there was a shift from character to appearance.

In academic life at the turn of the 20th century the best and brightest faculty often taught ethics courses. It was a plumb to be treasured. For some institutions that perspective has changed. Today it could be claimed that although the highest formal degree in higher education is the Doctorate of Philosophy, or Ph.D., many doctoral students never reach deep enough to go to the *philosophy* of their discipline.

More generally, ethics is a study of right/wrong, good/bad, proper/improper moral imperatives and their codification in professional settings. But just *who* decides what is right or wrong, good or bad, and proper or improper, and on *what basis*?

Not long ago, a School of Communication was approached by faculty members in the Philosophy Department. "You ought to let us teach the course in Media Ethics," they claimed. "After all, we have been asked to do so by the faculty members of the business school, who have little desire to delve into the subject matter of ancient philosophers and patterns of analyzing ethical dilemmas. Ethics is a branch of philosophy and has been for thousands of years."

Undeterred, the school stated a firm commitment to work at a focused, unique, applied kind of ethics that would be of direct consequence and interest to communication majors. Perhaps other departments try to get in on the growing recognized need for ethics in the professions and the consequential robust enrollments for such courses. In most major communication programs in many institutions, there have been bursts of enrollment in these courses. A look at the list of texts at the end of this chapter reveals many recent works designed to address the needs of growing enrollments in media ethics courses. A good media ethics text usually generates many actual case studies of ethical dilemmas or problems associated with moral judgments.

A recent survey of courses at two- and four-year institutions found that 43 percent of the schools sampled teach media ethics, a basic understanding of which is "essential to any curriculum" (Kock et al., 1999). Not many courses have such a uniform offering across the communication curriculum. Such interest may reflect a younger generation's concern for the media doing the right thing. Perhaps it's a passing fad—or the dramatic and visible problems of the media creating a demand for solutions. Certainly there is no lack of subject matter, enrollment, or faculty interest in this course.

Similar Courses

The discussion here relates to courses in Media Ethics but is not limited to courses in Press Ethics or Journalism Ethics. The difference is that the former includes not only the ethics of journalism—questions of privacy, loyalty to confidential sources, etc.—but also issues of ethics in advertising, public relations, and entertainment. Many journalism programs have courses in Press Ethics; some programs broaden the considerations to include the ancillary functions of advertising, ownership and entertainment. Although there are many good texts in Press/Journalism Ethics, fewer exist in these ancillary areas. This is, perhaps, indicative of how the courses focus on the subject matter, most being courses in press ethics.

On several occasions over the last generation of instructors, professional organizations have furnished surveys about how similar courses are taught, and ideas about approaching the teaching of various courses in communication. In surveys conducted by Broadcast Education Association (BEA), curricular designs in various kinds of courses have been sought.

In assessing the common features of this course, it seems imperative to look at the BEA's efforts. In 1969, its Courses and Curriculum Committee undertook a syllabus project to find as many syllabi of the major courses taught in broadcasting as possible. As a young faculty member, this author remembers both contributing to (Beginning TV Studio Production) and profiting from the model syllabi and composite information found in the committee's subsequent publication of its findings.

There have been further attempts through the years since then as well. More recently, the BEA has undertaken another ambitious master curriculum project. It's now possible to do larger-scale projects; it's easier to communicate with colleagues at other schools, thanks to such innovations as fax, Listserves and e-mail, Web sites, and Internet search engines. Such collated information offers further insight to those who have this teaching interest in common and is bound to trigger further ideas for effective teaching.

The call for syllabi for the course in media ethics was first delivered in the Courses Curricula and Administration Division of the BEA at the 1999 annual meetings in Las Vegas. Afterward, a call was made through the general BEA Listserve. Numerous faculty responded and furnished syllabi by regular mail, fax, and e-mail. Web sites with syllabi and valuable links were furnished. In addition, syllabi were exchanged at the Association for Education in Journalism and Mass Communication (AEJMC) conference in August (where a Media Ethics Interest Group was approved to become a division). All these resources provided about 25 syllabi from various schools.[1] Not all schools teaching courses in Media Ethics are listed here, but just the schools that responded to the call.

A listing of each syllabus or ideas from every school is not attempted, but rather a digest is offered of the major ideas therein. Many of the schools also offered their Web sites for further information and links to information and resources used in their courses. Frequently, however, the sites weren't current and had links that were outdated or otherwise unworkable. The results are found on the BEA Web site (beaweb.org) under "Syllabus Project."

Ancillary/Related Courses

The mixed structure of the departments' orientations made a difference in the way any ethics course was placed in the curriculum and the appearance of ancillary or related courses. In many communication curricula where a self-standing ethics course is not found, ancillary or related courses are found mostly as instructional segments in other media courses. As a matter of fact, most reporting and/or editing courses will include a segment on ethics, whether or not there is a self-standing ethics course in the curriculum. Some have expressed concern as to whether there would be sufficient emphasis on the critical topic of ethics when piled up with scores of other important principles necessary for aspiring reporters or communication professionals to remember.

Some curricula have chosen to place Media Ethics together in the same course as Media Law, and there is a text (Moore, 1999) specifically designed for this combination. The point of such a combination is that there is an ongoing comparison for future journalists and media practitioners of what they *must* or *must not* do (law) and *should* or *should not* do (ethics). The consideration of the history and social differences arriving at these distinctions can bring a solid understanding of many aspects of communication study. As Moore (1999) notes, "Every journalist must establish a personal code of ethics, but the standards can best be understood within the context of mass media law" (p. xvi).

A few schools with specialized concentrations offer ethics together with specialized functions: advertising ethics, entertainment ethics, broadcast ethics, public relations ethics, or ethics and new media technology. Certainly those in broadcasting and electronic media might take comfort in the growing number of broadcast or electronic media courses in ethics. Many would include ethical behavior in such areas as the Internet, a diverse and difficult, if not impossible quagmire in which one could scarcely expect any standardized code of ethics.

In addition, another orientation, already noted, is where some schools have determined that ethics is a philosophy and should be taught with that orientation, sometimes with mention of the applied ethics in such fields as journalism or mass media. Another instructor uses the course in a strictly applied way, working on the rules and responsibilities of media workers. One school uses the course early in the curriculum as a required one for advanced reporting; another uses it as a capstone course, giving a final ethical spin on the fundamental professional skills learned earlier by students. Another school uses it as part of its religious approach in their Christian school. One large university offers this as a required course in many sections, taught by five or six different faculty members.

Another orientation in the teaching of Media Ethics is its use as a qualitative methodology course for graduate students, with a focus on analysis possibly more complicated than most quantitative methodologies.

Comparative Features

Many instructors teach the course using a Socratic method, always probing, always questioning, allowing the students to learn the principles from their own discovery in trying to answer the questions the instructor puts before them. But such an approach works only when the course is not too large, and this is an increasing problem with this ever-popular offering.

In an age where curricular design often takes *diversity* into consideration, media ethics is studied as part of an examination of the assortment of values in our culture or society. Much like the assortment of values each individual holds, the assortment of orientations is wide and varied.

One of the age-old problems haunting the teaching of this course is how and whether to incorporate classical ethics concepts from philosophy. Does one include discussion of Socrates, Plato and Aristotle? What of deontological and teleological approaches to the study of ethics? What of all the philosophies that define truth in various ways that have bearing on ethics analysis? Can those be ignored? What of more contemporary contributors to the evaluative process: Milton Rokeach, Walter Lippmann, Sessela Bok, Lawrence Kohlberg or John Rawls? And what of media professionals such as Edward R. Murrow, who have had impact on the way the media define ethics? And should all these kinds of considerations be included in a course, would there be room for the study of applied ethics through such explorations as case studies?

Special Features

Many instructors attempt to provide small pieces of traditional ethics as they focus on contemporary issues and case studies. One class begins by giving thumbnail profiles of key figures from ethics/philosophy and then goes on to implement that philosophy in analyzing case studies. Altschull's work, *From Milton to McLuhan: The Ideas Behind American Journalism* (1990), seems suitable for such a strategy. Most respondents to the syllabus survey revealed that some discussion of defining terms and philosophical concepts is necessary for an intelligent analysis of ethical media situations.

Other courses take the first two or three weeks studying the classical concepts and then proceed to current media dilemmas that may be found in professional publications such as *Columbia Journalism Review* or *American Journalism Review*. Current breaking stories will often furnish the most problematic analysis, for there is not yet structured reaction or litigation. In attempts to encourage students to pay attention to media activities, particularly those of questionable ethics, students may be instructed to find their own ethical dilemmas and analyze them. (There may be a danger here of lack of independent work; ethics courses are not immune from plagiarism.)

Common Goals and Objectives

Nearly all courses and the syllabi examined contained either one or more *goals* or *objectives*. Although these varied, most were designed around the idea of *ethics analysis*. Call it *moral reasoning* if you like. Some more specific objectives for the student included

- Recognize moral issues and the various frames of reference in assessing media values.
- Develop critical reasoning skills.
- Learn models of ethics analysis.
- Learn to recognize ethical problems in current issues.
- Exercise moral imagination in working toward solutions of ethical dilemmas.
- Learn the design of professional expectations.
- Demonstrate an awareness of the evolution of the value in the media.
- Learn to tolerate other values or viewpoints.
- Learn to ask questions that are fundamental to ethics analysis.
- Learn to resist ambiguity by using values as fundamental tools in analysis.
- Develop a keen sense of moral obligation that can be justified rationally.

In addition, graduate-level courses may demand extensive literature searches or an extensive tracing of some facet of the history of value development.

There were other objectives, of course, or those worded differently. Often they were couched in behavioral terms such as "Student will perform these objectives as evidenced in" (written assignment, exams, etc.). Instructors who have been oriented to student *learning* (as opposed to simply teaching) may seek out *behavioral* objectives—knowing that students have learned from some demonstrable behavior, such as performance on exams, or oral or written presentations. Assignments, then, often are keyed to the aforementioned objectives or goals.

Since a frequently identified objective deals with ethics analysis, a common theme is the use of one or more analytic models, such as the Potter's Box, Bok's scheme for determining honesty, or other models sometimes developed by the instructors themselves. Even those courses that focus on case studies or instructors that are reluctant to delve into abstract theory may find such models useful if students are ever to go beyond simple subjective reactions to media dilemmas.

In applying their course objectives, some instructors of the media ethics course approach the subject by examining the individual (analyzer or student) as a moral agent before examining media issues. It could be argued that before one can effectively evaluate or analyze the ethics process or the values in a dilemma, one must be aware of his or her own values. One instructor begins his course with a thorough discussion of this Socratic notion: "An unexamined life is not worth living." The first assignment is one where the student identifies his or her most important values in life and then traces their origin—family, friends, church, media heroes, etc. A list of common values (e.g., Rokeach, 1972) is provided. Students are asked to trace how early values evolved during their life and then apply how those values might be applied to the media, either as future media professionals or as media consumers. Students can then refer back to these basic values they have identified. It makes the experience of identifying, evaluating and analyzing values in media scenarios more meaningful to each individual.

Students might hold on to their dearly held values, or they might learn reasons to change one or more. They might observe how their own values coincide or differ from those of the professional expectations as articulated in codes of good practice. They might also learn how some basic values evolve in the media and evaluate whether the changes are more important than holding to the earlier traditions. If students hold to values such as decency and respect for individuals, they may draw on those to evaluate the problems found in tabloid newspapers or a Howard Stern radio program; or they may believe that in this new millennium we now see things differently, and "that's all right."

Instructor Philosophy

It would be easy for a professor (one who professes a position) to impose her or his own values in a course studying values and ethics. To do so blatantly seems wrong at the onset. As Black points out, "There is a major difference between helping students learn how to become autonomous moral agents and imposing our value systems on them. It is the difference between moral philosophy and moralizing, and there is little room in the university setting for the latter" (1992, p. 235). Yet most courses deliberately point out expectations of professional codes that often have strict moral values so obvious that their acceptance seems to go without questioning: honesty, respect for individual privacy, social justice, or lines of propriety in regard to violence or censorship. Try as one may, the efforts to uphold some values (e.g., honesty) cannot remain hidden. Should they?

It has been suggested that it is more insidious to pretend that the course is not imposing values when, in fact, there are obvious ones expected of student behavior. Regardless of how students may feel about honesty or integrity, most instructors will expect a display of those values by not tolerate cheating, for example.

One instructor goes so far in this respect as to post, at the beginning of the course, a list, à la Letterman, of "(Instructor's) Top 10 Values." These values and the behavior that demonstrates them include the following: *Responsibility*—attend class, be on time, turn assignments in on time, etc. *Initiative*—complete assignments without undue supervision and get involved! *Honesty and integrity*—cheating in all its forms such as plagiarism is not tolerated and may earn the student expulsion from school. *Intelligence and industry*—"It may be true that not everyone has a high capacity to quickly grasp and understand difficult concepts. But successful people learn that dogged pursuit of learning can condition one to have greater learning capacities. Such efforts lead to a better understanding and the great trait pursued through the ages—*wisdom*" (from a course syllabus submitted). *Imagination*—"The world is full of drones that copy each others' ideas. Imagination is perhaps the best index of genius!" And others such as *enthusiasm, tolerance*, and *leadership* may be included.

While this idea may seem self-imposing, this instructor points out that when she receives requests for references for letters of recommendation, prospective employers will often ask about such character traits or values, rather than how much a student knows about a particular subject.

Common Emphases

A lot can be told about a course by looking at the schedule of topics offered each class. Many instructors stay close to the progress as outlined in a well-structured text such as that by Christians et al. (1998). This text, developed over several editions, is one of those widely used from the wide assortment of available publications. The first half focuses on press ethics, and then the text goes on to the subjects of ethics in advertising, public relations, and media entertainment. To many instructors, it seems logical to use the structure these authors furnish, starting with some basic instructions on how to analyze using the simple model of the Potter's Box for analysis. The elements of value identification and fundamental principles based on philosophical notions are carefully laid out. It is not certain in just which texts authors first set the major premises of principles or philosophies. However, there are *five ethical guidelines* (Aristotle's Golden Mean, Kant's Categorical Imperative, Mill's Principle of Utility, Rawl's Veil of Ignorance, and the Judeo-Christian Persons as Ends) that can be found in many of the texts used, setting a pattern for the universal perspectives learned by students.

Then comes a description of how to determine loyalties or to whom moral duty is owed. The progression of topics seems to make sense but may be too all-encompassing for some courses that cover only press or information ethics without advertising, etc. The breadth of focus is, of course, a curricular decision and may well determine both the progression of lecture topics and course text.

Typical of the subjects found in most syllabi and texts include truth telling, objectivity, confidentiality, respect for privacy, and freedom of expression. In addition, the texts (or they) considers social justice, advertising practices, business practices (Where does one draw the line between the vital need for profit and greed?), service to community, influence of entertainment, censorship, and image ethics or photojournalism. A few distinct subjects include "the role of conscience," "the role of reason," and "the ethics of advocacy."

Like most other topics within disciplines, course instructors have their areas of strength, special interest or expertise. Some spend several lectures on a subject that others treat more lightly. In one or two instances the course was team taught, giving perhaps a different perspective from each instructor and thus avoiding the possibility of a single bias.

At least one course describes the duties of established press councils, since they commonly make value judgments about what is fair or proper, a process not unlike ethics analysis. A few courses include the ethics of new media, including the Internet or cyberspace. But many do not, perhaps because of its newness, or perhaps because it's an area where the ethical problems and law are not yet clearly structured or are still evolving.

Some schools include looks at foreign systems and global communication, but such perspectives are rare or are mingled with courses that study international and foreign communication. More common is the topic of media economics and how the financial structure is becoming a universal in a world of otherwise diverse systems.

A few of the syllabi submitted for the project indicated that there was a deliberate inclusion of aesthetics and the ethics of "art," since art analysis is a logical approach when entertainment is considered.

One of the common traits across this course's offerings can be seen in the typical assignments. Most courses placed weight on participation in class discussion of case analyses. Most had exams, although their nature or format was not always clear. Some of the assignments worthy of note include the following:

- Students are required to interview a media person on the subject of "What I Believe" and then analyze the person's value set.
- Students choose a current media issue with two or more sides, find its ethical aspects, and then participate as debate teams in a formal debate.
- Students are assigned a case where there are clear value differences in the parties involved, then role-play assigned parts. They then discuss how that role's values differ from or are similar to their own.
- Students develop term papers that demonstrate careful research of a contemporary media issue and then demonstrate some method of analysis identified in class.
- Students are required to write an evaluative book report on a book that takes a value position in or about the media.
- Students are assigned to "rewrite one of the professional codes of the media" in a way that recognizes changes that have come into play in what is acceptable media performance.
- Class members form a panel to research and discuss an issue, much as might be expected at a panel of a professional conference.
- Students write several short position papers on an assigned media issue and give a careful rationale for their position.
- Students find issues in trade publication (e.g., *Columbia Journalism Review*) and frame them in a brief Potter's Box analysis.
- Students must keep a clip file of stories they find that raise ethical problems. Each is accompanied by an analysis of values and principles therein.
- Students attend a movie and find episodes, language, graphic depictions, etc., that have ethical implications.
- Students note the ratings of television shows and watch them—even though they may never have previously seen them—and observe how values are reflected therein and whether these are *reflective* of our culture or whether they *project* those values into our culture.
- Students analyze advertising (print and broadcast) and determine how the advertiser defines the consumer—to what basic value in the consumer does the ad appeal? Then evaluate.

- Students analyze the characters in a TV sitcom (or drama) and describe their values, comparing with that student's own perception of what normal values are in such settings.
- Students view a video of a biography and determine that featured media person's values and their likely origin.
- Perhaps most sublime of all were assignments of *community service*. These require students to demonstrate their values by serving some aspect of the community. This might include cleaning up the environment, helping at rest homes, helping elementary schools develop a short video about their school, or creating public service announcements for some local nonprofit group. The premise here is that one lives values, not just professes them.

Common Challenges/Solutions

What is the training and orientation of those instructors who teach media ethics? Have they had a strong professional media background? Is their academic graduate work in the area of communication theory? Journalism? Ethics? Law? An area tangent to media studies? Have instructors attended workshops or conferences that focus on media ethics? Is the instructor simply textbook educated in this subject? Does the instructor's terminal degree (likely a doctorate of philosophy) focus on philosophy? And, after all, what difference might any of these questions make? Perhaps there is a fear that the same fools that display a violation of good ethics in the media are the same ones who teach it.

John Seigenthaler once indicated how important ethics training is for wannabe media professionals. If one accepts that premise, it seems logical that informed instruction in this area is also critical. For those who may have unknowingly wandered into the subject of media ethics, or have been arbitrarily assigned to teach such a course, and who feel unprepared, there are workshops and materials to enhance the teaching.

One of the growing problems observed among those who discussed their teaching of the media ethics course was that of enrollment. One instructor indicated that his course began as a seminar with 12 to 15 students, then grew to 30 and then to 60. Apparently this instructor was popular in the dynamic method of teaching in addition to the growing popularity and exposure of this subject. At last report, he was pondering how to handle 120 students. The course really begs for student participation, a difficult if not impossible task with that many. Students are reluctant to talk in front of that many peers or, when they do, they don't always have the best contributions. The instructor may be tempted merely to put everything on PowerPoint presentation, blab on through lectures, simply pour information from the instructor's big bucket of knowledge to the smaller buckets of the students, and then end with an objective exam. (Essay exams are so time consuming!) In such a setting there would seem to be a terrible waste in the spillage of vital knowledge.

The solution? Hold to controllable enrollment, an idea easier said than done in a era of enrollment-driven department budgets. One school sees the critical nature of this vital course and simply invests its resources by offering several smaller sections, each taught by qualified faculty, not teaching assistants.

Another challenge would be to have students learn to develop critical reasoning skills to the extent that not only could solutions be found for existing problems, but insight could be shown to develop strategies of *proactive ethics*, where problems could be anticipated and policies or codes could be designed to handle them before they become problematic. Some courses consider proactive ethics as an extension of solutions found in ethics analysis.

Another common challenge would be the selection of suitable texts. Which approach by which author? Each instructor should study different approaches to determine which text fits the curricular demands and his or her interests.

In addition to the texts, already mentioned or listed hereafter, instructors may use a list of their own readings and resources. This might include packets or copies of journal or news articles. Such a packet is often prepared and copied by a service within the university system. Usually, permission is sought for such copying. But where it is not, the instructor simply makes a list, puts the materials at a reserve checkout station, and lets the student copy his or her own materials. Does that violate the intent of copyright? If not literally and legally, then perhaps there is an ethical compromise in the integrity of the use of intellectual property unless there is a clear indication of the source of ideas and writings. Otherwise, this situation could then present the appearance of impropriety, a common problem in ethical dilemmas.

Some instructors have their students participate in chat-room discussions of issues via cyberspace. It would seem to be a good idea, but such attempts are met with mixed results. No one is quite sure whether it's just a matter of adjusting age-old teaching techniques to new ways of doing things. Another use of applying the ancient discipline of ethics to modern techniques deals with submitting assignments by e-mail. Experiences with such submission often prove frustrating to instructors who find that reading monitors is much more difficult than reading from the printed page.

Another challenge is grading. Although grading seems to be no problem in most courses where grading criteria are carefully defined and laid out in advance, there can be a pitfall in the grading of ethics courses. When students reveal their values, even those that may not be in keeping with conventional norms, some instructors may be tempted to reflect the student's differing values as *mistakes* when grading assignments or determining course grades. The problem is often covert, and instructors may administer such punishment unknowingly. The path of ethics instruction may be fraught with such temptation, but total objectivity in such matters seems critical.

Most instructors incorporate *class participation* in student grades. The idea seems sound, but the problem always looms that some students are reluctant to participate for reasons of communication apprehension, shyness or, with some foreign students, cultural conditioning. Other students participate freely but may have little of substance to offer.

Another pedagogical problem becoming more universal in many courses across the curriculum is *reading*. Although instructors find importance and often place grading weight on the reading of texts and other articles, students may not read the material unless they see that they will be tested in some way on assigned reading. Instructors handle this in a variety of ways, including pop quizzes and/or random selection from the class roll to have students explain and evaluate what they were assigned to read.

Sometimes there is awkwardness, but students usually will rise to the expectation of their instructor as they come to recognize the importance of course readings.

Yet another challenge is determining whether the students are internalizing the values and principles they discover to be vital in media practices. In one class, students were surveyed at the beginning of the semester to identify the values they hold dearly. When it was determined that the dominant value was *honesty*, the instructor gave a midterm exam and either overscored (gave more points than really earned) or underscored (gave fewer points than earned) exam grades by "making mistakes" with the math. Students were told to take a minute to check their scores and let him know whether there were any errors. He found it interesting that, in the underscored exam grades, all the students let him know, but only a few of the overscoring students let him know. At the end of the semester, he explained what he had done, and that the students who confessed were given a few extra points on their exam scores, but students who did not let him know got the actual lower scores for their exams. (Consequently, he came under criticism from his colleagues for "deceptive" or "dishonest" practices by such a scheme of fooling the students to test the veracity of their values.)

Outside Resources

A variety of resources is available for instructors of media/journalism ethics courses. Workshops on a national level bring enlightening experiences and knowledge of the various perspectives of media ethics. Perhaps the best known and most focused is the Poynter Institute in St. Petersburg, Florida. The institute is funded for the specific training of both media professionals and teachers of future media professionals in areas of writing, editorial judgment and, most importantly, ethics training. The workshops may last for three days or so, and are geared to practical problems—case studies that have traditionally presented problems for professionals. What is often enlightening is the association with others who are seeking the best and most effective teaching methods for this course. Such networking is invaluable in keeping abreast of ideas about teaching ethics.

Another valuable workshop, exhausting in its examination of the presentation of ethical issues, was offered a few years ago. It was the Gannett workshop, sponsored by the School of Journalism at the University of Kentucky and the Association for Education in Journalism and Mass Communication, and funded by the Gannett Foundation. Its facilitator was Ed Lambeth, who has been at the forefront in Journalism Ethics for many years and has been one of the figures genuinely concerned with the training of media ethics instructors. Now Gannett has established Freedom Forum, which includes panels, speakers, forums, newsletters, scholarships, and the offering of materials for instruction. Media Ethics is a frequent subject of deliberations among the Forum's participants. Although the Gannett workshop is no longer running, the Poynter Institute continues to have its workshops.

Perhaps the best networking occurs at professional meetings: those of the AEJMC, the BEA, the NCA (National Communication Association), the ICA (International Communication Association), and other such organizations comprised mostly of teachers in this and related fields. The AEJMC now has an Ethics Division and provides an ongoing dialogue about the teaching of ethics. The BEA offers such panels every year, usually sponsored by the Courses, Curricula and Administration Division, the same organization that organized the syllabus project already described. Anyone not involved in any of these organizations would certainly be at a disadvantage in uncovering resources in the teaching of media/journalism ethics.

There are other conferences where one may tailor a presentation to an organization's interest and use the perspective of media ethics. This has been done by this author for conferences of the National Association of Broadcasters, Visual Communication Association, Society of Professional Journalists, Ethics in Technology workshops, and conferences on archival and history subjects, as well as regional conferences for journalists and broadcasters.

In addition to the liaison with media professionals, there is the possibility of association with professional ethicists. One such organization bringing together professionals from various disciplines is the Association for Practical and Professional Ethics. Its purpose is "to discuss common concerns in practical and professional ethics" at annual meetings that bring together those in the various fields of public administration, law, the environment, accounting, engineering, computer science, research, business, medicine, journalism and the academy, on issues that cut across the professions. Part of its activities include a miniconference on research ethics, a colloquium directed to an ethics center representative or those considering establishing an ethics center, and an intercollegiate ethics bowl addressing ethical topics in the classroom, personal relationships, and professional ethics.

The Literature

Some of the more popular texts, as cited in the sampling of course syllabi, included that of Christians et al. (1998), Black et al. (1999), Day (2000), and Patterson and Wilkins (1998). Each of these works could be considered useful, substantial, and popular among instructors of media ethics; they have all had three or more editions. However, as noted above and cited below, still numerous other texts are available, more than a score having direct bearing as a text for this course, plus a number of others (not cited) that could be used as supplemental text (e.g., using a philosophy, law, or business approach).

More than half of the syllabi obtained in the syllabus project revealed that instructors like to pull out their own case studies, either in a course workbook, or with cases happening concurrently during the semester, as issues arise. Resources for such case studies include the periodicals and journals cited below, as well as general news publications.

Conclusions

It is heartening for those concerned with ethics instruction, especially Media Ethics instruction, to see the growth of courses and design of curricula around this vital course. It is a discipline and a unique analysis, even becoming included in the conventional study of qualitative research methodology. It is also encouraging to see it as a refined mixture of current issues and classic philosophy.

Although courses began mostly as Journalism Ethics or Press Ethics, they are moving beyond that into other important functions, such as advertising, programming, business practices, and regulatory control. Some observers ask whether we need to consider ethics in *media entertainment*; after all, we are talking mostly of a nonexistent, fictitious world apart from that of the real world with which journalism usually deals. Yet, our perceptions of existence are partly formed from our heroes and villains, and the stories from the world of imagination. There is concern that we ought to continue to care as much about those influencing values as the others that shape us. The more narrowly focused texts in these areas ought to be a welcomed addition to our curricular development in media ethics.

Certainly the need continues for more refinement in Media Ethics, including the study of the ethics that are specific and peculiar in the wide range of media functions. The question continues: Are media ethics to be taught by those with a vision of the importance of analyzing the values carried by mass media that shape our culture, or by others—or are they to be taught in our curricula at all?

Note

1. *Schools participating* in the call for syllabi were Washington State University, Whitworth College, Oklahoma State University, LaSalle University, the University of Kansas, the University of Wisconsin at Eau Claire, Stanford University, Emerson College, Ball State University, the University of Florida, the University of South Florida, the University of North Carolina, Cedarville College, Washington and Lee University, the University of Minnesota, the University of Hawaii, Florida International University, Western Michigan University, North Dakota State University, the University of Illinois, Brigham Young University, the University of Nevada at Reno, Colorado State University, and the University of Iowa.

Works Cited

Altschull, J. Herbert. 1990. *From Milton to McLuhan: The ideas behind American journalism.* New York: Longman.

Black, Jay. 1992. Media ethics. In *Teaching mass communication: A guide to better instruction.* Ed. Michael D. Murray and Anthony J. Ferri. New York: Praeger, p. 235.

Black, Jay, Bob Steele, and Ralph Barney. 1999. *Doing ethics in journalism: A handbook with case studies.* 3rd ed. Boston: Allyn and Bacon.

Christians, Clifford, Mark Fackler, Kim Rotzoll, and Brittain McKee. 1998. *Media ethics: Cases and moral reasoning.* 5th ed. New York: Longman.

Covey, Stephen R. 1997. Forward. In *The power principle: Influence with honor,* by Blaine Lee. New York: Simon and Schuster.

Day, Louis A. 2000. *Ethics in media communications: Cases and controversies.* 3rd ed. Belmont, Calif.: Wadsworth.

Kock, Erin, John G. Kang, and David S. Allen. 1999. Broadcast education curricula in 2-year and 4-year colleges. *Journalism Educator* 54, no. 1:13.

Moore, Roy L. 1999. *Mass communication law and ethics.* Mahwah, N.J.: Lawrence Erlbaum.

Patterson, Philip, and Less Wilkins. 1998. *Media ethics: Issues and cases.* New York: McGraw-Hill.

Rokeach, Milton. 1972. *Beliefs, attitudes, and values: A theory of organization and change.* San Francisco: Jossey-Bass.

Further Resources

Media Ethics Texts

Arant, David, ed. 1999. *Ethics, issues and controversies in mass media.* Boston: Houghton Mifflin/Coursewise.

Bowie, Norman E. 1985. *Making ethical decisions.* New York: McGraw-Hill.

Bugeja, Michael J. 1996. *Living ethics: Developing values in mass communication.* Boston: Allyn and Bacon.

Christians, Clifford, John Ferré, and P. Mark Fackler. 1993. *Good news: Social ethics and the press.* New York: Oxford University Press.

Christians, Clifford, and Michael Traber. 1997. *Communication ethics and universal values.* Thousand Oaks, Calif.: Sage.

Cohen, Elliot D., ed. 1992. *Philosophical issues in journalism.* New York: Oxford University Press.

Fink, Conrad. 1995. *Media ethics.* Boston: Allyn and Bacon.

Gardner, Howard, Mihaly Csikszentmihalyi, and William Damon. 2001. *Good work: When excellence and ethics meet.* New York: Basic.

Gordon, A. David, and John Michael Kittross. 1999. *Controversies in media ethics.* 2nd ed. New York: Longman.

Hausman, Carl. 1992. *Crisis of conscience: Perspectives on journalism ethics.* New York: Harper Collins.

Jaksa, James A., and Michael S. Pritchard. 1988. *Communication ethics: Methods of analysis.* Belmont, Calif.: Wadsworth.

Klaidman, Stephen, and Tom L. Beauchamp. 1987. *The virtuous journalist.* New York: Oxford University Press.

Knowlton, Steven R., and Patrick R. Parsons. 1995. *The journalist's moral compass: Basic principles.* Westport, Conn.: Praeger.

Lambeth, Edmund B. 1986. *Committed journalism: An ethic for the profession.* Bloomington: Indiana University Press.

Limburg, Val E. 1994. *Electronic media ethics.* Boston: Focal.

Lynch, Dianne, ed. 1999. *Stand! Virtual ethics: Debating media values in a digital age.* Boulder, Colo.: Coursewise.

Matelski, Marilyn J. 1991. *TV news ethics.* Boston: Focal.

Merrill, John C. 1994. *Legacy of wisdom: Great thinkers and journalism.* Ames: Iowa State University Press.

Meyer, Phillip. 1987. *Ethical journalism.* New York: Longman.

Moore, Roy L. 1999. *Mass communication law and ethics.* Mahwah, N.J.: Lawrence Erlbaum.

Rivers, William L., and Cleve Matthews. 1988. *Ethics for the media.* Englewood Cliffs, N.J.: Prentice Hall.

Seib, Philip, and Kathy Fitzpatrick. 1997. *Journalism ethics.* New York: Harcourt Brace.

Smith, Ron F. 1999. *Groping for ethics in journalism.* Ames: Iowa State University Press.

Periodicals and Journals

American Journalism Review. Published 10 times a year by the College of Journalism of the University of Maryland at College Park, through the University of Maryland Foundation.

Columbia Journalism Review. "To assess the performance of journalism . . . to help stimulate continuing improvement in the profession, and to speak out for what is right, fair and decent." Published bimonthly by Columbia University, New York.

Communicator. Monthly publication of the Radio-Television News Directors' Association, which "offers lots of in-depth features on technological advances and innovative newsroom practices, plus regular departments on newswriting, legal issues and management."

Feedback. "A correspondence journal published quarterly by the Broadcast Education Association . . . Publishes articles or essays—especially those of pedagogical value—on any aspect of electronic media."

Journal of Broadcasting and Electronic Media. Carries scholarly articles from time to time on ethics in broadcasting and electronic media. Published quarterly by the Broadcast Education Association, Washington, D.C.

Journal of Mass Media Ethics. "Devoted to explorations of ethics problems and issues in the various field of mass communication." Published quarterly by Lawrence Erlbaum Associates, Inc., 10 Industrial Avenue, Mahwah, NJ 07430.

Journalism and Mass Communication Quarterly. "Devoted to Research and Commentary in Journalism and Mass Communication." Published by the Association for Education in Journalism and Mass Communication, with editorial offices at the University of South Carolina.

Journalism and Mass Communication Educator. "A Journal devoted to research and commentary on instruction, curriculum, and educational leadership in journalism and mass communication." Published quarterly by the AEJMC, Columbia, South Carolina.

Media Ethics. "The Magazine Serving Mass Communications Ethics." "Media Ethics is independent. It is eclectic in content, and edited on the basis of quality and space, not ideology or economics. It strives to provide a forum for opinion and research articles on media ethics, and to service readers in the form of announcements, and reviews of meetings, opportunities, and publications." Published twice yearly by Department of Visual and Media Arts, Emerson College, Boston.

Quill. "For more than 85 years, Quill has been a respected and sought-after resource for journalists, industry leaders, students and educators on issues central to journalism." Monthly publication of the Society of Professional Journalists.

Selected Web Sites

American Family Association. Fundamentalist media watchdog group that traces objectionable values displayed in the media. www.afa.net.

Associated Press Managing Editors. "Dedicated to the improvement, advancement and promotion of journalism by our own newspapers and through our relationship with the Associated Press." Also, access the APME Red Book, Statement of Ethical Principles, and the Newspaper Ethics Policy: A Proposal. www.apme.com.

Association for Practical and Professional Ethics. Goes beyond media ethics. php.ucs.indiana.edu/~appe/home.html.

Broadcast Education Association. "The Broadcast Education Association (BEA) was established in 1955. It was initially established as the Association for Professional Broadcast Education. While the BEA organizational name reflects our historic roots in preparing college students to enter the radio & TV business, the members share a diversity of interests involving all aspects of telecommunications and electronic media." www.beaweb.org.

Computer Professionals for Social Responsibility. Ten Commandments of Computer Ethics. www.cpsr.org/program/ethics/cei.html.

EthicNet. Databank for European Codes of Journalism Ethics. uta.fi/ethicnet.

Fairness and Accuracy in Reporting (FAIR). This media watchdog group's site includes articles from the group's publication *Extra!*, special reports, and online resources. www.fair.org.

Freedom Forum. A forum for the exchange of information and ideas promoting free press, free speech, and free spirit. www.freedomforum.org.

Journalism Ethics. Sample of a good Web site of a journalism ethics course by Tom Brislin, University of Hawaii. www2.hawaii.edu/~tbrislin/jethics.html.

Minnesota News Council. Information on disputes involving journalists. mtn.org/~newscncl/.

National Press Photographers Association. Information about the organization and articles on current topics. sunsite.unc.edu/nppa/.

Organization of News Ombudsmen. A roster of members and examples of their work. www5.infi.net/ono/.

Parents Television Council. "Bringing responsibility to the entertainment industry." www.ParentsTV.org.

Poynter Online. This institute for media studies examines cases in journalism ethics. www.poynter.org/index.htm.

RTNDA (Radio-Television News Directors Association). Professional codes, etc. www.rtnda.org/prodev/rtndf/ethics.htm.

SPJ (Society of Professional Journalists). This site includes organization news, links to online journalism resources, articles from *Quill*, SPJ's Code of Ethics, etc. www.spj.org/ethics.

CHAPTER 21

Mass Communication Law

Penelope Bradley Summers and Roy L. Moore

This (the press) formidable censor of the public functionaries; by arraigning them at the tribunal of public opinion, produces reform peaceably, which must otherwise be done by revolution. . . . It is also the best instrument for enlightening the mind of man and improving him as a rational, moral, and social being.

—THOMAS JEFFERSON[1]

Introduction

Freedom of the press, as Jefferson so eloquently wrote, serves as more than just a check on public officials. Its necessity lies at the heart of public enlightenment and the ability to self-govern. Such a charge puts a heavy responsibility on media professionals, as well as on those who prepare them for their positions.

Recognizing that a working knowledge of laws and regulations governing media is a must for practicing journalists, the Accrediting Council on Education in Journalism and Mass Communication (ACEJMC) notes this in its mission statement: "The mission of journalism and mass communications professions in a democratic society is to inform, to enlighten and to champion the freedoms guaranteed by the First Amendment."[2] To that end, according to the ACEJMC Principles of Accreditation, "Individual professions in journalism and mass communication may require certain specialized values and competencies. Irrespective of their particular specialization, all graduates should be aware of certain core values and competencies and be able to . . . understand and apply First Amendment principles and the law appropriate to professional practice."[3]

With the emphasis the ACEJMC puts on media law as a core value for graduates, each of the 109 accredited U.S. journalism programs has a required law component in the curriculum, usually at the upper-division level. A vast majority of the more than

450 journalism and mass communication programs are listed in *the Journalism and Mass Communication Directory*, published by the Association for Education in Journalism and Mass Communication. They are also included in the Dow Jones Newspaper Fund's *The Journalist's Road to Success, A Career and Scholarship Guide*, which includes law, or some combination of law and ethics, as an important requirement in preparing students as media professionals and as informed media consumers.[4]

A study of the university-wide role of journalism programs across the country reported in *Journalism Educator*[5] suggests eight strategies journalism and mass communication programs can adopt to improve their status and value to their institutions. Foremost, according to the authors, is "Making themselves more central to the mission of their institution."[6] The media law course certainly provides an avenue to do this. Political science departments, in particular, value this course for their majors, and are often open to cross-listing it. Additionally, some institutions have proposed the media law course with its focus on First Amendment law and related regulations as a general studies curriculum option.

The study of the science or philosophy of law can be divided parsimoniously into four major areas.[7] Most traditional law school textbooks and legal resources are based on a scholarship that analyzes, criticizes, explains and classifies bodies of law. A second type of scholarship focuses on comparing and contrasting laws with other areas of study such as economics, the arts and the social sciences. A third type attempts to discover and discuss the historical and cultural bases for particular legal concepts. Finally, the fourth type centers on abstract questions about different types of decision making and the definition of law itself.

In alliance with these major types of jurisprudence, there are schools of thought that examine how decisions are made. The formalist school assumes judges identify pertinent legal issues in a case and apply them objectively to resolve a dispute. This approach verges on an almost logical/mathematical method. In stark contrast is the realist school, which assumes judges must balance the issues and interests in a particular case and decide the outcome within its context and subject to the judge's own perspective.

The syllabi reviewed for this chapter include class discussion at some point of the various methods of jurisprudence. However, the traditional scholarship of the case analytical method is used most often, using both formalist and realist approaches.

A sample of 21 communication law syllabi and 12 course descriptions from online catalogs were examined for this chapter. Syllabi sampled include those from the University of North Carolina, the University of Alabama, Central Washington University, and State University of New York (Oswega and Freedonia campuses). In addition, Northern Kentucky University, Louisiana State University, the University of Kentucky, California State University, Washington State University, the University of Montana, the University of Tennessee, Ohio University, the University of Memphis, and Purdue University were also sampled. Some of these universities offer a general mass communication law course in addition to special topic law courses. Of the 21 syllabi examined, 12 were for general courses covering a range of legal topics and issues, four were for courses combining the study of media law and ethics, and five were for courses covering specific areas such as telecommunications and the creative and performing arts. This chapter focuses on the general, stand-alone law course offered at most schools.

Position of the Course in the Curriculum

The law course is offered as an upper-division course for media students across all areas of specialization, journalism, telecommunications, advertising, and public relations. Students coming into the course have likely been introduced to some legal concepts in prerequisite skills and/or theory classes. It is usual, for example, for a beginning newswriting textbook to include a chapter on legal issues, such as libel, and for an advertising textbook to contain a chapter on commercial speech regulation. By the same token most broadcast texts have a chapter on telecommunications regulations; public relations texts also include a discussion of regulations governing annual reports or insider trading. While these are essential to a student's specific field of study, most of those classes and texts provide only a cursory coverage of the legal issues and do so in a narrow way. Hence, the capstone legal course serves to combine the various areas of communication law, furnishing more context and depth than an aside in a specialized class can offer. The depth and breadth of the freestanding course also enhances the student's ability to predict legal directions necessary as media are transformed. A regularly mentioned side benefit of offering the course late in the student's academic career is that the course fosters consideration of the public policies under which media professionals must practice.

Although there are no similar courses in the curriculum per se, lower division courses touch on the basic principles to be studied in depth in the law course. Ethics courses could be considered most closely related to law courses in that both are rooted in moral philosophy, and many students take these two classes simultaneously. The study of the history and philosophy behind First Amendment law reads almost like the study of the ethical foundations of media-related professions. Such concepts as the societal utility involved in the search for truth(s), the tyranny of the majority, the marketplace of ideas, the presumed public right to know, the general will, and the leviathan are instrumental to the understanding of both.

However, the spirit and rule of American law diverge from that of professional ethics primarily in the consensual or perhaps "communitarian" nature of the latter and the more precise nature of the former, which threatens the loss of liberty, property or life in consequence of violation. The divergence in the two courses correspondingly is obviated in the questions "What should one do?" and "What can one do?"

While the answers to those two questions at times intersect at one point, there may be available legal options that are professionally unethical or available ethical options that are illegal. In addition, if students follow solely the rule of law, they are likely to mistake that for ethical behavior in media practices, when in fact disobedience of a law, such as refusing to reveal one's sources, may be the ethical behavior.

Common Objectives and Method

Almost without exception, the course goals and objectives in all variations of the course emphasize understanding the application of laws important to media practitioners and consumers. These include First Amendment principles, defamation, intellectual property, privacy, telecommunications regulations, commercial and corporate speech, freedom of information, media access, emerging mass media technologies, and a working knowledge of the legal system. First Amendment principles, including the philosophical and theoretical underpinnings, are typically covered during the first meetings of the class. These sessions include lectures and discussions on prior restraint; the functions and values served by a public policy that protects freedom of speech, expression and the press; the conflicts presented under differing amendments to the constitution; and the machinations of the judicial system in which these rights exist.

As mentioned earlier, most courses are taught in the traditional case analytical style requiring extensive reading prior to class with lecture/discussion as the primary in-class activity. Most syllabi note that students will be called upon in class, or in some cases prior to class, to address hypothetical situations posed by the professor using the Socratic method of inquiry. Reading lists vary depending on the professor, but there is always a required basic textbook. The texts cover a multitude of areas and issues in mass communication law. Those courses combining law and ethics use a textbook that addresses both areas, and the specialty courses require topic specific textbooks rather than a general textbook.

In addition to basic texts, all syllabi call for the reading of some case law. Some syllabi require a case reader as well as a primary text, and others refer students to *U.S. Reports* and regional reporters, where students must read some or all of the opinions written for particular cases. Some syllabi call for a reading of only the majority opinion in a case, whereas others expect students to read dissenting and concurring opinions as well. This seems to vary according to issues and opinions involved in a case. For example, Justice Byron White's *concurring* opinion in *R.A.V. v. City of St. Paul*[8] provides resolutely different reasoning from the court's majority opinion authored by Justice Antonin Scalia.

All syllabi note the importance of class attendance. Some instructors count attendance as part of the grade, and others strongly urge students to attend class regularly or risk lower test and assignment scores. A few give intermittent unannounced quizzes that may not be made up later. Because media law is dynamic and its study is, by nature, cumulative, especially in a case analytic setting, it is necessary for students to understand how one case builds on another, expanding or limiting previous interpretations. Without regular attendance, students often miss nuances and distinctions.

Grading, with a few exceptions, is based primarily on exam performance, with between 75 percent and 95 percent of the final grade coming from the averages of the exams. Three exams during the term is the norm among those syllabi examined. Most of those exams are short essay, with only one syllabus promising multiple-choice exams. The remaining 5 percent to 25 percent of the grading is based on attendance, out-of-class assignments (e.g., case briefs, hypothetical case arguments, petitions for *certiorari*, or moot court briefs), and in class performance (e.g., arguing cases in a moot court setting, quizzes, or class hypotheticals).

Common Emphases

The First Amendment and Prior Restraint

The initial topics covered in all the syllabi are general First Amendment theories and principles (e.g., governmental prior restraint versus subsequent punishment) and judicial structures and workings. The average amount of time spent on these is about one month (six to eight meetings for classes meeting twice a week). Accompanying case readings and discussions in this area vary widely, but all are landmark cases argued before the Supreme Court. Some of the case readings follow:

Near v. Minnesota ex rel. Olson.[9] This early First Amendment case provides a good foundation discussion of the court's presumption against prior restraint, and outlines reasons that may be acceptable for the government to practice it.

Brandenburg v. Ohio.[10] This involves incendiary speech and provides insight into First Amendment doctrine for both hate speech and speech that may or may not produce an action (e.g., violence in media as a causal element of violence in society.)

New York Times Co. v. U.S.[11] This case is a good example of a *per curiam* decision of the Court, and it reinforces the heavy presumption against governmental prior restraint.

Hazelwood School District v. Kuhlmeier.[12] This case involving a high school student newspaper provides for lively discussion on the First Amendment rights of students in public school settings.

Texas v. Johnson.[13] This case discusses actions as speech (symbolic speech) and opens the doors to class discussion about how the government may not distinguish between "bad speech" and "good speech."

Many other excellent cases can be used as a springboard for discussion, but these appeared most frequently in the syllabi examined.

Defamation and Privacy

Fortunately for law teachers, but not so fortunately for the media industry, every term there seems to be a major libel case in the news. That can help with the discussion of libel as a civil rather than a criminal matter, emphasizing the subsequent punishment approach as preferable to prior restraint and seditious libel. Most of the case law readings on syllabi in this area involve a local case, but two U.S. Supreme Court decisions are on every syllabus:

New York Times Co. v. Sullivan.[14] This eloquently written opinion reveals so many layers of beliefs and practices regarding a policy that protects freedom of the press. It affords students the opportunity to see an in-depth analysis of First Amendment issues from the concept of strict liability to the overturning of the Alien and Sedition Acts and the necessity of a free press in an open society.

Gertz v. Robert Welch, Inc.[15] This case expands on the preceding case, further delineating those individuals whose activities are open to public scrutiny versus those who are not public figures and how to tell the difference.

The Four Common Law Privacy Torts

These are also covered in general media law courses. This is increasingly important as the public becomes more critical of media intrusions on those who may or may not be unwitting subjects of public interest, as technological developments enable media to become even more invasive. These torts are illustrated in a number of cases, with more cases emerging each day. It is impractical to list them all here. Students typically have strong opinions regarding the publication of sensitive personal information, and an ensuing debate can offer the opportunity to distinguish legal arguments from emotional ones. Several cases, including two rape cases, appeared on the syllabi examined:

Florida Star v. B.J.F.[16] This case deals with legally obtaining and publishing a rape victim's identity in violation of a state statute. The case also provides an example of how the Court will often stop short of overturning a statute on First Amendment grounds when there are other viable flaws.

Cox Broadcasting Company v. Cohn.[17] This case is a predecessor to *B.J.F.* but contains similar reasoning regarding the state's interest in protecting names of crime victims when the accused has a right to face his/her accuser in a courtroom open to the public.

Bartnicki et al. v. Vopper, a.k.a. Williams, et al.[18] This case, similar to the first two, deals with the constitutional protection afforded to an innocent third party who lawfully obtains and broadcasts a recording of a private telephone conversation that was illegally recorded by another party. It is a limited opinion, but one that generates discussion of legal and ethical obligations of the media.

Wilson v. Layne.[19] This case revolves around media ride-alongs at the invitation of law enforcement officers who are executing search warrants.

Intellectual Property

The intellectual property sessions of the course typically engage students in a rapidly evolving area of law affected substantially by technology. Students are surprisingly unenlightened about the importance of this area of the law to daily media practices. Although they may be aware of some of the well-publicized conflicts, those cases are more salient to them as consumers than as creators. Many media law instructors rely on *Harper & Row Publishers, Inc. v. Nation Enterprises*[20] for a discussion of philosophical principles underlying the protection of intellectual property, and for a clearly written application of Fair Use exceptions. More recent cases that can serve as a pivotal discussion point follow:

Campbell v. Acuff-Rose Music, Inc.[21] This decision focuses on parody and the defense of fair comment and criticism. It also sheds light on the nature of the market value consideration in intellectual property analysis.

New York Times Company, Inc. v. Jonathan Tasini.[22] This opinion deals with freelance work and the right of ownership privileges in collective works. This case was originally brought as a direct result of online publication and is a good example of how new case law is emerging.

Corporate and Commercial Speech

Most, but not all, of the general law courses include a separate section on corporate speech, whereas others incorporate the topic into other areas of law. Some professors discuss corporate speech in sessions on business libel, privacy rights of businesses in private venues versus public venues, commercial speech, or administrative and regulatory law. Three Court decisions with an extensive discussion of corporate speech follow:

Buckley v. Valeo.[23] This is the premier case in which the Court set up constitutional standards for differentiating party speech from individual speech for political campaign contributions.

Nixon v. Shrink Missouri PAC.[24] This more recent case discusses campaign spending limits as they relate to contributions considered as speech.

United States v. O'Hagan.[25] This decision deals with stock trading and profiteering from confidential information and is based on the Securities and Exchange Commission rules 10b-5 and 14e-3(a).

Board of Regents of University of Wisconsin System v. Southworth.[26] This opinion is appealing to students because it involves a state speaker (the university) and its discriminatory funding (speech) of student organizations.

Supplemental Case Readings

In the syllabi reviewed for this chapter, commercial speech sessions seem to revolve around discussion of the level of protection afforded such speech (a speech value approach), and regulatory actions regarding false, misleading and/or deceptive speech. Most general texts adequately cover both, but many of the instructors require students to read court opinions and other resources for more depth. A compact disk produced in 2001 by the Federal Trade Commission contains cases since 1970 that can serve as a resource for students required to argue moot cases on these topics. Supplemental case readings include the following:

Central Hudson Gas & Electric Corporation v. Public Service Commission of N.Y.[27] This case introduces a four-pronged test for determining whether regulations on commercial speech are valid under the First Amendment. Although there have been some minor changes by the Court in terms of how reasonable the fit must be, many teachers consider the case student friendly.

44 Liquormart, Inc. et al. v. Rhode Island et al.[28] This opinion discusses the error of the Court's reasoning in *Posadas de Puerto Rico Associates v. Tourism Co. of Puerto Rico.*[29] A subsequent decision, *Greater New Orleans Broadcasting Association, Inc. v. United States*[30] is in stark contrast to *Posadas.*

One professor related that she teaches corporate speech as a form of compelled speech by framing it within the context of Securities and Exchange Commission filing requirements and Federal Drug Administration or Federal Trade Commission disclosure stipulations. She said this also enhances the relevance of First Amendment issues for students in ancillary media majors.

Pornography, Obscenity, and Indecency

The obscenity section of the course may include media violence and indecency materials as well. Most students are very interested in this topic and eager to share their observations and opinions. Nevertheless, some cases bring the issue of distinctions between obscenity and indecency (the former has no protection under the First Amendment) and between indecency standards for print and electronic media, respectively. This is also a good point to bring in a discussion of feminism and the law, because it frames it within a provocative context. The basic case for analysis is *Miller v. California*,[31] which establishes the constitutional test to determine obscenity. *FCC v. Pacifica Foundation*[32] provides the reasoning behind the less stringent indecency standard for broadcast media. More recent cases that delineate the issues follow:

Denver Area Educational Telecommunications Consortium, Inc. v. FCC.[33] This opinion discusses the regulation and responsibility of cable operators to exercise editorial control over public access channels.

United States v. Playboy Entertainment Group, Inc.[34] This decision involves the scrambling by cable operators of sexually explicit material and provides an insightful discussion of the government's constitutional burden in justifying content regulations.

Reno v. American Civil Liberties Union.[35] This case focuses on the constitutionality of two sections of the Communications Decency Act of 1996, which regulate sexually explicit or indecent materials on the Internet.

Renton v. Playtime Theatres, Inc.[36] This case evaluates the arguments both for and against the use of time, place and manner restrictions on sex-related businesses.

The Media on Both Sides of the Judicial Process

The American Bar Association serves as a very good resource for materials on the press and the judiciary. Its online site (www.abanet.org) lists a number of ABA publications that illuminate the tension between the Third Estate and the Fourth Estate, including the reporters' privilege and conflicts between the First and Sixth amendments. Pertinent cases that focus on these issues follow:

Sheppard v. Maxwell.[37] This opinion delineates what a trial court judge may do to control the effects of media publicity on the trial, including such steps as extensive *voir dire*, jury sequestration, jury admonishment, and restraining orders on officers of the court, including attorneys. Most students are familiar with the O. J. Simpson trial, and this case can help them understand the restrictions taken by the judge in the case to assure a fair trial.

Branzburg v. Hayes.[38] Coupled with two companion cases, this decision involves reporter's privilege, including how this concept clashes with the business of law enforcement and the authority of the courts.

Timothy James McVeigh v. U.S.[39] From the 10th Circuit Court of Appeals, this case provides a good discussion of pretrial publicity considerations based on presumed prejudice and actual prejudice standards of analysis.

Access to Information

In covering freedom of information and open meeting issues, most instructors in the media law course emphasize state and federal open record and government in the sunshine statutes. Students relate well to the Family Educational Rights and Privacy Act (also known as the Buckley Amendment or FERPA) because it protects their educational records, and so this may serve as a starting point for discussion on exemptions from open records. The exclusion of campus crime reports from educational records is especially of interest to those who have worked on the campus newspaper and have been frustrated in obtaining crime reports from campus security officers.

Resources for this section of the course include publications by state press associations, the Society of Professional Journalists, which has a freedom of information director, or state and federal offices of the attorney general. A new Web site, the Citizen Access Project, created by the Brechner Center at the University of Florida, went online (cap2.jou.ufl.edu) in 2002. It contains information about open records and open meetings laws in every state and provides other resource links.

Although a number of cases available will be pertinent to the particular state in which you are teaching, a classic federal case for study is *U.S. Department of Justice v. Reporters Committee for Freedom of the Press.*[40] This case involves an attempt by a media organization to obtain the criminal records of a suspect in an organized crime case.

Following the September 11, 2001, attacks, there have been several freedom of information cases working through the judicial system. These cases, involving military tribunals, deportation hearings, and names of federal detainees, may be found at federal circuit court Web sites. The Reporters Committee for Freedom of the Press Web site (www.rcfp.org/index.html) also contains up to date information on such issues.

Telecommunications and Electronic Media Regulations

The electronic media and telecommunications sessions of the course generally begin with a discussion of the somewhat different footing of print and electronic media under the First Amendment, including the obscenity standards applied to print versus the indecency standards applied to electronic media, including telecommunications. It is also a good opportunity for reinforcing the discussion of administrative law previously introduced, the impact of technological developments on legal interpretations, and the current lack of clarity in regulating Internet content. Many of these issues will have been previously introduced under topics such as commercial speech, pornography, and access. The general media law course should tie those topics together in this section. Some schools, as noted earlier, offer entirely separate courses on the regulation of telecommunications and electronic media.

Several cases that illustrate major principles regarding this area of the law include *Red Lion Broadcasting Co. v. FCC.*[41] This landmark case outlines the differences between broadcast and print media as an access issue and sets forth the reasoning for the Federal Communications Commission (FCC) requirement that came to be known as the Fairness Doctrine, which was subsequently dropped by the FCC many years later. The opinion discusses the requirement of balanced coverage of controversial issues in the electronic media. Other cases include:

Arkansas Educational Television Commission v. Forbes.[42] In this case a third-party candidate was denied participation in a candidate debate broadcast on a state public television network. It discusses taxpayer-supported broadcast licensees, the equal opportunity provision of FCC regulations, and political speech in the marketplace of ideas.

Turner Broadcasting System, Inc. v. FCC (I, 1994,[43] and II, 1997[44]). These cases deal with the FCC requirement that cable operators must carry local broadcast stations.

Some media law instructors integrate new technology and its developing body of law into related topic areas, whereas others devote a separate section in the course to such information.

Common Challenges and Possible Solutions

Probably the largest challenge those who teach the general media law course face is that of students with diverse academic backgrounds. Because the course is positioned as an upper-division offering it is safe to assume that more than half of a student's college coursework is completed and a certain level of academic maturity exists. As a capstone course, however, the course also draws together students from different areas of specialization and majors, which, in turn, creates great variation in students' ability to read and understand case law.

One solution employed is to require each student to *brief* a case. In this exercise, students select an acceptable media case. They then must write a single-spaced, one-page summary of the case that encompasses the case's significant media law aspects and the specific rationale behind the court's holding. Other requirements include compelling the student to provide a brief court history of the case (that is, what lower courts found) and frame the pertinent appeal question asked in the case as a requiring a "yes" or "no" answer. Instructors report a good deal of success in overcoming a *fear of legalese* in their students with just briefing one clear-cut decision. Some instructors have done such a brief together during the first day of class with a preselected case. They suggest that a case related to a recent news event such as campaign finance or pornography interests students, and such cases are available on line for classroom analysis.

Another way to overcome student fear of legal reading is the most common type of assignment found in syllabi and involves a hypothetical case in which students are asked to analyze and prepare a written brief with their legal arguments. Such an exercise not only requires that students examine several other cases to determine their legal arguments, making notes and briefs along the way, but also requires them to apply precedents correctly to a practical situation. This twofold purpose of both practical and philosophical analysis appeals to the student as well as the teacher. It provides them with the connection of esoteric discussion of First Amendment principles to everyday media practice.

Most instructors do not require that students write a brief for each side. However, those instructors who do require briefs for both sides of an argument reason that this provides students with an understanding of the difficult nature of deciding First Amendment cases. Some textbooks provide sample hypothetical cases in the instructor's guide, but most do not, leaving it up to the instructor to write the scenarios for the students.

One way to prepare a hypothetical case is to draw from cases the U.S. Supreme Court has already decided, using fictional names and elaborating on circumstances to fit the pedagogy of the class. This may be the simplest type to grade, because the courts already have accepted or rejected various arguments from the parties.

The risk in making it too similar to a decided case is that students may simply copy the opinion and then argue the points most pleasing to the court. One media law professor suggests using cases that have been granted *certiorari* by the U.S. Supreme Court but have not yet been argued. Although the petition for *certiorari* and case history are readily available to students through online resources, they still must research earlier arguments from each side in order to select those that are likely to have an impact at the federal level. One excellent source is C-Span in the Classroom, whose programs include judicial resources and a curriculum complete with an oral argument lesson plan.

A third option is to invent a situation that contains legal questions pertinent to the particular topics being studied. For example, a copyright case involving sexually explicit commercial material would encompass the three areas of intellectual property, pornography/obscenity/indecency and commercial speech. Depending upon how the case is drafted, a defendant might have copied a substantial portion of pictures for a marital aid product that he then uses to sell his/her own product (based heavily on the already created product). The hypothetical can be compounded by including the artistic nature of the photos, posting of the ad on the internet, mass mailing of the ad, or the use of cable access channels to produce infomercials. Such a case requires students to dig through cases on point and get a taste of what legal research entails.

The second most common challenge faced by media law instructors is student perception that the First Amendment and regulatory issues are not relevant to what the student will be doing professionally. Telecommunications students complain that print journalism and reporting issues have nothing to do with how they will do their jobs. Public relations and advertising students bemoan the task of learning access law that they claim is not pertinent to them. And general editorial students grumble they will never need to know about Federal Trade Commission procedures. Media practitioners in this technologically rich environment should be more concerned than ever about legal obstacles, pitfalls and policies that could serve to enhance or hinder their operations, so these student perceptions could not be further from the truth.

Although this challenge is resoundingly articulated by those who teach media law, procedures to dispel these student myths and to reinforce the relevance of the First Amendment as media and their auxiliary professions change are not so easily delineated. The best answer likely lies in the instructor's ability to update and examine a variety of cases continually that relate directly to each of the professions that students in the class will be entering. Asking students to respond orally or in written form to current issues and policy formation in their areas seems to be the method of choice.

Sometimes that assignment comes in the configuration of requiring students to prepare essays or response papers on a particular issue. One professor requires students to periodically respond without warning to a statement he makes in class, such as "Computer pornography containing 'morphed' children is child pornography, and therefore obscene." These response papers are limited to one page and are due during that class period. This, he says, encourages students to keep up with class readings, rewards those who attend class on a regular basis and, because the lowest grade for these responses is dropped, it teaches them how to think about these issues as they occur, a skill many will need as media professionals.

Although many of the syllabi examined require a brief or analysis of a current media case or policy to demonstrate understanding of legal applications, only two require that students actually provide oral arguments to be presented in a moot court setting in the class. These are often based on actual cases that have been argued before the courts or regulatory agencies or cases that are either pending or have been settled prior to hearing.

In this assignment, students are given roles of attorneys for the plaintiff (state, if criminal) or the defendant, and the judge (or panel, if regulatory in nature). The attorneys are charged with preparing briefs, arguing motions, and presenting arguments to the court. The judge must render decisions and opinions on motions, instruct the jury on points of law, and maintain the decorum of the proceeding, according to the applicable rules. The jury is comprised of the rest of the class, and they must decide the facts on the basis of preponderance of evidence, beyond a reasonable doubt or clear and convincing evidence, as instructed by the judge. Some believe it is best for the instructor to serve as the judge. Students are graded on their legal research, on the strength of their legal arguments, on the use of cases on point, and on their oral and written presentation skills. As one can imagine, this is a complicated assignment requiring sliding deadlines for summary briefs, responses, oral arguments, and decisions. But, from all reports, it is one that students seem to enjoy. If there is time during the term to conduct a mock hearing, many advise doing so. The mock hearing reinforces the importance of public policy on the everyday practice of media professionals.

A final challenge worthy of mention is that of overcoming individual biases against protecting unpopular speech. Students, like most American citizens, find First Amendment press and speech freedoms fit for protection as long as they cover speech with which they agree, but they are hesitant to accept the same level of protection for speech they don't value. The dismissal of at least one state university professor following the World Trade Center and Pentagon attacks makes it evident that colleagues as well as students would not protect speech they find distasteful.

Examples of speech in the popularly repugnant category include pornography, hate speech, reports of personal information, and even government criticism during times of national stress. These are sensitive areas especially because many students have experienced, either firsthand or vicariously, the hurt feelings resulting from such speech. This is a nexus where law and ethics at first glance appear at odds, and can actually serve as a springboard for meaningful class discussion of consistency in jurisprudence.

Everyone would censor something. Even John Milton, who wrote a definitive treatise against licensing of the press, *Aeropagetica*, worked as a government censor. However, for students to leave the class with a sense of what a strong First Amendment really means to a society, it is necessary to help them identify values in allowing publication of what popular opinion may find disdainful. Some of those values are articulated eloquently in decisions regarding hate speech ordinances and public officials mentioned previously. One instructor examines her state university's hate speech provision in the student handbook, which, like many, would not withstand constitutional scrutiny if put to the test. Another suggests weighing the harms done to the individual against the harms done to society when such reports are suppressed. The values versus harms approach, an economic type of analysis, is not a new one in the study of law, but can be especially useful in pinpointing how expensive true press freedom must be.

One instructor suggests dealing with these delicate areas by using self-deprecating humor. Drawing on her own characteristics, she generalizes hateful comments about people who possess similar characteristics, such as "Short people have no place on this earth" or "Short people are stupid." She further confesses membership in the Flat Earth Society, an organization her university derides as a group of ignorant miscreants. Throughout the term the instructor's shortness or memberships emerge in discussions of suppression of her expression, ownership of her research, privacy of her beliefs in relation to her public performance, libel in her profession, or the videotaping and broadcasting of Flat Earth Society naked dancing rituals. She asks students to share their experiences that may reflect what Professor "Short" has encountered and says they remarkably respond with true stories to add to her repertoire. Although humor is difficult to carry across different audiences and must be moderated, it can serve well in the classroom and relieve tension resulting from uncomfortable topics.

As mentioned earlier, most of the syllabi examined calculate grades based entirely on exam scores, probably because of the large amount of reading already required for such a course. Instructors who also require out-of-class assignments generally count them as 10 percent to 30 percent of the student's grade. A few syllabi allow students to prepare a written assignment for extra credit.

Outside Resources (Students)

Students have access to a wealth of free Web sites that provide information on media law. Here are a few of the most helpful sites:

Legal Information Institute. Located at Cornell University, this site contains decisions, dockets and filings of the U.S. Supreme Court, U.S. Circuit Courts, and other federal and state courts. It has a database searchable by parties, topics or authors of opinions and contains constitutions, codes and statutes. The site also provides links to other sites, including the U.S. Supreme Court home page, and contains directories of law journals and legal organizations.

The Freedom Forum's First Amendment Center at Vanderbilt University. This is a good site to find current First Amendment case news, which may also be accessed through other links on the site.

Law Library of Congress: Guide to Law Online. This site is a jewel. It is indexed by countries and by topics. For example, clicking on *law reviews* provides a list of law reviews, most with full text. Clicking on *Enron* or *Terrorism* provides information on government actions and links to sites with further information.

Findlaw and Findlaw Law Crawler. This is a general site with Web and databases capable of connecting to other law-related sites, cases, codes, forms, law reviews and government documents.

The Reporters Committee for Freedom of the Press. This site singles out cases dealing with the press across a wide range of issues. The Committee also produces a number of handbooks available for online reading only. Some of its publications make good supplemental texts on special topics, with the cost of most around $5 or less.

Students navigating these sites will find an extensive variety of information on media law and can begin to establish their own bookless law libraries by bookmarking those of interest to them.

Outside Resources (Faculty)

First, a word about copyright is warranted. The instructor in this course especially must be aware of and comply with copyright laws, particularly when displaying examples in class or on links for online courses. When in doubt, obtain the express permission of the copyright holder. Even with the Fair Use education exception under the Copyright Act of 1976, distribution can be risky, especially with online use. Copyright abuse not only subjects you to possible civil and criminal repercussions under the law, but it also demonstrates to students a lack of regard for the exclusive rights of creators of original works of authorship. Sharing copies of a current news story is generally considered permissible under the Fair Use guidelines because of the timeliness and relatively low quantity of the material used, but distributing or displaying copies of that same story in subsequent terms should be done only with the explicit permission of the copyright holder.

Supplemental texts recommended by various instructors include specific relevant law review articles; case notes from law reviews; American Bar Association publications such as *The First Amendment: A Journalist's Guide to Freedom of Speech*, *Reporter's Key*, *A Journalist's Primer on Locating Legal Documents* or *Law and the Courts*; the Reporters Committee on Freedom of the Press publications such as *The First Amendment Handbook* or one of the Committee's access books; or West Publishing's nutshell books on *Mass Communications Law* and *First Amendment Law*. The latter supplemental materials may also serve as review and study guides for students.

In addition to the aforementioned sources to which students have access, instructors may supplement the textbook with outside speakers, such as local attorneys for media,

American Civil Liberties Union attorneys, or local prosecutors or local judges who deal with First Amendment cases. Advertising and public relations professionals who daily deal with intellectual property and federal regulatory issues also make welcome speakers, and they have proven especially adamant about student awareness of these issues prior to entering the workforce.

If it is possible, supplementing the class with electronic slide presentations that have sound effects can make the subject matter more interesting for students. Sound effects such as applause, whistles, cash registers, chimes, and screeching brakes can really wake them up. Don't be gratuitous about it, but use those that apply to the subject matter or viewpoint at hand. Traveling to online sites during class to demonstrate points is an enhancement that should be used if available in your classroom. The best way to find sites that are copyright safe is to travel through government and nonprofit sites subscribed to by your school. Many libraries now have access to bundles of online publications and video resources that may not have been available in the past, plus federal and state document sites provide a bounty of examples from which to choose.

Conclusions

The traditional media law class, which is required in most journalism and mass media programs, is a reading-intensive course primarily taught through case analyses. Most instructors in the course require discussion by the students, and in their syllabi many strongly advise students meet to form study groups to examine the various cases for further understanding.

All accredited programs and most nonaccredited programs offer a general media law course, and some also offer other courses covering more specialized areas such as telecommunications law and policy or performing and creative arts law. Other programs offer a combined media law and ethics course, a logical choice, given that both are based on moral philosophy.

The syllabi examined for this chapter are remarkably similar in terms of delivery methods and content topics covered. Most of the variance occurs in the cases and supplemental readings assigned and in the nature of out-of-class assignments given.

Notes

1. Taken from an 1823 letter from Thomas Jefferson to Adamantios Coray, cited in Vincent Blasi, "The Checking Value in First Amendment Theory," *American Bar Foundation Research Journal* 521 (1977):528–538.

2. Accrediting Council on Education in Journalism and Mass Communications, *Principles of Accreditation* (revised September 2001), found at www.ukans.edu/~acejmc/PROGRAM/PRINCIPLES.SHTML.

3. Ibid.

4. These publications are those used for the annual enrollment report of students studying journalism and mass communication. The most recent report by Lee B. Becker, Tudor Vlad, Jisu Huh, and Joelle Prine is available at the home page of the

AEJMC (AEJMC.org), and the article appears in *Journalism & Mass Communication Educator* 56, no. 3 (Autumn 2001):28–60.

5. Fred Fedler, Arlen Carey, and Tim Counts, "Journalism's Status in Academia: A Candidate for Elimination?" *Journalism Educator* 53, no. 2 (1998).

6. Ibid., p. 39.

7. This grouping is done purely for simplification and is taken from the Administrative Office of the Courts' Web site on Understanding Federal Courts (www.uscourts.gov). It is not intended to discount other equally important types of legal scholarship, such as critical legal studies, pragmatism, economics, and the like, but provides a consensual standard on various methods of jurisprudence.

8. *R.A.V. v. City of St. Paul*, 505 U.S. 377 (1992).

9. *Near v. Minnesota ex rel. Olson*, 283 U.S. 697 (1931).

10. *Brandenburg v. Ohio*, 395 U.S. 444 (1969).

11. *New York Times Co. v. United States*, 403 U.S. 713 (1971) (*per curiam*).

12. *Hazelwood School Disrict. v. Kuhlmeier*, 484 U.S. 260 (1988).

13. *Texas v. Johnson*, 491 U.S. 397 (1989).

14. *New York Times Co. v. Sullivan*, 376 U.S. 254 (1964).

15. *Gertz v. Robert Welch, Inc.*, 418 U.S. 323 (1974).

16. *Florida Star v. B.J.F.*, 491 U.S. 524 (1989).

17. *Cox Broadcasting Corp. v. Cohn*, 420 U.S. 469 (1975).

18. *Bartnicki et al. v. Vopper, a.k.a. Williams, et al.*, 532 U.S. 514 (2001).

19. *Wilson v. Layne*, 526 U.S. 603 (1999).

20. *Harper & Row Publishers, Inc. v. Nation Enterprises*, 471 U.S. 539 (1985).

21. *Campbell v. Acuff-Rose Music, Inc.*, 510 U.S. 569 (1994).

22. *New York Times Company, Inc. v. Jonathan Tasini*, 533 U.S. 483 (2001).

23. *Buckley v. Valeo*, 424 U.S. 1 (1976) (*per curiam*).

24. *Nixon v. Shrink Missouri Government PAC*, 528 U.S. 377 (2000).

25. *United States v. O'Hagan*, 521 U.S. 642 (1997).

26. *Board of Regents of University of Wisconsin System v. Southworth*, 529 U.S. 217 (2000).

27. *Central Hudson Gas & Electric Corporation v. Public Service Commission of N.Y.*, 447 U.S. 557 (1980).

28. *44 Liquormart, Inc. et al. v. Rhode Island et al.*, 517 U.S. 484 (1996).

29. *Posadas de Puerto Rico Associates v. Tourism Co. of Puerto Rico*, 478 U.S. 328 (1986).

30. *Greater New Orleans Broadcasting Association, Inc. v. United States*, 527 U.S. 173 (1999).

31. *Miller v. California*, 418 U.S. 915 (1974).

32. *FCC v. Pacifica Foundation*, 438 U.S. 726 (1978).

33. *Denver Area Educational Telecommunications Consortium, Inc. v. FCC*, 518 U.S. 727 (1996).

34. *United States v. Playboy Entertainment Group, Inc.*, 529 U. S. 803 (2000).

35. *Reno v. American Civil Liberties Union*, 117 S.Ct. 2329, 138 L.Ed.2d874 (1997).

36. *Renton v. Playtime Theatres, Inc.*, 475 U.S. 41 (1986).

37. *Sheppard v. Maxwell*, 384 U.S. 333 (1966).

38. *Branzburg v. Hayes*, 408 U.S. 665 (1972).

39. *Timothy James McVeigh v. U.S.*, www.kscourts.org/ca10/cases/1998/09/97–1287.htm (1999).

40. *U.S. Department of Justice v. Reporters Committee for Freedom of the Press*, 489 U.S. 749 (1989).

41. *Red Lion Broadcasting Co. v. FCC*, 395 U.S. 367 (1969).

42. *Arkansas Educational Television Commission v. Forbes*, 523 U.S. 666 (1998).

43. *Turner Broadcasting System, Inc. v. FCC*, 512 U.S. 622 (1994).

44. *Turner Broadcasting System, Inc. v. FCC*, 520 U. S. 180 (1997).

CHAPTER 22

International Media

Mary E. Beadle

Introduction

As the importance of global awareness increased during the 1990s, more communication programs began offering courses in international media. Even today, course offerings in this field are not widespread. For example, in a survey of two- and four-year institutions by Kock, Kang and Allen (1999), international courses were not mentioned in the list of the top 10 courses offered by communication departments. Teaching guides to instruction are also an indication of the areas taught in communication departments. Previous books in the field, including both *Teaching Mass Communication* (Murray and Ferri, 1992) and the second edition of *Teaching Communication* (Vangelisti et al., 1999), do not include chapters on teaching international media. So, while more schools are offering international media courses, these are largely elective, taught by a single faculty member, and may not be fully integrated into the core curricula of communication departments.

In states with large university systems, governments have had an impact on the development of international courses. For example, the Board of Directors at the University of Georgia, mandated that 2 percent of the curriculum be internationalized. Leonard Teel reports that at Georgia State University they are beyond that level. He credits this mandate for allowing professors to ask for and receive support for international courses. According to Mark Tolstedt at the University of Wisconsin at Stevens Point, the former governor established a Global Education Conference for the state university system. The yearly conference provides opportunity for the state's professors to meet and share common interests and resources.

Despite the limited number of departments that offer international media courses, a major academic organization—the Broadcast Education Association (BEA)—decided to include international media as part of a syllabus project. That project provided course descriptions for such courses as ethics, sales and marketing, and television production taught in communication departments. The syllabi provided a very useful resource for those teaching in communication areas. It also offered a way for those who have taught in this area to share their ideas and methods, both with those who are just beginning or those who are interested in updating a course. The inclusion of this topic in the project demonstrates that scholars and leaders in the field of mass communication education especially in the broadcast area believe in the importance of international media in the communication curriculum.

Syllabi gathered for an analysis of international media courses were obtained by requests on the BEA Listserve and through the *BEA International Division Newsletter*. A total of 16 syllabi were collected, two of which were for graduate courses. The most frequently mentioned undergraduate course was offered at the introductory level and taught at either the 300 or the 400 level. Follow-up interviews were conducted with five instructors. All but one professor had originally submitted syllabi earlier.

The follow-up interviews resulted in a great deal of additional information for both undergraduate-level and graduate-level courses. Also, more international media courses are being offered as cross-listed at both graduate/undergraduate levels or with other departments. This may indicate a trend that international media courses are becoming more fully integrated into the broader communication curriculum.

Syllabi used to provide this analysis were from the University of Texas, the University of Minnesota, the University of Wisconsin at Stevens Point, the University of Florida, California State University at Long Beach, California State University at Fullerton, and the University of Kentucky. Also examined were the University of Wisconsin at Eau Claire, State University of New York at Fredonia, the University of Arizona, the Annenberg School at the University of Southern California, Georgia State University, and John Carroll University.

Not all schools that teach International Media courses are listed here, but only those that answered the call. It is interesting to note the types of institutions that submitted course information for this project. All the schools, except one, were larger state universities. This may demonstrate the difficulty in offering courses with this specialty or that this content area is now just being integrated into the curricula of many schools.

This chapter describes a variety of courses taught under the heading of international media. The primary focus is on the introductory-level courses that have a variety of emphases and titles. Some follow a traditional organizational pattern of comparative systems but more are offering courses with the themes of globalization and understanding of cultural influences. Upper-division and graduate-level courses will be included where appropriate, especially when courses are cross-listed with the undergraduate class. Instructor philosophy, common problems and solutions in teaching this course, and instructional resources are also presented.

Much of the attention on international mass media occurs within the broadcasting curriculum, and most of the courses in international media are offered on a senior or graduate level. However, junior-level students frequently take a course, and some of the senior-level courses are combined with graduate students. Courses are usually elective, primarily intended for majors and minors. Some courses are included in core requirements, part of a sequence, listed with other departments, or are included in other departments' list of acceptable courses. Departments that offer a sequence of international courses schedule these on rotation. Enrollments vary from seven to 120 in a large lecture format.

Position of the Course in the Curriculum

According to Mark Tolstedt at the University of Wisconsin at Stevens Point, his department offers a sequence of three courses on a rotation: International Media, Comparative Systems, and Special Topics. Don Browne, at the University of Minnesota, offers a three-course sequence: Comparing Electronic Media, Electronic Media in National Development, and Ethnic Minority Media. Both graduates and undergraduates take these classes, but most students are junior and seniors. All courses are electives in the Department of Communication Studies. One course is offered every year, and enrollment is about 20 students. Non-majors do enroll, but primarily in the National Development course, as there are no prerequisites.

Course material is often presented in a geographic structure. Issues of culture, ownership, financing, news, or developing world concerns, such as lack of technology or flow of information, are essential aspects of all international media courses. Most of the courses applied the term *media* to the study of radio, television and the Internet. One course did approach the material from a journalistic (press) perspective, and a few included advertising and film. All of the courses provided some discussion of technological factors, such as shortwave radio, Digital Broadcast System, and digital broadcasting. However, these varied in length from a part of a class period to a week of material.

Most of the syllabi included an overview of the U.S. media system. This was done to establish a basis for comparison with other systems from around the world and to develop an understanding of the unique features of the U.S. system. Another typical element of the courses was the inclusion of the cultural, political, legal, economic and technological aspects that influence the media in specific countries or regions. For example, the effects of a poorly developed infrastructure have a major impact in many African countries, as does the influence of fundamentalist religious groups on programming in the Middle East. One professor indicated a multidimensional approach was taken in the syllabus simultaneously considering factors such as culture, geography, economics and, of course, politics.

Awareness and the understanding of world trends, issues and problems are also considered critically important to these instructors. Topics included global news flow, culture and communication, privatization, external services, authoritarian media, clandestine radio, transnational corporations (TNCs), media imperialism, trade laws, current problems, the public service model versus the commercial model, press theories, and the New World Information and Communication Order (NWICO). The history of international media systems and research approaches to the study of major issues was indicated on several syllabi. A common thread in all syllabi was influences on national systems from a variety of sources beyond national borders.

Introductory Course

The introductory course often uses a comparative-systems approach. The use of a geographic organizational pattern was the most common, beginning in North America and then moving to Europe, Africa, Asia, the Middle East, South America, and Australia/Micronesia. Doug Boyd, at the University of Kentucky, teaches World Media Systems as a 300-level course, cross-listed with the Telecommunications Department using this structure. The course is offered every fall semester. It is a prerequisite for upper-level courses and is one of four classes offered on rotation: two undergraduate courses and two at the graduate level.

Boyd uses Don Browne's *Electronic Media and Industrialized Nations* (1999) as the text. Additional readings are also used. Boyd also emphasizes the importance of understanding the broadcasting system within "its cultural and political context." Media that are discussed include radio, television, cable, satellite and the Internet. He also emphasizes the importance of understanding the influence of large international corporations like AOL Time Warner and Newscorp and the various administrative systems such as BBC or RAI.

Craig Allen uses a different approach at the University of Arizona: "The course concentrates more broadly on a global media revolution, in which technology, language, culture and privatization are binding themes." The influence of English is a major component of the class. The syllabus indicates a structure that is political rather than geographic. The areas of analysis are described as English-speaking countries, Western countries, post-Communist countries, and developing countries. The course is listed as a 400-level introductory course "designed for the student with little or no background in mass media outside the United States."

No other similar course is offered at that university, so there is no prerequisite. The course is uniquely placed within the university's curriculum. It fulfills a minor requirement in the Business College, the International Studies Department, the Human Communication Department, and the Honors College. It fulfills a *media analysis* requirement for mass communication majors. It also can be used to meet the university's General Studies requirement in global awareness, so it is part of the General Studies program. Therefore, the course is reviewed by the General Studies Council every three years. The course is taught every fall semester as a large lecture with about 120 students, some of them graduate students. Allen has developed his own reading material and uses Robert Stevenson's *Global Communication in the Twenty-First Century* as optional reading (1994).

Once every two years, Mark Tolstedt, at the University of Wisconsin at Stevens Point, teaches an upper-division elective, International Communication, which is also cross-listed as a graduate course. Introduction to Broadcasting is a prerequisite for this class. The course is limited to students who are communication majors and also has a writing emphasis, so it is limited to 17 students. This introductory course has units on history, international organizations like the International Telecommunication Union, and bilateral agreements.

Tolstedt uses Robert Fortner's *International Communication: History, Conflict and Control of the Global Metropolis* (1994) as one textbook. He likes the book because it provides a good history of the development of media, with an international perspective. *Global Broadcasting Systems* (Hilliard and Keith, 1996) and additional readings are also used.

Common Emphasis

The primary goal in the introductory course is to develop student awareness and understanding of the cultural, political, economic and technological context in which media develop. Globalization is a key concept in reaching this goal. Related to this concept are objectives such as to understand the principles, history, and organizational and operational structures of media systems that are organized differently from those in the United States. They also strive to understand the role of U.S. media in the world; to understand the role and effect of global media companies in various countries; and to know about international media agencies and their global impact. Instructors are also interested in having students examine issues and problems faced by international and intercultural communication. This may lead to students becoming better practitioners of international and intercultural communication, possibly in a media-related career.

International Media course assignments include, as might be expected, exams, papers, and reports on books and articles or Web sites. Some other assignments were less typical. One instructor required participation on a course Listserve. Doug Boyd requires students to provide "a minimum of one meaningful e-mail contribution to [the] class listserv each week starting the third week of school." In many classes, students were expected to listen and to view both audio and videotapes of various countries' media. The use of speakers from the countries that were studied is an important component of many classes.

The author of this chapter, at John Carroll University, requires students to listen to international broadcasts. Shortwave radios were provided to students or Web sites were given that provide international audio programs. Suggested frequencies were given so students could more easily find an English-speaking broadcast, for example the BBC. The assignments included a cultural report, a description of the broadcast, and a comparison with U.S. radio broadcasts. Another assignment requires students to watch a program on SCOLA. International television programs are provided by SCOLA, a nonprofit educational consortium that receives and rebroadcasts programming from 55 countries to over 10 million viewers in North America. Originally known as Satellite Communication for Learning, SCOLA is operated by Creighton University in Omaha, Nebraska, and uses satellite feeds (C-Band) on three 24-hour satellite channels. Channel 1 provides news from 35 countries; Channel 2 provides variety, entertainment and arts from 10 countries; and Channel 3 is the China Channel.

The broadcasts are offered through campus cable television systems or may be available on local cable systems. The SCOLA Web site includes a schedule and scripts for the newscasts in both the original language and an English translation. Students need to download Acrobat Reader to obtain the translations. Streaming video of the broadcasts is also available. Class assignments included a cultural report, an analysis of the differences in news coverage, and the visual presentation of news. The quality of the video can be a problem and not all of the broadcasts are translated.

Don Browne suggests that students read foreign newspapers and magazines available in the library. However, few students do, since many students lack skill in a foreign language. Almost all syllabi indicated the use of outside readings assigned to keep students current in the material. As noted on some syllabi, international media change rapidly, and textbooks do not always keep pace. Some of these readings were provided to students; others were on reserve in the library.

A common assignment is a paper exploring a country or region's communication system, an international communication system like Reuters or VOA, pirate stations, clandestine radio, international advertising, individuals such as Ted Turner or Rupert Murdoch, or a concept such as cultural imperialism or TV flow. Another type of paper that is about a country's media system uses sources such as embassies, consulates, Web sites, *Cultrgrams*, or *CIA World Factbook* (www.odci.gov/cia/publications/factbook). The areas to be included are general background, history, financing, audience, programming, the legal and political systems, and problem areas.

Upper-Division and Graduate-Level Courses

As might be expected, graduate courses tend to organize material on a theoretical basis rather than on comparative systems or by countries. Themes of economic, political, social and cultural development are included. The common goal is an understanding and awareness of different media systems and similar issues faced by media in all countries, such as transnational media companies and the influence of U.S. media. Another goal is to understand the role of media in national and international development.

Assignments include midterm and final exams and a paper. Presentations of research and class participation are expected in the graduate classes. Book reviews are also listed an as assignment. The choice of books reflects this comprehensive theoretical approach. The syllabi list from two to five books and include a number of articles or a reading list. In general, the syllabi are less legalistic than the undergraduate syllabi and do not include descriptions of plagiarism, detailed assignments, or warnings about grade penalties. None had the practical assignments using international media that are included in some of the undergraduate courses.

Leonard Teel teaches an 800-level course and a cross-listed graduate/undergraduate course. Graduate students are required to teach or do additional papers. The first half of the 800-level class focuses on the Arab region, and the second half of the class focuses on a region of the students' choosing. In examining culture, Teel uses the PERSIA model examining the six fundamental categories of civilized activity: politics, economics, religion, society, intellect and aesthetics. Laws, standards of ethics, press freedom, and writing styles also are examined. Newspapers are included. The five textbooks for the 800-level course include a bound volume of Collected Essays and Stories and books that explain the Middle East context, such as *The Modern Middle East* (Hourani, 1993) and *Approaching the Qur'an* (Sells, 1999).

Another graduate class offered by Dr. Teel is a 600-level communication course, also cross-listed as a 400-level journalism course. The textbooks are John Merrill's *Global Journalism* (1996) and *Goode's World Atlas* (Espenshade, 1995). Supplemental readings include selected articles from international newspapers and magazines and the *World Press Encyclopedia*, published in 1982, which is used to show historical contrasts: "The object of this course is to travel widely in the mind." Teel describes the course as research intensive, blending theory and practice. The intention of the course is to develop critical thinking about media "reach," media impact, diversity of cultures, and stereotypes. Media are studied on three levels: global, regional and national.

Browne teaches a 400/500-level course Electronic Media and National Development. It qualifies as writing intensive and also fulfills the Department of Communication Senior Seminar requirement. The focus of this class is the use of the electronic media to resolve certain societal problems such as political disunity, lack of formal educational opportunities, and underproductive agriculture. Students use a case-study method to investigate a problem and offer solutions using the media.

Global Communication and Information Perspectives is a 600-level course taught by Doug Boyd. The course, which is open to graduate students in all colleges of the university, focuses on "international and intercultural communication . . . as it relates to the organization and impact of media in an international context." Boyd hopes that this course will "foster cross-cultural understanding since we must be willing to work with a variety of people from different backgrounds and cultures." Students complete formal research, give a formal report to the class, and post a minimum of one message per week to the class Listserve.

Instructor Philosophy

Doug Boyd, at the University of Kentucky, states that his purpose is to educate students about other systems to learn more about our own. Craig Allen, at Arizona State University, believes his course helps prepare students for a career with an emphasis on the concepts of globalization. According to Mark Tolstedt, at the University of Wisconsin at Stevens Point, students have a gap in understanding contextual factors that create situations for media. Don Browne, at the University of Minnesota, believes the role of a course like this is to help students think out of a narrow box, to help students learn about alternative uses of media and that even our own history was different in the past.

Special Features

An 800-level course, Seminar in International Media and Culture, taught by Leonard Teel, uses WebCT technology in a unique way. The class is linked via WebCT using chat rooms and bulletin boards with students at Modern Science and Arts University in Cairo, a university with English-language instruction. One research topic that students exchanged research material about was the media coverage for the Arab-Israeli wars of 1948 and 1967. Teel also makes the point that much of what they are able to do has been a result of institutional support for internationalizing the curriculum. As already noted, Teel uses the PERSIA model to analyze media and culture. He presents one application of the model that students then apply to another country. Students are then responsible for teaching this to the class. Occasionally this work becomes a conference presentation.

Don Browne teaches Electronic Media and National Development, a 500-level course, that seniors may take for their seminar requirement. Students in this class develop a case study. Each student chooses one medium of mass communication and one area of national development in a particular country. The student describes whether the media are adequate to help with the chosen country's national development. Students then present case studies of situations in which the medium chosen has been used in other countries for national development. They must present their own plan for use of media for national development and why it will succeed.

Craig Allen stresses in his introductory class the importance of English in globalization. He uses the television series *The History of English* to demonstrate the worldwide impact of English.

Common Challenges/Solutions

Instructors teaching courses in International Media describe two problems. The first problem is in acquiring materials for the course; the second is the students' lack of background or experience in international issues. Leonard Teel includes print media in his course since it is much easier to acquire. Don Browne indicates that there are many foreign-language newspapers available, but students' lack of foreign language skills limits what they can experience. Although recently more student bodies have diverse populations, it is still difficult to find people who have experienced other cultures. International students in the class help.

Mark Tolstedt believes that the university's semester-abroad programs help since 12 to 15 percent of the students now spend at least one semester studying abroad. This lack of experience among students is made more difficult by the lack of easily available teaching material. All of the instructors travel and collect material when they are abroad and believe in the importance of getting out of the classroom. For example, Leonard Teel said that when he started teaching international media in the 1980s he felt like an imposter since he had only been to Canada, Cuba, Great Britain, and France. Since that time, he has traveled and taught all over the world.

He believes that extensive travel and international teaching experience make him more credible, and the students appreciate his experience. Instructors usually videotape, purchase magazines and newspapers, and collect material to use in the classroom when traveling. There currently is no common storehouse for material to be shared, although Don Browne recalls many discussions of doing this in the past. Material also becomes outdated quickly and can be expensive. One resource that will become available in 2003 is an international database for journalists and journalism educators that is located at Georgia State University's Center for International Media Education (www.gsu.edu/cime).

Outside Resources

Personal contacts are very useful and important resources. Craig Allen teaches in Phoenix, so Spanish media are important topics in classes. He is a volunteer for the Sister Cities program and serves as the Teacher Exchange coordinator between

Phoenix and Hermosillo, Mexico. Through this organization, he is able to obtain up-to-date material. Leonard Teel, located in Atlanta, has benefited from the interest of international journalists at CNN and his association with the Arab/US Association for Communication Educators. During conferences of the AUSACE, professors meet and become valuable resources for one another. Georgia State has developed the Center for International Media Studies.

In Wisconsin, the former governor established the Institute for Global Studies program, which sponsors an annual conference for sister institutions in the state. Here professors have a chance to exchange ideas. Mark Tolstedt reports that technical writers have a relationship with writers at the University of Finland, and they exchange writing projects, including translation. This is especially important to introduce the idea of rhetoric and the meaning of words.

For both Mark Tolstedt and Leonard Teel, support from state government began the development of international resources. Dr. Teel also received grants from the U.S. State Department Bureau of Education and Culture and from the Office of University Affiliation. For all the instructors, associations, both formal and informal, with other universities and institutions are critical in making the course relevant and interesting to the students.

Doug Boyd stated that written material is much more available now than in the 1980s. However, none of the instructors viewed the Internet as a real help in providing updated visual material. The Internet has provided more information but not the video resources necessary for students to experience the media firsthand. All of the professors believed this firsthand experience to be critical for students in an international course.

Conclusions

This analysis of courses in International Media indicates two common approaches to the teaching of this subject to undergraduate students: comparative systems or a cultural/political analysis. Within these two broad categories, courses include a wide range of topics. The most frequent topics include transnational media companies, globalization, information flow, the NWICO, and technology. The particular study of various countries and regions and descriptions of their media systems also attract a great deal of attention today. These descriptions include the history and culture of a country or region, the legal and political structures, programming, financial support, and future directions.

Assignments included traditional requirements such as tests, papers and reports. However, students also were expected to use international media through the Internet, shortwave radio, SCOLA broadcasts, or international newspapers and magazines. Speakers and the use of videotape also provided international experiences for the students. Although more schools may be teaching international media courses, the responses to inquiries for this chapter revealed that most of the schools responding were the larger state institutions.

It may be that, at smaller schools, these types of courses constitute electives and as such are offered less frequently. The expense of having a specialist may not be warranted. It also may be that the smaller schools did not respond to this call for syllabi. It may be that this area of teaching is one that has developed at research institutions and may take time to become more widespread.

It is interesting to note that many of the scholars whose textbooks are used to teach these classes were also those who submitted syllabi for this project. Of the 16 original syllabi submitted, almost half were from people well known in the field as contributors to books and research. Globalization, the Internet, and continued development of media systems seem to suggest that international media courses will be important to the future of broadcast education. This project may help to provide general guidelines and identify themes, categories and resources necessary for effective curricular development.

Works Cited

Browne, Donald R. 1999. *Electronic media and industrialized nations.* Ames: Iowa State University Press.

Espenshade, E., ed. 1995. *Goode's world atlas.* 19th ed. Chicago: Rand McNally.

Fortner, Robert. 1994. *International communication: History, conflict and control of the global metropolis.* Belmont, Calif.: Wadsworth.

Merrill, John C. 1996. *Global journalism: A survey of the world's mass media.* 3rd ed. New York: Longman.

Hilliard, Robert, and Michael Keith. 1996. *Global broadcasting systems.* Boston: Focal.

Hourani, A., ed. 1993. *The modern Middle East.* Berkeley: University of California Press.

Kock, E., J. Kang, and D. Allen. 1999. Broadcast education curricula in 2-year and 4-year colleges. *Journalism Educator* 54(1):4–15.

Murray, M., and A. Ferri, eds. 1992. *Teaching mass communication: A guide to better instruction.* New York: Praeger.

Sells, Michael, trans. 1999. *Approaching the Qur'an: The early revelations.* Ashland, Ore.: White Cloud.

Stevenson, Robert L. 1994. *Global communication in the twenty-first century.* New York: Longman.

Vangelisti, A., J. Daly, and G. Friedrich. 1999. *Teaching communication.* 2nd ed. Mawah, N.J.: Lawrence Erlbaum.

Additional Resources

The following sections provide additional resources for teaching an international mass communication course. The list is intended to provide examples for a variety of courses and is not comprehensive. It includes the textbooks mentioned in the chapter, other books, Web sites, periodicals and journals, and videotapes. The videotapes vary in quality and, although some are dated, provide background information about various countries.

International Media Textbooks

Edwards, L. 2001. *MediaPolitik: How the mass media have transformed world politics.* Washington, D.C.: Catholic University Press.

Gershon, Richard. 1997. *The Transnational Media Corporation: Global messages and free market competition.* Hillsdale, N.J.: LEA.

Gross, Lynne Schafer. 1995. *The international world of electronic media.* Belmont, Calif.: Wadsworth.

Kamalipour, Y., ed. 2002. *Global communication.* Belmont, Calif.: Wadsworth.

Sinclair, John, Elizabeth Jacka, and Stuart Cunningham. 1996. *New patterns in global television.* Oxford: Oxford University Press.

Weaver, Gary R., ed. 1998. *Culture, communication and conflict: Readings in intercultural relations.* Needham Heights, Mass.: Simon and Schuster.

Books

Albarran, Alan B., and Sylvia M. Chan-Olmsted. 1998. *Global media economics: Commercialization, concentration and integration of world media markets.* Ames: Iowa State University Press.

Boyd, Douglas. 1999. *Broadcasting in the Arab world.* 3rd ed. Ames: Iowa State University Press.

Browne, D. 1996. *Electronic media and indigenous peoples: A voice of our own?* Ames: Iowa State University Press.

Comor, E. A., ed. 1994. *The global political economy of communication: Hegemony, telecommunication and the information economy.* New York: Free.

Demers, David. 1999. *Global media: Menace or messiah?* Cresskill, N.J.: Hampton.

Frederick, Howard H. 1993. *Global communication and international relations.* Belmont, Calif.: Wadsworth.

Herman, Edward S., and Robert W. McChesney. 1997. *The global media: The new missionaries of global capitalism.* London: Cassell, 1997.

Hugill, Peter J. 1999. *Global communications since 1844: Geopolitics and technology.* Baltimore: Johns Hopkins University Press.

Morley, David, and Kevin Robbins. 1993. *Spaces of identity: Global media, electronic landscapes and cultural boundaries.* London: Routledge.

Mowlana, Hamid. 1998. *Global information and world communication.* 2nd ed. Thousand Oaks, Calif.: Sage.

Sreberny-Mohammadi, Annabell, Dwayne Winseck, Jim McKenna, and Oliver Boyd-Barrett, eds. *Media in global context: A reader.* London: Arnold, 1997.

Sussman, Gerald, and John Lent, eds. 1991. *Transnational communications: Wiring the Third World.* Newbury Park, Calif.: Sage.

Thompson, J. B. 1995. *The media and modernity: A social theory of the media.* Stanford: Stanford University Press.

Vincent, Richard C., Kaarle Nordenstreng, and Michael Traber, eds. 1997. *Towards equity in global communication: MacBride update.* Cresskill, N.J.: Hampton.

Web Sites

www.aber.ac.uk/media/Functions/mcs.html.
www.ard.de. German radio, non-English.
www.bbc.co.uk or www.bbci. BBC online.
www.bertelsmann.de. Bertelsmann Media—German language.

www.bertelsmann.com/index.cfm. Bertelsmann Media—English language.
www.cgms.org. Center for Global Media Studies, Dr. David Demers.
www.scola.org. Video streaming of international news available.
www.tbsjournal.org.
www.ugs.edu/cime. Center for International Media Educators.
www.unesco.org/webworld/observatory/index.html. Notes from around the world on the information society by the United Nations.
www.voa.gov. Voice of America on-line, 32 languages.
www.zonalatina.com.

Periodicals and Journals

Asian Journal of Communication. The process of communication in the Asian-Pacific region is examined. Published biannually by the Asian Media Information and Communication Centre. www.amic.org.sg/amic/.

Australian Journalism Review. All aspects of communication research, theory and practice are addressed. It is published three times per year by the Australian and New Zealand Communication Association.

Canadian Journal of Communication Research. This contains scholarship in the field of communication and journalism. It is published quarterly by Simon Fraser University. www.ccsp.sfu.ca/calj/cjc.

Communication: South African Journal of Communication Theory and Research. This is published biannually by the South African Communication Association. www.unisa.ac.za/dept/kom/broseng.html.

Continuum: Journal of Media and Cultural Studies. Modern and historical approaches to media and cultural studies are covered. It is published three times per year by the Cultural Studies Association of Australia. www.carfax.co.uk/nfc/con-nfc.htm.

Critical Studies in Mass Communication. This provides interpretive approaches to mass communication and theory. It usually includes international articles and is published quarterly by the National Communication Association.

European Journal of Communication. This includes some media research and theory focusing on different European traditional and national backgrounds. It is published quarterly by Sage and is available electronically for institutions. www.sagepub.co.uk/journals/details/j0050.html.

Feedback. This is especially interested in pedagogical articles, including occasional international content. It is published quarterly by the BEA.

Gazette: The International Journal for Communication Studies. This includes treatment of the role of communication in world politics, world trade and contribution to international understanding, peace and security, as well as theoretical implications of human rights standards and the relationship between communication and development. It is published by Sage in February, April, June, August, October and December. www.sagepub.co.uk/journals/details/j0184.html.

The Global Network. Media and public communication development are addressed primarily in Central and Eastern Europe. It is published three times per year by the Faculty of Journalism and Mass Communication Studies, Bucharest University.

The Howard Journal of Communications. Ethnicity, gender and culture are addressed as domestic and international concerns. It is published quarterly by Howard University. www.tandf.co.uk/jnls/hjc.htm.

International Communication Bulletin. International mass communications are covered, including commentary and short notes on preliminary findings or research in progress. It is published by the International Communication Division of the Association for Education in Journalism and Mass Communication (AEJMC) quarterly.

Journal of Broadcasting and Electronic Media. This includes articles that are international in their scholarly focus. It is published quarterly by the BEA. www.beaweb.org/jobem.html.

Journal of Communication. This is an official publication of the International Communication Association. Articles and book reviews examine a wide range of issues in communication theory and research. It is published quarterly. www.icahdq.org/publications/publications.html.

Journal of Radio Studies. Interdisciplinary studies focusing on radio's contemporary and historical subject matter are addressed. International radio often has its own section. It is published biannually by the BEA. www.beaweb.org/pubs1.html.

Mass Communication & Society. This covers mass communication processes and effects with a goal of contributing to a theoretical base of knowledge and includes organizational, institutional, societal, cross-cultural, or global perspectives. It is published two to four times a year by the AEJMC. www.erlbaum.com/2082.htm.

Media Culture & Society. This provides an international forum for research and discussion, including new information on communication technologies. It is published bimonthly by Sage and is available electronically for institutions. www.sagepub.co.uk/journals/detailsj0088.html.

Nordicom Review. This documents media trends in Nordic countries and publishes comparative media statistics. It is published by the Journal of the Nordic Information Centre for Media and Communication Research, located in Sweden. www.nordicom.gu.se.

World Communication. This contains refereed articles exploring human communication and also complements the purposes of the World Communication Association. It is published quarterly by the WCA in affiliation with Western Kentucky University.

Videotapes

And the Dish Ran Away with the Spoon (BBC/TVE, 1992, 48 minutes). This highlights the effects of U.S. television on cultures in the Caribbean, including Cuba.

Distress Signal (Canadian Film Board; First Run Icarus Films, 1990, 55 minutes). Global television and the market for it are addressed. It shows attitudes and inequalities in different areas of the world, including Canada and Africa.

The Effect of TV on Culture in India (Films for Humanities and Sciences, 1998, 30 minutes). This covers cultural effects of television programming in India with the rapid rise of satellite TV and cable channels, and discusses the role of TV in altering Indian perceptions, both in urban and in rural settings.

Export TV (Center for Cuban Studies, Cinema Guild, 1990, 25 minutes). The relationship of U.S. television programming and TV Marti into Cuba is discussed.

Global Communication (Films for the Humanities and Sciences, 1994, 23 minutes). The technology of global communications, including fiber optic, satellite and cable distribution systems, is described.

Lifeline: The History of International Radio (Films for the Humanities and Sciences, 1998, 50 minutes). This traces development of international radio from 1927 through the end of the Cold War to the Gulf War. It contains some subtitles with English narration.

Prime Time South Africa (California Newsreel, 1995–1996, 110 minutes). Six television segments from the public service and entertainment series demonstrate ways in which media are portraying the post-apartheid society. Used are some English, as well as some South African languages with English subtitles.

Satellite Dreaming (Films for the Humanities and Sciences, 1993, 48 minutes). This shows how aboriginal people of Australia use television to preserve culture.

Starting Fire with Gunpowder (First Run Icarus Films, 1991, 54 minutes). Episode 4 of *As Long As the River Flows* chronicles the origin and achievements of the Inuit Broadcasting Company (IBC) and its efforts to preserve Inuit culture.

Tokyo Rose (Arts & Entertainment Network, 50 minutes). This covers the life of American Iva Taguri, who was one of many women described as Tokyo Rose during the Second World War. This *A & E Biography* provides a context for the development of international radio for propaganda purposes.

CHAPTER 23

Media Management

Max V. Grubb and Walter S. McDowell

Introduction

Unlike most courses in the field, Media Management is still seeking an identity in terms of objectives and level of sophistication. Among current instructors, there is no broad consensus as to what exactly a Media Management course should entail. Instead, there is a continuum of approaches ranging from courses that take an applied "nuts and bolts" training approach to courses that focus on academic theory and critical thinking. Within this continuum are two essential areas of divergence, each offering meaningful but different perspectives.

The first departure occurs at the beginning of the teaching process where the overall direction of the course is defined in terms of managing business issues versus managing people. Although not mutually exclusive, most courses tend to lean in one direction. Some professors prefer to emphasize the financial machinery that makes media companies work. Students are introduced to basic accounting, audience research techniques, sales, and strategic planning. The alternative perspective dwells on human resources and the art and science of organizational communications, leadership, consensus building, and negotiating.

A second pivotal issue deals with the relevance of the course within the context of a larger media management program. Whereas some universities offer one management course, others provide an array of courses, including programming, promotion, research and sales. The content of a management course will be dependent on the content of surrounding required courses.

Through the examination of course syllabi from around the country and personal interviews with professors within the discipline, the authors have identified some salient concepts and methods for constructing a viable course in Media Management. Course titles included Telecommunications Management, Broadcast and Cable Management, Media Management, and Media Management and Economics.

Media Management courses and curriculum depend on the institutional mission for a respective mass communication major, specialty, or concentration. This is the starting point in considering the course design.

Position of the Course in the Curriculum

Generally speaking, most Media Management courses are situated within either (1) an electronic media (broadcast/telecommunications) unit or (2) a journalism unit. Many university programs offer a *major*, *specialization*, *concentration*, or *focus* in some aspect of media management, where courses concerning this area can be found. The typical class size is 20 to 25 but can be larger. This course is often an element of this media management specialization, focus or major. However, there are exceptions.

Recent discussions within the academy concerning Media Management courses at the undergraduate level differ as to their importance. Ann Hollifield of the University of Georgia observed that all students in the Department of Telecommunications at that school are required to take a course titled Introduction to Telecommunications Programming and Management. This is a core course for all majors regardless of whether they are pursuing a broadcast news, broadcast production, or broadcast management focus based on awareness that students need to have an understanding that most media are businesses. Students need to understand business implications in terms of budgets, marketing, and demonstrated profit potential. They need to understand how to talk to media companies in business management terminology.

Anne Hoag of Penn State University describes a similar arrangement whereby all telecommunication majors are required to take Introduction to Broadcast/Cable Management. Students in the Penn State University program who desire to pursue the management track must complete a basic telecommunication course before they can pursue the upper-level-related courses.

Some mass communication faculty have noted that undergraduate students often enter a media program with only a vague notion of working in the field. Most student knowledge of career opportunities comes from their role as consumers. They enter school desiring to follow in the footsteps of Dave Berry, Howard Stern, Steven Spielberg, Katie Couric or Leslie Stahl.

As students approach graduation, they realize that this may not be feasible. Requiring that all mass media students take a course in Media Management or a business course, regardless of whether they are pursuing careers, gives students insight into business issues and long-range goals they desire to pursue.

Alan Albarran, Chair of the Department of Radio, Television, and Film at the University of North Texas, states that you are not telling students "that they are going to get a job as a manager when you get out of school," but preparing them "mentally so they have an understanding as to what management is all about . . . then hopefully if they want to go that route they can pursue it as a logical career path within 3 to 5 years."

Most university programs in mass media offer media management courses either as an upper-level elective or as core course for a specialization in media management. Prerequisites require students usually to take required core courses such as introduction to mass media or introduction to broadcasting courses. At Southern Illinois University at Carbondale, students desiring to pursue a focus in broadcast management must first successfully complete both the general introductory broadcasting course and an audience research course. At the University of Miami, students in the new media management track must take courses in research, sales or programming before taking the Media Management course.

For those programs that offer a master's and/or doctorate in mass media, journalism or broadcast/telecommunication, specialized courses in Media Management are often offered with a mix of undergraduates and graduate students, at least for basic instruction. Graduate students then have an additional Media Management seminar, usually focusing on theory and scholarship concerning that field. Such courses normally are geared with the student working on a research paper to be submitted to one of the related academic conferences of the Broadcast Education Association (BEA), the Association for Education in Journalism and Mass Communication (AEJMC), the National Communication Association (NCA), or the International Communication Association (ICA).

Common Goals and Objectives

Goals and objectives address the desired outcome of a course. At the conclusion of the course experience, what knowledge or skills will the student have learned? As stated earlier, the answer to this question depends greatly on the overall approach. The more applied end of our continuum looks at the student's first job and the training necessary to become a meaningful contributor to a media business. The more theoretical approach looks at enduring principles and tries to prepare students for future high-level decision-making positions and encourages appreciation for the long view. Additionally, the curriculum context in which the course is offered will influence the stated goals and objectives.

For Sylvia Chan-Olmsted at the University of Florida, her course in Media Management is defined by her Telecommunications Department as a senior capstone course, where students have already been exposed to several specialized courses in areas such as audience research, programming and sales. The overall objective is to "put all the pieces together" into an integrated course that emphasizes strategic planning. In addition to administering conventional tests, Chan-Olmsted introduces a major case-study project where small student groups compete for the best comprehensive strategic plan for problem solving.

The course is so specialized that she no longer uses a textbook but rather a custom-tailored course packet. A similar capstone approach can be found at the University of Alabama in a Telecommunications Media Management course offered by James A Brown. This course, intended exclusively for seniors and graduate students, seeks to "synthesize material covered in previous courses by majors in broadcasting." The aforementioned courses are seen as a culmination experience for students who have taken several related specialized courses.

For schools where media management is not a separate major or concentration, the course objectives tend to be broader, encompassing topics that in a larger program would be stand-alone courses. Here the objectives are intended to give students as much exposure as possible to many aspects of contemporary media management. In many respects, these could be designated as *survey courses*.

Of course, the notion of *media* is also conceptualized differently, depending on the school and the assigned professor. For example, many schools exclude *print media* from their definition of media, focusing primarily on electronic media. Furthermore, even among these electronic-based courses, there are varying conceptualizations. Some courses take a wide swath by including conventional radio, TV and cable but also satellite, common-carrier and Internet management issues.

For instance, Richard Gershon at Western Michigan University maintains that his students are interested in a total media environment and "are as likely to work for AT&T as for a broadcast station." As a consequence, the objectives of the course are to "diversify" students so that they have an appreciation of all sides of the telecommunications industry. On the other hand, at the University of Miami, the official course title is Broadcast and Cable Management, and the objectives are narrowly focused on specific problem-solving experiences relevant to these two core industries. Also, after examining many syllabi, it seems fair to say that courses that embrace the most media are often the most theoretical in their objectives. Courses targeting a smaller range of media such as broadcast and cable tend to emphasize the more applied aspects of management.

Another area where the overriding approach to the subject matter influences course objectives is the propensity to emphasize either economic or personnel issues. As mentioned in the introduction, this dichotomy is not absolute, but the evidence of a kind of duality in approaches is quite evident when examining syllabi.

For example, here is a sampling of some of the course learning goals for Randy Beam's course at Indiana University. Upon successfully completing the course, students will be able (1) to identify the characteristics of effective and ineffective teams, (2) to discuss the benefits and challenges of having a culturally diverse workplace, and (3) to describe how to foster a good relationship between an employee and supervisor. While this course also includes some business-oriented goals, such as the ability to write a simple business plan, the major thrust is toward human relations.

The other side of the coin can be seen by looking at the course objectives of a Media Management course offered by the University of Miami, where students receive a heavy dose of media economics, including practical exercises in accounting and finance procedures, marketing research, and Federal Communications Commission (FCC) policies pertaining to the ownership and operation of broadcast stations. The study of human resource management is not ignored but plays a secondary role to the business side of media.

Clyde Bentley at the University of Oregon provides a unique hybrid approach with a course entitled Media Management and Economics. Here students take "an intense but understandable plunge" into media management from a multidimensional perspective that looks at both people and economics. Portions of the course curriculum address such eclectic issues as personnel issues, budgeting, cost containment, financial reporting, freedom of the press, and libel.

Instructor Philosophy

Obviously, the philosophy in teaching Media Management courses is influenced and dependent on the institution's mission and overall instructional approach to its respective mass media degree. Therefore, the instructor needs to keep in mind how his or her respective course in Media Management falls within the department or school's curriculum and available major or specialization. Albarran notes that his Broadcasting and Cable Management course highlights the different levels and areas of media management. Furthermore, the course stresses a contemporary understanding of the different and pressing issues and constraints that confront electronic media managers daily. He prefers to err on the practical side of teaching media management, focusing less on management theory, with the rest of time reinforcing application issues.

Chan-Olmsted observes that her approach to their undergraduate course in media management focuses on economics and business as opposed to management of human resources. However, she does note that some management theory is included in the course. She states that "students should know how all the pieces fit together and interact." Hollifield believes the key to teaching this course is to keep an eye toward application, "helping students make the connection to the real world. ... to think like a professional and work like a professional." The introductory course into telecommunications programming and management stresses basic economics, management strategies, industry models, and programming issues. It is primarily an overview.

The philosophy for the other—theoretical—perspective of media management takes on a more human resource focus. While not devoid of the practical emphasis, instructors seek to develop the critical, analytical and strategic skills of their students. Often taught as a seminar course for undergraduates and master's graduate students, this level of media management course goes beyond basic station or newspaper operations or business management. Hollifield observes that she "spends a long time on personnel, leadership, managing difficult people, managing people to enhance activities, managing artistic personalities, managing small groups," etc. She notes that this course also examines organizational and professional culture.

Faculty who model this approach to Media Management courses seek to provide students an environment to explore fundamental management and leadership theories, strategies, and team-building skills. In some course descriptions, instructors note that students will explore the theories of what constitutes good management, leadership, decision making, etc., and how well media organizations put them into practice.

For purely graduate-level Media Management courses, the obvious approach is to emphasize the academic scholarship on management theories, media economics, and industry models. Taught as a seminar course, instructors have students explore various issues of media management through available scholarship, often with the goal of conducting primary research, writing a paper and submitting it to a conference.

Hollifield has her students conduct a major literature review on a Media Management topic, requiring them to use Roger's methodology for meta-analysis. Students are required to find out what is known from the academic literature and how it applies to the real world of management. Applied casework is emphasized to complement the theoretical aspects.

Common Emphasis

Despite the recognized disparities among Media Management courses, there are some common components. All courses examined for this chapter acknowledged that most students were seeking professional careers in media, and therefore the course needed a real-world connection. Even courses emphasizing more theory than practice proclaim that these abstract principles can have a direct bearing on how business is conducted. Except for a handful of graduate courses that stressed a more detached and scholarly understanding of media, the majority of courses had a common overarching theme of preparing students for life after college. Many courses attempt to replicate this future world in the classroom. A typical statement from a syllabus prepared by Chan-Olmsted might indicate an effort to include speakers, role playing, case studies, and team projects from stations to make the class "as realistic as possible."

A common attribute found in many courses, regardless of the conceptual approach, was the notion of problem solving. Hands-on training can solve problems but so can theories if they are indeed theoretically sound. Most Media Management courses in one way or another want students to learn how to provide solutions to problems. Hollifield typifies most Media Management instructors when she states in her course syllabus the objective to "introduce students to current issues and approaches" to understand and solve practical management problems.

Comparative Features

This section discusses the common or comparative features of Media Management courses, along with some unique approaches. Of course, common or comparative features follow or resemble the perspectives discussed earlier. Initial features of Media Management courses indicate that those classes that approach the subject from the practical, nuts-and-bolts perspective usually present an overview of economics, management and programming practices of media industries.

A focus on contemporary issues and trends is confronting today's mass media managers. On the other hand, the more theoretical approach for Media Management courses usually covers such areas as leadership, decision making, organizational behavior, group dynamics, motivation, change management, financial management, and industry research. Although these approaches can be pictured as two ends of a continuum, numerous Media Management courses fall between the two, dominated by one approach but including elements of the other.

Almost all syllabi emphasized the use of case studies. Depending on the level of instruction (introduction to advanced or graduate level), students are required to read and analyze media management case studies as a part of the course. Introductory classes into media management have a lesser emphasis on case studies, whereas advanced and graduate levels have considerable case-study requirements. Most basic classes in Media Management create a learning environment that includes lectures, case studies, and guest speakers.

A number and variety of textbooks are used in media management courses. Some textbooks use a case-studies approach, others approach topics from a practical perspective, and then there are those that emphasize management theory. Among the media management texts are those that are dominant in one of these approaches but include elements of the others. Based on discussions among media management instructors, most indicated that they were not totally happy with any of the texts that are available. Thus, a number of instructors have developed their own materials and/or case studies for student instruction. Instructors find that case studies permit students to apply the management theories and principles learned in class to cases, enabling them to critique and analyze various management situations and issues. Students often analyze one to three case studies as part of the class requirements.

Another prevalent feature of basic Media Management courses is the use of guest speakers. Faculty interviewed and a number of Media Management syllabi examined for this chapter emphasized guest speakers as an important part of the course. Albarran observes that the geographic location of the University of North Texas in the proximity of the sixth or seventh largest market, Dallas, gave him wonderful access to media professionals and the market.

Guest speakers offer students an excellent opportunity to gain realistic insight into management issues and challenges. Often guest speakers can make up for the dated text material, providing fresh information on current trends and problems confronting media managers. Albarran notes that often as an instructor he is as busy taking notes as the students are, since speakers often provide new information.

However, some instructors add a caveat to the use of guest speakers. They caution that sometimes guest speakers come to class loaded with old "war stories" that may lack relevancy to contemporary management issues. It is advised that instructors get to know beforehand prospective guest speakers and their potential contribution to media management studies.

The authors also found that Media Management courses frequently used small group exercises and projects. These experiences give students the opportunity to experience firsthand issues of group and organizational dynamics while working together either to study and report on specific Media Management issues or to participate in a role-playing exercise. Group exercises involving role playing or case analysis attempt to place students in a particular management dilemma and let them experience their response to it. Such exercises offer students the chance to make decisions on a particular management situation and then defend their solution based on the application of what they have learned. In classes where students in the group are assigned a marketing project or case, the group is required to make a report to the class, besides submitting a final paper.

Media Management classes tend to use groups on both the basic and the advanced levels. However, the use of groups in advanced Media Management courses often went further than small exercises, requiring the groups to work on a major project. Most of these major projects usually involved, for example, developing a business plan for a media company or organization, a strategic plan for some media endeavor, or a SWOT (strengths, weaknesses, opportunities and threats) analysis of some media business or corporation. Some group projects required by instructors involve student research into the history, organizational structure, financial performance, and strategic issues of a selected media business or corporation.

One group project used by Hollifield involves students conducting audience research for an actual broadcast station. The term ends with students making a presentation before the client. In her advanced broadcast management class, one assignment involves students "shadowing" (spending time) with a broadcast professional. The student then has to write a case study on the assignment. According to Hollifield, students often get internship or job offers as a result.

Graduate-level Media Management courses always involve a research paper component along with case studies and group projects. At this level of study, students inevitably ground themselves with management and organizational theory with the intention of working on a research paper for the class and a possible conference submission.

Generally, Media Management courses offer the traditional quizzes and exams as part of student evaluation. Graduate courses in Media Management rely less on testing and place more emphasis on evaluation of case-study analyses, group projects, and final research papers. As to unique aspects in teaching media management, the geographic location of the school can be a major factor. University programs located within or near major media markets have the advantage of capitalizing on media-company professionals, market research, etc. Instructors and students frequently can observe firsthand various media management issues and challenges as they play out before them. Often, they have will have the persons involved with these situations come to class to discuss the media management dilemma that is occurring, which offers students an inside look as it unfolds.

Unfortunately, this is an element beyond the control of media management instructors who are at universities located in smaller markets or rural areas. One alternative is to tap into alumni who are willing to take the time and spend the money to make the trip to their respective institutions.

Common Challenges/Solutions

The biggest challenge confronting those who teach media management is determining what is the appropriate content for a course. Even within the same university program, instructors may approach the course differently. Gershon observes that "the big issue as a whole is what do we come up with as a common approach to the teaching of media and telecommunications management" courses? As he sees it, the problem is that "we are trying to be all things to all people." Some programs teach media management from either a print orientation, generally in the journalism disciplines, or an electronic media orientation. Even within the electronic orientation, one can find a broadcast management emphasis and in others a telecommunications orientation that adds telephony to the broadcast orientation.

In a review of various Media Management syllabi, few such courses taught it all—that is, print, broadcast and telecommunications. Albarran believes that print management contains a different set of issues along with a different set of constraints. He notes that there is little enough time to cover broadcast management issues and constraints without burdening it with the addition of print.

Paul Driscoll, Director of the Broadcast Division at the University of Miami, observes that "different professors teach the course from different conceptual frameworks and personal experience." An indication of this is the different approaches used by texts and their content. Some have a strict nuts-and-bolts operational approach to media management instruction whereas other texts offer more of a management theory perspective.

An example of a nuts-and-bolts text would be Peter Pringle, Michael Starr, and William McCavitt's book, *Electronic Media Management* (1999), whereas a more theoretical text would be James Redmond and Robert Trager's *Balancing on the Wire: The Art of Managing Media Organizations* (1998). We do not advocate any particular text, but offer examples of the dichotomy. This lack of a consensus has become fodder for discussion on the AEJMC Media Management and Economics Division Listserve, with signs that discussion will continue in the form of conference panels and research.

Another challenge is the need to keep material current and topical. From corporate mergers to FCC rulings, almost every month the industry experiences a development that should be discussed by media management faculty and students. This particular issue is more acute for courses focusing on contemporary management issues rather than more theoretically oriented courses.

One solution has been for instructors to have students subscribe to industry trade magazines. This enables students to follow current events and key into what is on the horizon while getting them in the habit of keeping up on the industry. In addition, Albarran notes that he focuses on fundamental management "skill sets that will serve students well regardless of the changes that come about." Students are taught the rudiments of understanding different marketing approaches such as branding and segmentation and the difference in a profit-and-loss statement, a balance sheet, statement of cash flow, etc. Even though there maybe different competitors and new types of challenges, Media Management fundamentals remain the same, permitting students to navigate changing terrain and make the necessary adjustments for growth in their mass media careers.

On the graduate level, the major challenge is to bring students who have absolutely no background in management up to speed on media business fundamentals and issues. At Southern Illinois University at Carbondale, graduate students often are required to take undergraduate courses covering the basics if they are lacking a media or media management background.

A frustrating challenge that confronts many media management faculty is the failure of students to retain basic knowledge gained from prior classes such as audience research, promotion, or sales. This apparent amnesia compels media management instructors to backtrack over course content. Chan-Olmsted observes that the time spent "refreshing students on fundamentals of other required courses" is sometimes exasperating.

Outside Resources

The most obvious outside resource that instructors tap into are guest speakers, discussed earlier in this chapter. Related is the access to ratings books and other professional market research material. These items are provided free or for a minimum charge. Usually, the information is dated and of no proprietary value to a business but a resource for classroom instruction. Some instructors take students to industry trade shows, such as the National Association of Broadcasters or the National Association of Programmers and Television Executives.

Additional resources that instructors rely on are student subscriptions to mass media trade magazines. Most, such as *Broadcasting and Cable* and *Electronic Media*, offer special student rates. Additionally, many trade publications can now be found online;

most notably, www.tvinsight.com offers a wonderful survey of most of the electronic media trade magazines. Users must register (free) and access Web content from such magazines as *Multichannel News* and *Broadcasting and Cable*. Users can subscribe to an e-mail service through this Web site and have daily updates e-mailed to them with links back to the relevant articles, all for free.

Other resources include the use of industry and trade association Web sites, such as the Newspaper Association, the National Association of Broadcasters and the National Cable Association, Nielsen, Arbitron, the Television Bureau, and the Radio Advertising Bureau. These and other Web sites offer considerable information and materials for instructors and students. One unique example is Arbitron's corporate Web site, which offers a free tutorial on audience ratings. The authors provide information on texts, trade publications, and online resources at chapter's end.

Conclusions

The most obvious determination is that courses in Media Management are taught in a variety of ways depending on several factors. The size and mission of the department in which the course is offered are two interconnected controlling variables. For example, if the course is an integral part of a larger media management major or concentration that features ancillary courses in programming, research and sales, the management course will probably take a narrow in-depth capstone approach aimed at graduating seniors.

On the other hand, if the course is more of an isolated elective with few or no appropriate "nearby" courses in the departmental curriculum, it will probably take a much broader approach, attempting to take a cursory look at a full range of topics. Both approaches have their place within the academic discipline of media management. In addition, the variety in course content and teaching methods is a result of how much emphasis is placed on economic versus human resource management. Again, both have their rightful place in the all-inclusive definition of media management.

Depending on the school, the depth and breadth of *Media Management* can vary greatly, which can be a problem for students. Because of course approaches and objectives, it is imperative that departments and instructors publish detailed course descriptions in syllabi and catalog listings.

Finally, one cannot ignore the tension between the applied side versus the theoretical side of teaching this course. As mentioned earlier in this chapter, this issue is more of a continuum where courses can be placed anywhere between two poles. Some professors maintain that to appreciate fully the rewards of economic and management theory, a student or entry-level manager first must have practical understanding of the essential mechanics of a business. Others disagree, proposing that theory should come first, that there are key principles applied to any business situation. The debate goes on.

Resources

Books
Albarran, A. 2002. *Management of electronic media.* Belmont, Calif.: Wadsworth; Wadsworth/Thompson Learning.

Brown, J., and W. Quaal. 1998. *Radio-television-cable management.* Boston: McGraw-Hill.

Croteau, D., and W. Hoynes. 2001. *The business of media: Corporate media and the public interest.* Thousand Oaks, Calif.: Pine Forge.

Gershon, R. 2001. *Telecommunications management: Industry structures and planning strategies.* Mahwah, N.J.: Lawrence Erlbaum.

Mouritsen, R. 2001. *Case studies in media management.* Boston: McGraw-Hill.

Pringle, P., M. Starr, and W. McCavitt. 1999. *Electronic media management.* Boston: Focal.

Redmond, J., and R. Trager. 1998. *Balancing on the wire: The art of managing media.* Boulder, Colo.: Coursewise.

Scott, R. 1998. *Human resource management in the electronic media.* Westport, Conn.: Quorum.

Sherman, B. 1995. *Telecommunications management: Broadcasting/cable and the new technologies.* New York: McGraw-Hill.

Sohn, A., and S. Lacy. 1999. *Media management: A casebook approach.* Mahwah, N.J.: Lawrence Erlbaum.

Useful Web Sites

Arbitron Ratings. www.arbitron.com.

Federal Communications Commission. www.fcc.gov.

Findlaw.com. www.findlaw.com.

Edgar: Company Financial Data. www.freeedgar.com.

Media Central. www.mediacentral.com.

National Association of Broadcasters. www.nab.org.

National Association of Television Program Executives. www.natpe.org.

National Cable Television Association. www.ncta.com.

Newspaper Association of America. www.naa.org.

Nielsen Media Ratings. www.nielsen-netratings.com.

R&R ONLINE. www.rronline.com.

Radio Advertising Association. www.rab.com.

SRDS. www.srds.com.

Television Bureau of Advertising. www.tvb.org.

Tvinsite. www.tvinsite.com.

Zap2it.com. tv.zap2it.com.

CHAPTER 24

Mass Communication History

Kimberly Wilmot Voss and Maurine H. Beasley

Introduction

This chapter offers a brief introduction to current practice in the teaching of journalism and mass communication history. A review shows that mass communication history courses may be losing some ground in relation to the total curriculum, but that they retain an important position based on the premise that they are needed to broaden student understanding of the societal power and importance of the mass communication fields they aspire to enter.

In recent decades the teaching of journalism and mass communication history has been a contentious subject. As journalism programs increasingly have become integrated into colleges of communication, some educators have argued that history courses, based traditionally on the history of development of the American newspaper, have little relevance to broader study of communications theory and methodology. On the other hand, some of those committed to the teaching of professional practice have seen history courses as taking up space in a curriculum better devoted to intensive "skills" instruction. In some cases students, who are far more likely to ask for more job-oriented instruction than for more theory or liberal arts coursework, have complained that history courses are boring and perhaps inconsequential.

Yet the picture is not totally negative. Journalism and mass communication courses have their fervent advocates. These educators argue that journalism and mass communication history, if taught well, enhances students' intellectual development. They contend that its study enriches life experience and enables students to understand the values and institutions of the fields they are studying. They insist that journalism and related occupations can never reach professional status without their practitioners having a clear idea of the history of mass media institutions. Ethical challenges often serve to reinforce this position. Educators in this camp include instructors who have developed innovative ways of engaging students in subject matter that some students formerly had found dry and devoid of meaning.

Position of the Course in the Curriculum

When the world's first school of journalism opened its doors in 1908 at the University of Missouri in Columbia, it used press history as the cornerstone for the curriculum. Over the course of the 20th century, social science theories and methodology gradually replaced the humanistic field of history as the philosophical underpinnings of the professional curriculum. This occurred as broadcasting challenged print, and new forms of the media emerged along with new media-related fields like public relations that employed techniques of persuasive communication. Journalism schools, however, continued to teach history, insisting that students could not understand the changing role of media without an understanding of the development of journalism. For example, they insisted that students would not be able to grasp the power and responsibility given to the press in the United States without studying the First Amendment from an historical perspective.

In 1978 Fred Endres conducted a national survey of journalism history, in the wake of accusations that the subject had become ossified because it was taught from a narrow perspective that enshrined the newspaper without critical examination. Endres identified two major rationales for offering the classes. The first was to pass on the traditions of journalism. The second was to demonstrate the connection between journalism and America's economic political and cultural history (Endres, 1978, p. 1). A similar argument appeared nearly two decades later in an issue of *Journalism and Mass Communication Quarterly* that was devoted to history (a change from the quantitative research orientation generally associated with the journal). Editor Jean Folkerts, herself an historian, and two associates wrote that the media have become a foundation of this country and because of their role deserve study as much as the other social institutions of education, politics, religion and labor (Folkerts et al., 1997, p. 458).

These rationales, no matter how much they may resonate with faculty members who are oriented to the humanities, have not kept journalism and mass communication history alive at a majority of the 400+ institutions in the United States that offer journalism and mass communication programs. Once required of all students seeking journalism degrees, free-standing history courses now are being taught as electives, if taught at all.

Part of the problem, some educators say, may be accreditation rules for journalism programs. About one-fourth of the 400+ programs meet accreditation standards for journalism requiring students to take roughly three-fourths of their coursework outside their major. This leaves them with the equivalent of only about two actual semesters of instruction in journalism foundation and skills courses. According to William David Sloan, a professor at the University of Alabama and both founder and former president of the American Journalism Historians Association (AJHA), 60 percent of college programs in journalism and mass communication do not offer any history course at all. Sloan, editor of the most widely used history of journalism textbook, laments this trend and calls for schools to teach history as part of the undergraduate as well as the graduate curriculum.

The picture is not altogether bleak. At some institutions, particularly large state universities, it appears likely that history courses will remain a viable part of the journalism/mass communication curriculum in the years ahead, although there may not be a concurrence on what these courses should be named or on their content. At the end of the 20th century some two of five students who majored in journalism/mass communication continued to have history courses available to them as part of their programs.

The total number of history offerings represented a downward trend from the early 1980s, when a survey of nonaccredited programs found that history courses were "alive and well," and another survey of accredited programs found journalism history continued to be a popular offering (Westmoreland, 1981, p. 12; Smythe, 1981, p. 1). Many universities, however, integrated material about history into courses on mass media and society as they enlarged focus from print journalism to an array of mass media-related subjects.

Similar/Ancillary Courses

To determine different pedagogical approaches to the teaching of journalism and mass communication history, a sample of 18 syllabi and descriptions of seven other history courses were collected from journalism and mass communication programs that regularly offer courses in mass communication history. Most of the sample syllabi were accessed online through departmental Web sites at large state universities. Sampled universities included Boston University, Georgia State University, Indiana University, Michigan State University, Pennsylvania State University, Towson University, the University of Florida, and the University of California at Berkeley. Also included were the University of Central Florida, the University of Maryland, the University of Minnesota, the University of Missouri, the University of Oregon, the University of Texas at Austin, and the University of Wisconsin. The schools were chosen mostly on journalism and mass communication enrollment size.

Examination of the syllabi and course descriptions showed a range of pedagogical methods, as individual faculty members attempted to vary conventional teaching practices to make history more meaningful to students. It appeared that instructors frequently employed a traditional structured format to impart information and then tested students to see if they could recall it. Most likely the lecture format was chosen because of the large class sizes that predominated at several of the universities. Frequently, however, instructors endeavored to supplement lecturing with small group meetings or projects, and some went to great lengths to stimulate student involvement in learning the subject matter.

Comparative/Special Features

Although it is beyond the scope of this chapter to offer a critique of lecturing in general, it should be noted that critics of journalism and mass communication history classes have sometimes found lecturing a troubling pedagogical technique. While a gifted instructor may be able to hold student attention and impart stimulating mental content, some critics contend that a lecture format in large mass communication history courses forces instructors to dwell on trivia to gain student attention.

They note that instructors in such a context can pass on meaningless details, such as the facts that James Gordon Bennett Jr., publisher of the *New York Herald*, shocked society by getting drunk and acting inappropriately at a fashionable party or that William Randolph Hearst was called "Randy Randy." In addition, large lecture class sizes usually mean a reliance on using objective "names and dates" tests, which often are unpopular with students and may increase their resistance to studying history. Seeking to find ways to improve their teaching, instructors have turned to less structure in an attempt to foster learning.

Review of the syllabi showed that instructors frequently attempted to enhance lecturing by breaking large classes down into small groups or by giving students individual opportunities to showcase their work. Team projects were common with students asked to create presentations based on journalistic practices at different time periods or on the lives of important journalists.

Focus groups sometimes were used to facilitate student interaction with different groups assigned to study particular chapters of texts. These students then were required to assist in leading the class discussion. Unusual assignments included a role-playing element in which students were called upon to do improvisational skits representing journalism personalities. Another offered students an opportunity to publish papers in a journalism history journal originating at their particular university.

Common Goals and Objectives

The most commonly stated objective of the journalism/mass communication history course in various syllabi was examination of the writings and ideologies of individuals in journalism who changed journalism and who influenced social, economic and political issues of their day. Other common objectives included studying the major developments in technology and society that impacted on the news media in America, evaluating the impact of ideologies and movements upon the news media, and analyzing the historic interaction between the media and American society. Some syllabi note the goal of exploring the role of the press in American society and assessing its influence on government, with emphasis on connection between origins of the democratic experience and functioning of democracy.

Instructor Philosophy

Some schools combined journalism history with other topics to create an interdisciplinary approach. One example was a course on The Journalist as Novelist: Journalism and Imaginative Writing in America, drawing on literary history as well as social, cultural and literary criticism. It was cross-listed by journalism, English and American Studies departments. Another example was a course that looked at the development of the mass media since the widespread use of printing five centuries ago. Housed in the history department, the course also drew content from journalism and English.

Common Emphasis

A majority of the syllabi for journalism/mass communication history courses showed that they covered the history of newspapers, magazines, radio, film, television, public relations, advertising and the Internet. Exceptions at several schools were courses limited to the history of a specific medium. One university listed three specific courses—broadcast history, history of film, and women and gender in film—but no survey course in journalism/mass communications in general. At other schools history classes combined case studies of law with journalism history or focused on themes such as the First Amendment and the media.

The most commonly covered subjects included the impact of the First Amendment, the role of the press in wartime, the penny press, muckraking, the emergence of electronic media, and the creation of a mass audience. There was limited coverage of alternative media, usually defined as publications for women or African-Americans. Often, as they have for many years, courses focused on "great men" in publishing: James Gordon Bennett, Horace Greeley, Adolph Ochs, Joseph Pulitzer, William Randolph Hearst, and Henry Luce, although some added broadcasters David Sarnoff and William S. Paley.

To some degree the courses also covered historical developments in ethics, law, and the business of journalism and mass communication. Although they varied in their organization, the courses tended to follow a chronological or a reverse chronological theme, tying developments in the media to a description of changes in American social, economic and political life. Some focused on the specific relationship of the media to particular social or political events, such as civil rights, the Vietnam War or Watergate. A few were organized around the development of mass media.

Common Challenges/Solutions

Syllabi showed that attempts were made in most classes to draw attention to issues of diversity. Most syllabi included at least a few references to African-American newspapers and women journalists, although these topics often were covered as part of a one-class or two-class-period lesson. These lessons often featured "Nelly Bly" (Elizabeth Cochrane), the 19th-century investigative reporter, or Ida B. Wells, an African-American journalist who crusaded against lynching. In other classes an effort was made to integrate the work of women and minorities with material covered throughout the course. In one class 10 of the 16 term-paper topics that students could choose to write about were related to women or minorities. Other courses devoted significant time to the history of women's magazines, the media coverage of Native Americans, and the development of the gay and lesbian press.

Most courses involved a combination of teaching devices: exams, student presentations, projects and papers. In several classes efforts were made to get students to do personal primary research, if only in a very limited way, in the media. Students were directed to write a paper, typically five to seven pages long, focused on a particular newspaper or television program published or broadcast on the day of the student's birth, a parent's birth, and sometimes a grandparent's birth. The assignment was to examine the portrayal of news events on these days and then analyze the changes in presentation between generations.

Common assignments were book reviews and research papers. In doing book reviews students were instructed to summarize the contents of a book and then explore the place of its subject in journalism and mass communication history. Book subjects included the development of various areas within the communications industry, such as public relations, the rise and/or fall of a publication or broadcast program, and biographies of journalists.

Research term papers were required in many classes. Assignments required students to do original research by conducting oral history interviews or searching archival materials. Topics for these assignments appeared to have expanded with the addition of online archives. Sample topics include Frederick Douglass' newspapers, the career of Lincoln Steffens, the lives of early women war correspondents, public reaction to the "War of the Worlds" broadcast, and the birth of ARPNET (the early Internet). Other topical selections include the television quiz-show scandal, lawsuits brought by women staff members on grounds of sex discrimination, the rise and fall of the "Fairness Doctrine" in political broadcasting, radio and television ratings, the formation of National Public Radio, and the voluntary broadcast ban on hard-liquor advertising.

Outside Resources

One element in student research was the encouragement of the use of archives of local publications. Local access sometimes becomes an issue in such cases. One class called on students to conduct original research by selecting a local newspaper or magazine and tracing its history. As an incentive in another class the instructor chose a panel of referees to determine the top papers in the class for the semester and then honored the top authors with an awards pot-luck dinner at the end of the semester.

In one case an instructor asked students to use a journalistic form in writing their research papers by preparing essays based on imaginary interviews with prominent figures from journalism history. Students more commonly were instructed to explain the activities of prominent figures in the context of social, political and mass media trends during their time periods.

All classes included examinations, but the type of questions varied from objective multichoice tests to essay questions designed to test critical thinking skills. Some instructors gave sample questions in advance to help students prepare for the examinations. One journalism professor's Web page included the following sample questions: (1) Some historians argue that freedom of speech was limited by the government in the 19th century despite the protection of the First Amendment. Would that be true or false? Cite three examples to support your answers. (2) Prior to the Civil War, how did Americans learn about and debate political issues? Compare the pre-Civil War "party press" with the kind of newspaper created by Joseph Pulitzer in the 1880s in terms of (a) news content, (b) financing, (c) audience, and (d) political orientation. (3) Historian Daniel Boorstin suggests that new technologies make possible "communities of communication" based on ideas as well as location. Briefly describe three different kinds of these "communities" that emerged in the 19th century and their relationships to their audiences. Several instructors required students to submit their own questions based on readings and discussions to be included in quizzes and examinations.

Textbooks were listed in more than half of the syllabi examined, along with additional readings from packets or reserved publications. The dominant text was William David Sloan, ed., *The Media in America*, 5th edition (Northport, Ala.: Vision, 2002). Also used were Jean Folkerts and Dwight L. Teeter, *Voices of a Nation: A History of the Media in the United States*, 4th edition (Needham Heights, Mass.: Allyn and Bacon/Longman, 2002); and Michael Emery, Edwin Emery, and Nancy L. Roberts, *The Press in America: An Interpretative History of the Mass Media*, 9th edition (Englewood Cliffs, N.J.: Prentice-Hall, 1999). Additional adoptions included Barbara Tuchman, *Practicing History: Selected Essays* (New York: Ballantine, reissue of 1981 edition); and Rodger Streitmatter, *Mightier than the Sword: How the News Media Have Shaped American History* (Boulder, Colo.: Westview, 1997).

Several instructors did not use traditional textbooks and chose other readings instead. Two of the most commonly used books were Carl Bernstein and Bob Woodward, *All the President's Men* (New York: Simon and Schuster, 1974); and Timothy Crouse, *The Boys on the Bus: Riding with the Campaign Press Corps* (New York: Random House, 1973).

Course instructors frequently supplement texts with other books. In some cases these are biographies of famous journalists. In others they are books they deal with specific subjects and/or periods. Among those most commonly used in journalism and mass communication history courses are the following: J. Cutler Andrews, *The South Reports the Civil War* (Pittsburgh: University of Pittsburg Press, 1985); Edwin R. Bayley, *Joe McCarthy and the Press* (Madison: University of Wisconsin Press, 1981); Erik Barnouw, *Tube of Plenty: The Evolution of American Television* (New York: Oxford University Press, 1990); Maurine Beasley and Sheila Gibbons, *Taking Their Place: A Documentary History of Women and Journalism* (Washington, D.C.: American University Press (republished, 2003; State College, Pa.: Strata).

Other works include Robert Draper, *Rolling Stone Magazine: The Uncensored History* (New York: Doubleday, 1990); Marc Gunther, *The House That Roone Built: The Inside Story of ABC News* (Boston: Little, Brown, 1994); David Halberstam, *The Powers That Be* (New York: Alfred A. Knopf, 1979); and Richard Kluger, *The Paper: The Life and Death of the New York Herald Tribune* (New York: Alfred A. Knopf, 1986).

Other influential selections are Tom Lewis, *Empire of the Air: The Men Who Made Radio* (New York: Edward Burlingame, 1991); Joe Alex Morris, *Deadline Every Minute: The Story of the United Press* (Garden City, N.Y.: Doubleday, 1957); Garland Penn, *The Afro-American Press and Its Editors* (1891; rept. Springfield, Mass.: Wiley, 1969); Nan Robertson, *The Girls in the Balcony: Women, Men and the New York Times* (New York: Random House, 1992); and Martha Solomon, ed., *A Voice of Their Own: The Women's Suffrage Press, 1840–1910* (Tuscaloosa: University of Alabama Press, 1991).

Other books include Mitchell Stephens, *A History of News* (Ft. Worth: Harcourt Brace, 1997); Henry Lewis Suggs, *The Black Press in the South* (Westport, Conn.: Greenwood, 1983); Gay Talese, *The Kingdom and the Power* (New York: World, 1969); Hunter S. Thompson, *Fear and Loathing on the Campaign Trail '72* (San Francisco:

Straight Arrow, 1973); Larry Tye, *The Father of Spin: Edward L. Bernays and the Birth of Public Relations* (New York: Crown, 1998); and Arthur and Lila Weinberg, *The Muckrakers: The Era in Journalism That Moved America to Reform* (New York: Capricorn, 1964).

According to the syllabi reviewed, the Internet was used in different ways in teaching journalism and mass communication courses. Some professors required students to communicate electronically about course material via e-mail lists and Listserves. A few professors had links to journalism history sites on their personal Web pages. One class allowed students to create a media history Web page as an option for a term project.

Among sites frequently used for journalism history is the Media History Project (www.mediahistory.umn.edu) formerly located at the University of Colorado and now at the University of Minnesota. It contains time lines and material to facilitate understanding of the chronology of the field, as well as links to numerous other resources.

Another source of links to journalism history resources is the University of Missouri School of Journalism Media History Links Web site (www.missouir.edu/ !jourss/mediahist.html).

Syllabi indicated that instructors are increasingly urging students to take advantage of archival resources now available on the Internet as primary source material for papers. Sites listed for journalism and mass communication history classes included the following:

Broadcast Pioneers/Library of American Broadcasting at the University of Maryland. www.lib.umd.edu/UMCP/LAB/subjects.html.
News Events Collection of the Library of Congress. www.lcweb.loc.gov/spcoll/ snews/html.
Radio Program Archive of the University of Memphis. www.people.memphis. edu/~mbensman/welcome.html.
Freedom Forum. www.freedomforum.org.
Radio Smithsonian Program Black Radio. www.si.edu/resource/topics/onair/ blakrad.htm.
Washington Press Club Foundation Oral History Project. www.npc.press.org/ wpforal, which contains oral history interviews with some 60 women journalists.

Instructors made use of home pages devoted to the lives of past journalists and to the histories of numerous newspapers.

Textbooks for journalism and mass communication history classes contain voluminous bibliographies. In addition, two academic journals are solely devoted to journalism and mass communication history. The oldest, started in 1974, is *Journalism History*, currently published at Ohio University. The other is *American Journalism*, the journal of the AJHA, which publishes essays on "great ideas" in journalism as well as refereed articles, currently published at the University of Alabama. The Broadcast Education Association and the Freedom Forum Media Studies Center also have published materials for use in history classrooms. Of special interest to instructors is a quarterly newsletter, *CLIO*, published by the History Division of AEJMC, which regularly runs articles on ways to improve teaching. *Media History Monographs* is an online journal devoted to scholarly work in journalism history.

Conclusions

Growth in journalism and mass communication history appears today in specific subjects such as broadcasting or the history of advertising and public relations. In terms of the field as a whole, it appears that those committed to the teaching of these courses need to continue to band together in professional organizations to define their mission clearly and to work for coherence in coursework. This already is being done in the AJHA and the History Division of the AEJMC, but it always imperative to step up efforts in this direction to keep mass communication history courses vital elements in the curriculum.

A wide array of material now available electronically, as well as in traditional repositories, may make it possible to stimulate students to do more work with primary source material in the study of mass communication history. As more printed material becomes digital and archived, it seems likely that there will be increased emphasis on using the Internet in media history classes. Growth in online publications can lead to emphasis on the history of new media itself. Opportunities appear on the horizon but, as in other areas, change is called for if mass communication history courses are to continue to survive and prosper.

References

Endres, Fred F. 1978. Philosophies, practices and problems in teaching journalism history. *Journalism History* 5 (Spring):1–3, 30–31.

Folkerts, Jean, Douglas Gomery, and Janet Steele. 1997. An editorial comment. *Journalism and Mass Communication Quarterly* 74 (Autumn):458–459.

Smythe, Ted Curtis. 1981. Journalism history enrollment trends. *CLIO* (newsletter of the AEJMC History Division) 13 (Summer):1.

Westmoreland, Reg. 1981. J-History course very much alive and well in AASDJ schools. *Journalism Educator* 35 (January):12–13.

Selected Bibliography

Books

Alexander, A., and J. Hanson. 2003. *Taking sides: Clashing views on controversial issues in mass media and society.* 6th ed. Guilford, Conn.: McGraw-Hill.

Anderson, R., and V. Ross. 2002. *Questions of communication: A practical introduction to theory.* 3rd ed. Boston: Bedford/St. Martin's.

Bagdikian, B. 1983. *The media monopoly.* Boston: Beacon.

Baran, S. 2001. *Introduction to mass communication: Media literacy and culture.* Mountain View, Calif.: Mayfield.

Baran, S., and D. Davis. 2000. *Mass communication theory: Foundations, ferment, and future.* 2nd ed. Belmont, Calif.: Wadsworth/Thomson Learning.

Barnouw, E. 1975. *Tube of plenty.* New York: Oxford University Press.

Beasley, M., and S. Gibbons. 1993. *Taking their place: A history of women and journalism.* Washington, D.C.: American University Press.

Biagi, S. 2003. *Media/impact.* 6th ed. Belmont, Calif.: Wadsworth/Thomson Learning.

Blanchard, R. O., and W. G. Christ. 1993. *Media education and the liberal arts: A blueprint for the new professionalism.* Mawah, N.J.: Lawrence Erlbaum.

Boyd, A. 1997. *Broadcast journalism: Techniques of radio and TV news.* 4th ed. Boston: Focal.

Burton, G. 2000. *Talking television: An introduction to the study of television.* New York: Oxford University Press.

Butler, J. 2002. *Television: Critical methods and applications.* Mahwah, N.J.: Lawrence Erlbaum.

Center, A., and P. Jackson. 1995. *Public relations practice: Managerial case studies and problems.* Englewood Cliffs, N.J.: Prentice-Hall.

Creedon, P., ed. 1993. *Women in mass communication.* 2nd ed. Newbury Park, Calif.: Sage.

Cremer, C. F., et al. 1995. *ENG: Television news.* 3rd ed. New York: McGraw-Hill.

Cutlip, S., A. Center, and A. Broom. 1985. *Effective public relations.* 6th ed. Englewood Cliffs, N.J.: Prentice-Hall.

Dayan, D., and E. Katz. 1992. *Media events: The live broadcasting of history.* Cambridge: Harvard University Press.

Dixon, T. 2000. *Mass media education in transition.* Mahwah, N.J.: Lawrence Erlbaum.

Edgerton, G., and P. Rollins. 2001. *Television histories: Shaping collective memory in the media age.* Lexington: University of Kentucky Press.

Fiske, J. 1996. *Media matters.* Minneapolis: University of Minnesota Press.

Fox, R. F. 1996. *Harvesting minds: How TV commercials control kids.* Westport, Conn.: Praeger.

Geraghty, C., and D. Lusted. 1998. *The television studies book.* London: Arnold.

Gerbner, G., H. Mowlana, and K. Nordenstreng, eds. 1993. *The global media debate.* Norwood, N.J.: Ablex.

Griffin, E. 2003. *A first look at communication theory.* 5th ed. New York: McGraw-Hill.

Gitlin, T. 1986. *Watching television.* New York: Pantheon.

Grossberg, L., E. Wartella, and D. C. Whitney. 1998. *MediaMaking: Mass media in a popular culture.* Thousand Oaks, Calif.: Sage.

Hartley, J. 1999. *Uses of television.* London: Routledge.

Hausman, C. 1999. *Crafting the news for the electronic media: Writing, reporting, and producing.* Belmont, Calif.: Wadsworth/Thomson Learning.

Hewitt, J. 2002. *Airwords: Writing for broadcast news.* 3rd ed. Mountain View, Calif.: Mayfield. Himmelstein, H. 1994. *Television myth and the American mind.* Westport, Conn.: Praeger.

Jeffres, L., and R. Perloff. 1997. *Mass media effects.* 2nd ed. Prospect Heights, Ill.: Waveland, 494 pp.

Kalbfeld, B. 2000. *The Associated Press broadcast news handbook.* New York: McGraw-Hill.

Kessler, L., and D. McDonald. 2000. *When words collide: A media writer's guide to grammar and style.* 5th ed. Belmont, Calif.: Wadsworth/Thomson Learning.

Lacey, N. 1998. *Image and representation: Key concepts in media study.* New York: St. Martin's.

Leslie, L. 2000. *Mass communication ethics.* Boston: Houghton Mifflin.

Lester, P. 1998. *Visual communication images with messages.* Belmont, Calif.: Wadsworth/Thomson Learning.

Lind, R., ed. In Press. *Race/gender/media: Considering diversity across audiences, content, and producers.* Boston: Allyn and Bacon.

Littlejohn, S. 2002. *Theories of human communication.* 7th ed. Belmont, Calif.: Wadsworth/Thomson Learning.

Looker, T. 1995. *The sound and the story: NPR and the art of radio.* Boston: Houghton Mifflin.

Lowery, S., and M. DeFleur. 1995. *Milestones in mass communications research: Media effects.* 3rd ed. White Plains, N.Y.: Longman.

Lont, C., ed. 1995. *Women and media: Content/careers/criticism.* Belmont, Calif.: Wadsworth/Thomson Learning.

Marlane, J. 1999. *Women in television news revisited: Into the twenty-first century.* Austin: University of Texas Press.

McChesney, R. 2000. *Rich media, poor democracy: Communication politics in dubious times.* New York: New Press.

McQuail, D. 2000. *Mass communication theory.* 4th ed. London: Sage.

Meyrowitz, J. 1985. *No sense of place: The impact of electronic media on social behavior.* New York: Oxford University Press.

Moore, R. 1999. *Mass communication law and ethics.* 2nd ed. Mawah, N.J.: Lawrence Erlbaum.

Murray, M., and A. Ferri, eds. 1992. *Teaching mass communication: A guide to better instruction.* New York: Praeger.

Nelson, J. 1994. *The disabled, the media and the information age.* Westport, Conn.: Greenwood.

O'Keefe, D. 2002. *Persuasion theory and research.* 2nd ed. Thousand Oaks, Calif.: Sage.

Papper, R. A. 2002. *Broadcast news writing stylebook.* 2nd ed. Boston: Allyn and Bacon.

Postman, N. 1985. *Amusing ourselves to death.* New York: Viking Penguin.

Potter, W. 1998. *Media literacy.* Thousand Oaks, Calif.: Sage.

Rubin, R., A. Rubin, and L. Piele. 2000. *Communication research: Strategies and sources.* 5th ed. Belmont, Calif.: Wadsworth/Thomson Learning.

Schilpp, M., and S. Murphy. 1983. *Great women of the press.* Carbondale: Southern Illinois University Press.

Schudson, M. 1984. *Advertising: The uneasy persuasion.* New York: Basic.

Severin, W., and J. Tankard. 2001. *Communication theories: Origins, methods and uses in the mass media.* 5th ed. New York: Longman.

Shook, F., and Lattimore, D. 2001. *The broadcast news process.* 6th ed. Englewood, Colo.: Morton.

Siebert, F., T. Peterson, and W. Schramm. 1963. *The four theories of the press.* Urbana: University of Illinois Press.

Sillars, M. O. 1991. *Messages, meanings, and culture: Approaches to communication criticism.* New York: HarperCollins.

Silverblatt, A., J. Ferry, and B. Finan. 1999. *Approaches to media literacy: A handbook.* Armonk, N.Y.: M. E. Sharpe.

Sklar, R. 1975. *Movie-made America.* New York: Random House.

Sparks, G. 2002. *Media effects research: A basic overview.* Belmont, Calif.: Wadsworth/Thomson Learning.

Squires, J. 1993. *Read all about it: The corporate takeover of America's newspapers.* New York: Times Books.

Sterling, C., and Kittross, J. 1990. *Stay tuned: A concise history of American broadcasting.* 2nd ed. Belmont, Calif.: Wadsworth.

Tuggle, C. A., F. Carr, and S. Huffman. 2001. *Broadcast news handbook: Writing, reporting, and producing.* New York: McGraw-Hill.

Valdivia, A. 2000. *A Latina in the land of Hollywood and other essays on media culture.* Tuscon: University of Arizona Press.

Vande Berg, L., L. Wenner, and B. Gronbeck. 1998. *Critical approaches to television.* Boston: Houghton Mifflin.

Vangelisti, A., J. Daly, and G. Friedrich. 1999. *Teaching communication.* 2nd ed. Mawah, N.J.: Lawrence Erlbaum.

Wendland, M. 1999. *Wired journalist: Newsroom guide to the Internet.* 3rd ed. Washington, D.C.: RTNDA.

White, T. 2001. *Broadcast news writing, reporting, and producing.* 3rd ed. Boston: Focal.

Wood, J. 2000. *Communication theories in action: An introduction.* 2nd ed. Belmont, Calif.: Wadsworth/ Thomson Learning.

Journal Articles and Chapters in Edited Volumes

Becker, L. B., T. Vlad, J. Hu, and J. Prine. 2001. Annual enrollment report: Number of students studying journalism and mass communication at all-time high. *Journalism and Mass Communication Educator* 56, no. 3:28–60. Online at www.grady.uga.edu/annualsurveys/Enrollment00/educatorsummary.htm.

Blaney, J., and G. Donnelly. 2000. Relationships between academic broadcast facilities and pedagogical outcomes. *Feedback* 41, no. 1:1–8.

Cohen, J. 2001. Symposium: Journalism and mass communication education at the crossroads. *Journalism and Mass Communication Educator* 56:4–6.

Domke, D. 1997. Journalists, framing, and discourse about race relations. *Journalism and Mass Communication Monographs* 164:1–55.

Duhé, S. F., and L. A. Zukowski. 1997. Radio-TV journalism curriculum: First jobs and career preparation. *Journalism and Mass Communication Educator* 52, no. 1:4–15.

Entman, R. M. 1990. Modern racism and the images of blacks in local television news. *Critical Studies in Mass Communication* 7:332–345.

Fisher, H. A. 1978. Broadcast journalists' perceptions of appropriate career preparation. *Journalism Quarterly* 55, no. 1:140–144.

Gotfredson, D., and E. Engstrom. 1996. Video essay: Teaching and learning with alternative news presentations. *Journalism and Mass Communication Educator* 51, no. 2:55–62.

Hammond, S., D. Petersen, and S. Thomsen. 2000. Print, broadcast and online convergence in the newsroom. *Journalism and Mass Communication Educator* 55:16–26.

Kock, E., J. Kang, and D. Allen. 1999. Broadcast education curricula in 2-year and 4-Year colleges. *Journalism Educator* 54, no. 1:4–15.

Lind, R. A., and C. Salo. 2002. The framing of feminists and feminism in news and public affairs programs in U.S. electronic media. *Journal of Communication* 52:211–228.

Outing, S. 1999. Preparing J-school students for new media convergence. *Editor and Publisher* 132:49.

Shoemaker, P., with E. Mayfield. 1987. Building a theory of news content: A synthesis of current approaches. *Journalism Monographs* 103:1–34.

Utsler, M. 2001. The convergence curriculum: We got it now what are we gonna do with it? *Feedback* 42, no. 3:1–5.

———. 2002. The convergence curriculum: Lessons from year one. *Feedback* 43, no. 2:22–27.

Wong, W. 1994. Covering the invisible "model minority." *Media Studies Journal* 8:49–59.

Web Sites

American Journalism Review. ajr.org. The online presence of the *American Journalism Review*.

American Society of Newspaper Editors. www.asne.org.

American Women in Radio and Television. www.awrt.org.

Asian American Journalists Association. www.aaja.org.

Center for Media Literacy. www.medialit.org.

Citizens for Media Literacy. www.main.nc.us/cml/.

Directory of Media Literacy Sites Worldwide. www.chebucto.ns.ca/Community Support/AMLNS/internet.html.

Fairness and Accuracy in Reporting. www.fair.org.

Freedom Forum. www.freedomforum.org.

Freedom of Information Center, University of Missouri, Columbia. www.missouri.edu~foiwww/index.html.

Irby, J. 2000. "Journalism educators seeking partnerships." *American Editor* [online]. www.asne.org/index.cfm?id=530.

Journalist's Toolbox. www.journaliststoolbox.com/.

Media Awareness Network. www.media-awareness.ca/eng/.

Media Watch. www.mediawatch.com/.

Media Education Foundation. www.mediaed.org.

Media Studies. www.mediastudies.com/.

The Minorities and Media Project at the London School of Economics. www.lse.ac.uk/Depts/Media/EMTEL/Minorities/.

Project for Excellence in Journalism. An initiative by journalists concerned about the standards of the news media. www.journalism.org/publ_research/local-tv/.

National Association of Black Journalists. www.nabj.org.

National Association of Hispanic Journalists. www.nahj.org.

Native American Journalists Association. www.naja.org.

National Lesbian and Gay Journalists Association. www.nlgja.org.

National Press Photographers Association. www.nppa.org/.

Newslab. Nonprofit, focused on research and training. www.NewsLab.org.

Pew Research Center. 2000. Media Credibility. www.people-press.org/media00rpt.html.

Poynter Institute. www.poynter.org.

The Quill. The Society of Professional Journalists' national magazine. www.spj.org/quill_list.asp.

Radio-TV News Directors Association and Foundation. www.rtnda.org.

Sandeen, R. 2000. How much multimedia should students learn? *American Editor* [online]. www.asne.org/kiosk/editor/00.march/sandeen1.htm.

Silha Center for the Study of Media Ethics and Law (University of Minnesota). silha.cla.umn.edu.

Society of Professional Journalists. www.spj.org.

Stone, V. (employment issues in broadcast news). www.missouri.edu/~jourvs/.

Student Press Law Center. www.splc.org.

Media Report to Women. www.mediareporttowomen.com.

Media Resources Center of the Library at the University of California at Berkeley. Films by and about people of color. www.lib.berkeley.edu/MRC/Ethnic ImagesVid.html.

Radio-Television News Directors Association (RTNDA). www.rtnda.com.

Unity: Journalists of Color. www.unityjournalists.org.

University of Iowa, Communication Studies Department. Information about gender, race, and mass communication. www.uiowa.edu/~commstud/resources/Gender Media/.

Women's Studies and the Media. www.library.wisc.edu/libraries/WomensStudies/ others.htm.

Index